The Privacy Law Sourcebook 2016

United States Law, International Law and Recent Developments

MARC ROTENBERG

Electronic Privacy Information Center
WASHINGTON DC

Electronic Privacy Information Center
1718 Connecticut Ave. NW
Suite 200
Washington, DC 20009

Visit the EPIC Bookstore
http://www.epic.org/bookstore/

First edition 2016
Printed in the United States of America
All Rights Reserved

ISBN: 978-1-893044-02-9

Preface to the 2016 Edition

More than a decade has passed since the last publication of *The Privacy Law Sourcebook*. Although much has happened in the privacy world, we remain committed to providing an accurate and timely collection of the main legal instruments for privacy protection in the modern age, as well as useful resources to aid further research.

In the current version of *The Sourcebook*, we include the recently adopted General Data Protection Regulation of the European Union that will soon replace the EU Data Protection Directive. The GDPR is perhaps the most significant development in modern privacy law, reflecting the ongoing challenge of enabling new technology and new business practices while safeguarding a fundamental right.

Post Snowden, the United Nations has refocused its efforts on privacy and data protection, created a Special Rapporteur on the Right to Privacy, and passed several important resolutions. The 2014 resolution of the General Assembly on the Right to Privacy in the Modern Age is included, as are related texts from the UN. In this edition of *The Privacy Law Sourcebook*, as in previous editions, Article 12 of the UN Universal Declaration of Human Rights provides the starting point for the establishment of privacy as a fundamental right.

We also draw attention in this edition to regional frameworks for privacy protection, including the Cairo Declaration on Human Rights in Islam, the Declaration of Principles on Freedom of Expression in Africa, and the Declaration of Santa Cruz de la Sierra.

Over the past decade, there was not as much privacy activity in the United States as one might have hoped. The section on US materials, but for a few amendments (some favorable, some not) remains largely unchanged, though the passage of the USA Freedom Act in 2015 did bring about the end of the bulk record collection program in the United States. And recent legislation points to emerging privacy safeguards for automated vehicles and new techniquies for deidentification.

NGOs and experts continue to play an important role shaping the contours of the modern right to privacy. We note both the Madrid Privacy Declaration and the Necessary and Proportionate Principles.

The *2016 Privacy Law Sourcebook* was prepared with the assistance of Caitriona Fitzgerald, John Tran, and Kimberly Miller. Please send comments, corrections, and suggestions to pls@epic.org. Related resources will be found also at privacy.org and privacylawandsociety.org.

> Marc Rotenberg
> Washington, DC
> September 2016

Preface to 2004 Edition

The 2004 edition of the *Privacy Law Sourcebook* chronicles recent developments in the privacy and data protection world. New US legislation includes the Video Voyeurism Prevention Act, the Do-Not-Call Implementation Act, and the CAN-SPAM Act. New reports from the Article 29 Working Group examine the technology of Radio Frequency Identification (RFID), the impact on methods to protect intellectual property rights on data protection, and the application of European privacy law to unsolicited marketing communications. The APEC Privacy Framework, adopted in 2004, is a significant new development as is the new Mexican Information Law. We have updated the privacy resources section and added links to new laws for many countries, including the new member states of the European Union.

As we have noted in previous editions, our goal is to keep the *Privacy Law Sourcebook* to a single volume. As a result, we do not reprint certain materials that can be found in earlier editions. These include (from the *Privacy Law Sourcebook 2003*) the Argentina Data Protection Act and EU materials on the transfer of Passenger Name Record (PNR) Data; (from the *Privacy Law Sourcebook 2002*) the proposed consent decree between Microsoft and the US Federal Trade Commission; (from the *Privacy Law Sourcebook 2001*) materials on the Safe Harbor Arrangement, the Personal Data Protection Law for Latvia, the Protection of Personal Data Act for the Czech Republic; (from the *Privacy Law Sourcebook 2000*) the Italian Data Protection Act, the Council of European Guidelines for Internet Privacy, the Privacy Law of Chile, the Personal Information Protection Act of Canada, the UK Regulation of Investigative Powers Act; and (from the *Privacy Law Sourcebook 1999*) the Freedom of Information and Protection of Privacy Act for British Columbia, the German Law for Information and Communication, and the Hong Kong Personal Data (Privacy) Ordinance. Readers are encouraged to consult earlier editions of the Privacy Law Sourcebook for these materials. Significant reports from the Article 29 Working Group may also be found in earlier editions of the Privacy Law Sourcebook. The annual *Privacy and Human Rights* report contains extensive country reports and thematic materials. We have also removed the text of the US Freedom of Information Act from the *Privacy Law Sourcebook*. That law and detailed legal commentary will be found in the EPIC publication *Litigation Under the Federal Open Government Laws*.

The 2004 *Privacy Law Sourcebook* was prepared with the assistance of Charles Duan, Ula Galster, Cédric Laurant, Katitza Rodriguez Pereda, and Nerisha Singh. Please send comments, corrections, and suggestions to pls@epic.org.

Marc Rotenberg
Washington, DC
August 2005

Preface to First Edition

This collection provides a basic set of privacy materials for the United States and the international sphere. The materials are current as of the time of publication. Application of U.S. statutes and international instruments, such as the Council of Europe Convention, are subject to judicial interpretation and case decisions that are not included in this volume. Certain U.S. privacy laws, such as the Privacy Act of 1974, are qualified by federal regulations, which are also not included. The section on privacy resources provides information about how to locate additional legal material on privacy.

Several points should be made about the development of privacy laws. In the United States, privacy statutes have typically resulted from an effort by the legislative branch to address a matter left unresolved by the judicial branch or they have resulted from an attempt to codify a legal standard for privacy for commercial transactions in new technological services.

In the first category are such laws as the Right to Financial Privacy Act of 1978, the Privacy Protection Act of 1980, and to some extent, the Electronic Communication Privacy Act of 1986. These laws came about in response to decisions of the United States Supreme Court where the Court chose not establish a privacy right. Part of the development of privacy law in the United States is, therefore, the dialogue between the courts and the legislature on the proper scope of privacy as a legal claim.

In the second category are such laws as the Privacy Act of 1974, the Video Privacy Protection Act of 1988, the Employee Polygraph Protection Act of 1988, and the Telephone Consumer Protection Act of 1991. These statutes came about in direct response to new technologies that raised public concern and called for the establishment of legal standards to protect privacy.

The Electronic Communications Privacy Act is, in many respects, the most complex of US privacy laws. Its roots can be found in the dissent of Justice Brandeis in *Olmstead v. United States*, the first case in which the United States Supreme Court considered the Constitutionality of electronic surveillance. Title III of the Omnibus Crime Control Act of 1968, the precursor to ECPA, codified two decisions of the Supreme Court from the 1967 term and established the legislative framework for regulating electronic surveillance. In 1986 Title III was amended to include stored electronic mail and data in transit, and the name was changed to the "Electronic Communications Privacy Act." Then in 1994, the Act was once again amended to provide law enforcement access to electronic communications.

The Privacy Act of 1974 and the Freedom of Information Act, first enacted in 1966 and then significantly expanded in 1974, are a special case. These two laws were passed to give citizens rights of privacy and rights of access, two complimentary legal claims, in government record-keeping systems. They fall into a hybrid of the two categories described above: an attempt by Congress to establish legal rights in the absence of judicial decision-making and a response to new developments in technology.

The privacy materials provided here from the international sphere are of a different origin. In the first instance, they reflect a fundamental concern with human rights. This can be seen, for example, in Article 12 of the Universal Declaration of Human Rights that established privacy as a fundamental human right shortly after the end of World War II. Language similar to that found in Article 12 will be found in other international instruments on human rights, not included in this volume, such as the International Covenant on Civil and Political Rights (Article 17), the European Convention on Human Rights (Article 8), and the American Convention on Human Rights (Article 11). Many of these documents can be found at the web site of Privacy International.

In the second instance, international privacy law attempts to address the problem of privacy protection across national borders, what is sometimes called "transborder data flows." The Council of Europe Convention, for example, and the European Data Directive set out privacy standards so that personal information is protected when it moves between nations. Commentators on international privacy law have often noted that the paradox of privacy is found in this need to protect data so that it may be exchanged more freely.

The guidelines of the Organization for Economic Cooperation and Development do not of themselves have the force of law. However, OECD principles have played an important role in directing the development of national law and helping to establish international legal norms. By way of example, the subscriber privacy provisions of the Cable Communications Policy Act adopted in the United States in 1984 follow closely the OECD Privacy Guidelines of 1980.

The Data Protection Directive of the European Union is the most significant development in privacy law in many years. It draws together several of the traditions in privacy law. Based on the precept that privacy is a fundamental human right, it establishes a common standard for privacy protection for the benefit of European citizens among the member states of the European Union. It also seeks to extend privacy standards to the new, rapidly evolving commercial environment. The critical question of how the European Commission will determine whether data may be transferred to countries that lack similar privacy standards is taken up in the Recent Developments section in a short piece prepared by a working group of the European Commission on the problem of "adequacy."

The Recent Developments section also looks at several attempts to extend privacy principles in the age of the Internet. The German Telecommunications law is the first privacy law specifically tailored to recent on-line developments. It is noteworthy in that it both applies traditional Fair Information Practices to new commercial services and also encourages the use of anonymous payment techniques.

The OECD Cryptography Guidelines cover one of the most interesting and rapidly developing areas in privacy law and policy. The technique to encode digital data offers the possibility that technology could protect privacy, a belief that runs contrary to the premise supporting most privacy law to date. An appropriate role for public policy may be to encourage its adoption. Cryptography also raises some new privacy issues. Both dimensions were considered in the development of the OECD Cryptography Guidelines.

Also included in this section is the pledge of database firms concerning the protection of personal privacy. This might not generally be considered appropriate for a volume of legal materials. It is included here to show one approach to privacy protection.

The Freedom of Information and Protection of Privacy Act for British Columbia is one of the most recent privacy laws adopted in North America. Its structure and scope provides a helpful example of the role of privacy and access law in our modern society. Recent developments include the growing presence of the US Federal Trade Commission in the enforcement of privacy policies. Excerpts from the Federal Trade Commission Act are included.

I am grateful to the Georgetown University Law Center for the opportunity to develop my course on information privacy law over the last several years and to the Washington College of Law. Shauna Van Dongen, Lisa Harrinanan, and Dan Lin helped with the production of this volume. Privacy International and the Electronic Privacy Information Center provided excellent resources for privacy materials.

Marc Rotenberg
Washington, DC
August 1998

TABLE OF CONTENTS

UNITED STATES LAW   **1**

FEDERAL TRADE COMMISSION ACT (1914)   1
COMMUNICATIONS ACT (1934) [EXCERPT]   36
FAIR CREDIT REPORTING ACT (1970)   41
PRIVACY ACT (1974)   129
FAMILY EDUCATIONAL RIGHTS AND PRIVACY ACT (1974)   153
FOREIGN INTELLIGENCE SURVEILLANCE ACT (1978)   164
RIGHT TO FINANCIAL PRIVACY ACT (1978)   223
PRIVACY PROTECTION ACT (1980)   248
CABLE COMMUNICATIONS POLICY ACT (1984) [EXCERPT]   254
ELECTRONIC COMMUNICATIONS PRIVACY ACT (1986)   258
VIDEO PRIVACY PROTECTION ACT (1988)   319
EMPLOYEE POLYGRAPH PROTECTION ACT (1988)   323
TELEPHONE CONSUMER PROTECTION ACT (1991)   333
DRIVER'S PRIVACY PROTECTION ACT (1994)   350
TELECOMMUNICATIONS ACT (1996) [EXCERPT]   355
CHILDREN'S ONLINE PRIVACY PROTECTION ACT (1998)   359
IDENTITY THEFT AND ASSUMPTION DETERRENCE ACT (1998)   369
FINANCIAL SERVICES MODERNIZATION ACT (1999) [EXCERPTS]   374
NO CHILD LEFT BEHIND ACT (2001) [EXCERPT]   393
US HOMELAND SECURITY ACT (2002) [EXCERPTS]   399
US E-GOVERNMENT ACT (2002) [EXCERPT]   409
DO-NOT-CALL IMPLEMENTATION ACT (2003)   412
CAN-SPAM ACT (2003)   416
VIDEO VOYEURISM PREVENTION ACT (2004)   438
IDENTITY THEFT PENALTY ENHANCEMENT ACT (2004)   439
INTELLIGENCE REFORM AND TERRORISM
PREVENTION ACT (2004) [EXCERPTS]   443
HEALTH INFORMATION TECHNOLOGY FOR
CLINICAL AND ECONOMIC HEALTH (HITECH) ACT (2009) [EXCERPT] 458

INTERNATIONAL PRIVACY LAW   **471**

UNIVERSAL DECLARATION OF HUMAN RIGHTS (1948)   471
COUNCIL OF EUROPE CONVENTION FOR
THE PROTECTION OF HUMAN RIGHTS AND
FUNDAMENTAL FREEDOMS (1950)   476
OECD PRIVACY GUIDELINES (1980)   482
COUNCIL OF EUROPE CONVENTION ON PRIVACY (1981)   509
UNITED NATIONS GUIDELINES FOR THE REGULATION OF
COMPUTERIZED PERSONAL FILES (1990)   519
EUROPEAN UNION DATA PROTECTION DIRECTIVE (1995)   523
OECD CRYPTOGRAPHY GUIDELINES (1997)   551
GENERAL AGREEMENT ON TRADE IN SERVICES (1994) [EXCERPT]   561

EUROPEAN UNION DIRECTIVE ON PRIVACY AND ELECTRONIC
COMMUNICATIONS (2002)   563
CHARTER OF FUNDAMENTAL RIGHTS OF THE
EUROPEAN UNION (2000) [EXCERPT]   581
APEC PRIVACY FRAMEWORK   586
CAIRO DECLARATION OF HUMAN RIGHTS IN ISLAM [EXCERPT]   603
DECLARATION OF PRINCIPLES ON FREEDOM OF
EXPRESSION IN AFRICA [EXCERPT]   605
DECLARATION OF SANTA CRUZ DE LA SIERRA   607
MADRID DECLARATION   608

RECENT DEVELOPMENTS   **611**

UN RESOLUTION ON RIGHT TO PRIVACY (2014)   611
EU-US "UMBRELLA AGREEMENT" (2015)   616
US CYBERSECURITY INFORMATION SHARING ACT OF 2015   630
US DRIVER PRIVACY ACT OF 2015   655
EU-US "PRIVACY SHIELD"   657
EU GENERAL DATA PROTECTION REGULATION (2016)   666

SELECTED BIBLIOGRAPHY   **735**

PRIVACY RESOURCES   **741**

PRIVACY YEAR IN REVIEW 2015–2016   741
AGENCIES   751
NATIONAL LEGISLATION   758
ORGANIZATIONS   767
PUBLICATIONS   776
WEBSITES   779

DETAILED TABLE OF CONTENTS

UNITED STATES LAW	**1**
FEDERAL TRADE COMMISSION ACT (1914)	1
Summary	1
References	1
§ 45. Unfair methods of competition unlawful; prevention by Commission	1
(a) Declaration of unlawfulness; power to prohibit unfair practices; inapplicability to foreign trade	1
(b) Proceeding by Commission; modifying and setting aside orders	2
(c) Review of order; rehearing	3
(d) Jurisdiction of court	4
(e) Exemption from liability	4
(f) Service of complaints, orders and other processes; return	4
(g) Finality of order	5
(h) Modification or setting aside of order by Supreme Court	6
(i) Modification or setting aside of order by Court of Appeals	6
(j) Rehearing upon order or remand	6
(k) "Mandate" defined	6
(l) Penalty for violation of order; injunctions and other appropriate equitable relief	6
(m) Civil actions for recovery of penalties for knowing violations of rules and cease and desist orders respecting unfair or deceptive acts or practices; jurisdiction; maximum amount of penalties; continuing violations; de novo determinations; compromise or settlement procedure	7
(n) Standard of proof; public policy consideration	8
§ 46. Additional powers of Commission	8
(a) Investigation of persons, partnerships, or corporations	8
(b) Reports of persons, partnerships, and corporations	9
(c) Investigation of compliance with antitrust decrees	9
(d) Investigations of violations of antitrust statutes	9
(e) Readjustment of business of corporations violating antitrust statutes.	9
(f) Publication of information; reports	9
(g) Classification of corporations; regulations	10
(h) Investigations of foreign trade conditions; reports	10
(i) Investigations of foreign antitrust law violations	10
§ 57a. Unfair or deceptive acts or practices rulemaking proceedings	11
§ 57b. Civil actions for violations of rules and cease and desist orders respecting unfair or deceptive acts or practices	20
§ 57b-1. Civil investigative demands	21
§ 57b-2. Confidentiality	28
§ 57b-3. Rulemaking process	33
COMMUNICATIONS ACT (1934) [EXCERPT]	36
Summary	36
References	36
§605. Unauthorized publication or use of communications	36
FAIR CREDIT REPORTING ACT (1970)	41
Summary	41
References	42
§ 601. Short title	42
15 U.S.C. § 1681. Congressional findings and statement of purpose	42
§ 1681a. Definitions; rules of construction	43
§ 1681b. Permissible purposes of consumer reports	50
§ 1681c. Requirements relating to information contained in consumer reports	60

§ 1681c-1. Identity theft prevention; fraud alerts and active duty alerts 63
§ 1681c-2. Block of information resulting from identity theft 67
§ 1681d. Disclosure of investigative consumer reports 69
§ 1681e. Compliance procedures 70
§ 1681f. Disclosures to governmental agencies 72
§ 1681g. Disclosures to consumers 72
§ 1681h. Conditions and form of disclosure to consumers 82
§ 1681i. Procedure in case of disputed accuracy 84
§ 1681j. Charges for certain disclosures 90
§ 1681k. Public record information for employment purposes 93
§ 1681l. Restrictions on investigative consumer reports 94
§ 1681m. Requirements on users of consumer reports 94
§ 1681n. Civil liability for willful noncompliance 101
§ 1681o. Civil liability for negligent noncompliance 102
§ 1681p. Jurisdiction of courts; limitation of actions 102
§ 1681q. Obtaining information under false pretenses 102
§ 1681r. Unauthorized disclosures by officers or employees 103
§ 1681s. Administrative enforcement 103
§ 1681s-1. Information on overdue child support obligations 108
§ 1681s-2. Responsibilities of furnishers of information to consumer
reporting agencies 108
§ 1681s-3. Affiliate sharing 116
§ 1681t. Relation to State laws 119
§ 1681u. Disclosures to FBI for counterintelligence purposes 121
§ 1681v. Disclosures to governmental agencies for counterterrorism purposes 125
§ 1681w. Disposal of records 128
§ 1681x. Corporate and technological circumvention prohibited 128
PRIVACY ACT (1974) 129
Summary 129
References 130
Congressional findings and statement of purpose 130
5 U.S.C. § 552a Public information; agency rules, opinions, orders, records,
and proceedings 131
SECTION 1. SHORT TITLE. 149
SEC. 2. EXTENSION OF PRIVACY ACT REMEDIES TO CITIZENS OF
DESIGNATED COUNTRIES. 149
FAMILY EDUCATIONAL RIGHTS AND PRIVACY ACT (1974) 153
Summary 153
References 153
20 U.S.C. § 1232g. Family educational and privacy rights 154
a) Conditions for availability of funds to educational agencies or institutions;
inspection and review of education records; specific information to be made
available; procedure for access to education records; reasonableness of time for
such access; hearings; written explanations by parents; definitions 154
(b) Release of education records; parental consent requirement; exceptions;
compliance with judicial orders and subpoenas; audit and evaluation of
federally-supported education programs; recordkeeping 156
(c) Surveys or data-gathering activities; regulations 160
(d) Students' rather than parents' permission or consent 161
(e) Informing parents or students of rights under this section 161
(f) Enforcement; termination of assistance 161
(g) Office and review board; creation; functions 161
(h) Disciplinary records; disclosure 161
(i) Drug and alcohol violation disclosures 162

(j) Investigation and prosecution of terrorism 162
FOREIGN INTELLIGENCE SURVEILLANCE ACT (1978) 164
 Summary 164
 References 164
  50 U.S.C. § 1801. Definitions 165
  50 U.S.C. § 1802. Electronic surveillance authorization without court order;
  certification by Attorney General; reports to Congressional committees;
  transmittal under seal; duties and compensation of
  communication common carrier; applications; jurisdiction of court 169
  50 U.S.C. § 1803. Designation of judges 170
  50 U.S.C. § 1804. Applications for court orders 176
  50 U.S.C. § 1805. Issuance of order 178
  50 U.S.C. § 1806. Use of information 184
  50 U.S.C. § 1807. Report to Administrative Office
  of the United States Court and to Congress 187
  50 U.S.C. § 1808. Report of Attorney General to Congressional committees;
  limitation on authority or responsibility of information gathering activities of
  Congressional committees; report of Congressional committees to Congress 187
  50 U.S.C. § 1809. Criminal sanctions 188
  50 U.S.C. § 1810. Civil liability 189
  50 U.S.C. § 1811. Authorization during time of war 189
  50 U.S.C. § 1821. Definitions 189
  50 U.S.C. § 1822. Authorization of physical searches for foreign
  intelligence purposes 191
  50 U.S.C. § 1823. Application for order 193
  50 U.S.C. § 1824. Issuance of order 195
  50 U.S.C. § 1825. Use of information 198
  50 U.S.C. § 1826. Congressional oversight 201
  50 U.S.C. § 1827. Penalties 202
  50 U.S.C. § 1828. Civil liability 202
  50 U.S.C. § 1829. Authorization during time of war 203
  50 U.S.C. § 1841. Definitions 203
  50 U.S.C. § 1842. Pen registers and trap and trace devices for
  foreign intelligence and international terrorism investigations 204
  50 U.S.C. § 1843. Authorization during emergencies 207
  50 U.S.C. § 1844. Authorization during time of war 209
  50 U.S.C. § 1845. Use of information 209
  50 U.S.C. § 1846. Congressional oversight 211
  50 U.S.C. § 1861. Access to Certain Business Records for
  Foreign Intelligence and International Terrorism Investigations 212
  50 U.S.C. § 1862. Congressional Oversight 221
RIGHT TO FINANCIAL PRIVACY ACT (1978) 223
 Summary 223
 References 224
 12 U.S.C. § 3401. Definitions 224
 Sec. 3402. Access to financial records by Government
 authorities prohibited; exceptions 225
 Sec. 3403. Confidentiality of financial records 225
 Sec. 3404. Customer authorizations 226
 Sec. 3405. Administrative subpoena and summons 227
 Sec. 3406. Search warrants 228
 Sec. 3407. Judicial subpoena 229
 Sec. 3408. Formal written request 230
 Sec. 3409. Delayed notice 231

Sec. 3410. Customer challenges   232
Sec. 3411. Duty of financial institutions   234
Sec. 3412. Use of information   234
Sec. 3413. Exceptions   236
Sec. 3414. Special procedures   241
Sec. 3415. Cost reimbursement   244
Sec. 3416. Jurisdiction   245
Sec. 3417. Civil penalties   245
Sec. 3418. Injunctive relief   246
Sec. 3419. Suspension of limitations   246
Sec. 3420. Grand jury information; notification of certain persons prohibited 246
Sec. 3421. [Repealed]   247
Sec. 3422. Applicability to Securities and Exchange Commission   247
PRIVACY PROTECTION ACT (1980)   248
Summary   248
References   248
42 U.S.C. 2000aa. Searches and seizures by government officers and
employees in connection with investigation or prosecution of criminal offenses 248
Sec. 2000aa-5. Border and customs searches   250
Sec. 2000aa-6. Civil actions by aggrieved persons   250
Sec. 2000aa-7. Definitions   251
Sec. 2000aa-11. Guidelines for Federal officers and employees   252
Sec. 2000aa-12. Binding nature of guidelines; disciplinary actions for
violations; legal proceedings for non-compliance prohibited   253
CABLE COMMUNICATIONS POLICY ACT (1984) [EXCERPT]   254
Summary   254
References   254
47 U.S.C. § 551. Protection of subscriber privacy   254
ELECTRONIC COMMUNICATIONS PRIVACY ACT (1986)   258
Summary   258
References   258
Congressional Findings (1968)   259
18 U.S.C. § 2510. Definitions   259
Sec. 2511. Interception and disclosure of wire, oral, or electronic
communications prohibited   262
Sec. 2512. Manufacture, distribution, possession, and advertising of wire,
oral, or electronic communication intercepting devices prohibited   268
Sec. 2513. Confiscation of wire, oral, or electronic communication
intercepting devices   269
Sec. 2514. [Repealed]   269
Sec. 2515. Prohibition of use as evidence of intercepted wire or oral communications 269
Sec. 2516. Authorization for interception of wire, oral, or electronic communications 270
Sec. 2517. Authorization for disclosure and use of intercepted wire, oral,
or electronic communications   273
Sec. 2518. Procedure for interception of wire, oral, or electronic communications 275
Sec. 2519. Reports concerning intercepted wire, oral, or electronic communications 281
Sec. 2520. Recovery of civil damages authorized   282
Sec. 2521. Injunction against illegal interception   284
Sec. 2522. Enforcement of the Communications Assistance for
Law Enforcement Act   284
Sec. 2701. Unlawful access to stored communications   285
Sec. 2702. Voluntary Disclosure of Customer Communications or Records   286
Sec. 2703. Required Disclosure of Customer Communications or Records   288
Sec. 2704. Backup preservation   290

Sec. 2705. Delayed notice 292
Sec. 2706. Cost reimbursement 294
Sec. 2707. Civil action 295
Sec. 2708. Exclusivity of remedies 296
Sec. 2709. Counterintelligence access to telephone toll and transactional records 296
Sec. 2711. Definitions for chapter 298
Sec. 3121. General prohibition on pen register and trap and trace device use; exception 299
Sec. 3122. Application for an order for a pen register or a trap and trace device 300
Sec. 3123. Issuance of an order for a pen register or a trap and trace device 300
Sec. 3124. Assistance in installation and use of a pen register or a trap and trace device 302
Sec. 3125. Emergency pen register and trap and trace device installation 303
Sec. 3126. Reports concerning pen registers and trap and trace devices 304
Sec. 3127. Definitions for chapter 304
47 U.S.C. Sec. 1001. Definitions 305
Sec. 1002. Assistance capability requirements 306
Sec. 1003. Notices of capacity requirements 308
Sec. 1004. Systems security and integrity 310
Sec. 1005. Cooperation of equipment manufacturers and providers of
telecommunications support services 310
Sec. 1006. Technical requirements and standards; extension of compliance date 311
Sec. 1007. Enforcement orders 313
Sec. 1008. Payment of costs of telecommunications carriers to
comply with capability requirements 314
Sec. 1009. Authorization of appropriations 316
Sec. 1010. Reports 316
Sec. 1021. Department of Justice Telecommunications Carrier Compliance Fund 317
VIDEO PRIVACY PROTECTION ACT (1988) 319
Summary 319
References 319
18 U.S.C. § 2710. Wrongful disclosure of video tape rental or sale records 319
EMPLOYEE POLYGRAPH PROTECTION ACT (1988) 323
Summary 323
References 323
29 U.S.C. Sec. 2001. Definitions 324
Sec. 2002. Prohibitions on lie detector use 324
Sec. 2003. Notice of protection 325
Sec. 2004. Authority of Secretary 325
Sec. 2005. Enforcement provisions 325
Sec. 2006. Exemptions 326
Sec. 2007. Restrictions on use of exemptions 329
Sec. 2008. Disclosure of information 332
Sec. 2009. Effect on other law and agreements 332
TELEPHONE CONSUMER PROTECTION ACT (1991) 333
Summary 333
References 334
Congressional Statement of Findings 334
47 U.S.C. Sec. 227. Restrictions on use of telephone equipment 335
DRIVER'S PRIVACY PROTECTION ACT (1994) 350
Summary 350
References 350
18 U.S.C. § 2721. Prohibition on release and use of certain
personal information from State motor vehicle records 351
Sec. 2722. Additional unlawful acts 353
Sec. 2723. Penalties 353

Sec. 2724. Civil action   353
Sec. 2725. Definitions   354
TELECOMMUNICATIONS ACT (1996) [EXCERPT]   355
Summary   355
References   355
47 U.S.C. Sec. 222. Privacy of customer information   355
CHILDREN'S ONLINE PRIVACY PROTECTION ACT (1998)   359
Summary   359
References   359
15 U.S.C. § 6501. Definitions   359
§ 6502. Regulation of unfair and deceptive acts and practices in
connection with the collection and use of personal information from
and about children on the Internet   361
§ 6503. Safe harbors   364
§ 6504. Actions by States   365
§ 6505. Administration and applicability of Act   366
§ 6506. Review   367
IDENTITY THEFT AND ASSUMPTION DETERRENCE ACT (1998)   369
Summary   369
References   369
§1028. Fraud and related activity in connection with identification documents,
authentication features, and information   369
FINANCIAL SERVICES MODERNIZATION ACT (1999) [EXCERPTS]   374
Summary   374
References   375
§ 6801. Protection of nonpublic personal information   375
§ 6802. Obligations with respect to disclosures of personal information 375
§ 6803. Disclosure of institution privacy policy   378
§ 6804. Rulemaking   380
§ 6805. Enforcement   381
§ 6806. Relation to other provisions   383
§ 6807. Relation to State laws   383
§ 6808. Study of information sharing among financial affiliates   383
§ 6809. Definitions   384
§ 6821. Privacy protection for customer information of financial institutions 387
§ 6822. Administrative enforcement   388
§ 6823. Criminal penalty   389
§ 6824. Relation to State laws   389
§ 6825. Agency guidance   390
§ 6826. Reports   390
§ 6827. Definitions   391
NO CHILD LEFT BEHIND ACT (2001) [EXCERPT]   393
Summary   393
References   393
20 U.S.C. § 1232h   393
US HOMELAND SECURITY ACT (2002) [EXCERPTS]   399
Summary   399
References   399
§ 131 Definitions   399
§ 132. Designation of critical infrastructure protection program   401
§ 133. Protection of voluntarily shared critical infrastructure information 401
§ 134. No private right of action   404
§ 142. Privacy officer   405
§ 460. Prohibition of the Terrorism Information and Prevention System   408

§ 554. National identification system not authorized 408
US E-GOVERNMENT ACT (2002) [EXCERPT] 409
   Summary 409
   References 409
   44 U.S.C. § 3501 Note. Sec. 208. Privacy provisions. 409
DO-NOT-CALL IMPLEMENTATION ACT (2003) 412
   Summary 412
   References 412
   16 C.F.R. § 310.4 412
   Public Law 108-10 413
      § 1. Short Title. 413
      § 2. Telemarketing Sales Rule; Do-Not-Call Registry Fees. 413
      § 3. Federal Communications Commission Do-Not-Call Regulations. .. 414
      § 4. Reporting Requirements. 414
CAN-SPAM ACT (2003) 416
   Summary 416
   References 416
   15 U.S.C. § 7701. Congressional Findings and Policy 416
   15 U.S.C. § 7702. Definitions 418
   15 U.S.C. § 7703. Prohibition Against Predatory And Abusive Commercial E-Mail. .. 421
   15 U.S.C. § 7704. Other Protections for Users of Commercial Electronic Mail. 421
   15 U.S.C. § 7705. Businesses Knowingly Promoted By
   Electronic Mail With False Or Misleading Transmission Information. ... 426
   15 U.S.C. § 7706. Enforcement Generally. 427
   15 U.S.C. § 7707. Effect on Other Laws. 432
   15 U.S.C. § 7708. Do-Not-E-Mail Registry 433
   15 U.S.C. § 7709. Study Of Effects Of Commercial Electronic Mail ... 433
   15 U.S.C. § 7710. Improving Enforcement By Providing Rewards
   For Information About Violations; Labeling. 434
   15 U.S.C. § 7711. Regulations. 434
   15 U.S.C. § 7712. Application to Wireless 435
   15 U.S.C. § 7713. Separability 436
   18 U.S.C. § 1037. Fraud and related activity in connection with electronic mail .. 436
VIDEO VOYEURISM PREVENTION ACT (2004) 438
   Summary 438
   References 438
   18 U.S.C. § 1801. Video voyeurism 438
IDENTITY THEFT PENALTY ENHANCEMENT ACT (2004) 439
   Summary 439
   References 439
   18 U.S.C. § 1028A. Aggravated identity theft 439
   18 U.S.C. § 1028. Fraud and related activity in connection with
   identification documents and information 440
   18 U.S.C. § 641. Public money, property or records 442
INTELLIGENCE REFORM AND TERRORISM
PREVENTION ACT (2004) [EXCERPTS] 443
   Summary 443
   References 443
   § 7211 (5 U.S.C. § 301 note). Standards for Birth Certificates. 443
   § 7212 (49 U.S.C. § 30301 note). Driver's Licenses and Personal
   Identification Cards. 445
   § 7213 (42 U.S.C. § 405 note). Social Security Cards And Numbers. ... 448
   § 7214. Prohibition Of The Display Of Social Security Account
   Numbers On Driver's Licenses Or Motor Vehicle Registrations. 450

§ 7217. Study On Allegedly Lost Or Stolen Passports. 451
§ 7218 (22 U.S.C. § 4807). Establishment Of Visa And Passport Security
Program In The Department Of State. 451
§ 7220 (49 U.S.C. § 44901 note). Identification Standards. 453
HEALTH INFORMATION TECHNOLOGY FOR CLINICAL AND
ECONOMIC HEALTH (HITECH) ACT (2009) [EXCERPT] 458
Summary 458
Reference 458
42 U.S.C. § 17932. Notification in the case of breach 458
§17934. Application of privacy provisions and penalties to
business associates of covered entities 462
§17935. Restrictions on certain disclosures and sales of health information;
accounting of certain protected health information disclosures; access to
certain information in electronic format 462
§17937. Temporary breach notification requirement for vendors of personal
health records and other non-HIPAA covered entities 467
§17939. Improved enforcement 469

INTERNATIONAL PRIVACY LAW **471**

UNIVERSAL DECLARATION OF HUMAN RIGHTS (1948) 471
Summary 471
References 471
COUNCIL OF EUROPE CONVENTION FOR THE PROTECTION OF
HUMAN RIGHTS AND FUNDAMENTAL FREEDOMS (1950) 476
Summary 476
References 476
Article 1 – Obligation to respect human rights 477
Article 2 – Right to life 477
Article 3 – Prohibition of torture 477
Article 4 – Prohibition of slavery and forced labour 477
Article 5 – Right to liberty and security 477
Article 6 – Right to a fair trial 478
Article 7 – No punishment without law 479
Article 8 – Right to respect for private and family life 479
Article 9 – Freedom of thought, conscience and religion 479
Article 10 – Freedom of expression 479
Article 11 – Freedom of assembly and association 480
Article 12 – Right to marry 480
Article 13 – Right to an effective remedy 480
Article 14 – Prohibition of discrimination 480
Article 15 – Derogation in time of emergency 480
Article 16 – Restrictions on political activity of aliens 481
Article 17 – Prohibition of abuse of rights 481
Article 18 – Limitation on use of restrictions on rights 481
OECD PRIVACY GUIDELINES (1980) 482
Summary 482
References 482
GENERAL 484
Definitions 484
Scope of Guidelines 484
BASIC PRINCIPLES OF NATIONAL APPLICATION 485
Collection Limitation Principle 485
Data Quality Principle 485
Purpose Specification Principle 485

Use Limitation Principle   485
Security Safeguards Principle   485
Openness Principle   485
Individual Participation Principle   485
Accountability Principle   486
BASIC PRINCIPLES OF INTERNATIONAL APPLICATION: FREE FLOW
AND LEGITIMATE RESTRICTIONS   486
NATIONAL IMPLEMENTATION   486
INTERNATIONAL CO-OPERATION   487
APPENDIX   487
    Introduction   487
    I GENERAL BACKGROUND   488
    The Problems   488
    Activities at national level   489
    International aspects of privacy and data banks   490
    Relevant international activities   490
    Activities of the OECD   491
    II. THE GUIDELINES   494
    A. Purpose and Scope   494
    General   494
    Objectives   494
    Level of detail   495
    Non-Member countries   495
    The broader regulatory perspective   495
    Legal persons, groups and similar entities   496
    Automated and non-automated data   496
    B. Detailed Comments   497
    General   497
COUNCIL OF EUROPE CONVENTION ON PRIVACY (1981)   509
    Summary   509
    References   509
    CHAPTER I – GENERAL PROVISIONS   510
    Article 1: Object and purpose   510
    Article 2: Definitions   510
    Article 3: Scope   510
    CHAPTER II - BASIC PRINCIPLES FOR DATA PROTECTION   511
    Article 4: Duties of the Parties   511
    Article 5: Quality of data   511
    Article 6: Special categories of data   511
    Article 7: Data security   512
    Article 8: Additional safeguards for the data subject   512
    Article 9: Exceptions and restrictions   512
    Article 10: Sanctions and remedies   512
    Article 11: Extended protection   513
    CHAPTER III – TRANSBORDER DATA FLOWS   513
    Article 12: Transborder flows of personal data and domestic law   513
    CHAPTER IV – MUTUAL ASSISTANCE   513
    Article 13: Co-operation between Parties   513
    Article 14: Assistance to data subjects resident abroad   514
    Article 15: Safeguards concerning assistance rendered by designated authorities   514
    Article 16: Refusal of requests for assistance   514
    Article 17: Costs and procedures of assistance   514
    CHAPTER V – CONSULTATIVE COMMITTEE   515
    Article 18: Composition of the committee   515

Article 19: Functions of the committee 515
Article 20: Procedure 515
CHAPTER VI – AMENDMENTS 516
Article 21: Amendments 516
CHAPTER VII – FINAL CLAUSES 516
Article 22: Entry into force 516
Article 23: Accession by non-member States 516
Article 24: Territorial clause 517
Article 25: Reservations 517
Article 26: Denunciation 517
Article 27: Notifications 517
UNITED NATIONS GUIDELINES FOR THE REGULATION OF
COMPUTERIZED PERSONAL FILES (1990) 519
Summary 519
A. PRINCIPLES CONCERNING THE MINIMUM GUARANTEES THAT
SHOULD BE PROVIDED IN NATIONAL LEGISLATIONS 519
1. Principle of lawfulness and fairness 519
2. Principle of accuracy 520
3. Principle of the purpose-specification 520
4. Principle of interested-person access 520
5. Principle of non-discrimination 520
6. Power to make exceptions 520
7. Principle of security 521
8. Supervision and sanctions 521
9. Transborder data flows 521
10. Field of application 521
B. APPLICATION OF THE GUIDELINES TO PERSONAL DATA FILES KEPT
BY GOVERNMENTAL INTERNATIONAL ORGANIZATIONS . . . 521
EUROPEAN UNION DATA PROTECTION DIRECTIVE (1995) 523
Summary 523
References 523
CHAPTER I: GENERAL PROVISIONS 533
Article 1 Object of the Directive 533
Article 2 Definitions 534
Article 3 Scope 535
Article 4 National law applicable 535
CHAPTER II: GENERAL RULES ON THE LAWFULNESS OF THE
PROCESSING OF PERSONAL DATA 535
SECTION I PRINCIPLES RELATING TO DATA QUALITY 536
Article 6 536
SECTION II PRINCIPLES RELATING TO THE REASONS FOR
MAKING DATA PROCESSING LEGITIMATE 536
Article 7 536
SECTION III SPECIAL CATEGORIES OF PROCESSING 537
Article 8 The processing of special categories of data 537
Article 9 Processing of personal data and freedom of expression . . 538
SECTION IV INFORMATION TO BE GIVEN TO THE DATA SUBJECT 538
Article 10 Information in cases of collection of data from the data subject 538
Article 11 Information where the data have not been obtained from
the data subject 538
SECTION V THE DATA SUBJECT'S RIGHT OF ACCESS TO DATA 539
Article 12 Right of access 539
SECTION VI: EXEMPTIONS AND RESTRICTIONS 539
Article 13: Exemptions and restrictions 539

SECTION VII: THE DATA SUBJECT'S RIGHT TO OBJECT   540
    Article 14 The data subject's right to object   540
    Article 15: Automated individual decisions   540
SECTION VIII: CONFIDENTIALITY AND SECURITY OF PROCESSING   541
    Article 16 Confidentiality of processing   541
    Article 17 Security of processing   541
SECTION IX: NOTIFICATION   541
    Article 18 Obligation to notify the supervisory authority   541
    Article 19 Contents of notification   542
    Article 20 Prior checking   543
    Article 21 Publicizing of processing operations   543
CHAPTER III JUDICIAL REMEDIES, LIABILITY AND PENALTIES   543
    Article 22 Remedies   543
    Article 23 Liability   543
    Article 24 Sanctions   544
CHAPTER IV TRANSFER OF PERSONAL DATA TO
THIRD COUNTRIES   544
    Article 25 Principles   544
    Article 26 Derogations   545
CHAPTER V CODES OF CONDUCT   546
    Article 27   546
CHAPTER VI SUPERVISORY AUTHORITY AND WORKING PARTY
ON THE PROTECTION OF INDIVIDUALS WITH REGARD TO THE
PROCESSING OF PERSONAL DATA   546
    Article 28 Supervisory authority   546
    Article 29 Working Party on the Protection of Individuals with
    regard to the Processing of Personal Data   547
    Article 30   548
CHAPTER VII COMMUNITY IMPLEMENTING MEASURES   549
    Article 31 The Committee   549
FINAL PROVISIONS   549
    Article 32   549
    Article 33   550
    Article 34   550
OECD CRYPTOGRAPHY GUIDELINES (1997)   551
    Summary   551
    References   551
    I. AIMS   555
    II. SCOPE   555
    III. DEFINITIONS   555
    IV. INTEGRATION   557
    V. PRINCIPLES   557
      1. TRUST IN CRYPTOGRAPHIC METHODS   557
      2. CHOICE OF CRYPTOGRAPHIC METHODS   557
      3. MARKET DRIVEN DEVELOPMENT OF
      CRYPTOGRAPHIC METHODS   558
      4. STANDARDS FOR CRYPTOGRAPHIC METHODS   558
      5. PROTECTION OF PRIVACY AND PERSONAL DATA   558
      6. LAWFUL ACCESS   559
      7. LIABILITY   560
      8. INTERNATIONAL CO-OPERATION   560
GENERAL AGREEMENT ON TRADE IN SERVICES (1994) [EXCERPT]   561
    Reference   561
    Article XIV General Exceptions   561

EUROPEAN UNION DIRECTIVE ON PRIVACY AND
ELECTRONIC COMMUNICATIONS (2002)   563
    Article 1 - Scope and aim   572
    Article 2 - Definitions   572
    Article 3 - Services concerned   573
    Article 4 - Security   573
    Article 5 - Confidentiality of the communications   574
    Article 6 - Traffic data   574
    Article 7 - Itemised billing   575
    Article 8 - Presentation and restriction of calling and
connected line identification   575
    Article 9 - Location data other than traffic data   576
    Article 10 - Exceptions   576
    Article 11 - Automatic call forwarding   576
    Article 12 - Directories of subscribers   577
    Article 13 - Unsolicited communications   577
    Article 14 - Technical features and standardisation   578
    Article 15 - Application of certain provisions of Directive 95/46/EC   578
    Article 16 - Transitional arrangements   579
    (2) OJ L 36, 7.2.1987, p. 31.   579
    Article 17 - Transposition   579
    Article 18 - Review   579
    Article 20 - Entry into force   580
    Article 21 - Addressees   580
CHARTER OF FUNDAMENTAL RIGHTS OF THE
EUROPEAN UNION (2000) [EXCERPT]   581
    Reference   581
    PREAMBLE   581
    CHAPTER I DIGNITY   582
    Article 1 - Human dignity   582
    Article 2 - Right to life   582
    Article 3 - Right to the integrity of the person   582
    Article 4 - Prohibition of torture and inhuman or degrading
treatment or punishment   582
    Article 5 - Prohibition of slavery and forced labour   582
    CHAPTER II FREEDOMS   583
    Article 6 - Right to liberty and security   583
    Article 7 - Respect for private and family life   583
    Article 8 - Protection of personal data   583
    Article 9 - Right to marry and right to found a family   583
    Article 10 - Freedom of thought, conscience and religion   583
    Article 11 - Freedom of expression and information   583
    Article 12 - Freedom of assembly and of association   583
    Article 13 - Freedom of the arts and sciences   584
    Article 14 - Right to education   584
    Article 15 - Freedom to choose an occupation and right to engage in work   584
    Article 16 - Freedom to conduct a business   584
    Article 17 - Right to property   584
    Article 18 - Right to asylum   585
    Article 19 - Protection in the event of removal, expulsion or extradition   585
APEC PRIVACY FRAMEWORK   586
    References   586
    Part I. Preamble   586
    Part II. Scope   588

Definitions   588
   Application   589
Part III. APEC Information Privacy Principles   590
   I. Preventing Harm   590
   II. Notice   590
   III. Collection Limitation   592
   IV. Uses of Personal Information   592
   V.   Choice   593
   VI. Integrity of Personal Information   594
   VII. Security Safeguards   594
   VIII. Access and Correction   595
   IX. Accountability   597
Part IV. Implementation   598
   A. Guidance for Domestic Implementation   598
     I. Maximizing Benefits of Privacy Protections and Information Flows   598
     II. Giving Effect to the APEC Privacy Framework   598
     III. Educating and publicising domestic privacy protections   599
     IV. Cooperation between the Public and Private Sectors   599
     V. Providing for appropriate remedies in situations where
     privacy protections are violated   599
     VI. Mechanism for Reporting Domestic Implementation of the
     APEC Privacy Framework   600
   B. Guidance for International Implementation   600
     I. Information sharing among Member Economies   600
     II. Cross-border Cooperation in Investigation and Enforcement   600
     III. Cooperative Development of Cross-border Privacy Rules   601
CAIRO DECLARATION OF HUMAN RIGHTS IN ISLAM [EXCERPT]   603
   References   603
DECLARATION OF PRINCIPLES ON FREEDOM OF
EXPRESSION IN AFRICA [EXCERPT]   605
   References   605
   Preamble   605
   IV. Freedom of Information   606
DECLARATION OF SANTA CRUZ DE LA SIERRA   607
   References   607
MADRID DECLARATION   608
   References   608

RECENT DEVELOPMENTS   **611**

UN RESOLUTION ON RIGHT TO PRIVACY (2014)   611
   References   611
EU-US "UMBRELLA AGREEMENT" (2015)   616
   Summary   616
   References   616
   Article 1: Purpose of the Agreement   617
   Article 2: Definitions   617
   Article 3: Scope   618
   Article 4: Non-Discrimination   618
   Article 5: Effect of the Agreement   618
   Article 6: Purpose and Use Limitations   619
   Article 7: Onward Transfer   619
   Article 8: Maintaining Quality and Integrity of Information   620
   Article 9: Information Security   621
   Article 10: Notification of an information security incident   621

Article 11: Maintaining Records 622
Article 12: Retention Period 622
Article 13: Special Categories of Personal Information 622
Article 14: Accountability 623
Article 15: Automated Decisilons 623
Article 16: Access 623
Article 17: Rectification 624
Article 18: Administrative Redress 625
Article 19: Judicial Redress 625
Article 20: Transparency 626
Article 21: Effective Oversight 626
Article 22: Cooperation between oversight authorities 627
Article 23: Joint Review 627
Article 24: Notification 627
Article 25: Consultation 627
Article 26: Suspension 628
Article 27: Territorial application 628
Article 28: Duration of the Agreement 628
Article 29: Entry into force and Termination 628
US CYBERSECURITY INFORMATION SHARING ACT OF 2015 630
Summary 630
References 630
§1501. Definitions 630
§1502. Sharing of information by the Federal Government 633
§1503. Authorizations for preventing, detecting, analyzing, and
mitigating cybersecurity threats 635
§1504. Sharing of cyber threat indicators and defensive
measures with the Federal Government 639
§1505. Protection from liability 647
§1506. Oversight of government activities 648
§1507. Construction and preemption 650
§1508. Report on cybersecurity threats 653
§1509. Exception to limitation on authority of Secretary of Defense
to disseminate certain information 654
§1510. Effective period 654
US DRIVER PRIVACY ACT OF 2015 655
Summary 655
References 655
SEC. 24301. SHORT TITLE. 655
SEC. 24302. LIMITATIONS ON DATA RETRIEVAL FROM
VEHICLE EVENT DATA RECORDERS 655
SEC. 24303. VEHICLE EVENT DATA RECORDER STUDY. 656
EU-US "PRIVACY SHIELD" 657
Summary 657
References 657
I. OVERVIEW 657
II. PRINCIPLES 660
1. Notice 660
2. Choice 661
3. Accountability for Onward Transfer 662
4. Security 662
5. Data Integrity and Purpose Limitation 662
6. Access 663
7. Recourse, Enforcement and Liability 663

EU GENERAL DATA PROTECTION REGULATION (2016)   666
  Summary   666
  References   666
  CHAPTER I: General provisions   666
    Article 1: Subject-matter and objectives   666
    Article 2: Material scope   667
    Article 3: Territorial scope   667
    Article 4: Definitions   668
  CHAPTER II: Principles   671
    Article 5: Principles relating to processing of personal data   671
    Article 6: Lawfulness of processing   671
    Article 7: Conditions for consent   673
    Article 8: Conditions applicable to child's consent in relation to
    information society services   673
    Article 9: Processing of special categories of personal data   674
    Article 10: Processing of personal data relating to criminal
    convictions and offences   675
    Article 11: Processing which does not require identification   675
  CHAPTER III: Rights of the data subject   676
  Section 1: Transparency and modalities   676
    Article 12: Transparent information, communication and modalities for
    the exercise of the rights of the data subject   676
  Section 2: Information and access to personal data   677
    Article 13: Information to be provided where personal data are collected
    from the data subject   677
    Article 14: Information to be provided where personal data have not
    been obtained
    from the data subject   678
    Article 15: Right of access by the data subject   680
  Section 3: Rectification and erasure   681
    Article 16: Right to rectification   681
    Article 17: Right to erasure ('right to be forgotten')   681
    Article 18: Right to restriction of processing   682
    Article 19: Notification obligation regarding rectification or erasure of
    personal data or restriction of processing   682
    Article 20: Right to data portability   682
  Section 4: Right to object and automated individual decision-making   683
    Article 21: Right to object   683
    Article 22: Automated individual decision-making, including profiling   684
  Section 5: Restrictions   684
    Article 23: Restrictions   684
  CHAPTER IV: Controller and processor   685
  Section 1: General obligations   685
    Article 24: Responsibility of the controller   685
    Article 25: Data protection by design and by default   685
    Article 26: Joint controllers   686
    Article 27: Representatives of controllers or processors not
    established in the Union   686
    Article 28: Processor   687
    Article 29: Processing under the authority of the controller or processor   689
    Article 30: Records of processing activities   689
    Article 31: Cooperation with the supervisory authority   690
  Section 2: Security of personal data   690
    Article 32: Security of processing   690

Article 33: Notification of a personal data breach to the
supervisory authority   691
Article 34: Communication of a personal data breach to the data subject   691
Section 3: Data protection impact assessment and prior consultation   692
Article 35: Data protection impact assessment   692
Article 36: Prior consultation   694
Section 4: Data protection officer   694
Article 37: Designation of the data protection officer   694
Article 38: Position of the data protection officer   695
Article 39: Tasks of the data protection officer   696
Section 5: Codes of conduct and certification   696
Article 40: Codes of conduct   696
Article 41: Monitoring of approved codes of conduct   698
Article 42: Certification   699
Article 43: Certification bodies   700
CHAPTER V: Transfers of personal data to third countries or
international organisations   701
Article 44: General principle for transfers   701
Article 45: Transfers on the basis of an adequacy decision   701
Article 46: Transfers subject to appropriate safeguards   703
Article 47: Binding corporate rules   704
Article 48: Transfers or disclosures not authorised by Union law   705
Article 49: Derogations for specific situations   706
Article 50: International cooperation for the protection of personal data 707
CHAPTER VI: Independent supervisory authorities   707
Section 1: Independent status   707
Article 51: Supervisory authority   707
Article 52: Independence   708
Article 53: General conditions for the members of the supervisory authority 708
Article 54: Rules on the establishment of the supervisory authority   709
Section 2: Competence, tasks and powers   710
Article 55: Competence   710
Article 56: Competence of the lead supervisory authority   710
Article 57: Tasks   711
Article 58: Powers   712
Article 59: Activity reports   714
CHAPTER VII: Cooperation and consistency   714
Section 1: Cooperation   714
Article 60: Cooperation between the lead supervisory authority and the
other supervisory authorities concerned   714
Article 61: Mutual assistance   716
Article 62: Joint operations of supervisory authorities   717
Section 2: Consistency   718
Article 63: Consistency mechanism   718
Article 64: Opinion of the Board   718
Article 65: Dispute resolution by the Board   719
Article 66: Urgency procedure   720
Article 67: Exchange of information   721
Section 3: European data protection board   721
Article 68: European Data Protection Board   721
Article 69: Independence   721
Article 70: Tasks of the Board   721
Article 71: Reports   724
Article 72: Procedure   724

Article 73: Chair   724
Article 74: Tasks of the Chair   724
Article 75: Secretariat   725
Article 76: Confidentiality   725
CHAPTER VIII: Remedies, liability and penalties   725
Article 77: Right to lodge a complaint with a supervisory authority   725
Article 78: Right to an effective judicial remedy against a
supervisory authority   726
Article 79: Right to an effective judicial remedy against a
controller or processor   726
Article 80: Representation of data subjects   726
Article 81: Suspension of proceedings   727
Article 82: Right to compensation and liability   727
Article 83: General conditions for imposing administrative fines   728
Article 84: Penalties   730
CHAPTER IX: Provisions relating to specific processing situations   730
Article 85: Processing and freedom of expression and information   730
Article 86: Processing and public access to official documents   730
Article 87: Processing of the national identification number   730
Article 88: Processing in the context of employment   731
Article 89: Safeguards and derogations relating to processing for
archiving purposes in the public interest, scientific or historical research
purposes or statistical purposes   731
Article 90: Obligations of secrecy   732
Article 91: Existing data protection rules of churches and
religious associations   732
CHAPTER X: Delegated acts and implementing acts   732
Article 92: Exercise of the delegation   732
Article 93: Committee procedure   733
CHAPTER XI: Final provisions   733
Article 94: Repeal of Directive 95/46/EC   733
Article 95: Relationship with Directive 2002/58/EC   733
Article 96: Relationship with previously concluded Agreements   733
Article 97: Commission reports   734
Article 98: Review of other Union legal acts on data protection   734
Article 99: Entry into force and application   734

SELECTED BIBLIOGRAPHY   **735**

PRIVACY RESOURCES   **741**

PRIVACY YEAR IN REVIEW 2015–2016   741

AGENCIES   751
  Angola   751
  Argentina   751
  Australia   751
  Austria   751
  Belgium   751
  Bosnia and Herzegovina   751
  Brazil   751
  Bulgaria   751
  Canada   751
  Cape Verde   752
  Croatia   752
  Cyprus   752

Czech Republic   752
Denmark   752
Estonia   752
Finland   752
France   752
Germany   752
Ghana   753
Gibraltar   753
Greece   753
Hong Kong   753
Hungary   753
Iceland   753
Ireland   753
Israel   753
Italy   753
Japan   754
Latvia   754
Luxembourg   754
Lithuania   754
Macau   754
Macedonia   754
Malaysia   754
Malta   754
Mauritius   754
Mexico   754
Monaco   755
Montenegro   755
Morocco   755
Netherlands   755
New Zealand   755
Norway   755
Peru   755
Poland   755
Portugal   755
Romania   756
Russia   756
Serbia   756
Singapore   756
Slovak Republic   756
Spain   756
Sweden   756
Switzerland   756
Taiwan   756
United Kingdom   757
Uruguay   757
NATIONAL LEGISLATION   758
    References   758
ORGANIZATIONS   767
    US Organizations   767
    International Organizations   773
PUBLICATIONS   776
    US Publications   776
    International Publications   776
    Reports   777

WEBSITES   779
    General Interest   779
    Government   780
    Legal   781

United States Law

FEDERAL TRADE COMMISSION ACT
(1914)

Summary

In 1914 Congress passed the Federal Trade Commission Act (FTCA) to protect consumers from deceptive practices and unfair methods of competition. An unfair method of competition is defined under section 45(n) as "one that causes or is likely to cause substantial injury to consumers which is not reasonably avoidable by consumers themselves and not outweighed by countervailing benefits to consumers or to competition."

The Act created the Federal Trade Commission to regulate and enforce its provisions. It gave the FTC authority to investigate unfair practices, to pursue complaints, to issue reports, and to enforce orders. Thus, if the FTC finds that a practice violates the Act it may issue an order requiring the individual or entity to cease from using such method or practice. The individual or entity subject to the order may request to a court to review the order. If the court finds the practice to be unfair or deceptive it may impose preliminary/permanent injunctions or a penalty of no more than $10,000 for each violation of the FTC order.

References

Federal Trade Commission, Privacy Initiatives
[https://www.ftc.gov/tips-advice/business-center/privacy-and-security]

EPIC, Federal Trade Commission
[https://www.epic.org/privacy/internet/ftc/]

§ 45. Unfair methods of competition unlawful; prevention by Commission

(a) Declaration of unlawfulness; power to prohibit unfair practices; inapplicability to foreign trade

> (1) Unfair methods of competition in or affecting commerce, and unfair or deceptive acts or practices in or affecting commerce, are hereby declared unlawful.
> (2) The Commission is hereby empowered and directed to prevent persons, partnerships, or corporations, except banks, savings and loan institutions described in section 57a(f)(3) of this title, Federal credit unions described in section 57a(f)(4) of this title, common carriers subject to the Acts to regulate commerce, air carriers and foreign air carriers subject to part A of subtitle VII of title 49, and persons, partnerships, or corporations insofar as they are subject to the Packers and Stockyards Act, 1921, as amended (7 U.S.C. 181 et seq.), except as provided in section 406(b) of said Act (7 U.S.C. 227(b)), from using unfair methods of

competition in or affecting commerce and unfair or deceptive acts or practices in or affecting commerce.

(3) This subsection shall not apply to unfair methods of competition involving commerce with foreign nations (other than import commerce) unless -

(A) such methods of competition have a direct, substantial, and reasonably foreseeable effect -

(i) on commerce which is not commerce with foreign nations, or on import commerce with foreign nations; or

(ii) on export commerce with foreign nations, of a person engaged in such commerce in the United States; and

(B) such effect gives rise to a claim under the provisions of this subsection, other than this paragraph. If this subsection applies to such methods of competition only because of the operation of subparagraph (A)(ii), this subsection shall apply to such conduct only for injury to export business in the United States.

(b) Proceeding by Commission; modifying and setting aside orders

Whenever the Commission shall have reason to believe that any such person, partnership, or corporation has been or is using any unfair method of competition or unfair or deceptive act or practice in or affecting commerce, and if it shall appear to the Commission that a proceeding by it in respect thereof would be to the interest of the public, it shall issue and serve upon such person, partnership, or corporation a complaint stating its charges in that respect and containing a notice of a hearing upon a day and at a place therein fixed at least thirty days after the service of said complaint. The person, partnership, or corporation so complained of shall have the right to appear at the place and time so fixed and show cause why an order should not be entered by the Commission requiring such person, partnership, or corporation to cease and desist from the violation of the law so charged in said complaint. Any person, partnership, or corporation may make application, and upon good cause shown may be allowed by the Commission to intervene and appear in said proceeding by counsel or in person. The testimony in any such proceeding shall be reduced to writing and filed in the office of the Commission. If upon such hearing the Commission shall be of the opinion that the method of competition or the act or practice in question is prohibited by this subchapter, it shall make a report in writing in which it shall state its findings as to the facts and shall issue and cause to be served on such person, partnership, or corporation an order requiring such person, partnership, or corporation to cease and desist from using such method of competition or such act or practice. Until the expiration of the time allowed for filing a petition for review, if no such petition has been duly filed within such time, or, if a petition for review has been filed within such time then until the record in the proceeding has been filed in a court of appeals of the United States, as hereinafter provided, the Commission may at any time, upon such notice and in such manner as it shall deem proper, modify or set aside, in whole or in part, any report or any order made or issued by it under this section. After the expiration of the time allowed for filing a petition for review, if no such petition has been duly filed within such time, the Commission may at any time, after notice and opportunity for hearing, reopen and alter, modify, or set aside, in whole or in part any report or order made or issued by it under this section, whenever in the opinion of the Commission conditions of fact or of law have so changed as to require such action or if the public interest shall so require, except that (1) the said person, partnership, or corporation may, within sixty days after service upon him or it of said report or order entered after such a reopening, obtain a review thereof in the appropriate court of appeals of the United States, in the manner provided in subsection (c) of this section; and (2) in the case of an order, the Commission shall reopen any such order to consider whether such order (including any affirmative relief provision contained in such order) should be altered, modified, or set aside, in whole or in part, if the person, partnership, or corporation involved files a request with the Commission which makes a satisfactory showing that changed conditions of law or fact require such order to be altered, modified, or set aside, in whole or in part. The Commission shall determine whether to alter, modify, or set aside any order of the Commission in response to a request made by a person, partnership, or corporation under paragraph (2) not later than 120 days after the date of the filing of such request.

(c) Review of order; rehearing

Any person, partnership, or corporation required by an order of the Commission to cease and desist from using any method of competition or act or practice may obtain a review of such order in the court of appeals of the United States, within any circuit where the method of competition or the act or practice in question was used or where such person, partnership, or corporation resides or carries on business, by filing in the court, within sixty days from the date of the service of such order, a written petition praying that the order of the Commission be set aside. A copy of such petition shall be forthwith transmitted by the clerk of the court to the Commission, and thereupon the Commission shall file in the court the record in the proceeding, as provided in section 2112 of title 28. Upon such filing of the petition the court shall have jurisdiction of the proceeding and of the question determined therein concurrently with the Commission until the filing of the record and shall have power to make and enter a decree affirming, modifying, or setting aside the order of the Commission, and enforcing the same to the extent that such order is affirmed and to issue such writs as are ancillary to its jurisdiction or are necessary in its judgment to prevent injury to the public or to competitors pendente lite. The findings of the Commission as to the facts, if supported by evidence, shall be conclusive. To the extent that the order of the Commission is affirmed, the court shall thereupon issue its own order commanding obedience to the terms of such order of the Commission. If either party shall apply to the court for leave to adduce additional evidence, and shall show to the satisfaction of the court that such additional evidence is material and that there were reasonable grounds for the failure to adduce such evidence in the proceeding before the Commission, the court may order such additional evidence to be taken before the Commission and to be adduced upon the hearing in such manner and upon such terms and conditions as to the court may seem proper. The Commission may modify its findings as to the facts, or make new findings, by reason of the additional evidence so taken, and it shall file such modified or new findings, which, if supported by evidence, shall be conclusive, and its recommendation, if any, for the modification or setting aside of its original order, with the return of such additional evidence. The judgment and decree of the court shall be final, except that the same shall be subject to review by the Supreme Court upon certiorari, as provided in section 1254 of title 28.

(d) Jurisdiction of court

Upon the filing of the record with it the jurisdiction of the court of appeals of the United States to affirm, enforce, modify, or set aside orders of the Commission shall be exclusive.

(e) Exemption from liability

No order of the Commission or judgment of court to enforce the same shall in anywise relieve or absolve any person, partnership, or corporation from any liability under the Antitrust Acts.

(f) Service of complaints, orders and other processes; return

Complaints, orders, and other processes of the Commission under this section may be served by anyone duly authorized by the Commission, either (a) by delivering a copy thereof to the person to be served, or to a member of the partnership to be served, or the president, secretary, or other executive officer or a director of the corporation to be served; or (b) by leaving a copy thereof at the residence or the principal office or place of business of such person, partnership, or corporation; or (c) by mailing a copy thereof by registered mail or by certified mail addressed to such person, partnership, or corporation at his or its residence or principal office or place of business. The verified return by the person so serving said complaint, order, or other process setting forth the manner of said service shall be proof of the same, and the return post office receipt for said complaint, order, or other process mailed by registered mail or by certified mail as aforesaid shall be proof of the service of the same.

(g) Finality of order

An order of the Commission to cease and desist shall become final -

(1) Upon the expiration of the time allowed for filing a petition for review, if no such petition has been duly filed within such time; but the Commission may thereafter modify or set aside its order to the extent provided in the last sentence of subsection (b).

(2) Except as to any order provision subject to paragraph (4), upon the sixtieth day after such order is served, if a petition for review has been duly filed; except that any such order may be stayed, in whole or in part and subject to such conditions as may be appropriate, by -

(A) the Commission;

(B) an appropriate court of appeals of the United States, if

(i) a petition for review of such order is pending in such court, and (ii) an application for such a stay was previously submitted to the Commission and the Commission, within the 30-day period beginning on the date the application was received by the Commission, either denied the application or did not grant or deny the application; or

(C) the Supreme Court, if an applicable petition for certiorari is pending.

(3) For purposes of subsection (m)(1)(B) of this section and of section 57b(a)(2) of this title, if a petition for review of the order of the Commission has been filed -

(A) upon the expiration of the time allowed for filing a petition for certiorari, if the order of the Commission has been affirmed or the petition for review has been dismissed by the court of appeals and no petition for certiorari has been duly filed;

(B) upon the denial of a petition for certiorari, if the order of the Commission has been affirmed or the petition for review has been dismissed by the court of appeals; or

(C) upon the expiration of 30 days from the date of issuance of a mandate of the Supreme Court directing that the order of the Commission be affirmed or the petition for review be dismissed.

(4) In the case of an order provision requiring a person, partnership, or corporation to divest itself of stock, other share capital, or assets, if a petition for review of such order of the Commission has been filed -

(A) upon the expiration of the time allowed for filing a petition for certiorari, if the order of the Commission has been affirmed or the petition for review has been dismissed by the court of appeals and no petition for certiorari has been duly filed;

(B) upon the denial of a petition for certiorari, if the order of the Commission has been affirmed or the petition for review has been dismissed by the court of appeals; or

(C) upon the expiration of 30 days from the date of issuance of a mandate of the Supreme Court directing that the order of the Commission be affirmed or the petition for review be dismissed.

(h) Modification or setting aside of order by Supreme Court

If the Supreme Court directs that the order of the Commission be modified or set aside, the order of the Commission rendered in accordance with the mandate of the Supreme Court shall become final upon the expiration of thirty days from the time it was rendered, unless within such thirty days either party has instituted proceedings to have such order corrected to accord with the mandate, in which event the order of the Commission shall become final when so corrected.

(i) Modification or setting aside of order by Court of Appeals

If the order of the Commission is modified or set aside by the court of appeals, and if (1) the time allowed for filing a petition for certiorari has expired and no such petition has been duly filed, or (2) the petition for certiorari has been denied, or (3) the decision of the court has been affirmed by the Supreme Court, then the order of the Commission rendered in accordance with the mandate of the court of appeals shall become final on the expiration of thirty days from the time such order of the Commission was rendered, unless within such thirty days either party has instituted proceedings to have such order corrected so that it will accord with the mandate, in which event the order of the Commission shall become final when so corrected.

(j) Rehearing upon order or remand

If the Supreme Court orders a rehearing; or if the case is remanded by the court of appeals to the Commission for a rehearing, and if (1) the time allowed for filing a petition for certiorari has expired, and no such petition has been duly filed, or (2) the petition for certiorari has been denied, or (3) the decision of the court has been affirmed by the Supreme Court, then the order of the Commission rendered upon such rehearing shall become final in the same manner as though no prior order of the Commission had been rendered.

(k) "Mandate" defined

As used in this section the term "mandate", in case a mandate has been recalled prior to the expiration of thirty days from the date of issuance thereof, means the final mandate.

(l) Penalty for violation of order; injunctions and other appropriate equitable relief

Any person, partnership, or corporation who violates an order of the Commission after it has become final, and while such order is in effect, shall forfeit and pay to the United States a civil penalty of not more than $10,000 for each violation, which shall accrue to the United States and may be recovered in a civil action brought by the Attorney General of the United States. Each separate violation of such an order shall be a separate offense, except that in a case of a violation through continuing failure to obey or neglect to obey a final order of the Commission, each day of continuance of such failure or neglect shall be deemed a separate offense. In such actions, the United States district courts are empowered to grant mandatory injunctions and such other and further equitable relief as they deem appropriate in the enforcement of such final orders of the Commission.

(m) Civil actions for recovery of penalties for knowing violations of rules and cease and desist orders respecting unfair or deceptive acts or practices; jurisdiction; maximum amount of penalties; continuing violations; de novo determinations; compromise or settlement procedure

(1)(A) The Commission may commence a civil action to recover a civil penalty in a district court of the United States against any person, partnership, or corporation which violates any rule under this chapter respecting unfair or deceptive acts or practices (other than an interpretive rule or a rule violation of which the Commission has provided is not an unfair or deceptive act or practice in violation of subsection (a)(1) of this section) with actual knowledge or knowledge fairly implied on the basis of objective circumstances that such act is unfair or deceptive and is prohibited by such rule. In such action, such person, partnership, or corporation shall be liable for a civil penalty of not more than $10,000 for each violation.

(B) If the Commission determines in a proceeding under subsection (b) of this section that any act or practice is unfair or deceptive, and issues a final cease and desist order, other than a consent order, with respect to such act or practice, then the Commission may commence a civil action to obtain a civil penalty in a district court of the United States against any person, partnership, or corporation which engages in such act or practice -

(1) after such cease and desist order becomes final (whether or not such person, partnership, or corporation was subject to such cease and desist order), and

(2) with actual knowledge that such act or practice is unfair or deceptive and is unlawful under subsection (a)(1)

of this section. In such action, such person, partnership, or corporation shall be liable for a civil penalty of not more than $10,000 for each violation.

(C) In the case of a violation through continuing failure to comply with a rule or with subsection (a)(1) of this section, each day of continuance of such failure shall be treated as a separate violation, for purposes of subparagraphs (A) and

(B). In determining the amount of such a civil penalty, the court shall take into account the degree of culpability, any history of prior such conduct, ability to pay, effect on ability to continue to do business, and such other matters as justice may require.

(2) If the cease and desist order establishing that the act or practice is unfair or deceptive was not issued against the defendant in a civil penalty action under paragraph (1)(B) the issues of fact in such action against such defendant shall be tried de novo. Upon request of any party to such an action against such defendant, the court shall also review the determination of law made by the Commission in the proceeding under subsection (b) of this section that the act or practice which was the subject of such proceeding constituted an unfair or deceptive act or practice in violation of subsection (a) of this section.

(3) The Commission may compromise or settle any action for a civil penalty if such compromise or settlement is accompanied by a public statement of its reasons and is approved by the court.

(n) Standard of proof; public policy consideration

The Commission shall have no authority under this section or section 57a of this title to declare unlawful an act or practice on the grounds that such act or practice is unfair unless the act or practice causes or is likely to cause substantial injury to consumers which is not reasonably avoidable by consumers themselves and not outweighed by countervailing benefits to consumers or to competition. In determining whether an act or practice is unfair, the Commission may consider established public policies as evidence to be considered with all other evidence. Such public policy considerations may not serve as a primary basis for such determination.

§ 46. Additional powers of Commission

The Commission shall also have power -

(a) Investigation of persons, partnerships, or corporations

To gather and compile information concerning, and to investigate from time to time the organization, business, conduct, practices, and management of any person, partnership, or corporation engaged in or whose business affects commerce, excepting banks, savings and loan institutions described in section 57a(f)(3) of this title, Federal credit unions described in section 57a(f)(4) of this title, and common carriers subject to the Act to regulate commerce, and its relation to other persons, partnerships, and corporations.

(b) Reports of persons, partnerships, and corporations

To require, by general or special orders, persons, partnerships, and corporations, engaged in or whose business affects commerce, excepting banks, savings and loan institutions described in section 57a(f)(3) of this title, Federal credit unions described in section 57a(f)(4) of this title, and common carriers subject to the Act to regulate commerce, or any class of them, or any of them, respectively, to file with the Commission in such form as the Commission may prescribe annual or special, or both annual and special, reports, or answers in writing to specific questions, furnishing to the Commission such information as it may require as to the organization, business, conduct, practices, management, and relation to other corporations, partnerships, and individuals of the respective persons, partnerships, and corporations filing such reports or answers in writing. Such reports and answers shall be made under oath, or otherwise, as the Commission may prescribe, and shall be filed with the Commission within such reasonable period as the Commission may prescribe, unless additional time be granted in any case by the Commission.

(c) Investigation of compliance with antitrust decrees

Whenever a final decree has been entered against any defendant corporation in any suit brought by the United States to prevent and restrain any violation of the antitrust Acts, to make investigation, upon its own initiative, of the manner in which the decree has been or is being carried out, and upon the application of the Attorney General it shall be its duty to make such investigation. It shall transmit to the Attorney General a report embodying its findings and recommendations as a result of any such investigation, and the report shall be made public in the discretion of the Commission.

(d) Investigations of violations of antitrust statutes

Upon the direction of the President or either House of Congress to investigate and report the facts relating to any alleged violations of the antitrust Acts by any corporation.

(e) Readjustment of business of corporations violating antitrust statutes.

Upon the application of the Attorney General to investigate and make recommendations for the readjustment of the business of any corporation alleged to be violating the antitrust Acts in order that the corporation may thereafter maintain its organization, management, and conduct of business in accordance with law.

(f) Publication of information; reports

To make public from time to time such portions of the information obtained by it hereunder as are in the public interest; and to make annual and special reports to the Congress and to submit therewith recommendations for additional legislation; and to provide for the publication of its reports and decisions in such form and manner as may be best adapted for public information and use: Provided, That the Commission shall not have any authority to make public any trade secret or any commercial or financial information which is obtained from any person and which is privileged or confidential, except that the Commission may disclose such information to officers and employees of appropriate Federal law enforcement agencies or to any officer or employee of any State law enforcement agency upon the prior certification of an officer of any such Federal or State law enforcement agency that such information will be maintained in confidence and will be used only for official law enforcement purposes.

(g) Classification of corporations; regulations

From time to time classify corporations and (except as provided in section 57a(a)(2) of this title) to make rules and regulations for the purpose of carrying out the provisions of this subchapter.

(h) Investigations of foreign trade conditions; reports

To investigate, from time to time, trade conditions in and with foreign countries where associations, combinations, or practices of manufacturers, merchants, or traders, or other conditions, may affect the foreign trade of the United States, and to report to Congress thereon, with such recommendations as it deems advisable.

(i) Investigations of foreign antitrust law violations

With respect to the International Antitrust Enforcement Assistance Act of 1994 (15 U.S.C. 6201 et seq.), to conduct investigations of possible violations of foreign antitrust laws (as defined in section 12 of such Act (15 U.S.C. 6211)). Provided, That the exception of "banks, savings and loan institutions described in section 57a(f)(3) of this title, Federal credit unions described in section 57a(f)(4) of this title, and common carriers subject to the Act to regulate commerce" from the Commission's powers defined in clauses (a) and (b) of this section, shall not be construed to limit the Commission's authority to gather and compile information, to investigate, or to require reports or answers from, any person, partnership, or corporation to the extent that such action is necessary to the investigation of any person, partnership, or corporation, group of persons, partnerships, or corporations, or industry which is not engaged or is engaged only incidentally in banking, in business as a savings and loan institution, in business as a Federal credit union, or in business as a common carrier subject to the Act to regulate commerce.

The Commission shall establish a plan designed to substantially reduce burdens imposed upon small businesses as a result of requirements established by the Commission under clause (b) relating to the filing of quarterly financial reports. Such plan shall (1) be established after consultation with small businesses and persons who use the information contained in such quarterly financial reports; (2) provide for a reduction of the number of small businesses required to file such quarterly financial reports; and (3) make revisions in the forms used for such quarterly financial reports for the purpose of reducing the complexity of such forms. The Commission, not later than December 31, 1980, shall submit such plan to the Committee on Commerce, Science, and Transportation of the Senate and to the Committee on Energy and Commerce of the House of Representatives. Such plan shall take effect not later than October 31, 1981.

No officer or employee of the Commission or any Commissioner may publish or disclose information to the public, or to any Federal agency, whereby any line-of-business data furnished by a particular establishment or individual can be identified. No one other than designated sworn officers and employees of the Commission may examine the line-of-business reports from individual firms, and information provided in the line-of-business program administered by the Commission shall be used only for statistical purposes.

Information for carrying out specific law enforcement responsibilities of the Commission shall be obtained under practices and procedures in effect on May 28, 1980, or as changed by law.

Nothing in this section (other than the provisions of clause (c) and clause (d)) shall apply to the business of insurance, except that the Commission shall have authority to conduct studies and prepare reports relating to the business of insurance. The Commission may exercise such authority only upon receiving a request which is agreed to by a majority of the members of the Committee on Commerce, Science, and Transportation of the Senate or the Committee on Energy and Commerce of the House of Representatives. The authority to conduct any such study shall expire at the end of the Congress during which the request for such study was made.

§ 57a. Unfair or deceptive acts or practices rulemaking proceedings

(a) Authority of Commission to prescribe rules and general statements of policy

(1) Except as provided in subsection (h) of this section, the Commission may prescribe -

(A) interpretive rules and general statements of policy with respect to unfair or deceptive acts or practices in or affecting commerce (within the meaning of section 45(a)(1) of this title), and

(B) rules which define with specificity acts or practices which are unfair or deceptive acts or practices in or affecting commerce (within the meaning of section 45(a)(1) of this title), except that the Commission shall not develop or promulgate any trade rule or regulation with regard to the regulation of the development and utilization of the standards and certification activities pursuant to this section. Rules under this subparagraph may include requirements prescribed for the purpose of preventing such acts or practices.

(2) The Commission shall have no authority under this subchapter, other than its authority under this section, to prescribe any rule with respect to unfair or deceptive acts or practices in or affecting commerce (within the meaning of section 45(a)(1) of this title). The preceding sentence shall not affect any authority of the Commission to prescribe rules (including interpretive rules), and general statements of policy, with respect to unfair methods of competition in or affecting commerce.

(b) Procedures applicable

(1) When prescribing a rule under subsection (a)(1)(B) of this section, the Commission shall proceed in accordance with section 553 of title 5 (without regard to any reference in such section to sections 556 and 557 of such title), and shall also

(A) publish a notice of proposed rulemaking stating with particularity the text of the rule, including any alternatives, which the Commission proposes to promulgate, and the reason for the proposed rule;

(B) allow interested persons to submit written data, views, and arguments, and make all such submissions publicly available;

(C) provide an opportunity for an informal hearing in accordance with subsection (c) of this section; and

(D) promulgate, if appropriate, a final rule based on the matter in the rulemaking record (as defined in subsection (e)(1)(B) of section), together with a statement of basis and purpose.

(2)(A) Prior to the publication of any notice of proposed rulemaking pursuant to paragraph (1)(A), Commission shall publish an advance notice of proposed rulemaking in the Federal Register. Such advance notice shall -

(i) contain a brief description of the area of inquiry under consideration, the objectives which the Commission seeks to achieve, and possible regulatory alternatives under consideration by the Commission; and

(ii) invite the response of interested parties with respect to such proposed rulemaking, including any suggestions or alternative methods for achieving such objectives.

(B) The Commission shall submit such advance notice of proposed rulemaking to the Committee on Commerce, Science, and Transportation of the Senate and to the Committee on Energy and Commerce of the House of Representatives. The Commission may use such additional mechanisms as the Commission considers useful to obtain suggestions regarding the content of the area of inquiry before the publication of a general notice of proposed rulemaking under paragraph (1)(A).

(C) The Commission shall, 30 days before the publication of a notice of proposed rulemaking pursuant to paragraph (1)(A), submit such notice to the Committee on Commerce, Science, and Transportation of the Senate and to the Committee on Energy and Commerce of the House of Representatives.

(3) The Commission shall issue a notice of proposed rulemaking pursuant to paragraph (1)(A) only where it has reason to believe that the unfair or deceptive acts or practices which are the subject of the proposed rulemaking are prevalent. The Commission shall make a determination that unfair or deceptive acts or practices are prevalent under this paragraph only if -

(A) it has issued cease and desist orders regarding such acts or practices, or

(B) any other information available to the Commission indicates a widespread pattern of unfair or deceptive acts or practices.

(c) Informal hearing procedure

The Commission shall conduct any informal hearings required by subsection (b)(1)(C) of this section in accordance with the following procedure:

(1) (A) The Commission shall provide for the conduct of proceedings under this subsection by hearing officers who shall perform their functions in accordance with the requirements of this subsection

(B) The officer who presides over the rulemaking proceedings shall be responsible to a chief presiding officer who shall not be responsible to any other officer or employee of the Commission. The officer who presides over the rulemaking proceeding shall make a recommended decision based upon the findings and conclusions of such officer as to all relevant and material evidence, except that such recommended decision may be made by another officer if the officer who presided over the proceeding is no longer available to the Commission.

(C) Except as required for the disposition of ex parte matters as authorized by law, no presiding officer shall consult any person or party with respect to any fact in issue unless such officer gives notice and opportunity for all parties to participate.

(2) Subject to paragraph (3) of this subsection, an interested person is entitled -

(A) to present his position orally or by documentary submission (or both), and

(B) if the Commission determines that there are disputed issues of material fact it is necessary to resolve, to present such rebuttal submissions and to conduct (or have conducted under paragraph (3)(B)) such cross-examination of persons as the Commission determines

(i) to be appropriate, and

(ii) to be required for a full and true disclosure with respect to such issues.

(3) The Commission may prescribe such rules and make such rulings concerning proceedings in such hearings as may tend to avoid unnecessary costs or delay. Such rules or rulings may include

(A) imposition of reasonable time limits on each interested person's oral presentations, and (B) requirements that any cross-examination to which a person may be entitled under paragraph (2) be conducted by the Commission on behalf of that person in such manner as the Commission determines

(i) to be appropriate, and

(ii) to be required for a full and true disclosure with respect to disputed issues of material fact.

(4) (A) Except as provided in subparagraph (B), if a group of persons each of whom under paragraphs (2) and (3) would be entitled to conduct (or have conducted) cross-examination and who are determined by the Commission to have the same or similar interests in the proceeding cannot agree upon a single representative of such interests for purposes of cross-examination, the Commission may make rules and rulings

(i) limiting the representation of such interest, for such purposes, and (ii) governing the manner in which such cross-examination shall be limited.

(B) When any person who is a member of a group with respect to which the Commission has made a determination under subparagraph (A) is unable to agree upon group representation with the other members of the group, then such person shall not be denied under the authority of subparagraph (A) the opportunity to conduct (or have conducted) cross-examination as to issues affecting his particular interests if

(i) he satisfies the Commission that he has made a reasonable and good faith effort to reach agreement upon group representation with the other members of the group and

(ii) the Commission determines that there are substantial and relevant issues which are not adequately presented by the group representative.

(5) A verbatim transcript shall be taken of any oral presentation, and cross-examination, in an informal hearing to which this subsection applies. Such transcript shall be available to the public.

(d) Statement of basis and purpose accompanying rule; "Commission" defined; judicial review of amendment or repeal of rule; violation of rule

(1) The Commission's statement of basis and purpose to accompany a rule promulgated under subsection (a)(1)(B) of this section shall include

(A) a statement as to the prevalence of the acts or practices treated by the rule;

(B) a statement as to the manner and context in which such acts or practices are unfair or deceptive; and

(C) a statement as to the economic effect of the rule, taking into account the effect on small business and consumers.

(2) (A) The term "Commission" as used in this subsection and subsections (b) and (c) of this section includes any person authorized to act in behalf of the Commission in any part of the rulemaking proceeding.

(B) A substantive amendment to, or repeal of, a rule promulgated under subsection (a)(1)(B) of this section shall be prescribed, and subject to judicial review, in the same manner as a rule prescribed under such subsection. An exemption under subsection (g) of this section shall not be treated as an amendment or repeal of a rule.

(3) When any rule under subsection (a)(1)(B) of this section takes effect a subsequent violation thereof shall constitute an unfair or deceptive act or practice in violation of section 45(a)(1) of this title, unless the Commission otherwise expressly provides in such rule.

(e) Judicial review; petition; jurisdiction and venue; rulemaking record; additional submissions and presentations; scope of review and relief; review by Supreme Court; additional remedies

(1) (A) Not later than 60 days after a rule is promulgated under subsection (a)(1)(B) of this section by the Commission, any interested person (including a consumer or consumer organization) may file a petition, in the United States Court of Appeals for the District of Columbia circuit or for the circuit in which such person resides or has his principal place of business, for judicial review of such rule. Copies of the petition shall be forthwith transmitted by the clerk of the court to the Commission or other officer designated by it for that purpose. The provisions of section 2112 of title 28 shall apply to the filing of the rulemaking record of proceedings on which the Commission based its rule and to the transfer of proceedings in the courts of appeals.

(B) For purposes of this section, the term "rulemaking record" means the rule, its statement of basis and purpose, the transcript required by subsection (c)(5) of this section, any written submissions, and any other information which the Commission considers relevant to such rule.

(2) If the petitioner or the Commission applies to the court for leave to make additional oral submissions or written presentations and shows to the satisfaction of the court that such submissions and presentations would be material and that there were reasonable grounds for the submissions and failure to make such submissions and presentations in the proceeding before the Commission, the court may order the Commission to provide additional opportunity to make such submissions and presentations. The Commission may modify or set aside its rule or make a new rule by reason of the additional submissions and presentations and shall file such modified or new rule, and the rule's statement of basis of purpose,

with the return of such submissions and presentations. The court shall thereafter review such new or modified rule.

(3) Upon the filing of the petition under paragraph (1) of this subsection, the court shall have jurisdiction to review the rule in accordance with chapter 7 of title 5 and to grant appropriate relief, including interim relief, as provided in such chapter. The court shall hold unlawful and set aside the rule on any ground specified in subparagraphs (A), (B), (C), or (D) of section 706(2) of title 5 (taking due account of the rule of prejudicial error), or if -

> (A) the court finds that the Commission's action is not supported by substantial evidence in the rulemaking record (as defined in paragraph (1)(B) of this subsection) taken as a whole, or

> (B) the court finds that -

>> (i) a Commission determination under subsection (c) of this section that the petitioner is not entitled to conduct cross-examination or make rebuttal submissions, or

>> (ii) a Commission rule or ruling under subsection (c) of this section limiting the petitioner's cross-examination or rebuttal submissions, has precluded disclosure of disputed material facts which was necessary for fair determination by the Commission of the rulemaking proceeding taken as a whole. The term "evidence", as used in this paragraph, means any matter in the rulemaking record.

(4) The judgment of the court affirming or setting aside, in whole or in part, any such rule shall be final, subject to review by the Supreme Court of the United States upon certiorari or certification, as provided in section 1254 of title 28.

(5) (A) Remedies under the preceding paragraphs of this subsection are in addition to and not in lieu of any other remedies provided by law.

> (B) The United States Courts of Appeal shall have exclusive jurisdiction of any action to obtain judicial review (other than in an enforcement proceeding) of a rule prescribed under subsection (a)(1)(B) of this section, if any district court of the United States would have had jurisdiction of such action but for this subparagraph. Any such action shall be brought in the United States Court of Appeals for the District of Columbia circuit, or for any circuit which includes a judicial district in which the action could have been brought but for this subparagraph.

> (C) A determination, rule, or ruling of the Commission described in paragraph (3)(B)(i) or (ii) may be reviewed only in a proceeding under this subsection and only in accordance with paragraph (3)(B). Section 706(2)(E) of title 5 shall not apply to any rule promulgated under subsection (a)(1)(B) of this section. The contents and adequacy of any statement required by subsection (b)(1)(D) of this section shall not be subject to judicial review in any respect.

(f) Unfair or deceptive acts or practices by banks, savings and loan institutions, or Federal credit unions; promulgation of regulations by Board of Governors of Federal Reserve System, Federal Home Loan Bank Board, and National Credit Union Administration Board; agency enforcement and compliance proceedings; violations; power of other Federal agencies unaffected; reporting requirements

(1) In order to prevent unfair or deceptive acts or practices in or affecting commerce (including acts or practices which are unfair or deceptive to consumers) by banks or savings and loan institutions described in paragraph (3), each agency specified in paragraph (2) or (3) of this subsection shall establish a separate division of consumer affairs which shall receive and take appropriate action upon complaints with respect to such acts or practices by banks or savings and loan institutions described in paragraph (3) subject to its jurisdiction. The Board of Governors of the Federal Reserve System (with respect to banks) and the Federal Home Loan Bank Board (with respect to savings and loan institutions described in paragraph (3)) and the National Credit Union Administration Board (with respect to Federal credit unions described in paragraph (4)) shall prescribe regulations to carry out the purposes of this section, including regulations defining with specificity such unfair or deceptive acts or practices, and containing requirements prescribed for the purpose of preventing such acts or practices. Whenever the Commission prescribes a rule under subsection (a)(1)(B) of this section, then within 60 days after such rule takes effect each such Board shall promulgate substantially similar regulations prohibiting acts or practices of banks or savings and loan institutions described in paragraph (3), or Federal credit unions described in paragraph (4), as the case may be, which are substantially similar to those prohibited by rules of the Commission and which impose substantially similar requirements, unless (A) any such Board finds that such acts or practices of banks or savings and loan institutions described in paragraph (3), or Federal credit unions described in paragraph (4), as the case may be, are not unfair or deceptive, or (B) the Board of Governors of the Federal Reserve System finds that implementation of similar regulations with respect to banks, savings and loan institutions or Federal credit unions would seriously conflict with essential monetary and payments systems policies of such Board, and publishes any such finding, and the reasons therefor, in the Federal Register.

(2) Enforcement. - Compliance with regulations prescribed under this subsection shall be enforced under section 1818 of title 12, in the case of - (A) national banks, banks operating under the code of law for the District of Columbia, and Federal branches and Federal agencies of foreign banks, by the division of consumer affairs established by the Office of the Comptroller of the Currency; (B) member banks of the Federal Reserve System (other than national banks and banks operating under the code of law for the District of Columbia), branches and

agencies of foreign banks (other than Federal branches, Federal agencies, and insured State branches of foreign banks), commercial lending companies owned or controlled by foreign banks, and organizations operating under section 25 or 25(a)[1] of the Federal Reserve Act (12 U.S.C. 601 et seq., 611 et seq.), by the division of consumer affairs established by the Board of Governors of the Federal Reserve System; and (C) banks insured by the Federal Deposit Insurance Corporation (other[2] banks referred to in subparagraph (A) or (B)) and insured State branches of foreign banks, by the division of consumer affairs established by the Board of Directors of the Federal Deposit Insurance Corporation.

(3) Compliance with regulations prescribed under this subsection shall be enforced under section 1818 of title 12 with respect to savings associations as defined in section 1813 of title 12.

(4) Compliance with regulations prescribed under this subsection shall be enforced with respect to Federal credit unions under sections 1766 and 1786 of title 12.

(5) For the purpose of the exercise by any agency referred to in paragraph (2) of its powers under any Act referred to in that paragraph, a violation of any regulation prescribed under this subsection shall be deemed to be a violation of a requirement imposed under that Act. In addition to its powers under any provision of law specifically referred to in paragraph (2), each of the agencies referred to in that paragraph may exercise, for the purpose of enforcing compliance with any regulation prescribed under this subsection, any other authority conferred on it by law.

(6) The authority of the Board of Governors of the Federal Reserve System to issue regulations under this subsection does not impair the authority of any other agency designated in this subsection to make rules respecting its own procedures in enforcing compliance with regulations prescribed under this subsection.

(7) Each agency exercising authority under this subsection shall transmit to the Congress each year a detailed report on its activities under this paragraph during the preceding calendar year. The terms used in this paragraph that are not defined in this subchapter or otherwise defined in section 1813(s) of title 12 shall have the meaning given to them in section 3101 of title 12.

(g) Exemptions and stays from application of rules; procedures

---

[1] Section 25(a) of the Federal Reserve Act, referred to in subsec. (f)(2)(B), which is classified to subchapter II (Sec. 611 et seq.) of chapter 6 of Title 12, Banks and Banking, was renumbered section 25A of that act by Pub. L. 102-242, title I, Sec. 142(e)(2), Dec. 19, 1991, 105 Stat. 2281. Section 25 of the Federal Reserve Act is classified to subchapter I (Sec. 601 et seq.) of chapter 6 of Title 12.

[2] So in original. Probably should be "(other than".

(1) Any person to whom a rule under subsection (a)(1)(B) of this section applies may petition the Commission for an exemption from such rule.

(2) If, on its own motion or on the basis of a petition under paragraph (1), the Commission finds that the application of a rule prescribed under subsection (a)(1)(B) of this section to any person or class or[3] persons is not necessary to prevent the unfair or deceptive act or practice to which the rule relates, the Commission may exempt such person or class >from all or part of such rule. Section 553 of title 5 shall apply to action under this paragraph.

(3) Neither the pendency of a proceeding under this subsection respecting an exemption from a rule, nor the pendency of judicial proceedings to review the Commission's action or failure to act under this subsection, shall stay the applicability of such rule under subsection (a)(1)(B) of this section.

(h) Restriction on rulemaking authority of Commission respecting children's advertising proceedings pending on May 28, 1980 The Commission shall not have any authority to promulgate any rule in the children's advertising proceeding pending on May 28, 1980, or in any substantially similar proceeding on the basis of a determination by the Commission that such advertising constitutes an unfair act or practice in or affecting commerce.

(i) Meetings with outside parties

(1) For purposes of this subsection, the term "outside party" means any person other than

(A) a Commissioner;

(B) an officer or employee of the Commission; or

(C) any person who has entered into a contract or any other agreement or arrangement with the Commission to provide any goods or services (including consulting services) to the Commission.

(2) Not later than 60 days after May 28, 1980, the Commission shall publish a proposed rule, and not later than 180 days after May 28, 1980, the Commission shall promulgate a final rule, which shall authorize the Commission or any Commissioner to meet with any outside party concerning any rulemaking proceeding of the Commission. Such rule shall provide that -

(A) notice of any such meeting shall be included in any weekly calendar prepared by the Commission; and

(B) a verbatim record or a summary of any such meeting, or of any communication relating to any such meeting, shall be kept, made available to the public, and included in the rulemaking record.

(j) Communications by investigative personnel with staff of Commission concerning matters outside rulemaking record prohibited Not later than 60 days after May 28,

---

[3] So in original. Probably should be "of".

United States
Federal Trade Commission Act

1980, the Commission shall publish a proposed rule, and not later than 180 days after May 28, 1980, the Commission shall promulgate a final rule, which shall prohibit any officer, employee, or agent of the Commission with any investigative responsibility or other responsibility relating to any rulemaking proceeding within any operating bureau of the Commission, from communicating or causing to be communicated to any Commissioner or to the personal staff of any Commissioner any fact which is relevant to the merits of such proceeding and which is not on the rulemaking record of such proceeding, unless such communication is made available to the public and is included in the rulemaking record. The provisions of this subsection shall not apply to any communication to the extent such communication is required for the disposition of ex parte matters as authorized by law.

§ 57b. Civil actions for violations of rules and cease and desist orders respecting unfair or deceptive acts or practices

(a) Suits by Commission against persons, partnerships, or corporations; jurisdiction; relief for dishonest or fraudulent acts

(1) If any person, partnership, or corporation violates any rule under this subchapter respecting unfair or deceptive acts or practices (other than an interpretive rule, or a rule violation of which the Commission has provided is not an unfair or deceptive act or practice in violation of section 45(a) of this title), then the Commission may commence a civil action against such person, partnership, or corporation for relief under subsection (b) of this section in a United States district court or in any court of competent jurisdiction of a State.

(2) If any person, partnership, or corporation engages in any unfair or deceptive act or practice (within the meaning of section 45(a)(1) of this title) with respect to which the Commission has issued a final cease and desist order which is applicable to such person, partnership, or corporation, then the Commission may commence a civil action against such person, partnership, or corporation in a United States district court or in any court of competent jurisdiction of a State. If the Commission satisfies the court that the act or practice to which the cease and desist order relates is one which a reasonable man would have known under the circumstances was dishonest or fraudulent, the court may grant relief under subsection (b) of this section.

(b) Nature of relief available The court in an action under subsection (a) of this section shall have jurisdiction to grant such relief as the court finds necessary to redress injury to consumers or other persons, partnerships, and corporations resulting from the rule violation or the unfair or deceptive act or practice, as the case may be. Such relief may include, but shall not be limited to, rescission or reformation of contracts, the refund of money or return of property, the payment of damages, and public notification respecting the rule violation or the unfair or deceptive act or practice, as the case may be; except that nothing in this subsection is intended to authorize the imposition of any exemplary or punitive damages.

(c) Conclusiveness of findings of Commission in cease and desist proceedings; notice of judicial proceedings to injured persons, etc.

(1) If

(A) a cease and desist order issued under section 45(b) of this title has become final under section 45(g) of this title with respect to any person's, partnership's, or corporation's rule violation or unfair or deceptive act or practice, and

(B) an action under this section is brought with respect to such person's, partnership's, or corporation's rule violation or act or practice, then the findings of the Commission as to the material facts in the proceeding under section 45(b) of this title with respect to such person's, partnership's, or corporation's rule violation or act or practice, shall be conclusive unless

(i) the terms of such cease and desist order expressly provide that the Commission's findings shall not be conclusive, or

(ii) the order became final by reason of section 45(g)(1) of this title, in which case such finding shall be conclusive if supported by evidence.

(2) The court shall cause notice of an action under this section to be given in a manner which is reasonably calculated, under all of the circumstances, to apprise the persons, partnerships, and corporations allegedly injured by the defendant's rule violation or act or practice of the pendency of such action. Such notice may, in the discretion of the court, be given by publication.

(d) Time for bringing of actions No action may be brought by the Commission under this section more than 3 years after the rule violation to which an action under subsection (a)(1) of this section relates, or the unfair or deceptive act or practice to which an action under subsection (a)(2) of this section relates; except that if a cease and desist order with respect to any person's, partnership's, or corporation's rule violation or unfair or deceptive act or practice has become final and such order was issued in a proceeding under section 45(b) of this title which was commenced not later than 3 years after the rule violation or act or practice occurred, a civil action may be commenced under this section against such person, partnership, or corporation at any time before the expiration of one year after such order becomes final.

(e) Availability of additional Federal or State remedies; other authority of Commission unaffected Remedies provided in this section are in addition to, and not in lieu of, any other remedy or right of action provided by State or Federal law. Nothing in this section shall be construed to affect any authority of the Commission under any other provision of law.

§ 57b-1. Civil investigative demands

(a) Definitions For purposes of this section:

United States
Federal Trade Commission Act

(1) The terms "civil investigative demand" and "demand" mean any demand issued by the commission under subsection (c)(1) of this section.

(2) The term "Commission investigation" means any inquiry conducted by a Commission investigator for the purpose of ascertaining whether any person is or has been engaged in any unfair or deceptive acts or practices in or affecting commerce (within the meaning of section 45(a)(1) of this title) or in any antitrust violations.

(3) The term "Commission investigator" means any attorney or investigator employed by the Commission who is charged with the duty of enforcing or carrying into effect any provisions relating to unfair or deceptive acts or practices in or affecting commerce (within the meaning of section 45(a)(1) of this title) or any provisions relating to antitrust violations.

(4) The term "custodian" means the custodian or any deputy custodian designated under section 57b-2(b)(2)(A) of this title.

(5) The term "documentary material" includes the original or any copy of any book, record, report, memorandum, paper, communication, tabulation, chart, or other document.

(6) The term "person" means any natural person, partnership, corporation, association, or other legal entity, including any person acting under color or authority of State law.

(7) The term "violation" means any act or omission constituting an unfair or deceptive act or practice in or affecting commerce (within the meaning of section 45(a)(1) of this title) or any antitrust violation.

(8) The term "antitrust violation" means -

   (A) any unfair method of competition (within the meaning of section 45(a)(1) of this title);

   (B) any violation of the Clayton Act (15 U.S.C. 12 et seq.) or of any other Federal statute that prohibits, or makes available to the Commission a civil remedy with respect to, any restraint upon or monopolization of interstate or foreign trade or commerce;

   (C) with respect to the International Antitrust Enforcement Assistance Act of 1994 (15 U.S.C. 6201 et seq.), any violation of any of the foreign antitrust laws (as defined in section 12 of such Act (15 U.S.C. 6211)) with respect to which a request is made under section 3 of such Act (15 U.S.C. 6202); or

   (D) any activity in preparation for a merger, acquisition, joint venture, or similar transaction, which if consummated, may result in any such unfair method of competition or in any such violation.

(b) Actions conducted by Commission respecting unfair or deceptive acts or practices in or affecting commerce For the purpose of investigations performed pursuant to this section with respect to unfair or deceptive acts or practices in or affecting commerce (within the meaning of section 45(a)(1) of this title); all actions of the Commission taken under section 46 and section 49 of this title shall be conducted pursuant to subsection (c) of this section.

(c) Issuance of demand; contents; service; verified return; sworn certificate; answers; taking of oral testimony

(1) Whenever the Commission has reason to believe that any person may be in possession, custody, or control of any documentary material or tangible things, or may have any information, relevant to unfair or deceptive acts or practices in or affecting commerce (within the meaning of section 45(a)(1) of this title), or to antitrust violations, the Commission may, before the institution of any proceedings under this subchapter, issue in writing, and cause to be served upon such person, a civil investigative demand requiring such person to produce such documentary material for inspection and copying or reproduction, to submit such tangible things, to file written reports or answers to questions, to give oral testimony concerning documentary material or other information, or to furnish any combination of such material, answers, or testimony.

(2) Each civil investigative demand shall state the nature of the conduct constituting the alleged violation which is under investigation and the provision of law applicable to such violation.

(3) Each civil investigative demand for the production of documentary material shall -

(A) describe each class of documentary material to be produced under the demand with such definiteness and certainty as to permit such material to be fairly identified;

(B) prescribe a return date or dates which will provide a reasonable period of time within which the material so demanded may be assembled and made available for inspection and copying or reproduction; and

(C) identify the custodian to whom such material shall be made available.

(4) Each civil investigative demand for the submission of tangible things shall -

(A) describe each class of tangible things to be submitted under the demand with such definiteness and certainty as to permit such things to be fairly identified;

(B) prescribe a return date or dates which will provide a reasonable period of time within which the things so demanded may be assembled and submitted; and

(C) identify the custodian to whom such things shall be submitted.

(5) Each civil investigative demand for written reports or answers to questions shall -

(A) propound with definiteness and certainty the reports to be produced or the questions to be answered;

(B) prescribe a date or dates at which time written reports or answers to questions shall be submitted; and

(C) identify the custodian to whom such reports or answers shall be submitted.

(6) Each civil investigative demand for the giving of oral testimony shall -

(A) prescribe a date, time, and place at which oral testimony shall be commenced; and

(B) identify a Commission investigator who shall conduct the investigation and the custodian to whom the transcript of such investigation shall be submitted.

(7) (A) Any civil investigative demand may be served by any Commission investigator at any place within the territorial jurisdiction of any court of the United States.

(B) Any such demand or any enforcement petition filed under this section may be served upon any person who is not found within the territorial jurisdiction of any court of the United States, in such manner as the Federal Rules of Civil Procedure prescribe for service in a foreign nation.

(C) To the extent that the courts of the United States have authority to assert jurisdiction over such person consistent with due process, the United States District Court for the District of Columbia shall have the same jurisdiction to take any action respecting compliance with this section by such person that such district court would have if such person were personally within the jurisdiction of such district court.

(8) Service of any civil investigative demand or any enforcement petition filed under this section may be made upon a partnership, corporation, association, or other legal entity by -

(A) delivering a duly executed copy of such demand or petition to any partner, executive officer, managing agent, or general agent of such partnership, corporation, association, or other legal entity, or to any agent of such partnership, corporation, association, or other legal entity authorized by appointment or by law to receive service of process on behalf of such partnership, corporation, association, or other legal entity;

(B) delivering a duly executed copy of such demand or petition to the principal office or place of business of the partnership, corporation, association, or other legal entity to be served; or

(C) depositing a duly executed copy in the United States mails, by registered or certified mail, return receipt requested, duly addressed to such partnership, corporation, association, or other legal entity at its principal office or place of business.

(9) Service of any civil investigative demand or of any enforcement petition filed under this section may be made upon any natural person by -

(A) delivering a duly executed copy of such demand or petition to the person to be served; or

(B) depositing a duly executed copy in the United States mails by registered or certified mail, return receipt requested, duly addressed to such person at his residence or principal office or place of business.

(10) A verified return by the individual serving any civil investigative demand or any enforcement petition filed under this section setting forth the manner of such service shall be proof of such service. In the case of service by registered or certified mail, such return shall be accompanied by the return post office receipt of delivery of such demand or enforcement petition.

(11) The production of documentary material in response to a civil investigative demand shall be made under a sworn certificate, in such form as the demand designates, by the person, if a natural person, to whom the demand is directed or, if not a natural person, by any person having knowledge of the facts and circumstances relating to such production, to the effect that all of the documentary material required by the demand and in the possession, custody, or control of the person to whom the demand is directed has been produced and made available to the custodian.

(12) The submission of tangible things in response to a civil investigative demand shall be made under a sworn certificate, in such form as the demand designates, by the person to whom the demand is directed or, if not a natural person, by any person having knowledge of the facts and circumstances relating to such production, to the effect that all of the tangible things required by the demand and in the possession, custody, or control of the person to whom the demand is directed have been submitted to the custodian.

(13) Each reporting requirement or question in a civil investigative demand shall be answered separately and fully in writing under oath, unless it is objected to, in which event the reasons for the objection shall be stated in lieu of an answer, and it shall be submitted under a sworn certificate, in such form as the demand designates, by the person, if a natural person, to whom the demand is directed or, if not a natural person, by any person responsible for answering each reporting requirement or question, to the effect that all information required by the demand and in the possession, custody, control, or knowledge of the person to whom the demand is directed has been submitted.

(14) (A) Any Commission investigator before whom oral testimony is to be taken shall put the witness on oath or affirmation and shall personally, or by any individual acting under his direction and in his presence, record the testimony of the witness. The testimony shall be taken stenographically and transcribed. After the testimony is fully transcribed, the Commission investigator before whom the

testimony is taken shall promptly transmit a copy of the transcript of the testimony to the custodian.

(B) Any Commission investigator before whom oral testimony is to be taken shall exclude from the place where the testimony is to be taken all other persons except the person giving the testimony, his attorney, the officer before whom the testimony is to be taken, and any stenographer taking such testimony.

(C) The oral testimony of any person taken pursuant to a civil investigative demand shall be taken in the judicial district of the United States in which such person resides, is found, or transacts business, or in such other place as may be agreed upon by the Commission investigator before whom the oral testimony of such person is to be taken and such person.

(D) (i) Any person compelled to appear under a civil investigative demand for oral testimony pursuant to this section may be accompanied, represented, and advised by an attorney. The attorney may advise such person, in confidence, either upon the request of such person or upon the initiative of the attorney, with respect to any question asked of such person.

(ii) Such person or attorney may object on the record to any question, in whole or in part, and shall briefly state for the record the reason for the objection. An objection may properly be made, received, and entered upon the record when it is claimed that such person is entitled to refuse to answer the question on grounds of any constitutional or other legal right or privilege, including the privilege against self-incrimination. Such person shall not otherwise object to or refuse to answer any question, and shall not himself or through his attorney otherwise interrupt the oral examination. If such person refuses to answer any question, the Commission may petition the district court of the United States pursuant to this section for an order compelling such person to answer such question.

(iii) If such person refuses to answer any question on grounds of the privilege against self-incrimination, the testimony of such person may be compelled in accordance with the provisions of section 6004 of title 18.

(E) (i) After the testimony of any witness is fully transcribed, the Commission investigator shall afford the witness (who may be accompanied by an attorney) a reasonable opportunity to examine the transcript. The transcript shall be read to or by the witness, unless such examination and reading are waived by the witness. Any changes in form or substance which the witness desires to make shall be entered and identified upon the transcript by the Commission investigator with a statement of the reasons given by the witness for making such changes. The transcript shall then be signed by the witness, unless the witness in writing waives the signing, is ill, cannot be found, or refuses to sign.

(ii) If the transcript is not signed by the witness during the 30-day period following the date upon which the witness is first afforded a reasonable opportunity to examine it, the Commission investigator shall sign the transcript and state on the record the fact of the waiver, illness, absence of the witness, or the refusal to sign, together with any reasons given for the failure to sign.

(F) The Commission investigator shall certify on the transcript that the witness was duly sworn by him and that the transcript is a true record of the testimony given by the witness, and the Commission investigator shall promptly deliver the transcript or send it by registered or certified mail to the custodian.

(G) The Commission investigator shall furnish a copy of the transcript (upon payment of reasonable charges for the transcription) to the witness only, except that the Commission may for good cause limit such witness to inspection of the official transcript of his testimony.

(H) Any witness appearing for the taking of oral testimony pursuant to a civil investigative demand shall be entitled to the same fees and mileage which are paid to witnesses in the district courts of the United States.

(d) Procedures for demand material Materials received as a result of a civil investigative demand shall be subject to the procedures established in section 57b-2 of this title.

(e) Petition for enforcement Whenever any person fails to comply with any civil investigative demand duly served upon him under this section, or whenever satisfactory copying or reproduction of material requested pursuant to the demand cannot be accomplished and such person refuses to surrender such material, the Commission, through such officers or attorneys as it may designate, may file, in the district court of the United States for any judicial district in which such person resides, is found, or transacts business, and serve upon such person, a petition for an order of such court for the enforcement of this section. All process of any court to which application may be made as provided in this subsection may be served in any judicial district.

(f) Petition for order modifying or setting aside demand

(1) Not later than 20 days after the service of any civil investigative demand upon any person under subsection (c) of this section, or at any time before the return date specified in the demand, whichever period is shorter, or within such period exceeding 20 days after service or in excess of such return date as may be prescribed in writing, subsequent to service, by any Commission investigator named in the demand, such person may file with the Commission a petition for an order by the Commission modifying or setting aside the demand.

(2) The time permitted for compliance with the demand in whole or in part, as deemed proper and ordered by the Commission, shall not run during the pendency

of such petition at the Commission, except that such person shall comply with any portions of the demand not sought to be modified or set aside. Such petition shall specify each ground upon which the petitioner relies in seeking such relief, and may be based upon any failure of the demand to comply with the provisions of this section, or upon any constitutional or other legal right or privilege of such person.

(g) Custodial control of documentary material, tangible things, reports, etc. At any time during which any custodian is in custody or control of any documentary material, tangible things, reports, answers to questions, or transcripts of oral testimony given by any person in compliance with any civil investigative demand, such person may file, in the district court of the United States for the judicial district within which the office of such custodian is situated, and serve upon such custodian, a petition for an order of such court requiring the performance by such custodian of any duty imposed upon him by this section or section 57b-2 of this title.

(h) Jurisdiction of court Whenever any petition is filed in any district court of the United States under this section, such court shall have jurisdiction to hear and determine the matter so presented, and to enter such order or orders as may be required to carry into effect the provisions of this section. Any final order so entered shall be subject to appeal pursuant to section 1291 of title 28. Any disobedience of any final order entered under this section by any court shall be punished as a contempt of such court.

(i) Commission authority to issue subpoenas or make demand for information Notwithstanding any other provision of law, the Commission shall have no authority to issue a subpoena or make a demand for information, under authority of this subchapter or any other provision of law, unless such subpoena or demand for information is signed by a Commissioner acting pursuant to a Commission resolution. The Commission shall not delegate the power conferred by this section to sign subpoenas or demands for information to any other person.

(j) Applicability of this section The provisions of this section shall not -

(1) apply to any proceeding under section 45(b) of this title, any proceeding under section 11(b) of the Clayton Act (15 U.S.C. 21(b)), or any adjudicative proceeding under any other provision of law; or

(2) apply to or affect the jurisdiction, duties, or powers of any agency of the Federal Government, other than the Commission, regardless of whether such jurisdiction, duties, or powers are derived in whole or in part, by reference to this subchapter.

§ 57b-2. Confidentiality

(a) Definitions For purposes of this section:

(1) The term "material" means documentary material, tangible things, written reports or answers to questions, and transcripts of oral testimony.

(2) The term "Federal agency" has the meaning given it in section 552(e) of title 5.[1]

(b) Procedures respecting documents, tangible things, or transcripts of oral testimony received pursuant to compulsory process or investigation

(1) With respect to any document, tangible thing, or transcript of oral testimony received by the Commission pursuant to compulsory process in an investigation, a purpose of which is to determine whether any person may have violated any provision of the laws administered by the Commission, the procedures established in paragraph (2) through paragraph (7) shall apply.

(2) (A) The Commission shall designate a duly authorized agent to serve as custodian of documentary material, tangible things, or written reports or answers to questions, and transcripts of oral testimony, and such additional duly authorized agents as the Commission shall determine from time to time to be necessary to serve as deputies to the custodian.

(B) Any person upon whom any demand for the production of documentary material has been duly served shall make such material available for inspection and copying or reproduction to the custodian designated in such demand at the principal place of business of such person (or at such other place as such custodian and such person thereafter may agree or prescribe in writing or as the court may direct pursuant to section 57b-1(h) of this title) on the return date specified in such demand (or on such later date as such custodian may prescribe in writing). Such person may upon written agreement between such person and the custodian substitute copies for originals of all or any part of such material.

(3) (A) The custodian to whom any documentary material, tangible things, written reports or answers to questions, and transcripts of oral testimony are delivered shall take physical possession of such material, reports or answers, and transcripts, and shall be responsible for the use made of such material, reports or answers, and transcripts, and for the return of material, pursuant to the requirements of this section.

(B) The custodian may prepare such copies of the documentary material, written reports or answers to questions, and transcripts of oral testimony, and may make tangible things available, as may be required for official use by any duly authorized officer or employee of the Commission under regulations which shall be promulgated by the Commission. Notwithstanding subparagraph (C), such material, things, and transcripts may be used by any such officer or employee in connection with the taking of oral testimony under this section.

(C) Except as otherwise provided in this section, while in the possession of the custodian, no documentary material, tangible things, reports or answers to

---

[1] See References in Text note below.

questions, and transcripts of oral testimony shall be available for examination by any individual other than a duly authorized officer or employee of the Commission without the consent of the person who produced the material, things, or transcripts. Nothing in this section is intended to prevent disclosure to either House of the Congress or to any committee or subcommittee of the Congress, except that the Commission immediately shall notify the owner or provider of any such information of a request for information designated as confidential by the owner or provider.

(D) While in the possession of the custodian and under such reasonable terms and conditions as the Commission shall prescribe -

(i) documentary material, tangible things, or written reports shall be available for examination by the person who produced the material, or by any duly authorized representative of such person; and

(ii) answers to questions in writing and transcripts of oral testimony shall be available for examination by the person who produced the testimony or by his attorney.

(4) Whenever the Commission has instituted a proceeding against a person, partnership, or corporation, the custodian may deliver to any officer or employee of the Commission documentary material, tangible things, written reports or answers to questions, and transcripts of oral testimony for official use in connection with such proceeding. Upon the completion of the proceeding, the officer or employee shall return to the custodian any such material so delivered which has not been received into the record of the proceeding.

(5) If any documentary material, tangible things, written reports or answers to questions, and transcripts of oral testimony have been produced in the course of any investigation by any person pursuant to compulsory process and -

(A) any proceeding arising out of the investigation has been completed; or

(B) no proceeding in which the material may be used has been commenced within a reasonable time after completion of the examination and analysis of all such material and other information assembled in the course of the investigation; then the custodian shall, upon written request of the person who produced the material, return to the person any such material which has not been received into the record of any such proceeding (other than copies of such material made by the custodian pursuant to paragraph (3)(B)).

(6) The custodian of any documentary material, written reports or answers to questions, and transcripts of oral testimony may deliver to any officers or employees of appropriate Federal law enforcement agencies, in response to a written request, copies of such material for use in connection with an investigation or proceeding under the jurisdiction of any such agency. The custodian of any tangible things may make such things available for inspection to such persons on

the same basis. Such materials shall not be made available to any such agency until the custodian received certification of any officer of such agency that such information will be maintained in confidence and will be used only for official law enforcement purposes. Such documentary material, results of inspections of tangible things, written reports or answers to questions, and transcripts of oral testimony may be used by any officer or employee of such agency only in such manner and subject to such conditions as apply to the Commission under this section. The custodian may make such materials available to any State law enforcement agency upon the prior certification of any officer of such agency that such information will be maintained in confidence and will be used only for official law enforcement purposes.

(7) In the event of the death, disability, or separation from service in the Commission of the custodian of any documentary material, tangible things, written reports or answers to questions, and transcripts of oral testimony produced under any demand issued under this subchapter, or the official relief of the custodian from responsibility for the custody and control of such material, the Commission promptly shall -

    (A) designate under paragraph (2)(A) another duly authorized agent to serve as custodian of such material; and

    (B) transmit in writing to the person who produced the material or testimony notice as to the identity and address of the successor so designated. Any successor designated under paragraph (2)(A) as a result of the requirements of this paragraph shall have (with regard to the material involved) all duties and responsibilities imposed by this section upon his predecessor in office with regard to such material, except that he shall not be held responsible for any default or dereliction which occurred before his designation.

(c) Information considered confidential

    (1) All information reported to or otherwise obtained by the Commission which is not subject to the requirements of subsection (b) of this section shall be considered confidential when so marked by the person supplying the information and shall not be disclosed, except in accordance with the procedures established in paragraph (2) and paragraph (3).

    (2) If the Commission determines that a document marked confidential by the person supplying it may be disclosed because it is not a trade secret or commercial or financial information which is obtained from any person and which is privileged or confidential, within the meaning of section 46(f) of this title, then the Commission shall notify such person in writing that the Commission intends to disclose the document at a date not less than 10 days after the date of receipt of notification.

(3) Any person receiving such notification may, if he believes disclosure of the document would cause disclosure of a trade secret, or commercial or financial information which is obtained from any person and which is privileged or confidential, within the meaning of section 46(f) of this title, before the date set for release of the document, bring an action in the district court of the United States for the district within which the documents are located or in the United States District Court for the District of Columbia to restrain disclosure of the document. Any person receiving such notification may file with the appropriate district court or court of appeals of the United States, as appropriate, an application for a stay of disclosure. The documents shall not be disclosed until the court has ruled on the application for a stay.

(d) Particular disclosures allowed

(1) The provisions of subsection (c) of this section shall not be construed to prohibit -

(A) the disclosure of information to either House of the Congress or to any committee or subcommittee of the Congress, except that the Commission immediately shall notify the owner or provider of any such information of a request for information designated as confidential by the owner or provider;

(B) the disclosure of the results of any investigation or study carried out or prepared by the Commission, except that no information shall be identified nor shall information be disclosed in such a manner as to disclose a trade secret of any person supplying the trade secret, or to disclose any commercial or financial information which is obtained from any person and which is privileged or confidential;

(C) the disclosure of relevant and material information in Commission adjudicative proceedings or in judicial proceedings to which the Commission is a party; or

(D) the disclosure to a Federal agency of disaggregated information obtained in accordance with section 3512[1] of title 44, except that the recipient agency shall use such disaggregated information for economic, statistical, or policymaking purposes only, and shall not disclose such information in an individually identifiable form.

(2) Any disclosure of relevant and material information in Commission adjudicative proceedings or in judicial proceedings to which the Commission is a party shall be governed by the rules of the Commission for adjudicative proceedings or by court rules or orders, except that the rules of the Commission shall not be amended in a manner inconsistent with the purposes of this section.

(e) Effect on other statutory provisions limiting disclosure

Nothing in this section shall supersede any statutory provision which expressly prohibits or limits particular disclosures by the Commission, or which authorizes disclosures to any other Federal agency.

(f) Exemption from disclosure

Any material which is received by the Commission in any investigation, a purpose of which is to determine whether any person may have violated any provision of the laws administered by the Commission, and which is provided pursuant to any compulsory process under this subchapter or which is provided voluntarily in place of such compulsory process shall be exempt from disclosure under section 552 of title 5.

§ 57b-3. Rulemaking process

(a) Definitions For purposes of this section:

(1) The term "rule" means any rule promulgated by the Commission under section 46 or section 57a of this title, except that such term does not include interpretive rules, rules involving Commission management or personnel, general statements of policy, or rules relating to Commission organization, procedure, or practice. Such term does not include any amendment to a rule unless the Commission -

(A) estimates that such amendment will have an annual effect on the national economy of $100,000,000 or more;

(B) estimates that such amendment will cause a substantial change in the cost or price of goods or services which are used extensively by particular industries, which are supplied extensively in particular geographic regions, or which are acquired in significant quantities by the Federal Government, or by State or local governments; or

(C) otherwise determines that such amendment will have a significant impact upon persons subject to regulation under such amendment and upon consumers.

(2) The term "rulemaking" means any Commission process for formulating or amending a rule.

(b) Notice of proposed rulemaking; regulatory analysis; contents; issuance

(1) In any case in which the Commission publishes notice of a proposed rulemaking, the Commission shall issue a preliminary regulatory analysis relating to the proposed rule involved. Each preliminary regulatory analysis shall contain -

(A) a concise statement of the need for, and the objectives of, the proposed rule;

(B) a description of any reasonable alternatives to the proposed rule which may accomplish the stated objective of the rule in a manner consistent with applicable law; and

(C) for the proposed rule, and for each of the alternatives described in the analysis, a preliminary analysis of the projected benefits and any adverse economic effects and any other effects, and of the effectiveness of the proposed rule and each alternative in meeting the stated objectives of the proposed rule.

(2) In any case in which the Commission promulgates a final rule, the Commission shall issue a final regulatory analysis relating to the final rule. Each final regulatory analysis shall contain -

(A) a concise statement of the need for, and the objectives of, the final rule;

(B) a description of any alternatives to the final rule which were considered by the Commission;

(C) an analysis of the projected benefits and any adverse economic effects and any other effects of the final rule;

(D) an explanation of the reasons for the determination of the Commission that the final rule will attain its objectives in a manner consistent with applicable law and the reasons the particular alternative was chosen; and

(E) a summary of any significant issues raised by the comments submitted during the public comment period in response to the preliminary regulatory analysis, and a summary of the assessment by the Commission of such issues.

(3) (A) In order to avoid duplication or waste, the Commission is authorized to -
(i) consider a series of closely related rules as one rule for purposes of this subsection; and

(ii) whenever appropriate, incorporate any data or analysis contained in a regulatory analysis issued under this subsection in the statement of basis and purpose to accompany any rule promulgated under section 57a(a)(1)(B) of this title, and incorporate by reference in any preliminary or final regulatory analysis information contained in a notice of proposed rulemaking or a statement of basis and purpose.

(B) The Commission shall include, in each notice of proposed rulemaking and in each publication of a final rule, a statement of the manner in which the public may obtain copies of the preliminary and final regulatory analyses. The Commission may charge a reasonable fee for the copying and mailing of regulatory analyses. The regulatory analyses shall be furnished without charge or at a reduced charge if the Commission determines that waiver or reduction of the fee is in the public interest because furnishing the information primarily benefits the general public.

(4) The Commission is authorized to delay the completion of any of the requirements established in this subsection by publishing in the Federal Register, not later than the date of publication of the final rule involved, a finding that the final rule is being promulgated in response to an emergency which makes timely compliance with the provisions of this subsection impracticable. Such publication shall include a statement of the reasons for such finding.

(5) The requirements of this subsection shall not be construed to alter in any manner the substantive standards applicable to any action by the Commission, or the procedural standards otherwise applicable to such action.

(c) Judicial review

(1) The contents and adequacy of any regulatory analysis prepared or issued by the Commission under this section, including the adequacy of any procedure involved in such preparation or issuance, shall not be subject to any judicial review in any court, except that a court, upon review of a rule pursuant to section 57a(e) of this title, may set aside such rule if the Commission has failed entirely to prepare a regulatory analysis.

(2) Except as specified in paragraph (1), no Commission action may be invalidated, remanded, or otherwise affected by any court on account of any failure to comply with the requirements of this section.

(3) The provisions of this subsection do not alter the substantive or procedural standards otherwise applicable to judicial review of any action by the Commission.

(d) Regulatory agenda; contents; publication dates in Federal Register

(1) The Commission shall publish at least semiannually a regulatory agenda. Each regulatory agenda shall contain a list of rules which the Commission intends to propose or promulgate during the 12-month period following the publication of the agenda. On the first Monday in October of each year, the Commission shall publish in the Federal Register a schedule showing the dates during the current fiscal year on which the semiannual regulatory agenda of the Commission will be published. (2) For each rule listed in a regulatory agenda, the Commission shall -

(A) describe the rule;

(B) state the objectives of and the legal basis for the rule; and

(C) specify any dates established or anticipated by the Commission for taking action, including dates for advance notice of proposed rulemaking, notices of proposed rulemaking, and final action by the Commission.

(3) Each regulatory agenda shall state the name, office address, and office telephone number of the Commission officer or employee responsible for responding to any inquiry relating to each rule listed.

(4) The Commission shall not propose or promulgate a rule which was not listed on a regulatory agenda unless the Commission publishes with the rule an explanation of the reasons the rule was omitted from such agenda.

COMMUNICATIONS ACT (1934)
[EXCERPT]

Summary

Section 605 of the Communications Act followed from the dissent of Justice Brandeis in Olmstead v. U.S. (1928). The provision established a clear prohibition against the interception and subsequent publication of a wire communication.

References

June 19, 1934, ch. 652, title VII, § 705, formerly title VI, § 605, 48 Stat. 1103, as amended by Pub. L. 90–351, Pub. L. 97–259, Pub. L. 98–549, Pub. L. 100–626, Pub. L. 100–667, Pub. L. 103–414, and Pub. L. 104–104. Codified at 47 U.S.C. § 605. [https://www.law.cornell.edu/uscode/text/47/605]

§605. Unauthorized publication or use of communications

(a) Practices prohibited

Except as authorized by chapter 119, title 18, no person receiving, assisting in receiving, transmitting, or assisting in transmitting, any interstate or foreign communication by wire or radio shall divulge or publish the existence, contents, substance, purport, effect, or meaning thereof, except through authorized channels of transmission or reception, (1) to any person other than the addressee, his agent, or attorney, (2) to a person employed or authorized to forward such communication to its destination, (3) to proper accounting or distributing officers of the various communicating centers over which the communication may be passed, (4) to the master of a ship under whom he is serving, (5) in response to a subpena issued by a court of competent jurisdiction, or (6) on demand of other lawful authority. No person not being authorized by the sender shall intercept any radio communication and divulge or publish the existence, contents, substance, purport, effect, or meaning of such intercepted communication to any person. No person not being entitled thereto shall receive or assist in receiving any interstate or foreign communication by radio and use such communication (or any information therein contained) for his own benefit or for the benefit of another not entitled thereto. No person having received any intercepted radio communication or having become acquainted with the contents, substance, purport, effect, or meaning of such communication (or any part thereof) knowing that such communication was intercepted, shall divulge or publish the existence, contents, substance, purport, effect, or meaning of such communication (or any part thereof) or use such communication (or any information therein contained) for his own benefit or for the benefit of another not entitled thereto. This section shall not apply to the receiving, divulging, publishing, or utilizing the contents of any radio communication which is transmitted by any station for the use of the general public, which relates to ships, aircraft, vehicles, or persons in distress, or which is transmitted by an amateur radio station operator or by a citizens band radio operator.

(b) Exceptions

The provisions of subsection (a) shall not apply to the interception or receipt by any individual, or the assisting (including the manufacture or sale) of such interception or receipt, of any satellite cable programming for private viewing if-

(1) the programming involved is not encrypted; and

(2)(A) a marketing system is not established under which-

(i) an agent or agents have been lawfully designated for the purpose of authorizing private viewing by individuals, and

(ii) such authorization is available to the individual involved from the appropriate agent or agents; or

(B) a marketing system described in subparagraph (A) is established and the individuals receiving such programming has obtained authorization for private viewing under that system.

(c) Scrambling of Public Broadcasting Service programming

No person shall encrypt or continue to encrypt satellite delivered programs included in the National Program Service of the Public Broadcasting Service and intended for public viewing by retransmission by television broadcast stations; except that as long as at least one unencrypted satellite transmission of any program subject to this subsection is provided, this subsection shall not prohibit additional encrypted satellite transmissions of the same program.

(d) Definitions

For purposes of this section-

(1) the term "satellite cable programming" means video programming which is transmitted via satellite and which is primarily intended for the direct receipt by cable operators for their retransmission to cable subscribers;

(2) the term "agent", with respect to any person, includes an employee of such person;

(3) the term "encrypt", when used with respect to satellite cable programming, means to transmit such programming in a form whereby the aural and visual characteristics (or both) are modified or altered for the purpose of preventing the unauthorized receipt of such programming by persons without authorized equipment which is designed to eliminate the effects of such modification or alteration;

(4) the term "private viewing" means the viewing for private use in an individual's dwelling unit by means of equipment, owned or operated by such individual, capable of receiving satellite cable programming directly from a satellite;

(5) the term "private financial gain" shall not include the gain resulting to any individual for the private use in such individual's dwelling unit of any

programming for which the individual has not obtained authorization for that use; and

(6) the term "any person aggrieved" shall include any person with proprietary rights in the intercepted communication by wire or radio, including wholesale or retail distributors of satellite cable programming, and, in the case of a violation of paragraph (4) of subsection (e), shall also include any person engaged in the lawful manufacture, distribution, or sale of equipment necessary to authorize or receive satellite cable programming.

(e) Penalties; civil actions; remedies; attorney's fees and costs; computation of damages; regulation by State and local authorities

(1) Any person who willfully violates subsection (a) shall be fined not more than $2,000 or imprisoned for not more than 6 months, or both.

(2) Any person who violates subsection (a) willfully and for purposes of direct or indirect commercial advantage or private financial gain shall be fined not more than $50,000 or imprisoned for not more than 2 years, or both, for the first such conviction and shall be fined not more than $100,000 or imprisoned for not more than 5 years, or both, for any subsequent conviction.

(3)(A) Any person aggrieved by any violation of subsection (a) or paragraph (4) of this subsection may bring a civil action in a United States district court or in any other court of competent jurisdiction.

(B) The court-

(i) may grant temporary and final injunctions on such terms as it may deem reasonable to prevent or restrain violations of subsection (a);

(ii) may award damages as described in subparagraph (C); and

(iii) shall direct the recovery of full costs, including awarding reasonable attorneys' fees to an aggrieved party who prevails.

(C)(i) Damages awarded by any court under this section shall be computed, at the election of the aggrieved party, in accordance with either of the following subclauses;

(I) the party aggrieved may recover the actual damages suffered by him as a result of the violation and any profits of the violator that are attributable to the violation which are not taken into account in computing the actual damages; in determining the violator's profits, the party aggrieved shall be required to prove only the violator's gross revenue, and the violator shall be required to prove his deductible expenses and the elements of profit attributable to factors other than the violation; or

(II) the party aggrieved may recover an award of statutory damages for each violation of subsection (a) involved in the action in a sum of not less than $1,000 or more than $10,000, as the court considers just, and for each violation of paragraph (4) of this subsection involved in the action an aggrieved party may recover statutory damages in a sum not less than $10,000, or more than $100,000, as the court considers just.

(ii) In any case in which the court finds that the violation was committed willfully and for purposes of direct or indirect commercial advantage or private financial gain, the court in its discretion may increase the award of damages, whether actual or statutory, by an amount of not more than $100,000 for each violation of subsection (a).

(iii) In any case where the court finds that the violator was not aware and had no reason to believe that his acts constituted a violation of this section, the court in its discretion may reduce the award of damages to a sum of not less than $250.

(4) Any person who manufactures, assembles, modifies, imports, exports, sells, or distributes any electronic, mechanical, or other device or equipment, knowing or having reason to know that the device or equipment is primarily of assistance in the unauthorized decryption of satellite cable programming, or direct-to-home satellite services, or is intended for any other activity prohibited by subsection (a), shall be fined not more than $500,000 for each violation, or imprisoned for not more than 5 years for each violation, or both. For purposes of all penalties and remedies established for violations of this paragraph, the prohibited activity established herein as it applies to each such device shall be deemed a separate violation.

(5) The penalties under this subsection shall be in addition to those prescribed under any other provision of this subchapter.

(6) Nothing in this subsection shall prevent any State, or political subdivision thereof, from enacting or enforcing any laws with respect to the importation, sale, manufacture, or distribution of equipment by any person with the intent of its use to assist in the interception or receipt of radio communications prohibited by subsection (a).

(f) Rights, obligations, and liabilities under other laws unaffected

Nothing in this section shall affect any right, obligation, or liability under title 17, any rule, regulation, or order thereunder, or any other applicable Federal, State, or local law.

(g) Universal encryption standard

The Commission shall initiate an inquiry concerning the need for a universal encryption standard that permits decryption of satellite cable programming intended for private viewing. In conducting such inquiry, the Commission shall take into account-

(1) consumer costs and benefits of any such standard, including consumer investment in equipment in operation;

(2) incorporation of technological enhancements, including advanced television formats;

(3) whether any such standard would effectively prevent present and future unauthorized decryption of satellite cable programming;

(4) the costs and benefits of any such standard on other authorized users of encrypted satellite cable programming, including cable systems and satellite master antenna television systems;

(5) the effect of any such standard on competition in the manufacture of decryption equipment; and

(6) the impact of the time delay associated with the Commission procedures necessary for establishment of such standards.

(h) Rulemaking for encryption standard

If the Commission finds, based on the information gathered from the inquiry required by subsection (g), that a universal encryption standard is necessary and in the public interest, the Commission shall initiate a rulemaking to establish such a standard.

FAIR CREDIT REPORTING ACT (1970)

Summary

Congress passed the Fair Credit Reporting Act of 1970 to protect individuals from the misuse of personal information by Credit Reporting Agencies, or CRAs. Under the Act, CRAs may only disclose personal information to persons whom they have reason to believe intend to use the information to evaluate an application for credit, employment, insurance, license, or governmental benefit. Notice must be given to an individual when the CRA is asked to procure extensive information on the individual's character and habits, if this information is being procured to evaluate initial eligibility for a benefit. Individuals are entitled to a copy of their credit report, and if errors or discrepancies are found, the CRA must investigate and correct them.

The Act also provides guidelines for the information that can be gathered, and how long it may be maintained within a credit report. For example, bankruptcy can only be reported for ten years, and other negative information is removed from the report after seven. A private action may be brought for any violation of the act, regardless of damages. The Federal Trade Commission is charged with enforcement of the Act.

By the 1990s, many commentators believed the FCRA needed to be updated to bring it into line with new developments in banking and in technology. In 1996, Congress amended the FCRA, in the Consumer Credit Reporting Reform Act. The CCRRA allows for greater sharing of information between affiliate-entities without their becoming CRAs within the meaning of the Act. The CCRRA also tightens some loopholes in the pre-existing FCRA, imposes new obligations on businesses to ensure the accuracy of reports, and increases civil and criminal penalties. The CCRRA also provides for extensive preemption of state laws dealing with credit reporting; this preemption expires on January 1, 2004 unless the Congress renews those provisions.

In 2003 Congress enacted the Fair and Accurate Credit Transactions Act (FACTA), which substantially amended much of the FCRA. The Act establishes remedial rights for identity theft victims, but does little to actually prevent the crime. For example, the FACTA requires merchants to truncate credit and debit card numbers printed on receipts, it gives individuals the right to free annual credit reports, it requires credit agencies to block credit information that was recorded as a result of identity theft, and it creates new document destruction procedures for personal information. The FACTA also preempts state laws that would provide greater privacy safeguards. For example, the FACTA provides that credit agencies must disclose credit scores to individuals for a "reasonable fee"; the states would not be permitted to grant consumers the right to free credit score disclosures.

United States
Fair Credit Reporting Act

References

Public Law 91-508, as amended by Public Law 102-537, Public Law 104–208, Public Law 105–347, Public Law 108–159, and Public Law 111–203. Codified at 15 U.S.C. § 1681.

[https://www.law.cornell.edu/uscode/text/15/1681]

[https://www.ftc.gov/enforcement/rules/rulemaking-regulatory-reform-proceedings/fair-credit-reporting-act]

FTC, Credit Reporting

[https://www.ftc.gov/news-events/media-resources/consumer-finance/credit-reporting]

FTC, Consumer's Brochure on the FCRA

[http://www.ftc.gov/bcp/conline/pubs/credit/fcra.htm]

EPIC, Fair Credit Reporting Act

[https://www.epic.org/privacy/fcra/]

§ 601. Short title

This title may be cited as the Fair Credit Reporting Act.

15 U.S.C. § 1681. Congressional findings and statement of purpose

(a) Accuracy and fairness of credit reporting. The Congress makes the following findings:

(1) The banking system is dependent upon fair and accurate credit reporting. Inaccurate credit reports directly impair the efficiency of the banking system, and unfair credit reporting methods undermine the public confidence which is essential to the continued functioning of the banking system.

(2) An elaborate mechanism has been developed for investigating and evaluating the credit worthiness, credit standing, credit capacity, character, and general reputation of consumers.

(3) Consumer reporting agencies have assumed a vital role in assembling and evaluating consumer credit and other information on consumers.

(4) There is a need to insure that consumer reporting agencies exercise their grave responsibilities with fairness, impartiality, and a respect for the consumer's right to privacy.

(b) Reasonable procedures. It is the purpose of this title to require that consumer reporting agencies adopt reasonable procedures for meeting the needs of commerce for consumer credit, personnel, insurance, and other information in a manner which is fair and equitable to the consumer, with regard to the confidentiality, accuracy, relevancy, and proper utilization of such information in accordance with the requirements of this title.

§ 1681a. Definitions; rules of construction

(a) Definitions and rules of construction set forth in this section are applicable for the purposes of this subchapter.

(b) The term "person" means any individual, partnership, corporation, trust, estate, cooperative, association, government or governmental subdivision or agency, or other entity.

(c) The term "consumer" means an individual.

(d) Consumer Report. -

(1) In general. - The term "consumer report" means any written, oral, or other communication of any information by a consumer reporting agency bearing on a consumer's credit worthiness, credit standing, credit capacity, character, general reputation, personal characteristics, or mode of living which is used or expected to be used or collected in whole or in part for the purpose of serving as a factor in establishing the consumer's eligibility for-

(A) credit or insurance to be used primarily for personal, family, or household purposes;

(B) employment purposes; or

(C) any other purpose authorized under section 1681b of this title.

(2) Exclusions. - Except as provided in paragraph (3), the term "consumer report" does not include-

(A) subject to section 1681s–3 of this title, any -

(i) report containing information solely as to transactions or experiences between the consumer and the person making the report;

(ii) communication of that information among persons related by common ownership or affiliated by corporate control; or

(iii) communication of other information among persons related by common ownership or affiliated by corporate control, if it is clearly and conspicuously disclosed to the consumer that the information may be communicated among such persons and the consumer is given the opportunity, before the time that the information is initially communicated, to direct that such information not be communicated among such persons;

(B) any authorization or approval of a specific extension of credit directly or indirectly by the issuer of a credit card or similar device;

(C) any report in which a person who has been requested by a third party to make a specific extension of credit directly or indirectly to a consumer conveys his or her decision with respect to such request, if the third party advises the consumer of the name and address of the person to whom the request was made, and such person makes the disclosures to the consumer required under section 1681m of this title; or

(D) a communication described in subsection (o) or (x).

(3) Restriction on sharing of medical information. - Except for information or any communication of information disclosed as provided in section 1681b(g)(3) of this title, the exclusions in paragraph (2) shall not apply with respect to information disclosed to any person related by common ownership or affiliated by corporate control, if the information is -

(A) medical information;

(B) an individualized list or description based on the payment transactions of the consumer for medical products or services; or

(C) an aggregate list of identified consumers based on payment transactions for medical products or services.

(e) The term "investigative consumer report" means a consumer report or portion thereof in which information on a consumer's character, general reputation, personal characteristics, or mode of living is obtained through personal interviews with neighbors, friends, or associates of the consumer reported on or with others with whom he is acquainted or who may have knowledge concerning any such items of information. However, such information shall not include specific factual information on a consumer's credit record obtained directly from a creditor of the consumer or from a consumer reporting agency when such information was obtained directly from a creditor of the consumer or from the consumer.

(f) The term "consumer reporting agency" means any person which, for monetary fees, dues, or on a cooperative nonprofit basis, regularly engages in whole or in part in the practice of assembling or evaluating consumer credit information or other information on consumers for the purpose of furnishing consumer reports to third parties, and which uses any means or facility of interstate commerce for the purpose of preparing or furnishing consumer reports.

(g) The term "file", when used in connection with information on any consumer, means all of the information on that consumer recorded and retained by a consumer reporting agency regardless of how the information is stored.

(h) The term "employment purposes" when used in connection with a consumer report means a report used for the purpose of evaluating a consumer for employment, promotion, reassignment or retention as an employee.

(i) Medical Information. - The term "medical information" -

(1) means information or data, whether oral or recorded, in any form or medium, created by or derived from a health care provider or the consumer, that relates to-

(A) the past, present, or future physical, mental, or behavioral health or condition of an individual;

(B) the provision of health care to an individual; or

(C) the payment for the provision of health care to an individual.

(2) does not include the age or gender of a consumer, demographic information about the consumer, including a consumer's residence address or e-mail address, or any other information about a consumer that does not relate to the physical, mental, or behavioral health or condition of a consumer, including the existence or value of any insurance policy.

(j) Definitions Relating to Child Support Obligations. -

(1) Overdue support. - The term "overdue support" has the meaning given to such term in section 666(e) of title 42.

(2) State or local child support enforcement agency.-The term "State or local child support enforcement agency" means a State or local agency which administers a State or local program for establishing and enforcing child support obligations.

(k) Adverse Action. -

(1) Actions included.-The term "adverse action"-

(A) has the same meaning as in section 1691(d)(6) of this title; and

(B) means-

(i) a denial or cancellation of, an increase in any charge for, or a reduction or other adverse or unfavorable change in the terms of coverage or amount of, any insurance, existing or applied for, in connection with the underwriting of insurance;

(ii) a denial of employment or any other decision for employment purposes that adversely affects any current or prospective employee;

(iii) a denial or cancellation of, an increase in any charge for, or any other adverse or unfavorable change in the terms of, any license or benefit described in section 1681b(a)(3)(D) of this title; and

(iv) an action taken or determination that is-

(I) made in connection with an application that was made by, or a transaction that was initiated by, any consumer, or in connection with a review of an account under section 1681b(a)(3)(F)(ii) of this title; and

(II) adverse to the interests of the consumer.

(2) Applicable findings, decisions, commentary, and orders. - For purposes of any determination of whether an action is an adverse action under paragraph (1)(A), all appropriate final findings, decisions, commentary, and orders issued under section 1691(d)(6) of this title by the Bureau or any court shall apply.

(l) Firm Offer of Credit or Insurance. - The term "firm offer of credit or insurance" means any offer of credit or insurance to a consumer that will be honored if the consumer is determined, based on information in a consumer report on the consumer, to meet the specific criteria used to select the consumer for the offer, except that the offer may be further conditioned on one or more of the following:

(1) The consumer being determined, based on information in the consumer's application for the credit or insurance, to meet specific criteria bearing on credit worthiness or insurability, as applicable, that are established-

(A) before selection of the consumer for the offer; and

(B) for the purpose of determining whether to extend credit or insurance pursuant to the offer.

(2) Verification -

(A) that the consumer continues to meet the specific criteria used to select the consumer for the offer, by using information in a consumer report on the consumer, information in the consumer's application for the credit or insurance, or other information bearing on the credit worthiness or insurability of the consumer; or

(B) of the information in the consumer's application for the credit or insurance, to determine that the consumer meets the specific criteria bearing on credit worthiness or insurability.

(3) The consumer furnishing any collateral that is a requirement for the extension of the credit or insurance that was-

(A) established before selection of the consumer for the offer of credit or insurance; and

(B) disclosed to the consumer in the offer of credit or insurance.

(m) Credit or Insurance Transaction That Is Not Initiated by the Consumer.-The term "credit or insurance transaction that is not initiated by the consumer" does not include the use of a consumer report by a person with which the consumer has an account or insurance policy, for purposes of-

(1) reviewing the account or insurance policy; or

(2) collecting the account.

(n) State. - The term "State" means any State, the Commonwealth of Puerto Rico, the District of Columbia, and any territory or possession of the United States.

(o) Excluded Communications.-A communication is described in this subsection if it is a communication-

(1) that, but for subsection (d)(2)(D), would be an investigative consumer report;

(2) that is made to a prospective employer for the purpose of-

(A) procuring an employee for the employer; or

(B) procuring an opportunity for a natural person to work for the employer;

(3) that is made by a person who regularly performs such procurement;

(4) that is not used by any person for any purpose other than a purpose described in subparagraph (A) or (B) of paragraph (2); and

(5) with respect to which-

(A) the consumer who is the subject of the communication-

(i) consents orally or in writing to the nature and scope of the communication, before the collection of any information for the purpose of making the communication;

(ii) consents orally or in writing to the making of the communication to a prospective employer, before the making of the communication; and

(iii) in the case of consent under clause (i) or (ii) given orally, is provided written confirmation of that consent by the person making the communication, not later than 3 business days after the receipt of the consent by that person;

(B) the person who makes the communication does not, for the purpose of making the communication, make any inquiry that if made by a prospective employer of the consumer who is the subject of the communication would violate any applicable Federal or State equal employment opportunity law or regulation; and

(C) the person who makes the communication-

(i) discloses in writing to the consumer who is the subject of the communication, not later than 5 business days after receiving any request from the consumer for such disclosure, the nature and substance of all information in the consumer's file at the time of the request, except that the sources of any information that is acquired solely for use in making the communication and is actually used for no other purpose, need not be disclosed other than under appropriate discovery procedures in any court of competent jurisdiction in which an action is brought; and

(ii) notifies the consumer who is the subject of the communication, in writing, of the consumer's right to request the information described in clause (i).

(p) Consumer Reporting Agency That Compiles and Maintains Files on Consumers on a Nationwide Basis. - The term "consumer reporting agency that compiles and maintains files on consumers on a nationwide basis" means a consumer reporting agency that regularly engages in the practice of assembling or evaluating, and maintaining, for the purpose of furnishing consumer reports to third parties bearing on a consumer's credit worthiness, credit standing, or credit capacity, each of the following regarding consumers residing nationwide:

(1) Public record information.

(2) Credit account information from persons who furnish that information regularly and in the ordinary course of business.

(q) Definitions Relating to Fraud Alerts. -

(1) Active duty military consumer. - The term "active duty military consumer" means a consumer in military service who -

United States
Fair Credit Reporting Act

(A) is on active duty (as defined in section 101(d)(1) of title 10) or is a reservist performing duty under a call or order to active duty under a provision of law referred to in section 101(a)(13) of title 10; and

(B) is assigned to service away from the usual duty station of the consumer.

(2) Fraud alert; active duty alert.-The terms "fraud alert" and "active duty alert" mean a statement in the file of a consumer that-

(A) notifies all prospective users of a consumer report relating to the consumer that the consumer may be a victim of fraud, including identity theft, or is an active duty military consumer, as applicable; and

(B) is presented in a manner that facilitates a clear and conspicuous view of the statement described in subparagraph (A) by any person requesting such consumer report.

(3) Identity theft. - The term "identity theft" means a fraud committed using the identifying information of another person, subject to such further definition as the Bureau may prescribe, by regulation.

(4) Identity theft report.-The term "identity theft report" has the meaning given that term by rule of the Bureau, and means, at a minimum, a report-

(A) that alleges an identity theft;

(B) that is a copy of an official, valid report filed by a consumer with an appropriate Federal, State, or local law enforcement agency, including the United States Postal Inspection Service, or such other government agency deemed appropriate by the Bureau; and

(C) the filing of which subjects the person filing the report to criminal penalties relating to the filing of false information if, in fact, the information in the report is false.

(5) New credit plan. - The term "new credit plan" means a new account under an open end credit plan (as defined in section 1602(i) 1 of this title) or a new credit transaction not under an open end credit plan.

(r) Credit and Debit Related Terms -

(1) Card issuer. - The term "card issuer" means-

(A) a credit card issuer, in the case of a credit card; and

(B) a debit card issuer, in the case of a debit card.

(2) Credit card. - The term "credit card" has the same meaning as in section 1602 of this title.

(3) Debit card. - The term "debit card" means any card issued by a financial institution to a consumer for use in initiating an electronic fund transfer from the account of the consumer at such financial institution, for the purpose of transferring money between accounts or obtaining money, property, labor, or services.

(4) Account and electronic fund transfer.-The terms "account" and "electronic fund transfer" have the same meanings as in section 1693a of this title.

(5) Credit and creditor. - The terms "credit" and "creditor" have the same meanings as in section 1691a of this title.

(s) Federal Banking Agency. - The term "Federal banking agency" has the same meaning as in section 1813 of title 12.

(t) Financial Institution. - The term "financial institution" means a State or National bank, a State or Federal savings and loan association, a mutual savings bank, a State or Federal credit union, or any other person that, directly or indirectly, holds a transaction account (as defined in section 461(b) of title 12) belonging to a consumer.

(u) Reseller. - The term "reseller" means a consumer reporting agency that -

(1) assembles and merges information contained in the database of another consumer reporting agency or multiple consumer reporting agencies concerning any consumer for purposes of furnishing such information to any third party, to the extent of such activities; and

(2) does not maintain a database of the assembled or merged information from which new consumer reports are produced.

(v) Commission. - The term "Commission" means the Bureau.

(w) The term "Bureau" means the Bureau of Consumer Financial Protection.

(x) Nationwide Specialty Consumer Reporting Agency. - The term "nationwide specialty consumer reporting agency" means a consumer reporting agency that compiles and maintains files on consumers on a nationwide basis relating to-

(1) medical records or payments;

(2) residential or tenant history;

(3) check writing history;

(4) employment history; or

(5) insurance claims.

(y) Exclusion of Certain Communications for Employee Investigations. -

(1) Communications described in this subsection.-A communication is described in this subsection if-

(A) but for subsection (d)(2)(D), the communication would be a consumer report;

(B) the communication is made to an employer in connection with an investigation of-

(i) suspected misconduct relating to employment; or

(ii) compliance with Federal, State, or local laws and regulations, the rules of a self-regulatory organization, or any preexisting written policies of the employer;

(C) the communication is not made for the purpose of investigating a consumer's credit worthiness, credit standing, or credit capacity; and

(D) the communication is not provided to any person except-

(i) to the employer or an agent of the employer;

(ii) to any Federal or State officer, agency, or department, or any officer, agency, or department of a unit of general local government;

(iii) to any self-regulatory organization with regulatory authority over the activities of the employer or employee;

(iv) as otherwise required by law; or

(v) pursuant to section 1681f of this title.

(2) Subsequent disclosure. - After taking any adverse action based in whole or in part on a communication described in paragraph (1), the employer shall disclose to the consumer a summary containing the nature and substance of the communication upon which the adverse action is based, except that the sources of information acquired solely for use in preparing what would be but for subsection (d)(2)(D) an investigative consumer report need not be disclosed.

(3) Self-regulatory organization defined.-For purposes of this subsection, the term "self-regulatory organization" includes any self-regulatory organization (as defined in section 78c(a)(26) of this title), any entity established under title I of the Sarbanes-Oxley Act of 2002 [15 U.S.C. 7211 et seq.], any board of trade designated by the Commodity Futures Trading Commission, and any futures association registered with such Commission.

§ 1681b. Permissible purposes of consumer reports

(a) In general. Subject to subsection (c), any consumer reporting agency may furnish a consumer report under the following circumstances and no other:

(1) In response to the order of a court having jurisdiction to issue such an order, or a subpoena issued in connection with proceedings before a Federal grand jury.

(2) In accordance with the written instructions of the consumer to whom it relates.

(3) To a person which it has reason to believe-

(A) intends to use the information in connection with a credit transaction involving the consumer on whom the information is to be furnished and involving the extension of credit to, or review or collection of an account of, the consumer; or

(B) intends to use the information for employment purposes; or

(C) intends to use the information in connection with the underwriting of insurance involving the consumer; or

(D) intends to use the information in connection with a determination of the consumer's eligibility for a license or other benefit granted by a governmental instrumentality required by law to consider an applicant's financial responsibility or status; or

(E) intends to use the information, as a potential investor or servicer, or current insurer, in connection with a valuation of, or an assessment of the credit or prepayment risks associated with, an existing credit obligation; or

(F) otherwise has a legitimate business need for the information-

(i) in connection with a business transaction that is initiated by the consumer; or

(ii) to review an account to determine whether the consumer continues to meet the terms of the account.

(G) executive departments and agencies in connection with the issuance of government-sponsored individually-billed travel charge cards.

(4) In response to a request by the head of a State or local child support enforcement agency (or a State or local government official authorized by the head of such an agency), if the person making the request certifies to the consumer reporting agency that-

(A) the consumer report is needed for the purpose of establishing an individual's capacity to make child support payments, determining the appropriate level of such payments, or enforcing a child support order, award, agreement, or judgment;

(B) the parentage of the consumer for the child to which the obligation relates has been established or acknowledged by the consumer in accordance with State laws under which the obligation arises (if required by those laws); and

(C) the consumer report will be kept confidential, will be used solely for a purpose described in subparagraph (A), and will not be used in connection with any other civil, administrative, or criminal proceeding, or for any other purpose.

(5) To an agency administering a State plan under section 654 of title 42 for use to set an initial or modified child support award.

(6) To the Federal Deposit Insurance Corporation or the National Credit Union Administration as part of its preparation for its appointment or as part of its exercise of powers, as conservator, receiver, or liquidating agent for an insured depository institution or insured credit union under the Federal Deposit Insurance Act [12 U.S.C. 1811 et seq.] or the Federal Credit Union Act [12 U.S.C. 1751 et seq.], or other applicable Federal or State law, or in connection with the resolution or liquidation of a failed or failing insured depository institution or insured credit union, as applicable.

(b) Conditions for furnishing and using consumer reports for employment purposes

(1) Certification from user

A consumer reporting agency may furnish a consumer report for employment purposes only if-

(A) the person who obtains such report from the agency certifies to the agency that-

(i) the person has complied with paragraph (2) with respect to the consumer report, and the person will comply with paragraph (3) with respect to the consumer report if paragraph (3) becomes applicable; and

(ii) information from the consumer report will not be used in violation of any applicable Federal or State equal employment opportunity law or regulation; and

(B) the consumer reporting agency provides with the report, or has previously provided, a summary of the consumer's rights under this subchapter, as prescribed by the Bureau under section 1681g(c)(3) 1 of this title.

(2) Disclosure to consumer

(A) In general

Except as provided in subparagraph (B), a person may not procure a consumer report, or cause a consumer report to be procured, for employment purposes with respect to any consumer, unless-

(i) a clear and conspicuous disclosure has been made in writing to the consumer at any time before the report is procured or caused to be procured, in a document that consists solely of the disclosure, that a consumer report may be obtained for employment purposes; and

(ii) the consumer has authorized in writing (which authorization may be made on the document referred to in clause (i)) the procurement of the report by that person.

(B) Application by mail, telephone, computer, or other similar means

If a consumer described in subparagraph (C) applies for employment by mail, telephone, computer, or other similar means, at any time before a consumer report is procured or caused to be procured in connection with that application-

(i) the person who procures the consumer report on the consumer for employment purposes shall provide to the consumer, by oral, written, or electronic means, notice that a consumer report may be obtained for employment purposes, and a summary of the consumer's rights under section 1681m(a)(3) 1 of this title; and

(ii) the consumer shall have consented, orally, in writing, or electronically to the procurement of the report by that person.

(C) Scope

Subparagraph (B) shall apply to a person procuring a consumer report on a consumer in connection with the consumer's application for employment only if-

(i) the consumer is applying for a position over which the Secretary of Transportation has the power to establish qualifications and maximum hours of service pursuant to the provisions of section 31502 of title 49, or a position subject to safety regulation by a State transportation agency; and

(ii) as of the time at which the person procures the report or causes the report to be procured the only interaction between the consumer and the person in connection with that employment application has been by mail, telephone, computer, or other similar means.

(3) Conditions on use for adverse actions

(A) In general

Except as provided in subparagraph (B), in using a consumer report for employment purposes, before taking any adverse action based in whole or in part on the report, the person intending to take such adverse action shall provide to the consumer to whom the report relates -

(i) a copy of the report; and

(ii) a description in writing of the rights of the consumer under this subchapter, as prescribed by the Bureau under section 1681g(c)(3) 1 of this title.

(B) Application by mail, telephone, computer, or other similar means

(i) If a consumer described in subparagraph (C) applies for employment by mail, telephone, computer, or other similar means, and if a person who has procured a consumer report on the consumer for employment purposes takes adverse action on the employment application based in whole or in part on the report, then the person must provide to the consumer to whom the report relates, in lieu of the notices required under subparagraph (A) of this section and under section 1681m(a) of this title, within 3 business days of taking such action, an oral, written or electronic notification-

(I) that adverse action has been taken based in whole or in part on a consumer report received from a consumer reporting agency;

(II) of the name, address and telephone number of the consumer reporting agency that furnished the consumer report (including a toll-free telephone number established by the agency if the agency compiles and maintains files on consumers on a nationwide basis);

(III) that the consumer reporting agency did not make the decision to take the adverse action and is unable to provide to the consumer the specific reasons why the adverse action was taken; and

(IV) that the consumer may, upon providing proper identification, request a free copy of a report and may dispute with the consumer reporting agency the accuracy or completeness of any information in a report.

(ii) If, under clause (B)(i)(IV), the consumer requests a copy of a consumer report from the person who procured the report, then, within 3 business days of receiving the consumer's request, together with proper identification, the person must send or provide to the consumer a copy of a report and a copy of the consumer's rights as prescribed by the Bureau under section 1681g(c)(3) 1 of this title.

(C) Scope

Subparagraph (B) shall apply to a person procuring a consumer report on a consumer in connection with the consumer's application for employment only if-

(i) the consumer is applying for a position over which the Secretary of Transportation has the power to establish qualifications and maximum hours of service pursuant to the provisions of section 31502 of title 49, or a position subject to safety regulation by a State transportation agency; and

(ii) as of the time at which the person procures the report or causes the report to be procured the only interaction between the consumer and the person in connection with that employment application has been by mail, telephone, computer, or other similar means.

(4) Exception for national security investigations

(A) In general

In the case of an agency or department of the United States Government which seeks to obtain and use a consumer report for employment purposes, paragraph (3) shall not apply to any adverse action by such agency or department which is based in part on such consumer report, if the head of such agency or department makes a written finding that -

(i) the consumer report is relevant to a national security investigation of such agency or department;

(ii) the investigation is within the jurisdiction of such agency or department;

(iii) there is reason to believe that compliance with paragraph (3) will-

(I) endanger the life or physical safety of any person;

(II) result in flight from prosecution;

(III) result in the destruction of, or tampering with, evidence relevant to the investigation;

(IV) result in the intimidation of a potential witness relevant to the investigation;

(V) result in the compromise of classified information; or

(VI) otherwise seriously jeopardize or unduly delay the investigation or another official proceeding.

(B) Notification of consumer upon conclusion of investigation

Upon the conclusion of a national security investigation described in subparagraph (A), or upon the determination that the exception under subparagraph (A) is no longer required for the reasons set forth in such subparagraph, the official exercising the authority in such subparagraph shall provide to the consumer who is the subject of the consumer report with regard to which such finding was made-

(i) a copy of such consumer report with any classified information redacted as necessary;

(ii) notice of any adverse action which is based, in part, on the consumer report; and

(iii) the identification with reasonable specificity of the nature of the investigation for which the consumer report was sought.

(C) Delegation by head of agency or department

For purposes of subparagraphs (A) and (B), the head of any agency or department of the United States Government may delegate his or her authorities under this paragraph to an official of such agency or department who has personnel security responsibilities and is a member of the Senior Executive Service or equivalent civilian or military rank.

(D) Definitions

For purposes of this paragraph, the following definitions shall apply:

(i) Classified information

The term "classified information" means information that is protected from unauthorized disclosure under Executive Order No. 12958 or successor orders.

(ii) National security investigation

The term "national security investigation" means any official inquiry by an agency or department of the United States Government to determine the eligibility of a consumer to receive access or continued access to classified information or to determine whether classified information has been lost or compromised.

(c) Furnishing reports in connection with credit or insurance transactions that are not initiated by consumer

(1) In general

A consumer reporting agency may furnish a consumer report relating to any consumer pursuant to subparagraph (A) or (C) of subsection (a)(3) in connection with any credit or insurance transaction that is not initiated by the consumer only if-

(A) the consumer authorizes the agency to provide such report to such person; or

(B)(i) the transaction consists of a firm offer of credit or insurance;

(ii) the consumer reporting agency has complied with subsection (e);

(iii) there is not in effect an election by the consumer, made in accordance with subsection (e), to have the consumer's name and address excluded from lists of names provided by the agency pursuant to this paragraph; and

(iv) the consumer report does not contain a date of birth that shows that the consumer has not attained the age of 21, or, if the date of birth on the consumer report shows that the consumer has not attained the age of 21, such consumer consents to the consumer reporting agency to such furnishing.

(2) Limits on information received under paragraph (1)(B)

A person may receive pursuant to paragraph (1)(B) only-

(A) the name and address of a consumer;

(B) an identifier that is not unique to the consumer and that is used by the person solely for the purpose of verifying the identity of the consumer; and

(C) other information pertaining to a consumer that does not identify the relationship or experience of the consumer with respect to a particular creditor or other entity.

(3) Information regarding inquiries

Except as provided in section 1681g(a)(5) of this title, a consumer reporting agency shall not furnish to any person a record of inquiries in connection with a credit or insurance transaction that is not initiated by a consumer.

(d) Reserved

(e) Election of consumer to be excluded from lists

(1) In general

A consumer may elect to have the consumer's name and address excluded from any list provided by a consumer reporting agency under subsection (c)(1)(B) in connection with a credit or insurance transaction that is not initiated by the consumer, by notifying the agency in accordance with paragraph (2) that the consumer does not consent to any use of a consumer report relating to the consumer in connection with any credit or insurance transaction that is not initiated by the consumer.

(2) Manner of notification

A consumer shall notify a consumer reporting agency under paragraph (1)-

(A) through the notification system maintained by the agency under paragraph (5); or

(B) by submitting to the agency a signed notice of election form issued by the agency for purposes of this subparagraph.

(3) Response of agency after notification through system

Upon receipt of notification of the election of a consumer under paragraph (1) through the notification system maintained by the agency under paragraph (5), a consumer reporting agency shall-

(A) inform the consumer that the election is effective only for the 5-year period following the election if the consumer does not submit to the agency a signed notice of election form issued by the agency for purposes of paragraph (2)(B); and

(B) provide to the consumer a notice of election form, if requested by the consumer, not later than 5 business days after receipt of the notification of the election through the system established under paragraph (5), in the case of a request made at the time the consumer provides notification through the system.

(4) Effectiveness of election

An election of a consumer under paragraph (1)-

(A) shall be effective with respect to a consumer reporting agency beginning 5 business days after the date on which the consumer notifies the agency in accordance with paragraph (2);

(B) shall be effective with respect to a consumer reporting agency-

(i) subject to subparagraph (C), during the 5-year period beginning 5 business days after the date on which the consumer notifies the agency of the election, in the case of an election for which a consumer notifies the agency only in accordance with paragraph (2)(A); or

(ii) until the consumer notifies the agency under subparagraph (C), in the case of an election for which a consumer notifies the agency in accordance with paragraph (2)(B);

(C) shall not be effective after the date on which the consumer notifies the agency, through the notification system established by the agency under paragraph (5), that the election is no longer effective; and

(D) shall be effective with respect to each affiliate of the agency.

(5) Notification system

(A) In general

Each consumer reporting agency that, under subsection (c)(1)(B), furnishes a consumer report in connection with a credit or insurance transaction that is not initiated by a consumer, shall-

(i) establish and maintain a notification system, including a toll-free telephone number, which permits any consumer whose consumer report is maintained by the agency to notify the agency, with appropriate identification, of the consumer's election to have the consumer's name and address excluded from any such list of names and addresses provided by the agency for such a transaction; and

(ii) publish by not later than 365 days after September 30, 1996, and not less than annually thereafter, in a publication of general circulation in the area served by the agency-

(I) a notification that information in consumer files maintained by the agency may be used in connection with such transactions; and

(II) the address and toll-free telephone number for consumers to use to notify the agency of the consumer's election under clause (i).

(B) Establishment and maintenance as compliance

Establishment and maintenance of a notification system (including a toll-free telephone number) and publication by a consumer reporting agency on the agency's own behalf and on behalf of any of its affiliates in accordance with this paragraph is deemed to be compliance with this paragraph by each of those affiliates.

(6) Notification system by agencies that operate nationwide

Each consumer reporting agency that compiles and maintains files on consumers on a nationwide basis shall establish and maintain a notification system for purposes of paragraph (5) jointly with other such consumer reporting agencies.

(f) Certain use or obtaining of information prohibited

A person shall not use or obtain a consumer report for any purpose unless-

(1) the consumer report is obtained for a purpose for which the consumer report is authorized to be furnished under this section; and

(2) the purpose is certified in accordance with section 1681e of this title by a prospective user of the report through a general or specific certification.

(g) Protection of medical information

(1) Limitation on consumer reporting agencies

A consumer reporting agency shall not furnish for employment purposes, or in connection with a credit or insurance transaction, a consumer report that contains medical information (other than medical contact information treated in the manner required under section 1681c(a)(6) of this title) about a consumer, unless-

(A) if furnished in connection with an insurance transaction, the consumer affirmatively consents to the furnishing of the report;

(B) if furnished for employment purposes or in connection with a credit transaction-

(i) the information to be furnished is relevant to process or effect the employment or credit transaction; and

(ii) the consumer provides specific written consent for the furnishing of the report that describes in clear and conspicuous language the use for which the information will be furnished; or

(C) the information to be furnished pertains solely to transactions, accounts, or balances relating to debts arising from the receipt of medical services, products, or devises, where such information, other than account status or amounts, is restricted or reported using codes that do not identify, or do not provide information sufficient to infer, the specific provider or the nature of such services, products, or devices, as provided in section 1681c(a)(6) of this title.

(2) Limitation on creditors

Except as permitted pursuant to paragraph (3)(C) or regulations prescribed under paragraph (5)(A), a creditor shall not obtain or use medical information (other than medical information treated in the manner required under section 1681c(a)(6) of this title) pertaining to a consumer in connection with any determination of the consumer's eligibility, or continued eligibility, for credit.

(3) Actions authorized by Federal law, insurance activities and regulatory determinations

Section 1681a(d)(3) of this title shall not be construed so as to treat information or any communication of information as a consumer report if the information or communication is disclosed-

(A) in connection with the business of insurance or annuities, including the activities described in section 18B of the model Privacy of Consumer Financial and Health Information Regulation issued by the National Association of Insurance Commissioners (as in effect on January 1, 2003);

(B) for any purpose permitted without authorization under the Standards for Individually Identifiable Health Information promulgated by the Department of Health and Human Services pursuant to the Health Insurance Portability and Accountability Act of 1996, or referred to under section 1179 of such Act,1 or described in section 6802(e) of this title; or

(C) as otherwise determined to be necessary and appropriate, by regulation or order, by the Bureau or the applicable State insurance authority (with respect to any person engaged in providing insurance or annuities).

(4) Limitation on redisclosure of medical information

Any person that receives medical information pursuant to paragraph (1) or (3) shall not disclose such information to any other person, except as necessary to carry out the purpose for which the information was initially disclosed, or as otherwise permitted by statute, regulation, or order.

(5) Regulations and effective date for paragraph (2)

(A) Regulations required

The Bureau may, after notice and opportunity for comment, prescribe regulations that permit transactions under paragraph (2) that are determined to be necessary and appropriate to protect legitimate operational, transactional, risk, consumer, and other needs (and which shall include permitting actions necessary for administrative verification purposes), consistent with the intent of paragraph (2) to restrict the use of medical information for inappropriate purposes.

(6) Coordination with other laws

No provision of this subsection shall be construed as altering, affecting, or superseding the applicability of any other provision of Federal law relating to medical confidentiality.

§ 1681c. Requirements relating to information contained in consumer reports

(a) Information excluded from consumer reports

Except as authorized under subsection (b), no consumer reporting agency may make any consumer report containing any of the following items of information:

(1) Cases under title 11 or under the Bankruptcy Act that, from the date of entry of the order for relief or the date of adjudication, as the case may be, antedate the report by more than 10 years.

(2) Civil suits, civil judgments, and records of arrest that, from date of entry, antedate the report by more than seven years or until the governing statute of limitations has expired, whichever is the longer period.

(3) Paid tax liens which, from date of payment, antedate the report by more than seven years.

(4) Accounts placed for collection or charged to profit and loss which antedate the report by more than seven years.

(5) Any other adverse item of information, other than records of convictions of crimes which antedates the report by more than seven years.

(6) The name, address, and telephone number of any medical information furnisher that has notified the agency of its status, unless-

(A) such name, address, and telephone number are restricted or reported using codes that do not identify, or provide information sufficient to infer, the specific provider or the nature of such services, products, or devices to a person other than the consumer; or

(B) the report is being provided to an insurance company for a purpose relating to engaging in the business of insurance other than property and casualty insurance.

(b) Exempted cases

The provisions of paragraphs (1) through (5) of subsection (a) are not applicable in the case of any consumer credit report to be used in connection with-

(1) a credit transaction involving, or which may reasonably be expected to involve, a principal amount of $150,000 or more;

(2) the underwriting of life insurance involving, or which may reasonably be expected to involve, a face amount of $150,000 or more; or

(3) the employment of any individual at an annual salary which equals, or which may reasonably be expected to equal $75,000, or more.

(c) Running of reporting period

(1) In general

The 7-year period referred to in paragraphs (4) and (6) of subsection (a) shall begin, with respect to any delinquent account that is placed for collection (internally or by referral to a third party, whichever is earlier), charged to profit and loss, or subjected to any similar action, upon the expiration of the 180-day period beginning on the date of the commencement of the delinquency which immediately preceded the collection activity, charge to profit and loss, or similar action.

(2) Effective date

Paragraph (1) shall apply only to items of information added to the file of a consumer on or after the date that is 455 days after September 30, 1996.

(d) Information required to be disclosed

(1) Title 11 information

Any consumer reporting agency that furnishes a consumer report that contains information regarding any case involving the consumer that arises under title 11 shall include in the report an identification of the chapter of such title 11 under which such case arises if provided by the source of the information. If any case arising or filed under title 11 is withdrawn by the consumer before a final judgment, the consumer reporting agency shall include in the report that such case or filing was withdrawn upon receipt of documentation certifying such withdrawal.

(2) Key factor in credit score information

Any consumer reporting agency that furnishes a consumer report that contains any credit score or any other risk score or predictor on any consumer shall include in the report a clear and conspicuous statement that a key factor (as defined in section 1681g(f)(2)(B) of this title) that adversely affected such score or predictor was the number of enquiries, if such a predictor was in fact a key factor that adversely affected such score. This paragraph shall not apply to a check services company, acting as such, which issues authorizations for the purpose of approving or processing negotiable instruments, electronic fund transfers, or similar methods of payments, but only to the extent that such company is engaged in such activities.

(e) Indication of closure of account by consumer

If a consumer reporting agency is notified pursuant to section 1681s–2(a)(4) of this title that a credit account of a consumer was voluntarily closed by the consumer, the agency shall indicate that fact in any consumer report that includes information related to the account.

(f) Indication of dispute by consumer

If a consumer reporting agency is notified pursuant to section 1681s–2(a)(3) of this title that information regarding a consumer who was furnished to the agency is disputed by the consumer, the agency shall indicate that fact in each consumer report that includes the disputed information.

(g) Truncation of credit card and debit card numbers

    (1) In general

Except as otherwise provided in this subsection, no person that accepts credit cards or debit cards for the transaction of business shall print more than the last 5 digits of the card number or the expiration date upon any receipt provided to the cardholder at the point of the sale or transaction.

    (2) Limitation

This subsection shall apply only to receipts that are electronically printed, and shall not apply to transactions in which the sole means of recording a credit card or debit card account number is by handwriting or by an imprint or copy of the card.

    (3) Effective date

This subsection shall become effective-

        (A) 3 years after December 4, 2003, with respect to any cash register or other machine or device that electronically prints receipts for credit card or debit card transactions that is in use before January 1, 2005; and

        (B) 1 year after December 4, 2003, with respect to any cash register or other machine or device that electronically prints receipts for credit card or debit card transactions that is first put into use on or after January 1, 2005.

(h) Notice of discrepancy in address

    (1) In general

If a person has requested a consumer report relating to a consumer from a consumer reporting agency described in section 1681a(p) of this title, the request includes an address for the consumer that substantially differs from the addresses in the file of the consumer, and the agency provides a consumer report in response to the request, the consumer reporting agency shall notify the requester of the existence of the discrepancy.

    (2) Regulations

        (A) Regulations required

The Bureau shall, in consultation with the Federal banking agencies, the National Credit Union Administration, and the Federal Trade Commission,,2 prescribe regulations providing guidance regarding reasonable policies and procedures that a user of a consumer report should employ when such user has received a notice of discrepancy under paragraph (1).

        (B) Policies and procedures to be included

The regulations prescribed under subparagraph (A) shall describe reasonable policies and procedures for use by a user of a consumer report-

            (i) to form a reasonable belief that the user knows the identity of the person to whom the consumer report pertains; and

            (ii) if the user establishes a continuing relationship with the consumer, and the user regularly and in the ordinary course of business furnishes information to the consumer reporting agency from which the notice of discrepancy pertaining to the consumer was obtained, to reconcile the address of the consumer with the consumer reporting agency by furnishing such address to such consumer reporting agency as part of information regularly furnished by the user for the period in which the relationship is established.

§ 1681c-1. Identity theft prevention; fraud alerts and active duty alerts

(a) One-call fraud alerts

(1) Initial alerts

Upon the direct request of a consumer, or an individual acting on behalf of or as a personal representative of a consumer, who asserts in good faith a suspicion that the consumer has been or is about to become a victim of fraud or related crime, including identity theft, a consumer reporting agency described in section 1681a(p) of this title that maintains a file on the consumer and has received appropriate proof of the identity of the requester shall-

(A) include a fraud alert in the file of that consumer, and also provide that alert along with any credit score generated in using that file, for a period of not less than 90 days, beginning on the date of such request, unless the consumer or such representative requests that such fraud alert be removed before the end of such period, and the agency has received appropriate proof of the identity of the requester for such purpose; and

(B) refer the information regarding the fraud alert under this paragraph to each of the other consumer reporting agencies described in section 1681a(p) of this title, in accordance with procedures developed under section 1681s(f) of this title.

(2) Access to free reports

In any case in which a consumer reporting agency includes a fraud alert in the file of a consumer pursuant to this subsection, the consumer reporting agency shall-

(A) disclose to the consumer that the consumer may request a free copy of the file of the consumer pursuant to section 1681j(d) of this title; and

(B) provide to the consumer all disclosures required to be made under section 1681g of this title, without charge to the consumer, not later than 3 business days after any request described in subparagraph (A).

(b) Extended alerts

(1) In general

Upon the direct request of a consumer, or an individual acting on behalf of or as a personal representative of a consumer, who submits an identity theft report to a consumer reporting agency described in section 1681a(p) of this title that maintains a file on the consumer, if the agency has received appropriate proof of the identity of the requester, the agency shall-

(A) include a fraud alert in the file of that consumer, and also provide that alert along with any credit score generated in using that file, during the 7-year period beginning on the date of such request, unless the consumer or such representative requests that such fraud alert be removed before the end of such period and the agency has received appropriate proof of the identity of the requester for such purpose;

(B) during the 5-year period beginning on the date of such request, exclude the consumer from any list of consumers prepared by the consumer reporting agency and provided to any third party to offer credit or insurance to the consumer as part of a transaction that was not initiated by the consumer, unless the consumer or such representative requests that such exclusion be rescinded before the end of such period; and

(C) refer the information regarding the extended fraud alert under this paragraph to each of the other consumer reporting agencies described in section 1681a(p) of this title, in accordance with procedures developed under section 1681s(f) of this title.

(2) Access to free reports

In any case in which a consumer reporting agency includes a fraud alert in the file of a consumer pursuant to this subsection, the consumer reporting agency shall-

(A) disclose to the consumer that the consumer may request 2 free copies of the file of the consumer pursuant to section 1681j(d) of this title during the 12-month period beginning on the date on which the fraud alert was included in the file; and

(B) provide to the consumer all disclosures required to be made under section 1681g of this title, without charge to the consumer, not later than 3 business days after any request described in subparagraph (A).

(c) Active duty alerts

Upon the direct request of an active duty military consumer, or an individual acting on behalf of or as a personal representative of an active duty military consumer, a consumer reporting agency described in section 1681a(p) of this title that maintains a file on the active duty military consumer and has received appropriate proof of the identity of the requester shall-

(1) include an active duty alert in the file of that active duty military consumer, and also provide that alert along with any credit score generated in using that file, during a period of not less than 12 months, or such longer period as the Bureau shall determine, by regulation, beginning on the date of the request, unless the active duty military consumer or such representative requests that such fraud alert

be removed before the end of such period, and the agency has received appropriate proof of the identity of the requester for such purpose;

(2) during the 2-year period beginning on the date of such request, exclude the active duty military consumer from any list of consumers prepared by the consumer reporting agency and provided to any third party to offer credit or insurance to the consumer as part of a transaction that was not initiated by the consumer, unless the consumer requests that such exclusion be rescinded before the end of such period; and

(3) refer the information regarding the active duty alert to each of the other consumer reporting agencies described in section 1681a(p) of this title, in accordance with procedures developed under section 1681s(f) of this title.

(d) Procedures

Each consumer reporting agency described in section 1681a(p) of this title shall establish policies and procedures to comply with this section, including procedures that inform consumers of the availability of initial, extended, and active duty alerts and procedures that allow consumers and active duty military consumers to request initial, extended, or active duty alerts (as applicable) in a simple and easy manner, including by telephone.

(e) Referrals of alerts

Each consumer reporting agency described in section 1681a(p) of this title that receives a referral of a fraud alert or active duty alert from another consumer reporting agency pursuant to this section shall, as though the agency received the request from the consumer directly, follow the procedures required under-

(1) paragraphs (1)(A) and (2) of subsection (a), in the case of a referral under subsection (a)(1)(B);

(2) paragraphs (1)(A), (1)(B), and (2) of subsection (b), in the case of a referral under subsection (b)(1)(C); and

(3) paragraphs (1) and (2) of subsection (c), in the case of a referral under subsection (c)(3).

(f) Duty of reseller to reconvey alert

A reseller shall include in its report any fraud alert or active duty alert placed in the file of a consumer pursuant to this section by another consumer reporting agency.

(g) Duty of other consumer reporting agencies to provide contact information

If a consumer contacts any consumer reporting agency that is not described in section 1681a(p) of this title to communicate a suspicion that the consumer has been or is about to become a victim of fraud or related crime, including identity theft, the agency shall provide information to the consumer on how to contact the Bureau and the consumer reporting agencies described in section 1681a(p) of this title to obtain more detailed information and request alerts under this section.

(h) Limitations on use of information for credit extensions

United States
Fair Credit Reporting Act

(1) Requirements for initial and active duty alerts

(A) Notification

Each initial fraud alert and active duty alert under this section shall include information that notifies all prospective users of a consumer report on the consumer to which the alert relates that the consumer does not authorize the establishment of any new credit plan or extension of credit, other than under an open-end credit plan (as defined in section 1602(i) 1 of this title), in the name of the consumer, or issuance of an additional card on an existing credit account requested by a consumer, or any increase in credit limit on an existing credit account requested by a consumer, except in accordance with subparagraph (B).

(B) Limitation on users

(i) In general

No prospective user of a consumer report that includes an initial fraud alert or an active duty alert in accordance with this section may establish a new credit plan or extension of credit, other than under an open-end credit plan (as defined in section 1602(i) 1 of this title), in the name of the consumer, or issue an additional card on an existing credit account requested by a consumer, or grant any increase in credit limit on an existing credit account requested by a consumer, unless the user utilizes reasonable policies and procedures to form a reasonable belief that the user knows the identity of the person making the request.

(ii) Verification

If a consumer requesting the alert has specified a telephone number to be used for identity verification purposes, before authorizing any new credit plan or extension described in clause (i) in the name of such consumer, a user of such consumer report shall contact the consumer using that telephone number or take reasonable steps to verify the consumer's identity and confirm that the application for a new credit plan is not the result of identity theft.

(2) Requirements for extended alerts

(A) Notification

Each extended alert under this section shall include information that provides all prospective users of a consumer report relating to a consumer with-

(i) notification that the consumer does not authorize the establishment of any new credit plan or extension of credit described in clause (i), other than under an open-end credit plan (as defined in section 1602(i) 1 of this title), in the name of the consumer, or issuance of an additional card on an existing credit account requested by a consumer, or any increase in credit limit on an existing credit account requested by a consumer, except in accordance with subparagraph (B); and

(ii) a telephone number or other reasonable contact method designated by the consumer.

(B) Limitation on users

No prospective user of a consumer report or of a credit score generated using the information in the file of a consumer that includes an extended fraud alert in accordance with this section may establish a new credit plan or extension of credit, other than under an open-end credit plan (as defined in section 1602(i) of this title), in the name of the consumer, or issue an additional card on an existing credit account requested by a consumer, or any increase in credit limit on an existing credit account requested by a consumer, unless the user contacts the consumer in person or using the contact method described in subparagraph (A)(ii) to confirm that the application for a new credit plan or increase in credit limit, or request for an additional card is not the result of identity theft.

§ 1681c-2. Block of information resulting from identity theft

(a) Block

Except as otherwise provided in this section, a consumer reporting agency shall block the reporting of any information in the file of a consumer that the consumer identifies as information that resulted from an alleged identity theft, not later than 4 business days after the date of receipt by such agency of-

(1) appropriate proof of the identity of the consumer;

(2) a copy of an identity theft report;

(3) the identification of such information by the consumer; and

(4) a statement by the consumer that the information is not information relating to any transaction by the consumer.

(b) Notification

A consumer reporting agency shall promptly notify the furnisher of information identified by the consumer under subsection (a)-

(1) that the information may be a result of identity theft;

(2) that an identity theft report has been filed;

(3) that a block has been requested under this section; and

(4) of the effective dates of the block.

(c) Authority to decline or rescind

(1) In general

A consumer reporting agency may decline to block, or may rescind any block, of information relating to a consumer under this section, if the consumer reporting agency reasonably determines that-

(A) the information was blocked in error or a block was requested by the consumer in error;

(B) the information was blocked, or a block was requested by the consumer, on the basis of a material misrepresentation of fact by the consumer relevant to the request to block; or

(C) the consumer obtained possession of goods, services, or money as a result of the blocked transaction or transactions.

(2) Notification to consumer

If a block of information is declined or rescinded under this subsection, the affected consumer shall be notified promptly, in the same manner as consumers are notified of the reinsertion of information under section 1681i(a)(5)(B) of this title.

(3) Significance of block

For purposes of this subsection, if a consumer reporting agency rescinds a block, the presence of information in the file of a consumer prior to the blocking of such information is not evidence of whether the consumer knew or should have known that the consumer obtained possession of any goods, services, or money as a result of the block.

(d) Exception for resellers

(1) No reseller file

This section shall not apply to a consumer reporting agency, if the consumer reporting agency-

(A) is a reseller;

(B) is not, at the time of the request of the consumer under subsection (a), otherwise furnishing or reselling a consumer report concerning the information identified by the consumer; and

(C) informs the consumer, by any means, that the consumer may report the identity theft to the Bureau to obtain consumer information regarding identity theft.

(2) Reseller with file

The sole obligation of the consumer reporting agency under this section, with regard to any request of a consumer under this section, shall be to block the consumer report maintained by the consumer reporting agency from any subsequent use, if-

(A) the consumer, in accordance with the provisions of subsection (a), identifies, to a consumer reporting agency, information in the file of the consumer that resulted from identity theft; and

(B) the consumer reporting agency is a reseller of the identified information.

(3) Notice

In carrying out its obligation under paragraph (2), the reseller shall promptly provide a notice to the consumer of the decision to block the file. Such notice shall contain the name, address, and telephone number of each consumer reporting agency from which the consumer information was obtained for resale.

(e) Exception for verification companies

The provisions of this section do not apply to a check services company, acting as such, which issues authorizations for the purpose of approving or processing negotiable instruments, electronic fund transfers, or similar methods of payments, except that, beginning 4 business days after receipt of information described in paragraphs (1) through (3) of subsection (a), a check services company shall not report to a national consumer reporting agency described in section 1681a(p) of this title, any information identified in the subject identity theft report as resulting from identity theft.

(f) Access to blocked information by law enforcement agencies

No provision of this section shall be construed as requiring a consumer reporting agency to prevent a Federal, State, or local law enforcement agency from accessing blocked information in a consumer file to which the agency could otherwise obtain access under this subchapter.

§ 1681d. Disclosure of investigative consumer reports

(a) Disclosure of fact of preparation

A person may not procure or cause to be prepared an investigative consumer report on any consumer unless-

(1) it is clearly and accurately disclosed to the consumer that an investigative consumer report including information as to his character, general reputation, personal characteristics, and mode of living, whichever are applicable, may be made, and such disclosure (A) is made in a writing mailed, or otherwise delivered, to the consumer, not later than three days after the date on which the report was first requested, and (B) includes a statement informing the consumer of his right to request the additional disclosures provided for under subsection (b) of this section and the written summary of the rights of the consumer prepared pursuant to section 1681g(c) of this title; and

(2) the person certifies or has certified to the consumer reporting agency that-

(A) the person has made the disclosures to the consumer required by paragraph (1); and

(B) the person will comply with subsection (b).

(b) Disclosure on request of nature and scope of investigation

Any person who procures or causes to be prepared an investigative consumer report on any consumer shall, upon written request made by the consumer within a reasonable period of time after the receipt by him of the disclosure required by subsection (a)(1), make a complete and accurate disclosure of the nature and scope of the investigation requested. This disclosure shall be made in a writing mailed, or otherwise delivered, to the consumer not later than five days after the date on which the request for such disclosure was received from the consumer or such report was first requested, whichever is the later.

(c) Limitation on liability upon showing of reasonable procedures for compliance with provisions

No person may be held liable for any violation of subsection (a) or (b) of this section if he shows by a preponderance of the evidence that at the time of the violation he maintained reasonable procedures to assure compliance with subsection (a) or (b).

(d) Prohibitions

(1) Certification

A consumer reporting agency shall not prepare or furnish an investigative consumer report unless the agency has received a certification under subsection (a)(2) from the person who requested the report.

(2) Inquiries

A consumer reporting agency shall not make an inquiry for the purpose of preparing an investigative consumer report on a consumer for employment purposes if the making of the inquiry by an employer or prospective employer of the consumer would violate any applicable Federal or State equal employment opportunity law or regulation.

(3) Certain public record information

Except as otherwise provided in section 1681k of this title, a consumer reporting agency shall not furnish an investigative consumer report that includes information that is a matter of public record and that relates to an arrest, indictment, conviction, civil judicial action, tax lien, or outstanding judgment, unless the agency has verified the accuracy of the information during the 30-day period ending on the date on which the report is furnished.

(4) Certain adverse information

A consumer reporting agency shall not prepare or furnish an investigative consumer report on a consumer that contains information that is adverse to the interest of the consumer and that is obtained through a personal interview with a neighbor, friend, or associate of the consumer or with another person with whom the consumer is acquainted or who has knowledge of such item of information, unless-

(A) the agency has followed reasonable procedures to obtain confirmation of the information, from an additional source that has independent and direct knowledge of the information; or

(B) the person interviewed is the best possible source of the information.

§ 1681e. Compliance procedures

(a) Identity and purposes of credit users

Every consumer reporting agency shall maintain reasonable procedures designed to avoid violations of section 1681c of this title and to limit the furnishing of consumer reports to the purposes listed under section 1681b of this title. These procedures shall require that prospective users of the information identify themselves, certify the purposes for which the information is sought, and certify that the information will be used for no other purpose. Every consumer reporting agency shall make a reasonable effort to verify the identity of a new prospective user and the uses certified by such prospective user prior to furnishing such user a consumer report. No consumer reporting agency may furnish a consumer report to any person if it has reasonable grounds for believing that the consumer report will not be used for a purpose listed in section 1681b of this title.

(b) Accuracy of report

Whenever a consumer reporting agency prepares a consumer report it shall follow reasonable procedures to assure maximum possible accuracy of the information concerning the individual about whom the report relates.

(c) Disclosure of consumer reports by users allowed

A consumer reporting agency may not prohibit a user of a consumer report furnished by the agency on a consumer from disclosing the contents of the report to the consumer, if adverse action against the consumer has been taken by the user based in whole or in part on the report.

(d) Notice to users and furnishers of information

(1) Notice requirement

A consumer reporting agency shall provide to any person-

(A) who regularly and in the ordinary course of business furnishes information to the agency with respect to any consumer; or

(B) to whom a consumer report is provided by the agency;

a notice of such person's responsibilities under this subchapter.

(2) Content of notice

The Bureau shall prescribe the content of notices under paragraph (1), and a consumer reporting agency shall be in compliance with this subsection if it provides a notice under paragraph (1) that is substantially similar to the Bureau prescription under this paragraph.

(e) Procurement of consumer report for resale

(1) Disclosure

A person may not procure a consumer report for purposes of reselling the report (or any information in the report) unless the person discloses to the consumer reporting agency that originally furnishes the report-

(A) the identity of the end-user of the report (or information); and

(B) each permissible purpose under section 1681b of this title for which the report is furnished to the end-user of the report (or information).

(2) Responsibilities of procurers for resale

A person who procures a consumer report for purposes of reselling the report (or any information in the report) shall-

(A) establish and comply with reasonable procedures designed to ensure that the report (or information) is resold by the person only for a purpose for which the report may be furnished under section 1681b of this title, including by requiring that each person to which the report (or information) is resold and that resells or provides the report (or information) to any other person-

(i) identifies each end user of the resold report (or information);

(ii) certifies each purpose for which the report (or information) will be used; and

(iii) certifies that the report (or information) will be used for no other purpose; and

(B) before reselling the report, make reasonable efforts to verify the identifications and certifications made under subparagraph (A).

(3) Resale of consumer report to a Federal agency or department

Notwithstanding paragraph (1) or (2), a person who procures a consumer report for purposes of reselling the report (or any information in the report) shall not disclose the identity of the end-user of the report under paragraph (1) or (2) if-

(A) the end user is an agency or department of the United States Government which procures the report from the person for purposes of determining the eligibility of the consumer concerned to receive access or continued access to classified information (as defined in section 1681b(b)(4)(E)(i) of this title); and

(B) the agency or department certifies in writing to the person reselling the report that nondisclosure is necessary to protect classified information or the safety of persons employed by or contracting with, or undergoing investigation for work or contracting with the agency or department.

§ 1681f. Disclosures to governmental agencies

Notwithstanding the provisions of section 1681b of this title, a consumer reporting agency may furnish identifying information respecting any consumer, limited to his name, address, former addresses, places of employment, or former places of employment, to a governmental agency.

§ 1681g. Disclosures to consumers

(a) Information on file; sources; report recipients

Every consumer reporting agency shall, upon request, and subject to section 1681h(a)(1) of this title, clearly and accurately disclose to the consumer:

(1) All information in the consumer's file at the time of the request, except that-

(A) if the consumer to whom the file relates requests that the first 5 digits of the social security number (or similar identification number) of the consumer not be included in the disclosure and the consumer reporting agency has received appropriate proof of the identity of the requester, the consumer reporting agency shall so truncate such number in such disclosure; and

(B) nothing in this paragraph shall be construed to require a consumer reporting agency to disclose to a consumer any information concerning credit scores or any other risk scores or predictors relating to the consumer.

(2) The sources of the information; except that the sources of information acquired solely for use in preparing an investigative consumer report and actually used for no other purpose need not be disclosed: Provided, That in the event an action is brought under this subchapter, such sources shall be available to the plaintiff under appropriate discovery procedures in the court in which the action is brought.

(3)(A) Identification of each person (including each end-user identified under section 1681e(e)(1) of this title) that procured a consumer report-

(i) for employment purposes, during the 2-year period preceding the date on which the request is made; or

(ii) for any other purpose, during the 1-year period preceding the date on which the request is made.

(B) An identification of a person under subparagraph (A) shall include-

(i) the name of the person or, if applicable, the trade name (written in full) under which such person conducts business; and

(ii) upon request of the consumer, the address and telephone number of the person.

(C) Subparagraph (A) does not apply if-

(i) the end user is an agency or department of the United States Government that procures the report from the person for purposes of determining the eligibility of the consumer to whom the report relates to receive access or continued access to classified information (as defined in section 1681b(b)(4)(E)(i) of this title); and

(ii) the head of the agency or department makes a written finding as prescribed under section 1681b(b)(4)(A) of this title.

(4) The dates, original payees, and amounts of any checks upon which is based any adverse characterization of the consumer, included in the file at the time of the disclosure.

(5) A record of all inquiries received by the agency during the 1-year period preceding the request that identified the consumer in connection with a credit or insurance transaction that was not initiated by the consumer.

(6) If the consumer requests the credit file and not the credit score, a statement that the consumer may request and obtain a credit score.

(b) Exempt information

The requirements of subsection (a) respecting the disclosure of sources of information and the recipients of consumer reports do not apply to information received or consumer reports furnished prior to the effective date of this subchapter except to the extent that the matter involved is contained in the files of the consumer reporting agency on that date.

(c) Summary of rights to obtain and dispute information in consumer reports and to obtain credit scores

    (1) Commission summary of rights required

        (A) In general

        The Commission shall prepare a model summary of the rights of consumers under this subchapter.

        (B) Content of summary

        The summary of rights prepared under subparagraph (A) shall include a description of-

            (i) the right of a consumer to obtain a copy of a consumer report under subsection (a) from each consumer reporting agency;

            (ii) the frequency and circumstances under which a consumer is entitled to receive a consumer report without charge under section 1681j of this title;

            (iii) the right of a consumer to dispute information in the file of the consumer under section 1681i of this title;

            (iv) the right of a consumer to obtain a credit score from a consumer reporting agency, and a description of how to obtain a credit score;

            (v) the method by which a consumer can contact, and obtain a consumer report from, a consumer reporting agency without charge, as provided in the regulations of the Bureau prescribed under section 211(c) of the Fair and Accurate Credit Transactions Act of 2003; and

            (vi) the method by which a consumer can contact, and obtain a consumer report from, a consumer reporting agency described in section 1681a(w) of this title, as provided in the regulations of the Bureau prescribed under section 1681j(a)(1)(C) of this title.

        (C) Availability of summary of rights

        The Commission shall-

            (i) actively publicize the availability of the summary of rights prepared under this paragraph;

            (ii) conspicuously post on its Internet website the availability of such summary of rights; and

            (iii) promptly make such summary of rights available to consumers, on request.

    (2) Summary of rights required to be included with agency disclosures

A consumer reporting agency shall provide to a consumer, with each written disclosure by the agency to the consumer under this section-

(A) the summary of rights prepared by the Bureau under paragraph (1);

(B) in the case of a consumer reporting agency described in section 1681a(p) of this title, a toll-free telephone number established by the agency, at which personnel are accessible to consumers during normal business hours;

(C) a list of all Federal agencies responsible for enforcing any provision of this subchapter, and the address and any appropriate phone number of each such agency, in a form that will assist the consumer in selecting the appropriate agency;

(D) a statement that the consumer may have additional rights under State law, and that the consumer may wish to contact a State or local consumer protection agency or a State attorney general (or the equivalent thereof) to learn of those rights; and

(E) a statement that a consumer reporting agency is not required to remove accurate derogatory information from the file of a consumer, unless the information is outdated under section 1681c of this title or cannot be verified.

(d) Summary of rights of identity theft victims

(1) In general

The Commission, in consultation with the Federal banking agencies and the National Credit Union Administration, shall prepare a model summary of the rights of consumers under this subchapter with respect to the procedures for remedying the effects of fraud or identity theft involving credit, an electronic fund transfer, or an account or transaction at or with a financial institution or other creditor.

(2) Summary of rights and contact information

Beginning 60 days after the date on which the model summary of rights is prescribed in final form by the Bureau pursuant to paragraph (1), if any consumer contacts a consumer reporting agency and expresses a belief that the consumer is a victim of fraud or identity theft involving credit, an electronic fund transfer, or an account or transaction at or with a financial institution or other creditor, the consumer reporting agency shall, in addition to any other action that the agency may take, provide the consumer with a summary of rights that contains all of the information required by the Bureau under paragraph (1), and information on how to contact the Bureau to obtain more detailed information.

(e) Information available to victims

(1) In general

For the purpose of documenting fraudulent transactions resulting from identity theft, not later than 30 days after the date of receipt of a request from a victim in accordance with paragraph (3), and subject to verification of the identity of the victim and the claim of identity theft in accordance with paragraph (2), a business entity that has provided credit to, provided for consideration products, goods, or services to, accepted payment from, or otherwise entered into a commercial transaction for consideration with, a person who has allegedly made unauthorized use of the means of identification of the victim, shall provide a copy of application and business transaction records in the control of the business entity, whether maintained by the business entity or by another person on behalf of the business entity, evidencing any transaction alleged to be a result of identity theft to-

(A) the victim;

(B) any Federal, State, or local government law enforcement agency or officer specified by the victim in such a request; or

(C) any law enforcement agency investigating the identity theft and authorized by the victim to take receipt of records provided under this subsection.

(2) Verification of identity and claim

Before a business entity provides any information under paragraph (1), unless the business entity, at its discretion, otherwise has a high degree of confidence that it knows the identity of the victim making a request under paragraph (1), the victim shall provide to the business entity-

(A) as proof of positive identification of the victim, at the election of the business entity-

(i) the presentation of a government-issued identification card;

(ii) personally identifying information of the same type as was provided to the business entity by the unauthorized person; or

(iii) personally identifying information that the business entity typically requests from new applicants or for new transactions, at the time of the victim's request for information, including any documentation described in clauses (i) and (ii); and

(B) as proof of a claim of identity theft, at the election of the business entity-

(i) a copy of a police report evidencing the claim of the victim of identity theft; and

(ii) a properly completed-

(I) copy of a standardized affidavit of identity theft developed and made available by the Bureau; or

(II) an affidavit of fact that is acceptable to the business entity for that purpose.

(3) Procedures

The request of a victim under paragraph (1) shall-

(A) be in writing;

(B) be mailed to an address specified by the business entity, if any; and

(C) if asked by the business entity, include relevant information about any transaction alleged to be a result of identity theft to facilitate compliance with this section including-

(i) if known by the victim (or if readily obtainable by the victim), the date of the application or transaction; and

(ii) if known by the victim (or if readily obtainable by the victim), any other identifying information such as an account or transaction number.

(4) No charge to victim

Information required to be provided under paragraph (1) shall be so provided without charge.

(5) Authority to decline to provide information

A business entity may decline to provide information under paragraph (1) if, in the exercise of good faith, the business entity determines that-

(A) this subsection does not require disclosure of the information;

(B) after reviewing the information provided pursuant to paragraph (2), the business entity does not have a high degree of confidence in knowing the true identity of the individual requesting the information;

(C) the request for the information is based on a misrepresentation of fact by the individual requesting the information relevant to the request for information; or

(D) the information requested is Internet navigational data or similar information about a person's visit to a website or online service.

(6) Limitation on liability

Except as provided in section 1681s of this title, sections 1681n and 1681o of this title do not apply to any violation of this subsection.

(7) Limitation on civil liability

No business entity may be held civilly liable under any provision of Federal, State, or other law for disclosure, made in good faith pursuant to this subsection.

(8) No new recordkeeping obligation

Nothing in this subsection creates an obligation on the part of a business entity to obtain, retain, or maintain information or records that are not otherwise required to be obtained, retained, or maintained in the ordinary course of its business or under other applicable law.

(9) Rule of construction

(A) In general

No provision of subtitle A of title V of Public Law 106–102 [15 U.S.C. 6801 et seq.], prohibiting the disclosure of financial information by a business entity to third parties shall be used to deny disclosure of information to the victim under this subsection.

(B) Limitation

Except as provided in subparagraph (A), nothing in this subsection permits a business entity to disclose information, including information to law enforcement under subparagraphs (B) and (C) of paragraph (1), that the business entity is otherwise prohibited from disclosing under any other applicable provision of Federal or State law.

(10) Affirmative defense

In any civil action brought to enforce this subsection, it is an affirmative defense (which the defendant must establish by a preponderance of the evidence) for a business entity to file an affidavit or answer stating that-

(A) the business entity has made a reasonably diligent search of its available business records; and

(B) the records requested under this subsection do not exist or are not reasonably available.

(11) Definition of victim

For purposes of this subsection, the term "victim" means a consumer whose means of identification or financial information has been used or transferred (or has been alleged to have been used or transferred) without the authority of that consumer, with the intent to commit, or to aid or abet, an identity theft or a similar crime.

(12) Effective date

This subsection shall become effective 180 days after December 4, 2003.

(13) Effectiveness study

Not later than 18 months after December 4, 2003, the Comptroller General of the United States shall submit a report to Congress assessing the effectiveness of this provision.

(f) Disclosure of credit scores

(1) In general

Upon the request of a consumer for a credit score, a consumer reporting agency shall supply to the consumer a statement indicating that the information and credit scoring model may be different than the credit score that may be used by the lender, and a notice which shall include-

(A) the current credit score of the consumer or the most recent credit score of the consumer that was previously calculated by the credit reporting agency for a purpose related to the extension of credit;

(B) the range of possible credit scores under the model used;

(C) all of the key factors that adversely affected the credit score of the consumer in the model used, the total number of which shall not exceed 4, subject to paragraph (9);

(D) the date on which the credit score was created; and

(E) the name of the person or entity that provided the credit score or credit file upon which the credit score was created.

(2) Definitions

For purposes of this subsection, the following definitions shall apply:

  (A) Credit score

  The term "credit score"-

    (i) means a numerical value or a categorization derived from a statistical tool or modeling system used by a person who makes or arranges a loan to predict the likelihood of certain credit behaviors, including default (and the numerical value or the categorization derived from such analysis may also be referred to as a "risk predictor" or "risk score"); and

    (ii) does not include-

      (I) any mortgage score or rating of an automated underwriting system that considers one or more factors in addition to credit information, including the loan to value ratio, the amount of down payment, or the financial assets of a consumer; or

      (II) any other elements of the underwriting process or underwriting decision.

  (B) Key factors

  The term "key factors" means all relevant elements or reasons adversely affecting the credit score for the particular individual, listed in the order of their importance based on their effect on the credit score.

(3) Timeframe and manner of disclosure

The information required by this subsection shall be provided in the same timeframe and manner as the information described in subsection (a).

(4) Applicability to certain uses

This subsection shall not be construed so as to compel a consumer reporting agency to develop or disclose a score if the agency does not-

  (A) distribute scores that are used in connection with residential real property loans; or

  (B) develop scores that assist credit providers in understanding the general credit behavior of a consumer and predicting the future credit behavior of the consumer.

(5) Applicability to credit scores developed by another person

  (A) In general

  This subsection shall not be construed to require a consumer reporting agency that distributes credit scores developed by another person or entity to provide a further explanation of them, or to process a dispute arising pursuant to section 1681i of this title, except that the consumer reporting agency shall provide the consumer with the name and address and website for contacting the person or entity who developed the score or developed the methodology of the score.

  (B) Exception

This paragraph shall not apply to a consumer reporting agency that develops or modifies scores that are developed by another person or entity.

(6) Maintenance of credit scores not required

This subsection shall not be construed to require a consumer reporting agency to maintain credit scores in its files.

(7) Compliance in certain cases

In complying with this subsection, a consumer reporting agency shall-

(A) supply the consumer with a credit score that is derived from a credit scoring model that is widely distributed to users by that consumer reporting agency in connection with residential real property loans or with a credit score that assists the consumer in understanding the credit scoring assessment of the credit behavior of the consumer and predictions about the future credit behavior of the consumer; and

(B) a statement indicating that the information and credit scoring model may be different than that used by the lender.

(8) Fair and reasonable fee

A consumer reporting agency may charge a fair and reasonable fee, as determined by the Bureau, for providing the information required under this subsection.

(9) Use of enquiries as a key factor

If a key factor that adversely affects the credit score of a consumer consists of the number of enquiries made with respect to a consumer report, that factor shall be included in the disclosure pursuant to paragraph (1)(C) without regard to the numerical limitation in such paragraph.

(g) Disclosure of credit scores by certain mortgage lenders

(1) In general

Any person who makes or arranges loans and who uses a consumer credit score, as defined in subsection (f), in connection with an application initiated or sought by a consumer for a closed end loan or the establishment of an open end loan for a consumer purpose that is secured by 1 to 4 units of residential real property (hereafter in this subsection referred to as the "lender") shall provide the following to the consumer as soon as reasonably practicable:

(A) Information required under subsection (f)

(i) In general

A copy of the information identified in subsection (f) that was obtained from a consumer reporting agency or was developed and used by the user of the information.

(ii) Notice under subparagraph (D)

In addition to the information provided to it by a third party that provided the credit score or scores, a lender is only required to provide the notice contained in subparagraph (D).

(B) Disclosures in case of automated underwriting system

    (i) In general

If a person that is subject to this subsection uses an automated underwriting system to underwrite a loan, that person may satisfy the obligation to provide a credit score by disclosing a credit score and associated key factors supplied by a consumer reporting agency.

    (ii) Numerical credit score

However, if a numerical credit score is generated by an automated underwriting system used by an enterprise, and that score is disclosed to the person, the score shall be disclosed to the consumer consistent with subparagraph (C).

    (iii) Enterprise defined

For purposes of this subparagraph, the term "enterprise" has the same meaning as in paragraph (6) of section 4502 of title 12.

(C) Disclosures of credit scores not obtained from a consumer reporting agency

A person that is subject to the provisions of this subsection and that uses a credit score, other than a credit score provided by a consumer reporting agency, may satisfy the obligation to provide a credit score by disclosing a credit score and associated key factors supplied by a consumer reporting agency.

(D) Notice to home loan applicants

A copy of the following notice, which shall include the name, address, and telephone number of each consumer reporting agency providing a credit score that was used:

"notice to the home loan applicant

"In connection with your application for a home loan, the lender must disclose to you the score that a consumer reporting agency distributed to users and the lender used in connection with your home loan, and the key factors affecting your credit scores.

"The credit score is a computer generated summary calculated at the time of the request and based on information that a consumer reporting agency or lender has on file. The scores are based on data about your credit history and payment patterns. Credit scores are important because they are used to assist the lender in determining whether you will obtain a loan. They may also be used to determine what interest rate you may be offered on the mortgage. Credit scores can change over time, depending on your conduct, how your credit history and payment patterns change, and how credit scoring technologies change.

"Because the score is based on information in your credit history, it is very important that you review the credit-related information that is being furnished to make sure it is accurate. Credit records may vary from one company to another.

"If you have questions about your credit score or the credit information that is furnished to you, contact the consumer reporting agency at the address and telephone number provided with this notice, or contact the lender, if the lender developed or generated the credit score. The consumer reporting agency plays no part in the decision to take any action on the loan application and is unable to provide you with specific reasons for the decision on a loan application.

"If you have questions concerning the terms of the loan, contact the lender.".

(E) Actions not required under this subsection

This subsection shall not require any person to-

    (i) explain the information provided pursuant to subsection (f);

    (ii) disclose any information other than a credit score or key factors, as defined in subsection (f);

    (iii) disclose any credit score or related information obtained by the user after a loan has closed;

    (iv) provide more than 1 disclosure per loan transaction; or

    (v) provide the disclosure required by this subsection when another person has made the disclosure to the consumer for that loan transaction.

(F) No obligation for content

    (i) In general

The obligation of any person pursuant to this subsection shall be limited solely to providing a copy of the information that was received from the consumer reporting agency.

    (ii) Limit on liability

 (No person has liability under this subsection for the content of that information or for the omission of any information within the report provided by the consumer reporting agency.

(G) Person defined as excluding enterprise

As used in this subsection, the term "person" does not include an enterprise (as defined in paragraph (6) of section 4502 of title 12).

(2) Prohibition on disclosure clauses null and void

(A) In general

Any provision in a contract that prohibits the disclosure of a credit score by a person who makes or arranges loans or a consumer reporting agency is void.

(B) No liability for disclosure under this subsection

A lender shall not have liability under any contractual provision for disclosure of a credit score pursuant to this subsection.

§ 1681h. Conditions and form of disclosure to consumers

    (a) In general

        (1) Proper identification

A consumer reporting agency shall require, as a condition of making the disclosures required under section 1681g of this title, that the consumer furnish proper identification.

(2) Disclosure in writing

Except as provided in subsection (b), the disclosures required to be made under section 1681g of this title shall be provided under that section in writing.

(b) Other forms of disclosure

(1) In general

If authorized by a consumer, a consumer reporting agency may make the disclosures required under 1681g of this title-

(A) other than in writing; and

(B) in such form as may be-

(i) specified by the consumer in accordance with paragraph (2); and

(ii) available from the agency.

(2) Form

A consumer may specify pursuant to paragraph (1) that disclosures under section 1681g of this title shall be made-

(A) in person, upon the appearance of the consumer at the place of business of the consumer reporting agency where disclosures are regularly provided, during normal business hours, and on reasonable notice;

(B) by telephone, if the consumer has made a written request for disclosure by telephone;

(C) by electronic means, if available from the agency; or

(D) by any other reasonable means that is available from the agency.

(c) Trained personnel

Any consumer reporting agency shall provide trained personnel to explain to the consumer any information furnished to him pursuant to section 1681g of this title.

(d) Persons accompanying consumer

The consumer shall be permitted to be accompanied by one other person of his choosing, who shall furnish reasonable identification. A consumer reporting agency may require the consumer to furnish a written statement granting permission to the consumer reporting agency to discuss the consumer's file in such person's presence.

(e) Limitation of liability

Except as provided in sections 1681n and 1681o of this title, no consumer may bring any action or proceeding in the nature of defamation, invasion of privacy, or negligence with respect to the reporting of information against any consumer reporting agency, any user of information, or any person who furnishes information to a consumer reporting agency, based on information disclosed pursuant to section 1681g, 1681h, or 1681m of this title, or based on information disclosed by a user of a consumer report to or for a consumer against whom the user has taken adverse action, based in whole or in part on the reportexcept as to false information furnished with malice or willful intent to injure such consumer.

§ 1681i. Procedure in case of disputed accuracy

(a) Reinvestigations of disputed information

    (1) Reinvestigation required

        (A) In general

Subject to subsection (f), if the completeness or accuracy of any item of information contained in a consumer's file at a consumer reporting agency is disputed by the consumer and the consumer notifies the agency directly, or indirectly through a reseller, of such dispute, the agency shall, free of charge, conduct a reasonable reinvestigation to determine whether the disputed information is inaccurate and record the current status of the disputed information, or delete the item from the file in accordance with paragraph (5), before the end of the 30-day period beginning on the date on which the agency receives the notice of the dispute from the consumer or reseller.

        (B) Extension of period to reinvestigate

Except as provided in subparagraph (C), the 30-day period described in subparagraph (A) may be extended for not more than 15 additional days if the consumer reporting agency receives information from the consumer during that 30-day period that is relevant to the reinvestigation.

        (C) Limitations on extension of period to reinvestigate

Subparagraph (B) shall not apply to any reinvestigation in which, during the 30-day period described in subparagraph (A), the information that is the subject of the reinvestigation is found to be inaccurate or incomplete or the consumer reporting agency determines that the information cannot be verified.

    (2) Prompt notice of dispute to furnisher of information

        (A) In general

Before the expiration of the 5-business-day period beginning on the date on which a consumer reporting agency receives notice of a dispute from any consumer or a reseller in accordance with paragraph (1), the agency shall provide notification of the dispute to any person who provided any item of information in dispute, at the address and in the manner established with the person. The notice shall include all relevant information regarding the dispute that the agency has received from the consumer or reseller.

        (B) Provision of other information

The consumer reporting agency shall promptly provide to the person who provided the information in dispute all relevant information regarding the dispute that is received by the agency from the consumer or the reseller after the period referred to in subparagraph (A) and before the end of the period referred to in paragraph (1)(A).

(3) Determination that dispute is frivolous or irrelevant

(A) In general

Notwithstanding paragraph (1), a consumer reporting agency may terminate a reinvestigation of information disputed by a consumer under that paragraph if the agency reasonably determines that the dispute by the consumer is frivolous or irrelevant, including by reason of a failure by a consumer to provide sufficient information to investigate the disputed information.

(B) Notice of determination

Upon making any determination in accordance with subparagraph (A) that a dispute is frivolous or irrelevant, a consumer reporting agency shall notify the consumer of such determination not later than 5 business days after making such determination, by mail or, if authorized by the consumer for that purpose, by any other means available to the agency.

(C) Contents of notice

A notice under subparagraph (B) shall include-

(i) the reasons for the determination under subparagraph (A); and

(ii) identification of any information required to investigate the disputed information, which may consist of a standardized form describing the general nature of such information.

(4) Consideration of consumer information

In conducting any reinvestigation under paragraph (1) with respect to disputed information in the file of any consumer, the consumer reporting agency shall review and consider all relevant information submitted by the consumer in the period described in paragraph (1)(A) with respect to such disputed information.

(5) Treatment of inaccurate or unverifiable information

(A) In general

If, after any reinvestigation under paragraph (1) of any information disputed by a consumer, an item of the information is found to be inaccurate or incomplete or cannot be verified, the consumer reporting agency shall-

(i) promptly delete that item of information from the file of the consumer, or modify that item of information, as appropriate, based on the results of the reinvestigation; and

(ii) promptly notify the furnisher of that information that the information has been modified or deleted from the file of the consumer.

(B) Requirements relating to reinsertion of previously deleted material

(i) Certification of accuracy of information

If any information is deleted from a consumer's file pursuant to subparagraph (A), the information may not be reinserted in the file by the consumer reporting agency unless the person who furnishes the information certifies that the information is complete and accurate.

(ii) Notice to consumer

If any information that has been deleted from a consumer's file pursuant to subparagraph (A) is reinserted in the file, the consumer reporting agency shall notify the consumer of the reinsertion in writing not later than 5 business days after the reinsertion or, if authorized by the consumer for that purpose, by any other means available to the agency.

(iii) Additional information

As part of, or in addition to, the notice under clause (ii), a consumer reporting agency shall provide to a consumer in writing not later than 5 business days after the date of the reinsertion-

(I) a statement that the disputed information has been reinserted;

(II) the business name and address of any furnisher of information contacted and the telephone number of such furnisher, if reasonably available, or of any furnisher of information that contacted the consumer reporting agency, in connection with the reinsertion of such information; and

(III) a notice that the consumer has the right to add a statement to the consumer's file disputing the accuracy or completeness of the disputed information.

(C) Procedures to prevent reappearance

A consumer reporting agency shall maintain reasonable procedures designed to prevent the reappearance in a consumer's file, and in consumer reports on the consumer, of information that is deleted pursuant to this paragraph (other than information that is reinserted in accordance with subparagraph (B)(i)).

(D) Automated reinvestigation system

Any consumer reporting agency that compiles and maintains files on consumers on a nationwide basis shall implement an automated system through which furnishers of information to that consumer reporting agency may report the results of a reinvestigation that finds incomplete or inaccurate information in a consumer's file to other such consumer reporting agencies.

(6) Notice of results of reinvestigation

(A) In general

A consumer reporting agency shall provide written notice to a consumer of the results of a reinvestigation under this subsection not later than 5 business days after the completion of the reinvestigation, by mail or, if authorized by the consumer for that purpose, by other means available to the agency.

(B) Contents

As part of, or in addition to, the notice under subparagraph (A), a consumer reporting agency shall provide to a consumer in writing before the expiration of the 5-day period referred to in subparagraph (A)-

(i) a statement that the reinvestigation is completed;

(ii) a consumer report that is based upon the consumer's file as that file is revised as a result of the reinvestigation;

(iii) a notice that, if requested by the consumer, a description of the procedure used to determine the accuracy and completeness of the information shall be provided to the consumer by the agency, including the business name and address of any furnisher of information contacted in connection with such information and the telephone number of such furnisher, if reasonably available;

(iv) a notice that the consumer has the right to add a statement to the consumer's file disputing the accuracy or completeness of the information; and

(v) a notice that the consumer has the right to request under subsection (d) that the consumer reporting agency furnish notifications under that subsection.

(7) Description of reinvestigation procedure

A consumer reporting agency shall provide to a consumer a description referred to in paragraph (6)(B)(iii) by not later than 15 days after receiving a request from the consumer for that description.

(8) Expedited dispute resolution

If a dispute regarding an item of information in a consumer's file at a consumer reporting agency is resolved in accordance with paragraph (5)(A) by the deletion of the disputed information by not later than 3 business days after the date on which the agency receives notice of the dispute from the consumer in accordance with paragraph (1)(A), then the agency shall not be required to comply with paragraphs (2), (6), and (7) with respect to that dispute if the agency-

(A) provides prompt notice of the deletion to the consumer by telephone;

(B) includes in that notice, or in a written notice that accompanies a confirmation and consumer report provided in accordance with subparagraph (C), a statement of the consumer's right to request under subsection (d) that the agency furnish notifications under that subsection; and

(C) provides written confirmation of the deletion and a copy of a consumer report on the consumer that is based on the consumer's file after the deletion, not later than 5 business days after making the deletion.

(b) Statement of dispute

If the reinvestigation does not resolve the dispute, the consumer may file a brief statement setting forth the nature of the dispute. The consumer reporting agency may limit such statements to not more than one hundred words if it provides the consumer with assistance in writing a clear summary of the dispute.

(c) Notification of consumer dispute in subsequent consumer reports

Whenever a statement of a dispute is filed, unless there is reasonable grounds to believe that it is frivolous or irrelevant, the consumer reporting agency shall, in any subsequent consumer report containing the information in question, clearly note that it is disputed by the consumer and provide either the consumer's statement or a clear and accurate codification or summary thereof.

(d) Notification of deletion of disputed information

Following any deletion of information which is found to be inaccurate or whose accuracy can no longer be verified or any notation as to disputed information, the consumer reporting agency shall, at the request of the consumer, furnish notification that the item has been deleted or the statement, codification or summary pursuant to subsection (b) or (c) to any person specifically designated by the consumer who has within two years prior thereto received a consumer report for employment purposes, or within six months prior thereto received a consumer report for any other purpose, which contained the deleted or disputed information.

(e) Treatment of complaints and report to Congress

    (1) In general

    The Commission shall-

        (A) compile all complaints that it receives that a file of a consumer that is maintained by a consumer reporting agency described in section 1681a(p) of this title contains incomplete or inaccurate information, with respect to which, the consumer appears to have disputed the completeness or accuracy with the consumer reporting agency or otherwise utilized the procedures provided by subsection (a); and

        (B) transmit each such complaint to each consumer reporting agency involved.

    (2) Exclusion

Complaints received or obtained by the Bureau pursuant to its investigative authority under the Consumer Financial Protection Act of 2010 shall not be subject to paragraph (1).

    (3) Agency responsibilities

Each consumer reporting agency described in section 1681a(p) of this title that receives a complaint transmitted by the Bureau pursuant to paragraph (1) shall-

        (A) review each such complaint to determine whether all legal obligations imposed on the consumer reporting agency under this subchapter (including any obligation imposed by an applicable court or administrative order) have been met with respect to the subject matter of the complaint;

(B) provide reports on a regular basis to the Bureau regarding the determinations of and actions taken by the consumer reporting agency, if any, in connection with its review of such complaints; and

(C) maintain, for a reasonable time period, records regarding the disposition of each such complaint that is sufficient to demonstrate compliance with this subsection.

(4) Rulemaking authority

The Commission may prescribe regulations, as appropriate to implement this subsection.

(5) Annual report

The Commission shall submit to the Committee on Banking, Housing, and Urban Affairs of the Senate and the Committee on Financial Services of the House of Representatives an annual report regarding information gathered by the Bureau under this subsection.

(f) Reinvestigation requirement applicable to resellers

(1) Exemption from general reinvestigation requirement

Except as provided in paragraph (2), a reseller shall be exempt from the requirements of this section.

(2) Action required upon receiving notice of a dispute

If a reseller receives a notice from a consumer of a dispute concerning the completeness or accuracy of any item of information contained in a consumer report on such consumer produced by the reseller, the reseller shall, within 5 business days of receiving the notice, and free of charge-

(A) determine whether the item of information is incomplete or inaccurate as a result of an act or omission of the reseller; and

(B) if-

(i) the reseller determines that the item of information is incomplete or inaccurate as a result of an act or omission of the reseller, not later than 20 days after receiving the notice, correct the information in the consumer report or delete it; or

(ii) if the reseller determines that the item of information is not incomplete or inaccurate as a result of an act or omission of the reseller, convey the notice of the dispute, together with all relevant information provided by the consumer, to each consumer reporting agency that provided the reseller with the information that is the subject of the dispute, using an address or a notification mechanism specified by the consumer reporting agency for such notices.

(3) Responsibility of consumer reporting agency to notify consumer through reseller

Upon the completion of a reinvestigation under this section of a dispute concerning the completeness or accuracy of any information in the file of a consumer by a consumer reporting agency that received notice of the dispute from a reseller under paragraph (2)-

(A) the notice by the consumer reporting agency under paragraph (6), (7), or (8) of subsection (a) shall be provided to the reseller in lieu of the consumer; and

(B) the reseller shall immediately reconvey such notice to the consumer, including any notice of a deletion by telephone in the manner required under paragraph (8)(A).

(4) Reseller reinvestigations

No provision of this subsection shall be construed as prohibiting a reseller from conducting a reinvestigation of a consumer dispute directly.

§ 1681j. Charges for certain disclosures

(a) Free annual disclosure

(1) Nationwide consumer reporting agencies

(A) In general

All consumer reporting agencies described in subsections (p) and (w) of section 1681a of this title shall make all disclosures pursuant to section 1681g of this title once during any 12-month period upon request of the consumer and without charge to the consumer.

(B) Centralized source

Subparagraph (A) shall apply with respect to a consumer reporting agency described in section 1681a(p) of this title only if the request from the consumer is made using the centralized source established for such purpose in accordance with section 211(c) of the Fair and Accurate Credit Transactions Act of 2003.

(C) Nationwide specialty consumer reporting agency

(i) In general

The Commission shall prescribe regulations applicable to each consumer reporting agency described in section 1681a(w) of this title to require the establishment of a streamlined process for consumers to request consumer reports under subparagraph (A), which shall include, at a minimum, the establishment by each such agency of a toll-free telephone number for such requests.

(ii) Considerations

In prescribing regulations under clause (i), the Bureau shall consider-

(b) the significant demands that may be placed on consumer reporting agencies in providing such consumer reports;

(II) appropriate means to ensure that consumer reporting agencies can satisfactorily meet those demands, including the efficacy of a system of staggering the availability to consumers of such consumer reports; and

(III) the ease by which consumers should be able to contact consumer reporting agencies with respect to access to such consumer reports.

(iii) Date of issuance

The Commission shall issue the regulations required by this subparagraph in final form not later than 6 months after December 4, 2003.

(iv) Consideration of ability to comply

The regulations of the Bureau under this subparagraph shall establish an effective date by which each nationwide specialty consumer reporting agency (as defined in section 1681a(w) of this title) shall be required to comply with subsection (a), which effective date-

(b) shall be established after consideration of the ability of each nationwide specialty consumer reporting agency to comply with subsection (a); and

(II) shall be not later than 6 months after the date on which such regulations are issued in final form (or such additional period not to exceed 3 months, as the Bureau determines appropriate).

(2) Timing

A consumer reporting agency shall provide a consumer report under paragraph (1) not later than 15 days after the date on which the request is received under paragraph (1).

(3) Reinvestigations

Notwithstanding the time periods specified in section 1681i(a)(1) of this title, a reinvestigation under that section by a consumer reporting agency upon a request of a consumer that is made after receiving a consumer report under this subsection shall be completed not later than 45 days after the date on which the request is received.

(4) Exception for first 12 months of operation

This subsection shall not apply to a consumer reporting agency that has not been furnishing consumer reports to third parties on a continuing basis during the 12-month period preceding a request under paragraph (1), with respect to consumers residing nationwide.

(b) Free disclosure after adverse notice to consumer

Each consumer reporting agency that maintains a file on a consumer shall make all disclosures pursuant to section 1681g of this title without charge to the consumer if, not later than 60 days after receipt by such consumer of a notification pursuant to section 1681m of this title, or of a notification from a debt collection agency affiliated with that consumer reporting agency stating that the consumer's credit rating may be or has been adversely affected, the consumer makes a request under section 1681g of this title.

(c) Free disclosure under certain other circumstances

Upon the request of the consumer, a consumer reporting agency shall make all disclosures pursuant to section 1681g of this title once during any 12-month period without charge to that consumer if the consumer certifies in writing that the consumer-

(1) is unemployed and intends to apply for employment in the 60-day period beginning on the date on which the certification is made;

(2) is a recipient of public welfare assistance; or

(3) has reason to believe that the file on the consumer at the agency contains inaccurate information due to fraud.

(d) Free disclosures in connection with fraud alerts

Upon the request of a consumer, a consumer reporting agency described in section 1681a(p) of this title shall make all disclosures pursuant to section 1681g of this title without charge to the consumer, as provided in subsections (a)(2) and (b)(2) of section 1681c–1 of this title, as applicable.

(e) Other charges prohibited

A consumer reporting agency shall not impose any charge on a consumer for providing any notification required by this subchapter or making any disclosure required by this subchapter, except as authorized by subsection (f).

(f) Reasonable charges allowed for certain disclosures

(1) In general

In the case of a request from a consumer other than a request that is covered by any of subsections (a) through (d), a consumer reporting agency may impose a reasonable charge on a consumer-

(A) for making a disclosure to the consumer pursuant to section 1681g of this title, which charge-

(i) shall not exceed $8; and

(ii) shall be indicated to the consumer before making the disclosure; and

(B) for furnishing, pursuant to section 1681i(d) of this title, following a reinvestigation under section 1681i(a) of this title, a statement, codification, or summary to a person designated by the consumer under that section after the 30-day period beginning on the date of notification of the consumer under paragraph (6) or (8) of section 1681i(a) of this title with respect to the reinvestigation, which charge-

(i) shall not exceed the charge that the agency would impose on each designated recipient for a consumer report; and

(ii) shall be indicated to the consumer before furnishing such information.

(2) Modification of amount

The Bureau shall increase the amount referred to in paragraph (1)(A)(i) on January 1 of each year, based proportionally on changes in the Consumer Price Index, with fractional changes rounded to the nearest fifty cents.

(g) Prevention of deceptive marketing of credit reports

(1) In general

Subject to rulemaking pursuant to section 205(b) of the Credit CARD Act of 2009, any advertisement for a free credit report in any medium shall prominently disclose in such advertisement that free credit reports are available under Federal law at: "AnnualCreditReport.com" (or such other source as may be authorized under Federal law).

(2) Television and radio advertisement

In the case of an advertisement broadcast by television, the disclosures required under paragraph (1) shall be included in the audio and visual part of such advertisement. In the case of an advertisement broadcast by televison or radio, the disclosure required under paragraph (1) shall consist only of the following: "This is not the free credit report provided for by Federal law".

§ 1681k. Public record information for employment purposes

(a) In general

A consumer reporting agency which furnishes a consumer report for employment purposes and which for that purpose compiles and reports items of information on consumers which are matters of public record and are likely to have an adverse effect upon a consumer's ability to obtain employment shall-

(1) at the time such public record information is reported to the user of such consumer report, notify the consumer of the fact that public record information is being reported by the consumer reporting agency, together with the name and address of the person to whom such information is being reported; or

(2) maintain strict procedures designed to insure that whenever public record information which is likely to have an adverse effect on a consumer's ability to obtain employment is reported it is complete and up to date. For purposes of this paragraph, items of public record relating to arrests, indictments, convictions, suits, tax liens, and outstanding judgments shall be considered up to date if the current public record status of the item at the time of the report is reported.

(b) Exemption for national security investigations

Subsection (a) does not apply in the case of an agency or department of the United States Government that seeks to obtain and use a consumer report for employment purposes, if the head of the agency or department makes a written finding as prescribed under section 1681b(b)(4)(A) of this title.

United States
Fair Credit Reporting Act

§ 1681l. Restrictions on investigative consumer reports

Whenever a consumer reporting agency prepares an investigative consumer report, no adverse information in the consumer report (other than information which is a matter of public record) may be included in a subsequent consumer report unless such adverse information has been verified in the process of making such subsequent consumer report, or the adverse information was received within the three-month period preceding the date the subsequent report is furnished.

§ 1681m. Requirements on users of consumer reports

(a) Duties of users taking adverse actions on basis of information contained in consumer reports

If any person takes any adverse action with respect to any consumer that is based in whole or in part on any information contained in a consumer report, the person shall-

(1) provide oral, written, or electronic notice of the adverse action to the consumer;

(2) provide to the consumer written or electronic disclosure-

(A) of a numerical credit score as defined in section 1681g(f)(2)(A) of this title used by such person in taking any adverse action based in whole or in part on any information in a consumer report; and

(B) of the information set forth in subparagraphs (B) through (E) of section 1681g(f)(1) of this title;

(3) provide to the consumer orally, in writing, or electronically-

(A) the name, address, and telephone number of the consumer reporting agency (including a toll-free telephone number established by the agency if the agency compiles and maintains files on consumers on a nationwide basis) that furnished the report to the person; and

(B) a statement that the consumer reporting agency did not make the decision to take the adverse action and is unable to provide the consumer the specific reasons why the adverse action was taken; and

(4) provide to the consumer an oral, written, or electronic notice of the consumer's right-

(A) to obtain, under section 1681j of this title, a free copy of a consumer report on the consumer from the consumer reporting agency referred to in paragraph (3), which notice shall include an indication of the 60-day period under that section for obtaining such a copy; and

(B) to dispute, under section 1681i of this title, with a consumer reporting agency the accuracy or completeness of any information in a consumer report furnished by the agency.

(b) Adverse action based on information obtained from third parties other than consumer reporting agencies

(1) In general

Whenever credit for personal, family, or household purposes involving a consumer is denied or the charge for such credit is increased either wholly or partly because of information obtained from a person other than a consumer reporting agency bearing upon the consumer's credit worthiness, credit standing, credit capacity, character, general reputation, personal characteristics, or mode of living, the user of such information shall, within a reasonable period of time, upon the consumer's written request for the reasons for such adverse action received within sixty days after learning of such adverse action, disclose the nature of the information to the consumer. The user of such information shall clearly and accurately disclose to the consumer his right to make such written request at the time such adverse action is communicated to the consumer.

(2) Duties of person taking certain actions based on information provided by affiliate

(A) Duties, generally

If a person takes an action described in subparagraph (B) with respect to a consumer, based in whole or in part on information described in subparagraph (C), the person shall-

(i) notify the consumer of the action, including a statement that the consumer may obtain the information in accordance with clause (ii); and

(ii) upon a written request from the consumer received within 60 days after transmittal of the notice required by clause (i), disclose to the consumer the nature of the information upon which the action is based by not later than 30 days after receipt of the request.

(B) Action described

An action referred to in subparagraph (A) is an adverse action described in section 1681a(k)(1)(A) of this title, taken in connection with a transaction initiated by the consumer, or any adverse action described in clause (i) or (ii) of section 1681a(k)(1)(B) of this title.

(C) Information described

Information referred to in subparagraph (A)-

(i) except as provided in clause (ii), is information that-

(I) is furnished to the person taking the action by a person related by common ownership or affiliated by common corporate control to the person taking the action; and

(II) bears on the credit worthiness, credit standing, credit capacity, character, general reputation, personal characteristics, or mode of living of the consumer; and

(ii) does not include-

(I) information solely as to transactions or experiences between the consumer and the person furnishing the information; or

(II) information in a consumer report.

(c) Reasonable procedures to assure compliance

No person shall be held liable for any violation of this section if he shows by a preponderance of the evidence that at the time of the alleged violation he maintained reasonable procedures to assure compliance with the provisions of this section.

(d) Duties of users making written credit or insurance solicitations on basis of information contained in consumer files

(1) In general

Any person who uses a consumer report on any consumer in connection with any credit or insurance transaction that is not initiated by the consumer, that is provided to that person under section 1681b(c)(1)(B) of this title, shall provide with each written solicitation made to the consumer regarding the transaction a clear and conspicuous statement that-

(A) information contained in the consumer's consumer report was used in connection with the transaction;

(B) the consumer received the offer of credit or insurance because the consumer satisfied the criteria for credit worthiness or insurability under which the consumer was selected for the offer;

(C) if applicable, the credit or insurance may not be extended if, after the consumer responds to the offer, the consumer does not meet the criteria used to select the consumer for the offer or any applicable criteria bearing on credit worthiness or insurability or does not furnish any required collateral;

(D) the consumer has a right to prohibit information contained in the consumer's file with any consumer reporting agency from being used in connection with any credit or insurance transaction that is not initiated by the consumer; and

(E) the consumer may exercise the right referred to in subparagraph (D) by notifying a notification system established under section 1681b(e) of this title.

(2) Disclosure of address and telephone number; format

A statement under paragraph (1) shall-

(A) include the address and toll-free telephone number of the appropriate notification system established under section 1681b(e) of this title; and

(B) be presented in such format and in such type size and manner as to be simple and easy to understand, as established by the Bureau, by rule, in consultation with the Federal Trade Commission, the Federal banking agencies, and the National Credit Union Administration.

(3) Maintaining criteria on file

A person who makes an offer of credit or insurance to a consumer under a credit or insurance transaction described in paragraph (1) shall maintain on file the criteria used to select the consumer to receive the offer, all criteria bearing on credit worthiness or insurability, as applicable, that are the basis for determining whether or not to extend credit or insurance pursuant to the offer, and any requirement for the furnishing of collateral as a condition of the extension of credit or insurance, until the expiration of the 3-year period beginning on the date on which the offer is made to the consumer.

(4) Authority of Federal agencies regarding unfair or deceptive acts or practices not affected

This section is not intended to affect the authority of any Federal or State agency to enforce a prohibition against unfair or deceptive acts or practices, including the making of false or misleading statements in connection with a credit or insurance transaction that is not initiated by the consumer.

(e) Red flag guidelines and regulations required

(1) Guidelines

The Federal banking agencies, the National Credit Union Administration, the Federal Trade Commission, the Commodity Futures Trading Commission, and the Securities and Exchange Commission shall jointly, with respect to the entities that are subject to their respective enforcement authority under section 1681s of this title-

(A) establish and maintain guidelines for use by each financial institution and each creditor regarding identity theft with respect to account holders at, or customers of, such entities, and update such guidelines as often as necessary;

(B) prescribe regulations requiring each financial institution and each creditor to establish reasonable policies and procedures for implementing the guidelines established pursuant to subparagraph (A), to identify possible risks to account holders or customers or to the safety and soundness of the institution or customers; and

(C) prescribe regulations applicable to card issuers to ensure that, if a card issuer receives notification of a change of address for an existing account, and within a short period of time (during at least the first 30 days after such notification is received) receives a request for an additional or replacement card for the same account, the card issuer may not issue the additional or replacement card, unless the card issuer, in accordance with reasonable policies and procedures-

(i) notifies the cardholder of the request at the former address of the cardholder and provides to the cardholder a means of promptly reporting incorrect address changes;

(ii) notifies the cardholder of the request by such other means of communication as the cardholder and the card issuer previously agreed to; or

(iii) uses other means of assessing the validity of the change of address, in accordance with reasonable policies and procedures established by the card issuer in accordance with the regulations prescribed under subparagraph (B).

(2) Criteria

(A) In general

In developing the guidelines required by paragraph (1)(A), the agencies described in paragraph (1) shall identify patterns, practices, and specific forms of activity that indicate the possible existence of identity theft.

(B) Inactive accounts

In developing the guidelines required by paragraph (1)(A), the agencies described in paragraph (1) shall consider including reasonable guidelines providing that when a transaction occurs with respect to a credit or deposit account that has been inactive for more than 2 years, the creditor or financial institution shall follow reasonable policies and procedures that provide for notice to be given to a consumer in a manner reasonably designed to reduce the likelihood of identity theft with respect to such account.

(3) Consistency with verification requirements

Guidelines established pursuant to paragraph (1) shall not be inconsistent with the policies and procedures required under section 5318(l) of title 31.

(4) Definitions

As used in this subsection, the term "creditor"-

(A) means a creditor, as defined in section 1691a of this title, that regularly and in the ordinary course of business-

(i) obtains or uses consumer reports, directly or indirectly, in connection with a credit transaction;

(ii) furnishes information to consumer reporting agencies, as described in section 1681s–2 of this title, in connection with a credit transaction; or

(iii) advances funds to or on behalf of a person, based on an obligation of the person to repay the funds or repayable from specific property pledged by or on behalf of the person;

(B) does not include a creditor described in subparagraph (A)(iii) that advances funds on behalf of a person for expenses incidental to a service provided by the creditor to that person; and

(C) includes any other type of creditor, as defined in that section 1691a of this title, as the agency described in paragraph (1) having authority over that creditor may determine appropriate by rule promulgated by that agency, based on a determination that such creditor offers or maintains accounts that are subject to a reasonably foreseeable risk of identity theft.

(f) Prohibition on sale or transfer of debt caused by identity theft

(1) In general

No person shall sell, transfer for consideration, or place for collection a debt that such person has been notified under section 1681c–2 of this title has resulted from identity theft.

(2) Applicability

The prohibitions of this subsection shall apply to all persons collecting a debt described in paragraph (1) after the date of a notification under paragraph (1).

(3) Rule of construction

Nothing in this subsection shall be construed to prohibit-

(A) the repurchase of a debt in any case in which the assignee of the debt requires such repurchase because the debt has resulted from identity theft;

(B) the securitization of a debt or the pledging of a portfolio of debt as collateral in connection with a borrowing; or

(C) the transfer of debt as a result of a merger, acquisition, purchase and assumption transaction, or transfer of substantially all of the assets of an entity.

(g) Debt collector communications concerning identity theft

If a person acting as a debt collector (as that term is defined in subchapter V) on behalf of a third party that is a creditor or other user of a consumer report is notified that any information relating to a debt that the person is attempting to collect may be fraudulent or may be the result of identity theft, that person shall-

(1) notify the third party that the information may be fraudulent or may be the result of identity theft; and

(2) upon request of the consumer to whom the debt purportedly relates, provide to the consumer all information to which the consumer would otherwise be entitled if the consumer were not a victim of identity theft, but wished to dispute the debt under provisions of law applicable to that person.

(h) Duties of users in certain credit transactions

(1) In general

Subject to rules prescribed as provided in paragraph (6), if any person uses a consumer report in connection with an application for, or a grant, extension, or other provision of, credit on material terms that are materially less favorable than the most favorable terms available to a substantial proportion of consumers from or through that person, based in whole or in part on a consumer report, the person shall provide an oral, written, or electronic notice to the consumer in the form and manner required by regulations prescribed in accordance with this subsection.

(2) Timing

The notice required under paragraph (1) may be provided at the time of an application for, or a grant, extension, or other provision of, credit or the time of communication of an approval of an application for, or grant, extension, or other provision of, credit, except as provided in the regulations prescribed under paragraph (6).

(3) Exceptions

No notice shall be required from a person under this subsection if-

(A) the consumer applied for specific material terms and was granted those terms, unless those terms were initially specified by the person after the transaction was initiated by the consumer and after the person obtained a consumer report; or

(B) the person has provided or will provide a notice to the consumer under subsection (a) in connection with the transaction.

(4) Other notice not sufficient

A person that is required to provide a notice under subsection (a) cannot meet that requirement by providing a notice under this subsection.

(5) Content and delivery of notice

A notice under this subsection shall, at a minimum-

(A) include a statement informing the consumer that the terms offered to the consumer are set based on information from a consumer report;

(B) identify the consumer reporting agency furnishing the report;

(C) include a statement informing the consumer that the consumer may obtain a copy of a consumer report from that consumer reporting agency without charge;

(D) include the contact information specified by that consumer reporting agency for obtaining such consumer reports (including a toll-free telephone number established by the agency in the case of a consumer reporting agency described in section 1681a(p) of this title); and

(E) include a statement informing the consumer of-

(i) a numerical credit score as defined in section 1681g(f)(2)(A) of this title, used by such person in making the credit decision described in paragraph (1) based in whole or in part on any information in a consumer report; and

(ii) the information set forth in subparagraphs (B) through (E) of section 1681g(f)(1) of this title.

(6) Rulemaking

(A) Rules required

The Bureau shall prescribe rules to carry out this subsection.

(B) Content

Rules required by subparagraph (A) shall address, but are not limited to-

(i) the form, content, time, and manner of delivery of any notice under this subsection;

(ii) clarification of the meaning of terms used in this subsection, including what credit terms are material, and when credit terms are materially less favorable;

(iii) exceptions to the notice requirement under this subsection for classes of persons or transactions regarding which the agencies determine that notice would not significantly benefit consumers;

(iv) a model notice that may be used to comply with this subsection; and

(v) the timing of the notice required under paragraph (1), including the circumstances under which the notice must be provided after the terms offered to the consumer were set based on information from a consumer report.

(7) Compliance

A person shall not be liable for failure to perform the duties required by this section if, at the time of the failure, the person maintained reasonable policies and procedures to comply with this section.

(8) Enforcement

(A) No civil actions

Sections 1681n and 1681o of this title shall not apply to any failure by any person to comply with this section.

(B) Administrative enforcement

This section shall be enforced exclusively under section 1681s of this title by the Federal agencies and officials identified in that section.

§ 1681n. Civil liability for willful noncompliance

(a) In general

Any person who willfully fails to comply with any requirement imposed under this subchapter with respect to any consumer is liable to that consumer in an amount equal to the sum of-

(1)(A) any actual damages sustained by the consumer as a result of the failure or damages of not less than $100 and not more than $1,000; or

(B) in the case of liability of a natural person for obtaining a consumer report under false pretenses or knowingly without a permissible purpose, actual damages sustained by the consumer as a result of the failure or $1,000, whichever is greater;

(2) such amount of punitive damages as the court may allow; and

(3) in the case of any successful action to enforce any liability under this section, the costs of the action together with reasonable attorney's fees as determined by the court.

(b) Civil liability for knowing noncompliance

Any person who obtains a consumer report from a consumer reporting agency under false pretenses or knowingly without a permissible purpose shall be liable to the consumer reporting agency for actual damages sustained by the consumer reporting agency or $1,000, whichever is greater.

(c) Attorney's fees

Upon a finding by the court that an unsuccessful pleading, motion, or other paper filed in connection with an action under this section was filed in bad faith or for purposes of harassment, the court shall award to the prevailing party attorney's fees reasonable in relation to the work expended in responding to the pleading, motion, or other paper.

(d) Clarification of willful noncompliance

For the purposes of this section, any person who printed an expiration date on any receipt provided to a consumer cardholder at a point of sale or transaction between December 4, 2004, and June 3, 2008, but otherwise complied with the requirements of section 1681c(g) of this title for such receipt shall not be in willful noncompliance with section 1681c(g) of this title by reason of printing such expiration date on the receipt.

§ 1681o. Civil liability for negligent noncompliance

(a) In general

Any person who is negligent in failing to comply with any requirement imposed under this subchapter with respect to any consumer is liable to that consumer in an amount equal to the sum of-

(1) any actual damages sustained by the consumer as a result of the failure; and

(2) in the case of any successful action to enforce any liability under this section, the costs of the action together with reasonable attorney's fees as determined by the court.

(b) Attorney's fees

On a finding by the court that an unsuccessful pleading, motion, or other paper filed in connection with an action under this section was filed in bad faith or for purposes of harassment, the court shall award to the prevailing party attorney's fees reasonable in relation to the work expended in responding to the pleading, motion, or other paper.

§ 1681p. Jurisdiction of courts; limitation of actions

An action to enforce any liability created under this subchapter may be brought in any appropriate United States district court, without regard to the amount in controversy, or in any other court of competent jurisdiction, not later than the earlier of-

(1) 2 years after the date of discovery by the plaintiff of the violation that is the basis for such liability; or

(2) 5 years after the date on which the violation that is the basis for such liability occurs.

§ 1681q. Obtaining information under false pretenses

Any person who knowingly and willfully obtains information on a consumer from a consumer reporting agency under false pretenses shall be fined under title 18, imprisoned for not more than 2 years, or both.

§ 1681r. Unauthorized disclosures by officers or employees

Any officer or employee of a consumer reporting agency who knowingly and willfully provides information concerning an individual from the agency's files to a person not authorized to receive that information shall be fined under title 18, imprisoned for not more than 2 years, or both.

§ 1681s. Administrative enforcement

(a) Enforcement by Federal Trade Commission

(1) In general

The Federal Trade Commission shall be authorized to enforce compliance with the requirements imposed by this subchapter under the Federal Trade Commission Act (15 U.S.C. 41 et seq.), with respect to consumer reporting agencies and all other persons subject thereto, except to the extent that enforcement of the requirements imposed under this subchapter is specifically committed to some other Government agency under any of subparagraphs (A) through (G) of subsection (b)(1), and subject to subtitle B of the Consumer Financial Protection Act of 2010 [12 U.S.C. 5511 et seq.], subsection (b). For the purpose of the exercise by the Federal Trade Commission of its functions and powers under the Federal Trade Commission Act, a violation of any requirement or prohibition imposed under this subchapter shall constitute an unfair or deceptive act or practice in commerce, in violation of section 5(a) of the Federal Trade Commission Act (15 U.S.C. 45(a)), and shall be subject to enforcement by the Federal Trade Commission under section 5(b) of that Act [15 U.S.C. 45(b)] with respect to any consumer reporting agency or person that is subject to enforcement by the Federal Trade Commission pursuant to this subsection, irrespective of whether that person is engaged in commerce or meets any other jurisdictional tests under the Federal Trade Commission Act. The Federal Trade Commission shall have such procedural, investigative, and enforcement powers, including the power to issue procedural rules in enforcing compliance with the requirements imposed under this subchapter and to require the filing of reports, the production of documents, and the appearance of witnesses, as though the applicable terms and conditions of the Federal Trade Commission Act were part of this subchapter. Any person violating any of the provisions of this subchapter shall be subject to the penalties and entitled to the privileges and immunities provided in the Federal Trade Commission Act as though the applicable terms and provisions of such Act are part of this subchapter.

(2) Penalties

(A) Knowing violations

Except as otherwise provided by subtitle B of the Consumer Financial Protection Act of 2010, in the event of a knowing violation, which constitutes a pattern or practice of violations of this subchapter, the Federal Trade Commission may commence a civil action to recover a civil penalty in a district court of the United States against any person that violates this subchapter. In such action, such person shall be liable for a civil penalty of not more than $2,500 per violation.

(B) Determining penalty amount

In determining the amount of a civil penalty under subparagraph (A), the court shall take into account the degree of culpability, any history of such prior conduct, ability to pay, effect on ability to continue to do business, and such other matters as justice may require.

(C) Limitation

Notwithstanding paragraph (2), a court may not impose any civil penalty on a person for a violation of section 1681s–2(a)(1) of this title, unless the person has been enjoined from committing the violation, or ordered not to commit the violation, in an action or proceeding brought by or on behalf of the Federal Trade Commission, and has violated the injunction or order, and the court may not impose any civil penalty for any violation occurring before the date of the violation of the injunction or order.

(b) Enforcement by other agencies

(1) In general

Subject to subtitle B of the Consumer Financial Protection Act of 2010, compliance with the requirements imposed under this subchapter with respect to consumer reporting agencies, persons who use consumer reports from such agencies, persons who furnish information to such agencies, and users of information that are subject to section 1681m(d) of this title shall be enforced under-

(A) section 8 of the Federal Deposit Insurance Act (12 U.S.C. 1818), by the appropriate Federal banking agency, as defined in section 3(q) of the Federal Deposit Insurance Act (12 U.S.C. 1813(q)), with respect to-

(i) any national bank or State savings association, and any Federal branch or Federal agency of a foreign bank;

(ii) any member bank of the Federal Reserve System (other than a national bank), a branch or agency of a foreign bank (other than a Federal branch, Federal agency, or insured State branch of a foreign bank), a commercial lending company owned or controlled by a foreign bank, and any organization operating under section 25 or 25A of the Federal Reserve Act [12 U.S.C. 601 et seq., 611 et seq.]; and

(iii) any bank or Federal savings association insured by the Federal Deposit Insurance Corporation (other than a member of the Federal Reserve System) and any insured State branch of a foreign bank;

(B) the Federal Credit Union Act (12 U.S.C. 1751 et seq.), by the Administrator of the National Credit Union Administration with respect to any Federal credit union;

(C) subtitle IV of title 49, by the Secretary of Transportation, with respect to all carriers subject to the jurisdiction of the Surface Transportation Board;

(D) part A of subtitle VII of title 49, by the Secretary of Transportation, with respect to any air carrier or foreign air carrier subject to that part;

(E) the Packers and Stockyards Act, 1921 (7 U.S.C. 181 et seq.) (except as provided in section 406 of that Act [7 U.S.C. 226, 227]), by the Secretary of Agriculture, with respect to any activities subject to that Act;

(F) the Commodity Exchange Act [7 U.S.C. 1 et seq.], with respect to a person subject to the jurisdiction of the Commodity Futures Trading Commission;

(G) the Federal securities laws, and any other laws that are subject to the jurisdiction of the Securities and Exchange Commission, with respect to a person that is subject to the jurisdiction of the Securities and Exchange Commission; and

(H) subtitle E of the Consumer Financial Protection Act of 2010 [12 U.S.C. 5561 et seq.], by the Bureau, with respect to any person subject to this subchapter.

(2) Incorporated definitions

The terms used in paragraph (1) that are not defined in this subchapter or otherwise defined in section 3(s) of the Federal Deposit Insurance Act (12 U.S.C. 1813(s)) have the same meanings as in section 1(b) of the International Banking Act of 1978 (12 U.S.C. 3101).

(c) State action for violations

(1) Authority of States

In addition to such other remedies as are provided under State law, if the chief law enforcement officer of a State, or an official or agency designated by a State, has reason to believe that any person has violated or is violating this subchapter, the State-

(A) may bring an action to enjoin such violation in any appropriate United States district court or in any other court of competent jurisdiction;

(B) subject to paragraph (5), may bring an action on behalf of the residents of the State to recover-

(i) damages for which the person is liable to such residents under sections 1681n and 1681o of this title as a result of the violation;

(ii) in the case of a violation described in any of paragraphs (1) through (3) of section 1681s–2(c) of this title, damages for which the person would, but for section 1681s–2(c) of this title, be liable to such residents as a result of the violation; or

(iii) damages of not more than $1,000 for each willful or negligent violation; and

(C) in the case of any successful action under subparagraph (A) or (B), shall be awarded the costs of the action and reasonable attorney fees as determined by the court.

(2) Rights of Federal regulators

The State shall serve prior written notice of any action under paragraph (1) upon the Bureau and the Federal Trade Commission or the appropriate Federal regulator determined under subsection (b) and provide the Bureau and the Federal Trade Commission or appropriate Federal regulator with a copy of its complaint, except in any case in which such prior notice is not feasible, in which case the State shall serve such notice immediately upon instituting such action. The Bureau and the Federal Trade Commission or appropriate Federal regulator shall have the right-

(A) to intervene in the action;

(B) upon so intervening, to be heard on all matters arising therein;

(C) to remove the action to the appropriate United States district court; and

(D) to file petitions for appeal.

(3) Investigatory powers

For purposes of bringing any action under this subsection, nothing in this subsection shall prevent the chief law enforcement officer, or an official or agency designated by a State, from exercising the powers conferred on the chief law enforcement officer or such official by the laws of such State to conduct investigations or to administer oaths or affirmations or to compel the attendance of witnesses or the production of documentary and other evidence.

(4) Limitation on State action while Federal action pending

If the Bureau, the Federal Trade Commission, or the appropriate Federal regulator has instituted a civil action or an administrative action under section 8 of the Federal Deposit Insurance Act [12 U.S.C. 1818] for a violation of this subchapter, no State may, during the pendency of such action, bring an action under this section against any defendant named in the complaint of the Bureau, the Federal Trade Commission, or the appropriate Federal regulator for any violation of this subchapter that is alleged in that complaint.

(5) Limitations on State actions for certain violations

(A) Violation of injunction required

A State may not bring an action against a person under paragraph (1)(B) for a violation described in any of paragraphs (1) through (3) of section 1681s–2(c) of this title, unless-

(i) the person has been enjoined from committing the violation, in an action brought by the State under paragraph (1)(A); and

(ii) the person has violated the injunction.

(B) Limitation on damages recoverable

In an action against a person under paragraph (1)(B) for a violation described in any of paragraphs (1) through (3) of section 1681s–2(c) of this title, a State may not recover any damages incurred before the date of the violation of an injunction on which the action is based.

(d) Enforcement under other authority

For the purpose of the exercise by any agency referred to in subsection (b) of its powers under any Act referred to in that subsection, a violation of any requirement imposed under this subchapter shall be deemed to be a violation of a requirement imposed under that Act. In addition to its powers under any provision of law specifically referred to in subsection (b), each of the agencies referred to in that subsection may exercise, for the purpose of enforcing compliance with any requirement imposed under this subchapter any other authority conferred on it by law.

(e) Regulatory authority

(1) In general

The Bureau shall prescribe such regulations as are necessary to carry out the purposes of this subchapter, except with respect to sections 1681m(e) and 1681w of this title. The Bureau may prescribe regulations as may be necessary or appropriate to administer and carry out the purposes and objectives of this subchapter, and to prevent evasions thereof or to facilitate compliance therewith. Except as provided in section 1029(a) of the Consumer Financial Protection Act of 2010 [12 U.S.C. 5519(a)], the regulations prescribed by the Bureau under this subchapter shall apply to any person that is subject to this subchapter, notwithstanding the enforcement authorities granted to other agencies under this section.

(2) Deference

Notwithstanding any power granted to any Federal agency under this subchapter, the deference that a court affords to a Federal agency with respect to a determination made by such agency relating to the meaning or interpretation of any provision of this subchapter that is subject to the jurisdiction of such agency shall be applied as if that agency were the only agency authorized to apply, enforce, interpret, or administer the provisions of this subchapter. The regulations prescribed by the Bureau under this subchapter shall apply to any person that is subject to this subchapter, notwithstanding the enforcement authorities granted to other agencies under this section.

(f) Coordination of consumer complaint investigations

(1) In general

Each consumer reporting agency described in section 1681a(p) of this title shall develop and maintain procedures for the referral to each other such agency of any consumer complaint received by the agency alleging identity theft, or requesting a fraud alert under section 1681c–1 of this title or a block under section 1681c–2 of this title.

(2) Model form and procedure for reporting identity theft

The Commission, in consultation with the Federal Trade Commission, the Federal banking agencies, and the National Credit Union Administration, shall develop a model form and model procedures to be used by consumers who are victims of identity theft for contacting and informing creditors and consumer reporting agencies of the fraud.

(3) Annual summary reports

Each consumer reporting agency described in section 1681a(p) of this title shall submit an annual summary report to the Bureau on consumer complaints received by the agency on identity theft or fraud alerts.

(g) Bureau regulation of coding of trade names

If the Bureau determines that a person described in paragraph (9) of section 1681s–2(a) of this title has not met the requirements of such paragraph, the Bureau shall take action to ensure the person's compliance with such paragraph, which may include issuing model guidance or prescribing reasonable policies and procedures, as necessary to ensure that such person complies with such paragraph.

§ 1681s-1. Information on overdue child support obligations

Notwithstanding any other provision of this subchapter, a consumer reporting agency shall include in any consumer report furnished by the agency in accordance with section 1681b of this title, any information on the failure of the consumer to pay overdue support which-

(1) is provided-

(A) to the consumer reporting agency by a State or local child support enforcement agency; or

(B) to the consumer reporting agency and verified by any local, State, or Federal Government agency; and

(2) antedates the report by 7 years or less.

§ 1681s-2. Responsibilities of furnishers of information to consumer reporting agencies

(a) Duty of furnishers of information to provide accurate information

(1) Prohibition

(A) Reporting information with actual knowledge of errors

A person shall not furnish any information relating to a consumer to any consumer reporting agency if the person knows or has reasonable cause to believe that the information is inaccurate.

(B) Reporting information after notice and confirmation of errors

A person shall not furnish information relating to a consumer to any consumer reporting agency if-

> (i) the person has been notified by the consumer, at the address specified by the person for such notices, that specific information is inaccurate; and
>
> (ii) the information is, in fact, inaccurate.

(C) No address requirement

A person who clearly and conspicuously specifies to the consumer an address for notices referred to in subparagraph (B) shall not be subject to subparagraph (A); however, nothing in subparagraph (B) shall require a person to specify such an address.

(D) Definition

For purposes of subparagraph (A), the term "reasonable cause to believe that the information is inaccurate" means having specific knowledge, other than solely allegations by the consumer, that would cause a reasonable person to have substantial doubts about the accuracy of the information.

(2) Duty to correct and update information

A person who-

(A) regularly and in the ordinary course of business furnishes information to one or more consumer reporting agencies about the person's transactions or experiences with any consumer; and

(B) has furnished to a consumer reporting agency information that the person determines is not complete or accurate, shall promptly notify the consumer reporting agency of that determination and provide to the agency any corrections to that information, or any additional information, that is necessary to make the information provided by the person to the agency complete and accurate, and shall not thereafter furnish to the agency any of the information that remains not complete or accurate.

(3) Duty to provide notice of dispute

If the completeness or accuracy of any information furnished by any person to any consumer reporting agency is disputed to such person by a consumer, the person may not furnish the information to any consumer reporting agency without notice that such information is disputed by the consumer.

(4) Duty to provide notice of closed accounts

A person who regularly and in the ordinary course of business furnishes information to a consumer reporting agency regarding a consumer who has a credit account with that person shall notify the agency of the voluntary closure of the account by the consumer, in information regularly furnished for the period in which the account is closed.

(5) Duty to provide notice of delinquency of accounts

(A) In general

A person who furnishes information to a consumer reporting agency regarding a delinquent account being placed for collection, charged to profit or loss, or subjected to any similar action shall, not later than 90 days after furnishing the information, notify the agency of the date of delinquency on the account, which shall be the month and year of the commencement of the delinquency on the account that immediately preceded the action.

(B) Rule of construction

For purposes of this paragraph only, and provided that the consumer does not dispute the information, a person that furnishes information on a delinquent account that is placed for collection, charged for profit or loss, or subjected to any similar action, complies with this paragraph, if-

(i) the person reports the same date of delinquency as that provided by the creditor to which the account was owed at the time at which the commencement of the delinquency occurred, if the creditor previously reported that date of delinquency to a consumer reporting agency;

(ii) the creditor did not previously report the date of delinquency to a consumer reporting agency, and the person establishes and follows reasonable procedures to obtain the date of delinquency from the creditor or another reliable source and reports that date to a consumer reporting agency as the date of delinquency; or

(iii) the creditor did not previously report the date of delinquency to a consumer reporting agency and the date of delinquency cannot be reasonably obtained as provided in clause (ii), the person establishes and follows reasonable procedures to ensure the date reported as the date of delinquency precedes the date on which the account is placed for collection, charged to profit or loss, or subjected to any similar action, and reports such date to the credit reporting agency.

(6) Duties of furnishers upon notice of identity theft-related information

(A) Reasonable procedures

A person that furnishes information to any consumer reporting agency shall have in place reasonable procedures to respond to any notification that it receives from a consumer reporting agency under section 1681c-2 of this title relating to information resulting from identity theft, to prevent that person from refurnishing such blocked information.

(B) Information alleged to result from identity theft

If a consumer submits an identity theft report to a person who furnishes information to a consumer reporting agency at the address specified by that person for receiving such reports stating that information maintained by such person that purports to relate to the consumer resulted from identity theft, the person may not furnish such information that purports to relate to the consumer to any consumer reporting agency, unless the person subsequently knows or is informed by the consumer that the information is correct.

(7) Negative information

    (A) Notice to consumer required

        (i) In general

        If any financial institution that extends credit and regularly and in the ordinary course of business furnishes information to a consumer reporting agency described in section 1681a(p) of this title furnishes negative information to such an agency regarding credit extended to a customer, the financial institution shall provide a notice of such furnishing of negative information, in writing, to the customer.

        (ii) Notice effective for subsequent submissions

        After providing such notice, the financial institution may submit additional negative information to a consumer reporting agency described in section 1681a(p) of this title with respect to the same transaction, extension of credit, account, or customer without providing additional notice to the customer.

    (B) Time of notice

        (i) In general

        The notice required under subparagraph (A) shall be provided to the customer prior to, or no later than 30 days after, furnishing the negative information to a consumer reporting agency described in section 1681a(p) of this title.

        (ii) Coordination with new account disclosures

        If the notice is provided to the customer prior to furnishing the negative information to a consumer reporting agency, the notice may not be included in the initial disclosures provided under section 1637(a) of this title.

    (C) Coordination with other disclosures

The notice required under subparagraph (A)-

        (i) may be included on or with any notice of default, any billing statement, or any other materials provided to the customer; and

        (ii) must be clear and conspicuous.

    (D) Model disclosure

        (i) Duty of Bureau

        The Bureau shall prescribe a brief model disclosure that a financial institution may use to comply with subparagraph (A), which shall not exceed 30 words.

        (ii) Use of model not required

No provision of this paragraph may be construed to require a financial institution to use any such model form prescribed by the Bureau.

(iii) Compliance using model

A financial institution shall be deemed to be in compliance with subparagraph (A) if the financial institution uses any model form prescribed by the Bureau under this subparagraph, or the financial institution uses any such model form and rearranges its format.

(E) Use of notice without submitting negative information

No provision of this paragraph shall be construed as requiring a financial institution that has provided a customer with a notice described in subparagraph (A) to furnish negative information about the customer to a consumer reporting agency.

(F) Safe harbor

A financial institution shall not be liable for failure to perform the duties required by this paragraph if, at the time of the failure, the financial institution maintained reasonable policies and procedures to comply with this paragraph or the financial institution reasonably believed that the institution is prohibited, by law, from contacting the consumer.

(G) Definitions

For purposes of this paragraph, the following definitions shall apply:

(i) Negative information

The term "negative information" means information concerning a customer's delinquencies, late payments, insolvency, or any form of default.

(ii) Customer; financial institution

The terms "customer" and "financial institution" have the same meanings as in section 6809 of this title.

(8) Ability of consumer to dispute information directly with furnisher

(A) In general

The Bureau, in consultation with the Federal Trade Commission, the Federal banking agencies, and the National Credit Union Administration, shall prescribe regulations that shall identify the circumstances under which a furnisher shall be required to reinvestigate a dispute concerning the accuracy of information contained in a consumer report on the consumer, based on a direct request of a consumer.

(B) Considerations

In prescribing regulations under subparagraph (A), the agencies shall weigh-

(i) the benefits to consumers with the costs on furnishers and the credit reporting system;

(ii) the impact on the overall accuracy and integrity of consumer reports of any such requirements;

(iii) whether direct contact by the consumer with the furnisher would likely result in the most expeditious resolution of any such dispute; and

(iv) the potential impact on the credit reporting process if credit repair organizations, as defined in section 1679a(3) of this title, including entities that would be a credit repair organization, but for section 1679a(3)(B)(i) of this title, are able to circumvent the prohibition in subparagraph (G).

(C) Applicability

Subparagraphs (D) through (G) shall apply in any circumstance identified under the regulations promulgated under subparagraph (A).

(D) Submitting a notice of dispute

A consumer who seeks to dispute the accuracy of information shall provide a dispute notice directly to such person at the address specified by the person for such notices that-

(i) identifies the specific information that is being disputed;

(ii) explains the basis for the dispute; and

(iii) includes all supporting documentation required by the furnisher to substantiate the basis of the dispute.

(E) Duty of person after receiving notice of dispute

After receiving a notice of dispute from a consumer pursuant to subparagraph (D), the person that provided the information in dispute to a consumer reporting agency shall-

(i) conduct an investigation with respect to the disputed information;

(ii) review all relevant information provided by the consumer with the notice;

(iii) complete such person's investigation of the dispute and report the results of the investigation to the consumer before the expiration of the period under section 1681i(a)(1) of this title within which a consumer reporting agency would be required to complete its action if the consumer had elected to dispute the information under that section; and

(iv) if the investigation finds that the information reported was inaccurate, promptly notify each consumer reporting agency to which the person furnished the inaccurate information of that determination and provide to the agency any correction to that information that is necessary to make the information provided by the person accurate.

(F) Frivolous or irrelevant dispute

(i) In general

This paragraph shall not apply if the person receiving a notice of a dispute from a consumer reasonably determines that the dispute is frivolous or irrelevant, including-

(I) by reason of the failure of a consumer to provide sufficient information to investigate the disputed information; or

(II) the submission by a consumer of a dispute that is substantially the same as a dispute previously submitted by or for the consumer, either directly to the person or through a consumer reporting agency under subsection (b), with respect to which the person has already performed the person's duties under this paragraph or subsection (b), as applicable.

(ii) Notice of determination

Upon making any determination under clause (i) that a dispute is frivolous or irrelevant, the person shall notify the consumer of such determination not later than 5 business days after making such determination, by mail or, if authorized by the consumer for that purpose, by any other means available to the person.

(iii) Contents of notice

A notice under clause (ii) shall include-

(I) the reasons for the determination under clause (i); and

(II) identification of any information required to investigate the disputed information, which may consist of a standardized form describing the general nature of such information.

(G) Exclusion of credit repair organizations

This paragraph shall not apply if the notice of the dispute is submitted by, is prepared on behalf of the consumer by, or is submitted on a form supplied to the consumer by, a credit repair organization, as defined in section 1679a(3) of this title, or an entity that would be a credit repair organization, but for section 1679a(3)(B)(i) of this title.

(9) Duty to provide notice of status as medical information furnisher

A person whose primary business is providing medical services, products, or devices, or the person's agent or assignee, who furnishes information to a consumer reporting agency on a consumer shall be considered a medical information furnisher for purposes of this subchapter, and shall notify the agency of such status.

(b) Duties of furnishers of information upon notice of dispute

(1) In general

After receiving notice pursuant to section 1681i(a)(2) of this title of a dispute with regard to the completeness or accuracy of any information provided by a person to a consumer reporting agency, the person shall-

(A) conduct an investigation with respect to the disputed information;

(B) review all relevant information provided by the consumer reporting agency pursuant to section 1681i(a)(2) of this title;

(C) report the results of the investigation to the consumer reporting agency;

(D) if the investigation finds that the information is incomplete or inaccurate, report those results to all other consumer reporting agencies to which the person furnished the information and that compile and maintain files on consumers on a nationwide basis; and

(E) if an item of information disputed by a consumer is found to be inaccurate or incomplete or cannot be verified after any reinvestigation under paragraph (1), for purposes of reporting to a consumer reporting agency only, as appropriate, based on the results of the reinvestigation promptly-

(i) modify that item of information;

(ii) delete that item of information; or

(iii) permanently block the reporting of that item of information.

(2) Deadline

A person shall complete all investigations, reviews, and reports required under paragraph (1) regarding information provided by the person to a consumer reporting agency, before the expiration of the period under section 1681i(a)(1) of this title within which the consumer reporting agency is required to complete actions required by that section regarding that information.

(c) Limitation on liability

Except as provided in section 1681s(c)(1)(B) of this title, sections 1681n and 1681o of this title do not apply to any violation of-

(1) subsection (a) of this section, including any regulations issued thereunder;

(2) subsection (e) of this section, except that nothing in this paragraph shall limit, expand, or otherwise affect liability under section 1681n or 1681o of this title, as applicable, for violations of subsection (b) of this section; or

(3) subsection (e) of section 1681m of this title.

(d) Limitation on enforcement

The provisions of law described in paragraphs (1) through (3) of subsection (c) (other than with respect to the exception described in paragraph (2) of subsection (c)) shall be enforced exclusively as provided under section 1681s of this title by the Federal agencies and officials and the State officials identified in section 1681s of this title.

(e) Accuracy guidelines and regulations required

(1) Guidelines

The Bureau shall, with respect to persons or entities that are subject to the enforcement authority of the Bureau under section 1681s of this title-

(A) establish and maintain guidelines for use by each person that furnishes information to a consumer reporting agency regarding the accuracy and integrity of the information relating to consumers that such entities furnish to consumer reporting agencies, and update such guidelines as often as necessary; and

(B) prescribe regulations requiring each person that furnishes information to a consumer reporting agency to establish reasonable policies and procedures for implementing the guidelines established pursuant to subparagraph (A).

(2) Criteria

In developing the guidelines required by paragraph (1)(A), the Bureau shall-

(A) identify patterns, practices, and specific forms of activity that can compromise the accuracy and integrity of information furnished to consumer reporting agencies;

(B) review the methods (including technological means) used to furnish information relating to consumers to consumer reporting agencies;

(C) determine whether persons that furnish information to consumer reporting agencies maintain and enforce policies to ensure the accuracy and integrity of information furnished to consumer reporting agencies; and

(D) examine the policies and processes that persons that furnish information to consumer reporting agencies employ to conduct reinvestigations and correct inaccurate information relating to consumers that has been furnished to consumer reporting agencies.

§ 1681s-3. Affiliate sharing

(a) Special rule for solicitation for purposes of marketing

(1) Notice

Any person that receives from another person related to it by common ownership or affiliated by corporate control a communication of information that would be a consumer report, but for clauses (i), (ii), and (iii) of section 1681a(d)(2)(A) of this title, may not use the information to make a solicitation for marketing purposes to a consumer about its products or services, unless-

(A) it is clearly and conspicuously disclosed to the consumer that the information may be communicated among such persons for purposes of making such solicitations to the consumer; and

(B) the consumer is provided an opportunity and a simple method to prohibit the making of such solicitations to the consumer by such person.

(2) Consumer choice

(A) In general

The notice required under paragraph (1) shall allow the consumer the opportunity to prohibit all solicitations referred to in such paragraph, and may allow the consumer to choose from different options when electing to prohibit the sending of such solicitations, including options regarding the types of entities and information covered, and which methods of delivering solicitations the consumer elects to prohibit.

(B) Format

Notwithstanding subparagraph (A), the notice required under paragraph (1) shall be clear, conspicuous, and concise, and any method provided under paragraph (1)(B) shall be simple. The regulations prescribed to implement this section shall provide specific guidance regarding how to comply with such standards.

(3) Duration

(A) In general

The election of a consumer pursuant to paragraph (1)(B) to prohibit the making of solicitations shall be effective for at least 5 years, beginning on the date on which the person receives the election of the consumer, unless the consumer requests that such election be revoked.

(B) Notice upon expiration of effective period

At such time as the election of a consumer pursuant to paragraph (1)(B) is no longer effective, a person may not use information that the person receives in the manner described in paragraph (1) to make any solicitation for marketing purposes to the consumer, unless the consumer receives a notice and an opportunity, using a simple method, to extend the opt-out for another period of at least 5 years, pursuant to the procedures described in paragraph (1).

(4) Scope

This section shall not apply to a person-

(A) using information to make a solicitation for marketing purposes to a consumer with whom the person has a pre-existing business relationship;

(B) using information to facilitate communications to an individual for whose benefit the person provides employee benefit or other services pursuant to a contract with an employer related to and arising out of the current employment relationship or status of the individual as a participant or beneficiary of an employee benefit plan;

(C) using information to perform services on behalf of another person related by common ownership or affiliated by corporate control, except that this subparagraph shall not be construed as permitting a person to send solicitations on behalf of another person, if such other person would not be permitted to send the solicitation on its own behalf as a result of the election of the consumer to prohibit solicitations under paragraph (1)(B);

(D) using information in response to a communication initiated by the consumer;

(E) using information in response to solicitations authorized or requested by the consumer; or

(F) if compliance with this section by that person would prevent compliance by that person with any provision of State insurance laws pertaining to unfair discrimination in any State in which the person is lawfully doing business.

(5) No retroactivity

This subsection shall not prohibit the use of information to send a solicitation to a consumer if such information was received prior to the date on which persons are required to comply with regulations implementing this subsection.

(b) Notice for other purposes permissible

A notice or other disclosure under this section may be coordinated and consolidated with any other notice required to be issued under any other provision of law by a person that is subject to this section, and a notice or other disclosure that is equivalent to the notice required by subsection (a), and that is provided by a person described in subsection (a) to a consumer together with disclosures required by any other provision of law, shall satisfy the requirements of subsection (a).

(c) User requirements

Requirements with respect to the use by a person of information received from another person related to it by common ownership or affiliated by corporate control, such as the requirements of this section, constitute requirements with respect to the exchange of information among persons affiliated by common ownership or common corporate control, within the meaning of section 1681t(b)(2) of this title.

(d) Definitions

For purposes of this section, the following definitions shall apply:

(1) Pre-existing business relationship

The term "pre-existing business relationship" means a relationship between a person, or a person's licensed agent, and a consumer, based on-

(A) a financial contract between a person and a consumer which is in force;

(B) the purchase, rental, or lease by the consumer of that person's goods or services, or a financial transaction (including holding an active account or a policy in force or having another continuing relationship) between the consumer and that person during the 18-month period immediately preceding the date on which the consumer is sent a solicitation covered by this section;

(C) an inquiry or application by the consumer regarding a product or service offered by that person, during the 3-month period immediately preceding the date on which the consumer is sent a solicitation covered by this section; or

(D) any other pre-existing customer relationship defined in the regulations implementing this section.

(2) Solicitation

The term "solicitation" means the marketing of a product or service initiated by a person to a particular consumer that is based on an exchange of information described in subsection (a), and is intended to encourage the consumer to purchase such product or service, but does not include communications that are directed at the general public or determined not to be a solicitation by the regulations prescribed under this section.

§ 1681t. Relation to State laws

(a) In general

Except as provided in subsections (b) and (c), this subchapter does not annul, alter, affect, or exempt any person subject to the provisions of this subchapter from complying with the laws of any State with respect to the collection, distribution, or use of any information on consumers, or for the prevention or mitigation of identity theft, except to the extent that those laws are inconsistent with any provision of this subchapter, and then only to the extent of the inconsistency.

(b) General exceptions

No requirement or prohibition may be imposed under the laws of any State-

   (1) with respect to any subject matter regulated under-

      (A) subsection (c) or (e) of section 1681b of this title, relating to the prescreening of consumer reports;

      (B) section 1681i of this title, relating to the time by which a consumer reporting agency must take any action, including the provision of notification to a consumer or other person, in any procedure related to the disputed accuracy of information in a consumer's file, except that this subparagraph shall not apply to any State law in effect on September 30, 1996;

      (C) subsections (a) and (b) of section 1681m of this title, relating to the duties of a person who takes any adverse action with respect to a consumer;

      (D) section 1681m(d) of this title, relating to the duties of persons who use a consumer report of a consumer in connection with any credit or insurance transaction that is not initiated by the consumer and that consists of a firm offer of credit or insurance;

      (E) section 1681c of this title, relating to information contained in consumer reports, except that this subparagraph shall not apply to any State law in effect on September 30, 1996;

      (F) section 1681s-2 of this title, relating to the responsibilities of persons who furnish information to consumer reporting agencies, except that this paragraph shall not apply-

         (i) with respect to section 54A(a) of chapter 93 of the Massachusetts Annotated Laws (as in effect on September 30, 1996); or

         (ii) with respect to section 1785.25(a) of the California Civil Code (as in effect on September 30, 1996);

      (G) section 1681g(e) of this title, relating to information available to victims under section 1681g(e) of this title;

(H) section 1681s–3 of this title, relating to the exchange and use of information to make a solicitation for marketing purposes; or

(I) section 1681m(h) of this title, relating to the duties of users of consumer reports to provide notice with respect to terms in certain credit transactions;

(2) with respect to the exchange of information among persons affiliated by common ownership or common corporate control, except that this paragraph shall not apply with respect to subsection (a) or (c)(1) of section 2480e of title 9, Vermont Statutes Annotated (as in effect on September 30, 1996);

(3) with respect to the disclosures required to be made under subsection (c), (d), (e), or (g) of section 1681g of this title, or subsection (f) of section 1681g of this title relating to the disclosure of credit scores for credit granting purposes, except that this paragraph-

(A) shall not apply with respect to sections 1785.10, 1785.16, and 1785.20.2 of the California Civil Code (as in effect on December 4, 2003) and section 1785.15 through section 1785.15.2 of such Code (as in effect on such date);

(B) shall not apply with respect to sections 5–3–106(2) and 212–14.3–104.3 of the Colorado Revised Statutes (as in effect on December 4, 2003); and

(C) shall not be construed as limiting, annulling, affecting, or superseding any provision of the laws of any State regulating the use in an insurance activity, or regulating disclosures concerning such use, of a credit-based insurance score of a consumer by any person engaged in the business of insurance;

(4) with respect to the frequency of any disclosure under section 1681j(a) of this title, except that this paragraph shall not apply-

(A) with respect to section 12–14.3–105(1)(d) of the Colorado Revised Statutes (as in effect on December 4, 2003);

(B) with respect to section 10–1–393(29)(C) of the Georgia Code (as in effect on December 4, 2003);

(C) with respect to section 1316.2 of title 10 of the Maine Revised Statutes (as in effect on December 4, 2003);

(D) with respect to sections 14–1209(a)(1) and 14–1209(b)(1)(i) of the Commercial Law Article of the Code of Maryland (as in effect on December 4, 2003);

(E) with respect to section 59(d) and section 59(e) of chapter 93 of the General Laws of Massachusetts (as in effect on December 4, 2003);

(F) with respect to section 56:11–37.10(a)(1) of the New Jersey Revised Statutes (as in effect on December 4, 2003); or

(G) with respect to section 2480c(a)(1) of title 9 of the Vermont Statutes Annotated (as in effect on December 4, 2003); or

(5) with respect to the conduct required by the specific provisions of-

(A) section 1681c(g) of this title;

(B) section 1681c–1 of this title;

(C) section 1681c–2 of this title;

(D) section 1681g(a)(1)(A) of this title;

(E) section 1681j(a) of this title;

(F) subsections (e), (f), and (g) of section 1681m of this title;

(G) section 1681s(f) of this title;

(H) section 1681s–2(a)(6) of this title; or

(I) section 1681w of this title.

(c) "Firm offer of credit or insurance" defined

Notwithstanding any definition of the term "firm offer of credit or insurance" (or any equivalent term) under the laws of any State, the definition of that term contained in section 1681a(l) of this title shall be construed to apply in the enforcement and interpretation of the laws of any State governing consumer reports.

(d) Limitations

Subsections (b) and (c) do not affect any settlement, agreement, or consent judgment between any State Attorney General and any consumer reporting agency in effect on September 30, 1996.

§ 1681u. Disclosures to FBI for counterintelligence purposes

(a) Identity of financial institutions

Notwithstanding section 1681b of this title or any other provision of this subchapter, a consumer reporting agency shall furnish to the Federal Bureau of Investigation the names and addresses of all financial institutions (as that term is defined in section 3401 of title 12) at which a consumer maintains or has maintained an account, to the extent that information is in the files of the agency, when presented with a written request for that information that includes a term that specifically identifies a consumer or account to be used as the basis for the production of that information, signed by the Director of the Federal Bureau of Investigation, or the Director's designee in a position not lower than Deputy Assistant Director at Bureau headquarters or a Special Agent in Charge of a Bureau field office designated by the Director, which certifies compliance with this section. The Director or the Director's designee may make such a certification only if the Director or the Director's designee has determined in writing, that such information is sought for the conduct of an authorized investigation to protect against international terrorism or clandestine intelligence activities, provided that such an investigation of a United States person is not conducted solely upon the basis of activities protected by the first amendment to the Constitution of the United States.

(b) Identifying information

Notwithstanding the provisions of section 1681b of this title or any other provision of this subchapter, a consumer reporting agency shall furnish identifying information respecting a consumer, limited to name, address, former addresses, places of employment, or former places of employment, to the Federal Bureau of Investigation when presented with a written request that includes a term that specifically identifies a consumer or account to be used as the basis for the production of that information, signed by the Director or the Director's designee in a position not lower than Deputy Assistant Director at Bureau headquarters or a Special Agent in Charge of a Bureau field office designated by the Director, which certifies compliance with this subsection. The Director or the Director's designee may make such a certification only if the Director or the Director's designee has determined in writing that such information is sought for the conduct of an authorized investigation to protect against international terrorism or clandestine intelligence activities, provided that such an investigation of a United States person is not conducted solely upon the basis of activities protected by the first amendment to the Constitution of the United States.

(c) Court order for disclosure of consumer reports

Notwithstanding section 1681b of this title or any other provision of this subchapter, if requested in writing by the Director of the Federal Bureau of Investigation, or a designee of the Director in a position not lower than Deputy Assistant Director at Bureau headquarters or a Special Agent in Charge in a Bureau field office designated by the Director, a court may issue an order ex parte, which shall include a term that specifically identifies a consumer or account to be used as the basis for the production of the information, directing a consumer reporting agency to furnish a consumer report to the Federal Bureau of Investigation, upon a showing in camera that the consumer report is sought for the conduct of an authorized investigation to protect against international terrorism or clandestine intelligence activities, provided that such an investigation of a United States person is not conducted solely upon the basis of activities protected by the first amendment to the Constitution of the United States. The terms of an order issued under this subsection shall not disclose that the order is issued for purposes of a counterintelligence investigation.

(d) Prohibition of certain disclosure

    (1) Prohibition

        (A) In general

        If a certification is issued under subparagraph (B) and notice of the right to judicial review under subsection (e) is provided, no consumer reporting agency that receives a request under subsection (a) or (b) or an order under subsection (c), or officer, employee, or agent thereof, shall disclose or specify in any consumer report, that the Federal Bureau of Investigation has sought or obtained access to information or records under subsection (a), (b), or (c).

        (B) Certification

        The requirements of subparagraph (A) shall apply if the Director of the Federal Bureau of Investigation, or a designee of the Director whose rank shall be no lower than Deputy Assistant Director at Bureau headquarters or a Special

Agent in Charge of a Bureau field office, certifies that the absence of a prohibition of disclosure under this subsection may result in-

(i) a danger to the national security of the United States;

(ii) interference with a criminal, counterterrorism, or counterintelligence investigation;

(iii) interference with diplomatic relations; or

(iv) danger to the life or physical safety of any person.

(2) Exception

(A) In general

A consumer reporting agency that receives a request under subsection (a) or (b) or an order under subsection (c), or officer, employee, or agent thereof, may disclose information otherwise subject to any applicable nondisclosure requirement to-

(i) those persons to whom disclosure is necessary in order to comply with the request;

(ii) an attorney in order to obtain legal advice or assistance regarding the request; or

(iii) other persons as permitted by the Director of the Federal Bureau of Investigation or the designee of the Director.

(B) Application

A person to whom disclosure is made under subparagraph (A) shall be subject to the nondisclosure requirements applicable to a person to whom a request under subsection (a) or (b) or an order under subsection (c) is issued in the same manner as the person to whom the request is issued.

(C) Notice

Any recipient that discloses to a person described in subparagraph (A) information otherwise subject to a nondisclosure requirement shall inform the person of the applicable nondisclosure requirement.

(D) Identification of disclosure recipients

At the request of the Director of the Federal Bureau of Investigation or the designee of the Director, any person making or intending to make a disclosure under clause (i) or (iii) of subparagraph (A) shall identify to the Director or such designee the person to whom such disclosure will be made or to whom such disclosure was made prior to the request.

(e) Judicial review

(1) In general

A request under subsection (a) or (b) or an order under subsection (c) or a non-disclosure requirement imposed in connection with such request under subsection (d) shall be subject to judicial review under section 3511 of title 18.

(2) Notice

A request under subsection (a) or (b) or an order under subsection (c) shall include notice of the availability of judicial review described in paragraph (1).

(f) Payment of fees

The Federal Bureau of Investigation shall, subject to the availability of appropriations, pay to the consumer reporting agency assembling or providing report or information in accordance with procedures established under this section a fee for reimbursement for such costs as are reasonably necessary and which have been directly incurred in searching, reproducing, or transporting books, papers, records, or other data required or requested to be produced under this section.

(g) Limit on dissemination

The Federal Bureau of Investigation may not disseminate information obtained pursuant to this section outside of the Federal Bureau of Investigation, except to other Federal agencies as may be necessary for the approval or conduct of a foreign counterintelligence investigation, or, where the information concerns a person subject to the Uniform Code of Military Justice, to appropriate investigative authorities within the military department concerned as may be necessary for the conduct of a joint foreign counterintelligence investigation.

(h) Rules of construction

Nothing in this section shall be construed to prohibit information from being furnished by the Federal Bureau of Investigation pursuant to a subpoena or court order, in connection with a judicial or administrative proceeding to enforce the provisions of this subchapter. Nothing in this section shall be construed to authorize or permit the withholding of information from the Congress.

(i) Reports to Congress

(1) On a semiannual basis, the Attorney General shall fully inform the Permanent Select Committee on Intelligence and the Committee on Banking, Finance and Urban Affairs of the House of Representatives, and the Select Committee on Intelligence and the Committee on Banking, Housing, and Urban Affairs of the Senate concerning all requests made pursuant to subsections (a), (b), and (c).

(2) In the case of the semiannual reports required to be submitted under paragraph (1) to the Permanent Select Committee on Intelligence of the House of Representatives and the Select Committee on Intelligence of the Senate, the submittal dates for such reports shall be as provided in section 3106 of title 50.

(j) Damages

Any agency or department of the United States obtaining or disclosing any consumer reports, records, or information contained therein in violation of this section is liable to the consumer to whom such consumer reports, records, or information relate in an amount equal to the sum of-

(1) $100, without regard to the volume of consumer reports, records, or information involved;

(2) any actual damages sustained by the consumer as a result of the disclosure;

(3) if the violation is found to have been willful or intentional, such punitive damages as a court may allow; and

(4) in the case of any successful action to enforce liability under this subsection, the costs of the action, together with reasonable attorney fees, as determined by the court.

(k) Disciplinary actions for violations

If a court determines that any agency or department of the United States has violated any provision of this section and the court finds that the circumstances surrounding the violation raise questions of whether or not an officer or employee of the agency or department acted willfully or intentionally with respect to the violation, the agency or department shall promptly initiate a proceeding to determine whether or not disciplinary action is warranted against the officer or employee who was responsible for the violation.

(l) Good-faith exception

Notwithstanding any other provision of this subchapter, any consumer reporting agency or agent or employee thereof making disclosure of consumer reports or identifying information pursuant to this subsection in good-faith reliance upon a certification of the Federal Bureau of Investigation pursuant to provisions of this section shall not be liable to any person for such disclosure under this subchapter, the constitution of any State, or any law or regulation of any State or any political subdivision of any State.

(m) Limitation of remedies

Notwithstanding any other provision of this subchapter, the remedies and sanctions set forth in this section shall be the only judicial remedies and sanctions for violation of this section.

(n) Injunctive relief

In addition to any other remedy contained in this section, injunctive relief shall be available to require compliance with the procedures of this section. In the event of any successful action under this subsection, costs together with reasonable attorney fees, as determined by the court, may be recovered.

§ 1681v. Disclosures to governmental agencies for counterterrorism purposes

(a) Disclosure

Notwithstanding section 1681b of this title or any other provision of this subchapter, a consumer reporting agency shall furnish a consumer report of a consumer and all other information in a consumer's file to a government agency authorized to conduct investigations of, or intelligence or counterintelligence activities or analysis related to, international terrorism when presented with a written certification by such government agency that such information is necessary for the agency's conduct or such investigation, activity or analysis and that includes a term that specifically identifies a consumer or account to be used as the basis for the production of such information.

(b) Form of certification

The certification described in subsection (a) shall be signed by a supervisory official designated by the head of a Federal agency or an officer of a Federal agency whose appointment to office is required to be made by the President, by and with the advice and consent of the Senate.

(c) Prohibition of certain disclosure

    (1) Prohibition

        (A) In general

If a certification is issued under subparagraph (B) and notice of the right to judicial review under subsection (d) is provided, no consumer reporting agency that receives a request under subsection (a), or officer, employee, or agent thereof, shall disclose or specify in any consumer report, that a government agency described in subsection (a) has sought or obtained access to information or records under subsection (a).

        (B) Certification

The requirements of subparagraph (A) shall apply if the head of the government agency described in subsection (a), or a designee, certifies that the absence of a prohibition of disclosure under this subsection may result in-

            (i) a danger to the national security of the United States;

            (ii) interference with a criminal, counterterrorism, or counterintelligence investigation;

            (iii) interference with diplomatic relations; or

            (iv) danger to the life or physical safety of any person.

    (2) Exception

        (A) In general

A consumer reporting agency that receives a request under subsection (a), or officer, employee, or agent thereof, may disclose information otherwise subject to any applicable nondisclosure requirement to-

            (i) those persons to whom disclosure is necessary in order to comply with the request;

            (ii) an attorney in order to obtain legal advice or assistance regarding the request; or

            (iii) other persons as permitted by the head of the government agency described in subsection (a) or a designee.

        (B) Application

A person to whom disclosure is made under subparagraph (A) shall be subject to the nondisclosure requirements applicable to a person to whom a request under subsection (a) is issued in the same manner as the person to whom the request is issued.

(C) Notice

Any recipient that discloses to a person described in subparagraph (A) information otherwise subject to a nondisclosure requirement shall inform the person of the applicable nondisclosure requirement.

(D) Identification of disclosure recipients

At the request of the head of the government agency described in subsection (a) or a designee, any person making or intending to make a disclosure under clause (i) or (iii) of subparagraph (A) shall identify to the head or such designee the person to whom such disclosure will be made or to whom such disclosure was made prior to the request.

(d) Judicial review

(1) In general

A request under subsection (a) or a non-disclosure requirement imposed in connection with such request under subsection (c) shall be subject to judicial review under section 3511 of title 18.

(2) Notice

A request under subsection (a) shall include notice of the availability of judicial review described in paragraph (1).

(e) Rule of construction

Nothing in section 1681u of this title shall be construed to limit the authority of the Director of the Federal Bureau of Investigation under this section.

(f) Safe harbor

Notwithstanding any other provision of this subchapter, any consumer reporting agency or agent or employee thereof making disclosure of consumer reports or other information pursuant to this section in good-faith reliance upon a certification of a government agency pursuant to the provisions of this section shall not be liable to any person for such disclosure under this subchapter, the constitution of any State, or any law or regulation of any State or any political subdivision of any State.

(g) Reports to Congress

(1) On a semi-annual basis, the Attorney General shall fully inform the Committee on the Judiciary, the Committee on Financial Services, and the Permanent Select Committee on Intelligence of the House of Representatives and the Committee on the Judiciary, the Committee on Banking, Housing, and Urban Affairs, and the Select Committee on Intelligence of the Senate concerning all requests made pursuant to subsection (a).

(2) In the case of the semiannual reports required to be submitted under paragraph (1) to the Permanent Select Committee on Intelligence of the House of

Representatives and the Select Committee on Intelligence of the Senate, the submittal dates for such reports shall be as provided in section 3106 of title 50.

§ 1681w. Disposal of records

(a) Regulations

(1) In general

The Federal Trade Commission, the Securities and Exchange Commission, the Commodity Futures Trading Commission, the Federal banking agencies, and the National Credit Union Administration, with respect to the entities that are subject to their respective enforcement authority under section 1681s of this title, and in coordination as described in paragraph (2), shall issue final regulations requiring any person that maintains or otherwise possesses consumer information, or any compilation of consumer information, derived from consumer reports for a business purpose to properly dispose of any such information or compilation.

(2) Coordination

Each agency required to prescribe regulations under paragraph (1) shall-

(A) consult and coordinate with each other such agency so that, to the extent possible, the regulations prescribed by each such agency are consistent and comparable with the regulations by each such other agency; and

(B) ensure that such regulations are consistent with the requirements and regulations issued pursuant to Public Law 106–102 and other provisions of Federal law.

(3) Exemption authority

In issuing regulations under this section, the agencies identified in paragraph (1) may exempt any person or class of persons from application of those regulations, as such agency deems appropriate to carry out the purpose of this section.

(b) Rule of construction

Nothing in this section shall be construed-

(1) to require a person to maintain or destroy any record pertaining to a consumer that is not imposed under other law; or

(2) to alter or affect any requirement imposed under any other provision of law to maintain or destroy such a record.

§ 1681x. Corporate and technological circumvention prohibited

The Commission shall prescribe regulations, to become effective not later than 90 days after December 4, 2003, to prevent a consumer reporting agency from circumventing or evading treatment as a consumer reporting agency described in section 1681a(p) of this title for purposes of this subchapter, including-

(1) by means of a corporate reorganization or restructuring, including a merger, acquisition, dissolution, divestiture, or asset sale of a consumer reporting agency; or

(2) by maintaining or merging public record and credit account information in a manner that is substantially equivalent to that described in paragraphs (1) and (2) of section 1681a(p) of this title, in the manner described in section 1681a(p) of this title.

PRIVACY ACT (1974)

Summary

In enacting the Privacy Act of 1974, Congress's stated purpose was to promote governmental respect for citizens' privacy by requiring federal agencies to observe certain guidelines in the use and disclosure of citizens' personal information. The Act was to promote accountability and legislative oversight with respect to the use of computer databases and other information systems in managing personal data files. The Act was also meant to strengthen review within agencies of criteria for the collection and retention of personal data.

The Act implements a set of privacy principles known as 'Fair Information Practices.' The Code of Fair Information Practices was first articulated by the Department of Health, Education and Welfare Special Advisory Commission in its 1973 report on "Records, Computers and the Rights of Citizens." It includes five core principles: that there should be no secret record keeping systems; that information collected for one purpose should not be used for another purpose without the consent of the individual; that individuals should be given access to information held about them and the opportunity to correct or amend that information; that information is kept relevant, accurate, and up to date; and that information is protected against unauthorized loss, alteration or disclosure.

Accordingly, the Act requires each Federal agency to publish a description of each system of records maintained by that agency. It requires that surrender of personal information is made with informed consent or with some guarantees of the uses and confidentiality of the information. It grants individuals the right of access including the right to review, copy and amend the record. It requires that information is maintained with "accuracy, relevance, timeliness and completeness." Finally, it requires agencies to protect against any security breaches which could result in "substantial harm, embarrassment, inconvenience, or unfairness to any individual on whom information is maintained." To aid in the enforcement of these legislative restraints, the Act provides administrative and judicial machinery for oversight and for civil remedy of violations. The Act also provides a private cause of action to individuals denied access to their information.

As originally drafted, the Privacy Act would have created a Federal Privacy Board to act as an oversight and enforcement mechanism. The final Act, however, created a far more limited body, the Privacy Protection Study Commission which issued a report in 1977 examining the problems with both private and public sector record keeping systems and making numerous recommendations for change. The Commission was dissolved following the release of its report. In 2016, the Act was amended to permit non-US citizens to bring suit in limited circumstances, against a subset of federal agencies, where the Attorney General has determined that the individual is from a country that (1) shares information with the United States for law enforcement purposes, (2) permits the transfer of personal information to the United States for commercial use, and (3) such policies do not impede the national security interests of the United States. The Attorney General may also subsequently revoke the designation.

References

> Public Law 93-579, as amended by Pub. L. 94–183, Pub. L. 97–365, Pub. L. 97–375, Pub. L. 97–452, Pub. L. 98–477, Pub. L. 98–497, Pub. L. 100–503, Pub. L. 101–508, Pub. L. 103–66, Pub. L. 104–193, Pub. L. 104–226, Pub. L. 104–316, Pub. L. 105–34, Pub. L. 105–362, Pub. L. 106–170, Pub. L. 108–271, Pub. L. 111–148, Pub. L. 111–203, and Pub. L. 113–295. Codified at 5 U.S.C. § 552a.
> [https://www.law.cornell.edu/uscode/text/5/552a]
>
> Senate Report No. 93-1183, September 26, 1974
>
> U.S. Department of Health, Education & Welfare, Report of the Secretary's Advisory Committee on Automated Personal Data Systems, *Records Computers and the Rights of Citizens* (MIT 1973)
> [https://www.epic.org/privacy/hew1973report/]
>
> Privacy Protection Study Commission, *Personal Privacy in an Information Society* (GPO 1977)
> [https://www.epic.org/privacy/ppsc1977report/]
>
> EPIC, Privacy Act of 1974
> [https://www.epic.org/privacy/1974act/]

Congressional findings and statement of purpose

> (a) The Congress finds that--
>> (1) the privacy of an individual is directly affected by the collection, maintenance, use, and dissemination of personal information by Federal agencies;
>> (2) the increasing use of computers and sophisticated information technology, while essential to the efficient operations of the Government, has greatly magnified the harm to individual privacy that can occur from any collection, maintenance, use, or dissemination of personal information;
>> (3) the opportunities for an individual to secure employment, insurance, and credit, and his right to due process, and other legal protections are endangered by the misuse of certain information systems;
>> (4) the right to privacy is a personal and fundamental right protected by the Constitution of the United States; and
>> (5) in order to protect the privacy of individuals identified in information systems maintained by Federal agencies, it is necessary and proper for the Congress to

regulate the collection, maintenance, use, and dissemination of information by such agencies.

(b) The purpose of this Act is to provide certain safeguards for an individual against an invasion of personal privacy by requiring Federal agencies, except as otherwise provided by law, to--

(1) permit an individual to determine what records pertaining to him are collected, maintained, used, or disseminated by such agencies;

(2) permit an individual to prevent records pertaining to him obtained by such agencies for a particular purpose from being used or made available for another purpose without his consent;

(3) permit an individual to gain access to information pertaining to him in Federal agency records, to have a copy made of all or any portion thereof, and to correct or amend such records;

(4) collect, maintain, use, or disseminate any record of identifiable personal information in a manner that assures that such action is for a necessary and lawful purpose, that the information is current and accurate for its intended use, and that adequate safeguards are provided to prevent misuse of such information;

(5) permit exemptions from the requirements with respect to records provided in this Act only in those cases where there is an important public policy need for such exemption as has been determined by specific statutory authority; and

(6) be subject to civil suit for any damages which occur as a result of willful or intentional action which violates any individual's rights under this Act.

5 U.S.C. § 552a Public information; agency rules, opinions, orders, records, and proceedings

(a) Definitions.-For purposes of this section-

(1) the term "agency" means agency as defined in section 552(e) of this title;

(2) the term "individual" means a citizen of the United States or an alien lawfully admitted for permanent residence;

(3) the term "maintain" includes maintain, collect, use, or disseminate;

(4) the term "record" means any item, collection, or grouping of information about an individual that is maintained by an agency, including, but not limited to, his education, financial transactions, medical history, and criminal or employment history and that contains his name, or the identifying number, symbol, or other identifying particular assigned to the individual, such as a finger or voice print or a photograph;

(5) the term "system of records" means a group of any records under the control of any agency from which information is retrieved by the name of the individual or by some identifying number, symbol, or other identifying particular assigned to the individual;

(6) the term "statistical record" means a record in a system of records maintained for statistical research or reporting purposes only and not used in whole or in part in making any determination about an identifiable individual, except as provided by section 8 of title 13;

(7) the term "routine use" means, with respect to the disclosure of a record, the use of such record for a purpose which is compatible with the purpose for which it was collected;

(8) the term "matching program"-

(A) means any computerized comparison of-

(i) two or more automated systems of records or a system of records with non-Federal records for the purpose of-

(I) establishing or verifying the eligibility of, or continuing compliance with statutory and regulatory requirements by, applicants for, recipients or beneficiaries of, participants in, or providers of services with respect to, cash or in-kind assistance or payments under Federal benefit programs, or

(II) recouping payments or delinquent debts under such Federal benefit programs, or

(ii) two or more automated Federal personnel or payroll systems of records or a system of Federal personnel or payroll records with non-Federal records,

(B) but does not include-

(i) matches performed to produce aggregate statistical data without any personal identifiers;

(ii) matches performed to support any research or statistical project, the specific data of which may not be used to make decisions concerning the rights, benefits, or privileges of specific individuals;

(iii) matches performed, by an agency (or component thereof) which performs as its principal function any activity pertaining to the enforcement of criminal laws, subsequent to the initiation of a specific criminal or civil law enforcement investigation of a named person or persons for the purpose of gathering evidence against such person or persons;

(iv) matches of tax information (I) pursuant to section 6103(d) of the Internal Revenue Code of 1986, (II) for purposes of tax administration as defined in section 6103(b)(4) of such Code, (III) for the purpose of intercepting a tax refund due an individual under authority granted by section 404(e), 464, or 1137 of the Social Security Act; or (IV) for the purpose of intercepting a tax refund due an individual under any other tax refund intercept program authorized by statute which has been determined by the Director of the Office of Management and Budget to contain verification, notice, and hearing requirements that are substantially similar to the procedures in section 1137 of the Social Security Act;

(v) matches-

(I) using records predominantly relating to Federal personnel, that are performed for routine administrative purposes (subject to guidance provided by the Director of the Office of Management and Budget pursuant to subsection (v)); or

(II) conducted by an agency using only records from systems of records maintained by that agency;

if the purpose of the match is not to take any adverse financial, personnel, disciplinary, or other adverse action against Federal personnel;

(vi) matches performed for foreign counterintelligence purposes or to produce background checks for security clearances of Federal personnel or Federal contractor personnel;

(vii) matches performed incident to a levy described in section 6103(k)(8) of the Internal Revenue Code of 1986;

(viii) matches performed pursuant to section 202(x)(3) or 1611(e)(1) of the Social Security Act (42 U.S.C. 402(x)(3), 1382(e)(1));

(ix) matches performed by the Secretary of Health and Human Services or the Inspector General of the Department of Health and Human Services with respect to potential fraud, waste, and abuse, including matches of a system of records with non-Federal records; or

(x) matches performed pursuant to section 3(d)(4) of the Achieving a Better Life Experience Act of 2014;

(9) the term "recipient agency" means any agency, or contractor thereof, receiving records contained in a system of records from a source agency for use in a matching program;

(10) the term "non-Federal agency" means any State or local government, or agency thereof, which receives records contained in a system of records from a source agency for use in a matching program;

(11) the term "source agency" means any agency which discloses records contained in a system of records to be used in a matching program, or any State or local government, or agency thereof, which discloses records to be used in a matching program;

(12) the term "Federal benefit program" means any program administered or funded by the Federal Government, or by any agent or State on behalf of the

Federal Government, providing cash or in-kind assistance in the form of payments, grants, loans, or loan guarantees to individuals; and

(13) the term "Federal personnel" means officers and employees of the Government of the United States, members of the uniformed services (including members of the Reserve Components), individuals entitled to receive immediate or deferred retirement benefits under any retirement program of the Government of the United States (including survivor benefits).

(b) Conditions of Disclosure.-No agency shall disclose any record which is contained in a system of records by any means of communication to any person, or to another agency, except pursuant to a written request by, or with the prior written consent of, the individual to whom the record pertains, unless disclosure of the record would be-

(1) to those officers and employees of the agency which maintains the record who have a need for the record in the performance of their duties;

(2) required under section 552 of this title;

(3) for a routine use as defined in subsection (a)(7) of this section and described under subsection (e)(4)(D) of this section;

(4) to the Bureau of the Census for purposes of planning or carrying out a census or survey or related activity pursuant to the provisions of title 13;

(5) to a recipient who has provided the agency with advance adequate written assurance that the record will be used solely as a statistical research or reporting record, and the record is to be transferred in a form that is not individually identifiable;

(6) to the National Archives and Records Administration as a record which has sufficient historical or other value to warrant its continued preservation by the United States Government, or for evaluation by the Archivist of the United States or the designee of the Archivist to determine whether the record has such value;

(7) to another agency or to an instrumentality of any governmental jurisdiction within or under the control of the United States for a civil or criminal law enforcement activity if the activity is authorized by law, and if the head of the agency or instrumentality has made a written request to the agency which maintains the record specifying the particular portion desired and the law enforcement activity for which the record is sought;

(8) to a person pursuant to a showing of compelling circumstances affecting the health or safety of an individual if upon such disclosure notification is transmitted to the last known address of such individual;

(9) to either House of Congress, or, to the extent of matter within its jurisdiction, any committee or subcommittee thereof, any joint committee of Congress or subcommittee of any such joint committee;

(10) to the Comptroller General, or any of his authorized representatives, in the course of the performance of the duties of the Government Accountability Office;

(11) pursuant to the order of a court of competent jurisdiction; or

(12) to a consumer reporting agency in accordance with section 3711(e) of title 31.

(c) Accounting of Certain Disclosures.-Each agency, with respect to each system of records under its control, shall-

(1) except for disclosures made under subsections (b)(1) or (b)(2) of this section, keep an accurate accounting of-

(A) the date, nature, and purpose of each disclosure of a record to any person or to another agency made under subsection (b) of this section; and

(B) the name and address of the person or agency to whom the disclosure is made;

(2) retain the accounting made under paragraph (1) of this subsection for at least five years or the life of the record, whichever is longer, after the disclosure for which the accounting is made;

(3) except for disclosures made under subsection (b)(7) of this section, make the accounting made under paragraph (1) of this subsection available to the individual named in the record at his request; and

(4) inform any person or other agency about any correction or notation of dispute made by the agency in accordance with subsection (d) of this section of any record that has been disclosed to the person or agency if an accounting of the disclosure was made.

(d) Access to Records.-Each agency that maintains a system of records shall-

(1) upon request by any individual to gain access to his record or to any information pertaining to him which is contained in the system, permit him and upon his request, a person of his own choosing to accompany him, to review the record and have a copy made of all or any portion thereof in a form comprehensible to him, except that the agency may require the individual to furnish a written statement authorizing discussion of that individual's record in the accompanying person's presence;

(2) permit the individual to request amendment of a record pertaining to him and-

(A) not later than 10 days (excluding Saturdays, Sundays, and legal public holidays) after the date of receipt of such request, acknowledge in writing such receipt; and

(B) promptly, either-

(i) make any correction of any portion thereof which the individual believes is not accurate, relevant, timely, or complete; or

(ii) inform the individual of its refusal to amend the record in accordance with his request, the reason for the refusal, the procedures established by the agency for the individual to request a review of that refusal by the head of the agency or an officer designated by the head of the agency, and the name and business address of that official;

(3) permit the individual who disagrees with the refusal of the agency to amend his record to request a review of such refusal, and not later than 30 days (excluding Saturdays, Sundays, and legal public holidays) from the date on which the individual requests such review, complete such review and make a final determination unless, for good cause shown, the head of the agency extends such 30-day period; and if, after his review, the reviewing official also refuses to amend the record in accordance with the request, permit the individual to file with the agency a concise statement setting forth the reasons for his disagreement with the refusal of the agency, and notify the individual of the provisions for judicial review of the reviewing official's determination under subsection (g)(1)(A) of this section;

(4) in any disclosure, containing information about which the individual has filed a statement of disagreement, occurring after the filing of the statement under paragraph (3) of this subsection, clearly note any portion of the record which is disputed and provide copies of the statement and, if the agency deems it appropriate, copies of a concise statement of the reasons of the agency for not making the amendments requested, to persons or other agencies to whom the disputed record has been disclosed; and

(5) nothing in this section shall allow an individual access to any information compiled in reasonable anticipation of a civil action or proceeding.

(e) Agency Requirements.-Each agency that maintains a system of records shall-

(1) maintain in its records only such information about an individual as is relevant and necessary to accomplish a purpose of the agency required to be accomplished by statute or by executive order of the President;

(2) collect information to the greatest extent practicable directly from the subject individual when the information may result in adverse determinations about an individual's rights, benefits, and privileges under Federal programs;

(3) inform each individual whom it asks to supply information, on the form which it uses to collect the information or on a separate form that can be retained by the individual-

(A) the authority (whether granted by statute, or by executive order of the President) which authorizes the solicitation of the information and whether disclosure of such information is mandatory or voluntary;

(B) the principal purpose or purposes for which the information is intended to be used;

(C) the routine uses which may be made of the information, as published pursuant to paragraph (4)(D) of this subsection; and

(D) the effects on him, if any, of not providing all or any part of the requested information;

(4) subject to the provisions of paragraph (11) of this subsection, publish in the Federal Register upon establishment or revision a notice of the existence and character of the system of records, which notice shall include-

(A) the name and location of the system;

(B) the categories of individuals on whom records are maintained in the system;

(C) the categories of records maintained in the system;

(D) each routine use of the records contained in the system, including the categories of users and the purpose of such use;

(E) the policies and practices of the agency regarding storage, retrievability, access controls, retention, and disposal of the records;

(F) the title and business address of the agency official who is responsible for the system of records;

(G) the agency procedures whereby an individual can be notified at his request if the system of records contains a record pertaining to him;

(H) the agency procedures whereby an individual can be notified at his request how he can gain access to any record pertaining to him contained in the system of records, and how he can contest its content; and

(I) the categories of sources of records in the system;

(5) maintain all records which are used by the agency in making any determination about any individual with such accuracy, relevance, timeliness, and completeness as is reasonably necessary to assure fairness to the individual in the determination;

(6) prior to disseminating any record about an individual to any person other than an agency, unless the dissemination is made pursuant to subsection (b)(2) of this section, make reasonable efforts to assure that such records are accurate, complete, timely, and relevant for agency purposes;

(7) maintain no record describing how any individual exercises rights guaranteed by the First Amendment unless expressly authorized by statute or by the individual about whom the record is maintained or unless pertinent to and within the scope of an authorized law enforcement activity;

(8) make reasonable efforts to serve notice on an individual when any record on such individual is made available to any person under compulsory legal process when such process becomes a matter of public record;

(9) establish rules of conduct for persons involved in the design, development, operation, or maintenance of any system of records, or in maintaining any record, and instruct each such person with respect to such rules and the requirements of this section, including any other rules and procedures adopted pursuant to this section and the penalties for noncompliance;

(10) establish appropriate administrative, technical, and physical safeguards to insure the security and confidentiality of records and to protect against any anticipated threats or hazards to their security or integrity which could result in substantial harm, embarrassment, inconvenience, or unfairness to any individual on whom information is maintained;

(11) at least 30 days prior to publication of information under paragraph (4)(D) of this subsection, publish in the Federal Register notice of any new use or intended use of the information in the system, and provide an opportunity for interested persons to submit written data, views, or arguments to the agency; and

(12) if such agency is a recipient agency or a source agency in a matching program with a non-Federal agency, with respect to any establishment or revision of a matching program, at least 30 days prior to conducting such program, publish in the Federal Register notice of such establishment or revision.

(f) Agency Rules.-In order to carry out the provisions of this section, each agency that maintains a system of records shall promulgate rules, in accordance with the requirements (including general notice) of section 553 of this title, which shall-

(1) establish procedures whereby an individual can be notified in response to his request if any system of records named by the individual contains a record pertaining to him;

(2) define reasonable times, places, and requirements for identifying an individual who requests his record or information pertaining to him before the agency shall make the record or information available to the individual;

(3) establish procedures for the disclosure to an individual upon his request of his record or information pertaining to him, including special procedure, if deemed necessary, for the disclosure to an individual of medical records, including psychological records, pertaining to him;

(4) establish procedures for reviewing a request from an individual concerning the amendment of any record or information pertaining to the individual, for making a determination on the request, for an appeal within the agency of an initial adverse agency determination, and for whatever additional means may be necessary for each individual to be able to exercise fully his rights under this section; and

(5) establish fees to be charged, if any, to any individual for making copies of his record, excluding the cost of any search for and review of the record.

The Office of the Federal Register shall biennially compile and publish the rules promulgated under this subsection and agency notices published under subsection (e)(4) of this section in a form available to the public at low cost.

(g)(1) Civil Remedies.-Whenever any agency

(A) makes a determination under subsection (d)(3) of this section not to amend an individual's record in accordance with his request, or fails to make such review in conformity with that subsection;

(B) refuses to comply with an individual request under subsection (d)(1) of this section;

(C) fails to maintain any record concerning any individual with such accuracy, relevance, timeliness, and completeness as is necessary to assure fairness in any determination relating to the qualifications, character, rights, or opportunities of, or benefits to the individual that may be made on the basis of such record, and consequently a determination is made which is adverse to the individual; or

(D) fails to comply with any other provision of this section, or any rule promulgated thereunder, in such a way as to have an adverse effect on an individual,the individual may bring a civil action against the agency, and the district courts of the United States shall have jurisdiction in the matters under the provisions of this subsection.

(2)(A) In any suit brought under the provisions of subsection (g)(1)(A) of this section, the court may order the agency to amend the individual's record in accordance with his request or in such other way as the court may direct. In such a case the court shall determine the matter de novo.

(B) The court may assess against the United States reasonable attorney fees and other litigation costs reasonably incurred in any case under this paragraph in which the complainant has substantially prevailed.

(3)(A) In any suit brought under the provisions of subsection (g)(1)(B) of this section, the court may enjoin the agency from withholding the records and order the production to the complainant of any agency records improperly withheld from him. In such a case the court shall determine the matter de novo, and may examine the contents of any agency records in camera to determine whether the records or any portion thereof may be withheld under any of the exemptions set forth in subsection (k) of this section, and the burden is on the agency to sustain its action.

(B) The court may assess against the United States reasonable attorney fees and other litigation costs reasonably incurred in any case under this paragraph in which the complainant has substantially prevailed.

(4) In any suit brought under the provisions of subsection (g)(1)(C) or (D) of this section in which the court determines that the agency acted in a manner which was

intentional or willful, the United States shall be liable to the individual in an amount equal to the sum of-

(A) actual damages sustained by the individual as a result of the refusal or failure, but in no case shall a person entitled to recovery receive less than the sum of $1,000; and

(B) the costs of the action together with reasonable attorney fees as determined by the court.

(5) An action to enforce any liability created under this section may be brought in the district court of the United States in the district in which the complainant resides, or has his principal place of business, or in which the agency records are situated, or in the District of Columbia, without regard to the amount in controversy, within two years from the date on which the cause of action arises, except that where an agency has materially and willfully misrepresented any information required under this section to be disclosed to an individual and the information so misrepresented is material to establishment of the liability of the agency to the individual under this section, the action may be brought at any time within two years after discovery by the individual of the misrepresentation. Nothing in this section shall be construed to authorize any civil action by reason of any injury sustained as the result of a disclosure of a record prior to September 27, 1975.

(h) Rights of Legal Guardians.-For the purposes of this section, the parent of any minor, or the legal guardian of any individual who has been declared to be incompetent due to physical or mental incapacity or age by a court of competent jurisdiction, may act on behalf of the individual.

(i)(1) Criminal Penalties.-Any officer or employee of an agency, who by virtue of his employment or official position, has possession of, or access to, agency records which contain individually identifiable information the disclosure of which is prohibited by this section or by rules or regulations established thereunder, and who knowing that disclosure of the specific material is so prohibited, willfully discloses the material in any manner to any person or agency not entitled to receive it, shall be guilty of a misdemeanor and fined not more than $5,000.

(2) Any officer or employee of any agency who willfully maintains a system of records without meeting the notice requirements of subsection (e)(4) of this section shall be guilty of a misdemeanor and fined not more than $5,000.

(3) Any person who knowingly and willfully requests or obtains any record concerning an individual from an agency under false pretenses shall be guilty of a misdemeanor and fined not more than $5,000.

(j) General Exemptions.-The head of any agency may promulgate rules, in accordance with the requirements (including general notice) of sections 553(b)(1), (2), and (3), (c), and (e) of this title, to exempt any system of records within the agency from any part of this section except subsections (b), (c)(1) and (2), (e)(4)(A) through (F), (e)(6), (7), (9), (10), and (11), and (i) if the system of records is-

(1) maintained by the Central Intelligence Agency; or

(2) maintained by an agency or component thereof which performs as its principal function any activity pertaining to the enforcement of criminal laws, including police efforts to prevent, control, or reduce crime or to apprehend criminals, and the activities of prosecutors, courts, correctional, probation, pardon, or parole authorities, and which consists of (A) information compiled for the purpose of identifying individual criminal offenders and alleged offenders and consisting only of identifying data and notations of arrests, the nature and disposition of criminal charges, sentencing, confinement, release, and parole and probation status; (B) information compiled for the purpose of a criminal investigation, including reports of informants and investigators, and associated with an identifiable individual; or (C) reports identifiable to an individual compiled at any stage of the process of enforcement of the criminal laws from arrest or indictment through release from supervision.

At the time rules are adopted under this subsection, the agency shall include in the statement required under section 553(c) of this title, the reasons why the system of records is to be exempted from a provision of this section.

(k) Specific Exemptions.-The head of any agency may promulgate rules, in accordance with the requirements (including general notice) of sections 553(b)(1), (2), and (3), (c), and (e) of this title, to exempt any system of records within the agency from subsections (c)(3), (d), (e)(1), (e)(4)(G), (H), and (I) and (f) of this section if the system of records is-

    (1) subject to the provisions of section 552(b)(1) of this title;

    (2) investigatory material compiled for law enforcement purposes, other than material within the scope of subsection (j)(2) of this section: Provided, however, That if any individual is denied any right, privilege, or benefit that he would otherwise be entitled by Federal law, or for which he would otherwise be eligible, as a result of the maintenance of such material, such material shall be provided to such individual, except to the extent that the disclosure of such material would reveal the identity of a source who furnished information to the Government under an express promise that the identity of the source would be held in confidence, or, prior to the effective date of this section, under an implied promise that the identity of the source would be held in confidence;

(3) maintained in connection with providing protective services to the President of the United States or other individuals pursuant to section 3056 of title 18;

(4) required by statute to be maintained and used solely as statistical records;

(5) investigatory material compiled solely for the purpose of determining suitability, eligibility, or qualifications for Federal civilian employment, military service, Federal contracts, or access to classified information, but only to the extent that the disclosure of such material would reveal the identity of a source who furnished information to the Government under an express promise that the identity of the source would be held in confidence, or, prior to the effective date of this section, under an implied promise that the identity of the source would be held in confidence;

(6) testing or examination material used solely to determine individual qualifications for appointment or promotion in the Federal service the disclosure of which would compromise the objectivity or fairness of the testing or examination process; or

(7) evaluation material used to determine potential for promotion in the armed services, but only to the extent that the disclosure of such material would reveal the identity of a source who furnished information to the Government under an express promise that the identity of the source would be held in confidence, or, prior to the effective date of this section, under an implied promise that the identity of the source would be held in confidence.

At the time rules are adopted under this subsection, the agency shall include in the statement required under section 553(c) of this title, the reasons why the system of records is to be exempted from a provision of this section.

(l)(1) Archival Records.-Each agency record which is accepted by the Archivist of the United States for storage, processing, and servicing in accordance with section 3103 of title 44 shall, for the purposes of this section, be considered to be maintained by the agency which deposited the record and shall be subject to the provisions of this section. The Archivist of the United States shall not disclose the record except to the agency which maintains the record, or under rules established by that agency which are not inconsistent with the provisions of this section.

(2) Each agency record pertaining to an identifiable individual which was transferred to the National Archives of the United States as a record which has sufficient historical or other value to warrant its continued preservation by the United States Government, prior to the effective date of this section, shall, for the purposes of this section, be considered to be maintained by the National Archives and shall not be subject to the provisions of this section, except that a statement generally describing such records

(modeled after the requirements relating to records subject to subsections (e)(4)(A) through (G) of this section) shall be published in the Federal Register.

(3) Each agency record pertaining to an identifiable individual which is transferred to the National Archives of the United States as a record which has sufficient historical or other value to warrant its continued preservation by the United States Government, on or after the effective date of this section, shall, for the purposes of this section, be considered to be maintained by the National Archives and shall be exempt from the requirements of this section except subsections (e)(4)(A) through (G) and (e)(9) of this section.

(m)(1) Government Contractors.-When an agency provides by a contract for the operation by or on behalf of the agency of a system of records to accomplish an agency function, the agency shall, consistent with its authority, cause the requirements of this section to be applied to such system. For purposes of subsection (i) of this section any such contractor and any employee of such contractor, if such contract is agreed to on or after the effective date of this section, shall be considered to be an employee of an agency.

(2) A consumer reporting agency to which a record is disclosed under section 3711(e) of title 31 shall not be considered a contractor for the purposes of this section.

(n) Mailing Lists.-An individual's name and address may not be sold or rented by an agency unless such action is specifically authorized by law. This provision shall not be construed to require the withholding of names and addresses otherwise permitted to be made public.

(o) Matching Agreements.-(1) No record which is contained in a system of records may be disclosed to a recipient agency or non-Federal agency for use in a computer matching program except pursuant to a written agreement between the source agency and the recipient agency or non-Federal agency specifying-

(A) the purpose and legal authority for conducting the program;

(B) the justification for the program and the anticipated results, including a specific estimate of any savings;

(C) a description of the records that will be matched, including each data element that will be used, the approximate number of records that will be matched, and the projected starting and completion dates of the matching program;

(D) procedures for providing individualized notice at the time of application, and notice periodically thereafter as directed by the Data Integrity Board of such agency (subject to guidance provided by the Director of the Office of Management and Budget pursuant to subsection (v)), to-

(i) applicants for and recipients of financial assistance or payments under Federal benefit programs, and

(ii) applicants for and holders of positions as Federal personnel, that any information provided by such applicants, recipients, holders, and individuals may be subject to verification through matching programs;

(E) procedures for verifying information produced in such matching program as required by subsection (p);

(F) procedures for the retention and timely destruction of identifiable records created by a recipient agency or non-Federal agency in such matching program;

(G) procedures for ensuring the administrative, technical, and physical security of the records matched and the results of such programs;

(H) prohibitions on duplication and redisclosure of records provided by the source agency within or outside the recipient agency or the non-Federal agency, except where required by law or essential to the conduct of the matching program;

(I) procedures governing the use by a recipient agency or non-Federal agency of records provided in a matching program by a source agency, including procedures governing return of the records to the source agency or destruction of records used in such program;

(J) information on assessments that have been made on the accuracy of the records that will be used in such matching program; and

(K) that the Comptroller General may have access to all records of a recipient agency or a non-Federal agency that the Comptroller General deems necessary in order to monitor or verify compliance with the agreement.

(2)(A) A copy of each agreement entered into pursuant to paragraph (1) shall-

(i) be transmitted to the Committee on Governmental Affairs of the Senate and the Committee on Government Operations of the House of Representatives; and

(ii) be available upon request to the public.

(B) No such agreement shall be effective until 30 days after the date on which such a copy is transmitted pursuant to subparagraph (A)(i).

(C) Such an agreement shall remain in effect only for such period, not to exceed 18 months, as the Data Integrity Board of the agency determines is appropriate in light of the purposes, and length of time necessary for the conduct, of the matching program.

(D) Within 3 months prior to the expiration of such an agreement pursuant to subparagraph (C), the Data Integrity Board of the agency may, without additional review, renew the matching agreement for a current, ongoing matching program for not more than one additional year if-

(i) such program will be conducted without any change; and

(ii) each party to the agreement certifies to the Board in writing that the program has been conducted in compliance with the agreement.

(p) Verification and Opportunity to Contest Findings.-(1) In order to protect any individual whose records are used in a matching program, no recipient agency, non-Federal agency, or source agency may suspend, terminate, reduce, or make a final denial of any financial assistance or payment under a Federal benefit program to such individual, or take other adverse action against such individual, as a result of information produced by such matching program, until-

(A)(i) the agency has independently verified the information; or

(ii) the Data Integrity Board of the agency, or in the case of a non-Federal agency the Data Integrity Board of the source agency, determines in accordance with guidance issued by the Director of the Office of Management and Budget that-

(I) the information is limited to identification and amount of benefits paid by the source agency under a Federal benefit program; and

(II) there is a high degree of confidence that the information provided to the recipient agency is accurate;

(B) the individual receives a notice from the agency containing a statement of its findings and informing the individual of the opportunity to contest such findings; and

(C)(i) the expiration of any time period established for the program by statute or regulation for the individual to respond to that notice; or

(ii) in the case of a program for which no such period is established, the end of the 30-day period beginning on the date on which notice under subparagraph (B) is mailed or otherwise provided to the individual.

(2) Independent verification referred to in paragraph (1) requires investigation and confirmation of specific information relating to an individual that is used as a basis for an adverse action against the individual, including where applicable investigation and confirmation of-

(A) the amount of any asset or income involved;

(B) whether such individual actually has or had access to such asset or income for such individual's own use; and

(C) the period or periods when the individual actually had such asset or income.

(3) Notwithstanding paragraph (1), an agency may take any appropriate action otherwise prohibited by such paragraph if the agency determines that the public health or public safety may be adversely affected or significantly threatened during any notice period required by such paragraph.

(q) Sanctions.-(1) Notwithstanding any other provision of law, no source agency may disclose any record which is contained in a system of records to a recipient agency or non-Federal agency for a matching program if such source agency has reason to believe that the requirements of subsection (p), or any matching agreement entered into pursuant to subsection (o), or both, are not being met by such recipient agency.

(2) No source agency may renew a matching agreement unless-

(A) the recipient agency or non-Federal agency has certified that it has complied with the provisions of that agreement; and

(B) the source agency has no reason to believe that the certification is inaccurate.

(r) Report on New Systems and Matching Programs.-Each agency that proposes to establish or make a significant change in a system of records or a matching program shall provide adequate advance notice of any such proposal (in duplicate) to the Committee on Government Operations of the House of Representatives, the Committee on Governmental Affairs of the Senate, and the Office of Management and Budget in order to permit an evaluation of the probable or potential effect of such proposal on the privacy or other rights of individuals.

(s) Biennial Report.-The President shall biennially submit to the Speaker of the House of Representatives and the President pro tempore of the Senate a report-

(1) describing the actions of the Director of the Office of Management and Budget pursuant to section 6 of the Privacy Act of 1974 during the preceding 2 years;

(2) describing the exercise of individual rights of access and amendment under this section during such years;

(3) identifying changes in or additions to systems of records;

(4) containing such other information concerning administration of this section as may be necessary or useful to the Congress in reviewing the effectiveness of this section in carrying out the purposes of the Privacy Act of 1974.

(t)(1) Effect of Other Laws.-No agency shall rely on any exemption contained in section 552 of this title to withhold from an individual any record which is otherwise accessible to such individual under the provisions of this section.

(2) No agency shall rely on any exemption in this section to withhold from an individual any record which is otherwise accessible to such individual under the provisions of section 552 of this title.

(u) Data Integrity Boards.-(1) Every agency conducting or participating in a matching program shall establish a Data Integrity Board to oversee and coordinate among the various components of such agency the agency's implementation of this section.

(2) Each Data Integrity Board shall consist of senior officials designated by the head of the agency, and shall include any senior official designated by the head of the agency as responsible for implementation of this section, and the inspector general of the

agency, if any. The inspector general shall not serve as chairman of the Data Integrity Board.

(3) Each Data Integrity Board-

(A) shall review, approve, and maintain all written agreements for receipt or disclosure of agency records for matching programs to ensure compliance with subsection (o), and all relevant statutes, regulations, and guidelines;

(B) shall review all matching programs in which the agency has participated during the year, either as a source agency or recipient agency, determine compliance with applicable laws, regulations, guidelines, and agency agreements, and assess the costs and benefits of such programs;

(C) shall review all recurring matching programs in which the agency has participated during the year, either as a source agency or recipient agency, for continued justification for such disclosures;

(D) shall compile an annual report, which shall be submitted to the head of the agency and the Office of Management and Budget and made available to the public on request, describing the matching activities of the agency, including-

(i) matching programs in which the agency has participated as a source agency or recipient agency;

(ii) matching agreements proposed under subsection (o) that were disapproved by the Board;

(iii) any changes in membership or structure of the Board in the preceding year;

(iv) the reasons for any waiver of the requirement in paragraph (4) of this section for completion and submission of a cost-benefit analysis prior to the approval of a matching program;

(v) any violations of matching agreements that have been alleged or identified and any corrective action taken; and

(vi) any other information required by the Director of the Office of Management and Budget to be included in such report;

(E) shall serve as a clearinghouse for receiving and providing information on the accuracy, completeness, and reliability of records used in matching programs;

(F) shall provide interpretation and guidance to agency components and personnel on the requirements of this section for matching programs;

(G) shall review agency recordkeeping and disposal policies and practices for matching programs to assure compliance with this section; and

(H) may review and report on any agency matching activities that are not matching programs.

(4)(A) Except as provided in subparagraphs (B) and (C), a Data Integrity Board shall not approve any written agreement for a matching program unless the agency has completed and submitted to such Board a cost-benefit analysis of the proposed program and such analysis demonstrates that the program is likely to be cost effective.2

(B) The Board may waive the requirements of subparagraph (A) of this paragraph if it determines in writing, in accordance with guidelines prescribed by the Director of the Office of Management and Budget, that a cost-benefit analysis is not required.

(C) A cost-benefit analysis shall not be required under subparagraph (A) prior to the initial approval of a written agreement for a matching program that is specifically required by statute. Any subsequent written agreement for such a program shall not be approved by the Data Integrity Board unless the agency has submitted a cost-benefit analysis of the program as conducted under the preceding approval of such agreement.

(5)(A) If a matching agreement is disapproved by a Data Integrity Board, any party to such agreement may appeal the disapproval to the Director of the Office of Management and Budget. Timely notice of the filing of such an appeal shall be provided by the Director of the Office of Management and Budget to the Committee on Governmental Affairs of the Senate and the Committee on Government Operations of the House of Representatives.

(B) The Director of the Office of Management and Budget may approve a matching agreement notwithstanding the disapproval of a Data Integrity Board if the Director determines that-

(i) the matching program will be consistent with all applicable legal, regulatory, and policy requirements;

(ii) there is adequate evidence that the matching agreement will be cost-effective; and

(iii) the matching program is in the public interest.

(C) The decision of the Director to approve a matching agreement shall not take effect until 30 days after it is reported to committees described in subparagraph (A).

(D) If the Data Integrity Board and the Director of the Office of Management and Budget disapprove a matching program proposed by the inspector general of an agency, the inspector general may report the disapproval to the head of the agency and to the Congress.

(6) In the reports required by paragraph (3)(D), agency matching activities that are not matching programs may be reported on an aggregate basis, if and to the extent necessary to protect ongoing law enforcement or counterintelligence investigations.

(v) Office of Management and Budget Responsibilities.-The Director of the Office of Management and Budget shall-

(1) develop and, after notice and opportunity for public comment, prescribe guidelines and regulations for the use of agencies in implementing the provisions of this section; and

(2) provide continuing assistance to and oversight of the implementation of this section by agencies.

(w) Applicability to Bureau of Consumer Financial Protection.-Except as provided in the Consumer Financial Protection Act of 2010, this section shall apply with respect to the Bureau of Consumer Financial Protection.

Pub. L. 114–126, Feb. 24, 2016, 130 Stat. 282 , provided that:

SECTION 1. SHORT TITLE.

This Act may be cited as the 'Judicial Redress Act of 2015'.

SEC. 2. EXTENSION OF PRIVACY ACT REMEDIES TO CITIZENS OF DESIGNATED COUNTRIES.

(a) Civil Action; Civil Remedies.-With respect to covered records, a covered person may bring a civil action against an agency and obtain civil remedies, in the same manner, to the same extent, and subject to the same limitations, including exemptions and exceptions, as an individual may bring and obtain with respect to records under-

(1) section 552a(g)(1)(D) of title 5, United States Code, but only with respect to disclosures intentionally or willfully made in violation of section 552a(b) of such title; and

(2) subparagraphs (A) and (B) of section 552a(g)(1) of title 5, United States Code, but such an action may only be brought against a designated Federal agency or component.

(b) Exclusive Remedies.-The remedies set forth in subsection (a) are the exclusive remedies available to a covered person under this section.

(c) Application of the Privacy Act With Respect to a Covered Person.-For purposes of a civil action described in subsection (a), a covered person shall have the same rights, and be subject to the same limitations, including exemptions and exceptions, as an individual has and is subject to under section 552a of title 5, United States Code, when pursuing the civil remedies described in paragraphs (1) and (2) of subsection (a).

(d) Designation of Covered Country.-

(1) In general.-The Attorney General may, with the concurrence of the Secretary of State, the Secretary of the Treasury, and the Secretary of Homeland Security, designate a foreign country or regional economic integration organization, or member country of such organization, as a 'covered country' for purposes of this section if-

(A)(i) the country or regional economic integration organization, or member country of such organization, has entered into an agreement with the United States that provides for appropriate privacy protections for information shared for the purpose of preventing, investigating, detecting, or prosecuting criminal offenses; or

(ii) the Attorney General has determined that the country or regional economic integration organization, or member country of such organization, has effectively shared information with the United States for the purpose of preventing, investigating, detecting, or prosecuting criminal offenses and has appropriate privacy protections for such shared information;

(B) the country or regional economic integration organization, or member country of such organization, permits the transfer of personal data for commercial purposes between the territory of that country or regional economic organization and the territory of the United States, through an agreement with the United States or otherwise; and

(C) the Attorney General has certified that the policies regarding the transfer of personal data for commercial purposes and related actions of the country or regional economic integration organization, or member country of such organization, do not materially impede the national security interests of the United States.

(2) Removal of designation.-The Attorney General may, with the concurrence of the Secretary of State, the Secretary of the Treasury, and the Secretary of Homeland Security, revoke the designation of a foreign country or regional economic integration organization, or member country of such organization, as a 'covered country' if the Attorney General determines that such designated 'covered country'-

(A) is not complying with the agreement described under paragraph (1)(A)(i);

(B) no longer meets the requirements for designation under paragraph (1)(A)(ii);

(C) fails to meet the requirements under paragraph (1)(B);

(D) no longer meets the requirements for certification under paragraph (1)(C); or

(E) impedes the transfer of information (for purposes of reporting or preventing unlawful activity) to the United States by a private entity or person.

(e) Designation of Designated Federal Agency or Component.-

(1) In general.-The Attorney General shall determine whether an agency or component thereof is a 'designated Federal agency or component' for purposes of this section. The Attorney General shall not designate any agency or component thereof other than the Department of Justice or a component of the Department of

Justice without the concurrence of the head of the relevant agency, or of the agency to which the component belongs.

(2) Requirements for designation.-The Attorney General may determine that an agency or component of an agency is a 'designated Federal agency or component' for purposes of this section, if-

(A) the Attorney General determines that information exchanged by such agency with a covered country is within the scope of an agreement referred to in subsection (d)(1)(A); or

(B) with respect to a country or regional economic integration organization, or member country of such organization, that has been designated as a 'covered country' under subsection (d)(1)(B), the Attorney General determines that designating such agency or component thereof is in the law enforcement interests of the United States.

(f) Federal Register Requirement; Nonreviewable Determination.-The Attorney General shall publish each determination made under subsections (d) and (e). Such determination shall not be subject to judicial or administrative review.

(g) Jurisdiction.-The United States District Court for the District of Columbia shall have exclusive jurisdiction over any claim arising under this section.

(h) Definitions.-In this Act:

(1) Agency.-The term 'agency' has the meaning given that term in section 552(f) of title 5, United States Code.

(2) Covered country.-The term 'covered country' means a country or regional economic integration organization, or member country of such organization, designated in accordance with subsection (d).

(3) Covered person.-The term 'covered person' means a natural person (other than an individual) who is a citizen of a covered country.

(4) Covered record.-The term 'covered record' has the same meaning for a covered person as a record has for an individual under section 552a of title 5, United States Code, once the covered record is transferred-

(A) by a public authority of, or private entity within, a country or regional economic organization, or member country of such organization, which at the time the record is transferred is a covered country; and

(B) to a designated Federal agency or component for purposes of preventing, investigating, detecting, or prosecuting criminal offenses.

(5) Designated federal agency or component.-The term 'designated Federal agency or component' means a Federal agency or component of an agency designated in accordance with subsection (e).

(6) Individual.-The term 'individual' has the meaning given that term in section 552a(a)(2) of title 5, United States Code.

(i) Preservation of Privileges.-Nothing in this section shall be construed to waive any applicable privilege or require the disclosure of classified information. Upon an agency's request, the district court shall review in camera and ex parte any submission by the agency in connection with this subsection.

(j) Effective Date.-This Act shall take effect 90 days after the date of the enactment of this Act [Feb. 24, 2016]."

FAMILY EDUCATIONAL RIGHTS AND PRIVACY ACT (1974)

Summary

The Family Educational Rights and Privacy Act (FERPA) protects the confidentiality of student educational records. It states that educational institutions shall not disclose any information from those records without the written consent of the student, or, if the student is a minor, without the written consent of his or her parents. Under the Act, students have the right to inspect and review their own educational records, request corrections, stop the release of personally identifiable information, and obtain a copy of the institutional policy concerning access to educational records. The Act applies to primary, secondary, and post-secondary educational institutions.

Federal funding will be denied to any institution that discloses information without the student's prior written consent, or without his or her parent's consent if the student is under eighteen years of age. There are exceptions to allow certain personnel within the institution to see the records and to allow certain information to be disclosed to the public and to the parents. There are also certain exceptions allowing disclosure to aid in development, validation, and administration of standardized tests, to administer student aid programs, and to improve instruction. However, such information may be released only when it protects the personal identification of students. Written consent is needed for any disclosure of personally identifiable information.

Individuals who have grievances under the Act must petition the head of the educational institution for redress. If unsatisfied, they may petition the Secretary of Education, who is the only person authorized to limit federal funding for non-complying institutions.

In 2002, the Supreme Court decided two cases involving FERPA claims. In Owasso Independent School District , the Court held that the practice of "peer grading" did not violate the FERPA because the student papers in question had not yet been collected by the teacher and thus were not "maintained" by the school under § 1232(a)(4)(A). Furthermore, the Court concluded that a student grader is not a "person acting for" an educational institution under § 1232g(a)(4)(A). In Gonzaga University v. Doe, the Court reversed an award for damages, holding that the FERPA created no new private cause of action enforceable under 42 U.S.C. § 1983. Under Gonzaga, the FERPA is enforced through administrative review procedures under the Secretary of Education.

References

Public Law 90-247 as amended. Codified at 20 U.S.C. § 1232g
[https://www.law.cornell.edu/uscode/text/20/1232g]

Owasso Independent School District v. Falvo, 534 U.S. 426 (2002)
[http://supct.law.cornell.edu/supct/html/00-1073.ZO.html]

United States
Family Educational Rights and Privacy Act

Gonzaga Univ. v. Doe, 122 S. Ct. 2268 (2002)
[http://supct.law.cornell.edu/supct/html/01-679.ZS.html]

EPIC, EPIC Student Privacy Project
[http://www.epic.org/privacy/student/]

20 U.S.C. § 1232g. Family educational and privacy rights

a) Conditions for availability of funds to educational agencies or institutions; inspection and review of education records; specific information to be made available; procedure for access to education records; reasonableness of time for such access; hearings; written explanations by parents; definitions

(1)(A) No funds shall be made available under any applicable program to any educational agency or institution which has a policy of denying, or which effectively prevents, the parents of students who are or have been in attendance at a school of such agency or at such institution, as the case may be, the right to inspect and review the education records of their children. If any material or document in the education record of a student includes information on more than one student, the parents of one of such students shall have the right to inspect and review only such part of such material or document as relates to such student or to be informed of the specific information contained in such part of such material. Each educational agency or institution shall establish appropriate procedures for the granting of a request by parents for access to the education records of their children within a reasonable period of time, but in no case more than forty-five days after the request has been made.

(B) No funds under any applicable program shall be made available to any State educational agency (whether or not that agency is an educational agency or institution under this section) that has a policy of denying, or effectively prevents, the parents of students the right to inspect and review the education records maintained by the State educational agency on their children who are or have been in attendance at any school of an educational agency or institution that is subject to the provisions of this section.

(C) The first sentence of subparagraph (A) shall not operate to make available to students in institutions of postsecondary education the following materials:

(i) financial records of the parents of the student or any information contained therein;

(ii) confidential letters and statements of recommendation, which were placed in the education records prior to January 1, 1975, if such letters or statements are not used for purposes other than those for which they were specifically intended;

(iii) if the student has signed a waiver of the student's right of access under this subsection in accordance with subparagraph (D), confidential recommendations-

(I) respecting admission to any educational agency or institution,

(II) respecting an application for employment, and

(III) respecting the receipt of an honor or honorary recognition.

(D) A student or a person applying for admission may waive his right of access to confidential statements described in clause (iii) of subparagraph (C), except that such waiver shall apply to recommendations only if (i) the student is, upon request, notified of the names of all persons making confidential recommendations and (ii) such recommendations are used solely for the purpose for which they were specifically intended. Such waivers may not be required as a condition for admission to, receipt of financial aid from, or receipt of any other services or benefits from such agency or institution.

(2) No funds shall be made available under any applicable program to any educational agency or institution unless the parents of students who are or have been in attendance at a school of such agency or at such institution are provided an opportunity for a hearing by such agency or institution, in accordance with regulations of the Secretary, to challenge the content of such student's education records, in order to insure that the records are not inaccurate, misleading, or otherwise in violation of the privacy rights of students, and to provide an opportunity for the correction or deletion of any such inaccurate, misleading or otherwise inappropriate data contained therein and to insert into such records a written explanation of the parents respecting the content of such records.

(3) For the purposes of this section the term "educational agency or institution" means any public or private agency or institution which is the recipient of funds under any applicable program.

(4)(A) For the purposes of this section, the term "education records" means, except as may be provided otherwise in subparagraph (B), those records, files, documents, and other materials which-

(i) contain information directly related to a student; and

(ii) are maintained by an educational agency or institution or by a person acting for such agency or institution.

(B) The term "education records" does not include-

(i) records of instructional, supervisory, and administrative personnel and educational personnel ancillary thereto which are in the sole possession of the maker thereof and which are not accessible or revealed to any other person except a substitute;

(ii) records maintained by a law enforcement unit of the educational agency or institution that were created by that law enforcement unit for the purpose of law enforcement;

(iii) in the case of persons who are employed by an educational agency or institution but who are not in attendance at such agency or institution, records made and maintained in the normal course of business which relate exclusively to such person in that person's capacity as an employee and are not available for use for any other purpose; or

(iv) records on a student who is eighteen years of age or older, or is attending an institution of postsecondary education, which are made or maintained by a physician, psychiatrist, psychologist, or other recognized professional or paraprofessional acting in his professional or paraprofessional capacity, or assisting in that capacity, and which are made, maintained, or used only in connection with the provision of treatment to the student, and are not available to anyone other than persons providing such treatment, except that such records can be personally reviewed by a physician or other appropriate professional of the student's choice.

(5)(A) For the purposes of this section the term "directory information" relating to a student includes the following: the student's name, address, telephone listing, date and place of birth, major field of study, participation in officially recognized activities and sports, weight and height of members of athletic teams, dates of attendance, degrees and awards received, and the most recent previous educational agency or institution attended by the student.

(B) Any educational agency or institution making public directory information shall give public notice of the categories of information which it has designated as such information with respect to each student attending the institution or agency and shall allow a reasonable period of time after such notice has been given for a parent to inform the institution or agency that any or all of the information designated should not be released without the parent's prior consent.

(6) For the purposes of this section, the term "student" includes any person with respect to whom an educational agency or institution maintains education records or personally identifiable information, but does not include a person who has not been in attendance at such agency or institution.

(b) Release of education records; parental consent requirement; exceptions; compliance with judicial orders and subpoenas; audit and evaluation of federally-supported education programs; recordkeeping

(1) No funds shall be made available under any applicable program to any educational agency or institution which has a policy or practice of permitting the release of education records (or personally identifiable information contained therein other than directory information, as defined in paragraph (5) of subsection (a)) of students without the written consent of their parents to any individual, agency, or organization, other than to the following-

(A) other school officials, including teachers within the educational institution or local educational agency, who have been determined by such agency or institution to have legitimate educational interests, including the educational interests of the child for whom consent would otherwise be required;

(B) officials of other schools or school systems in which the student seeks or intends to enroll, upon condition that the student's parents be notified of the transfer, receive a copy of the record if desired, and have an opportunity for a hearing to challenge the content of the record;

(C)(i) authorized representatives of (I) the Comptroller General of the United States, (II) the Secretary, or (III) State educational authorities, under the conditions set forth in paragraph (3), or (ii) authorized representatives of the Attorney General for law enforcement purposes under the same conditions as apply to the Secretary under paragraph (3);

(D) in connection with a student's application for, or receipt of, financial aid;

(E) State and local officials or authorities to whom such information is specifically allowed to be reported or disclosed pursuant to State statute adopted-

(i) before November 19, 1974, if the allowed reporting or disclosure concerns the juvenile justice system and such system's ability to effectively serve the student whose records are released, or

(ii) after November 19, 1974, if-

(I) the allowed reporting or disclosure concerns the juvenile justice system and such system's ability to effectively serve, prior to adjudication, the student whose records are released; and

(II) the officials and authorities to whom such information is disclosed certify in writing to the educational agency or institution that the information will not be disclosed to any other party except as provided under State law without the prior written consent of the parent of the student.

(F) organizations conducting studies for, or on behalf of, educational agencies or institutions for the purpose of developing, validating, or administering predictive tests, administering student aid programs, and improving instruction, if such studies are conducted in such a manner as will not permit the personal identification of students and their parents by persons other than representatives of such organizations and such information will be destroyed when no longer needed for the purpose for which it is conducted;

(G) accrediting organizations in order to carry out their accrediting functions;

(H) parents of a dependent student of such parents, as defined in section 152 of title 26;

(I) subject to regulations of the Secretary, in connection with an emergency, appropriate persons if the knowledge of such information is necessary to protect the health or safety of the student or other persons;

(J)(i) the entity or persons designated in a Federal grand jury subpoena, in which case the court shall order, for good cause shown, the educational agency or institution (and any officer, director, employee, agent, or attorney for such agency or institution) on which the subpoena is served, to not disclose to any person the existence or contents of the subpoena or any information furnished to the grand jury in response to the subpoena; and

(ii) the entity or persons designated in any other subpoena issued for a law enforcement purpose, in which case the court or other issuing agency may order, for good cause shown, the educational agency or institution (and any officer, director, employee, agent, or attorney for such agency or institution) on which the subpoena is served, to not disclose to any person the existence or contents of the subpoena or any information furnished in response to the subpoena;

(K) the Secretary of Agriculture, or authorized representative from the Food and Nutrition Service or contractors acting on behalf of the Food and Nutrition Service, for the purposes of conducting program monitoring, evaluations, and performance measurements of State and local educational and other agencies and institutions receiving funding or providing benefits of 1 or more programs authorized under the Richard B. Russell National School Lunch Act (42 U.S.C. 1751 et seq.) or the Child Nutrition Act of 1966 (42 U.S.C. 1771 et seq.) for which the results will be reported in an aggregate form that does not identify any individual, on the conditions that-

> (i) any data collected under this subparagraph shall be protected in a manner that will not permit the personal identification of students and their parents by other than the authorized representatives of the Secretary; and

> (ii) any personally identifiable data shall be destroyed when the data are no longer needed for program monitoring, evaluations, and performance measurements; and

(L) an agency caseworker or other representative of a State or local child welfare agency, or tribal organization (as defined in section 5304 of title 25), who has the right to access a student's case plan, as defined and determined by the State or tribal organization, when such agency or organization is legally responsible, in accordance with State or tribal law, for the care and protection of the student, provided that the education records, or the personally identifiable information contained in such records, of the student will not be disclosed by such agency or organization, except to an individual or entity engaged in addressing the student's education needs and authorized by such agency or organization to receive such disclosure and such disclosure is consistent with the State or tribal laws applicable to protecting the confidentiality of a student's education records.

Nothing in subparagraph (E) of this paragraph shall prevent a State from further limiting the number or type of State or local officials who will continue to have access thereunder.

(2) No funds shall be made available under any applicable program to any educational agency or institution which has a policy or practice of releasing, or providing access to, any personally identifiable information in education records other than directory information, or as is permitted under paragraph (1) of this subsection, unless-

(A) there is written consent from the student's parents specifying records to be released, the reasons for such release, and to whom, and with a copy of the records to be released to the student's parents and the student if desired by the parents, or

(B) except as provided in paragraph (1)(J), such information is furnished in compliance with judicial order, or pursuant to any lawfully issued subpoena, upon condition that parents and the students are notified of all such orders or subpoenas in advance of the compliance therewith by the educational institution or agency, except when a parent is a party to a court proceeding involving child abuse and neglect (as defined in section 3 of the Child Abuse Prevention and Treatment Act (42 U.S.C. 5101 note)) or dependency matters, and the order is issued in the context of that proceeding, additional notice to the parent by the educational agency or institution is not required.

(3) Nothing contained in this section shall preclude authorized representatives of (A) the Comptroller General of the United States, (B) the Secretary, or (C) State educational authorities from having access to student or other records which may be necessary in connection with the audit and evaluation of Federally-supported education programs, or in connection with the enforcement of the Federal legal requirements which relate to such programs: Provided, That except when collection of personally identifiable information is specifically authorized by Federal law, any data collected by such officials shall be protected in a manner which will not permit the personal identification of students and their parents by other than those officials, and such personally identifiable data shall be destroyed when no longer needed for such audit, evaluation, and enforcement of Federal legal requirements.

(4)(A) Each educational agency or institution shall maintain a record, kept with the education records of each student, which will indicate all individuals (other than those specified in paragraph (1)(A) of this subsection), agencies, or organizations which have requested or obtained access to a student's education records maintained by such educational agency or institution, and which will indicate specifically the legitimate interest that each such person, agency, or organization has in obtaining this information. Such record of access shall be available only to parents, to the school official and his assistants who are responsible for the custody of such records, and to persons or organizations authorized in, and under the conditions of, clauses (A) and (C) of paragraph (1) as a means of auditing the operation of the system.

(B) With respect to this subsection, personal information shall only be transferred to a third party on the condition that such party will not permit any other party to have access to such information without the written consent of the parents of the student. If a third party outside the educational agency or institution permits access to information in violation of paragraph (2)(A), or fails to destroy information in violation of paragraph (1)(F), the educational agency or institution shall be prohibited from permitting access to information from education records to that third party for a period of not less than five years.

(5) Nothing in this section shall be construed to prohibit State and local educational officials from having access to student or other records which may be necessary in connection with the audit and evaluation of any federally or State supported education program or in connection with the enforcement of the Federal legal requirements which relate to any such program, subject to the conditions specified in the proviso in paragraph (3).

(6)(A) Nothing in this section shall be construed to prohibit an institution of postsecondary education from disclosing, to an alleged victim of any crime of violence (as that term is defined in section 16 of title 18), or a nonforcible sex offense, the final results of any disciplinary proceeding conducted by such institution against the alleged perpetrator of such crime or offense with respect to such crime or offense.

(B) Nothing in this section shall be construed to prohibit an institution of postsecondary education from disclosing the final results of any disciplinary proceeding conducted by such institution against a student who is an alleged perpetrator of any crime of violence (as that term is defined in section 16 of title 18), or a nonforcible sex offense, if the institution determines as a result of that disciplinary proceeding that the student committed a violation of the institution's rules or policies with respect to such crime or offense.

(C) For the purpose of this paragraph, the final results of any disciplinary proceeding-

(i) shall include only the name of the student, the violation committed, and any sanction imposed by the institution on that student; and

(ii) may include the name of any other student, such as a victim or witness, only with the written consent of that other student.

(7)(A) Nothing in this section may be construed to prohibit an educational institution from disclosing information provided to the institution under section 14071 of title 42 concerning registered sex offenders who are required to register under such section.

(B) The Secretary shall take appropriate steps to notify educational institutions that disclosure of information described in subparagraph (A) is permitted.

(c) Surveys or data-gathering activities; regulations

Not later than 240 days after October 20, 1994, the Secretary shall adopt appropriate regulations or procedures, or identify existing regulations or procedures, which protect the rights of privacy of students and their families in connection with any surveys or data-gathering activities conducted, assisted, or authorized by the Secretary or an administrative head of an education agency. Regulations established under this subsection shall include provisions controlling the use, dissemination, and protection of such data. No survey or data-gathering activities shall be conducted by the Secretary, or an administrative head of an education agency under an applicable program, unless such activities are authorized by law.

(d) Students' rather than parents' permission or consent

For the purposes of this section, whenever a student has attained eighteen years of age, or is attending an institution of postsecondary education, the permission or consent required of and the rights accorded to the parents of the student shall thereafter only be required of and accorded to the student.

(e) Informing parents or students of rights under this section

No funds shall be made available under any applicable program to any educational agency or institution unless such agency or institution effectively informs the parents of students, or the students, if they are eighteen years of age or older, or are attending an institution of postsecondary education, of the rights accorded them by this section.

(f) Enforcement; termination of assistance

The Secretary shall take appropriate actions to enforce this section and to deal with violations of this section, in accordance with this chapter, except that action to terminate assistance may be taken only if the Secretary finds there has been a failure to comply with this section, and he has determined that compliance cannot be secured by voluntary means.

(g) Office and review board; creation; functions

The Secretary shall establish or designate an office and review board within the Department for the purpose of investigating, processing, reviewing, and adjudicating violations of this section and complaints which may be filed concerning alleged violations of this section. Except for the conduct of hearings, none of the functions of the Secretary under this section shall be carried out in any of the regional offices of such Department.

(h) Disciplinary records; disclosure

Nothing in this section shall prohibit an educational agency or institution from-
(1) including appropriate information in the education record of any student concerning disciplinary action taken against such student for conduct that posed a significant risk to the safety or well-being of that student, other students, or other members of the school community; or

(2) disclosing such information to teachers and school officials, including teachers and school officials in other schools, who have legitimate educational interests in the behavior of the student.

(i) Drug and alcohol violation disclosures

(1) In general

Nothing in this Act or the Higher Education Act of 1965 [20 U.S.C. 1001 et seq., 42 U.S.C. 2751 et seq.] shall be construed to prohibit an institution of higher education from disclosing, to a parent or legal guardian of a student, information regarding any violation of any Federal, State, or local law, or of any rule or policy of the institution, governing the use or possession of alcohol or a controlled substance, regardless of whether that information is contained in the student's education records, if-

(A) the student is under the age of 21; and

(B) the institution determines that the student has committed a disciplinary violation with respect to such use or possession.

(2) State law regarding disclosure

Nothing in paragraph (1) shall be construed to supersede any provision of State law that prohibits an institution of higher education from making the disclosure described in subsection (a).

(j) Investigation and prosecution of terrorism

(1) In general

Notwithstanding subsections (a) through (i) or any provision of State law, the Attorney General (or any Federal officer or employee, in a position not lower than an Assistant Attorney General, designated by the Attorney General) may submit a written application to a court of competent jurisdiction for an ex parte order requiring an educational agency or institution to permit the Attorney General (or his designee) to-

(A) collect education records in the possession of the educational agency or institution that are relevant to an authorized investigation or prosecution of an offense listed in section 2332b(g)(5)(B) of title 18, or an act of domestic or international terrorism as defined in section 2331 of that title; and

(B) for official purposes related to the investigation or prosecution of an offense described in paragraph (1)(A), retain, disseminate, and use (including as evidence at trial or in other administrative or judicial proceedings) such records, consistent with such guidelines as the Attorney General, after consultation with the Secretary, shall issue to protect confidentiality.

(2) Application and approval

(A) In general.-An application under paragraph (1) shall certify that there are specific and articulable facts giving reason to believe that the education records are likely to contain information described in paragraph (1)(A).

(B) The court shall issue an order described in paragraph (1) if the court finds that the application for the order includes the certification described in subparagraph (A).

(3) Protection of educational agency or institution

An educational agency or institution that, in good faith, produces education records in accordance with an order issued under this subsection shall not be liable to any person for that production.

(4) Record-keeping

Subsection (b)(4) does not apply to education records subject to a court order under this subsection.

United States
Foreign Intelligence Surveillance Act

FOREIGN INTELLIGENCE
SURVEILLANCE ACT (1978)

Summary

Congress enacted the Foreign Intelligence Surveillance Act (FISA) in 1978 to establish a legal regime for "foreign intelligence" information gathering in the United States, independent from the rules that govern surveillance for ordinary law enforcement. The Supreme Court invited Congress to establish a separate regime for foreign intelligence surveillance in United States v. U.S District Court, 407 U.S. 297 (1972), stating: "Given these potential distinctions between Title III criminal surveillances and those involving the domestic security, Congress may wish to consider protective standards for the latter which differ from those already prescribed for specific crimes in Title III. Different standards may be compatible with the Fourth Amendment if they are reasonable both in relation to the legitimate needs of Government for intelligence information and the protected rights of our citizens."

Although ordinarily under the Fourth Amendment a search warrant will only be issued upon showing of probable cause to believe that a crime has been or is being committed, FISA requires only a showing of probable cause that the target is a foreign power or an agent of a foreign power. FISA also applies differently to "U.S. persons" and aliens; in order to be used against a U.S. person, there must be probable cause to believe that person's activities involve a violation of the criminal statutes of the United States. Furthermore, the information sought must be "necessary to" U.S. self-protective ability or U.S. national defense, national security, or foreign affairs. No such restrictions apply when the target or surveillance is not a U.S. person as defined in .50 U.S.C. § 1801(i).

FISA's reach was expanded by the USA Patriot Act, 107 PL 56 (2001). Prior to the amendments, FISA could only be used when foreign intelligence information gathering was the primary or sole purpose of an investigation. Under the USA Patriot Act, however, surveillance can be conducted under FISA when foreign counterintelligence is merely a "significant" purpose of the investigation. 50 U.S.C. §§ 1804(a)(7)(B), 1823(a)(7)(B). The Patriot Act also amended FISA to bar certain investigations of U.S. persons conducted solely on the basis of activities protected by the First Amendment. 50 U.S.C. §§ 1842, 1843, 1861. The Act was amended in 2015. The USA Freedom Act limited the bulk collection of telephone metadata of domestic communications, enhanced judicial oversight, narrows the scope of National Security Letters, promotes established amicus curiae for the Foreign Intelligence Surveillance Court ("FISC"), established declassification procedures for the FISC, and creates new reporting requirements

References

Public Law 95-511 as amended by Public Law 107-56, Public Law 107-108, Public Law 107-296, Public Law 108-458, Public Law 109–177, Public Law 110–261,

United States
Foreign Intelligence Surveillance Act

Public Law 111–259, and Public Law 114–23. Codified at 50 U.S.C. §§ 1801–1811, 1821–1829, 1841–1846, 1861–1862.

[https://www.law.cornell.edu/uscode/text/50/1801]

EPIC, Foreign Intelligence Surveillance Act (FISA)

[https://epic.org/privacy/terrorism/fisa/]

50 U.S.C. § 1801. Definitions

As used in this subchapter:

(a) "Foreign power" means-

(1) a foreign government or any component thereof, whether or not recognized by the United States;

(2) a faction of a foreign nation or nations, not substantially composed of United States persons;

(3) an entity that is openly acknowledged by a foreign government or governments to be directed and controlled by such foreign government or governments;

(4) a group engaged in international terrorism or activities in preparation therefor;

(5) a foreign-based political organization, not substantially composed of United States persons;

(6) an entity that is directed and controlled by a foreign government or governments; or

(7) an entity not substantially composed of United States persons that is engaged in the international proliferation of weapons of mass destruction.

(b) "Agent of a foreign power" means-

(1) any person other than a United States person, who-

(A) acts in the United States as an officer or employee of a foreign power, or as a member of a foreign power as defined in subsection (a)(4), irrespective of whether the person is inside the United States;

(B) acts for or on behalf of a foreign power which engages in clandestine intelligence activities in the United States contrary to the interests of the United States, when the circumstances indicate that such person may engage in such activities, or when such person knowingly aids or abets any person in the conduct of such activities or knowingly conspires with any person to engage in such activities;

(C) engages in international terrorism or activities in preparation therefore;

(D) engages in the international proliferation of weapons of mass destruction, or activities in preparation therefor; or

(E) engages in the international proliferation of weapons of mass destruction, or activities in preparation therefor, for or on behalf of a foreign power, or knowingly aids or abets any person in the conduct of such proliferation or activities in preparation therefor, or knowingly conspires with any person to engage in such proliferation or activities in preparation therefor; or

(2) any person who-

(A) knowingly engages in clandestine intelligence gathering activities for or on behalf of a foreign power, which activities involve or may involve a violation of the criminal statutes of the United States;

(B) pursuant to the direction of an intelligence service or network of a foreign power, knowingly engages in any other clandestine intelligence activities for or on behalf of such foreign power, which activities involve or are about to involve a violation of the criminal statutes of the United States;

(C) knowingly engages in sabotage or international terrorism, or activities that are in preparation therefor, for or on behalf of a foreign power;

(D) knowingly enters the United States under a false or fraudulent identity for or on behalf of a foreign power or, while in the United States, knowingly assumes a false or fraudulent identity for or on behalf of a foreign power; or

(E) knowingly aids or abets any person in the conduct of activities described in subparagraph (A), (B), or (C) or knowingly conspires with any person to engage in activities described in subparagraph (A), (B), or (C).

(c) "International terrorism" means activities that-

(1) involve violent acts or acts dangerous to human life that are a violation of the criminal laws of the United States or of any State, or that would be a criminal violation if committed within the jurisdiction of the United States or any State;

(2) appear to be intended-

(A) to intimidate or coerce a civilian population;

(B) to influence the policy of a government by intimidation or coercion; or

(C) to affect the conduct of a government by assassination or kidnapping; and

(3) occur totally outside the United States, or transcend national boundaries in terms of the means by which they are accomplished, the persons they appear intended to coerce or intimidate, or the locale in which their perpetrators operate or seek asylum.

(d) "Sabotage" means activities that involve a violation of chapter 105 of title 18, or that would involve such a violation if committed against the United States.

(e) "Foreign intelligence information" means-

(1) information that relates to, and if concerning a United States person is necessary to, the ability of the United States to protect against-

(A) actual or potential attack or other grave hostile acts of a foreign power or an agent of a foreign power;

(B) sabotage, international terrorism, or the international proliferation of weapons of mass destruction by a foreign power or an agent of a foreign power; or

(C) clandestine intelligence activities by an intelligence service or network of a foreign power or by an agent of a foreign power; or

(2) information with respect to a foreign power or foreign territory that relates to, and if concerning a United States person is necessary to-

(A) the national defense or the security of the United States; or

(B) the conduct of the foreign affairs of the United States.

(f) "Electronic surveillance" means-

(1) the acquisition by an electronic, mechanical, or other surveillance device of the contents of any wire or radio communication sent by or intended to be received by a particular, known United States person who is in the United States, if the contents are acquired by intentionally targeting that United States person, under circumstances in which a person has a reasonable expectation of privacy and a warrant would be required for law enforcement purposes;

(2) the acquisition by an electronic, mechanical, or other surveillance device of the contents of any wire communication to or from a person in the United States, without the consent of any party thereto, if such acquisition occurs in the United States, but does not include the acquisition of those communications of computer trespassers that would be permissible under section 2511(2)(i) of title 18;

(3) the intentional acquisition by an electronic, mechanical, or other surveillance device of the contents of any radio communication, under circumstances in which a person has a reasonable expectation of privacy and a warrant would be required for law enforcement purposes, and if both the sender and all intended recipients are located within the United States; or

(4) the installation or use of an electronic, mechanical, or other surveillance device in the United States for monitoring to acquire information, other than from a wire or radio communication, under circumstances in which a person has a reasonable expectation of privacy and a warrant would be required for law enforcement purposes.

(g) "Attorney General" means the Attorney General of the United States (or Acting Attorney General), the Deputy Attorney General, or, upon the designation of the Attorney General, the Assistant Attorney General designated as the Assistant Attorney General for National Security under section 507A of title 28.

(h) "Minimization procedures", with respect to electronic surveillance, means-

(1) specific procedures, which shall be adopted by the Attorney General, that are reasonably designed in light of the purpose and technique of the particular surveillance, to minimize the acquisition and retention, and prohibit the dissemination, of nonpublicly available information concerning unconsenting United States persons consistent with the need of the United States to obtain, produce, and disseminate foreign intelligence information;

(2) procedures that require that nonpublicly available information, which is not foreign intelligence information, as defined in subsection (e)(1), shall not be disseminated in a manner that identifies any United States person, without such person's consent, unless such person's identity is necessary to understand foreign intelligence information or assess its importance;

(3) notwithstanding paragraphs (1) and (2), procedures that allow for the retention and dissemination of information that is evidence of a crime which has been, is being, or is about to be committed and that is to be retained or disseminated for law enforcement purposes; and

(4) notwithstanding paragraphs (1), (2), and (3), with respect to any electronic surveillance approved pursuant to section 1802(a) of this title, procedures that require that no contents of any communication to which a United States person is a party shall be disclosed, disseminated, or used for any purpose or retained for longer than 72 hours unless a court order under section 1805 of this title is obtained or unless the Attorney General determines that the information indicates a threat of death or serious bodily harm to any person.

(i) "United States person" means a citizen of the United States, an alien lawfully admitted for permanent residence (as defined in section 1101(a)(20) of title 8), an unincorporated association a substantial number of members of which are citizens of the United States or aliens lawfully admitted for permanent residence, or a corporation which is incorporated in the United States, but does not include a corporation or an association which is a foreign power, as defined in subsection (a)(1), (2), or (3).

(j) "United States", when used in a geographic sense, means all areas under the territorial sovereignty of the United States and the Trust Territory of the Pacific Islands.

(k) "Aggrieved person" means a person who is the target of an electronic surveillance or any other person whose communications or activities were subject to electronic surveillance.

(l) "Wire communication" means any communication while it is being carried by a wire, cable, or other like connection furnished or operated by any person engaged as a common carrier in providing or operating such facilities for the transmission of interstate or foreign communications.

(m) "Person" means any individual, including any officer or employee of the Federal Government, or any group, entity, association, corporation, or foreign power.

(n) "Contents", when used with respect to a communication, includes any information concerning the identity of the parties to such communication or the existence, substance, purport, or meaning of that communication.

(o) "State" means any State of the United States, the District of Columbia, the Commonwealth of Puerto Rico, the Trust Territory of the Pacific Islands, and any territory or possession of the United States.

(p) "Weapon of mass destruction" means-

(1) any explosive, incendiary, or poison gas device that is designed, intended, or has the capability to cause a mass casualty incident;

(2) any weapon that is designed, intended, or has the capability to cause death or serious bodily injury to a significant number of persons through the release, dissemination, or impact of toxic or poisonous chemicals or their precursors;

(3) any weapon involving a biological agent, toxin, or vector (as such terms are defined in section 178 of title 18) that is designed, intended, or has the capability to cause death, illness, or serious bodily injury to a significant number of persons; or

(4) any weapon that is designed, intended, or has the capability to release radiation or radioactivity causing death, illness, or serious bodily injury to a significant number of persons.

50 U.S.C. § 1802. Electronic surveillance authorization without court order; certification by Attorney General; reports to Congressional committees; transmittal under seal; duties and compensation of communication common carrier; applications; jurisdiction of court

a)(1) Notwithstanding any other law, the President, through the Attorney General, may authorize electronic surveillance without a court order under this subchapter to acquire foreign intelligence information for periods of up to one year if the Attorney General certifies in writing under oath that-

(A) the electronic surveillance is solely directed at-

(i) the acquisition of the contents of communications transmitted by means of communications used exclusively between or among foreign powers, as defined in section 1801(a)(1), (2), or (3) of this title; or

(ii) the acquisition of technical intelligence, other than the spoken communications of individuals, from property or premises under the open and exclusive control of a foreign power, as defined in section 1801(a)(1), (2), or (3) of this title;

(B) there is no substantial likelihood that the surveillance will acquire the contents of any communication to which a United States person is a party; and

(C) the proposed minimization procedures with respect to such surveillance meet the definition of minimization procedures under section 1801(h) of this title; and if the Attorney General reports such minimization procedures and any changes thereto to the House Permanent Select Committee on Intelligence and the Senate Select Committee on Intelligence at least thirty days prior to their effective date, unless the Attorney General determines immediate action is required and notifies the committees immediately of such minimization procedures and the reason for their becoming effective immediately.

(2) An electronic surveillance authorized by this subsection may be conducted only in accordance with the Attorney General's certification and the minimization procedures adopted by him. The Attorney General shall assess compliance with such procedures and shall report such assessments to the House Permanent Select Committee on Intelligence and the Senate Select Committee on Intelligence under the provisions of section 1808(a) of this title.

(3) The Attorney General shall immediately transmit under seal to the court established under section 1803(a) of this title a copy of his certification. Such certification shall be maintained under security measures established by the Chief Justice with the concurrence of the Attorney General, in consultation with the Director of National Intelligence, and shall remain sealed unless-

(A) an application for a court order with respect to the surveillance is made under sections 1801(h)(4) and 1804 of this title; or

(B) the certification is necessary to determine the legality of the surveillance under section 1806(f) of this title.

(4) With respect to electronic surveillance authorized by this subsection, the Attorney General may direct a specified communication common carrier to-

(A) furnish all information, facilities, or technical assistance necessary to accomplish the electronic surveillance in such a manner as will protect its secrecy and produce a minimum of interference with the services that such carrier is providing its customers; and

(B) maintain under security procedures approved by the Attorney General and the Director of National Intelligence any records concerning the surveillance or the aid furnished which such carrier wishes to retain.

The Government shall compensate, at the prevailing rate, such carrier for furnishing such aid.

(b) Applications for a court order under this subchapter are authorized if the President has, by written authorization, empowered the Attorney General to approve applications to the court having jurisdiction under section 1803 of this title, and a judge to whom an application is made may, notwithstanding any other law, grant an order, in conformity with section 1805 of this title, approving electronic surveillance of a foreign power or an agent of a foreign power for the purpose of obtaining foreign intelligence information, except that the court shall not have jurisdiction to grant any order approving electronic surveillance directed solely as described in paragraph (1)(A) of subsection (a) unless such surveillance may involve the acquisition of communications of any United States person.

50 U.S.C. § 1803. Designation of judges

(a) Court to hear applications and grant orders; record of denial; transmittal to court of review

(1) The Chief Justice of the United States shall publicly designate 11 district court judges from at least seven of the United States judicial circuits of whom no fewer than 3 shall reside within 20 miles of the District of Columbia who shall constitute a court which shall have jurisdiction to hear applications for and grant orders approving electronic surveillance anywhere within the United States under the procedures set forth in this chapter, except that no judge designated under this subsection (except when sitting en banc under paragraph (2)) shall hear the same application for electronic surveillance under this chapter which has been denied previously by another judge designated under this subsection. If any judge so designated denies an application for an order authorizing electronic surveillance under this chapter, such judge shall provide immediately for the record a written statement of each reason for his decision and, on motion of the United States, the record shall be transmitted, under seal, to the court of review established in subsection (b).

(2)(A) The court established under this subsection may, on its own initiative, or upon the request of the Government in any proceeding or a party under section 1861(f) of this title or paragraph (4) or (5) of section 1881a(h) of this title, hold a hearing or rehearing, en banc, when ordered by a majority of the judges that constitute such court upon a determination that-

(i) en banc consideration is necessary to secure or maintain uniformity of the court's decisions; or

(ii) the proceeding involves a question of exceptional importance.

(B) Any authority granted by this chapter to a judge of the court established under this subsection may be exercised by the court en banc. When exercising such authority, the court en banc shall comply with any requirements of this chapter on the exercise of such authority.

(C) For purposes of this paragraph, the court en banc shall consist of all judges who constitute the court established under this subsection.

(b) Court of review; record, transmittal to Supreme Court

The Chief Justice shall publicly designate three judges, one of whom shall be publicly designated as the presiding judge, from the United States district courts or courts of appeals who together shall comprise a court of review which shall have jurisdiction to review the denial of any application made under this chapter. If such court determines that the application was properly denied, the court shall immediately provide for the record a written statement of each reason for its decision and, on petition of the United States for a writ of certiorari, the record shall be transmitted under seal to the Supreme Court, which shall have jurisdiction to review such decision.

(c) Expeditious conduct of proceedings; security measures for maintenance of records

Proceedings under this chapter shall be conducted as expeditiously as possible. The record of proceedings under this chapter, including applications made and orders granted, shall be maintained under security measures established by the Chief Justice in consultation with the Attorney General and the Director of National Intelligence.

(d) Tenure

Each judge designated under this section shall so serve for a maximum of seven years and shall not be eligible for redesignation, except that the judges first designated under subsection (a) shall be designated for terms of from one to seven years so that one term expires each year, and that judges first designated under subsection (b) shall be designated for terms of three, five, and seven years.

(e) Jurisdiction and procedures for review of petitions

(1) Three judges designated under subsection (a) who reside within 20 miles of the District of Columbia, or, if all of such judges are unavailable, other judges of the court established under subsection (a) as may be designated by the presiding judge of such court, shall comprise a petition review pool which shall have jurisdiction to review petitions filed pursuant to section 1861(f)(1) or 1881a(h)(4) of this title.

(2) Not later than 60 days after March 9, 2006, the court established under subsection (a) shall adopt and, consistent with the protection of national security, publish procedures for the review of petitions filed pursuant to section 1861(f)(1) or 1881a(h)(4) of this title by the panel established under paragraph (1). Such procedures shall provide that review of a petition shall be conducted in camera and shall also provide for the designation of an acting presiding judge.

(f) Stay of order

(1) A judge of the court established under subsection (a), the court established under subsection (b) or a judge of that court, or the Supreme Court of the United States or a justice of that court, may, in accordance with the rules of their respective courts, enter a stay of an order or an order modifying an order of the court established under subsection (a) or the court established under subsection (b) entered under any subchapter of this chapter, while the court established under subsection (a) conducts a rehearing, while an appeal is pending to the court established under subsection (b), or while a petition of certiorari is pending in the Supreme Court of the United States, or during the pendency of any review by that court.

(2) The authority described in paragraph (1) shall apply to an order entered under any provision of this chapter.

(g) Establishment and transmittal of rules and procedures

(1) The courts established pursuant to subsections (a) and (b) may establish such rules and procedures, and take such actions, as are reasonably necessary to administer their responsibilities under this chapter.

(2) The rules and procedures established under paragraph (1), and any modifications of such rules and procedures, shall be recorded, and shall be transmitted to the following:

(A) All of the judges on the court established pursuant to subsection (a).

(B) All of the judges on the court of review established pursuant to subsection (b).

(C) The Chief Justice of the United States.

(D) The Committee on the Judiciary of the Senate.

(E) The Select Committee on Intelligence of the Senate.

(F) The Committee on the Judiciary of the House of Representatives.

(G) The Permanent Select Committee on Intelligence of the House of Representatives.

(3) The transmissions required by paragraph (2) shall be submitted in unclassified form, but may include a classified annex.

(h) Compliance with orders, rules, and procedures

Nothing in this chapter shall be construed to reduce or contravene the inherent authority of the court established under subsection (a) to determine or enforce compliance with an order or a rule of such court or with a procedure approved by such court.

(i) Amicus curiae

(1) Designation

The presiding judges of the courts established under subsections (a) and (b) shall, not later than 180 days after June 2, 2015, jointly designate not fewer than 5 individuals to be eligible to serve as amicus curiae, who shall serve pursuant to rules the presiding judges may establish. In designating such individuals, the presiding judges may consider individuals recommended by any source, including members of the Privacy and Civil Liberties Oversight Board, the judges determine appropriate.

(2) Authorization

A court established under subsection (a) or (b), consistent with the requirement of subsection (c) and any other statutory requirement that the court act expeditiously or within a stated time-

(A) shall appoint an individual who has been designated under paragraph (1) to serve as amicus curiae to assist such court in the consideration of any application for an order or review that, in the opinion of the court, presents a novel or significant interpretation of the law, unless the court issues a finding that such appointment is not appropriate; and

(B) may appoint an individual or organization to serve as amicus curiae, including to provide technical expertise, in any instance as such court deems appropriate or, upon motion, permit an individual or organization leave to file an amicus curiae brief.

(3) Qualifications of amicus curiae

(A) Expertise

Individuals designated under paragraph (1) shall be persons who possess expertise in privacy and civil liberties, intelligence collection, communications technology, or any other area that may lend legal or technical expertise to a court established under subsection (a) or (b).

(B) Security clearance

Individuals designated pursuant to paragraph (1) shall be persons who are determined to be eligible for access to classified information necessary to participate in matters before the courts. Amicus curiae appointed by the court pursuant to paragraph (2) shall be persons who are determined to be eligible for access to classified information, if such access is necessary to participate in the matters in which they may be appointed.

(4) Duties

If a court established under subsection (a) or (b) appoints an amicus curiae under paragraph (2)(A), the amicus curiae shall provide to the court, as appropriate-

(A) legal arguments that advance the protection of individual privacy and civil liberties;

(B) information related to intelligence collection or communications technology; or

(C) legal arguments or information regarding any other area relevant to the issue presented to the court.

(5) Assistance

An amicus curiae appointed under paragraph (2)(A) may request that the court designate or appoint additional amici curiae pursuant to paragraph (1) or paragraph (2), to be available to assist the amicus curiae.

(6) Access to information

(A) In general

If a court established under subsection (a) or (b) appoints an amicus curiae under paragraph (2), the amicus curiae-

(i) shall have access to any legal precedent, application, certification, petition, motion, or such other materials that the court determines are relevant to the duties of the amicus curiae; and

(ii) may, if the court determines that it is relevant to the duties of the amicus curiae, consult with any other individuals designated pursuant to paragraph (1) regarding information relevant to any assigned proceeding.

(B) Briefings

The Attorney General may periodically brief or provide relevant materials to individuals designated pursuant to paragraph (1) regarding constructions and interpretations of this chapter and legal, technological, and other issues related to actions authorized by this chapter.

(C) Classified information

An amicus curiae designated or appointed by the court may have access to classified documents, information, and other materials or proceedings only if that individual is eligible for access to classified information and to the extent consistent with the national security of the United States.

(D) Rule of construction

Nothing in this section shall be construed to require the Government to provide information to an amicus curiae appointed by the court that is privileged from disclosure.

(7) Notification

A presiding judge of a court established under subsection (a) or (b) shall notify the Attorney General of each exercise of the authority to appoint an individual to serve as amicus curiae under paragraph (2).

(8) Assistance

A court established under subsection (a) or (b) may request and receive (including on a nonreimbursable basis) the assistance of the executive branch in the implementation of this subsection.

(9) Administration

A court established under subsection (a) or (b) may provide for the designation, appointment, removal, training, or other support for an individual designated to serve as amicus curiae under paragraph (1) or appointed to serve as amicus curiae under paragraph (2) in a manner that is not inconsistent with this subsection.

(10) Receipt of information

Nothing in this subsection shall limit the ability of a court established under subsection (a) or (b) to request or receive information or materials from, or otherwise communicate with, the Government or amicus curiae appointed under paragraph (2) on an ex parte basis, nor limit any special or heightened obligation in any ex parte communication or proceeding.

(j) Review of FISA court decisions

Following issuance of an order under this chapter, a court established under subsection (a) shall certify for review to the court established under subsection (b) any question of law that may affect resolution of the matter in controversy that the court determines warrants such review because of a need for uniformity or because consideration by the court established under subsection (b) would serve the interests of justice. Upon certification of a question of law under this subsection, the court established under subsection (b) may give binding instructions or require the entire record to be sent up for decision of the entire matter in controversy.

(k) Review of FISA court of review decisions

(1) Certification

For purposes of section 1254(2) of title 28, the court of review established under subsection (b) shall be considered to be a court of appeals.

(2) Amicus curiae briefing

Upon certification of an application under paragraph (1), the Supreme Court of the United States may appoint an amicus curiae designated under subsection (i)(1), or any other person, to provide briefing or other assistance.

50 U.S.C. § 1804. Applications for court orders

(a) Submission by Federal officer; approval of Attorney General; contents

Each application for an order approving electronic surveillance under this subchapter shall be made by a Federal officer in writing upon oath or affirmation to a judge having jurisdiction under section 1803 of this title. Each application shall require the approval of the Attorney General based upon his finding that it satisfies the criteria and requirements of such application as set forth in this subchapter. It shall include-

(1) the identity of the Federal officer making the application;

(2) the identity, if known, or a description of the specific target of the electronic surveillance;

(3) a statement of the facts and circumstances relied upon by the applicant to justify his belief that-

(A) the target of the electronic surveillance is a foreign power or an agent of a foreign power; and

(B) each of the facilities or places at which the electronic surveillance is directed is being used, or is about to be used, by a foreign power or an agent of a foreign power;

(4) a statement of the proposed minimization procedures;

(5) a description of the nature of the information sought and the type of communications or activities to be subjected to the surveillance;

(6) a certification or certifications by the Assistant to the President for National Security Affairs, an executive branch official or officials designated by the President from among those executive officers employed in the area of national security or defense and appointed by the President with the advice and consent of the Senate, or the Deputy Director of the Federal Bureau of Investigation, if designated by the President as a certifying official-

(A) that the certifying official deems the information sought to be foreign intelligence information;

(B) that a significant purpose of the surveillance is to obtain foreign intelligence information;

(C) that such information cannot reasonably be obtained by normal investigative techniques;

(D) that designates the type of foreign intelligence information being sought according to the categories described in section 1801(e) of this title; and

(E) including a statement of the basis for the certification that-

(i) the information sought is the type of foreign intelligence information designated; and

(ii) such information cannot reasonably be obtained by normal investigative techniques;

(7) a summary statement of the means by which the surveillance will be effected and a statement whether physical entry is required to effect the surveillance;

(8) a statement of the facts concerning all previous applications that have been made to any judge under this subchapter involving any of the persons, facilities, or places specified in the application, and the action taken on each previous application; and

(9) a statement of the period of time for which the electronic surveillance is required to be maintained, and if the nature of the intelligence gathering is such that the approval of the use of electronic surveillance under this subchapter should not automatically terminate when the described type of information has first been obtained, a description of facts supporting the belief that additional information of the same type will be obtained thereafter.

(b) Additional affidavits or certifications

The Attorney General may require any other affidavit or certification from any other officer in connection with the application.

(c) Additional information

The judge may require the applicant to furnish such other information as may be necessary to make the determinations required by section 1805 of this title.

(d) Personal review by Attorney General

(1)(A) Upon written request of the Director of the Federal Bureau of Investigation, the Secretary of Defense, the Secretary of State, the Director of National Intelligence, or the Director of the Central Intelligence Agency, the Attorney General shall personally review under subsection (a) an application under that subsection for a target described in section 1801(b)(2) of this title.

(B) Except when disabled or otherwise unavailable to make a request referred to in subparagraph (A), an official referred to in that subparagraph may not delegate the authority to make a request referred to in that subparagraph.

(C) Each official referred to in subparagraph (A) with authority to make a request under that subparagraph shall take appropriate actions in advance to ensure that delegation of such authority is clearly established in the event such official is disabled or otherwise unavailable to make such request.

(2)(A) If as a result of a request under paragraph (1) the Attorney General determines not to approve an application under the second sentence of subsection (a) for purposes of making the application under this section, the Attorney General shall provide written notice of the determination to the official making the request for the review of the application under that paragraph. Except when disabled or otherwise unavailable to make a determination under the preceding sentence, the Attorney General may not delegate the responsibility to make a determination under that sentence. The Attorney General shall take appropriate actions in advance to ensure that delegation of such responsibility is clearly established in the event the Attorney General is disabled or otherwise unavailable to make such determination.

(B) Notice with respect to an application under subparagraph (A) shall set forth the modifications, if any, of the application that are necessary in order for the Attorney General to approve the application under the second sentence of subsection (a) for purposes of making the application under this section.

(C) Upon review of any modifications of an application set forth under subparagraph (B), the official notified of the modifications under this paragraph shall modify the application if such official determines that such modification is warranted. Such official shall supervise the making of any modification under this subparagraph. Except when disabled or otherwise unavailable to supervise the making of any modification under the preceding sentence, such official may not delegate the responsibility to supervise the making of any modification under that preceding sentence. Each such official shall take appropriate actions in advance to ensure that delegation of such responsibility is clearly established in the event such official is disabled or otherwise unavailable to supervise the making of such modification.

50 U.S.C. § 1805. Issuance of order

(a) Necessary findings

Upon an application made pursuant to section 1804 of this title, the judge shall enter an ex parte order as requested or as modified approving the electronic surveillance if he finds that-

(1) the application has been made by a Federal officer and approved by the Attorney General;

(2) on the basis of the facts submitted by the applicant there is probable cause to believe that-

(A) the target of the electronic surveillance is a foreign power or an agent of a foreign power: Provided, That no United States person may be considered a foreign power or an agent of a foreign power solely upon the basis of activities protected by the first amendment to the Constitution of the United States; and

(B) each of the facilities or places at which the electronic surveillance is directed is being used, or is about to be used, by a foreign power or an agent of a foreign power;

(3) the proposed minimization procedures meet the definition of minimization procedures under section 1801(h) of this title; and

(4) the application which has been filed contains all statements and certifications required by section 1804 of this title and, if the target is a United States person, the certification or certifications are not clearly erroneous on the basis of the statement made under section 1804(a)(7)(E) of this title and any other information furnished under section 1804(d) of this title.

(b) Determination of probable cause

In determining whether or not probable cause exists for purposes of an order under subsection (a)(2), a judge may consider past activities of the target, as well as facts and circumstances relating to current or future activities of the target.

(c) Specifications and directions of orders

(1) Specifications

An order approving an electronic surveillance under this section shall specify-

(A) the identity, if known, or a description of the specific target of the electronic surveillance identified or described in the application pursuant to section 1804(a)(3) of this title;

(B) the nature and location of each of the facilities or places at which the electronic surveillance will be directed, if known;

(C) the type of information sought to be acquired and the type of communications or activities to be subjected to the surveillance;

(D) the means by which the electronic surveillance will be effected and whether physical entry will be used to effect the surveillance; and

(E) the period of time during which the electronic surveillance is approved.

(2) Directions

An order approving an electronic surveillance under this section shall direct-

(A) that the minimization procedures be followed;

(B) that, upon the request of the applicant, a specified communication or other common carrier, landlord, custodian, or other specified person, or in circumstances where the Court finds, based upon specific facts provided in the application, that the actions of the target of the application may have the effect of thwarting the identification of a specified person, such other persons, furnish the applicant forthwith all information, facilities, or technical assistance necessary to accomplish the electronic surveillance in such a manner as will protect its secrecy and produce a minimum of interference with the services that such carrier, landlord, custodian, or other person is providing that target of electronic surveillance;

(C) that such carrier, landlord, custodian, or other person maintain under security procedures approved by the Attorney General and the Director of National Intelligence any records concerning the surveillance or the aid furnished that such person wishes to retain; and

(D) that the applicant compensate, at the prevailing rate, such carrier, landlord, custodian, or other person for furnishing such aid.

(3) Special directions for certain orders

An order approving an electronic surveillance under this section in circumstances where the nature and location of each of the facilities or places at which the surveillance will be directed is unknown shall direct the applicant to provide notice to the court within ten days after the date on which surveillance begins to be directed at any new facility or place, unless the court finds good cause to justify a longer period of up to 60 days, of-

(A) the nature and location of each new facility or place at which the electronic surveillance is directed;

(B) the facts and circumstances relied upon by the applicant to justify the applicant's belief that each new facility or place at which the electronic surveillance is directed is or was being used, or is about to be used, by the target of the surveillance;

(C) a statement of any proposed minimization procedures that differ from those contained in the original application or order, that may be necessitated by a change in the facility or place at which the electronic surveillance is directed; and

(D) the total number of electronic surveillances that have been or are being conducted under the authority of the order.

(d) Duration of order; extensions; review of circumstances under which information was acquired, retained or disseminated

(1) An order issued under this section may approve an electronic surveillance for the period necessary to achieve its purpose, or for ninety days, whichever is less, except that (A) an order under this section shall approve an electronic surveillance targeted against a foreign power, as defined in section 1801(a)(1), (2), or (3) of this title, for the period specified in the application or for one year, whichever is less, and (B) an order under this chapter for a surveillance targeted against an agent of a foreign power who is not a United States person may be for the period specified in the application or for 120 days, whichever is less.

(2) Extensions of an order issued under this subchapter may be granted on the same basis as an original order upon an application for an extension and new findings made in the same manner as required for an original order, except that (A) an extension of an order under this chapter for a surveillance targeted against a foreign power, as defined in paragraph (5), (6), or (7) of section 1801(a) of this title, or against a foreign power as defined in section 1801(a)(4) of this title that is not a United States person, may be for a period not to exceed one year if the judge finds probable cause to believe that no communication of any individual United States person will be acquired during the period, and (B) an extension of an order

under this chapter for a surveillance targeted against an agent of a foreign power who is not a United States person may be for a period not to exceed 1 year.

(3) At or before the end of the period of time for which electronic surveillance is approved by an order or an extension, the judge may assess compliance with the minimization procedures by reviewing the circumstances under which information concerning United States persons was acquired, retained, or disseminated.

(e) Emergency orders

(1) Notwithstanding any other provision of this subchapter, the Attorney General may authorize the emergency employment of electronic surveillance if the Attorney General-

(A) reasonably determines that an emergency situation exists with respect to the employment of electronic surveillance to obtain foreign intelligence information before an order authorizing such surveillance can with due diligence be obtained;

(B) reasonably determines that the factual basis for the issuance of an order under this subchapter to approve such electronic surveillance exists;

(C) informs, either personally or through a designee, a judge having jurisdiction under section 1803 of this title at the time of such authorization that the decision has been made to employ emergency electronic surveillance; and

(D) makes an application in accordance with this subchapter to a judge having jurisdiction under section 1803 of this title as soon as practicable, but not later than 7 days after the Attorney General authorizes such surveillance.

(2) If the Attorney General authorizes the emergency employment of electronic surveillance under paragraph (1), the Attorney General shall require that the minimization procedures required by this subchapter for the issuance of a judicial order be followed.

(3) In the absence of a judicial order approving such electronic surveillance, the surveillance shall terminate when the information sought is obtained, when the application for the order is denied, or after the expiration of 7 days from the time of authorization by the Attorney General, whichever is earliest.

(4) A denial of the application made under this subsection may be reviewed as provided in section 1803 of this title.

(5) In the event that such application for approval is denied, or in any other case where the electronic surveillance is terminated and no order is issued approving the surveillance, no information obtained or evidence derived from such surveillance shall be received in evidence or otherwise disclosed in any trial, hearing, or other proceeding in or before any court, grand jury, department, office, agency, regulatory body, legislative committee, or other authority of the United States, a State, or political subdivision thereof, and no information concerning any United States person acquired from such surveillance shall subsequently be used

or disclosed in any other manner by Federal officers or employees without the consent of such person, except with the approval of the Attorney General if the information indicates a threat of death or serious bodily harm to any person.

(6) The Attorney General shall assess compliance with the requirements of paragraph (5).

(f) Emergencies involving non-United States persons

(1) Notwithstanding any other provision of this chapter, the lawfully authorized targeting of a non-United States person previously believed to be located outside the United States for the acquisition of foreign intelligence information may continue for a period not to exceed 72 hours from the time that the non-United States person is reasonably believed to be located inside the United States and the acquisition is subject to this subchapter or to subchapter II of this chapter, provided that the head of an element of the intelligence community-

(A) reasonably determines that a lapse in the targeting of such non-United States person poses a threat of death or serious bodily harm to any person;

(B) promptly notifies the Attorney General of a determination under subparagraph (A); and

(C) requests, as soon as practicable, the employment of emergency electronic surveillance under subsection (e) or the employment of an emergency physical search pursuant to section 1824(e) of this title, as warranted.

(2) The authority under this subsection to continue the acquisition of foreign intelligence information is limited to a period not to exceed 72 hours and shall cease upon the earlier of the following:

(A) The employment of emergency electronic surveillance under subsection (e) or the employment of an emergency physical search pursuant to section 1824(e) of this title.

(B) An issuance of a court order under this subchapter or subchapter II of this chapter.

(C) The Attorney General provides direction that the acquisition be terminated.

(D) The head of the element of the intelligence community conducting the acquisition determines that a request under paragraph (1)(C) is not warranted.

(E) When the threat of death or serious bodily harm to any person is no longer reasonably believed to exist.

(3) Nonpublicly available information concerning unconsenting United States persons acquired under this subsection shall not be disseminated during the 72 hour time period under paragraph (1) unless necessary to investigate, reduce, or eliminate the threat of death or serious bodily harm to any person.

(4) If the Attorney General declines to authorize the employment of emergency electronic surveillance under subsection (e) or the employment of an emergency physical search pursuant to section 1824(e) of this title, or a court order is not

obtained under this subchapter or subchapter II of this chapter, information obtained during the 72 hour acquisition time period under paragraph (1) shall not be retained, except with the approval of the Attorney General if the information indicates a threat of death or serious bodily harm to any person.

(5) Paragraphs (5) and (6) of subsection (e) shall apply to this subsection.

(g) Testing of electronic equipment; discovering unauthorized electronic surveillance; training of intelligence personnel

Notwithstanding any other provision of this subchapter, officers, employees, or agents of the United States are authorized in the normal course of their official duties to conduct electronic surveillance not targeted against the communications of any particular person or persons, under procedures approved by the Attorney General, solely to-

(1) test the capability of electronic equipment, if-

(A) it is not reasonable to obtain the consent of the persons incidentally subjected to the surveillance;

(B) the test is limited in extent and duration to that necessary to determine the capability of the equipment;

(C) the contents of any communication acquired are retained and used only for the purpose of determining the capability of the equipment, are disclosed only to test personnel, and are destroyed before or immediately upon completion of the test; and:

(D) Provided, That the test may exceed ninety days only with the prior approval of the Attorney General;

(2) determine the existence and capability of electronic surveillance equipment being used by persons not authorized to conduct electronic surveillance, if-

(A) it is not reasonable to obtain the consent of persons incidentally subjected to the surveillance;

(B) such electronic surveillance is limited in extent and duration to that necessary to determine the existence and capability of such equipment; and

(C) any information acquired by such surveillance is used only to enforce chapter 119 of title 18, or section 605 of title 47, or to protect information from unauthorized surveillance; or

(3) train intelligence personnel in the use of electronic surveillance equipment, if-

(A) it is not reasonable to-

(i) obtain the consent of the persons incidentally subjected to the surveillance;

(ii) train persons in the course of surveillances otherwise authorized by this subchapter; or

(iii) train persons in the use of such equipment without engaging in electronic surveillance;

(B) such electronic surveillance is limited in extent and duration to that necessary to train the personnel in the use of the equipment; and

(C) no contents of any communication acquired are retained or disseminated for any purpose, but are destroyed as soon as reasonably possible.

(h) Retention of certifications, applications and orders

Certifications made by the Attorney General pursuant to section 1802(a) of this title and applications made and orders granted under this subchapter shall be retained for a period of at least ten years from the date of the certification or application.

(i) Bar to legal action

No cause of action shall lie in any court against any provider of a wire or electronic communication service, landlord, custodian, or other person (including any officer, employee, agent, or other specified person thereof) that furnishes any information, facilities, or technical assistance in accordance with a court order or request for emergency assistance under this chapter for electronic surveillance or physical search.

(j) Pen registers and trap and trace devices

In any case in which the Government makes an application to a judge under this subchapter to conduct electronic surveillance involving communications and the judge grants such application, upon the request of the applicant, the judge shall also authorize the installation and use of pen registers and trap and trace devices, and direct the disclosure of the information set forth in section 1842(d)(2) of this title.

50 U.S.C. § 1806. Use of information

(a) Compliance with minimization procedures; privileged communications; lawful purposes

Information acquired from an electronic surveillance conducted pursuant to this subchapter concerning any United States person may be used and disclosed by Federal officers and employees without the consent of the United States person only in accordance with the minimization procedures required by this subchapter. No otherwise privileged communication obtained in accordance with, or in violation of, the provisions of this subchapter shall lose its privileged character. No information acquired from an electronic surveillance pursuant to this subchapter may be used or disclosed by Federal officers or employees except for lawful purposes.

(b) Statement for disclosure

No information acquired pursuant to this subchapter shall be disclosed for law enforcement purposes unless such disclosure is accompanied by a statement that such information, or any information derived therefrom, may only be used in a criminal proceeding with the advance authorization of the Attorney General.

(c) Notification by United States

Whenever the Government intends to enter into evidence or otherwise use or disclose in any trial, hearing, or other proceeding in or before any court, department, officer, agency, regulatory body, or other authority of the United States, against an aggrieved person, any information obtained or derived from an electronic surveillance of that aggrieved person pursuant to the authority of this subchapter, the Government shall, prior to the trial, hearing, or other proceeding or at a reasonable time prior to an effort to so disclose or so use that information or submit it in evidence, notify the aggrieved person and the court or other authority in which the information is to be disclosed or used that the Government intends to so disclose or so use such information.

(d) Notification by States or political subdivisions

Whenever any State or political subdivision thereof intends to enter into evidence or otherwise use or disclose in any trial, hearing, or other proceeding in or before any court, department, officer, agency, regulatory body, or other authority of a State or a political subdivision thereof, against an aggrieved person any information obtained or derived from an electronic surveillance of that aggrieved person pursuant to the authority of this subchapter, the State or political subdivision thereof shall notify the aggrieved person, the court or other authority in which the information is to be disclosed or used, and the Attorney General that the State or political subdivision thereof intends to so disclose or so use such information.

(e) Motion to suppress

Any person against whom evidence obtained or derived from an electronic surveillance to which he is an aggrieved person is to be, or has been, introduced or otherwise used or disclosed in any trial, hearing, or other proceeding in or before any court, department, officer, agency, regulatory body, or other authority of the United States, a State, or a political subdivision thereof, may move to suppress the evidence obtained or derived from such electronic surveillance on the grounds that-

    (1) the information was unlawfully acquired; or

    (2) the surveillance was not made in conformity with an order of authorization or approval.

Such a motion shall be made before the trial, hearing, or other proceeding unless there was no opportunity to make such a motion or the person was not aware of the grounds of the motion.

(f) In camera and ex parte review by district court

Whenever a court or other authority is notified pursuant to subsection (c) or (d), or whenever a motion is made pursuant to subsection (e), or whenever any motion or request is made by an aggrieved person pursuant to any other statute or rule of the United States or any State before any court or other authority of the United States or any State to discover or obtain applications or orders or other materials relating to electronic surveillance or to discover, obtain, or suppress evidence or information obtained or derived from electronic surveillance under this chapter, the United States district court or, where the motion is made before another authority, the United States district court in the same district as the authority, shall, notwithstanding any other law, if the Attorney General files an affidavit under oath that disclosure or an adversary hearing would harm the national security of the United States, review in camera and ex parte the application, order, and such other materials relating to the surveillance as may be necessary to determine whether the surveillance of the aggrieved person was lawfully authorized and conducted. In making this determination, the court may disclose to the aggrieved person, under appropriate security procedures and protective orders, portions of the application, order, or other materials relating to the surveillance only where such disclosure is necessary to make an accurate determination of the legality of the surveillance.

(g) Suppression of evidence; denial of motion

If the United States district court pursuant to subsection (f) determines that the surveillance was not lawfully authorized or conducted, it shall, in accordance with the requirements of law, suppress the evidence which was unlawfully obtained or derived from electronic surveillance of the aggrieved person or otherwise grant the motion of the aggrieved person. If the court determines that the surveillance was lawfully authorized and conducted, it shall deny the motion of the aggrieved person except to the extent that due process requires discovery or disclosure.

(h) Finality of orders

Orders granting motions or requests under subsection (g), decisions under this section that electronic surveillance was not lawfully authorized or conducted, and orders of the United States district court requiring review or granting disclosure of applications, orders, or other materials relating to a surveillance shall be final orders and binding upon all courts of the United States and the several States except a United States court of appeals and the Supreme Court.

(i) Destruction of unintentionally acquired information

In circumstances involving the unintentional acquisition by an electronic, mechanical, or other surveillance device of the contents of any communication, under circumstances in which a person has a reasonable expectation of privacy and a warrant would be required for law enforcement purposes, and if both the sender and all intended recipients are located within the United States, such contents shall be destroyed upon recognition, unless the Attorney General determines that the contents indicate a threat of death or serious bodily harm to any person.

(j) Notification of emergency employment of electronic surveillance; contents; postponement, suspension or elimination

If an emergency employment of electronic surveillance is authorized under subsection (e) or (f) of section 1805 of this title and a subsequent order approving the surveillance is not obtained, the judge shall cause to be served on any United States person named in the application and on such other United States persons subject to electronic surveillance as the judge may determine in his discretion it is in the interest of justice to serve, notice of-

(1) the fact of the application;

(2) the period of the surveillance; and

(3) the fact that during the period information was or was not obtained.

On an ex parte showing of good cause to the judge the serving of the notice required by this subsection may be postponed or suspended for a period not to exceed ninety days. Thereafter, on a further ex parte showing of good cause, the court shall forego ordering the serving of the notice required under this subsection.

(k) Coordination with law enforcement on national security matters

(1) Federal officers who conduct electronic surveillance to acquire foreign intelligence information under this subchapter may consult with Federal law enforcement officers or law enforcement personnel of a State or political subdivision of a State (including the chief executive officer of that State or political subdivision who has the authority to appoint or direct the chief law enforcement officer of that State or political subdivision) to coordinate efforts to investigate or protect against-

(A) actual or potential attack or other grave hostile acts of a foreign power or an agent of a foreign power;

(B) sabotage, international terrorism, or the international proliferation of weapons of mass destruction by a foreign power or an agent of a foreign power; or

(C) clandestine intelligence activities by an intelligence service or network of a foreign power or by an agent of a foreign power.

(2) Coordination authorized under paragraph (1) shall not preclude the certification required by section 1804(a)(7)(B) of this title or the entry of an order under section 1805 of this title.

50 U.S.C. § 1807. Report to Administrative Office of the United States Court and to Congress

In April of each year, the Attorney General shall transmit to the Administrative Office of the United States Court and to Congress a report setting forth with respect to the preceding calendar year -

(a) the total number of applications made for orders and extensions of orders approving electronic surveillance under this subchapter; and

(b) the total number of such orders and extensions either granted, modified, or denied.

50 U.S.C. § 1808. Report of Attorney General to Congressional committees; limitation on authority or responsibility of information gathering activities of Congressional committees; report of Congressional committees to Congress

(a)(1) On a semiannual basis the Attorney General shall fully inform the Permanent Select Committee on Intelligence and the Committee on the Judiciary of the House of

Representatives and the Select Committee on Intelligence and the Committee on the Judiciary of the Senate concerning all electronic surveillance under this subchapter. Nothing in this subchapter shall be deemed to limit the authority and responsibility of the appropriate committees of each House of Congress to obtain such information as they may need to carry out their respective functions and duties.

(2) Each report under the first sentence of paragraph (1) shall include a description of-

(A) the total number of applications made for orders and extensions of orders approving electronic surveillance under this subchapter where the nature and location of each facility or place at which the electronic surveillance will be directed is unknown;

(B) each criminal case in which information acquired under this chapter has been authorized for use at trial during the period covered by such report;

(C) the total number of emergency employments of electronic surveillance under section 1805(e) of this title and the total number of subsequent orders approving or denying such electronic surveillance; and

(D) the total number of authorizations under section 1805(f) of this title and the total number of subsequent emergency employments of electronic surveillance under section 1805(e) of this title or emergency physical searches pursuant to section 301(e).

(b) On or before one year after October 25, 1978, and on the same day each year for four years thereafter, the Permanent Select Committee on Intelligence and the Senate Select Committee on Intelligence shall report respectively to the House of Representatives and the Senate, concerning the implementation of this chapter. Said reports shall include but not be limited to an analysis and recommendations concerning whether this chapter should be (1) amended, (2) repealed, or (3) permitted to continue in effect without amendment.

50 U.S.C. § 1809. Criminal sanctions

(a) Prohibited activities

A person is guilty of an offense if he intentionally-

(1) engages in electronic surveillance under color of law except as authorized by this chapter, chapter 119, 121, or 206 of title 18, or any express statutory authorization that is an additional exclusive means for conducting electronic surveillance under section 1812 of this title;

(2) discloses or uses information obtained under color of law by electronic surveillance, knowing or having reason to know that the information was obtained through electronic surveillance not authorized by this chapter, chapter 119, 121, or 206 of title 18, or any express statutory authorization that is an additional exclusive means for conducting electronic surveillance under section 1812 of this title.

(b) Defense

It is a defense to a prosecution under subsection (a) that the defendant was a law enforcement or investigative officer engaged in the course of his official duties and the electronic surveillance was authorized by and conducted pursuant to a search warrant or court order of a court of competent jurisdiction.

(c) Penalties

An offense described in this section is punishable by a fine of not more than $10,000 or imprisonment for not more than five years, or both.

(d) Federal jurisdiction

There is Federal jurisdiction over an offense under this section if the person committing the offense was an officer or employee of the United States at the time the offense was committed.

50 U.S.C. § 1810. Civil liability

An aggrieved person, other than a foreign power or an agent of a foreign power, as defined in section 1801(a) or (b)(1)(A) of this title, respectively, who has been subjected to an electronic surveillance or about whom information obtained by electronic surveillance of such person has been disclosed or used in violation of section 1809 of this title shall have a cause of action against any person who committed such violation and shall be entitled to recover -

(a) actual damages, but not less than liquidated damages of $1,000 or $100 per day for each day of violation, whichever is greater;

(b) punitive damages; and

(c) reasonable attorney's fees and other investigation and litigation costs reasonably incurred.

50 U.S.C. § 1811. Authorization during time of war

Notwithstanding any other law, the President, through the Attorney General, may authorize electronic surveillance without a court order under this subchapter to acquire foreign intelligence information for a period not to exceed fifteen calendar days following a declaration of war by the Congress.

50 U.S.C. § 1821. Definitions

As used in this subchapter:

(1) The terms "foreign power", "agent of a foreign power", "international terrorism", "sabotage", "foreign intelligence information", "Attorney General", "United States person", "United States", "person", "weapon of mass destruction", and "State" shall have the same meanings as in section 1801 of this title, except as specifically provided by this subchapter.

United States
Foreign Intelligence Surveillance Act

(2) "Aggrieved person" means a person whose premises, property, information, or material is the target of physical search or any other person whose premises, property, information, or material was subject to physical search.

(3) "Foreign Intelligence Surveillance Court" means the court established by section 1803(a) of this title.

(4) "Minimization procedures" with respect to physical search, means-

(A) specific procedures, which shall be adopted by the Attorney General, that are reasonably designed in light of the purposes and technique of the particular physical search, to minimize the acquisition and retention, and prohibit the dissemination, of nonpublicly available information concerning unconsenting United States persons consistent with the need of the United States to obtain, produce, and disseminate foreign intelligence information;

(B) procedures that require that nonpublicly available information, which is not foreign intelligence information, as defined in section 1801(e)(1) of this title, shall not be disseminated in a manner that identifies any United States person, without such person's consent, unless such person's identity is necessary to understand such foreign intelligence information or assess its importance;

(C) notwithstanding subparagraphs (A) and (B), procedures that allow for the retention and dissemination of information that is evidence of a crime which has been, is being, or is about to be committed and that is to be retained or disseminated for law enforcement purposes; and

(D) notwithstanding subparagraphs (A), (B), and (C), with respect to any physical search approved pursuant to section 1822(a) of this title, procedures that require that no information, material, or property of a United States person shall be disclosed, disseminated, or used for any purpose or retained for longer than 72 hours unless a court order under section 1824 of this title is obtained or unless the Attorney General determines that the information indicates a threat of death or serious bodily harm to any person.

(5) "Physical search" means any physical intrusion within the United States into premises or property (including examination of the interior of property by technical means) that is intended to result in a seizure, reproduction, inspection, or alteration of information, material, or property, under circumstances in which a person has a reasonable expectation of privacy and a warrant would be required for law enforcement purposes, but does not include (A) "electronic surveillance", as defined in section 1801(f) of this title, or (B) the acquisition by the United States Government of foreign intelligence information from international or foreign communications, or foreign intelligence activities conducted in accordance with otherwise applicable Federal law involving a foreign electronic communications system, utilizing a means other than electronic surveillance as defined in section 1801(f) of this title.

50 U.S.C. § 1822. Authorization of physical searches for foreign intelligence purposes

(a) Presidential authorization

(1) Notwithstanding any other provision of law, the President, acting through the Attorney General, may authorize physical searches without a court order under this subchapter to acquire foreign intelligence information for periods of up to one year if-

(A) the Attorney General certifies in writing under oath that-

(i) the physical search is solely directed at premises, information, material, or property used exclusively by, or under the open and exclusive control of, a foreign power or powers (as defined in section 1801(a)(1), (2), or (3) of this title);

(ii) there is no substantial likelihood that the physical search will involve the premises, information, material, or property of a United States person; and

(iii) the proposed minimization procedures with respect to such physical search meet the definition of minimization procedures under paragraphs (1) through (4) of section 1821(4) of this title; and

(B) the Attorney General reports such minimization procedures and any changes thereto to the Permanent Select Committee on Intelligence of the House of Representatives and the Select Committee on Intelligence of the Senate at least 30 days before their effective date, unless the Attorney General determines that immediate action is required and notifies the committees immediately of such minimization procedures and the reason for their becoming effective immediately.

(2) A physical search authorized by this subsection may be conducted only in accordance with the certification and minimization procedures adopted by the Attorney General. The Attorney General shall assess compliance with such procedures and shall report such assessments to the Permanent Select Committee on Intelligence of the House of Representatives and the Select Committee on Intelligence of the Senate under the provisions of section 1826 of this title.

(3) The Attorney General shall immediately transmit under seal to the Foreign Intelligence Surveillance Court a copy of the certification. Such certification shall be maintained under security measures established by the Chief Justice of the United States with the concurrence of the Attorney General, in consultation with the Director of National Intelligence, and shall remain sealed unless-

(A) an application for a court order with respect to the physical search is made under section 1821(4) of this title and section 1823 of this title; or

(B) the certification is necessary to determine the legality of the physical search under section 1825(g) of this title.

(4)(A) With respect to physical searches authorized by this subsection, the Attorney General may direct a specified landlord, custodian, or other specified person to-

(i) furnish all information, facilities, or assistance necessary to accomplish the physical search in such a manner as will protect its secrecy and produce a minimum of interference with the services that such landlord, custodian, or other person is providing the target of the physical search; and

(ii) maintain under security procedures approved by the Attorney General and the Director of National Intelligence any records concerning the search or the aid furnished that such person wishes to retain.

(B) The Government shall compensate, at the prevailing rate, such landlord, custodian, or other person for furnishing such aid.

(b) Application for order; authorization

Applications for a court order under this subchapter are authorized if the President has, by written authorization, empowered the Attorney General to approve applications to the Foreign Intelligence Surveillance Court. Notwithstanding any other provision of law, a judge of the court to whom application is made may grant an order in accordance with section 1824 of this title approving a physical search in the United States of the premises, property, information, or material of a foreign power or an agent of a foreign power for the purpose of collecting foreign intelligence information.

(c) Jurisdiction of Foreign Intelligence Surveillance Court

The Foreign Intelligence Surveillance Court shall have jurisdiction to hear applications for and grant orders approving a physical search for the purpose of obtaining foreign intelligence information anywhere within the United States under the procedures set forth in this subchapter, except that no judge (except when sitting en banc) shall hear the same application which has been denied previously by another judge designated under section 1803(a) of this title. If any judge so designated denies an application for an order authorizing a physical search under this subchapter, such judge shall provide immediately for the record a written statement of each reason for such decision and, on motion of the United States, the record shall be transmitted, under seal, to the court of review established under section 1803(b) of this title.

(d) Court of review; record; transmittal to Supreme Court

The court of review established under section 1803(b) of this title shall have jurisdiction to review the denial of any application made under this subchapter. If such court determines that the application was properly denied, the court shall immediately provide for the record a written statement of each reason for its decision and, on petition of the United States for a writ of certiorari, the record shall be transmitted under seal to the Supreme Court, which shall have jurisdiction to review such decision.

(e) Expeditious conduct of proceedings; security measures for maintenance of records

Judicial proceedings under this subchapter shall be concluded as expeditiously as possible. The record of proceedings under this subchapter, including applications made and orders granted, shall be maintained under security measures established by the Chief Justice of the United States in consultation with the Attorney General and the Director of National Intelligence.

50 U.S.C. § 1823. Application for order

(a) Submission by Federal officer; approval of Attorney General; contents
Each application for an order approving a physical search under this subchapter shall be made by a Federal officer in writing upon oath or affirmation to a judge of the Foreign Intelligence Surveillance Court. Each application shall require the approval of the Attorney General based upon the Attorney General's finding that it satisfies the criteria and requirements for such application as set forth in this subchapter. Each application shall include-

(1) the identity of the Federal officer making the application;

(2) the identity, if known, or a description of the target of the search, and a description of the premises or property to be searched and of the information, material, or property to be seized, reproduced, or altered;

(3) a statement of the facts and circumstances relied upon by the applicant to justify the applicant's belief that-

(A) the target of the physical search is a foreign power or an agent of a foreign power;

(B) the premises or property to be searched contains foreign intelligence information; and

(C) the premises or property to be searched is or is about to be owned, used, possessed by, or is in transit to or from a foreign power or an agent of a foreign power;

(4) a statement of the proposed minimization procedures;

(5) a statement of the nature of the foreign intelligence sought and the manner in which the physical search is to be conducted;

(6) a certification or certifications by the Assistant to the President for National Security Affairs, an executive branch official or officials designated by the President from among those executive branch officers employed in the area of national security or defense and appointed by the President, by and with the advice and consent of the Senate, or the Deputy Director of the Federal Bureau of Investigation, if designated by the President as a certifying official-

(A) that the certifying official deems the information sought to be foreign intelligence information;

(B) that a significant purpose of the search is to obtain foreign intelligence information;

United States
Foreign Intelligence Surveillance Act

(C) that such information cannot reasonably be obtained by normal investigative techniques;

(D) that designates the type of foreign intelligence information being sought according to the categories described in section 1801(e) of this title; and

(E) includes a statement explaining the basis for the certifications required by subparagraphs (C) and (D);

(7) where the physical search involves a search of the residence of a United States person, the Attorney General shall state what investigative techniques have previously been utilized to obtain the foreign intelligence information concerned and the degree to which these techniques resulted in acquiring such information; and

(8) a statement of the facts concerning all previous applications that have been made to any judge under this subchapter involving any of the persons, premises, or property specified in the application, and the action taken on each previous application.

(b) Additional affidavits or certifications

The Attorney General may require any other affidavit or certification from any other officer in connection with the application.

(c) Additional information

The judge may require the applicant to furnish such other information as may be necessary to make the determinations required by section 1824 of this title.

(d) Personal review by Attorney General

(1)(A) Upon written request of the Director of the Federal Bureau of Investigation, the Secretary of Defense, the Secretary of State, the Director of National Intelligence, or the Director of the Central Intelligence Agency, the Attorney General shall personally review under subsection (a) an application under that subsection for a target described in section 1801(b)(2) of this title.

(B) Except when disabled or otherwise unavailable to make a request referred to in subparagraph (A), an official referred to in that subparagraph may not delegate the authority to make a request referred to in that subparagraph.

(C) Each official referred to in subparagraph (A) with authority to make a request under that subparagraph shall take appropriate actions in advance to ensure that delegation of such authority is clearly established in the event such official is disabled or otherwise unavailable to make such request.

(2)(A) If as a result of a request under paragraph (1) the Attorney General determines not to approve an application under the second sentence of subsection (a) for purposes of making the application under this section, the Attorney General shall provide written notice of the determination to the official making the request for the review of the application under that paragraph. Except when disabled or otherwise unavailable to make a determination under the preceding sentence, the Attorney General may not delegate the responsibility to make a determination under that sentence. The Attorney General shall take appropriate actions in advance to ensure that delegation of such responsibility is clearly established in the event the Attorney General is disabled or otherwise unavailable to make such determination.

(B) Notice with respect to an application under subparagraph (A) shall set forth the modifications, if any, of the application that are necessary in order for the Attorney General to approve the application under the second sentence of subsection (a) for purposes of making the application under this section.

(C) Upon review of any modifications of an application set forth under subparagraph (B), the official notified of the modifications under this paragraph shall modify the application if such official determines that such modification is warranted. Such official shall supervise the making of any modification under this subparagraph. Except when disabled or otherwise unavailable to supervise the making of any modification under the preceding sentence, such official may not delegate the responsibility to supervise the making of any modification under that preceding sentence. Each such official shall take appropriate actions in advance to ensure that delegation of such responsibility is clearly established in the event such official is disabled or otherwise unavailable to supervise the making of such modification.

50 U.S.C. § 1824. Issuance of order

(a) Necessary findings

Upon an application made pursuant to section 1823 of this title, the judge shall enter an ex parte order as requested or as modified approving the physical search if the judge finds that-

(1) the application has been made by a Federal officer and approved by the Attorney General;

(2) on the basis of the facts submitted by the applicant there is probable cause to believe that-

(A) the target of the physical search is a foreign power or an agent of a foreign power, except that no United States person may be considered an agent of a foreign power solely upon the basis of activities protected by the first amendment to the Constitution of the United States; and

(B) the premises or property to be searched is or is about to be owned, used, possessed by, or is in transit to or from an agent of a foreign power or a foreign power;

(3) the proposed minimization procedures meet the definition of minimization contained in this subchapter; and

(4) the application which has been filed contains all statements and certifications required by section 1823 of this title, and, if the target is a United States person, the certification or certifications are not clearly erroneous on the basis of the statement made under section 1823(a)(6)(E) of this title and any other information furnished under section 1823(c) of this title.

(b) Determination of probable cause

In determining whether or not probable cause exists for purposes of an order under subsection (a)(2), a judge may consider past activities of the target, as well as facts and circumstances relating to current or future activities of the target.

(c) Specifications and directions of orders

An order approving a physical search under this section shall-

    (1) specify-

        (A) the identity, if known, or a description of the target of the physical search;

        (B) the nature and location of each of the premises or property to be searched;

        (C) the type of information, material, or property to be seized, altered, or reproduced;

        (D) a statement of the manner in which the physical search is to be conducted and, whenever more than one physical search is authorized under the order, the authorized scope of each search and what minimization procedures shall apply to the information acquired by each search; and

        (E) the period of time during which physical searches are approved; and

    (2) direct-

        (A) that the minimization procedures be followed;

        (B) that, upon the request of the applicant, a specified landlord, custodian, or other specified person furnish the applicant forthwith all information, facilities, or assistance necessary to accomplish the physical search in such a manner as will protect its secrecy and produce a minimum of interference with the services that such landlord, custodian, or other person is providing the target of the physical search;

        (C) that such landlord, custodian, or other person maintain under security procedures approved by the Attorney General and the Director of National Intelligence any records concerning the search or the aid furnished that such person wishes to retain;

        (D) that the applicant compensate, at the prevailing rate, such landlord, custodian, or other person for furnishing such aid; and

        (E) that the Federal officer conducting the physical search promptly report to the court the circumstances and results of the physical search.

(d) Duration of order; extensions; assessment of compliance

    (1) An order issued under this section may approve a physical search for the period necessary to achieve its purpose, or for 90 days, whichever is less, except

that (A) an order under this section shall approve a physical search targeted against a foreign power, as defined in paragraph (1), (2), or (3) of section 1801(a) of this title, for the period specified in the application or for one year, whichever is less, and (B) an order under this section for a physical search targeted against an agent of a foreign power who is not a United States person may be for the period specified in the application or for 120 days, whichever is less.

(2) Extensions of an order issued under this subchapter may be granted on the same basis as the original order upon an application for an extension and new findings made in the same manner as required for the original order, except that an extension of an order under this chapter for a physical search targeted against a foreign power, as defined in paragraph (5), (6), or (7) of section 1801(a) of this title, or against a foreign power, as defined in section 1801(a)(4) of this title, that is not a United States person, or against an agent of a foreign power who is not a United States person, may be for a period not to exceed one year if the judge finds probable cause to believe that no property of any individual United States person will be acquired during the period.

(3) At or before the end of the period of time for which a physical search is approved by an order or an extension, or at any time after a physical search is carried out, the judge may assess compliance with the minimization procedures by reviewing the circumstances under which information concerning United States persons was acquired, retained, or disseminated.

(e) Emergency orders

(1) Notwithstanding any other provision of this subchapter, the Attorney General may authorize the emergency employment of a physical search if the Attorney General-

(A) reasonably determines that an emergency situation exists with respect to the employment of a physical search to obtain foreign intelligence information before an order authorizing such physical search can with due diligence be obtained;

(B) reasonably determines that the factual basis for issuance of an order under this subchapter to approve such physical search exists;

(C) informs, either personally or through a designee, a judge of the Foreign Intelligence Surveillance Court at the time of such authorization that the decision has been made to employ an emergency physical search; and

(D) makes an application in accordance with this subchapter to a judge of the Foreign Intelligence Surveillance Court as soon as practicable, but not more than 7 days after the Attorney General authorizes such physical search.

(2) If the Attorney General authorizes the emergency employment of a physical search under paragraph (1), the Attorney General shall require that the

minimization procedures required by this subchapter for the issuance of a judicial order be followed.

(3) In the absence of a judicial order approving such physical search, the physical search shall terminate when the information sought is obtained, when the application for the order is denied, or after the expiration of 7 days from the time of authorization by the Attorney General, whichever is earliest.

(4) A denial of the application made under this subsection may be reviewed as provided in section 1803 of this title.

(5) In the event that such application for approval is denied, or in any other case where the physical search is terminated and no order is issued approving the physical search, no information obtained or evidence derived from such physical search shall be received in evidence or otherwise disclosed in any trial, hearing, or other proceeding in or before any court, grand jury, department, office, agency, regulatory body, legislative committee, or other authority of the United States, a State, or political subdivision thereof, and no information concerning any United States person acquired from such physical search shall subsequently be used or disclosed in any other manner by Federal officers or employees without the consent of such person, except with the approval of the Attorney General if the information indicates a threat of death or serious bodily harm to any person.

(6) The Attorney General shall assess compliance with the requirements of paragraph (5).

(f) Retention of applications and orders

Applications made and orders granted under this subchapter shall be retained for a period of at least 10 years from the date of the application.

50 U.S.C. § 1825. Use of information

(a) Compliance with minimization procedures; lawful purposes

Information acquired from a physical search conducted pursuant to this subchapter concerning any United States person may be used and disclosed by Federal officers and employees without the consent of the United States person only in accordance with the minimization procedures required by this subchapter. No information acquired from a physical search pursuant to this subchapter may be used or disclosed by Federal officers or employees except for lawful purposes.

(b) Notice of search and identification of property seized, altered, or reproduced

Where a physical search authorized and conducted pursuant to section 1824 of this title involves the residence of a United States person, and, at any time after the search the Attorney General determines there is no national security interest in continuing to maintain the secrecy of the search, the Attorney General shall provide notice to the United States person whose residence was searched of the fact of the search conducted pursuant to this chapter and shall identify any property of such person seized, altered, or reproduced during such search.

(c) Statement for disclosure

No information acquired pursuant to this subchapter shall be disclosed for law enforcement purposes unless such disclosure is accompanied by a statement that such information, or any information derived therefrom, may only be used in a criminal proceeding with the advance authorization of the Attorney General.

(d) Notification by United States

Whenever the United States intends to enter into evidence or otherwise use or disclose in any trial, hearing, or other proceeding in or before any court, department, officer, agency, regulatory body, or other authority of the United States, against an aggrieved person, any information obtained or derived from a physical search pursuant to the authority of this subchapter, the United States shall, prior to the trial, hearing, or the other proceeding or at a reasonable time prior to an effort to so disclose or so use that information or submit it in evidence, notify the aggrieved person and the court or other authority in which the information is to be disclosed or used that the United States intends to so disclose or so use such information.

(e) Notification by States or political subdivisions

Whenever any State or political subdivision thereof intends to enter into evidence or otherwise use or disclose in any trial, hearing, or other proceeding in or before any court, department, officer, agency, regulatory body, or other authority of a State or a political subdivision thereof against an aggrieved person any information obtained or derived from a physical search pursuant to the authority of this subchapter, the State or political subdivision thereof shall notify the aggrieved person, the court or other authority in which the information is to be disclosed or used, and the Attorney General that the State or political subdivision thereof intends to so disclose or so use such information.

(f) Motion to suppress

(1) Any person against whom evidence obtained or derived from a physical search to which he is an aggrieved person is to be, or has been, introduced or otherwise used or disclosed in any trial, hearing, or other proceeding in or before any court, department, officer, agency, regulatory body, or other authority of the United States, a State, or a political subdivision thereof, may move to suppress the evidence obtained or derived from such search on the grounds that-

(A) the information was unlawfully acquired; or

(B) the physical search was not made in conformity with an order of authorization or approval.

(2) Such a motion shall be made before the trial, hearing, or other proceeding unless there was no opportunity to make such a motion or the person was not aware of the grounds of the motion.

(g) In camera and ex parte review by district court

Whenever a court or other authority is notified pursuant to subsection (d) or (e), or whenever a motion is made pursuant to subsection (f), or whenever any motion or request is made by an aggrieved person pursuant to any other statute or rule of the United States or any State before any court or other authority of the United States or any State to discover or obtain applications or orders or other materials relating to a physical search authorized by this subchapter or to discover, obtain, or suppress evidence or information obtained or derived from a physical search authorized by this subchapter, the United States district court or, where the motion is made before another authority, the United States district court in the same district as the authority shall, notwithstanding any other provision of law, if the Attorney General files an affidavit under oath that disclosure or any adversary hearing would harm the national security of the United States, review in camera and ex parte the application, order, and such other materials relating to the physical search as may be necessary to determine whether the physical search of the aggrieved person was lawfully authorized and conducted. In making this determination, the court may disclose to the aggrieved person, under appropriate security procedures and protective orders, portions of the application, order, or other materials relating to the physical search, or may require the Attorney General to provide to the aggrieved person a summary of such materials, only where such disclosure is necessary to make an accurate determination of the legality of the physical search.

(h) Suppression of evidence; denial of motion

If the United States district court pursuant to subsection (g) determines that the physical search was not lawfully authorized or conducted, it shall, in accordance with the requirements of law, suppress the evidence which was unlawfully obtained or derived from the physical search of the aggrieved person or otherwise grant the motion of the aggrieved person. If the court determines that the physical search was lawfully authorized or conducted, it shall deny the motion of the aggrieved person except to the extent that due process requires discovery or disclosure.

(i) Finality of orders

Orders granting motions or requests under subsection (h), decisions under this section that a physical search was not lawfully authorized or conducted, and orders of the United States district court requiring review or granting disclosure of applications, orders, or other materials relating to the physical search shall be final orders and binding upon all courts of the United States and the several States except a United States Court of Appeals or the Supreme Court.

(j) Notification of emergency execution of physical search; contents; postponement, suspension, or elimination

    (1) If an emergency execution of a physical search is authorized under section 1824(d) of this title and a subsequent order approving the search is not obtained,

the judge shall cause to be served on any United States person named in the application and on such other United States persons subject to the search as the judge may determine in his discretion it is in the interests of justice to serve, notice of-

(A) the fact of the application;

(B) the period of the search; and

(C) the fact that during the period information was or was not obtained.

(2) On an ex parte showing of good cause to the judge, the serving of the notice required by this subsection may be postponed or suspended for a period not to exceed 90 days. Thereafter, on a further ex parte showing of good cause, the court shall forego ordering the serving of the notice required under this subsection.

(k) Coordination with law enforcement on national security matters

(1) Federal officers who conduct physical searches to acquire foreign intelligence information under this subchapter may consult with Federal law enforcement officers or law enforcement personnel of a State or political subdivision of a State (including the chief executive officer of that State or political subdivision who has the authority to appoint or direct the chief law enforcement officer of that State or political subdivision) to coordinate efforts to investigate or protect against-

(A) actual or potential attack or other grave hostile acts of a foreign power or an agent of a foreign power;

(B) sabotage, international terrorism, or the international proliferation of weapons of mass destruction by a foreign power or an agent of a foreign power; or

(C) clandestine intelligence activities by an intelligence service or network of a foreign power or by an agent of a foreign power.

(2) Coordination authorized under paragraph (1) shall not preclude the certification required by section 1823(a)(6) of this title or the entry of an order under section 1824 of this title.

50 U.S.C. § 1826. Congressional oversight

On a semiannual basis the Attorney General shall fully inform the Permanent Select Committee on Intelligence and the Committee on the Judiciary of the House of Representatives and the Select Committee on Intelligence and the Committee on the Judiciary of the Senate concerning all physical searches conducted pursuant to this subchapter. On a semiannual basis the Attorney General shall also provide to those committees a report setting forth with respect to the preceding six-month period-

(1) the total number of applications made for orders approving physical searches under this subchapter;

(2) the total number of such orders either granted, modified, or denied;

(3) the number of physical searches which involved searches of the residences, offices, or personal property of United States persons, and the number of occasions, if any, where the Attorney General provided notice pursuant to section 1825(b) of this title; and

(4) the total number of emergency physical searches authorized by the Attorney General under section 1824(e) of this title and the total number of subsequent orders approving or denying such physical searches.

50 U.S.C. § 1827. Penalties

(a) Prohibited activities

A person is guilty of an offense if he intentionally -

(1) under color of law for the purpose of obtaining foreign intelligence information, executes a physical search within the United States except as authorized by statute; or

(2) discloses or uses information obtained under color of law by physical search within the United States, knowing or having reason to know that the information was obtained through physical search not authorized by statute, for the purpose of obtaining intelligence information.

(b) Defense

It is a defense to a prosecution under subsection (a) of this section that the defendant was a law enforcement or investigative officer engaged in the course of his official duties and the physical search was authorized by and conducted pursuant to a search warrant or court order of a court of competent jurisdiction.

(c) Fine or imprisonment

An offense described in this section is punishable by a fine of not more than $10,000 or imprisonment for not more than five years, or both.

(d) Federal jurisdiction

There is Federal jurisdiction over an offense under this section if the person committing the offense was an officer or employee of the United States at the time the offense was committed.

50 U.S.C. § 1828. Civil liability

An aggrieved person, other than a foreign power or an agent of a foreign power, as defined in section 1801(a) or (b)(1)(A), respectively, of this title, whose premises, property, information, or material has been subjected to a physical search within the United States or about whom information obtained by such a physical search has been disclosed or used in violation of section 1827 of this title shall have a cause of action against any person who committed such violation and shall be entitled to recover -

(1) actual damages, but not less than liquidated damages of $1,000 or $100 per day for each day of violation, whichever is greater;

(2) punitive damages; and

(3) reasonable attorney's fees and other investigative and litigation costs reasonably incurred.

50 U.S.C. § 1829. Authorization during time of war

Notwithstanding any other provision of law, the President, through the Attorney General, may authorize physical searches without a court order under this subchapter to acquire foreign intelligence information for a period not to exceed 15 calendar days following a declaration of war by the Congress.

50 U.S.C. § 1841. Definitions

As used in this subchapter:

(1) The terms "foreign power", "agent of a foreign power", "international terrorism", "foreign intelligence information", "Attorney General", "United States person", "United States", "person", and "State" shall have the same meanings as in section 1801 of this title.

(2) The terms "pen register" and "trap and trace device" have the meanings given such terms in section 3127 of title 18.

(3) The term "aggrieved person" means any person-

(A) whose telephone line was subject to the installation or use of a pen register or trap and trace device authorized by this subchapter; or

(B) whose communication instrument or device was subject to the use of a pen register or trap and trace device authorized by this subchapter to capture incoming electronic or other communications impulses.

(4)(A) The term "specific selection term"-

(i) is a term that specifically identifies a person, account, address, or personal device, or any other specific identifier; and

(ii) is used to limit, to the greatest extent reasonably practicable, the scope of information sought, consistent with the purpose for seeking the use of the pen register or trap and trace device.

(B) A specific selection term under subparagraph (A) does not include an identifier that does not limit, to the greatest extent reasonably practicable, the scope of information sought, consistent with the purpose for seeking the use of the pen register or trap and trace device, such as an identifier that-

(i) identifies an electronic communication service provider (as that term is defined in section 1881 of this title) or a provider of remote computing service (as that term is defined in section 2711 of title 18), when not used as part of a specific identifier as described in subparagraph (A), unless the provider is itself a subject of an authorized investigation for which the specific selection term is used as the basis for the use; or

(ii) identifies a broad geographic region, including the United States, a city, a county, a State, a zip code, or an area code, when not used as part of a specific identifier as described in subparagraph (A).

(C) For purposes of subparagraph (A), the term "address" means a physical address or electronic address, such as an electronic mail address or temporarily assigned network address (including an Internet protocol address).

(D) Nothing in this paragraph shall be construed to preclude the use of multiple terms or identifiers to meet the requirements of subparagraph (A).

50 U.S.C. § 1842. Pen registers and trap and trace devices for foreign intelligence and international terrorism investigations

(a) Application for authorization or approval

(1) Notwithstanding any other provision of law, the Attorney General or a designated attorney for the Government may make an application for an order or an extension of an order authorizing or approving the installation and use of a pen register or trap and trace device for any investigation to obtain foreign intelligence information not concerning a United States person or to protect against international terrorism or clandestine intelligence activities, provided that such investigation of a United States person is not conducted solely upon the basis of activities protected by the first amendment to the Constitution which is being conducted by the Federal Bureau of Investigation under such guidelines as the Attorney General approves pursuant to Executive Order No. 12333, or a successor order.

(2) The authority under paragraph (1) is in addition to the authority under subchapter I of this chapter to conduct the electronic surveillance referred to in that paragraph.

(b) Form of application; recipient

Each application under this section shall be in writing under oath or affirmation to-

(1) a judge of the court established by section 1803(a) of this title; or

(2) a United States Magistrate Judge under chapter 43 of title 28 who is publicly designated by the Chief Justice of the United States to have the power to hear applications for and grant orders approving the installation and use of a pen register or trap and trace device on behalf of a judge of that court.

(c) Executive approval; contents of application

Each application under this section shall require the approval of the Attorney General, or a designated attorney for the Government, and shall include-

(1) the identity of the Federal officer seeking to use the pen register or trap and trace device covered by the application;

(2) a certification by the applicant that the information likely to be obtained is foreign intelligence information not concerning a United States person or is

relevant to an ongoing investigation to protect against international terrorism or clandestine intelligence activities, provided that such investigation of a United States person is not conducted solely upon the basis of activities protected by the first amendment to the Constitution; and

(3) a specific selection term to be used as the basis for the use of the pen register or trap and trace device.

(d) Ex parte judicial order of approval

(1) Upon an application made pursuant to this section, the judge shall enter an ex parte order as requested, or as modified, approving the installation and use of a pen register or trap and trace device if the judge finds that the application satisfies the requirements of this section.

(2) An order issued under this section-

(A) shall specify-

(i) the identity, if known, of the person who is the subject of the investigation;

(ii) the identity, if known, of the person to whom is leased or in whose name is listed the telephone line or other facility to which the pen register or trap and trace device is to be attached or applied; and

(iii) the attributes of the communications to which the order applies, such as the number or other identifier, and, if known, the location of the telephone line or other facility to which the pen register or trap and trace device is to be attached or applied and, in the case of a trap and trace device, the geographic limits of the trap and trace order;

(B) shall direct that-

(i) upon request of the applicant, the provider of a wire or electronic communication service, landlord, custodian, or other person shall furnish any information, facilities, or technical assistance necessary to accomplish the installation and operation of the pen register or trap and trace device in such a manner as will protect its secrecy and produce a minimum amount of interference with the services that such provider, landlord, custodian, or other person is providing the person concerned;

(ii) such provider, landlord, custodian, or other person-

(I) shall not disclose the existence of the investigation or of the pen register or trap and trace device to any person unless or until ordered by the court; and

(II) shall maintain, under security procedures approved by the Attorney General and the Director of National Intelligence pursuant to section 1805(b)(2)(C) of this title, any records concerning the pen register or trap and trace device or the aid furnished; and

(iii) the applicant shall compensate such provider, landlord, custodian, or other person for reasonable expenses incurred by such provider, landlord, custodian, or other person in providing such information, facilities, or technical assistance; and

(C) shall direct that, upon the request of the applicant, the provider of a wire or electronic communication service shall disclose to the Federal officer using the pen register or trap and trace device covered by the order-

(i) in the case of the customer or subscriber using the service covered by the order (for the period specified by the order)-

(I) the name of the customer or subscriber;

(II) the address of the customer or subscriber;

(III) the telephone or instrument number, or other subscriber number or identifier, of the customer or subscriber, including any temporarily assigned network address or associated routing or transmission information;

(IV) the length of the provision of service by such provider to the customer or subscriber and the types of services utilized by the customer or subscriber;

(V) in the case of a provider of local or long distance telephone service, any local or long distance telephone records of the customer or subscriber;

(VI) if applicable, any records reflecting period of usage (or sessions) by the customer or subscriber; and

(VII) any mechanisms and sources of payment for such service, including the number of any credit card or bank account utilized for payment for such service; and

(ii) if available, with respect to any customer or subscriber of incoming or outgoing communications to or from the service covered by the order-

(I) the name of such customer or subscriber;

(II) the address of such customer or subscriber;

(III) the telephone or instrument number, or other subscriber number or identifier, of such customer or subscriber, including any temporarily assigned network address or associated routing or transmission information; and

(IV) the length of the provision of service by such provider to such customer or subscriber and the types of services utilized by such customer or subscriber.

(e) Time limitation

(1) Except as provided in paragraph (2), an order issued under this section shall authorize the installation and use of a pen register or trap and trace device for a

activities, provided that such investigation of a United States person is not conducted solely upon the basis of activities protected by the first amendment to the Constitution if-

(1) a judge referred to in section 1842(b) of this title is informed by the Attorney General or his designee at the time of such authorization that the decision has been made to install and use the pen register or trap and trace device, as the case may be, on an emergency basis; and

(2) an application in accordance with section 1842 of this title is made to such judge as soon as practicable, but not more than 7 days, after the Attorney General authorizes the installation and use of the pen register or trap and trace device, as the case may be, under this section.

(b) Determination of emergency and factual basis

A determination under this subsection is a reasonable determination by the Attorney General that-

(1) an emergency requires the installation and use of a pen register or trap and trace device to obtain foreign intelligence information not concerning a United States person or information to protect against international terrorism or clandestine intelligence activities, provided that such investigation of a United States person is not conducted solely upon the basis of activities protected by the first amendment to the Constitution before an order authorizing the installation and use of the pen register or trap and trace device, as the case may be, can with due diligence be obtained under section 1842 of this title; and

(2) the factual basis for issuance of an order under such section 1842 of this title to approve the installation and use of the pen register or trap and trace device, as the case may be, exists.

(c) Effect of absence of order

(1) In the absence of an order applied for under subsection (a)(2) approving the installation and use of a pen register or trap and trace device authorized under this section, the installation and use of the pen register or trap and trace device, as the case may be, shall terminate at the earlier of-

(A) when the information sought is obtained;

(B) when the application for the order is denied under section 1842 of this title; or

(C) 7 days after the time of the authorization by the Attorney General.

(2) In the event that an application for an order applied for under subsection (a)(2) is denied, or in any other case where the installation and use of a pen register or trap and trace device under this section is terminated and no order under section 1842 of this title is issued approving the installation and use of the pen register or trap and trace device, as the case may be, no information obtained or evidence derived from the use of the pen register or trap and trace device, as the case may

be, shall be received in evidence or otherwise disclosed in any trial, hearing, or other proceeding in or before any court, grand jury, department, office, agency, regulatory body, legislative committee, or other authority of the United States, a State, or political subdivision thereof, and no information concerning any United States person acquired from the use of the pen register or trap and trace device, as the case may be, shall subsequently be used or disclosed in any other manner by Federal officers or employees without the consent of such person, except with the approval of the Attorney General if the information indicates a threat of death or serious bodily harm to any person.

(d) Privacy procedures

Information collected through the use of a pen register or trap and trace device installed under this section shall be subject to the policies and procedures required under section 1842(h) of this title.

50 U.S.C. § 1844. Authorization during time of war

Notwithstanding any other provision of law, the President, through the Attorney General, may authorize the use of a pen register or trap and trace device without a court order under this subchapter to acquire foreign intelligence information for a period not to exceed 15 calendar days following a declaration of war by Congress.

50 U.S.C. § 1845. Use of information

(a) In general

(1) Information acquired from the use of a pen register or trap and trace device installed pursuant to this subchapter concerning any United States person may be used and disclosed by Federal officers and employees without the consent of the United States person only in accordance with the provisions of this section.

(2) No information acquired from a pen register or trap and trace device installed and used pursuant to this subchapter may be used or disclosed by Federal officers or employees except for lawful purposes.

(b) Disclosure for law enforcement purposes No information acquired pursuant to this subchapter shall be disclosed for law enforcement purposes unless such disclosure is accompanied by a statement that such information, or any information derived therefrom, may only be used in a criminal proceeding with the advance authorization of the Attorney General.

(c) Notification of intended disclosure by United States Whenever the United States intends to enter into evidence or otherwise use or disclose in any trial, hearing, or other proceeding in or before any court, department, officer, agency, regulatory body, or other authority of the United States against an aggrieved person any information obtained or derived from the use of a pen register or trap and trace device pursuant to this subchapter, the United States shall, before the trial, hearing, or the other proceeding or at a reasonable time before an effort to so disclose or so use that information or submit it in evidence, notify the aggrieved person and the court or other authority in which the information is to be disclosed or used that the United States intends to so disclose or so use such information.

(d) Notification of intended disclosure by State or political subdivision Whenever any State or political subdivision thereof intends to enter into evidence or otherwise use or disclose in any trial, hearing, or other proceeding in or before any court, department, officer, agency, regulatory body, or other authority of the State or political subdivision thereof against an aggrieved person any information obtained or derived from the use of a pen register or trap and trace device pursuant to this subchapter, the State or political subdivision thereof shall notify the aggrieved person, the court or other authority in which the information is to be disclosed or used, and the Attorney General that the State or political subdivision thereof intends to so disclose or so use such information.

(e) Motion to suppress

(1) Any aggrieved person against whom evidence obtained or derived from the use of a pen register or trap and trace device is to be, or has been, introduced or otherwise used or disclosed in any trial, hearing, or other proceeding in or before any court, department, officer, agency, regulatory body, or other authority of the United States, or a State or political subdivision thereof, may move to suppress the evidence obtained or derived from the use of the pen register or trap and trace device, as the case may be, on the grounds that -

(A) the information was unlawfully acquired; or

(B) the use of the pen register or trap and trace device, as the case may be, was not made in conformity with an order of authorization or approval under this subchapter.

(2) A motion under paragraph (1) shall be made before the trial, hearing, or other proceeding unless there was no opportunity to make such a motion or the aggrieved person concerned was not aware of the grounds of the motion.

(f) In camera and ex parte review

(1) Whenever a court or other authority is notified pursuant to subsection (c) or (d) of this section, whenever a motion is made pursuant to subsection (e) of this section, or whenever any motion or request is made by an aggrieved person pursuant to any other statute or rule of the United States or any State before any court or other authority of the United States or any State to discover or obtain applications or orders or other materials relating to the use of a pen register or trap and trace device authorized by this subchapter or to discover, obtain, or suppress evidence or information obtained or derived from the use of a pen register or trap and trace device authorized by this subchapter, the United States district court or, where the motion is made before another authority, the United States district court

in the same district as the authority shall, notwithstanding any other provision of law and if the Attorney General files an affidavit under oath that disclosure or any adversary hearing would harm the national security of the United States, review in camera and ex parte the application, order, and such other materials relating to the use of the pen register or trap and trace device, as the case may be, as may be necessary to determine whether the use of the pen register or trap and trace device, as the case may be, was lawfully authorized and conducted.

(2) In making a determination under paragraph (1), the court may disclose to the aggrieved person, under appropriate security procedures and protective orders, portions of the application, order, or other materials relating to the use of the pen register or trap and trace device, as the case may be, or may require the Attorney General to provide to the aggrieved person a summary of such materials, only where such disclosure is necessary to make an accurate determination of the legality of the use of the pen register or trap and trace device, as the case may be.

(g) Effect of determination of lawfulness

(1) If the United States district court determines pursuant to subsection (f) of this section that the use of a pen register or trap and trace device was not lawfully authorized or conducted, the court may, in accordance with the requirements of law, suppress the evidence which was unlawfully obtained or derived from the use of the pen register or trap and trace device, as the case may be, or otherwise grant the motion of the aggrieved person.

(2) If the court determines that the use of the pen register or trap and trace device, as the case may be, was lawfully authorized or conducted, it may deny the motion of the aggrieved person except to the extent that due process requires discovery or disclosure.

(h) Binding final orders

Orders granting motions or requests under subsection (g) of this section, decisions under this section that the use of a pen register or trap and trace device was not lawfully authorized or conducted, and orders of the United States district court requiring review or granting disclosure of applications, orders, or other materials relating to the installation and use of a pen register or trap and trace device shall be final orders and binding upon all courts of the United States and the several States except a United States Court of Appeals or the Supreme Court.

50 U.S.C. § 1846. Congressional oversight

(a) On a semiannual basis, the Attorney General shall fully inform the Permanent Select Committee on Intelligence of the House of Representatives and the Select Committee on Intelligence of the Senate, and the Committee on the Judiciary of the House of Representatives and the Committee on the Judiciary of the Senate, concerning all uses of pen registers and trap and trace devices pursuant to this subchapter.

(b) On a semiannual basis, the Attorney General shall also provide to the committees referred to in subsection (a) and |to the Committees on the Judiciary of the House of Representatives and the Senate a report setting forth with respect to the preceding 6-month period-

(1) the total number of applications made for orders approving the use of pen registers or trap and trace devices under this subchapter;

(2) the total number of such orders either granted, modified, or denied;

(3) the total number of pen registers and trap and trace devices whose installation and use was authorized by the Attorney General on an emergency basis under section 1843 of this title, and the total number of subsequent orders approving or denying the installation and use of such pen registers and trap and trace devices;

(4) each department or agency on behalf of which the Attorney General or a designated attorney for the Government has made an application for an order authorizing or approving the installation and use of a pen register or trap and trace device under this subchapter; and

(5) for each department or agency described in paragraph (4), each number described in paragraphs (1), (2), and (3).

50 U.S.C. § 1861. Access to Certain Business Records for Foreign Intelligence and International Terrorism Investigations

(a) Application for order; conduct of investigation generally

(1) Subject to paragraph (3), the Director of the Federal Bureau of Investigation or a designee of the Director (whose rank shall be no lower than Assistant Special Agent in Charge) may make an application for an order requiring the production of any tangible things (including books, records, papers, documents, and other items) for an investigation to obtain foreign intelligence information not concerning a United States person or to protect against international terrorism or clandestine intelligence activities, provided that such investigation of a United States person is not conducted solely upon the basis of activities protected by the first amendment to the Constitution.

(2) An investigation conducted under this section shall-

(A) be conducted under guidelines approved by the Attorney General under Executive Order 12333 (or a successor order); and

(B) not be conducted of a United States person solely upon the basis of activities protected by the first amendment to the Constitution of the United States.

(3) In the case of an application for an order requiring the production of library circulation records, library patron lists, book sales records, book customer lists,

firearms sales records, tax return records, educational records, or medical records containing information that would identify a person, the Director of the Federal Bureau of Investigation may delegate the authority to make such application to either the Deputy Director of the Federal Bureau of Investigation or the Executive Assistant Director for National Security (or any successor position). The Deputy Director or the Executive Assistant Director may not further delegate such authority.

(b) Recipient and contents of application

Each application under this section-

    (1) shall be made to-

        (A) a judge of the court established by section 1803(a) of this title; or

        (B) a United States Magistrate Judge under chapter 43 of title 28, who is publicly designated by the Chief Justice of the United States to have the power to hear applications and grant orders for the production of tangible things under this section on behalf of a judge of that court; and

    (2) shall include-

        (A) a specific selection term to be used as the basis for the production of the tangible things sought;

        (B) in the case of an application other than an application described in subparagraph (C) (including an application for the production of call detail records other than in the manner described in subparagraph (C)), a statement of facts showing that there are reasonable grounds to believe that the tangible things sought are relevant to an authorized investigation (other than a threat assessment) conducted in accordance with subsection (a)(2) to obtain foreign intelligence information not concerning a United States person or to protect against international terrorism or clandestine intelligence activities, such things being presumptively relevant to an authorized investigation if the applicant shows in the statement of the facts that they pertain to-

            (i) a foreign power or an agent of a foreign power;

            (ii) the activities of a suspected agent of a foreign power who is the subject of such authorized investigation; or

            (iii) an individual in contact with, or known to, a suspected agent of a foreign power who is the subject of such authorized investigation;

        (C) in the case of an application for the production on an ongoing basis of call detail records created before, on, or after the date of the application relating to an authorized investigation (other than a threat assessment) conducted in accordance with subsection (a)(2) to protect against international terrorism, a statement of facts showing that-

(i) there are reasonable grounds to believe that the call detail records sought to be produced based on the specific selection term required under subparagraph (A) are relevant to such investigation; and

(ii) there is a reasonable, articulable suspicion that such specific selection term is associated with a foreign power engaged in international terrorism or activities in preparation therefor, or an agent of a foreign power engaged in international terrorism or activities in preparation therefor; and

(D) an enumeration of the minimization procedures adopted by the Attorney General under subsection (g) that are applicable to the retention and dissemination by the Federal Bureau of Investigation of any tangible things to be made available to the Federal Bureau of Investigation based on the order requested in such application.

(c) Ex parte judicial order of approval

(1) Upon an application made pursuant to this section, if the judge finds that the application meets the requirements of subsections (a) and (b) and that the minimization procedures submitted in accordance with subsection (b)(2)(D) meet the definition of minimization procedures under subsection (g), the judge shall enter an ex parte order as requested, or as modified, approving the release of tangible things. Such order shall direct that minimization procedures adopted pursuant to subsection (g) be followed.

(2) An order under this subsection-

(A) shall describe the tangible things that are ordered to be produced with sufficient particularity to permit them to be fairly identified, including each specific selection term to be used as the basis for the production;

(B) shall include the date on which the tangible things must be provided, which shall allow a reasonable period of time within which the tangible things can be assembled and made available;

(C) shall provide clear and conspicuous notice of the principles and procedures described in subsection (d);

(D) may only require the production of a tangible thing if such thing can be obtained with a subpoena duces tecum issued by a court of the United States in aid of a grand jury investigation or with any other order issued by a court of the United States directing the production of records or tangible things;

(E) shall not disclose that such order is issued for purposes of an investigation described in subsection (a); and

(F) in the case of an application described in subsection (b)(2)(C), shall-

(i) authorize the production on a daily basis of call detail records for a period not to exceed 180 days;

(ii) provide that an order for such production may be extended upon application under subsection (b) and the judicial finding under paragraph (1) of this subsection;

(iii) provide that the Government may require the prompt production of a first set of call detail records using the specific selection term that satisfies the standard required under subsection (b)(2)(C)(ii);

(iv) provide that the Government may require the prompt production of a second set of call detail records using session-identifying information or a telephone calling card number identified by the specific selection term used to produce call detail records under clause (iii);

(v) provide that, when produced, such records be in a form that will be useful to the Government;

(vi) direct each person the Government directs to produce call detail records under the order to furnish the Government forthwith all information, facilities, or technical assistance necessary to accomplish the production in such a manner as will protect the secrecy of the production and produce a minimum of interference with the services that such person is providing to each subject of the production; and

(vii) direct the Government to-

(I) adopt minimization procedures that require the prompt destruction of all call detail records produced under the order that the Government determines are not foreign intelligence information; and

(II) destroy all call detail records produced under the order as prescribed by such procedures.

(3) No order issued under this subsection may authorize the collection of tangible things without the use of a specific selection term that meets the requirements of subsection (b)(2).

(d) Nondisclosure

(1) No person shall disclose to any other person that the Federal Bureau of Investigation has sought or obtained tangible things pursuant to an order issued or an emergency production required under this section, other than to-

(A) those persons to whom disclosure is necessary to comply with such order or such emergency production;

(B) an attorney to obtain legal advice or assistance with respect to the production of things in response to the order or the emergency production; or

(C) other persons as permitted by the Director of the Federal Bureau of Investigation or the designee of the Director.

(2)

(A) A person to whom disclosure is made pursuant to paragraph (1) shall be subject to the nondisclosure requirements applicable to a person to whom an order or emergency production is directed under this section in the same manner as such person.

(B) Any person who discloses to a person described in subparagraph (A), (B), or (C) of paragraph (1) that the Federal Bureau of Investigation has sought or obtained tangible things pursuant to an order or emergency production under this section shall notify such person of the nondisclosure requirements of this subsection.

(C) At the request of the Director of the Federal Bureau of Investigation or the designee of the Director, any person making or intending to make a disclosure under subparagraph (A) or (C) of paragraph (1) shall identify to the Director or such designee the person to whom such disclosure will be made or to whom such disclosure was made prior to the request.

(e) Liability for good faith disclosure; waiver

(1) No cause of action shall lie in any court against a person who-

(A) produces tangible things or provides information, facilities, or technical assistance in accordance with an order issued or an emergency production required under this section; or

(B) otherwise provides technical assistance to the Government under this section or to implement the amendments made to this section by the USA FREEDOM Act of 2015.

(2) A production or provision of information, facilities, or technical assistance described in paragraph (1) shall not be deemed to constitute a waiver of any privilege in any other proceeding or context.

(f) Judicial review of FISA orders

(1) In this subsection-

(A) the term "production order" means an order to produce any tangible thing under this section; and

(B) the term "nondisclosure order" means an order imposed under subsection (d).

(2)

(A)(i) A person receiving a production order may challenge the legality of the production order or any nondisclosure order imposed in connection with the production order by filing a petition with the pool established by section 1803(e)(1) of this title.

(ii) The presiding judge shall immediately assign a petition under clause (i) to 1 of the judges serving in the pool established by section 1803(e)(1) of this title. Not later than 72 hours after the assignment of such petition, the assigned judge shall conduct an initial review of the petition. If the assigned judge determines that the petition is frivolous, the assigned judge shall immediately deny the petition and affirm the production order or nondisclosure order. If the assigned judge determines the petition is not frivolous, the assigned judge shall promptly consider the petition in accordance with the procedures established under section 1803(e)(2) of this title.

(iii) The assigned judge shall promptly provide a written statement for the record of the reasons for any determination under this subsection. Upon the request of the Government, any order setting aside a nondisclosure order shall be stayed pending review pursuant to paragraph (3).

(B) A judge considering a petition to modify or set aside a production order may grant such petition only if the judge finds that such order does not meet the requirements of this section or is otherwise unlawful. If the judge does not modify or set aside the production order, the judge shall immediately affirm such order, and order the recipient to comply therewith.

(C)(i) A judge considering a petition to modify or set aside a nondisclosure order may grant such petition only if the judge finds that there is no reason to believe that disclosure may endanger the national security of the United States, interfere with a criminal, counterterrorism, or counterintelligence investigation, interfere with diplomatic relations, or endanger the life or physical safety of any person.

(ii) If the judge denies a petition to modify or set aside a nondisclosure order, the recipient of such order shall be precluded for a period of 1 year from filing another such petition with respect to such nondisclosure order.

(D) Any production or nondisclosure order not explicitly modified or set aside consistent with this subsection shall remain in full effect.

(3) A petition for review of a decision under paragraph (2) to affirm, modify, or set aside an order by the Government or any person receiving such order shall be made to the court of review established under section 1803(b) of this title, which shall have jurisdiction to consider such petitions. The court of review shall provide for the record a written statement of the reasons for its decision and, on petition by the Government or any person receiving such order for writ of certiorari, the record shall be transmitted under seal to the Supreme Court of the United States, which shall have jurisdiction to review such decision.

(4) Judicial proceedings under this subsection shall be concluded as expeditiously as possible. The record of proceedings, including petitions filed, orders granted, and statements of reasons for decision, shall be maintained under security measures established by the Chief Justice of the United States, in consultation with the Attorney General and the Director of National Intelligence.

(5) All petitions under this subsection shall be filed under seal. In any proceedings under this subsection, the court shall, upon request of the Government, review ex parte and in camera any Government submission, or portions thereof, which may include classified information.

United States
Foreign Intelligence Surveillance Act

(g) Minimization procedures

    (1) In general

The Attorney General shall adopt, and update as appropriate, specific minimization procedures governing the retention and dissemination by the Federal Bureau of Investigation of any tangible things, or information therein, received by the Federal Bureau of Investigation in response to an order under this subchapter.

    (2) Defined

In this section, the term "minimization procedures" means-

    (A) specific procedures that are reasonably designed in light of the purpose and technique of an order for the production of tangible things, to minimize the retention, and prohibit the dissemination, of nonpublicly available information concerning unconsenting United States persons consistent with the need of the United States to obtain, produce, and disseminate foreign intelligence information;

    (B) procedures that require that nonpublicly available information, which is not foreign intelligence information, as defined in section 1801(e)(1) of this title, shall not be disseminated in a manner that identifies any United States person, without such person's consent, unless such person's identity is necessary to understand foreign intelligence information or assess its importance; and

    (C) notwithstanding subparagraphs (A) and (B), procedures that allow for the retention and dissemination of information that is evidence of a crime which has been, is being, or is about to be committed and that is to be retained or disseminated for law enforcement purposes.

    (3) Rule of construction

Nothing in this subsection shall limit the authority of the court established under section 1803(a) of this title to impose additional, particularized minimization procedures with regard to the production, retention, or dissemination of nonpublicly available information concerning unconsenting United States persons, including additional, particularized procedures related to the destruction of information within a reasonable time period.

(h) Use of information

Information acquired from tangible things received by the Federal Bureau of Investigation in response to an order under this subchapter concerning any United States person may be used and disclosed by Federal officers and employees without the consent of the United States person only in accordance with the minimization procedures adopted pursuant to subsection (g). No otherwise privileged information acquired from tangible things received by the Federal Bureau of Investigation in accordance with the provisions of this subchapter shall lose its privileged character. No information acquired from tangible things received by the Federal Bureau of

Investigation in response to an order under this subchapter may be used or disclosed by Federal officers or employees except for lawful purposes.

(i) Emergency authority for production of tangible things

(1) Notwithstanding any other provision of this section, the Attorney General may require the emergency production of tangible things if the Attorney General-

(A) reasonably determines that an emergency situation requires the production of tangible things before an order authorizing such production can with due diligence be obtained;

(B) reasonably determines that the factual basis for the issuance of an order under this section to approve such production of tangible things exists;

(C) informs, either personally or through a designee, a judge having jurisdiction under this section at the time the Attorney General requires the emergency production of tangible things that the decision has been made to employ the authority under this subsection; and

(D) makes an application in accordance with this section to a judge having jurisdiction under this section as soon as practicable, but not later than 7 days after the Attorney General requires the emergency production of tangible things under this subsection.

(2) If the Attorney General requires the emergency production of tangible things under paragraph (1), the Attorney General shall require that the minimization procedures required by this section for the issuance of a judicial order be followed.

(3) In the absence of a judicial order approving the production of tangible things under this subsection, the production shall terminate when the information sought is obtained, when the application for the order is denied, or after the expiration of 7 days from the time the Attorney General begins requiring the emergency production of such tangible things, whichever is earliest.

(4) A denial of the application made under this subsection may be reviewed as provided in section 1803 of this title.

(5) If such application for approval is denied, or in any other case where the production of tangible things is terminated and no order is issued approving the production, no information obtained or evidence derived from such production shall be received in evidence or otherwise disclosed in any trial, hearing, or other proceeding in or before any court, grand jury, department, office, agency, regulatory body, legislative committee, or other authority of the United States, a State, or a political subdivision thereof, and no information concerning any United States person acquired from such production shall subsequently be used or disclosed in any other manner by Federal officers or employees without the consent of such person, except with the approval of the Attorney General if the information indicates a threat of death or serious bodily harm to any person.

(6) The Attorney General shall assess compliance with the requirements of paragraph (5).

(j) Compensation

The Government shall compensate a person for reasonable expenses incurred for-

(1) producing tangible things or providing information, facilities, or assistance in accordance with an order issued with respect to an application described in subsection (b)(2)(C) or an emergency production under subsection (i) that, to comply with subsection (i)(1)(D), requires an application described in subsection (b)(2)(C); or

(2) otherwise providing technical assistance to the Government under this section or to implement the amendments made to this section by the USA FREEDOM Act of 2015.

(k) Definitions

In this section:

(1) In general

The terms "foreign power", "agent of a foreign power", "international terrorism", "foreign intelligence information", "Attorney General", "United States person", "United States", "person", and "State" have the meanings provided those terms in section 1801 of this title.

(2) Address

The term "address" means a physical address or electronic address, such as an electronic mail address or temporarily assigned network address (including an Internet protocol address).

(3) Call detail record

The term "call detail record"-

(A) means session-identifying information (including an originating or terminating telephone number, an International Mobile Subscriber Identity number, or an International Mobile Station Equipment Identity number), a telephone calling card number, or the time or duration of a call; and

(B) does not include-

(i) the contents (as defined in section 2510(8) of title 18) of any communication;

(ii) the name, address, or financial information of a subscriber or customer; or

(iii) cell site location or global positioning system information.

(4) Specific selection term

(A) Tangible things

(i) In general

Except as provided in subparagraph (B), a "specific selection term"-

(I) is a term that specifically identifies a person, account, address, or personal device, or any other specific identifier; and

(II) is used to limit, to the greatest extent reasonably practicable, the scope of tangible things sought consistent with the purpose for seeking the tangible things.

(ii) Limitation

A specific selection term under clause (i) does not include an identifier that does not limit, to the greatest extent reasonably practicable, the scope of tangible things sought consistent with the purpose for seeking the tangible things, such as an identifier that-

(I) identifies an electronic communication service provider (as that term is defined in section 1881 of this title) or a provider of remote computing service (as that term is defined in section 2711 of title 18), when not used as part of a specific identifier as described in clause (i), unless the provider is itself a subject of an authorized investigation for which the specific selection term is used as the basis for the production; or

(II) identifies a broad geographic region, including the United States, a city, a county, a State, a zip code, or an area code, when not used as part of a specific identifier as described in clause (i).

(iii) Rule of construction

Nothing in this paragraph shall be construed to preclude the use of multiple terms or identifiers to meet the requirements of clause (i).

(B) Call detail record applications

For purposes of an application submitted under subsection (b)(2)(C), the term "specific selection term" means a term that specifically identifies an individual, account, or personal device.

50 U.S.C. § 1862. Congressional Oversight

(a) On an annual basis, the Attorney General shall fully inform the Permanent Select Committee on Intelligence and the Committee on the Judiciary of the House of Representatives and the Select Committee on Intelligence and the Committee on the Judiciary of the Senate concerning all requests for the production of tangible things under section 1861 of this title.

(b) In April of each year, the Attorney General shall submit to the House and Senate Committees on the Judiciary and the House Permanent Select Committee on Intelligence and the Senate Select Committee on Intelligence a report setting forth with respect to the preceding calendar year-

(1) a summary of all compliance reviews conducted by the Government for the production of tangible things under section 1861 of this title;

(2) the total number of applications described in section 1861(b)(2)(B) of this title made for orders approving requests for the production of tangible things;

(3) the total number of such orders either granted, modified, or denied;

(4) the total number of applications described in section 1861(b)(2)(C) of this title made for orders approving requests for the production of call detail records;

(5) the total number of such orders either granted, modified, or denied;

(6) the total number of applications made for orders approving requests for the production of tangible things under section 1861 of this title;

(7) the total number of such orders either granted, modified, or denied; and

(8) the number of such orders either granted, modified, or denied for the production of each of the following:

(A) Library circulation records, library patron lists, book sales records, or book customer lists.

(B) Firearms sales records.

(C) Tax return records.

(D) Educational records.

(E) Medical records containing information that would identify a person.

(c)(1) In April of each year, the Attorney General shall submit to Congress a report setting forth with respect to the preceding year-

(A) the total number of applications made for orders approving requests for the production of tangible things under section 1861 of this title;

(B) the total number of such orders either granted, modified, or denied;

(C) the total number of applications made for orders approving requests for the production of tangible things under section 1861 of this title in which the specific selection term does not specifically identify an individual, account, or personal device;

(D) the total number of orders described in subparagraph (C) either granted, modified, or denied; and

(E) with respect to orders described in subparagraph (D) that have been granted or modified, whether the court established under section 1803 of this title has directed additional, particularized minimization procedures beyond those adopted pursuant to section 1861(g) of this title.

(2) Each report under this subsection shall be submitted in unclassified form.

RIGHT TO FINANCIAL PRIVACY ACT
(1978)

Summary

The Right to Financial Privacy Act was precipitated by the Supreme Court's decision in United States v Miller, 425 U.S. 435 (1976) in which a customer challenged the disclosure of his personal financial information by his bank. The Court held that the records were the property of the bank and, therefore, that the customer did not have standing under the Fourth Amendment to challenge the disclosure. Furthermore, the Court ruled that the customer did not have a reasonable expectation of privacy regarding records of his checking account because in writing a check, the customer knew that the bank employees would see the information on it.

The Right to Financial Privacy Act sought to regulate disclosure of personal financial information to federal agencies, to recognize individuals' privacy interest in their bank records, and to give them rights regarding the disclosure of those records. The Act does not prohibit the disclosure of financial information to federal agencies. Instead it puts strict guidelines into place regarding such disclosures, and mandates a procedure for notice and challenge. The Act only applies to the federal government; it does not regulate disclosure of financial information to private parties or businesses.

The Right to Financial Privacy Act prohibits any Government authority from obtaining copies of, access to, or the information contained in, the financial records of any customer from a financial institution unless such records are reasonably described and: (1) such customer has authorized such disclosure in accordance with this Act; (2) such records are disclosed in response to an administrative subpoena or summons; (3) such records are disclosed in response to a court order; (4) such records are disclosed in response to a judicial subpoena; or (5) such financial records are disclosed in response to a formal written request meeting specified requirements. Requires in all cases that the customer be notified of the agency seeking such records, the purpose for which such records are sought, and the rights of customers under this Act.

The Act establishes specific conditions and procedures for the delay of notice to a customer. It states that no financial institution may provide to a Government authority copies of or the information contained in the financial records of any customer except in accordance with the requirements of this Act. It sets forth provisions governing customer authorization, administrative subpoenas and summons, judicial subpoenas, and search warrants. It establishes procedures for a customer to challenge the disclosure of financial records. It provides exceptions to the provisions of this Act and special procedures for the disclosure of records to the Secret Service and government authorities acting in the field of foreign intelligence.

The Act establishes civil penalties and the right to injunctive relief without regard to the amount in controversy for violation of the provisions of this Title. Actions may be brought within three years of a customer's discovery of violation. Injunctive relief and compensatory and punitive damages are available under the Act.

References

Public Law 95-630 as amended. Codified at 12 U.S.C. § 3401 et seq.
[https://www.law.cornell.edu/uscode/text/12/3401]

L. Richard Fischer, *The Law of Financial Privacy* (A.S. Pratt & Sons 2000)

EPIC, Right to Financial Privacy Act
[https://www.epic.org/privacy/rfpa/]

12 U.S.C. § 3401. Definitions

For the purpose of this chapter, the term-

(1) "financial institution", except as provided in section 3414 of this title, means any office of a bank, savings bank, card issuer as defined in section 1602(n) [1] of title 15, industrial loan company, trust company, savings association, building and loan, or homestead association (including cooperative banks), credit union, or consumer finance institution, located in any State or territory of the United States, the District of Columbia, Puerto Rico, Guam, American Samoa, or the Virgin Islands;

(2) "financial record" means an original of, a copy of, or information known to have been derived from, any record held by a financial institution pertaining to a customer's relationship with the financial institution;

(3) "Government authority" means any agency or department of the United States, or any officer, employee, or agent thereof;

(4) "person" means an individual or a partnership of five or fewer individuals;

(5) "customer" means any person or authorized representative of that person who utilized or is utilizing any service of a financial institution, or for whom a financial institution is acting or has acted as a fiduciary, in relation to an account maintained in the person's name;

(6) "holding company" means-

(A) any bank holding company (as defined in section 1841 of this title); and

(B) any company described in section 1843(f)(1) of this title;

(7) "supervisory agency" means with respect to any particular financial institution, holding company, or any subsidiary of a financial institution or holding company, any of the following which has statutory authority to examine the financial condition, business operations, or records or transactions of that institution, holding company, or subsidiary-

(A) the Federal Deposit Insurance Corporation;

(B) the Bureau of Consumer Financial Protection;

(C) the National Credit Union Administration;

(D) the Board of Governors of the Federal Reserve System;

(E) the Comptroller of the Currency;

(F) the Securities and Exchange Commission;

(G) the Commodity Futures Trading Commission;

(H) the Secretary of the Treasury, with respect to the Bank Secrecy Act (Public Law 91–508, title I) [12 U.S.C. 1951 et seq.] and subchapter II of chapter 53 of title 31; or

(I) any State banking or securities department or agency; and

(8) "law enforcement inquiry" means a lawful investigation or official proceeding inquiring into a violation of, or failure to comply with, any criminal or civil statute or any regulation, rule, or order issued pursuant thereto.

Sec. 3402. Access to financial records by Government authorities prohibited; exceptions

Except as provided by section 3403(c) or (d), 3413, or 3414 of this title, no Government authority may have access to or obtain copies of, or the information contained in the financial records of any customer from a financial institution unless the financial records are reasonably described and -

(1) such customer has authorized such disclosure in accordance with section 3404 of this title;

(2) such financial records are disclosed in response to an administrative subpoena or summons which meets the requirements of section 3405 of this title;

(3) such financial records are disclosed in response to a search warrant which meets the requirements of section 3406 of this title;

(4) such financial records are disclosed in response to a judicial subpoena which meets the requirements of section 3407 of this title; or

(5) such financial records are disclosed in response to a formal written request which meets the requirements of section 3408 of this title.

Sec. 3403. Confidentiality of financial records

(a) Release of records by financial institutions prohibited

No financial institution, or officer, employees, or agent of a financial institution, may provide to any Government authority access to or copies of, or the information contained in, the financial records of any customer except in accordance with the provisions of this chapter.

(b) Release of records upon certification of compliance with chapter

A financial institution shall not release the financial records of a customer until the Government authority seeking such records certifies in writing to the financial institution that it has complied with the applicable provisions of this chapter.

(c) Notification to Government authority of existence of relevant information in records

Nothing in this chapter shall preclude any financial institution, or any officer, employee, or agent of a financial institution, from notifying a Government authority that such institution, or officer, employee, or agent has information which may be relevant to a possible violation of any statute or regulation. Such information may include only the name or other identifying information concerning any individual, corporation, or account involved in and the nature of any suspected illegal activity. Such information may be disclosed notwithstanding any constitution, law, or regulation of any State or political subdivision thereof to the contrary. Any financial institution, or officer, employee, or agent thereof, making a disclosure of information pursuant to this subsection, shall not be liable to the customer under any law or regulation of the United States or any constitution, law, or regulation of any State or political subdivision thereof, for such disclosure or for any failure to notify the customer of such disclosure.

(d) Release of records as incident to perfection of security interest, proving a claim in bankruptcy, collecting a debt, or processing an application with regard to a Government loan, loan guarantee, etc.

(1) Nothing in this chapter shall preclude a financial institution, as an incident to perfecting a security interest, proving a claim in bankruptcy, or otherwise collecting on a debt owing either to the financial institution itself or in its role as a fiduciary, from providing copies of any financial record to any court or Government authority.

(2) Nothing in this chapter shall preclude a financial institution, as an incident to processing an application for assistance to a customer in the form of a Government loan, loan guaranty, or loan insurance agreement, or as an incident to processing a default on, or administering, a Government guaranteed or insured loan, from initiating contact with an appropriate Government authority for the purpose of providing any financial record necessary to permit such authority to carry out its responsibilities under a loan, loan guaranty, or loan insurance agreement.

Sec. 3404. Customer authorizations

(a) Statement furnished by customer to financial institution and Government authority; contents

A customer may authorize disclosure under section 3402(1) of this title if he furnishes to the financial institution and to the Government authority seeking to obtain such disclosure a signed and dated statement which -

(1) authorizes such disclosure for a period not in excess of three months;

(2) states that the customer may revoke such authorization at any time before the financial records are disclosed;

(3) identifies the financial records which are authorized to be disclosed;

(4) specifies the purposes for which, and the Government authority to which, such records may be disclosed; and

(5) states the customer's rights under this chapter.

(b) Authorization as condition of doing business prohibited

No such authorization shall be required as a condition of doing business with any financial institution.

(c) Right of customer to access to financial institution's record of disclosures

The customer has the right, unless the Government authority obtains a court order as provided in section 3409 of this title, to obtain a copy of the record which the financial institution shall keep of all instances in which the customer's record is disclosed to a Government authority pursuant to this section, including the identity of the Government authority to which such disclosure is made.

Sec. 3405. Administrative subpoena and summons

A Government authority may obtain financial records under section 3402(2) of this title pursuant to an administrative subpoena or summons otherwise authorized by law only if -

(1) there is reason to believe that the records sought are relevant to a legitimate law enforcement inquiry;

(2) a copy of the subpoena or summons has been served upon the customer or mailed to his last known address on or before the date on which the subpoena or summons was served on the financial institution together with the following notice which shall state with reasonable specificity the nature of the law enforcement inquiry:

"Records or information concerning your transactions held by the financial institution named in the attached subpoena or summons are being sought by this (agency or department) in accordance with the Right to Financial Privacy Act of 1978 (12 U.S.C. 3401 et seq.) for the following purpose: If you desire that such records or information not be made available, you must:

"1. Fill out the accompanying motion paper and sworn statement or write one of your own, stating that you are the customer whose records are being requested by the Government and either giving the reasons you believe that the records are not relevant to the legitimate law enforcement inquiry stated in this notice or any other legal basis for objecting to the release of the records.

"2. File the motion and statement by mailing or delivering them to the clerk of any one of the following United States district courts:

"3. Serve the Government authority requesting the records by mailing or delivering a copy of your motion and statement to .

"4. Be prepared to come to court and present your position in further detail.

"5. You do not need to have a lawyer, although you may wish to employ one to represent you and protect your rights.

If you do not follow the above procedures, upon the expiration of ten days from the date of service or fourteen days from the date of mailing of this notice, the records or information requested therein will be made available. These records may be transferred to other Government authorities for legitimate law enforcement inquiries, in which event you will be notified after the transfer."; and

(3) ten days have expired from the date of service of the notice or fourteen days have expired from the date of mailing the notice to the customer and within such time period the customer has not filed a sworn statement and motion to quash in an appropriate court, or the customer challenge provisions of section 3410 of this title have been complied with.

Sec. 3406. Search warrants

(a) Applicability of Federal Rules of Criminal Procedure

A Government authority may obtain financial records under section 3402(3) of this title only if it obtains a search warrant pursuant to the Federal Rules of Criminal Procedure.

(b) Mailing of copy and notice to customer

No later than ninety days after the Government authority serves the search warrant, it shall mail to the customer's last known address a copy of the search warrant together with the following notice:

"Records or information concerning your transactions held by the financial institution named in the attached search warrant were obtained by this (agency or department) on (date) for the following purpose: . You may have rights under the Right to Financial Privacy Act of 1978 (12 U.S.C. 3401 et seq.).".

(c) Court-ordered delays in mailing

Upon application of the Government authority, a court may grant a delay in the mailing of the notice required in subsection (b) of this section, which delay shall not exceed one hundred and eighty days following the service of the warrant, if the court makes the findings required in section 3409(a) of this title. If the court so finds, it shall enter an ex parte order granting the requested delay and an order prohibiting the financial institution from disclosing that records have been obtained or that a search warrant for such records has been executed. Additional delays of up to ninety days may be granted by the court upon application, but only in accordance with this subsection. Upon expiration of the period of delay of notification of the customer, the following notice shall be mailed to the customer along with a copy of the search warrant:

"Records or information concerning your transactions held by the financial institution named in the attached search warrant were obtained by this (agency or department) on (date). Notification was delayed beyond the statutory ninety-day delay period pursuant to a determination by the court that such notice would seriously jeopardize an investigation concerning . You may have rights under the Right to Financial Privacy Act of 1978 (12 U.S.C. 3401 et seq.).".

Sec. 3407. Judicial subpoena

A Government authority may obtain financial records under section 3402(4) of this title pursuant to judicial subpoena only if -

> (1) such subpoena is authorized by law and there is reason to believe that the records sought are relevant to a legitimate law enforcement inquiry;
> (2) a copy of the subpoena has been served upon the customer or mailed to his last known address on or before the date on which the subpoena was served on the financial institution together with the following notice which shall state with reasonable specificity the nature of the law enforcement inquiry:
>> "Records or information concerning your transactions which are held by the financial institution named in the attached subpoena are being sought by this (agency or department or authority) in accordance with the Right to Financial Privacy Act of 1978 (12 U.S.C. 3401 et seq.) for the following purpose: If you desire that such records or information not be made available, you must:
>> "1. Fill out the accompanying motion paper and sworn statement or write one of your own, stating that you are the customer whose records are being requested by the Government and either giving the reasons you believe that the records are not relevant to the legitimate law enforcement inquiry stated in this notice or any other legal basis for objecting to the release of the records.
>> "2. File the motion and statement by mailing or delivering them to the clerk of the Court.
>> "3. Serve the Government authority requesting the records by mailing or delivering a copy of your motion and statement to .
>> "4. Be prepared to come to court and present your position in further detail.
>> "5. You do not need to have a lawyer, although you may wish to employ one to represent you and protect your rights. If you do not follow the above procedures, upon the expiration of ten days from the date of service or fourteen days from the date of mailing of this notice, the records or information requested therein will be made available. These records may be transferred to other government authorities for legitimate law enforcement inquiries, in which event you will be notified after the transfer;" and
> (3) ten days have expired from the date of service or fourteen days from the date of mailing of the notice to the customer and within such time period the customer has not filed a sworn statement and motion to quash in an appropriate court, or the customer challenge provisions of section 3410 of this title have been complied with.

United States
Right to Financial Privacy Act

Sec. 3408. Formal written request

A Government authority may request financial records under section 3402(5) of this title pursuant to a formal written request only if -

(1) no administrative summons or subpoena authority reasonably appears to be available to that Government authority to obtain financial records for the purpose for which such records are sought;

(2) the request is authorized by regulations promulgated by the head of the agency or department;

(3) there is reason to believe that the records sought are relevant to a legitimate law enforcement inquiry; and

(4)(A) a copy of the request has been served upon the customer or mailed to his last known address on or before the date on which the request was made to the financial institution together with the following notice which shall state with reasonable specificity the nature of the law enforcement inquiry:

"Records or information concerning your transactions held by the financial institution named in the attached request are being sought by this (agency or department) in accordance with the Right to Financial Privacy Act of 1978 (12 U.S.C. 3401 et seq.) for the following purpose:

"If you desire that such records or information not be made available, you must:

"1. Fill out the accompanying motion paper and sworn statement or write one of your own, stating that you are the customer whose records are being requested by the Government and either giving the reasons you believe that the records are not relevant to the legitimate law enforcement inquiry stated in this notice or any other legal basis for objecting to the release of the records.

"2. File the motion and statement by mailing or delivering them to the clerk of any one of the following United States District Courts:

"3. Serve the Government authority requesting the records by mailing or delivering a copy of your motion and statement to .

"4. Be prepared to come to court and present your position in further detail.

"5. You do not need to have a lawyer, although you may wish to employ one to represent you and protect your rights. If you do not follow the above procedures, upon the expiration of ten days from the date of service or fourteen days from the date of mailing of this notice, the records or information requested therein may be made available. These records may be transferred to other Government authorities for legitimate law enforcement inquiries, in which event you will be notified after the transfer;" and

(B) ten days have expired from the date of service or fourteen days from the date of mailing of the notice by the customer and within such time period the customer has not filed a sworn statement and an application to enjoin the Government authority in an appropriate court, or the customer challenge provisions of section 3410 of this title have been complied with.

Sec. 3409. Delayed notice

(a) Application by Government authority; findings

Upon application of the Government authority, the customer notice required under section 3404(c), 3405(2), 3406(c), 3407(2), 3408(4), or 3412(b) of this title may be delayed by order of an appropriate court if the presiding judge or magistrate judge finds that -

(1) the investigation being conducted is within the lawful jurisdiction of the Government authority seeking the financial records;

(2) there is reason to believe that the records being sought are relevant to a legitimate law enforcement inquiry; and

(3) there is reason to believe that such notice will result in

(A) endangering life or physical safety of any person;

(B) flight from prosecution;

(C) destruction of or tampering with evidence;

(D) intimidation of potential witnesses; or

(E) otherwise seriously jeopardizing an investigation or official proceeding or unduly delaying a trial or ongoing official proceeding to the same extent as the circumstances in the preceding subparagraphs.

An application for delay must be made with reasonable specificity.

(b) Grant of delay order; duration and specifications; extensions; copy of request and notice to customer

(1) If the court makes the findings required in paragraphs (1), (2), and (3) of subsection (a) of this section, it shall enter an ex parte order granting the requested delay for a period not to exceed ninety days and an order prohibiting the financial institution from disclosing that records have been obtained or that a request for records has been made, except that, if the records have been sought by a Government authority exercising financial controls over foreign accounts in the United States under section 5(b) of the Trading with the Enemy Act (12 U.S.C. 95a, 50 App. U.S.C. 5(b)), the International Emergency Economic Powers Act (title II, Public Law 95-223) (50 U.S.C. 1701 et seq.), or section 287c of title 22, and the court finds that there is reason to believe that such notice may endanger the lives or physical safety of a customer or group of customers, or any person or group of persons associated with a customer, the court may specify that the delay be indefinite.

(2) Extensions of the delay of notice provided in paragraph (1) of up to ninety days each may be granted by the court upon application, but only in accordance with this subsection.

(3) Upon expiration of the period of delay of notification under paragraph (1) or (2), the customer shall be served with or mailed a copy of the process or request together with the following notice which shall state with reasonable specificity the nature of the law enforcement inquiry:

"Records or information concerning your transactions which are held by the financial institution named in the attached process or request were supplied to or requested by the Government authority named in the process or request on (date). Notification was withheld pursuant to a determination by the (title of court so ordering) under the Right to Financial Privacy Act of 1978 (12 U.S.C. 3401 et seq.) that such notice might (state reason). The purpose of the investigation or official proceeding was .".

(c) Notice requirement respecting emergency access to financial records

When access to financial records is obtained pursuant to section 3414(b) of this title (emergency access), the Government authority shall, unless a court has authorized delay of notice pursuant to subsections (a) and (b) of this section, as soon as practicable after such records are obtained serve upon the customer, or mail by registered or certified mail to his last known address, a copy of the request to the financial institution together with the following notice which shall state with reasonable specificity the nature of the law enforcement inquiry:

"Records concerning your transactions held by the financial institution named in the attached request were obtained by (agency or department) under the Right to Financial Privacy Act of 1978 (12 U.S.C. 3401 et seq.) on (date) for the following purpose: Emergency access to such records was obtained on the grounds that (state grounds).".

(d) Preservation of memorandums, affidavits, or other papers

Any memorandum, affidavit, or other paper filed in connection with a request for delay in notification shall be preserved by the court. Upon petition by the customer to whom such records pertain, the court may order disclosure of such papers to the petitioner unless the court makes the findings required in subsection (a) of this section.

Sec. 3410. Customer challenges

(a) Filing of motion to quash or application to enjoin; proper court; contents

Within ten days of service or within fourteen days of mailing of a subpoena, summons, or formal written request, a customer may file a motion to quash an administrative summons or judicial subpoena, or an application to enjoin a Government authority from obtaining financial records pursuant to a formal written request, with copies served upon the Government authority. A motion to quash a judicial subpoena shall be filed in the court which issued the subpoena. A motion to quash an administrative summons or an application to enjoin a Government authority from obtaining records pursuant to a formal written request shall be filed in the appropriate United States district court. Such motion or application shall contain an affidavit or sworn statement -

(1) stating that the applicant is a customer of the financial institution from which financial records pertaining to him have been sought; and

(2) stating the applicant's reasons for believing that the financial records sought are not relevant to the legitimate law enforcement inquiry stated by the Government authority in its notice, or that there has not been substantial compliance with the provisions of this chapter.

Service shall be made under this section upon a Government authority by delivering or mailing by registered or certified mail a copy of the papers to the person, office, or department specified in the notice which the customer has received pursuant to this chapter. For the purposes of this section, "delivery" has the meaning stated in rule 5(b) of the Federal Rules of Civil Procedure.

(b) Filing of response; additional proceedings

If the court finds that the customer has complied with subsection (a) of this section, it shall order the Government authority to file a sworn response, which may be filed in camera if the Government includes in its response the reasons which make in camera review appropriate. If the court is unable to determine the motion or application on the basis of the parties' initial allegations and response, the court may conduct such additional proceedings as it deems appropriate. All such proceedings shall be completed and the motion or application decided within seven calendar days of the filing of the Government's response.

(c) Decision of court

If the court finds that the applicant is not the customer to whom the financial records sought by the Government authority pertain, or that there is a demonstrable reason to believe that the law enforcement inquiry is legitimate and a reasonable belief that the records sought are relevant to that inquiry, it shall deny the motion or application, and, in the case of an administrative summons or court order other than a search warrant, order such process enforced. If the court finds that the applicant is the customer to whom the records sought by the Government authority pertain, and that there is not a demonstrable reason to believe that the law enforcement inquiry is legitimate and a reasonable belief that the records sought are relevant to that inquiry, or that there has not been substantial compliance with the provisions of this chapter, it shall order the process quashed or shall enjoin the Government authority's formal written request.

(d) Appeals

A court ruling denying a motion or application under this section shall not be deemed a final order and no interlocutory appeal may be taken therefrom by the customer. An appeal of a ruling denying a motion or application under this section may be taken by the customer

(1) within such period of time as provided by law as part of any appeal from a final order in any legal proceeding initiated against him arising out of or based upon the financial records, or

(2) within thirty days after a notification that no legal proceeding is contemplated against him. The Government authority obtaining the financial records shall promptly notify a customer when a determination has been made that no legal proceeding against him is contemplated. After one hundred and eighty days from the denial of the motion or application, if the Government authority obtaining the records has not initiated such a proceeding, a supervisory official of the Government authority shall certify to the appropriate court that no such determination has been made. The court may require that such certifications be made, at reasonable intervals thereafter, until either notification to the customer has occurred or a legal proceeding is initiated as described in clause (A).

(e) Sole judicial remedy available to customer

The challenge procedures of this chapter constitute the sole judicial remedy available to a customer to oppose disclosure of financial records pursuant to this chapter.

(f) Affect on challenges by financial institutions

Nothing in this chapter shall enlarge or restrict any rights of a financial institution to challenge requests for records made by a Government authority under existing law. Nothing in this chapter shall entitle a customer to assert the rights of a financial institution.

Sec. 3411. Duty of financial institutions

Upon receipt of a request for financial records made by a Government authority under section 3405 or 3407 of this title, the financial institution shall, unless otherwise provided by law, proceed to assemble the records requested and must be prepared to deliver the records to the Government authority upon receipt of the certificate required under section 3403(b) of this title.

Sec. 3412. Use of information

(a) Transfer of financial records to other agencies or departments; certification

Financial records originally obtained pursuant to this chapter shall not be transferred to another agency or department unless the transferring agency or department certifies in writing that there is reason to believe that the records are relevant to a legitimate law enforcement inquiry, or intelligence or counterintelligence activity, investigation or analysis related to international terrorism within the jurisdiction of the receiving agency or department.

(b) Mailing of copy of certification and notice to customer

When financial records subject to this chapter are transferred pursuant to subsection (a), the transferring agency or department shall, within fourteen days, send to the customer a copy of the certification made pursuant to subsection (a) and the following notice, which shall state the nature of the law enforcement inquiry with reasonable specificity: "Copies of, or information contained in, your financial records lawfully in possession of _____ have been furnished to _____ pursuant to the Right of Financial Privacy Act of 1978 [12 U.S.C. 3401 et seq.] for the following purpose: _____. If you believe that this transfer has not been made to further a legitimate law enforcement inquiry, you may have legal rights under the Financial Privacy Act of 1978 or the Privacy Act of 1974 [5 U.S.C. 552a]."

(c) Court-ordered delays in mailing

Notwithstanding subsection (b), notice to the customer may be delayed if the transferring agency or department has obtained a court order delaying notice pursuant to section 3409(a) and (b) of this title and that order is still in effect, or if the receiving agency or department obtains a court order authorizing a delay in notice pursuant to section 3409(a) and (b) of this title. Upon the expiration of any such period of delay, the transferring agency or department shall serve to the customer the notice specified in subsection (b) and the agency or department that obtained the court order authorizing a delay in notice pursuant to section 3409(a) and (b) of this title shall serve to the customer the notice specified in section 3409(b) of this title.

(d) Exchanges of examination reports by supervisory agencies; transfer of financial records to defend customer action; withholding of information

Nothing in this chapter prohibits any supervisory agency from exchanging examination reports or other information with another supervisory agency. Nothing in this chapter prohibits the transfer of a customer's financial records needed by counsel for a Government authority to defend an action brought by the customer. Nothing in this chapter shall authorize the withholding of information by any officer or employee of a supervisory agency from a duly authorized committee or subcommittee of the Congress.

(e) Exchange of records, reports, or other information

Notwithstanding section 3401(6) of this title or any other provision of law, the exchange of financial records, examination reports or other information with respect to a financial institution, holding company, or any subsidiary of a depository institution or holding company, among and between the five member supervisory agencies of the Federal Financial Institutions Examination Council, the Securities and Exchange Commission, the Federal Trade Commission, the Commodity Futures Trading Commission, and the Bureau of Consumer Financial Protection is permitted.

(f) Transfer to Attorney General or Secretary of the Treasury

(1) In general

Nothing in this chapter shall apply when financial records obtained by an agency or department of the United States are disclosed or transferred to the Attorney

General or the Secretary of the Treasury upon the certification by a supervisory level official of the transferring agency or department that-

(A) there is reason to believe that the records may be relevant to a violation of Federal criminal law; and

(B) the records were obtained in the exercise of the agency's or department's supervisory or regulatory functions.

(2) Limitation on use

Records so transferred shall be used only for criminal investigative or prosecutive purposes, for civil actions under section 1833a of this title, or for forfeiture under sections 981 or 982 of title 18 by the Department of Justice and only for criminal investigative purposes relating to money laundering and other financial crimes by the Department of the Treasury and shall, upon completion of the investigation or prosecution (including any appeal), be returned only to the transferring agency or department. No agency or department so transferring such records shall be deemed to have waived any privilege applicable to those records under law.

Sec. 3413. Exceptions

(a) Disclosure of financial records not identified with particular customers

Nothing in this chapter prohibits the disclosure of any financial records or information which is not identified with or identifiable as being derived from the financial records of a particular customer.

(b) Disclosure to, or examination by, supervisory agency pursuant to exercise of supervisory, regulatory, or monetary functions with respect to financial institutions, holding companies, subsidiaries, institution-affiliated parties, or other persons

This chapter shall not apply to the examination by or disclosure to any supervisory agency of financial records or information in the exercise of its supervisory, regulatory, or monetary functions, including conservatorship or receivership functions, with respect to any financial institution, holding company, subsidiary of a financial institution or holding company, institution-affiliated party (within the meaning of section 1813(u) of this title) with respect to a financial institution, holding company, or subsidiary, or other person participating in the conduct of the affairs thereof.

(c) Disclosure pursuant to title 26

Nothing in this chapter prohibits the disclosure of financial records in accordance with procedures authorized by title 26.

(d) Disclosure pursuant to Federal statute or rule promulgated thereunder

Nothing in this chapter shall authorize the withholding of financial records or information required to be reported in accordance with any Federal statute or rule promulgated thereunder.

(e) Disclosure pursuant to Federal Rules of Criminal Procedure or comparable rules of other courts

Nothing in this chapter shall apply when financial records are sought by a Government authority under the Federal Rules of Civil or Criminal Procedure or comparable rules of other courts in connection with litigation to which the Government authority and the customer are parties.

(f) Disclosure pursuant to administrative subpena issued by administrative law judge

Nothing in this chapter shall apply when financial records are sought by a Government authority pursuant to an administrative subpena issued by an administrative law judge in an adjudicatory proceeding subject to section 554 of title 5 and to which the Government authority and the customer are parties.

(g) Disclosure pursuant to legitimate law enforcement inquiry respecting name, address, account number, and type of account of particular customers

The notice requirements of this chapter and sections 3410 and 3412 of this title shall not apply when a Government authority by a means described in section 3402 of this title and for a legitimate law enforcement inquiry is seeking only the name, address, account number, and type of account of any customer or ascertainable group of customers associated (1) with a financial transaction or class of financial transactions, or (2) with a foreign country or subdivision thereof in the case of a Government authority exercising financial controls over foreign accounts in the United States under section 5(b) of the Trading with the Enemy Act [50 U.S.C. 4305(b)]; the International Emergency Economic Powers Act (title II, Public Law 95–223) [50 U.S.C. 1701 et seq.]; or section 287c of title 22.

(h) Disclosure pursuant to lawful proceeding, investigation, etc., directed at financial institution or legal entity or consideration or administration respecting Government loans, loan guarantees, etc.

(1) Nothing in this chapter (except sections 3403, 3417 and 3418 of this title) shall apply when financial records are sought by a Government authority-

(A) in connection with a lawful proceeding, investigation, examination, or inspection directed at a financial institution (whether or not such proceeding, investigation, examination, or inspection is also directed at a customer) or at a legal entity which is not a customer; or

(B) in connection with the authority's consideration or administration of assistance to the customer in the form of a Government loan, loan guaranty, or loan insurance program.

(2) When financial records are sought pursuant to this subsection, the Government authority shall submit to the financial institution the certificate required by section 3403(b) of this title. For access pursuant to paragraph (1)(B), no further certification shall be required for subsequent access by the certifying Government authority during the term of the loan, loan guaranty, or loan insurance agreement.

(3) After the effective date of this chapter, whenever a customer applies for participation in a Government loan, loan guaranty, or loan insurance program, the

Government authority administering such program shall give the customer written notice of the authority's access rights under this subsection. No further notification shall be required for subsequent access by that authority during the term of the loan, loan guaranty, or loan insurance agreement.

(4) Financial records obtained pursuant to this subsection may be used only for the purpose for which they were originally obtained, and may be transferred to another agency or department only when the transfer is to facilitate a lawful proceeding, investigation, examination, or inspection directed at a financial institution (whether or not such proceeding, investigation, examination, or inspection is also directed at a customer), or at a legal entity which is not a customer, except that-

(A) nothing in this paragraph prohibits the use or transfer of a customer's financial records needed by counsel representing a Government authority in a civil action arising from a Government loan, loan guaranty, or loan insurance agreement; and

(B) nothing in this paragraph prohibits a Government authority providing assistance to a customer in the form of a loan, loan guaranty, or loan insurance agreement from using or transferring financial records necessary to process, service or foreclose a loan, or to collect on an indebtedness to the Government resulting from a customer's default.

(5) Notification that financial records obtained pursuant to this subsection may relate to a potential civil, criminal, or regulatory violation by a customer may be given to an agency or department with jurisdiction over that violation, and such agency or department may then seek access to the records pursuant to the provisions of this chapter.

(6) Each financial institution shall keep a notation of each disclosure made pursuant to paragraph (1)(B) of this subsection, including the date of such disclosure and the Government authority to which it was made. The customer shall be entitled to inspect this information.

(i) Disclosure pursuant to issuance of subpena or court order respecting grand jury proceeding

Nothing in this chapter (except sections 3415 and 3420 of this title) shall apply to any subpena or court order issued in connection with proceedings before a grand jury, except that a court shall have authority to order a financial institution, on which a grand jury subpoena for customer records has been served, not to notify the customer of the existence of the subpoena or information that has been furnished to the grand jury, under the circumstances and for the period specified and pursuant to the procedures established in section 3409 of this title.

(j) Disclosure pursuant to proceeding, investigation, etc., instituted by Government Accountability Office and directed at a government authority

This chapter shall not apply when financial records are sought by the Government Accountability Office pursuant to an authorized proceeding, investigation, examination or audit directed at a government authority.

(k) Disclosure necessary for proper administration of programs of certain Government authorities

(1) Nothing in this chapter shall apply to the disclosure by the financial institution of the name and address of any customer to the Department of the Treasury, the Social Security Administration, or the Railroad Retirement Board, where the disclosure of such information is necessary to, and such information is used solely for the purpose of, the proper administration of section 1441 of title 26, title II of the Social Security Act [42 U.S.C. 401 et seq.], or the Railroad Retirement Act of 1974 [45 U.S.C. 231 et seq.].

(2) Nothing in this chapter shall apply to the disclosure by the financial institution of information contained in the financial records of any customer to any Government authority that certifies, disburses, or collects payments, where the disclosure of such information is necessary to, and such information is used solely for the purpose of-

(A) verification of the identity of any person or proper routing and delivery of funds in connection with the issuance of a Federal payment or collection of funds by a Government authority; or

(B) the investigation or recovery of an improper Federal payment or collection of funds or an improperly negotiated Treasury check.

(3) Notwithstanding any other provision of law, a request authorized by paragraph (1) or (2) (and the information contained therein) may be used by the financial institution or its agents solely for the purpose of providing information contained in the financial records of the customer to the Government authority requesting the information, and the financial institution and its agents shall be barred from redisclosure of such information. Any Government authority receiving information pursuant to paragraph (1) or (2) may not disclose or use the information, except for the purposes set forth in such paragraph.

(l) Crimes against financial institutions by insiders

Nothing in this chapter shall apply when any financial institution or supervisory agency provides any financial record of any officer, director, employee, or controlling shareholder (within the meaning of subparagraph (A) or (B) of section 1841(a)(2) of this title or subparagraph (A) or (B) of section 1730a(a)(2) of this title) of such institution, or of any major borrower from such institution who there is reason to believe may be acting in concert with any such officer, director, employee, or controlling shareholder, to the Attorney General of the United States, to a State law enforcement agency, or, in the case of a possible violation of subchapter II of chapter

53 of title 31, to the Secretary of the Treasury if there is reason to believe that such record is relevant to a possible violation by such person of-

(1) any law relating to crimes against financial institutions or supervisory agencies by directors, officers, employees, or controlling shareholders of, or by borrowers from, financial institutions; or

(2) any provision of subchapter II of chapter 53 of title 31 or of section 1956 or 1957 of title 18.

No supervisory agency which transfers any such record under this subsection shall be deemed to have waived any privilege applicable to that record under law.

(m) Disclosure to, or examination by, employees or agents of Board of Governors of Federal Reserve System or Federal Reserve Bank

This chapter shall not apply to the examination by or disclosure to employees or agents of the Board of Governors of the Federal Reserve System or any Federal Reserve Bank of financial records or information in the exercise of the Federal Reserve System's authority to extend credit to the financial institutions or others.

(n) Disclosure to, or examination by, Resolution Trust Corporation or its employees or agents

This chapter shall not apply to the examination by or disclosure to the Resolution Trust Corporation or its employees or agents of financial records or information in the exercise of its conservatorship, receivership, or liquidation functions with respect to a financial institution.

(o) Disclosure to, or examination by, Federal Housing Finance Agency or Federal home loan banks

This chapter shall not apply to the examination by or disclosure to the Federal Housing Finance Agency or any of the Federal home loan banks of financial records or information in the exercise of the Federal Housing Finance Agency's authority to extend credit (either directly or through a Federal home loan bank) to financial institutions or others.

(p) Access to information necessary for administration of certain veteran benefits laws

(1) Nothing in this chapter shall apply to the disclosure by the financial institution of the name and address of any customer to the Department of Veterans Affairs where the disclosure of such information is necessary to, and such information is used solely for the purposes of, the proper administration of benefits programs under laws administered by the Secretary.

(2) Notwithstanding any other provision of law, any request authorized by paragraph (1) (and the information contained therein) may be used by the financial institution or its agents solely for the purpose of providing the customer's name and address to the Department of Veterans Affairs and shall be barred from redisclosure by the financial institution or its agents.

(q) Disclosure pursuant to Federal contractor-issued travel charge card

Nothing in this chapter shall apply to the disclosure of any financial record or information to a Government authority in conjunction with a Federal contractor-issued travel charge card issued for official Government travel.

(r) Disclosure to the Bureau of Consumer Financial Protection

Nothing in this chapter shall apply to the examination by or disclosure to the Bureau of Consumer Financial Protection of financial records or information in the exercise of its authority with respect to a financial institution.

Sec. 3414. Special procedures

(a) Access to financial records for certain intelligence and protective purposes

(1) Nothing in this chapter (except sections 3415, 3417, 3418, and 3421 of this title) shall apply to the production and disclosure of financial records pursuant to requests from-

(A) a Government authority authorized to conduct foreign counter- or foreign positive-intelligence activities for purposes of conducting such activities;

(B) the Secret Service for the purpose of conducting its protective functions (18 U.S.C. 3056; 18 U.S.C. 3056A, Public Law 90–331, as amended); or

(C) a Government authority authorized to conduct investigations of, or intelligence or counterintelligence analyses related to, international terrorism for the purpose of conducting such investigations or analyses.

(2) In the instances specified in paragraph (1), the Government authority shall submit to the financial institution the certificate required in section 3403(b) of this title signed by a supervisory official of a rank designated by the head of the Government authority and a term that specifically identifies a customer, entity, or account to be used as the basis for the production and disclosure of financial records.

(3)(A) If the Government authority described in paragraph (1) or the Secret Service, as the case may be, certifies that otherwise there may result a danger to the national security of the United States, interference with a criminal, counterterrorism, or counterintelligence investigation, interference with diplomatic relations, or danger to the life or physical safety of any person, no financial institution, or officer, employee, or agent of such institution, shall disclose to any person (other than those to whom such disclosure is necessary to comply with the request or an attorney to obtain legal advice or legal assistance with respect to the request) that the Government authority or the Secret Service has sought or obtained access to a customer's financial records.

(B) The request shall notify the person or entity to whom the request is directed of the nondisclosure requirement under subparagraph (A).

(C) Any recipient disclosing to those persons necessary to comply with the request or to an attorney to obtain legal advice or legal assistance with respect to the request shall inform such persons of any applicable nondisclosure requirement. Any person who receives a disclosure under this subsection shall be subject to the same prohibitions on disclosure under subparagraph (A).

(D) At the request of the authorized Government authority or the Secret Service, any person making or intending to make a disclosure under this section shall identify to the requesting official of the authorized Government authority or the Secret Service the person to whom such disclosure will be made or to whom such disclosure was made prior to the request, except that nothing in this section shall require a person to inform the requesting official of the authorized Government authority or the Secret Service of the identity of an attorney to whom disclosure was made or will be made to obtain legal advice or legal assistance with respect to the request for financial records under this subsection.

(4) The Government authority specified in paragraph (1) shall compile an annual tabulation of the occasions in which this section was used.

(5)(A) Financial institutions, and officers, employees, and agents thereof, shall comply with a request for a customer's or entity's financial records made pursuant to this subsection by the Federal Bureau of Investigation when the Director of the Federal Bureau of Investigation (or the Director's designee in a position not lower than Deputy Assistant Director at Bureau headquarters or a Special Agent in Charge in a Bureau field office designated by the Director) certifies in writing to the financial institution that such records are sought for foreign counter intelligence purposes to protect against international terrorism or clandestine intelligence activities, provided that such an investigation of a United States person is not conducted solely upon the basis of activities protected by the first amendment to the Constitution of the United States.

(B) The Federal Bureau of Investigation may disseminate information obtained pursuant to this paragraph only as provided in guidelines approved by the Attorney General for foreign intelligence collection and foreign counterintelligence investigations conducted by the Federal Bureau of Investigation, and, with respect to dissemination to an agency of the United States, only if such information is clearly relevant to the authorized responsibilities of such agency.

(C) On the dates provided in section 3106 of title 50, the Attorney General shall fully inform the congressional intelligence committees (as defined in section 3003 of title 50) concerning all requests made pursuant to this paragraph.

(b) Emergency access to financial records

(1) Nothing in this chapter shall prohibit a Government authority from obtaining financial records from a financial institution if the Government authority determines that delay in obtaining access to such records would create imminent danger of-

(A) physical injury to any person;

(B) serious property damage; or

(C) flight to avoid prosecution.

(2) In the instances specified in paragraph (1), the Government shall submit to the financial institution the certificate required in section 3403(b) of this title signed by a supervisory official of a rank designated by the head of the Government authority.

(3) Within five days of obtaining access to financial records under this subsection, the Government authority shall file with the appropriate court a signed, sworn statement of a supervisory official of a rank designated by the head of the Government authority setting forth the grounds for the emergency access. The Government authority shall thereafter comply with the notice provisions of section 3409(c) of this title.

(4) The Government authority specified in paragraph (1) shall compile an annual tabulation of the occasions in which this section was used.

(c) Prohibition of certain disclosure

(1) Prohibition

(A) In general

If a certification is issued under subparagraph (B) and notice of the right to judicial review under subsection (d) is provided, no financial institution that receives a request under subsection (a), or officer, employee, or agent thereof, shall disclose to any person that the Federal Bureau of Investigation has sought or obtained access to information or records under subsection (a).

(B) Certification

The requirements of subparagraph (A) shall apply if the Director of the Federal Bureau of Investigation, or a designee of the Director whose rank shall be no lower than Deputy Assistant Director at Bureau headquarters or a Special Agent in Charge of a Bureau field office, certifies that the absence of a prohibition of disclosure under this subsection may result in-

(i) a danger to the national security of the United States;

(ii) interference with a criminal, counterterrorism, or counterintelligence investigation;

(iii) interference with diplomatic relations; or

(iv) danger to the life or physical safety of any person.

(2) Exception

(A) In general

A financial institution that receives a request under subsection (a), or officer, employee, or agent thereof, may disclose information otherwise subject to any applicable nondisclosure requirement to-

(i) those persons to whom disclosure is necessary in order to comply with the request;

(ii) an attorney in order to obtain legal advice or assistance regarding the request; or

(iii) other persons as permitted by the Director of the Federal Bureau of Investigation or the designee of the Director.

(B) Application

A person to whom disclosure is made under subparagraph (A) shall be subject to the nondisclosure requirements applicable to a person to whom a request is issued under subsection (a) in the same manner as the person to whom the request is issued.

(C) Notice

Any recipient that discloses to a person described in subparagraph (A) information otherwise subject to a nondisclosure requirement shall inform the person of the applicable nondisclosure requirement.

(D) Identification of disclosure recipients

At the request of the Director of the Federal Bureau of Investigation or the designee of the Director, any person making or intending to make a disclosure under clause (i) or (iii) of subparagraph (A) shall identify to the Director or such designee the person to whom such disclosure will be made or to whom such disclosure was made prior to the request.

(d) Judicial review

(1) In general

A request under subsection (a) or a nondisclosure requirement imposed in connection with such request under subsection (c) shall be subject to judicial review under section 3511 of title 18.

(2) Notice

A request under subsection (a) shall include notice of the availability of judicial review described in paragraph (1).

(e) Definition of "financial institution"

For purposes of this section, and sections 3415 and 3417 of this title insofar as they relate to the operation of this section, the term "financial institution" has the same meaning as in subsections (a)(2) and (c)(1) of section 5312 of title 31, except that, for purposes of this section, such term shall include only such a financial institution any part of which is located inside any State or territory of the United States, the District of Columbia, Puerto Rico, Guam, American Samoa, the Commonwealth of the Northern Mariana Islands, or the United States Virgin Islands.

Sec. 3415. Cost reimbursement

Except for records obtained pursuant to section 3403(d) or 3413(a) through (h) of this title, or as otherwise provided by law, a Government authority shall pay to the financial institution assembling or providing financial records pertaining to a customer and in accordance with procedures established by this chapter a fee for reimbursement for such costs as are reasonably necessary and which have been directly incurred in searching for, reproducing, or transporting books, papers, records, or other data required or requested to be produced. The Board of Governors of the Federal Reserve System shall, by regulation, establish the rates and conditions under which such payment may be made.

Sec. 3416. Jurisdiction

An action to enforce any provision of this chapter may be brought in any appropriate United States district court without regard to the amount in controversy within three years from the date on which the violation occurs or the date of discovery of such violation, whichever is later.

Sec. 3417. Civil penalties

(a) Liability of agencies or departments of United States or financial institutions
Any agency or department of the United States or financial institution obtaining or disclosing financial records or information contained therein in violation of this chapter is liable to the customer to whom such records relate in an amount equal to the sum of -

(1) $100 without regard to the volume of records involved;

(2) any actual damages sustained by the customer as a result of the disclosure;

(3) such punitive damages as the court may allow, where the violation is found to have been willful or intentional; and

(4) in the case of any successful action to enforce liability under this section, the costs of the action together with reasonable attorney's fees as determined by the court.

(b) Disciplinary action for willful or intentional violation of chapter by agents or employees of department or agency
Whenever the court determines that any agency or department of the United States has violated any provision of this chapter and the court finds that the circumstances surrounding the violation raise questions of whether an officer or employee of the department or agency acted willfully or intentionally with respect to the violation, the Director of the Office of Personnel Management shall promptly initiate a proceeding to determine whether disciplinary action is warranted against the agent or employee who was primarily responsible for the violation. The Director after investigation and consideration of the evidence submitted, shall submit his findings and recommendations to the administrative authority of the agency concerned and shall send copies of the findings and recommendations to the officer or employee or his representative. The administrative authority shall take the corrective action that the Director recommends.

(c) Good faith defense

United States
Right to Financial Privacy Act

Any financial institution or agent or employee thereof making a disclosure of financial records pursuant to this chapter in good-faith reliance upon a certificate by any Government authority or pursuant to the provisions of section 3413(l) of this title shall not be liable to the customer for such disclosure under this chapter, the constitution of any State, or any law or regulation of any State or any political subdivision of any State.

(d) Exclusive judicial remedies and sanctions

The remedies and sanctions described in this chapter shall be the only authorized judicial remedies and sanctions for violations of this chapter.

Sec. 3418. Injunctive relief

In addition to any other remedy contained in this chapter, injunctive relief shall be available to require that the procedures of this chapter are complied with. In the event of any successful action, costs together with reasonable attorney's fees as determined by the court may be recovered.

Sec. 3419. Suspension of limitations

If any individual files a motion or application under this chapter which has the effect of delaying the access of a Government authority to financial records pertaining to such individual, any applicable statute of limitations shall be deemed to be tolled for the period extending from the date such motion or application was filed until the date upon which the motion or application is decided.

Sec. 3420. Grand jury information; notification of certain persons prohibited

(a) Financial records about a customer obtained from a financial institution pursuant to a subpoena issued under the authority of a Federal grand jury -

(1) shall be returned and actually presented to the grand jury unless the volume of such records makes such return and actual presentation impractical in which case the grand jury shall be provided with a description of the contents of the records.;

(2) shall be used only for the purpose of considering whether to issue an indictment or presentment by that grand jury, or of prosecuting a crime for which that indictment or presentment is issued, or for a purpose authorized by rule 6(e) of the Federal Rules of Criminal Procedure or for a purpose authorized by section 1112(a);

(3) shall be destroyed or returned to the financial institution if not used for one of the purposes specified in paragraph (2); and

(4) shall not be maintained, or a description of the contents of such records shall not be maintained by any Government authority other than in the sealed records of the grand jury, unless such record has been used in the prosecution of a crime for

which the grand jury issued an indictment or presentment or for a purpose authorized by rule 6(e) of the Federal Rules of Criminal Procedure.

(b)

(1) No officer, director, partner, employee, or shareholder of, or agent or attorney for, a financial institution shall, directly or indirectly, notify any person named in a grand jury subpoena served on such institution in connection with an investigation relating to a possible -

(A) crime against any financial institution or supervisory agency or crime involving a violation of the Controlled Substance Act (21 U.S.C. 801 et seq.), the Controlled Substances Import and Export Act (21 U.S.C. 951 et seq.), section 1956 or 1957 of title 18, sections 5313, 5316 and 5324 of title 31, or section 6050I of title 26; or

(B) conspiracy to commit such a crime, about the existence or contents of such subpoena, or information that has been furnished to the grand jury in response to such subpoena.

(2) Section 1818 of this title and section 1786(k)(2) of this title shall apply to any violation of this subsection.

Sec. 3421. [Repealed]

Sec. 3422. Applicability to Securities and Exchange Commission

Except as provided in the Securities Exchange Act of 1934 (15 U.S.C. 78a et seq.), this chapter shall apply with respect to the Securities and Exchange Commission.

United States
Privacy Protection Act

PRIVACY PROTECTION ACT (1980)

Summary

The Privacy Protection Act of 1980 was passed in response to Zurcher v. Stanford Daily, 436 U.S. 547 (1978), which upheld broad law enforcement access to a newspaper's files. The Act establishes procedures for law enforcement seeking access to records and other information from the offices and employees of a media organization. In general, the Act prohibits both federal and state officers and employees from searching or seizing journalists' "work product" or the "documentary materials" in their possession. Under the Act, in order to gain access to journalists' information, law enforcement must obtain a court subpoena, rather than a simple search warrant.

The Act provides limited exceptions that allow the government to use a warrant, rather than a subpoena, to search for certain types of national security information, child pornography, evidence that the journalists themselves have committed a crime, or materials that must be immediately seized to prevent death or serious bodily injury. "Documentary materials" may also be seized if there is reason to believe that they would be destroyed in the time it took to obtain them using a subpoena, or if a court has ordered disclosure, the news organization has refused to release the materials, and all other remedies have been exhausted.

A search may be conducted only when there is probable cause to believe that an individual is involved in a crime. Also, only those who are involved with a particular investigation can do the searching. Although the statute specifically provides that its violation is not grounds to suppress evidence, it does provide a civil remedy in Federal court against either the government entity or individual officers involved in the search where a search warrant, rather than a subpoena, is used contrary to the Act's provisions.

References

Public 96-440 as amended 104-208. Codified at 42 U.S.C. § 2000aa et seq.
[https://www.law.cornell.edu/uscode/text/42/2000aa]

EPIC, Privacy Protection Act of 1980
[https://www.epic.org/privacy/ppa/]

42 U.S.C. 2000aa. Searches and seizures by government officers and employees in connection with investigation or prosecution of criminal offenses

(a) Work product materials

Notwithstanding any other law, it shall be unlawful for a government officer or employee, in connection with the investigation or prosecution of a criminal offense, to search for or seize any work product materials possessed by a person reasonably believed to have a purpose to disseminate to the public a newspaper, book, broadcast, or other similar form of public communication, in or affecting interstate or foreign commerce; but this provision shall not impair or affect the ability of any government officer or employee, pursuant to otherwise applicable law, to search for or seize such materials, if -

(1) there is probable cause to believe that the person possessing such materials has committed or is committing the criminal offense to which the materials relate: Provided, however, That a government officer or employee may not search for or seize such materials under the provisions of this paragraph if the offense to which the materials relate consists of the receipt, possession, communication, or withholding of such materials or the information contained therein (but such a search or seizure may be conducted under the provisions of this paragraph if the offense consists of the receipt, possession, or communication of information relating to the national defense, classified information, or restricted data under the provisions of section 793, 794, 797, or 798 of title 18, or section 2274, 2275, or 2277 of this title, or section 783 of title 50; or if the offense involves the production, possession, receipt, mailing, sale, distribution, shipment, or transportation of child pornography, the sexual exploitation of children, or the sale or purchase of children under section 2251, 2251A, 2252, or 2252A of title 18); or

(2) there is reason to believe that the immediate seizure of such materials is necessary to prevent the death of, or serious bodily injury to, a human being.

(b) Other documents

Notwithstanding any other law, it shall be unlawful for a government officer or employee, in connection with the investigation or prosecution of a criminal offense, to search for or seize documentary materials, other than work product materials, possessed by a person in connection with a purpose to disseminate to the public a newspaper, book, broadcast, or other similar form of public communication, in or affecting interstate or foreign commerce; but this provision shall not impair or affect the ability of any government officer or employee, pursuant to otherwise applicable law, to search for or seize such materials, if -

(1) there is probable cause to believe that the person possessing such materials has committed or is committing the criminal offense to which the materials relate: Provided, however, That a government officer or employee may not search for or seize such materials under the provisions of this paragraph if the offense to which the materials relate consists of the receipt, possession, communication, or withholding of such materials or the information contained therein (but such a search or seizure may be conducted under the provisions of this paragraph if the offense consists of the receipt, possession, or communication of information relating to the national defense, classified information, or restricted data under the provisions of section 793, 794, 797, or 798 of title 18, or section 2274, 2275, or 2277 of this title, or section 783 of title 50, or if the offense involves the production, possession, receipt, mailing, sale, distribution, shipment, or

transportation of child pornography, the sexual exploitation of children, or the sale or purchase of children under section 2251, 2251A, 2252, or 2252A of title 18);

(2) there is reason to believe that the immediate seizure of such materials is necessary to prevent the death of, or serious bodily injury to, a human being;

(3) there is reason to believe that the giving of notice pursuant to a subpoena duces tecum would result in the destruction, alteration, or concealment of such materials; or

(4) such materials have not been produced in response to a court order directing compliance with a subpoena duces tecum, and-

    (A) all appellate remedies have been exhausted; or

    (B) there is reason to believe that the delay in an investigation or trial occasioned by further proceedings relating to the subpoena would threaten the interests of justice.

(c) Objections to court ordered subpoenas; affidavits

In the event a search warrant is sought pursuant to paragraph (4)(B) of subsection (b) of this section, the person possessing the materials shall be afforded adequate opportunity to submit an affidavit setting forth the basis for any contention that the materials sought are not subject to seizure.

Sec. 2000aa-5. Border and customs searches

This chapter shall not impair or affect the ability of a government officer or employee, pursuant to otherwise applicable law, to conduct searches and seizures at the borders of, or at international points of entry into the United States in order to enforce the customs laws of the United States.

Sec. 2000aa-6. Civil actions by aggrieved persons

(a) Right of action

A person aggrieved by a search for or seizure of materials in violation of this chapter shall have a civil cause of action for damages for such search or seizure -

(1) against the United States, against a State which has waived its sovereign immunity under the Constitution to a claim for damages resulting from a violation of this chapter, or against any other governmental unit, all of which shall be liable for violations of this chapter by their officers or employees while acting within the scope or under color of their office or employment; and

(2) against an officer or employee of a State who has violated this chapter while acting within the scope or under color of his office or employment, if such State has not waived its sovereign immunity as provided in paragraph (1).

(b) Good faith defense

It shall be a complete defense to a civil action brought under paragraph (2) of subsection (a) of this section that the officer or employee had a reasonable good faith belief in the lawfulness of his conduct.

(c) Official immunity

The United States, a State, or any other governmental unit liable for violations of this chapter under subsection (a)(1) of this section, may not assert as a defense to a claim arising under this chapter the immunity of the officer or employee whose violation is complained of or his reasonable good faith belief in the lawfulness of his conduct, except that such a defense may be asserted if the violation complained of is that of a judicial officer.

(d) Exclusive nature of remedy

The remedy provided by subsection (a)(1) of this section against the United States, a State, or any other governmental unit is exclusive of any other civil action or proceeding for conduct constituting a violation of this chapter, against the officer or employee whose violation gave rise to the claim, or against the estate of such officer or employee.

(e) Admissibility of evidence

Evidence otherwise admissible in a proceeding shall not be excluded on the basis of a violation of this chapter.

(f) Damages; costs and attorneys' fees

A person having a cause of action under this section shall be entitled to recover actual damages but not less than liquidated damages of $1,000, and such reasonable attorneys' fees and other litigation costs reasonably incurred as the court, in its discretion, may award: Provided, however, That the United States, a State, or any other governmental unit shall not be liable for interest prior to judgment.

(g) Attorney General; claims settlement; regulations

The Attorney General may settle a claim for damages brought against the United States under this section, and shall promulgate regulations to provide for the commencement of an administrative inquiry following a determination of a violation of this chapter by an officer or employee of the United States and for the imposition of administrative sanctions against such officer or employee, if warranted.

(h) Jurisdiction

The district courts shall have original jurisdiction of all civil actions arising under this section.

Sec. 2000aa-7. Definitions

(a) "Documentary materials", as used in this chapter, means materials upon which information is recorded, and includes, but is not limited to, written or printed materials, photographs, motion picture films, negatives, video tapes, audio tapes, and other mechanically, magnetically[1] or electronically recorded cards, tapes, or discs, but does not include contraband or the fruits of a crime or things otherwise criminally possessed, or property designed or intended for use, or which is or has been used as, the means of committing a criminal offense.

(b) "Work product materials", as used in this chapter, means materials, other than contraband or the fruits of a crime or things otherwise criminally possessed, or property designed or intended for use, or which is or has been used, as the means of committing a criminal offense, and -

> (1) in anticipation of communicating such materials to the public, are prepared, produced, authored, or created, whether by the person in possession of the materials or by any other person;

> (2) are possessed for the purposes of communicating such materials to the public; and

> (3) include mental impressions, conclusions, opinions, or theories of the person who prepared, produced, authored, or created such material.

(c) "Any other governmental unit", as used in this chapter, includes the District of Columbia, the Commonwealth of Puerto Rico, any territory or possession of the United States, and any local government, unit of local government, or any unit of State government.

Sec. 2000aa-11. Guidelines for Federal officers and employees

(a) Procedures to obtain documentary evidence; protection of certain privacy interests
The Attorney General shall, within six months of October 13, 1980, issue guidelines for the procedures to be employed by any Federal officer or employee, in connection with the investigation or prosecution of an offense, to obtain documentary materials in the private possession of a person when the person is not reasonably believed to be a suspect in such offense or related by blood or marriage to such a suspect, and when the materials sought are not contraband or the fruits or instrumentalities of an offense. The Attorney General shall incorporate in such guidelines

> (1) a recognition of the personal privacy interests of the person in possession of such documentary materials;

> (2) a requirement that the least intrusive method or means of obtaining such materials be used which do not substantially jeopardize the availability or usefulness of the materials sought to be obtained;

> (3) a recognition of special concern for privacy interests in cases in which a search or seizure for such documents would intrude upon a known confidential relationship such as that which may exist between clergyman and parishioner; lawyer and client; or doctor and patient; and

---

[1] So in original. Probably should be "magnetically".

(4) a requirement that an application for a warrant to conduct a search governed by this subchapter be approved by an attorney for the government, except that in an emergency situation the application may be approved by another appropriate supervisory official if within 24 hours of such emergency the appropriate United States Attorney is notified.

(b) Use of search warrants; reports to Congress

The Attorney General shall collect and compile information on, and report annually to the Committees on the Judiciary of the Senate and the House of Representatives on the use of search warrants by Federal officers and employees for documentary materials described in subsection (a)(3) of this section.

Sec. 2000aa-12. Binding nature of guidelines; disciplinary actions for violations; legal proceedings for non-compliance prohibited

Guidelines issued by the Attorney General under this subchapter shall have the full force and effect of Department of Justice regulations and any violation of these guidelines shall make the employee or officer involved subject to appropriate administrative disciplinary action. However, an issue relating to the compliance, or the failure to comply, with guidelines issued pursuant to this subchapter may not be litigated, and a court may not entertain such an issue as the basis for the suppression or exclusion of evidence.

United States
Cable Communications Policy Act

CABLE COMMUNICATIONS POLICY
ACT (1984) [EXCERPT]

Summary

The Cable Communications Policy Act of 1984 provides a strong statutory framework for the protection of cable subscribers' personal information and incorporates the privacy principles set out in the OECD Privacy Guidelines of 1980.

Under the Act, cable providers must provide written notice to subscribers of their privacy rights at the time they first subscribe to the cable service and, thereafter, at least once a year. These notices must specify the kind of information that may be collected, how it will be used, to whom and how often it may be disclosed, how long it will be stored, how a subscriber may access this information and the liability imposed by the Act on providers.

Subject to limited exceptions, the Act requires providers to obtain the prior written or electronic consent of the cable subscriber before collecting or disclosing personally identifiable information. Cable providers do not need consent to collect personally identifiable information needed to offer or render cable service to a subscriber, or to detect cable piracy. Furthermore, they do not need consent to disclose subscriber information where disclosure is necessary to rendering a legitimate business activity related to a cable service or pursuant to a court order.

The Act grants cable subscribers the right to access the data collected about them and to correct any errors. It also provides for the destruction of personally identifiable information if that information is no longer necessary. Finally, it sets out a private right of action including actual and punitive damages, attorney's fees and litigation costs for violations of any of its provisions. State and local cable privacy laws are not preempted by the Act.

References

Public Law 98-549 as codified at 47 U.S.C. § 551 et seq.
[https://www.law.cornell.edu/uscode/text/47/551]

David H. Flaherty, *Protecting Privacy in Two-Way Electronic Services (1985)*

47 U.S.C. § 551. Protection of subscriber privacy

(a) Notice to subscriber regarding personally identifiable information; definitions

(1) At the time of entering into an agreement to provide any cable service or other service to a subscriber and at least once a year thereafter, a cable operator shall provide notice in the form of a separate, written statement to such subscriber which clearly and conspicuously informs the subscriber of -

(A) the nature of personally identifiable information collected or to be collected with respect to the subscriber and the nature of the use of such information;

(B) the nature, frequency, and purpose of any disclosure which may be made of such information, including an identification of the types of persons to whom the disclosure may be made;

(C) the period during which such information will be maintained by the cable operator;

(D) the times and place at which the subscriber may have access to such information in accordance with subsection (d) of this section; and

(E) the limitations provided by this section with respect to the collection and disclosure of information by a cable operator and the right of the subscriber under subsections (f) and (h) of this section to enforce such limitations.

In the case of subscribers who have entered into such an agreement before the effective date of this section, such notice shall be provided within 180 days of such date and at least once a year thereafter.

(2) For purposes of this section, other than subsection (h) of this section -

(A) the term "personally identifiable information" does not include any record of aggregate data which does not identify particular persons;

B) the term "other service" includes any wire or radio communications service provided using any of the facilities of a cable operator that are used in the provision of cable service; and

(C) the term "cable operator" includes, in addition to persons within the definition of cable operator in section 522 of this title, any person who

(i) is owned or controlled by, or under common ownership or control with, a cable operator, and

(ii) provides any wire or radio communications service.

(b) Collection of personally identifiable information using cable system

(1) Except as provided in paragraph (2), a cable operator shall not use the cable system to collect personally identifiable information concerning any subscriber without the prior written or electronic consent of the subscriber concerned.

(2) A cable operator may use the cable system to collect such information in order to -

(A) obtain information necessary to render a cable service or other service provided by the cable operator to the subscriber; or

(B) detect unauthorized reception of cable communications.

(c) Disclosure of personally identifiable information

(1) Except as provided in paragraph (2), a cable operator shall not disclose personally identifiable information concerning any subscriber without the prior written or electronic consent of the subscriber concerned and shall take such actions as are necessary to prevent unauthorized access to such information by a person other than the subscriber or cable operator.

(2) A cable operator may disclose such information if the disclosure is -

(A) necessary to render, or conduct a legitimate business activity related to, a cable service or other service provided by the cable operator to the subscriber;

(B) subject to subsection (h) of this section, made pursuant to a court order authorizing such disclosure, if the subscriber is notified of such order by the person to whom the order is directed;

(C) a disclosure of the names and addresses of subscribers to any cable service or other service, if -

    (i) the cable operator has provided the subscriber the opportunity to prohibit or limit such disclosure, and

    (ii) the disclosure does not reveal, directly or indirectly, the -

        (I) extent of any viewing or other use by the subscriber of a cable service or other service provided by the cable operator, or

        (II) the nature of any transaction made by the subscriber over the cable system of the cable operator; or

(D) to a government entity as authorized under chapters 119, 121, or 206 of title 18, United States Code, except that such disclosure shall not include records revealing cable subscriber selection of video programming from a cable operator.

(d) Subscriber access to information

A cable subscriber shall be provided access to all personally identifiable information regarding that subscriber which is collected and maintained by a cable operator. Such information shall be made available to the subscriber at reasonable times and at a convenient place designated by such cable operator. A cable subscriber shall be provided reasonable opportunity to correct any error in such information.

(e) Destruction of information

A cable operator shall destroy personally identifiable information if the information is no longer necessary for the purpose for which it was collected and there are no pending requests or orders for access to such information under subsection (d) of this section or pursuant to a court order.

(f) Civil action in United States district court; damages; attorney's fees and costs; nonexclusive nature of remedy

(1) Any person aggrieved by any act of a cable operator in violation of this section may bring a civil action in a United States district court.

(2) The court may award -

    (A) actual damages but not less than liquidated damages computed at the rate of $100 a day for each day of violation or $1,000, whichever is higher;

    (B) punitive damages; and

    (C) reasonable attorneys' fees and other litigation costs reasonably incurred.

(3) The remedy provided by this section shall be in addition to any other lawful remedy available to a cable subscriber.

(g) Regulation by States or franchising authorities

Nothing in this subchapter shall be construed to prohibit any State or any franchising authority from enacting or enforcing laws consistent with this section for the protection of subscriber privacy.

(h) Disclosure of information to governmental entity pursuant to court order

Except as provided in subsection (c)(2)(D), a governmental entity may obtain personally identifiable information concerning a cable subscriber pursuant to a court order only if, in the court proceeding relevant to such court order -

> (1) such entity offers clear and convincing evidence that the subject of the information is reasonably suspected of engaging in criminal activity and that the information sought would be material evidence in the case; and

> (2) the subject of the information is afforded the opportunity to appear and contest such entity's claim.

United States
Electronic Communications Privacy Act

ELECTRONIC COMMUNICATIONS
PRIVACY ACT (1986)

Summary

The Electronic Communications Privacy Act (ECPA) was enacted in 1986, as an amendment to the Omnibus Crime Control Act of 1968, to address technological advancements in communication networks and to bring "electronic communication" within the purview of federal law regarding wiretapping and bugging. ECPA covers wireless communication, email, and digitally transmitted conversations. ECPA criminalizes the interception of such communication, and provides civil remedies for violations. It also prevents government entities from requiring disclosure of electronic communications from a provider without proper procedure.

Title I of the Act protects electronic communications from unauthorized interception during transmission. In this way it mirrors the wiretap statute under the Omnibus Crime Control Act. Title II protects electronic data and messages in storage from unauthorized access and disclosure. Title II protects two kinds of data. First, it protects email and similar substantive electronic communications. Second, it protects data transfers between businesses and customers, such as fund transfers and computerized transfer of medical records.

It is useful to note that while the ECPA prohibits operators of electronic communications services from disclosing the content of messages in storage, this does not apply to purely internal email systems.

Both Title I and Title II mirror the principle of one-party consent found in the Omnibus Crime Control Act. Anyone may access electronic information if authorized by the user. Anyone may divulge such information with the consent of either the sender or recipient of the information. Sanctions under Title I include criminal penalties, a special injunction procedure, and a civil right of action. Penalties for Title II violations vary, but can include fines of up to $250,000 and prison sentences of no more than two years.

References

Public Law 90-351 (Omnibus Crime Control and Safe Streets Act of 1968)
[https://www.law.cornell.edu/uscode/text/18/2510]

Public Law 99-508 (Electronic Communications Privacy Act of 1986)
[https://www.law.cornell.edu/uscode/text/18/2701 html]

Public Law 103-414 (Communications Assistance for Law Enforcement
Act of 1994)
[https://www.law.cornell.edu/uscode/text/47/1001]

James G. Carr, *The Law of Electronic Surveillance* (Clark, Boardman &

Callaghan 2001)

Clifford S. Fishman & Anne T. McKenna, *Wiretapping and Eavesdropping* (Clark, Boardman & Callaghan 1995)

Congressional Findings (1968)

Section 801 of Pub. L. 90-351 provided that: "On the basis of its own investigations and of published studies, the Congress makes the following findings:

"(a) Wire communications are normally conducted through the use of facilities which form part of an interstate network. The same facilities are used for interstate and intrastate communications. There has been extensive wiretapping carried on without legal sanctions, and without the consent of any of the parties to the conversation. Electronic, mechanical, and other intercepting devices are being used to overhear oral conversations made in private, without the consent of any of the parties to such communications. The contents of these communications and evidence derived therefrom are being used by public and private parties as evidence in court and administrative proceedings, and by persons whose activities affect interstate commerce. The possession, manufacture, distribution, advertising, and use of these devices are facilitated by interstate commerce.

"(b) In order to protect effectively the privacy of wire and oral communications, to protect the integrity of court and administrative proceedings, and to prevent the obstruction of interstate commerce, it is necessary for Congress to define on a uniform basis the circumstances and conditions under which the interception of wire and oral communications may be authorized, to prohibit any unauthorized interception of such communications, and the use of the contents thereof in evidence in courts and administrative proceedings.

"(c) Organized criminals make extensive use of wire and oral communications in their criminal activities. The interception of such communications to obtain evidence of the commission of crimes or to prevent their commission is an indispensable aid to law enforcement and the administration of justice.

"(d) To safeguard the privacy of innocent persons, the interception of wire or oral communications where none of the parties to the communication has consented to the interception should be allowed only when authorized by a court of competent jurisdiction and should remain under the control and supervision of the authorizing court. Interception of wire and oral communications should further be limited to certain major types of offenses and specific categories of crime with assurances that the interception is justified and that the information obtained thereby will not be misused."

18 U.S.C. § 2510. Definitions

As used in this chapter -

United States
Electronic Communications Privacy Act

(1) "wire communication" means any aural transfer made in whole or in part through the use of facilities for the transmission of communications by the aid of wire, cable, or other like connection between the point of origin and the point of reception (including the use of such connection in a switching station) furnished or operated by any person engaged in providing or operating such facilities for the transmission of interstate or foreign communications or communications affecting interstate or foreign commerce;

(2) "oral communication" means any oral communication uttered by a person exhibiting an expectation that such communication is not subject to interception under circumstances justifying such expectation, but such term does not include any electronic communication;

(3) "State" means any State of the United States, the District of Columbia, the Commonwealth of Puerto Rico, and any territory or possession of the United States;

(4) "intercept" means the aural or other acquisition of the contents of any wire, electronic, or oral communication through the use of any electronic, mechanical, or other device.

(5) "electronic, mechanical, or other device" means any device or apparatus which can be used to intercept a wire, oral, or electronic communication other than -

(a) any telephone or telegraph instrument, equipment or facility, or any component thereof,

(i) furnished to the subscriber or user by a provider of wire or electronic communication service in the ordinary course of its business and being used by the subscriber or user in the ordinary course of its business or furnished by such subscriber or user for connection to the facilities of such service and used in the ordinary course of its business; or

(ii) being used by a provider of wire or electronic communication service in the ordinary course of its business, or by an investigative or law enforcement officer in the ordinary course of his duties;

(b) a hearing aid or similar device being used to correct subnormal hearing to not better than normal;

(6) "person" means any employee, or agent of the United States or any State or political subdivision thereof, and any individual, partnership, association, joint stock company, trust, or corporation;

(7) "Investigative or law enforcement officer" means any officer of the United States or of a State or political subdivision thereof, who is empowered by law to conduct investigations of or to make arrests for offenses enumerated in this chapter, and any attorney authorized by law to prosecute or participate in the prosecution of such offenses;

(8) "contents", when used with respect to any wire, oral, or electronic communication, includes any information concerning the substance, purport, or meaning of that communication;

(9) "Judge of competent jurisdiction" means -

(a) a judge of a United States district court or a United States court of appeals; and

(b) a judge of any court of general criminal jurisdiction of a State who is authorized by a statute of that State to enter orders authorizing interceptions of wire, oral, or electronic communications;

(10) "communication common carrier" has the meaning given that term in section 3 of the Communications Act of 1934;

(11) "aggrieved person" means a person who was a party to any intercepted wire, oral, or electronic communication or a person against whom the interception was directed;

(12) "electronic communication" means any transfer of signs, signals, writing, images, sounds, data, or intelligence of any nature transmitted in whole or in part by a wire, radio, electromagnetic, photoelectronic or photooptical system that affects interstate or foreign commerce, but does not include -

(A) any wire or oral communication;

(B) any communication made through a tone-only paging device;

(C) any communication from a tracking device (as defined in section 3117 of this title); or

(D) electronic funds transfer information stored by a financial institution in a communications system used for the electronic storage and transfer of funds;

(13) "user" means any person or entity who -

(A) uses an electronic communication service; and

(B) is duly authorized by the provider of such service to engage in such use;

(14) "electronic communications system" means any wire, radio, electromagnetic, photooptical or photoelectronic facilities for the transmission of wire or electronic communications, and any computer facilities or related electronic equipment for the electronic storage of such communications;

(15) "electronic communication service" means any service which provides to users thereof the ability to send or receive wire or electronic communications;

(16) "readily accessible to the general public" means, with respect to a radio communication, that such communication is not

(A) scrambled or encrypted;

(B) transmitted using modulation techniques whose essential parameters have been withheld from the public with the intention of preserving the privacy of such communication;

(C) carried on a subcarrier or other signal subsidiary to a radio transmission;

(D) transmitted over a communication system provided by a common carrier, unless the communication is a tone only paging system communication; or

(E) transmitted on frequencies allocated under part 25, subpart D, E, or F of part 74, or part 94 of the Rules of the Federal Communications Commission, unless, in the case of a communication transmitted on a frequency allocated under part 74 that is not exclusively allocated to broadcast auxiliary services, the communication is a two-way voice communication by radio;

(17) "electronic storage" means -

(A) any temporary, intermediate storage of a wire or electronic communication incidental to the electronic transmission thereof; and

(B) any storage of such communication by an electronic communication service for purposes of backup protection of such communication;

(18) "aural transfer" means a transfer containing the human voice at any point between and including the point of origin and the point of reception;

(19) "foreign intelligence information", for purposes of section 2517(6) of this title, means –

(A) information, whether or not concerning a United States person, that relates to the ability of the United States to protect against –

(i) actual or potential attack or other grave hostile acts of a foreign power or an agent of a foreign power;

(ii) sabotage or international terrorism by a foreign power or an agent of a foreign power; or

(iii) clandestine intelligence activities by an intelligence service or network of a foreign power or by an agent of a foreign power; or

(B) information, whether or not concerning a United States person, with respect to a foreign power or foreign territory that relates to –

(i) the national defense or the security of the United States; or

(ii) the conduct of the foreign affairs of the United States;

(20) "protected computer" has the meaning set forth in section 1030; and

(21) "computer trespasser" –

(A) means a person who accesses a protected computer without authorization and thus has no reasonable expectation of privacy in any communication transmitted to, through, or from the protected computer; and

(b) does not include a person known by the owner or operator of the protected computer to have an existing contractual relationship with the owner or operator of the protected computer for access to all or part of the protected computer.

Sec. 2511. Interception and disclosure of wire, oral, or electronic communications prohibited

(1) Except as otherwise specifically provided in this chapter any person who-

(a) intentionally intercepts, endeavors to intercept, or procures any other person to intercept or endeavor to intercept, any wire, oral, or electronic communication;

(b) intentionally uses, endeavors to use, or procures any other person to use or endeavor to use any electronic, mechanical, or other device to intercept any oral communication when-

(i) such device is affixed to, or otherwise transmits a signal through, a wire, cable, or other like connection used in wire communication; or

(ii) such device transmits communications by radio, or interferes with the transmission of such communication; or

(iii) such person knows, or has reason to know, that such device or any component thereof has been sent through the mail or transported in interstate or foreign commerce; or

(iv) such use or endeavor to use (A) takes place on the premises of any business or other commercial establishment the operations of which affect interstate or foreign commerce; or (B) obtains or is for the purpose of obtaining information relating to the operations of any business or other commercial establishment the operations of which affect interstate or foreign commerce; or

(v) such person acts in the District of Columbia, the Commonwealth of Puerto Rico, or any territory or possession of the United States;

(c) intentionally discloses, or endeavors to disclose, to any other person the contents of any wire, oral, or electronic communication, knowing or having reason to know that the information was obtained through the interception of a wire, oral, or electronic communication in violation of this subsection;

(d) intentionally uses, or endeavors to use, the contents of any wire, oral, or electronic communication, knowing or having reason to know that the information was obtained through the interception of a wire, oral, or electronic communication in violation of this subsection; or

(e)(i) intentionally discloses, or endeavors to disclose, to any other person the contents of any wire, oral, or electronic communication, intercepted by means authorized by sections 2511(2)(a)(ii), 2511(2)(b)–(c), 2511(2)(e), 2516, and 2518 of this chapter, (ii) knowing or having reason to know that the information was obtained through the interception of such a communication in connection with a criminal investigation, (iii) having obtained or received the information in connection with a criminal investigation, and (iv) with intent to improperly obstruct, impede, or interfere with a duly authorized criminal investigation, shall be punished as provided in subsection (4) or shall be subject to suit as provided in subsection (5).

(2)(a)(i) It shall not be unlawful under this chapter for an operator of a switchboard, or an officer, employee, or agent of a provider of wire or electronic communication service, whose facilities are used in the transmission of a wire or electronic communication, to intercept, disclose, or use that communication in the normal course of his employment while engaged in any activity which is a necessary incident to the rendition of his service or to the protection of the rights or property of the provider of that service, except that a provider of wire communication service to the public shall not utilize service observing or random monitoring except for mechanical or service quality control checks.

(ii) Notwithstanding any other law, providers of wire or electronic communication service, their officers, employees, and agents, landlords, custodians, or other persons, are authorized to provide information, facilities, or technical assistance to persons authorized by law to intercept wire, oral, or electronic communications or to conduct electronic surveillance, as defined in section 101 of the Foreign Intelligence Surveillance Act of 1978, if such provider, its officers, employees, or agents, landlord, custodian, or other specified person, has been provided with-

(A) a court order directing such assistance or a court order pursuant to section 704 of the Foreign Intelligence Surveillance Act of 1978 signed by the authorizing judge, or

(B) a certification in writing by a person specified in section 2518(7) of this title or the Attorney General of the United States that no warrant or court order is required by law, that all statutory requirements have been met, and that the specified assistance is required, setting forth the period of time during which the provision of the information, facilities, or technical assistance is authorized and specifying the information, facilities, or technical assistance required. No provider of wire or electronic communication service, officer, employee, or agent thereof, or landlord, custodian, or other specified person shall disclose the existence of any interception or surveillance or the device used to accomplish the interception or surveillance with respect to which the person has been furnished a court order or certification under this chapter, except as may otherwise be required by legal process and then only after prior notification to the Attorney General or to the principal prosecuting attorney of a State or any political subdivision of a State, as may be appropriate. Any such disclosure, shall render such person liable for the civil damages provided for in section 2520. No cause of action shall lie in any court against any provider of wire or electronic communication service, its officers, employees, or agents, landlord, custodian, or other specified person for providing information, facilities, or assistance in accordance with the terms of a court order, statutory authorization, or certification under this chapter.

(iii) If a certification under subparagraph (ii)(B) for assistance to obtain foreign intelligence information is based on statutory authority, the certification shall identify the specific statutory provision and shall certify that the statutory requirements have been met.

(b) It shall not be unlawful under this chapter for an officer, employee, or agent of the Federal Communications Commission, in the normal course of his employment and in discharge of the monitoring responsibilities exercised by the Commission in the enforcement of chapter 5 of title 47 of the United States Code, to intercept a wire or electronic communication, or oral communication transmitted by radio, or to disclose or use the information thereby obtained.

(c) It shall not be unlawful under this chapter for a person acting under color of law to intercept a wire, oral, or electronic communication, where such person is a party to the communication or one of the parties to the communication has given prior consent to such interception.

(d) It shall not be unlawful under this chapter for a person not acting under color of law to intercept a wire, oral, or electronic communication where such person is a party to the communication or where one of the parties to the communication has given prior consent to such interception unless such communication is intercepted for the purpose of committing any criminal or tortious act in violation of the Constitution or laws of the United States or of any State.

(e) Notwithstanding any other provision of this title or section 705 or 706 of the Communications Act of 1934, it shall not be unlawful for an officer, employee, or agent of the United States in the normal course of his official duty to conduct electronic surveillance, as defined in section 101 of the Foreign Intelligence Surveillance Act of 1978, as authorized by that Act.

(f) Nothing contained in this chapter or chapter 121 or 206 of this title, or section 705 of the Communications Act of 1934, shall be deemed to affect the acquisition by the United States Government of foreign intelligence information from international or foreign communications, or foreign intelligence activities conducted in accordance with otherwise applicable Federal law involving a foreign electronic communications system, utilizing a means other than electronic surveillance as defined in section 101 of the Foreign Intelligence Surveillance Act of 1978, and procedures in this chapter or chapter 121 and the Foreign Intelligence Surveillance Act of 1978 shall be the exclusive means by which electronic surveillance, as defined in section 101 of such Act, and the interception of domestic wire, oral, and electronic communications may be conducted.

(g) It shall not be unlawful under this chapter or chapter 121 of this title for any person-

(i) to intercept or access an electronic communication made through an electronic communication system that is configured so that such electronic communication is readily accessible to the general public;

(ii) to intercept any radio communication which is transmitted-

(I) by any station for the use of the general public, or that relates to ships, aircraft, vehicles, or persons in distress;

(II) by any governmental, law enforcement, civil defense, private land mobile, or public safety communications system, including police and fire, readily accessible to the general public;

(III) by a station operating on an authorized frequency within the bands allocated to the amateur, citizens band, or general mobile radio services; or

(IV) by any marine or aeronautical communications system;

(iii) to engage in any conduct which-

(I) is prohibited by section 633 of the Communications Act of 1934; or

(II) is excepted from the application of section 705(a) of the Communications Act of 1934 by section 705(b) of that Act;

(iv) to intercept any wire or electronic communication the transmission of which is causing harmful interference to any lawfully operating station or consumer electronic equipment, to the extent necessary to identify the source of such interference; or

(v) for other users of the same frequency to intercept any radio communication made through a system that utilizes frequencies monitored by individuals engaged in the provision or the use of such system, if such communication is not scrambled or encrypted.

(h) It shall not be unlawful under this chapter-

(i) to use a pen register or a trap and trace device (as those terms are defined for the purposes of chapter 206 (relating to pen registers and trap and trace devices) of this title); or

(ii) for a provider of electronic communication service to record the fact that a wire or electronic communication was initiated or completed in order to protect such provider, another provider furnishing service toward the completion of the wire or electronic communication, or a user of that service, from fraudulent, unlawful or abusive use of such service.

(i) It shall not be unlawful under this chapter for a person acting under color of law to intercept the wire or electronic communications of a computer trespasser transmitted to, through, or from the protected computer, if-

(I) the owner or operator of the protected computer authorizes the interception of the computer trespasser's communications on the protected computer;

(II) the person acting under color of law is lawfully engaged in an investigation;

(III) the person acting under color of law has reasonable grounds to believe that the contents of the computer trespasser's communications will be relevant to the investigation; and

(IV) such interception does not acquire communications other than those transmitted to or from the computer trespasser.

(3)(a) Except as provided in paragraph (b) of this subsection, a person or entity providing an electronic communication service to the public shall not intentionally divulge the contents of any communication (other than one to such person or entity, or an agent thereof) while in transmission on that service to any person or entity other than an addressee or intended recipient of such communication or an agent of such addressee or intended recipient.

(b) A person or entity providing electronic communication service to the public may divulge the contents of any such communication-

(i) as otherwise authorized in section 2511(2)(a) or 2517 of this title;

(ii) with the lawful consent of the originator or any addressee or intended recipient of such communication;

(iii) to a person employed or authorized, or whose facilities are used, to forward such communication to its destination; or

(iv) which were inadvertently obtained by the service provider and which appear to pertain to the commission of a crime, if such divulgence is made to a law enforcement agency.

(4)(a) Except as provided in paragraph (b) of this subsection or in subsection (5), whoever violates subsection (1) of this section shall be fined under this title or imprisoned not more than five years, or both.

(b) Conduct otherwise an offense under this subsection that consists of or relates to the interception of a satellite transmission that is not encrypted or scrambled and that is transmitted-

(i) to a broadcasting station for purposes of retransmission to the general public; or

(ii) as an audio subcarrier intended for redistribution to facilities open to the public, but not including data transmissions or telephone calls, is not an offense under this subsection unless the conduct is for the purposes of direct or indirect commercial advantage or private financial gain.

(5)(a)(i) If the communication is-

(A) a private satellite video communication that is not scrambled or encrypted and the conduct in violation of this chapter is the private viewing of that communication and is not for a tortious or illegal purpose or for purposes of direct or indirect commercial advantage or private commercial gain; or

(B) a radio communication that is transmitted on frequencies allocated under subpart D of part 74 of the rules of the Federal Communications Commission that is not scrambled or encrypted and the conduct in violation of this chapter is not for a tortious or illegal purpose or for purposes of direct or indirect commercial advantage or private commercial gain, then the person who engages in such conduct shall be subject to suit by the Federal Government in a court of competent jurisdiction.

(ii) In an action under this subsection-

(A) if the violation of this chapter is a first offense for the person under paragraph (a) of subsection (4) and such person has not been found liable in a civil action under section 2520 of this title, the Federal Government shall be entitled to appropriate injunctive relief; and

(B) if the violation of this chapter is a second or subsequent offense under paragraph (a) of subsection (4) or such person has been found liable in any prior civil action under section 2520, the person shall be subject to a mandatory $500 civil fine.

(b) The court may use any means within its authority to enforce an injunction issued under paragraph (ii)(A), and shall impose a civil fine of not less than $500 for each violation of such an injunction.

Sec. 2512. Manufacture, distribution, possession, and advertising of wire, oral, or electronic communication intercepting devices prohibited

(1) Except as otherwise specifically provided in this chapter, any person who intentionally

(a) sends through the mail, or sends or carries in interstate or foreign commerce, any electronic, mechanical, or other device, knowing or having reason to know that the design of such device renders it primarily useful for the purpose of the surreptitious interception of wire, oral, or electronic communications;

(b) manufactures, assembles, possesses, or sells any electronic, mechanical, or other device, knowing or having reason to know that the design of such device renders it primarily useful for the purpose of the surreptitious interception of wire, oral, or electronic communications, and that such device or any component thereof has been or will be sent through the mail or transported in interstate or foreign commerce; or

(c) places in any newspaper, magazine, handbill, or other publication or disseminates by electronic means any advertisement of

(i) any electronic, mechanical, or other device knowing or having reason to know that the design of such device renders it primarily useful for the purpose of the surreptitious interception of wire, oral, or electronic communications; or

(ii) any other electronic, mechanical, or other device, where such advertisement promotes the use of such device for the purpose of the surreptitious interception of wire, oral, or electronic communications, knowing the content of the advertisement and knowing or having reason to know that such advertisement will be sent through the mail or transported in interstate or foreign commerce, shall be fined under this title or imprisoned not more than five years, or both.

(2) It shall not be unlawful under this section for

(a) a provider of wire or electronic communication service or an officer, agent, or employee of, or a person under contract with, such a provider, in the normal course of the business of providing that wire or electronic communication service, or

(b) an officer, agent, or employee of, or a person under contract with, the United States, a State, or a political subdivision thereof, in the normal course of the activities of the United States, a State, or a political subdivision thereof, to send through the mail, send or carry in interstate or foreign commerce, or manufacture, assemble, possess, or sell any electronic, mechanical, or other device knowing or having reason to know that the design of such device renders it primarily useful for the purpose of the surreptitious interception of wire, oral, or electronic communications.

(3) It shall not be unlawful under this section to advertise for sale a device described in subsection (1) of this section if the advertisement is mailed, sent, or carried in interstate or foreign commerce solely to a domestic provider of wire or electronic communication service or to an agency of the United States, a State, or a political subdivision thereof which is duly authorized to use such device.

Sec. 2513. Confiscation of wire, oral, or electronic communication intercepting devices

Any electronic, mechanical, or other device used, sent, carried, manufactured, assembled, possessed, sold, or advertised in violation of section 2511 or section 2512 of this chapter may be seized and forfeited to the United States. All provisions of law relating to (1) the seizure, summary and judicial forfeiture, and condemnation of vessels, vehicles, merchandise, and baggage for violations of the customs laws contained in title 19 of the United States Code, (2) the disposition of such vessels, vehicles, merchandise, and baggage or the proceeds from the sale thereof, (3) the remission or mitigation of such forfeiture, (4) the compromise of claims, and (5) the award of compensation to informers in respect of such forfeitures, shall apply to seizures and forfeitures incurred, or alleged to have been incurred, under the provisions of this section, insofar as applicable and not inconsistent with the provisions of this section; except that such duties as are imposed upon the collector of customs or any other person with respect to the seizure and forfeiture of vessels, vehicles, merchandise, and baggage under the provisions of the customs laws contained in title 19 of the United States Code shall be performed with respect to seizure and forfeiture of electronic, mechanical, or other intercepting devices under this section by such officers, agents, or other persons as may be authorized or designated for that purpose by the Attorney General.

Sec. 2514. [Repealed]

Sec. 2515. Prohibition of use as evidence of intercepted wire or oral communications

Whenever any wire or oral communication has been intercepted, no part of the contents of such communication and no evidence derived therefrom may be received in evidence in any trial, hearing, or other proceeding in or before any court, grand jury, department, officer, agency, regulatory body, legislative committee, or other authority of the United States, a State, or a political subdivision thereof if the disclosure of that information would be in violation of this chapter.

United States
Electronic Communications Privacy Act

Sec. 2516. Authorization for interception of wire, oral, or electronic communications

(1) The Attorney General, Deputy Attorney General, Associate Attorney General, or any Assistant Attorney General, any acting Assistant Attorney General, or any Deputy Assistant Attorney General or acting Deputy Assistant Attorney General in the Criminal Division specially designated by the Attorney General, may authorize an application to a Federal judge of competent jurisdiction for, and such judge may grant in conformity with section 2518 of this chapter an order authorizing or approving the interception of wire or oral communications by the Federal Bureau of Investigation, or a Federal agency having responsibility for the investigation of the offense as to which the application is made, when such interception may provide or has provided evidence of -

(a) any offense punishable by death or by imprisonment for more than one year under sections 2122 and 2274 through 2277 of title 42 of the United States Code (relating to the enforcement of the Atomic Energy Act of 1954), section 2284 of title 42 of the United States Code (relating to sabotage of nuclear facilities or fuel), or under the following chapters of this title: chapter 37 (relating to espionage), chapter 55 (relating to kidnapping), chapter 90 (relating to protection of trade secrets), chapter 105 (relating to sabotage), chapter 115 (relating to treason), chapter 102 (relating to riots), chapter 65 (relating to malicious mischief), chapter 111 (relating to destruction of vessels), or chapter 81 (relating to piracy);

(b) a violation of section 186 or section 501(c) of title 29, United States Code (dealing with restrictions on payments and loans to labor organizations), or any offense which involves murder, kidnapping, robbery, or extortion, and which is punishable under this title;

(c) any offense which is punishable under the following sections of this title: section 201 (bribery of public officials and witnesses), section 215 (relating to bribery of bank officials), section 224 (bribery in sporting contests), subsection (d), (e), (f), (g), (h), or (i) of section 844 (unlawful use of explosives), section 1032 (relating to concealment of assets), section 1084 (transmission of wagering information), section 751 (relating to escape), section 1014 (relating to loans and credit applications generally; renewals and discounts), sections 1503, 1512, and 1513 (influencing or injuring an officer, juror, or witness generally), section 1510 (obstruction of criminal investigations), section 1511 (obstruction of State or local law enforcement), section 1591 (sex trafficking of children by force, fraud, or coercion), section 1751 (Presidential and Presidential staff assassination, kidnapping, and assault), section 1951 (interference with commerce by threats or violence), section 1952 (interstate and foreign travel or transportation in aid of racketeering enterprises), section 1958 (relating to use of interstate commerce facilities in the commission of murder for hire), section 1959 (relating to violent crimes in aid of racketeering activity), section 1954 (offer, acceptance, or solicitation to influence operations of employee benefit plan), section 1955 (prohibition of business enterprises of gambling), section 1956 (laundering of monetary instruments),section 1957 (relating to engaging in monetary transactions in property derived from specified unlawful activity), section 659 (theft from interstate shipment), section 664 (embezzlement from pension and welfare funds), section 1343 (fraud by wire, radio, or television), section 1344 (relating to bank fraud), sections 2251 and 2252 (sexual exploitation of children), section 2251A (selling or buying of children), section 2252A (relating to material constituting or containing child pornography), section 1466A (relating to child obscenity), section 2260 (production of sexually explicit depictions of a minor for importation into the United States), sections 2421, 2422, 2423, and 2425 (relating to transportation for illegal sexual activity and related crimes), sections 2312,2313, 2314, and 2315 (interstate transportation of stolen property), section 2321 (relating to trafficking in certain motor vehicles or motor vehicle parts), section 1203 (relating to hostage taking), section 1029 (relating to fraud and related activity in connection with access devices), section 3146 (relating to penalty for failure to appear), section 3521(b)(3) (relating to witness relocation and assistance), section 32 (relating to destruction of aircraft or aircraft facilities), section 38 (relating to aircraft parts fraud), section 1963 (violations with respect to racketeer influenced and corrupt organizations), section 115 (relating to threatening or retaliating against a Federal official), section 1341 (relating to mail fraud), a felony violation of section 1030 (relating to computer fraud and abuse), section 351 (violations with respect to congressional, Cabinet, or Supreme Court assassinations, kidnapping, and assault), section 831 (relating to prohibited transactions involving nuclear materials), section 33 (relating to destruction of motor vehicles or motor vehicle facilities), section 175 (relating to biological weapons), section 175c (relating to variola virus), section 1992 (relating to wrecking trains), a felony violation of section 1028 (relating to production of false identification documentation), section 1425 (relating to the procurement of citizenship or nationalization unlawfully), section 1426 (relating to the reproduction of naturalization or citizenship papers), section 1427 (relating to the sale of naturalization or citizenship papers), section 1541 (relating to passport issuance without authority), section 1542 (relating to false statements in passport applications), section 1543 (relating to forgery or false use of passports), section 1544 (relating to misuse of passports), or section 1546 (relating to fraud and misuse of visas, permits, and other documents);

(d) any offense involving counterfeiting punishable under section 471, 472, or 473 of this title;

(e) any offense involving fraud connected with a case under title 11 or the manufacture, importation, receiving, concealment, buying, selling, or otherwise dealing in narcotic drugs, marihuana, or other dangerous drugs, punishable under any law of the United States;

(f) any offense including extortionate credit transactions under sections 892, 893, or 894 of this title;

(g) a violation of section 5322 of title 31, United States Code (dealing with the reporting of currency transactions);

(h) any felony violation of sections 2511 and 2512 (relating to interception and disclosure of certain communications and to certain intercepting devices) of this title;

(i) any felony violation of chapter 71 (relating to obscenity) of this title;

(j) any violation of section 60123(b) (relating to destruction of a natural gas pipeline) or 46502 (relating to aircraft piracy) of title 49;

(k) any criminal violation of section 2778 of title 22 (relating to the Arms Export Control Act);

(l) the location of any fugitive from justice from an offense described in this section;

(m) a violation of section 274, 277, or 278 of the Immigration
and Nationality Act (8 U.S.C. 1324, 1327, or 1328) (relating to the smuggling of aliens);

(n) any felony violation of sections 922 and 924 of title 18, United States Code (relating to firearms);

(o) any violation of section 5861 of the Internal Revenue Code of 1986 (relating to firearms);

(p) a felony violation of section 1028 (relating to production of false identification documents), section 1542 (relating to false statements in passport applications), section 1546 (relating to fraud and misuse of visas, permits, and other documents) of this title or a violation of section 274, 277, or 278 of the Immigration and Nationality Act (relating to the smuggling of aliens);

(q) any criminal violation of section 229 (relating to chemical weapons); or sections 2332, 2332a, 2332b, 2332d, 2332f, 2332g, 2332h, 2339A, 2339B, or 2339C of this title (relating to terrorism); or

(r) any conspiracy to commit any offense described in any subparagraph of this paragraph.

(2) The principal prosecuting attorney of any State, or the principal prosecuting attorney of any political subdivision thereof, if such attorney is authorized by a statute of that State to make application to a State court judge of competent jurisdiction for an order authorizing or approving the interception of wire, oral, or electronic communications, may apply to such judge for, and such judge may grant in conformity with section 2518 of this chapter and with the applicable State statute an order authorizing, or approving the interception of wire, oral, or electronic communications

by investigative or law enforcement officers having responsibility for the investigation of the offense as to which the application is made, when such interception may provide or has provided evidence of the commission of the offense of murder, kidnapping, gambling, robbery, bribery, extortion, or dealing in narcotic drugs, marihuana or other dangerous drugs, or other crime dangerous to life, limb, or property, and punishable by imprisonment for more than one year, designated in any applicable State statute authorizing such interception, or any conspiracy to commit any of the foregoing offenses.

(3) Any attorney for the Government (as such term is defined for the purposes of the Federal Rules of Criminal Procedure) may authorize an application to a Federal judge of competent jurisdiction for, and such judge may grant, in conformity with section 2518 of this title, an order authorizing or approving the interception of electronic communications by an investigative or law enforcement officer having responsibility for the investigation of the offense as to which the application is made, when such interception may provide or has provided evidence of any Federal felony.

Sec. 2517. Authorization for disclosure and use of intercepted wire, oral, or electronic communications

(1) Any investigative or law enforcement officer who, by any means authorized by this chapter, has obtained knowledge of the contents of any wire, oral, or electronic communication, or evidence derived therefrom, may disclose such contents to another investigative or law enforcement officer to the extent that such disclosure is appropriate to the proper performance of the official duties of the officer making or receiving the disclosure.

(2) Any investigative or law enforcement officer who, by any means authorized by this chapter, has obtained knowledge of the contents of any wire, oral, or electronic communication or evidence derived therefrom may use such contents to the extent such use is appropriate to the proper performance of his official duties.

(3) Any person who has received, by any means authorized by this chapter, any information concerning a wire, oral, or electronic communication, or evidence derived therefrom intercepted in accordance with the provisions of this chapter may disclose the contents of that communication or such derivative evidence while giving testimony under oath or affirmation in any proceeding held under the authority of the United States or of any State or political subdivision thereof.

(4) No otherwise privileged wire, oral, or electronic communication intercepted in accordance with, or in violation of, the provisions of this chapter shall lose its privileged character.

(5) When an investigative or law enforcement officer, while engaged in intercepting wire, oral, or electronic communications in the manner authorized herein, intercepts wire, oral, or electronic communications relating to offenses other than those specified

in the order of authorization or approval, the contents thereof, and evidence derived therefrom, may be disclosed or used as provided in subsections (1) and (2) of this section. Such contents and any evidence derived therefrom may be used under subsection (3) of this section when authorized or approved by a judge of competent jurisdiction where such judge finds on subsequent application that the contents were otherwise intercepted in accordance with the provisions of this chapter. Such application shall be made as soon as practicable.

(6) Any investigative or law enforcement officer, or attorney for the Government, who by any means authorized by this chapter, has obtained knowledge of the contents of any wire, oral, or electronic communication, or evidence derived therefrom, may disclose such contents to any other Federal law enforcement, intelligence, protective, immigration, national defense, or national security official to the extent that such contents include foreign intelligence or counterintelligence (as defined in section 3 of the National Security Act of 1947 (50 U.S.C. 401a), or foreign intelligence information (as defined in subsection (19) of section 2510 of this title), to assist the official who is to receive that information in the performance of his official duties. Any Federal official who receives information pursuant to this provision may use that information only as necessary in the conduct of that person's official duties subject to any limitations on the unauthorized disclosure of such information.

(7) Any investigative or law enforcement officer, or other Federal official in carrying out official duties as such Federal official, who by any means authorized by this chapter, has obtained knowledge of the contents of any wire, oral, or electronic communication, or evidence derived therefrom, may disclose such contents or derivative evidence to a foreign investigative or law enforcement officer to the extent that such disclosure is appropriate to the proper performance of the official duties of the officer making or receiving the disclosure, and foreign investigative or law enforcement officers may use or disclose such contents or derivative evidence to the extent such use or disclosure is appropriate to the proper performance of their official duties.

(8) Any investigative or law enforcement officer, or other Federal official in carrying out official duties as such Federal official, who by any means authorized by this chapter, has obtained knowledge of the contents of any wire, oral, or electronic communication, or evidence derived therefrom, may disclose such contents or derivative evidence to any appropriate Federal, State, local, or foreign government official to the extent that such contents or derivative evidence reveals a threat of actual or potential attack or other grave hostile acts of a foreign power or an agent of a foreign power, domestic or international sabotage, domestic or international terrorism, or clandestine intelligence gathering activities by an intelligence service or network of a foreign power or by an agent of a foreign power, within the United States or elsewhere, for the purpose of preventing or responding to such a threat. Any official

who receives information pursuant to this provision may use that information only as necessary in the conduct of that person's official duties subject to any limitations on the unauthorized disclosure of such information, and any State, local, or foreign official who receives information pursuant to this provision may use that information only consistent with such guidelines as the Attorney General and Director of National Intelligence shall jointly issue.

Sec. 2518. Procedure for interception of wire, oral, or electronic communications

(1) Each application for an order authorizing or approving the interception of a wire, oral, or electronic communication under this chapter shall be made in writing upon oath or affirmation to a judge of competent jurisdiction and shall state the applicant's authority to make such application. Each application shall include the following information:

    (a) the identity of the investigative or law enforcement officer making the application, and the officer authorizing the application;

    (b) a full and complete statement of the facts and circumstances relied upon by the applicant, to justify his belief that an order should be issued, including

        (i) details as to the particular offense that has been, is being, or is about to be committed,

        (ii) except as provided in subsection (11), a particular description of the nature and location of the facilities from which or the place where the communication is to be intercepted,

        (iii) a particular description of the type of communications sought to be intercepted,

        (iv) the identity of the person, if known, committing the offense and whose communications are to be intercepted;

    (c) a full and complete statement as to whether or not other investigative procedures have been tried and failed or why they reasonably appear to be unlikely to succeed if tried or to be too dangerous;

    (d) a statement of the period of time for which the interception is required to be maintained. If the nature of the investigation is such that the authorization for interception should not automatically terminate when the described type of communication has been first obtained, a particular description of facts establishing probable cause to believe that additional communications of the same type will occur thereafter;

    (e) a full and complete statement of the facts concerning all previous applications known to the individual authorizing and making the application, made to any judge for authorization to intercept, or for approval of interceptions of, wire, oral, or electronic communications involving any of the same persons, facilities or places specified in the application, and the action taken by the judge on each such application; and

(f) where the application is for the extension of an order, a statement setting forth the results thus far obtained from the interception, or a reasonable explanation of the failure to obtain such results.

(2) The judge may require the applicant to furnish additional testimony or documentary evidence in support of the application.

(3) Upon such application the judge may enter an ex parte order, as requested or as modified, authorizing or approving interception of wire, oral, or electronic communications within the territorial jurisdiction of the court in which the judge is sitting (and outside that jurisdiction but within the United States in the case of a mobile interception device authorized by a Federal court within such jurisdiction), if the judge determines on the basis of the facts submitted by the applicant that -

(a) there is probable cause for belief that an individual is committing, has committed, or is about to commit a particular offense enumerated in section 2516 of this chapter;

(b) there is probable cause for belief that particular communications concerning that offense will be obtained through such interception;

(c) normal investigative procedures have been tried and have failed or reasonably appear to be unlikely to succeed if tried or to be too dangerous;

(d) except as provided in subsection (11), there is probable cause for belief that the facilities from which, or the place where, the wire, oral, or electronic communications are to be intercepted are being used, or are about to be used, in connection with the commission of such offense, or are leased to, listed in the name of, or commonly used by such person.

(4) Each order authorizing or approving the interception of any wire, oral, or electronic communication under this chapter shall specify -

(a) the identity of the person, if known, whose communications are to be intercepted;

(b) the nature and location of the communications facilities as to which, or the place where, authority to intercept is granted;

(c) a particular description of the type of communication sought to be intercepted, and a statement of the particular offense to which it relates;

(d) the identity of the agency authorized to intercept the communications, and of the person authorizing the application; and

(e) the period of time during which such interception is authorized, including a statement as to whether or not the interception shall automatically terminate when the described communication has been first obtained.

An order authorizing the interception of a wire, oral, or electronic communication under this chapter shall, upon request of the applicant, direct that a provider of wire or electronic communication service, landlord, custodian or other person shall furnish the applicant forthwith all information, facilities, and technical assistance necessary to accomplish the interception unobtrusively and with a minimum of interference with the services that such service provider, landlord, custodian, or person is according the person whose communications are to be intercepted. Any provider of wire or electronic communication service, landlord, custodian or other person furnishing such facilities or technical assistance shall be compensated therefor by the applicant for reasonable expenses incurred in providing such facilities or assistance. Pursuant to section 2522 of this chapter, an order may also be issued to enforce the assistance capability and capacity requirements under the Communications Assistance for Law Enforcement Act.

(5) No order entered under this section may authorize or approve the interception of any wire, oral, or electronic communication for any period longer than is necessary to achieve the objective of the authorization, nor in any event longer than thirty days. Such thirty-day period begins on the earlier of the day on which the investigative or law enforcement officer first begins to conduct an interception under the order or ten days after the order is entered. Extensions of an order may be granted, but only upon application for an extension made in accordance with subsection (1) of this section and the court making the findings required by subsection (3) of this section. The period of extension shall be no longer than the authorizing judge deems necessary to achieve the purposes for which it was granted and in no event for longer than thirty days. Every order and extension thereof shall contain a provision that the authorization to intercept shall be executed as soon as practicable, shall be conducted in such a way as to minimize the interception of communications not otherwise subject to interception under this chapter, and must terminate upon attainment of the authorized objective, or in any event in thirty days. In the event the intercepted communication is in a code or foreign language, and an expert in that foreign language or code is not reasonably available during the interception period, minimization may be accomplished as soon as practicable after such interception. An interception under this chapter may be conducted in whole or in part by Government personnel, or by an individual operating under a contract with the Government, acting under the supervision of an investigative or law enforcement officer authorized to conduct the interception.

(6) Whenever an order authorizing interception is entered pursuant to this chapter, the order may require reports to be made to the judge who issued the order showing what progress has been made toward achievement of the authorized objective and the need for continued interception. Such reports shall be made at such intervals as the judge may require.

(7) Notwithstanding any other provision of this chapter, any investigative or law enforcement officer, specially designated by the Attorney General, the Deputy Attorney General, the Associate Attorney General, or by the principal prosecuting

attorney of any State or subdivision thereof acting pursuant to a statute of that State, who reasonably determines that -

(a) an emergency situation exists that involves -

(i) immediate danger of death or serious physical injury to any person,

(ii) conspiratorial activities threatening the national security interest, or

(iii) conspiratorial activities characteristic of organized crime, that requires a wire, oral, or electronic communication to be intercepted before an order authorizing such interception can, with due diligence, be obtained, and

(b) there are grounds upon which an order could be entered under this chapter to authorize such interception, may intercept such wire, oral, or electronic communication if an application for an order approving the interception is made in accordance with this section within forty-eight hours after the interception has occurred, or begins to occur. In the absence of an order, such interception shall immediately terminate when the communication sought is obtained or when the application for the order is denied, whichever is earlier. In the event such application for approval is denied, or in any other case where the interception is terminated without an order having been issued, the contents of any wire, oral, or electronic communication intercepted shall be treated as having been obtained in violation of this chapter, and an inventory shall be served as provided for in subsection (d) of this section on the person named in the application.

(8)

(a) The contents of any wire, oral, or electronic communication intercepted by any means authorized by this chapter shall, if possible, be recorded on tape or wire or other comparable device. The recording of the contents of any wire, oral, or electronic communication under this subsection shall be done in such way as will protect the recording from editing or other alterations. Immediately upon the expiration of the period of the order, or extensions thereof, such recordings shall be made available to the judge issuing such order and sealed under his directions. Custody of the recordings shall be wherever the judge orders. They shall not be destroyed except upon an order of the issuing or denying judge and in any event shall be kept for ten years. Duplicate recordings may be made for use or disclosure pursuant to the provisions of subsections (1) and (2) of section 2517 of this chapter for investigations. The presence of the seal provided for by this subsection, or a satisfactory explanation for the absence thereof, shall be a prerequisite for the use or disclosure of the contents of any wire, oral, or electronic communication or evidence derived therefrom under subsection (3) of section 2517.

(b) Applications made and orders granted under this chapter shall be sealed by the judge. Custody of the applications and orders shall be wherever the judge directs. Such applications and orders shall be disclosed only upon a showing of good cause before a judge of competent jurisdiction and shall not be destroyed except on order of the issuing or denying judge, and in any event shall be kept for ten years.

(c) Any violation of the provisions of this subsection may be punished as contempt of the issuing or denying judge.

(d) Within a reasonable time but not later than ninety days after the filing of an application for an order of approval under section 2518(7)(b) which is denied or the termination of the period of an order or extensions thereof, the issuing or denying judge shall cause to be served, on the persons named in the order or the application, and such other parties to intercepted communications as the judge may determine in his discretion that is in the interest of justice, an inventory which shall include notice of -

(1) the fact of the entry of the order or the application;

(2) the date of the entry and the period of authorized, approved or disapproved interception, or the denial of the application; and

(3) the fact that during the period wire, oral, or electronic communications were or were not intercepted.

The judge, upon the filing of a motion, may in his discretion make available to such person or his counsel for inspection such portions of the intercepted communications, applications and orders as the judge determines to be in the interest of justice. On an ex parte showing of good cause to a judge of competent jurisdiction the serving of the inventory required by this subsection may be postponed.

(9) The contents of any wire, oral, or electronic communication intercepted pursuant to this chapter or evidence derived therefrom shall not be received in evidence or otherwise disclosed in any trial, hearing, or other proceeding in a Federal or State court unless each party, not less than ten days before the trial, hearing, or proceeding, has been furnished with a copy of the court order, and accompanying application, under which the interception was authorized or approved. This ten-day period may be waived by the judge if he finds that it was not possible to furnish the party with the above information ten days before the trial, hearing, or proceeding and that the party will not be prejudiced by the delay in receiving such information.

(10)

(a) Any aggrieved person in any trial, hearing, or proceeding in or before any court, department, officer, agency, regulatory body, or other authority of the United States, a State, or a political subdivision thereof, may move to suppress the contents of any wire or oral communication intercepted pursuant to this chapter, or evidence derived therefrom, on the grounds that -

(i) the communication was unlawfully intercepted;

(ii) the order of authorization or approval under which it was intercepted is insufficient on its face; or

(iii) the interception was not made in conformity with the order of authorization or approval.

Such motion shall be made before the trial, hearing, or proceeding unless there was no opportunity to make such motion or the person was not aware of the grounds of the motion. If the motion is granted, the contents of the intercepted wire or oral communication, or evidence derived therefrom, shall be treated as having been obtained in violation of this chapter. The judge, upon the filing of such motion by the aggrieved person, may in his discretion make available to the aggrieved person or his counsel for inspection such portions of the intercepted communication or evidence derived therefrom as the judge determines to be in the interests of justice.

(b) In addition to any other right to appeal, the United States shall have the right to appeal from an order granting a motion to suppress made under paragraph (a) of this subsection, or the denial of an application for an order of approval, if the United States attorney shall certify to the judge or other official granting such motion or denying such application that the appeal is not taken for purposes of delay. Such appeal shall be taken within thirty days after the date the order was entered and shall be diligently prosecuted.

(c) The remedies and sanctions described in this chapter with respect to the interception of electronic communications are the only judicial remedies and sanctions for nonconstitutional violations of this chapter involving such communications.

(11) The requirements of subsections (1)(b)(ii) and (3)(d) of this section relating to the specification of the facilities from which, or the place where, the communication is to be intercepted do not apply if -

(a) in the case of an application with respect to the interception of an oral communication -

(i) the application is by a Federal investigative or law enforcement officer and is approved by the Attorney General, the Deputy Attorney General, the Associate Attorney General, an Assistant Attorney General, or an acting Assistant Attorney General;

(ii) the application contains a full and complete statement as to why such specification is not practical and identifies the person committing the offense and whose communications are to be intercepted; and

(iii) the judge finds that such specification is not practical; and

(b) in the case of an application with respect to a wire or electronic communication -

(i) the application is by a Federal investigative or law enforcement officer and is approved by the Attorney General, the Deputy Attorney General, the

Associate Attorney General, an Assistant Attorney General, or an acting Assistant Attorney General;

(ii) the application identifies the person believed to be committing the offense and whose communications are to be intercepted and the applicant makes a showing that there is probable cause to believe that the person's actions could have the effect of thwarting interception from a specified facility;

(iii) the judge finds that such showing has been adequately made; and

(iv) the order authorizing or approving the interception is limited to interception only for such time as it is reasonable to presume that the person identified in the application is or was reasonably proximate to the instrument through which such communication will be or was transmitted.

(12) An interception of a communication under an order with respect to which the requirements of subsections (1)(b)(ii) and (3)(d) of this section do not apply by reason of subsection (11)(a) shall not begin until the place where the communication is to be intercepted is ascertained by the person implementing the interception order. A provider of wire or electronic communications service that has received an order as provided for in subsection (11)(b) may move the court to modify or quash the order on the ground that its assistance with respect to the interception cannot be performed in a timely or reasonable fashion. The court, upon notice to the government, shall decide such a motion expeditiously.

Sec. 2519. Reports concerning intercepted wire, oral, or electronic communications

(1) In January of each year, any judge who has issued an order (or an extension thereof) under section 2518 that expired during the preceding year, or who has denied approval of an interception during that year, shall report to the Administrative Office of the United States Courts-

(a) the fact that an order or extension was applied for;

(b) the kind of order or extension applied for (including whether or not the order was an order with respect to which the requirements of sections 2518(1)(b)(ii) and 2518(3)(d) of this title did not apply by reason of section 2518(11) of this title);

(c) the fact that the order or extension was granted as applied for, was modified, or was denied;

(d) the period of interceptions authorized by the order, and the number and duration of any extensions of the order;

(e) the offense specified in the order or application, or extension of an order;

(f) the identity of the applying investigative or law enforcement officer and agency making the application and the person authorizing the application; and

(g) the nature of the facilities from which or the place where communications were to be intercepted.

United States
Electronic Communications Privacy Act

(2) In March of each year the Attorney General, an Assistant Attorney General specially designated by the Attorney General, or the principal prosecuting attorney of a State, or the principal prosecuting attorney for any political subdivision of a State, shall report to the Administrative Office of the United States Courts-

(a) the information required by paragraphs (a) through (g) of subsection (1) of this section with respect to each application for an order or extension made during the preceding calendar year;

(b) a general description of the interceptions made under such order or extension, including (i) the approximate nature and frequency of incriminating communications intercepted, (ii) the approximate nature and frequency of other communications intercepted, (iii) the approximate number of persons whose communications were intercepted, (iv) the number of orders in which encryption was encountered and whether such encryption prevented law enforcement from obtaining the plain text of communications intercepted pursuant to such order, and (v) the approximate nature, amount, and cost of the manpower and other resources used in the interceptions;

(c) the number of arrests resulting from interceptions made under such order or extension, and the offenses for which arrests were made;

(d) the number of trials resulting from such interceptions;

(e) the number of motions to suppress made with respect to such interceptions, and the number granted or denied;

(f) the number of convictions resulting from such interceptions and the offenses for which the convictions were obtained and a general assessment of the importance of the interceptions; and

(g) the information required by paragraphs (b) through (f) of this subsection with respect to orders or extensions obtained in a preceding calendar year.

(3) In June of each year the Director of the Administrative Office of the United States Courts shall transmit to the Congress a full and complete report concerning the number of applications for orders authorizing or approving the interception of wire, oral, or electronic communications pursuant to this chapter and the number of orders and extensions granted or denied pursuant to this chapter during the preceding calendar year. Such report shall include a summary and analysis of the data required to be filed with the Administrative Office by subsections (1) and (2) of this section. The Director of the Administrative Office of the United States Courts is authorized to issue binding regulations dealing with the content and form of the reports required to be filed by subsections (1) and (2) of this section.

Sec. 2520. Recovery of civil damages authorized

(a) In General. - Except as provided in section 2511(2)(a)(ii), any person whose wire, oral, or electronic communication is intercepted, disclosed, or intentionally used in violation of this chapter may in a civil action recover from the person or entity, other than the United States, which engaged in that violation such relief as may be appropriate.

(b) Relief. - In an action under this section, appropriate relief includes -

(1) such preliminary and other equitable or declaratory relief as may be appropriate;

(2) damages under subsection (c) and punitive damages in appropriate cases; and

(3) a reasonable attorney's fee and other litigation costs reasonably incurred.

(c) Computation of Damages. -

(1) In an action under this section, if the conduct in violation of this chapter is the private viewing of a private satellite video communication that is not scrambled or encrypted or if the communication is a radio communication that is transmitted on frequencies allocated under subpart D of part 74 of the rules of the Federal Communications Commission that is not scrambled or encrypted and the conduct is not for a tortious or illegal purpose or for purposes of direct or indirect commercial advantage or private commercial gain, then the court shall assess damages as follows:

(A) If the person who engaged in that conduct has not previously been enjoined under section 2511(5) and has not been found liable in a prior civil action under this section, the court shall assess the greater of the sum of actual damages suffered by the plaintiff, or statutory damages of not less than $50 and not more than $500.

(B) If, on one prior occasion, the person who engaged in that conduct has been enjoined under section 2511(5) or has been found liable in a civil action under this section, the court shall assess the greater of the sum of actual damages suffered by the plaintiff, or statutory damages of not less than $100 and not more than $1000.

(2) In any other action under this section, the court may assess as damages whichever is the greater of -

(A) the sum of the actual damages suffered by the plaintiff and any profits made by the violator as a result of the violation; or

(B) statutory damages of whichever is the greater of $100 a day for each day of violation or $10,000.

(d) Defense. - A good faith reliance on -

(1) a court warrant or order, a grand jury subpoena, a legislative authorization, or a statutory authorization;

(2) a request of an investigative or law enforcement officer under section 2518(7) of this title; or

(3) a good faith determination that section 2511(3) or 2511(2)(i) of this title permitted the conduct complained of;

is a complete defense against any civil or criminal action brought under this chapter or any other law.

(e) Limitation. - A civil action under this section may not be commenced later than two years after the date upon which the claimant first has a reasonable opportunity to discover the violation.

(f) Administrative Discipline. - If a court or appropriate department or agency determines that the United States or any of its departments or agencies has violated any provision of this chapter, and the court or appropriate department or agency finds that the circumstances surrounding the violation raise serious questions about whether or not an officer or employee of the United States acted willfully or intentionally with respect to the violation, the department or agency shall, upon receipt of a true and correct copy of the decision and findings of the court or appropriate department or agency promptly initiate a proceeding to determine whether disciplinary action against the officer or employee is warranted. If the head of the department or agency involved determines that disciplinary action is not warranted, he or she shall notify the Inspector General with jurisdiction over the department or agency concerned and shall provide the Inspector General with the reasons for such determination.

(g) Improper Disclosure is Violation. - Any willful disclosure or use by an investigative or law enforcement officer or governmental entity of information beyond the extent permitted by section 2517 is a violation of this chapter for purposes of section 2520(a).

Sec. 2521. Injunction against illegal interception

Whenever it shall appear that any person is engaged or is about to engage in any act which constitutes or will constitute a felony violation of this chapter, the Attorney General may initiate a civil action in a district court of the United States to enjoin such violation. The court shall proceed as soon as practicable to the hearing and determination of such an action, and may, at any time before final determination, enter such a restraining order or prohibition, or take such other action, as is warranted to prevent a continuing and substantial injury to the United States or to any person or class of persons for whose protection the action is brought. A proceeding under this section is governed by the Federal Rules of Civil Procedure, except that, if an indictment has been returned against the respondent, discovery is governed by the Federal Rules of Criminal Procedure.

Sec. 2522. Enforcement of the Communications Assistance for Law Enforcement Act

(a) Enforcement by Court Issuing Surveillance Order. - If a court authorizing an interception under this chapter, a State statute, or the Foreign Intelligence Surveillance Act of 1978 (50 U.S.C. 1801 et seq.) or authorizing use of a pen register or a trap and trace device under chapter 206 or a State statute finds that a telecommunications carrier has failed to comply with the requirements of the Communications Assistance for Law

Enforcement Act, the court may, in accordance with section 108 of such Act, direct that the carrier comply forthwith and may direct that a provider of support services to the carrier or the manufacturer of the carrier's transmission or switching equipment furnish forthwith modifications necessary for the carrier to comply.

(b) Enforcement Upon Application by Attorney General. - The Attorney General may, in a civil action in the appropriate United States district court, obtain an order, in accordance with section 108 of the Communications Assistance for Law Enforcement Act, directing that a telecommunications carrier, a manufacturer of telecommunications transmission or switching equipment, or a provider of telecommunications support services comply with such Act.

(c) Civil Penalty. -

(1) In general. - A court issuing an order under this section against a telecommunications carrier, a manufacturer of telecommunications transmission or switching equipment, or a provider of telecommunications support services may impose a civil penalty of up to $10,000 per day for each day in violation after the issuance of the order or after such future date as the court may specify.

(2) Considerations. - In determining whether to impose a civil penalty and in determining its amount, the court shall take into account -

(A) the nature, circumstances, and extent of the violation;

(B) the violator's ability to pay, the violator's good faith efforts to comply in a timely manner, any effect on the violator's ability to continue to do business, the degree of culpability, and the length of any delay in undertaking efforts to comply; and

(C) such other matters as justice may require.

(d) Definitions. - As used in this section, the terms defined in section 102 of the Communications Assistance for Law Enforcement Act have the meanings provided, respectively, in such section.

Sec. 2701. Unlawful access to stored communications

(a) Offense. - Except as provided in subsection (c) of this section whoever -

(1) intentionally accesses without authorization a facility through which an electronic communication service is provided; or

(2) intentionally exceeds an authorization to access that facility; and thereby obtains, alters, or prevents authorized access to a wire or electronic communication while it is in electronic storage in such system shall be punished as provided in subsection (b) of this section.

(b) Punishment. - The punishment for an offense under subsection (a) of this section is -

(1) if the offense is committed for purposes of commercial advantage, malicious destruction or damage, or private commercial gain, or in furtherance of any

criminal or tortious act in violation of the Constitution or laws of the United States or any State -

(A) a fine under this title or imprisonment for not more than 5 years, or both, in the case of a first offense under this subparagraph; and

(B) a fine under this title or imprisonment for not more than 10 years, or both, for any subsequent offense under this subparagraph; and

(2) in any other case -

(A) a fine under this title or imprisonment for not more than 1 year or both, in the case of a first offense under this paragraph; and

(B) a fine under this title or imprisonment for not more than 5 years, or both, in the case of an offense under this subparagraph that occurs after a conviction of another offense under this section.

(c) Exceptions. - Subsection (a) of this section does not apply with respect to conduct authorized

(1) by the person or entity providing a wire or electronic communications service;

(2) by a user of that service with respect to a communication of or intended for that user; or

(3) in section 2703, 2704 or 2518 of this title.

Sec. 2702. Voluntary Disclosure of Customer Communications or Records

(a) Prohibitions.-Except as provided in subsection (b) or (c)-

(1) a person or entity providing an electronic communication service to the public shall not knowingly divulge to any person or entity the contents of a communication while in electronic storage by that service; and

(2) a person or entity providing remote computing service to the public shall not knowingly divulge to any person or entity the contents of any communication which is carried or maintained on that service-

(A) on behalf of, and received by means of electronic transmission from (or created by means of computer processing of communications received by means of electronic transmission from), a subscriber or customer of such service;

(B) solely for the purpose of providing storage or computer processing services to such subscriber or customer, if the provider is not authorized to access the contents of any such communications for purposes of providing any services other than storage or computer processing; and

(3) a provider of remote computing service or electronic communication service to the public shall not knowingly divulge a record or other information pertaining to a subscriber to or customer of such service (not including the contents of communications covered by paragraph (1) or (2)) to any governmental entity.

(b) Exceptions for disclosure of communications.-A provider described in subsection (a) may divulge the contents of a communication-

(1) to an addressee or intended recipient of such communication or an agent of such addressee or intended recipient;

(2) as otherwise authorized in section 2517, 2511(2)(a), or 2703 of this title;

(3) with the lawful consent of the originator or an addressee or intended recipient of such communication, or the subscriber in the case of remote computing service;

(4) to a person employed or authorized or whose facilities are used to forward such communication to its destination;

(5) as may be necessarily incident to the rendition of the service or to the protection of the rights or property of the provider of that service;

(6) to the National Center for Missing and Exploited Children, in connection with a report submitted thereto under section 2258A;

(7) to a law enforcement agency-

(A) if the contents-

(i) were inadvertently obtained by the service provider; and

(ii) appear to pertain to the commission of a crime; or

[(B) Repealed. Pub. L. 108–21, title V, §508(b)(1)(A), Apr. 30, 2003, 117 Stat. 684]

(8) to a governmental entity, if the provider, in good faith, believes that an emergency involving danger of death or serious physical injury to any person requires disclosure without delay of communications relating to the emergency.

(c) Exceptions for Disclosure of Customer Records.-A provider described in subsection (a) may divulge a record or other information pertaining to a subscriber to or customer of such service (not including the contents of communications covered by subsection (a)(1) or (a)(2))-

(1) as otherwise authorized in section 2703;

(2) with the lawful consent of the customer or subscriber;

(3) as may be necessarily incident to the rendition of the service or to the protection of the rights or property of the provider of that service;

(4) to a governmental entity, if the provider, in good faith, believes that an emergency involving danger of death or serious physical injury to any person requires disclosure without delay of information relating to the emergency;

(5) to the National Center for Missing and Exploited Children, in connection with a report submitted thereto under section 2258A; or

(6) to any person other than a governmental entity.

United States
Electronic Communications Privacy Act

(d) Reporting of Emergency Disclosures.-On an annual basis, the Attorney General shall submit to the Committee on the Judiciary of the House of Representatives and the Committee on the Judiciary of the Senate a report containing-

(1) the number of accounts from which the Department of Justice has received voluntary disclosures under subsection (b)(8);

(2) a summary of the basis for disclosure in those instances where-

(A) voluntary disclosures under subsection (b)(8) were made to the Department of Justice; and

(B) the investigation pertaining to those disclosures was closed without the filing of criminal charges; and

(3) the number of accounts from which the Department of Justice has received voluntary disclosures under subsection (c)(4).

Sec. 2703. Required Disclosure of Customer Communications or Records

(a) Contents of Wire or Electronic Communications in Electronic Storage.-A governmental entity may require the disclosure by a provider of electronic communication service of the contents of a wire or electronic communication, that is in electronic storage in an electronic communications system for one hundred and eighty days or less, only pursuant to a warrant issued using the procedures described in the Federal Rules of Criminal Procedure (or, in the case of a State court, issued using State warrant procedures) by a court of competent jurisdiction. A governmental entity may require the disclosure by a provider of electronic communications services of the contents of a wire or electronic communication that has been in electronic storage in an electronic communications system for more than one hundred and eighty days by the means available under subsection (b) of this section.

(b) Contents of Wire or Electronic Communications in a Remote Computing Service.-

(1) A governmental entity may require a provider of remote computing service to disclose the contents of any wire or electronic communication to which this paragraph is made applicable by paragraph (2) of this subsection-

(A) without required notice to the subscriber or customer, if the governmental entity obtains a warrant issued using the procedures described in the Federal Rules of Criminal Procedure (or, in the case of a State court, issued using State warrant procedures) by a court of competent jurisdiction; or

(B) with prior notice from the governmental entity to the subscriber or customer if the governmental entity-

(i) uses an administrative subpoena authorized by a Federal or State statute or a Federal or State grand jury or trial subpoena; or

(ii) obtains a court order for such disclosure under subsection (d) of this section;

except that delayed notice may be given pursuant to section 2705 of this title.

(2) Paragraph (1) is applicable with respect to any wire or electronic communication that is held or maintained on that service-

(A) on behalf of, and received by means of electronic transmission from (or created by means of computer processing of communications received by means of electronic transmission from), a subscriber or customer of such remote computing service; and

(B) solely for the purpose of providing storage or computer processing services to such subscriber or customer, if the provider is not authorized to access the contents of any such communications for purposes of providing any services other than storage or computer processing.

(c) Records Concerning Electronic Communication Service or Remote Computing Service.-

(1) A governmental entity may require a provider of electronic communication service or remote computing service to disclose a record or other information pertaining to a subscriber to or customer of such service (not including the contents of communications) only when the governmental entity-

(A) obtains a warrant issued using the procedures described in the Federal Rules of Criminal Procedure (or, in the case of a State court, issued using State warrant procedures) by a court of competent jurisdiction;

(B) obtains a court order for such disclosure under subsection (d) of this section;

(C) has the consent of the subscriber or customer to such disclosure;

(D) submits a formal written request relevant to a law enforcement investigation concerning telemarketing fraud for the name, address, and place of business of a subscriber or customer of such provider, which subscriber or customer is engaged in telemarketing (as such term is defined in section 2325 of this title); or

(E) seeks information under paragraph (2).

(2) A provider of electronic communication service or remote computing service shall disclose to a governmental entity the-

(A) name;

(B) address;

(C) local and long distance telephone connection records, or records of session times and durations;

(D) length of service (including start date) and types of service utilized;

(E) telephone or instrument number or other subscriber number or identity, including any temporarily assigned network address; and

(F) means and source of payment for such service (including any credit card or bank account number), of a subscriber to or customer of such service when the governmental entity uses an administrative subpoena authorized by a Federal or

United States
Electronic Communications Privacy Act

State statute or a Federal or State grand jury or trial subpoena or any means available under paragraph (1).

(3) A governmental entity receiving records or information under this subsection is not required to provide notice to a subscriber or customer.

(d) Requirements for Court Order.-A court order for disclosure under subsection (b) or (c) may be issued by any court that is a court of competent jurisdiction and shall issue only if the governmental entity offers specific and articulable facts showing that there are reasonable grounds to believe that the contents of a wire or electronic communication, or the records or other information sought, are relevant and material to an ongoing criminal investigation. In the case of a State governmental authority, such a court order shall not issue if prohibited by the law of such State. A court issuing an order pursuant to this section, on a motion made promptly by the service provider, may quash or modify such order, if the information or records requested are unusually voluminous in nature or compliance with such order otherwise would cause an undue burden on such provider.

(e) No Cause of Action Against a Provider Disclosing Information Under This Chapter.-No cause of action shall lie in any court against any provider of wire or electronic communication service, its officers, employees, agents, or other specified persons for providing information, facilities, or assistance in accordance with the terms of a court order, warrant, subpoena, statutory authorization, or certification under this chapter.

(f) Requirement To Preserve Evidence.-

(1) In general.-A provider of wire or electronic communication services or a remote computing service, upon the request of a governmental entity, shall take all necessary steps to preserve records and other evidence in its possession pending the issuance of a court order or other process.

(2) Period of retention.-Records referred to in paragraph (1) shall be retained for a period of 90 days, which shall be extended for an additional 90-day period upon a renewed request by the governmental entity.

(g) Presence of Officer Not Required.-Notwithstanding section 3105 of this title, the presence of an officer shall not be required for service or execution of a search warrant issued in accordance with this chapter requiring disclosure by a provider of electronic communications service or remote computing service of the contents of communications or records or other information pertaining to a subscriber to or customer of such service.

Sec. 2704. Backup preservation

(a) Backup Preservation. -

(1) A governmental entity acting under section 2703(b)(2) may include in its subpoena or court order a requirement that the service provider to whom the

request is directed create a backup copy of the contents of the electronic communications sought in order to preserve those communications. Without notifying the subscriber or customer of such subpoena or court order, such service provider shall create such backup copy as soon as practicable consistent with its regular business practices and shall confirm to the governmental entity that such backup copy has been made. Such backup copy shall be created within two business days after receipt by the service provider of the subpoena or court order.

(2) Notice to the subscriber or customer shall be made by the governmental entity within three days after receipt of such confirmation, unless such notice is delayed pursuant to section 2705(a).

(3) The service provider shall not destroy such backup copy until the later of -

(A) the delivery of the information; or

(B) the resolution of any proceedings (including appeals of any proceeding) concerning the government's subpoena or court order.

(4) The service provider shall release such backup copy to the requesting governmental entity no sooner than fourteen days after the governmental entity's notice to the subscriber or customer if such service provider -

(A) has not received notice from the subscriber or customer that the subscriber or customer has challenged the governmental entity's request; and

(B) has not initiated proceedings to challenge the request of the governmental entity.

(5) A governmental entity may seek to require the creation of a backup copy under subsection (a)(1) of this section if in its sole discretion such entity determines that there is reason to believe that notification under section 2703 of this title of the existence of the subpoena or court order may result in destruction of or tampering with evidence. This determination is not subject to challenge by the subscriber or customer or service provider.

(b) Customer Challenges. -

(1) Within fourteen days after notice by the governmental entity to the subscriber or customer under subsection (a)(2) of this section, such subscriber or customer may file a motion to quash such subpoena or vacate such court order, with copies served upon the governmental entity and with written notice of such challenge to the service provider. A motion to vacate a court order shall be filed in the court which issued such order. A motion to quash a subpoena shall be filed in the appropriate United States district court or State court. Such motion or application shall contain an affidavit or sworn statement-

(A) stating that the applicant is a customer or subscriber to the service from which the contents of electronic communications maintained for him have been sought; and

(B) stating the applicant's reasons for believing that the records sought are not relevant to a legitimate law enforcement inquiry or that there has not been substantial compliance with the provisions of this chapter in some other respect.

(2) Service shall be made under this section upon a governmental entity by delivering or mailing by registered or certified mail a copy of the papers to the person, office, or department specified in the notice which the customer has received pursuant to this chapter. For the purposes of this section, the term "delivery" has the meaning given that term in the Federal Rules of Civil Procedure.

(3) If the court finds that the customer has complied with paragraphs (1) and (2) of this subsection, the court shall order the governmental entity to file a sworn response, which may be filed in camera if the governmental entity includes in its response the reasons which make in camera review appropriate. If the court is unable to determine the motion or application on the basis of the parties' initial allegations and response, the court may conduct such additional proceedings as it deems appropriate. All such proceedings shall be completed and the motion or application decided as soon as practicable after the filing of the governmental entity's response.

(4) If the court finds that the applicant is not the subscriber or customer for whom the communications sought by the governmental entity are maintained, or that there is a reason to believe that the law enforcement inquiry is legitimate and that the communications sought are relevant to that inquiry, it shall deny the motion or application and order such process enforced. If the court finds that the applicant is the subscriber or customer for whom the communications sought by the governmental entity are maintained, and that there is not a reason to believe that the communications sought are relevant to a legitimate law enforcement inquiry, or that there has not been substantial compliance with the provisions of this chapter, it shall order the process quashed.

(5) A court order denying a motion or application under this section shall not be deemed a final order and no interlocutory appeal may be taken therefrom by the customer.

Sec. 2705. Delayed notice

(a) Delay of Notification. -

(1) A governmental entity acting under section 2703(b) of this title may -

(A) where a court order is sought, include in the application a request, which the court shall grant, for an order delaying the notification required under section 2703(b) of this title for a period not to exceed ninety days, if the court determines that there is reason to believe that notification of the existence of the court order may have an adverse result described in paragraph (2) of this subsection; or

(B) where an administrative subpoena authorized by a Federal or State statute or a Federal or State grand jury subpoena is obtained, delay the notification required under section 2703(b) of this title for a period not to exceed ninety days upon the execution of a written certification of a supervisory official that there is reason to believe that notification of the existence of the subpoena may have an adverse result described in paragraph (2) of this subsection.

(2) An adverse result for the purposes of paragraph (1) of this subsection is -

(A) endangering the life or physical safety of an individual;

(B) flight from prosecution;

(C) destruction of or tampering with evidence;

(D) intimidation of potential witnesses; or

(E) otherwise seriously jeopardizing an investigation or unduly delaying a trial.

(3) The governmental entity shall maintain a true copy of certification under paragraph (1)(B).

(4) Extensions of the delay of notification provided in section 2703 of up to ninety days each may be granted by the court upon application, or by certification by a governmental entity, but only in accordance with subsection (b) of this section.

(5) Upon expiration of the period of delay of notification under paragraph (1) or (4) of this subsection, the governmental entity shall serve upon, or deliver by registered or first-class mail to, the customer or subscriber a copy of the process or request together with notice that -

(A) states with reasonable specificity the nature of the law enforcement inquiry; and

(B) informs such customer or subscriber -

(i) that information maintained for such customer or subscriber by the service provider named in such process or request was supplied to or requested by that governmental authority and the date on which the supplying or request took place;

(ii) that notification of such customer or subscriber was delayed;

(iii) what governmental entity or court made the certification or determination pursuant to which that delay was made; and

(iv) which provision of this chapter allowed such delay.

(6) As used in this subsection, the term "supervisory official" means the investigative agent in charge or assistant investigative agent in charge or an equivalent of an investigating agency's headquarters or regional office, or the chief prosecuting attorney or the first assistant prosecuting attorney or an equivalent of a prosecuting attorney's headquarters or regional office.

(b) Preclusion of Notice to Subject of Governmental Access. -

United States
Electronic Communications Privacy Act

A governmental entity acting under section 2703, when it is not required to notify the subscriber or customer under section 2703(b)(1), or to the extent that it may delay such notice pursuant to subsection (a) of this section, may apply to a court for an order commanding a provider of electronic communications service or remote computing service to whom a warrant, subpoena, or court order is directed, for such period as the court deems appropriate, not to notify any other person of the existence of the warrant, subpoena, or court order. The court shall enter such an order if it determines that there is reason to believe that notification of the existence of the warrant, subpoena, or court order will result in -

(1) endangering the life or physical safety of an individual;

(2) flight from prosecution;

(3) destruction of or tampering with evidence;

(4) intimidation of potential witnesses; or

(5) otherwise seriously jeopardizing an investigation or unduly delaying a trial.

Sec. 2706. Cost reimbursement

(a) Payment. -

Except as otherwise provided in subsection (c), a governmental entity obtaining the contents of communications, records, or other information under section 2702, 2703, or 2704 of this title shall pay to the person or entity assembling or providing such information a fee for reimbursement for such costs as are reasonably necessary and which have been directly incurred in searching for, assembling, reproducing, or otherwise providing such information. Such reimbursable costs shall include any costs due to necessary disruption of normal operations of any electronic communication service or remote computing service in which such information may be stored.

(b) Amount. -

The amount of the fee provided by subsection (a) shall be as mutually agreed by the governmental entity and the person or entity providing the information, or, in the absence of agreement, shall be as determined by the court which issued the order for production of such information (or the court before which a criminal prosecution relating to such information would be brought, if no court order was issued for production of the information).

(c) Exception. -

The requirement of subsection (a) of this section does not apply with respect to records or other information maintained by a communications common carrier that relate to telephone toll records and telephone listings obtained under section 2703 of this title. The court may, however, order a payment as described in subsection (a) if the court determines the information required is unusually voluminous in nature or otherwise caused an undue burden on the provider.

Sec. 2707. Civil action

(a) Cause of Action. -

Except as provided in section 2703(e), any provider of electronic communication service, subscriber, or other person aggrieved by any violation of this chapter in which the conduct constituting the violation is engaged in with a knowing or intentional state of mind may, in a civil action, recover from the person or entity, other than the United States, which engaged in that violation such relief as may be appropriate.

(b) Relief. - In a civil action under this section, appropriate relief includes -

(1) such preliminary and other equitable or declaratory relief as may be appropriate;

(2) damages under subsection (c); and

(3) a reasonable attorney's fee and other litigation costs reasonably incurred.

(c) Damages. -

The court may assess as damages in a civil action under this section the sum of the actual damages suffered by the plaintiff and any profits made by the violator as a result of the violation, but in no case shall a person entitled to recover receive less than the sum of $1,000. If the violation is willful or intentional, the court may assess punitive damages. In the case of a successful action to enforce liability under this section, the court may assess the costs of the action, together with reasonable attorney fees determined by the court.

(d) Administrative Discipline. If a court or appropriate department or agency determines that the United States or any of its departments or agencies has violated any provision of this chapter, and the court or appropriate department or agency finds that the circumstances surrounding the violation raise serious questions about whether or not an officer or employee of the United States acted willfully or intentionally with respect to the violation, the department or agency shall, upon receipt of a true and correct copy of the decision and findings of the court or appropriate department or agency promptly initiate a proceeding to determine whether disciplinary action against the officer or employee is warranted. If the head of the department or agency involved determines that disciplinary action is not warranted, he or she shall notify the Inspector General with jurisdiction over the department or agency concerned and shall provide the Inspector General with the reasons for such determination.

(e) Defense. - A good faith reliance on -

(1) a court warrant or order, a grand jury subpoena, a legislative authorization, or a statutory authorization (including a request of a governmental entity under section 2703(f) of this title);

(2) a request of an investigative or law enforcement officer under section 2518(7) of this title; or

(3) a good faith determination that section 2511(3) of this title permitted the conduct complained of; is a complete defense to any civil or criminal action brought under this chapter or any other law.

(f) Limitation. - A civil action under this section may not be commenced later than two years after the date upon which the claimant first discovered or had a reasonable opportunity to discover the violation.

(g) Improper disclosure. Any willful disclosure of a "record", as that term is defined in section 552a(a) of title 5, United States Code, obtained by an investigative or law enforcement officer, or a governmental entity, pursuant to section 2703 of this title, or from a device installed pursuant to section 3123 or 3125 of this title, that is not a disclosure made in the proper performance of the official functions of the officer or governmental entity making the disclosure, is a violation of this chapter. This provision shall not apply to information previously lawfully disclosed (prior to the commencement of any civil or administrative proceeding under this chapter) to the public by a Federal, State, or local governmental entity or by the plaintiff in a civil action under this chapter.

Sec. 2708. Exclusivity of remedies

The remedies and sanctions described in this chapter are the only judicial remedies and sanctions for nonconstitutional violations of this chapter.

Sec. 2709. Counterintelligence access to telephone toll and transactional records

(a) Duty to Provide.-A wire or electronic communication service provider shall comply with a request for subscriber information and toll billing records information, or electronic communication transactional records in its custody or possession made by the Director of the Federal Bureau of Investigation under subsection (b) of this section.

(b) Required Certification.-The Director of the Federal Bureau of Investigation, or his designee in a position not lower than Deputy Assistant Director at Bureau headquarters or a Special Agent in Charge in a Bureau field office designated by the Director, may, using a term that specifically identifies a person, entity, telephone number, or account as the basis for a request-

(1) request the name, address, length of service, and local and long distance toll billing records of a person or entity if the Director (or his designee) certifies in writing to the wire or electronic communication service provider to which the request is made that the name, address, length of service, and toll billing records sought are relevant to an authorized investigation to protect against international terrorism or clandestine intelligence activities, provided that such an investigation of a United States person is not conducted solely on the basis of activities protected by the first amendment to the Constitution of the United States; and

(2) request the name, address, and length of service of a person or entity if the Director (or his designee) certifies in writing to the wire or electronic communication service provider to which the request is made that the information sought is relevant to an authorized investigation to protect against international terrorism or clandestine intelligence activities, provided that such an investigation of a United States person is not conducted solely upon the basis of activities protected by the first amendment to the Constitution of the United States.

(c) Prohibition of Certain Disclosure.-

(1) Prohibition.-

(A) In general.-If a certification is issued under subparagraph (B) and notice of the right to judicial review under subsection (d) is provided, no wire or electronic communication service provider that receives a request under subsection (b), or officer, employee, or agent thereof, shall disclose to any person that the Federal Bureau of Investigation has sought or obtained access to information or records under this section.

(B) Certification.-The requirements of subparagraph (A) shall apply if the Director of the Federal Bureau of Investigation, or a designee of the Director whose rank shall be no lower than Deputy Assistant Director at Bureau headquarters or a Special Agent in Charge of a Bureau field office, certifies that the absence of a prohibition of disclosure under this subsection may result in-

(i) a danger to the national security of the United States;

(ii) interference with a criminal, counterterrorism, or counterintelligence investigation;

(iii) interference with diplomatic relations; or

(iv) danger to the life or physical safety of any person.

(2) Exception.-

(A) In general.-A wire or electronic communication service provider that receives a request under subsection (b), or officer, employee, or agent thereof, may disclose information otherwise subject to any applicable nondisclosure requirement to-

(i) those persons to whom disclosure is necessary in order to comply with the request;

(ii) an attorney in order to obtain legal advice or assistance regarding the request; or

(iii) other persons as permitted by the Director of the Federal Bureau of Investigation or the designee of the Director.

(B) Application.-A person to whom disclosure is made under subparagraph (A) shall be subject to the nondisclosure requirements applicable to a person to whom a request is issued under subsection (b) in the same manner as the person to whom the request is issued.

(C) Notice.-Any recipient that discloses to a person described in subparagraph (A) information otherwise subject to a nondisclosure requirement shall notify the person of the applicable nondisclosure requirement.

(D) Identification of disclosure recipients.-At the request of the Director of the Federal Bureau of Investigation or the designee of the Director, any person making or intending to make a disclosure under clause (i) or (iii) of subparagraph (A) shall identify to the Director or such designee the person to whom such disclosure will be made or to whom such disclosure was made prior to the request.

(d) Judicial Review.-

(1) In general.-A request under subsection (b) or a nondisclosure requirement imposed in connection with such request under subsection (c) shall be subject to judicial review under section 3511.

(2) Notice.-A request under subsection (b) shall include notice of the availability of judicial review described in paragraph (1).

(e) Dissemination by Bureau.-The Federal Bureau of Investigation may disseminate information and records obtained under this section only as provided in guidelines approved by the Attorney General for foreign intelligence collection and foreign counterintelligence investigations conducted by the Federal Bureau of Investigation, and, with respect to dissemination to an agency of the United States, only if such information is clearly relevant to the authorized responsibilities of such agency.

(f) Requirement That Certain Congressional Bodies Be Informed.-On a semiannual basis the Director of the Federal Bureau of Investigation shall fully inform the Permanent Select Committee on Intelligence of the House of Representatives and the Select Committee on Intelligence of the Senate, and the Committee on the Judiciary of the House of Representatives and the Committee on the Judiciary of the Senate, concerning all requests made under subsection (b) of this section.

(g) Libraries.-A library (as that term is defined in section 213(1) of the Library Services and Technology Act (20 U.S.C. 9122(1)), the services of which include access to the Internet, books, journals, magazines, newspapers, or other similar forms of communication in print or digitally by patrons for their use, review, examination, or circulation, is not a wire or electronic communication service provider for purposes of this section, unless the library is providing the services defined in section 2510(15) ("electronic communication service") of this title.

Sec. 2711. Definitions for chapter

As used in this chapter-

(1) the terms defined in section 2510 of this title have, respectively, the definitions given such terms in that section;

(2) the term "remote computing service" means the provision to the public of computer storage or processing services by means of an electronic communications system;

(3) the term "court of competent jurisdiction" includes-

　(A) any district court of the United States (including a magistrate judge of such a court) or any United States court of appeals that-

　　(i) has jurisdiction over the offense being investigated;

　　(ii) is in or for a district in which the provider of a wire or electronic communication service is located or in which the wire or electronic communications, records, or other information are stored; or

　　(iii) is acting on a request for foreign assistance pursuant to section 3512 of this title; or

　(B) a court of general criminal jurisdiction of a State authorized by the law of that State to issue search warrants; and

(4) the term "governmental entity" means a department or agency of the United States or any State or political subdivision thereof.

Sec. 3121. General prohibition on pen register and trap and trace device use; exception

(a) In General. - Except as provided in this section, no person may install or use a pen register or a trap and trace device without first obtaining a court order under section 3123 of this title or under the Foreign Intelligence Surveillance Act of 1978 (50 U.S.C. 1801 et seq.).

(b) Exception. - The prohibition of subsection (a) does not apply with respect to the use of a pen register or a trap and trace device by a provider of electronic or wire communication service -

　(1) relating to the operation, maintenance, and testing of a wire or electronic communication service or to the protection of the rights or property of such provider, or to the protection of users of that service from abuse of service or unlawful use of service; or

　(2) to record the fact that a wire or electronic communication was initiated or completed in order to protect such provider, another provider furnishing service toward the completion of the wire communication, or a user of that service, from fraudulent, unlawful or abusive use of service; or (3) where the consent of the user of that service has been obtained.

(c) Limitation. - A government agency authorized to install and use a pen register or trap and trace device under this chapter or under State law shall use technology reasonably available to it that restricts the recording or decoding of electronic or other impulses to the dialing, routing, addressing, and signaling information utilized in the processing and transmitting of wire or electronic communications so as not to include the contents of any wire or electronic communications.

(d) Penalty. - Whoever knowingly violates subsection (a) shall be fined under this title or imprisoned not more than one year, or both.

Sec. 3122. Application for an order for a pen register or a trap and trace device

(a) Application. -

(1) An attorney for the Government may make application for an order or an extension of an order under section 3123 of this title authorizing or approving the installation and use of a pen register or a trap and trace device under this chapter, in writing under oath or equivalent affirmation, to a court of competent jurisdiction.

(2) Unless prohibited by State law, a State investigative or law enforcement officer may make application for an order or an extension of an order under section 3123 of this title authorizing or approving the installation and use of a pen register or a trap and trace device under this chapter, in writing under oath or equivalent affirmation, to a court of competent jurisdiction of such State.

(b) Contents of Application. - An application under subsection (a) of this section shall include -

(1) the identity of the attorney for the Government or the State law enforcement or investigative officer making the application and the identity of the law enforcement agency conducting the investigation; and

(2) a certification by the applicant that the information likely to be obtained is relevant to an ongoing criminal investigation being conducted by that agency.

Sec. 3123. Issuance of an order for a pen register or a trap and trace device

(a) In general.

(1) Attorney for the Government. Upon an application made under section 3122(a)(1), the court shall enter an ex parte order authorizing the installation and use of a pen register or trap and trace device anywhere within the United States, if the court finds that the attorney for the Government has certified to the court that the information likely to be obtained by such installation and use is relevant to an ongoing criminal investigation. The order, upon service of that order, shall apply to any person or entity providing wire or electronic communication service in the United States whose assistance may facilitate the execution of the order. Whenever such an order is served on any person or entity not specifically named in the order, upon request of such person or entity, the attorney for the Government or law enforcement or investigative officer that is serving the order shall provide written or electronic certification that the order applies to the person or entity being served.

(2) State investigative or law enforcement officer. Upon an application made under section 3122(a)(2), the court shall enter an ex parte order authorizing the installation and use of a pen register or trap and trace device within the jurisdiction of the court, if the court finds that the State law enforcement or investigative officer has certified to the court that the information likely to be obtained by such installation and use is relevant to an ongoing criminal investigation.

(3) (A) Where the law enforcement agency implementing an ex parte order under this subsection seeks to do so by installing and using its own pen register or trap and trace device on a packet-switched data network of a provider of electronic communication service to the public, the agency shall ensure that a record will be maintained which will identify--

(i) any officer or officers who installed the device and any officer or officers who accessed the device to obtain information from the network;

(ii) the date and time the device was installed, the date and time the device was uninstalled, and the date, time, and duration of each time the device is accessed to obtain information;

(iii) the configuration of the device at the time of its installation and any subsequent modification thereof; and

(iv) any information which has been collected by the device.

To the extent that the pen register or trap and trace device can be set automatically to record this information electronically, the record shall be maintained electronically throughout the installation and use of such device.

(B) The record maintained under subparagraph (A) shall be provided ex parte and under seal to the court which entered the ex parte order authorizing the installation and use of the device within 30 days after termination of the order (including any extensions thereof).

(b) Contents of order. An order issued under this section--

(1) shall specify--

(A) the identity, if known, of the person to whom is leased or in whose name is listed the telephone line or other facility to which the pen register or trap and trace device is to be attached or applied;

(B) the identity, if known, of the person who is the subject of the criminal investigation;

(C) the attributes of the communications to which the order applies, including the number or other identifier and, if known, the location of the telephone line or other facility to which the pen register or trap and trace device is to be attached or applied, and, in the case of an order authorizing installation and use of a trap and trace device under subsection (a)(2), the geographic limits of the order; and

(D) a statement of the offense to which the information likely to be obtained by the pen register or trap and trace device relates; and

(2) shall direct, upon the request of the applicant, the furnishing of information, facilities, and technical assistance necessary to accomplish the installation of the pen register or trap and trace device under section 3124 of this title.

(c) Time period and extensions.

(1) An order issued under this section shall authorize the installation and use of a pen register or a trap and trace device for a period not to exceed sixty days.

(2) Extensions of such an order may be granted, but only upon an application for an order under section 3122 of this title and upon the judicial finding required by subsection (a) of this section. The period of extension shall be for a period not to exceed sixty days.

(d) Nondisclosure of existence of pen register or a trap and trace device. An order authorizing or approving the installation and use of a pen register or a trap and trace device shall direct that--

(1) the order be sealed until otherwise ordered by the court; and

(2) the person owning or leasing the line or other facility to which the pen register or a trap and trace device is attached, or applied, or who is obligated by the order to provide assistance to the applicant, not disclose the existence of the pen register or trap and trace device or the existence of the investigation to the listed subscriber, or to any other person, unless or until otherwise ordered by the court.

Sec. 3124. Assistance in installation and use of a pen register or a trap and trace device

(a) Pen Registers. - Upon the request of an attorney for the Government or an officer of a law enforcement agency authorized to install and use a pen register under this chapter, a provider of wire or electronic communication service, landlord, custodian, or other person shall furnish such investigative or law enforcement officer forthwith all information, facilities, and technical assistance necessary to accomplish the installation of the pen register unobtrusively and with a minimum of interference with the services that the person so ordered by the court accords the party with respect to whom the installation and use is to take place, if such assistance is directed by a court order as provided in section 3123(b)(2) of this title.

(b) Trap and Trace Device. - Upon the request of an attorney for the Government or an officer of a law enforcement agency authorized to receive the results of a trap and trace device under this chapter, a provider of a wire or electronic communication service, landlord, custodian, or other person shall install such device forthwith on the appropriate line or other facility and shall furnish such investigative or law enforcement officer all additional information, facilities and technical assistance including installation and operation of the device unobtrusively and with a minimum of interference with the services that the person so ordered by the court accords the party with respect to whom the installation and use is to take place, if such installation and assistance is directed by a court order as provided in section 3123(b)(2) of this title. Unless otherwise ordered by the court, the results of the trap and trace device shall be furnished, pursuant to section 3123(b) or section 3125 of this title, to the officer of a law enforcement agency, designated in the court order, at reasonable intervals during regular business hours for the duration of the order.

(c) Compensation. - A provider of a wire or electronic communication service, landlord, custodian, or other person who furnishes facilities or technical assistance pursuant to this section shall be reasonably compensated for such reasonable expenses incurred in providing such facilities and assistance.

(d) No Cause of Action Against a Provider Disclosing Information Under This Chapter. - No cause of action shall lie in any court against any provider of a wire or electronic communication service, its officers, employees, agents, or other specified persons for providing information, facilities, or assistance in accordance with a court order under this chapter or request pursuant to section 3125 of this title.

(e) Defense. - A good faith reliance on a court order under this chapter, a request pursuant to section 3125 of this title, a legislative authorization, or a statutory authorization is a complete defense against any civil or criminal action brought under this chapter or any other law.

(f) Communications Assistance Enforcement Orders. - Pursuant to section 2522, an order may be issued to enforce the assistance capability and capacity requirements under the Communications Assistance for Law Enforcement Act.

Sec. 3125. Emergency pen register and trap and trace device installation

(a) Notwithstanding any other provision of this chapter, any investigative or law enforcement officer, specially designated by the Attorney General, the Deputy Attorney General, the Associate Attorney General, any Assistant Attorney General, any acting Assistant Attorney General, or any Deputy Assistant Attorney General, or by the principal prosecuting attorney of any State or subdivision thereof acting pursuant to a statute of that State, who reasonably determines that -

    (1) an emergency situation exists that involves -

        (A) immediate danger of death or serious bodily injury to any person;

        (B) conspiratorial activities characteristic of organized crime;

        (C) an immediate threat to a national security interest; or

        (D) an ongoing attack on a protected computer (as defined in section 1030) that constitutes a crime punishable by a term of imprisonment greater than one year;

        that requires the installation and use of a pen register or a trap and trace device before an order authorizing such installation and use can, with due diligence, be obtained, and

(2) there are grounds upon which an order could be entered under this chapter to authorize such installation and use; may have installed and use a pen register or trap and trace device if, within forty-eight hours after the installation has occurred, or begins to occur, an order approving the installation or use is issued in accordance with section 3123 of this title.

(b) In the absence of an authorizing order, such use shall immediately terminate when the information sought is obtained, when the application for the order is denied or when forty-eight hours have lapsed since the installation of the pen register or trap and trace device, whichever is earlier.

(c) The knowing installation or use by any investigative or law enforcement officer of a pen register or trap and trace device pursuant to subsection (a) without application for the authorizing order within forty-eight hours of the installation shall constitute a violation of this chapter.

(d) A provider of a wire or electronic service, landlord, custodian, or other person who furnished facilities or technical assistance pursuant to this section shall be reasonably compensated for such reasonable expenses incurred in providing such facilities and assistance.

Sec. 3126. Reports concerning pen registers and trap and trace devices

The Attorney General shall annually report to Congress on the number of pen register orders and orders for trap and trace devices applied for by law enforcement agencies of the Department of Justice, which report shall include information concerning--

(1) the period of interceptions authorized by the order, and the number and duration of any extensions of the order;

(2) the offense specified in the order or application, or extension of an order;

(3) the number of investigations involved;

(4) the number and nature of the facilities affected; and

(5) the identity, including district, of the applying investigative or law enforcement agency making the application and the person authorizing the order.

Sec. 3127. Definitions for chapter

As used in this chapter-

(1) the terms "wire communication", "electronic communication", "electronic communication service", and "contents" have the meanings set forth for such terms in section 2510 of this title;

(2) the term "court of competent jurisdiction" means-

(A) any district court of the United States (including a magistrate judge of such a court) or any United States court of appeals that-

(i) has jurisdiction over the offense being investigated;

(ii) is in or for a district in which the provider of a wire or electronic communication service is located;

(iii) is in or for a district in which a landlord, custodian, or other person subject to subsections (a) or (b) of section 3124 of this title is located; or

(iv) is acting on a request for foreign assistance pursuant to section 3512 of this title; or

(B) a court of general criminal jurisdiction of a State authorized by the law of that State to enter orders authorizing the use of a pen register or a trap and trace device;

(3) the term "pen register" means a device or process which records or decodes dialing, routing, addressing, or signaling information transmitted by an instrument or facility from which a wire or electronic communication is transmitted, provided, however, that such information shall not include the contents of any communication, but such term does not include any device or process used by a provider or customer of a wire or electronic communication service for billing, or recording as an incident to billing, for communications services provided by such provider or any device or process used by a provider or customer of a wire communication service for cost accounting or other like purposes in the ordinary course of its business;

(4) the term "trap and trace device" means a device or process which captures the incoming electronic or other impulses which identify the originating number or other dialing, routing, addressing, and signaling information reasonably likely to identify the source of a wire or electronic communication, provided, however, that such information shall not include the contents of any communication;

(5) the term "attorney for the Government" has the meaning given such term for the purposes of the Federal Rules of Criminal Procedure; and

(6) the term "State" means a State, the District of Columbia, Puerto Rico, and any other possession or territory of the United States.

47 U.S.C. Sec. 1001. Definitions

For purposes of this subchapter -

(1) The terms defined in section 2510 of title 18 have, respectively, the meanings stated in that section.

(2) The term "call-identifying information" means dialing or signaling information that identifies the origin, direction, destination, or termination of each communication generated or received by a subscriber by means of any equipment, facility, or service of a telecommunications carrier.

(3) The term "Commission" means the Federal Communications Commission.

(4) The term "electronic messaging services" means software-based services that enable the sharing of data, images, sound, writing, or other information among computing devices controlled by the senders or recipients of the messages.

(5) The term "government" means the government of the United States and any agency or instrumentality thereof, the District of Columbia, any commonwealth, territory, or possession of the United States, and any State or political subdivision thereof authorized by law to conduct electronic surveillance.

(6) The term "information services" –

(A) means the offering of a capability for generating, acquiring, storing, transforming, processing, retrieving, utilizing, or making available information via telecommunications; and (B) includes -

(i) a service that permits a customer to retrieve stored information from, or file information for storage in, information storage facilities;

(ii) electronic publishing; and

(iii) electronic messaging services; but

(C) does not include any capability for a telecommunications carrier's internal management, control, or operation of its telecommunications network.

(7) The term "telecommunications support services" means a product, software, or service used by a telecommunications carrier for the internal signaling or switching functions of its telecommunications network.

(8) The term "telecommunications carrier" -

(A) means a person or entity engaged in the transmission or switching of wire or electronic communications as a common carrier for hire; and

(B) includes -

(i) a person or entity engaged in providing commercial mobile service (as defined in section 332(d) of this title); or

(ii) a person or entity engaged in providing wire or electronic communication switching or transmission service to the extent that the Commission finds that such service is a replacement for a substantial portion of the local telephone exchange service and that it is in the public interest to deem such a person or entity to be a telecommunications carrier for purposes of this subchapter; but

(C) does not include -

(i) persons or entities insofar as they are engaged in providing information services; and

(ii) any class or category of telecommunications carriers that the Commission exempts by rule after consultation with the Attorney General.

Sec. 1002. Assistance capability requirements

(a) Capability requirements

Except as provided in subsections (b), (c), and (d) of this section and sections 1007(a) and 1008(b) and (d) of this title, a telecommunications carrier shall ensure that its equipment, facilities, or services that provide a customer or subscriber with the ability to originate, terminate, or direct communications are capable of -

(1) expeditiously isolating and enabling the government, pursuant to a court order or other lawful authorization, to intercept, to the exclusion of any other communications, all wire and electronic communications carried by the carrier within a service area to or from equipment, facilities, or services of a subscriber of such carrier concurrently with their transmission to or from the subscriber's equipment, facility, or service, or at such later time as may be acceptable to the government;

(2) expeditiously isolating and enabling the government, pursuant to a court order or other lawful authorization, to access call-identifying information that is reasonably available to the carrier -

(A) before, during, or immediately after the transmission of a wire or electronic communication (or at such later time as may be acceptable to the government); and

(B) in a manner that allows it to be associated with the communication to which it pertains, except that, with regard to information acquired solely pursuant to the authority for pen registers and trap and trace devices (as defined in section 3127 of title 18), such call-identifying information shall not include any information that may disclose the physical location of the subscriber (except to the extent that the location may be determined from the telephone number);

(3) delivering intercepted communications and call-identifying information to the government, pursuant to a court order or other lawful authorization, in a format such that they may be transmitted by means of equipment, facilities, or services procured by the government to a location other than the premises of the carrier; and

(4) facilitating authorized communications interceptions and access to call-identifying information unobtrusively and with a minimum of interference with any subscriber's telecommunications service and in a manner that protects -

(A) the privacy and security of communications and call-identifying information not authorized to be intercepted; and

(B) information regarding the government's interception of communications and access to call-identifying information.

(b) Limitations

(1) Design of features and systems configurations

This subchapter does not authorize any law enforcement agency or officer -

(A) to require any specific design of equipment, facilities, services, features, or system configurations to be adopted by any provider of a wire or electronic communication service, any manufacturer of telecommunications equipment, or any provider of telecommunications support services; or

(B) to prohibit the adoption of any equipment, facility, service, or feature by any provider of a wire or electronic communication service, any manufacturer of telecommunications equipment, or any provider of telecommunications support services.

(2) Information services; private networks and interconnection services and facilities The requirements of subsection (a) of this section do not apply to -

(A) information services; or

(B) equipment, facilities, or services that support the transport or switching of communications for private networks or for the sole purpose of interconnecting telecommunications carriers.

(3) Encryption

A telecommunications carrier shall not be responsible for decrypting, or ensuring the government's ability to decrypt, any communication encrypted by a subscriber or customer, unless the encryption was provided by the carrier and the carrier possesses the information necessary to decrypt the communication.

(c) Emergency or exigent circumstances

In emergency or exigent circumstances (including those described in sections 2518(7) or (11)(b) and 3125 of title 18 and section 1805(e) of title 50), a carrier at its discretion may comply with subsection (a)(3) of this section by allowing monitoring at its premises if that is the only means of accomplishing the interception or access.

(d) Mobile service assistance requirements

A telecommunications carrier that is a provider of commercial mobile service (as defined in section 332(d) of this title) offering a feature or service that allows subscribers to redirect, hand off, or assign their wire or electronic communications to another service area or another service provider or to utilize facilities in another service area or of another service provider shall ensure that, when the carrier that had been providing assistance for the interception of wire or electronic communications or access to call-identifying information pursuant to a court order or lawful authorization no longer has access to the content of such communications or call-identifying information within the service area in which interception has been occurring as a result of the subscriber's use of such a feature or service, information is made available to the government (before, during, or immediately after the transfer of such communications) identifying the provider of a wire or electronic communication service that has acquired access to the communications.

Sec. 1003. Notices of capacity requirements

(a) Notices of maximum and actual capacity requirements

(1) In general

Not later than 1 year after October 25, 1994, after consulting with State and local law enforcement agencies, telecommunications carriers, providers of telecommunications support services, and manufacturers of telecommunications equipment, and after notice and comment, the Attorney General shall publish in the Federal Register and provide to appropriate telecommunications industry associations and standard-setting organizations -

(A) notice of the actual number of communication interceptions, pen registers, and trap and trace devices, representing a portion of the maximum capacity set forth under subparagraph (B), that the Attorney General estimates that government agencies authorized to conduct electronic surveillance may conduct and use simultaneously by the date that is 4 years after October 25, 1994; and

(B) notice of the maximum capacity required to accommodate all of the communication interceptions, pen registers, and trap and trace devices that the Attorney General estimates that government agencies authorized to conduct electronic surveillance may conduct and use simultaneously after the date that is 4 years after October 25, 1994.

(2) Basis of notices

The notices issued under paragraph (1) -

(A) may be based upon the type of equipment, type of service, number of subscribers, type or size or[1] carrier, nature of service area, or any other measure; and

(B) shall identify, to the maximum extent practicable, the capacity require at specific geographic locations.

(b) Compliance with Capacity Notices

(1) Initial capacity

Within 3 years after the publication by the Attorney General of a notice of capacity requirements or within 4 years after October 25, 1994, whichever is longer, a telecommunications carrier shall, subject to subsection (e) of this section, ensure that its systems are capable of -

(A) accommodating simultaneously the number of interceptions, pen registers, and trap and trace devices set forth in the notice under subsection (a)(1)(A) of this section; and

(B) expanding to the maximum capacity set forth in the notice under subsection (a)(1)(B) of this section.

(2) Expansion to maximum capacity

After the date described in paragraph (1), a telecommunications carrier shall, subject to subsection (e) of this section, ensure that it can accommodate

---

[1] So in original. Probably should be "of".

expeditiously any increase in the actual number of communication interceptions, pen registers, and trap and trace devices that authorized agencies may seek to conduct and use, up to the maximum capacity requirement set forth in the notice under subsection (a)(1)(B) of this section.

(c) Notices of increased maximum capacity requirements

(1) Notice

The Attorney General shall periodically publish in the Federal Register, after notice and comment, notice of any necessary increases in the maximum capacity requirement set forth in the notice under subsection (a)(1)(B) of this section.

(2) Compliance

Within 3 years after notice of increased maximum capacity requirements is published under paragraph (1), or within such longer time period as the Attorney General may specify, a telecommunications carrier shall, subject to subsection (e) of this section, ensure that its systems are capable of expanding to the increased maximum capacity set forth in the notice.

(d) Carrier statement

Within 180 days after the publication by the Attorney General of a notice of capacity requirements pursuant to subsection (a) or (c) of this section, a telecommunications carrier shall submit to the Attorney General a statement identifying any of its systems or services that do not have the capacity to accommodate simultaneously the number of interceptions, pen registers, and trap and trace devices set forth in the notice under such subsection.

(e) Reimbursement required for compliance

The Attorney General shall review the statements submitted under subsection (d) of this section and may, subject to the availability of appropriations, agree to reimburse a telecommunications carrier for costs directly associated with modifications to attain such capacity requirement that are determined to be reasonable in accordance with section 1008(e) of this title. Until the Attorney General agrees to reimburse such carrier for such modification, such carrier shall be considered to be in compliance with the capacity notices under subsection (a) or (c) of this section.

Sec. 1004. Systems security and integrity

A telecommunications carrier shall ensure that any interception of communications or access to call-identifying information effected within its switching premises can be activated only in accordance with a court order or other lawful authorization and with the affirmative intervention of an individual officer or employee of the carrier acting in accordance with regulations prescribed by the Commission.

Sec. 1005. Cooperation of equipment manufacturers and providers of telecommunications support services

(a) Consultation

A telecommunications carrier shall consult, as necessary, in a timely fashion with manufacturers of its telecommunications transmission and switching equipment and its providers of telecommunications support services for the purpose of ensuring that current and planned equipment, facilities, and services comply with the capability requirements of section 1002 of this title and the capacity requirements identified by the Attorney General under section 1003 of this title.

(b) Cooperation

Subject to sections 1003(e), 1007(a), and 1008(b) and (d) of this title, a manufacturer of telecommunications transmission or switching equipment and a provider of telecommunications support services shall, on a reasonably timely basis and at a reasonable charge, make available to the telecommunications carriers using its equipment, facilities, or services such features or modifications as are necessary to permit such carriers to comply with the capability requirements of section 1002 of this title and the capacity requirements identified by the Attorney General under section 1003 of this title.

Sec. 1006. Technical requirements and standards; extension of compliance date

(a) Safe harbor

   (1) Consultation

   To ensure the efficient and industry-wide implementation of the assistance capability requirements under section 1002 of this title, the Attorney General, in coordination with other Federal, State, and local law enforcement agencies, shall consult with appropriate associations and standard-setting organizations of the telecommunications industry, with representatives of users of telecommunications equipment, facilities, and services, and with State utility commissions.

   (2) Compliance under accepted standards

   A telecommunications carrier shall be found to be in compliance with the assistance capability requirements under section 1002 of this title, and a manufacturer of telecommunications transmission or switching equipment or a provider of telecommunications support services shall be found to be in compliance with section 1005 of this title, if the carrier, manufacturer, or support service provider is in compliance with publicly available technical requirements or standards adopted by an industry association or standard-setting organization, or by the Commission under subsection (b) of this section, to meet the requirements of section 1002 of this title.

   (3) Absence of standards

   The absence of technical requirements or standards for implementing the assistance capability requirements of section 1002 of this title shall not -

(A) preclude a telecommunications carrier, manufacturer, or telecommunications support services provider from deploying a technology or service; or

(B) relieve a carrier, manufacturer, or telecommunications support services provider of the obligations imposed by section 1002 or 1005 of this title, as applicable.

(b) Commission authority

If industry associations or standard-setting organizations fail to issue technical requirements or standards or if a Government agency or any other person believes that such requirements or standards are deficient, the agency or person may petition the Commission to establish, by rule, technical requirements or standards that - (1) meet the assistance capability requirements of section 1002 of this title by cost-effective methods;

(2) protect the privacy and security of communications not authorized to be intercepted;

(3) minimize the cost of such compliance on residential ratepayers;

(4) serve the policy of the United States to encourage the provision of new technologies and services to the public; and

(5) provide a reasonable time and conditions for compliance with and the transition to any new standard, including defining the obligations of telecommunications carriers under section 1002 of this title during any transition period.

(c) Extension of compliance date for equipment, facilities, and services

(1) Petition

A telecommunications carrier proposing to install or deploy, or having installed or deployed, any equipment, facility, or service prior to the effective date of section 1002 of this title may petition the Commission for 1 or more extensions of the deadline for complying with the assistance capability requirements under section 1002 of this title.

(2) Grounds for extension

The Commission may, after consultation with the Attorney General, grant an extension under this subsection, if the Commission determines that compliance with the assistance capability requirements under section 1002 of this title is not reasonably achievable through application of technology available within the compliance period.

(3) Length of extension

An extension under this subsection shall extend for no longer than the earlier of -

(A) the date determined by the Commission as necessary for the carrier to comply with the assistance capability requirements under section 1002 of this title; or

(B) the date that is 2 years after the date on which the extension is granted.

(4) Applicability of extension

An extension under this subsection shall apply to only that part of the carrier's business on which the new equipment, facility, or service is used.

Sec. 1007. Enforcement orders

(a) Grounds for issuance

A court shall issue an order enforcing this subchapter under section 2522 of title 18 only if the court finds that -

(1) alternative technologies or capabilities or the facilities of another carrier are not reasonably available to law enforcement for implementing the interception of communications or access to call-identifying information; and

(2) compliance with the requirements of this subchapter is reasonably achievable through the application of available technology to the equipment, facility, or service at issue or would have been reasonably achievable if timely action had been taken.

(b) Time for compliance

Upon issuing an order enforcing this subchapter, the court shall specify a reasonable time and conditions for complying with its order, considering the good faith efforts to comply in a timely manner, any effect on the carrier's, manufacturer's, or service provider's ability to continue to do business, the degree of culpability or delay in undertaking efforts to comply, and such other matters as justice may require.

(c) Limitations

An order enforcing this subchapter may not -

(1) require a telecommunications carrier to meet the Government's [1] demand for interception of communications and acquisition of call-identifying information to any extent in excess of the capacity for which the Attorney General has agreed to reimburse such carrier;

(2) require any telecommunications carrier to comply with assistance capability requirement [2] of section 1002 of this title if the Commission has determined (pursuant to section 1008(b)(1) of this title) that compliance is not reasonably achievable, unless the Attorney General has agreed (pursuant to section 1008(b)(2) of this title) to pay the costs described in section 1008(b)(2)(A) of this title; or

(3) require a telecommunications carrier to modify, for the purpose of complying with the assistance capability requirements of section 1002 of this title, any equipment, facility, or service deployed on or before January 1, 1995, unless -

(A) the Attorney General has agreed to pay the telecommunications carrier for all reasonable costs directly associated with modifications necessary to bring the equipment, facility, or service into compliance with those requirements; or

(B) the equipment, facility, or service has been replaced or significantly upgraded or otherwise undergoes major modification.

United States
Electronic Communications Privacy Act

Sec. 1008. Payment of costs of telecommunications carriers to comply with capability requirements

(a) Equipment, facilities, and services deployed on or before January 1, 1995 The Attorney General may, subject to the availability of appropriations, agree to pay telecommunications carriers for all reasonable costs directly associated with the modifications performed by carriers in connection with equipment, facilities, and services installed or deployed on or before January 1, 1995, to establish the capabilities necessary to comply with section 1002 of this title.

(b) Equipment, facilities, and services deployed after January 1, 1995

(1) Determinations of reasonably achievable

The Commission, on petition from a telecommunications carrier or any other interested person, and after notice to the Attorney General, shall determine whether compliance with the assistance capability requirements of section 1002 of this title is reasonably achievable with respect to any equipment, facility, or service installed or deployed after January 1, 1995. The Commission shall make such determination within 1 year after the date such petition is filed. In making such determination, the Commission shall determine whether compliance would impose significant difficulty or expense on the carrier or on the users of the carrier's systems and shall consider the following factors:

(A) The effect on public safety and national security.

(B) The effect on rates for basic residential telephone service.

(C) The need to protect the privacy and security of communications not authorized to be intercepted.

(D) The need to achieve the capability assistance requirements of section 1002 of this title by cost-effective methods.

(E) The effect on the nature and cost of the equipment, facility, or service at issue.

(F) The effect on the operation of the equipment, facility, or service at issue.

(G) The policy of the United States to encourage the provision of new technologies and services to the public. (H) The financial resources of the telecommunications carrier.

(I) The effect on competition in the provision of telecommunications services.

(J) The extent to which the design and development of the equipment, facility, or service was initiated before January 1, 1995.

(K) Such other factors as the Commission determines are appropriate.

(2) Compensation

If compliance with the assistance capability requirements of section 1002 of this title is not reasonably achievable with respect to equipment, facilities, or services deployed after January 1, 1995 -

(A) the Attorney General, on application of a telecommunications carrier, may agree, subject to the availability of appropriations, to pay the telecommunications carrier for the additional reasonable costs of making compliance with such assistance capability requirements reasonably achievable; and

(B) if the Attorney General does not agree to pay such costs, the telecommunications carrier shall be deemed to be in compliance with such capability requirements.

(c) Allocation of funds for payment

The Attorney General shall allocate funds appropriated to carry out this subchapter in accordance with law enforcement priorities determined by the Attorney General.

(d) Failure to make payment with respect to equipment, facilities, and services deployed on or before January 1, 1995 If a carrier has requested payment in accordance with procedures promulgated pursuant to subsection (e) of this section, and the Attorney General has not agreed to pay the telecommunications carrier for all reasonable costs directly associated with modifications necessary to bring any equipment, facility, or service deployed on or before January 1, 1995, into compliance with the assistance capability requirements of section 1002 of this title, such equipment, facility, or service shall be considered to be in compliance with the assistance capability requirements of section 1002 of this title until the equipment, facility, or service is replaced or significantly upgraded or otherwise undergoes major modification.

(e) Cost control regulations

(1) In general

The Attorney General shall, after notice and comment, establish regulations necessary to effectuate timely and cost-efficient payment to telecommunications carriers under this subchapter, under chapters 119 and 121 of title 18, and under the Foreign Intelligence Surveillance Act of 1978 (50 U.S.C. 1801 et seq.).

(2) Contents of regulations

The Attorney General, after consultation with the Commission, shall prescribe regulations for purposes of determining reasonable costs under this subchapter. Such regulations shall seek to minimize the cost to the Federal Government and shall -

(A) permit recovery from the Federal Government of -

(i) the direct costs of developing the modifications described in subsection (a) of this section, of providing the capabilities requested under subsection (b)(2) of this section, or of providing the capacities requested under section 1003(e) of this title, but only to the extent that such costs have not been recovered from any other governmental or nongovernmental entity;

(ii) the costs of training personnel in the use of such capabilities or capacities; and

(iii) the direct costs of deploying or installing such capabilities or capacities;

(B) in the case of any modification that may be used for any purpose other than lawfully authorized electronic surveillance by a law enforcement agency of a government, permit recovery of only the incremental cost of making the modification suitable for such law enforcement purposes; and

(C) maintain the confidentiality of trade secrets.

(3) Submission of claims

Such regulations shall require any telecommunications carrier that the Attorney General has agreed to pay for modifications pursuant to this section and that has installed or deployed such modification to submit to the Attorney General a claim for payment that contains or is accompanied by such information as the Attorney General may require.

Sec. 1009. Authorization of appropriations

There are authorized to be appropriated to carry out this subchapter a total of $500,000,000 for fiscal years 1995, 1996, 1997, and 1998. Such sums are authorized to remain available until expended.

Sec. 1010. Reports

(a) Reports by Attorney General

(1) In general

On or before November 30, 1995, and on or before November 30 of each year thereafter, the Attorney General shall submit to Congress and make available to the public a report on the amounts paid during the preceding fiscal year to telecommunications carriers under sections 1003(e) and 1008 of this title.

(2) Contents

A report under paragraph (1) shall include -

(A) a detailed accounting of the amounts paid to each carrier and the equipment, facility, or service for which the amounts were paid; and

(B) projections of the amounts expected to be paid in the current fiscal year, the carriers to which payment is expected to be made, and the equipment, facilities, or services for which payment is expected to be made.

(b) Reports by Comptroller General and Inspector General

(1) On or before April 1, 1996, the Comptroller General of the United States, and every two years thereafter, the Inspector General of the Department of Justice, shall submit to the Congress a report, after consultation with the Attorney General and the telecommunications industry -

(A) describing the type of equipment, facilities, and services that have been brought into compliance under this subchapter; and

(B) reflecting its analysis of the reasonableness and cost-effectiveness of the payments made by the Attorney General to telecommunications carriers for modifications necessary to ensure compliance with this subchapter.

(2) Compliance cost estimates. - A report under paragraph (1) shall include findings and conclusions on the costs to be incurred by telecommunications carriers to comply with the assistance capability requirements of section 1002 of this title after the effective date of such section 1002 of this title, including projections of the amounts expected to be incurred and a description of the equipment, facilities, or services for which they are expected to be incurred.

Sec. 1021. Department of Justice Telecommunications Carrier Compliance Fund

(a) Establishment of Fund

There is hereby established in the United States Treasury a fund to be known as the Department of Justice Telecommunications Carrier Compliance Fund (hereafter referred to as "the Fund"), which shall be available without fiscal year limitation to the Attorney General for making payments to telecommunications carriers, equipment manufacturers, and providers of telecommunications support services pursuant to section 1008 of this title.

(b) Deposits to Fund

Notwithstanding any other provision of law, any agency of the United States with law enforcement or intelligence responsibilities may deposit as offsetting collections to the Fund any unobligated balances that are available until expended, upon compliance with any Congressional notification requirements for reprogrammings of funds applicable to the appropriation from which the deposit is to be made.

(c) Termination

(1) The Attorney General may terminate the Fund at such time as the Attorney General determines that the Fund is no longer necessary.

(2) Any balance in the Fund at the time of its termination shall be deposited in the General Fund of the Treasury.

(3) A decision of the Attorney General to terminate the Fund shall not be subject to judicial review.

(d) Availability of funds for expenditure

Funds shall not be available for obligation unless an implementation plan as set forth in subsection (e) of this section is submitted to each member of the Committees on the Judiciary and Appropriations of both the House of Representatives and the Senate and the Congress does not by law block or prevent the obligation of such funds. Such funds shall be treated as a reprogramming of funds under section 605 of the Department of Commerce, Justice, and State, the Judiciary, and Related Agencies Appropriations Act,

1997, and shall not be available for obligation or expenditure except in compliance with the procedures set forth in that section and this section.

(e) Implementation plan

The implementation plan shall include:

(1) the law enforcement assistance capability requirements and an explanation of law enforcement's recommended interface;

(2) the proposed actual and maximum capacity requirements for the number of simultaneous law enforcement communications intercepts, pen registers, and trap and trace devices that authorized law enforcement agencies may seek to conduct, set forth on a county-by-county basis for wireline services and on a market service area basis for wireless services, and the historical baseline of electronic surveillance activity upon which such capacity requirements are based;

(3) a prioritized list of carrier equipment, facilities, and services deployed on or before January 1, 1995, to be modified by carriers at the request of law enforcement based on its investigative needs;

(4) a projected reimbursement plan that estimates the cost for the coming fiscal year and for each fiscal year thereafter, based on the prioritization of law enforcement needs as outlined in (3),[1] of modification by carriers of equipment, facilities and services, installed on or before January 1, 1995.

(f) Annual report to Congress

The Attorney General shall submit to the Congress each year a report specifically detailing all deposits and expenditures made pursuant to subchapter I of this chapter in each fiscal year. This report shall be submitted to each member of the Committees on the Judiciary and Appropriations of both the House of Representatives and the Senate, and to the Speaker and minority leader of the House of Representatives and to the majority and minority leaders of the Senate, no later than 60 days after the end of each fiscal year.

---

[1] So in original. Probably should be "paragraph (3),".

VIDEO PRIVACY PROTECTION ACT
(1988)

Summary

The Video Privacy Protection Act of 1988 amends the Federal criminal code to prohibit the disclosure of video rental records containing personally identifiable information. The Act permits the disclosure of such information: (1) to the consumer; (2) with the written consent of the consumer (3) pursuant to a Federal criminal warrant, an equivalent State warrant, a grand jury subpoena, or a court order under specified guidelines; (4) to any person if such disclosure is solely the names and addresses of consumers and the consumer has had the opportunity to prohibit such disclosure; (5) to any person if such disclosure is incident to the ordinary course of business of the video tape service provider; or (6) pursuant to a civil court order.

The Act permits any person who is aggrieved by a violation of this Act to bring a civil action for damages. It establishes a two-year statute of limitations for such actions. It states that any such information unlawfully obtained may not be used in any court proceeding. It further requires the destruction of personally identifiable records within a specified period of time. The Act was amended in 2012 to modify the procedures for obtaining consent and for revoking consent.

References

Public Law 100-618 as amended by Public Law 112-258. Codified at 18 U.S.C. § 2710.
[https://www.law.cornell.edu/uscode/text/18/2710]

EPIC, Video Privacy Protection Act
[https://www.epic.org/privacy/vppa/]

18 U.S.C. § 2710. Wrongful disclosure of video tape rental or sale records

(a) Definitions. - For purposes of this section -

(1) the term "consumer" means any renter, purchaser, or subscriber of goods or services from a video tape service provider;

(2) the term "ordinary course of business" means only debt collection activities, order fulfillment, request processing, and the transfer of ownership;

(3) the term "personally identifiable information" includes information which identifies a person as having requested or obtained specific video materials or services from a video tape service provider; and

(4) the term "video tape service provider" means any person, engaged in the business, in or affecting interstate or foreign commerce, of rental, sale, or delivery of prerecorded video cassette tapes or similar audio visual materials, or any person

or other entity to whom a disclosure is made under subparagraph (D) or (E) of subsection (b)(2), but only with respect to the information contained in the disclosure.

(b) Video Tape Rental and Sale Records. -

(1) A video tape service provider who knowingly discloses, to any person, personally identifiable information concerning any consumer of such provider shall be liable to the aggrieved person for the relief provided in subsection (d).

(2) A video tape service provider may disclose personally identifiable information concerning any consumer-

(A) to the consumer;

(B) to any person with the informed, written consent (including through an electronic means using the Internet) of the consumer that-

(i) is in a form distinct and separate from any form setting forth other legal or financial obligations of the consumer;

(ii) at the election of the consumer-

(I) is given at the time the disclosure is sought; or

(II) is given in advance for a set period of time, not to exceed 2 years or until consent is withdrawn by the consumer, whichever is sooner; and

(iii) the video tape service provider has provided an opportunity, in a clear and conspicuous manner, for the consumer to withdraw on a case-by-case basis or to withdraw from ongoing disclosures, at the consumer's election;

(C) to a law enforcement agency pursuant to a warrant issued under the Federal Rules of Criminal Procedure, an equivalent State warrant, a grand jury subpoena, or a court order;

(D) to any person if the disclosure is solely of the names and addresses of consumers and if-

(i) the video tape service provider has provided the consumer with the opportunity, in a clear and conspicuous manner, to prohibit such disclosure; and

(ii) the disclosure does not identify the title, description, or subject matter of any video tapes or other audio visual material; however, the subject matter of such materials may be disclosed if the disclosure is for the exclusive use of marketing goods and services directly to the consumer;

(E) to any person if the disclosure is incident to the ordinary course of business of the video tape service provider; or

(F) pursuant to a court order, in a civil proceeding upon a showing of compelling need for the information that cannot be accommodated by any other means, if-

(i) the consumer is given reasonable notice, by the person seeking the disclosure, of the court proceeding relevant to the issuance of the court order; and

(ii) the consumer is afforded the opportunity to appear and contest the claim of the person seeking the disclosure.

If an order is granted pursuant to subparagraph (C) or (F), the court shall impose appropriate safeguards against unauthorized disclosure.

(3) Court orders authorizing disclosure under subparagraph (C) shall issue only with prior notice to the consumer and only if the law enforcement agency shows that there is probable cause to believe that the records or other information sought are relevant to a legitimate law enforcement inquiry. In the case of a State government authority, such a court order shall not issue if prohibited by the law of such State. A court issuing an order pursuant to this section, on a motion made promptly by the video tape service provider, may quash or modify such order if the information or records requested are unreasonably voluminous in nature or if compliance with such order otherwise would cause an unreasonable burden on such provider.

(c) Civil Action. -

(1) Any person aggrieved by any act of a person in violation of this section may bring a civil action in a United States district court.

(2) The court may award-

(A) actual damages but not less than liquidated damages in an amount of $2,500;

(B) punitive damages;

(C) reasonable attorneys' fees and other litigation costs reasonably incurred; and

(D) such other preliminary and equitable relief as the court determines to be appropriate.

(3) No action may be brought under this subsection unless such action is begun within 2 years from the date of the act complained of or the date of discovery.

(4) No liability shall result from lawful disclosure permitted by this section.

(d) Personally Identifiable Information. - Personally identifiable information obtained in any manner other than as provided in this section shall not be received in evidence in any trial, hearing, arbitration, or other proceeding in or before any court, grand jury, department, officer, agency, regulatory body, legislative committee, or other authority of the United States, a State, or a political subdivision of a State.

(e) Destruction of Old Records. - A person subject to this section shall destroy personally identifiable information as soon as practicable, but no later than one year from the date the information is no longer necessary for the purpose for which it was collected and there are no pending requests or orders for access to such information under subsection (b)(2) or (c)(2) or pursuant to a court order.

(f) Preemption. - The provisions of this section preempt only the provisions of State or local law that require disclosure prohibited by this section.

EMPLOYEE POLYGRAPH PROTECTION
ACT (1988)

Summary

The Employee Polygraph Protection Act of 1988 prohibits any employer from: (1) requiring or suggesting that an employee or prospective employee take a lie detector test; (2) using lie detector test results; or (3) taking employment action against an employee or prospective employee who refuses to take a lie detector test or institutes or testifies in a proceeding under or related to this Act. The Act requires the Secretary to Labor (the Secretary) to prepare notices setting forth such prohibitions, and requires employers to post such notices.

The Act provides civil penalties for violations of this Act, and grants the Secretary authority to restrain violations of the Act. It allows employees and prospective employees to bring civil actions against any employer who violates its provisions.

The Act exempts from coverage under this Act: (1) Federal, State, and local governments; (2) certain Federal contractors; (3) tests conducted pursuant to the performance of intelligence or counterintelligence functions or Federal security clearances; (4) certain security personnel and other security services; and (5) employers who are authorized to manufacture, distribute, or dispense controlled substances. It provides a limited exemption under which an employer may request certain employees to submit to a polygraph test if the test is administered in connection with an ongoing investigation involving economic loss or injury to the employer's business, including theft, embezzlement, misappropriation, or an act of unlawful industrial espionage or sabotage. The Act specifies reporting requirements of the employer under such circumstances. It further declares that such limited exemption does not apply if an employee is discharged, dismissed, disciplined, or discriminated against in any manner on the basis of the results of one or more polygraph tests or the refusal to take a polygraph test, without additional supporting evidence.

The Act sets forth the rights of an examinee during a pretest phase, the actual testing phase, and the post-test phase. It specifies the qualification of an examiner. It prohibits the disclosure of information obtained from a polygraph test, except as provided by the Act.

References

Public Law 100-347 codified at 29 U.S.C. § 2001 et seq.
[https://www.law.cornell.edu/uscode/text/29/2001

Conference report, House Report 100-659 (May 26, 1988)

EPIC, Polygraph Testing
[http://www.epic.org/privacy/polygraph/]

United States
Employee Polygraph Protection Act

29 U.S.C. Sec. 2001. Definitions

As used in this chapter:

(1) Commerce

The term "commerce" has the meaning provided by section 203(b) of this title.

(2) Employer

The term "employer" includes any person acting directly or indirectly in the interest of an employer in relation to an employee or prospective employee.

(3) Lie detector

The term "lie detector" includes a polygraph, deceptograph, voice stress analyzer, psychological stress evaluator, or any other similar device (whether mechanical or electrical) that is used, or the results of which are used, for the purpose of rendering a diagnostic opinion regarding the honesty or dishonesty of an individual.

(4) Polygraph

The term "polygraph" means an instrument that -

(A) records continuously, visually, permanently, and simultaneously changes in cardiovascular, respiratory, and electrodermal patterns as minimum instrumentation standards; and

(B) is used, or the results of which are used, for the

purpose of rendering a diagnostic opinion regarding the honesty or dishonesty of an individual.

(5) Secretary

The term "Secretary" means the Secretary of Labor.

Sec. 2002. Prohibitions on lie detector use

Except as provided in sections 2006 and 2007 of this title, it shall be unlawful for any employer engaged in or affecting commerce or in the production of goods for commerce -

(1) directly or indirectly, to require, request, suggest, or cause any employee or prospective employee to take or submit to any lie detector test;

(2) to use, accept, refer to, or inquire concerning the results of any lie detector test of any employee or prospective employee;

(3) to discharge, discipline, discriminate against in any manner, or deny employment or promotion to, or threaten to take any such action against -

(A) any employee or prospective employee who refuses, declines, or fails to take or submit to any lie detector test, or

(B) any employee or prospective employee on the basis of the results of any lie detector test; or

(4) to discharge, discipline, discriminate against in any manner, or deny employment or promotion to, or threaten to take any such action against, any employee or prospective employee because -

(A) such employee or prospective employee has filed any complaint or instituted or caused to be instituted any proceeding under or related to this chapter,

(B) such employee or prospective employee has testified or is about to testify in any such proceeding, or

(C) of the exercise by such employee or prospective employee, on behalf of such employee or another person, of any right afforded by this chapter.

Sec. 2003. Notice of protection

The Secretary shall prepare, have printed, and distribute a notice setting forth excerpts from, or summaries of, the pertinent provisions of this chapter. Each employer shall post and maintain such notice in conspicuous places on its premises where notices to employees and applicants to employment are customarily posted.

Sec. 2004. Authority of Secretary

(a) In general

The Secretary shall -

(1) issue such rules and regulations as may be necessary or appropriate to carry out this chapter;

(2) cooperate with regional, State, local, and other agencies, and cooperate with and furnish technical assistance to employers, labor organizations, and employment agencies to aid in effectuating the purposes of this chapter; and

(3) make investigations and inspections and require the keeping of records necessary or appropriate for the administration of this chapter.

(b) Subpoena authority

For the purpose of any hearing or investigation under this chapter, the Secretary shall have the authority contained in sections 49 and 50 of title 15.

Sec. 2005. Enforcement provisions

(a) Civil penalties

(1) In general

Subject to paragraph (2), any employer who violates any provision of this chapter may be assessed a civil penalty of not more than $10,000.

(2) Determination of amount

In determining the amount of any penalty under paragraph (1), the Secretary shall take into account the previous record of the person in terms of compliance with this chapter and the gravity of the violation.

(3) Collection

Any civil penalty assessed under this subsection shall be collected in the same manner as is required by subsections (b) through (e) of section 1853 of this title with respect to civil penalties assessed under subsection (a) of such section.

(b) Injunctive actions by Secretary

The Secretary may bring an action under this section to restrain violations of this chapter. The Solicitor of Labor may appear for and represent the Secretary in any litigation brought under this chapter. In any action brought under this section, the district courts of the United States shall have jurisdiction, for cause shown, to issue temporary or permanent restraining orders and injunctions to require compliance with this chapter, including such legal or equitable relief incident thereto as may be appropriate, including, but not limited to, employment, reinstatement, promotion, and the payment of lost wages and benefits.

(c) Private civil actions

(1) Liability

An employer who violates this chapter shall be liable to the employee or prospective employee affected by such violation. Such employer shall be liable for such legal or equitable relief as may be appropriate, including, but not limited to, employment, reinstatement, promotion, and the payment of lost wages and benefits.

(2) Court

An action to recover the liability prescribed in paragraph (1) may be maintained against the employer in any Federal or State court of competent jurisdiction by an employee or prospective employee for or on behalf of such employee, prospective employee, and other employees or prospective employees similarly situated. No such action may be commenced more than 3 years after the date of the alleged violation.

(3) Costs

The court, in its discretion, may allow the prevailing party (other than the United States) reasonable costs, including attorney's fees.

(d) Waiver of rights prohibited

The rights and procedures provided by this chapter may not be waived by contract or otherwise, unless such waiver is part of a written settlement agreed to and signed by the parties to the pending action or complaint under this chapter.

Sec. 2006. Exemptions

(a) No application to governmental employers

This chapter shall not apply with respect to the United States Government, any State or local government, or any political subdivision of a State or local government.

(b) National defense and security exemption

(1) National defense

Nothing in this chapter shall be construed to prohibit the administration, by the Federal Government, in the performance of any counterintelligence function, of any lie detector test to-

(A) any expert or consultant under contract to the Department of Defense or any employee of any contractor of such Department; or

(B) any expert or consultant under contract with the Department of Energy in connection with the atomic energy defense activities of such Department or any employee of any contractor of such Department in connection with such activities.

(2) Security

Nothing in this chapter shall be construed to prohibit the administration, by the Federal Government, in the performance of any intelligence or counterintelligence function, of any lie detector test to-

(A)(i) any individual employed by, assigned to, or detailed to, the National Security Agency, the Defense Intelligence Agency, the National Geospatial-Intelligence Agency, or the Central Intelligence Agency,

(ii) any expert or consultant under contract to any such agency,

(iii) any employee of a contractor to any such agency,

(iv) any individual applying for a position in any such agency, or

(v) any individual assigned to a space where sensitive cryptologic information is produced, processed, or stored for any such agency; or

(B) any expert, or consultant (or employee of such expert or consultant) under contract with any Federal Government department, agency, or program whose duties involve access to information that has been classified at the level of top secret or designated as being within a special access program under section 4.2(a) of Executive Order 12356 (or a successor Executive order).

(c) FBI contractors exemption

Nothing in this chapter shall be construed to prohibit the administration, by the Federal Government, in the performance of any counterintelligence function, of any lie detector test to an employee of a contractor of the Federal Bureau of Investigation of the Department of Justice who is engaged in the performance of any work under the contract with such Bureau.

(d) Limited exemption for ongoing investigations

Subject to sections 2007 and 2009 of this title, this chapter shall not prohibit an employer from requesting an employee to submit to a polygraph test if-

(1) the test is administered in connection with an ongoing investigation involving economic loss or injury to the employer's business, such as theft, embezzlement, misappropriation, or an act of unlawful industrial espionage or sabotage;

(2) the employee had access to the property that is the subject of the investigation;

(3) the employer has a reasonable suspicion that the employee was involved in the incident or activity under investigation; and

(4) the employer executes a statement, provided to the examinee before the test, that-

(A) sets forth with particularity the specific incident or activity being investigated and the basis for testing particular employees,

(B) is signed by a person (other than a polygraph examiner) authorized to legally bind the employer,

(C) is retained by the employer for at least 3 years, and

(D) contains at a minimum-

(i) an identification of the specific economic loss or injury to the business of the employer,

(ii) a statement indicating that the employee had access to the property that is the subject of the investigation, and

(iii) a statement describing the basis of the employer's reasonable suspicion that the employee was involved in the incident or activity under investigation.

(e) Exemption for security services

(1) In general

Subject to paragraph (2) and sections 2007 and 2009 of this title, this chapter shall not prohibit the use of polygraph tests on prospective employees by any private employer whose primary business purpose consists of providing armored car personnel, personnel engaged in the design, installation, and maintenance of security alarm systems, or other uniformed or plainclothes security personnel and whose function includes protection of-

(A) facilities, materials, or operations having a significant impact on the health or safety of any State or political subdivision thereof, or the national security of the United States, as determined under rules and regulations issued by the Secretary within 90 days after June 27, 1988, including-

(i) facilities engaged in the production, transmission, or distribution of electric or nuclear power,

(ii) public water supply facilities,

(iii) shipments or storage of radioactive or other toxic waste materials, and

(iv) public transportation, or

(B) currency, negotiable securities, precious commodities or instruments, or proprietary information.

(2) Access

The exemption provided under this subsection shall not apply if the test is administered to a prospective employee who would not be employed to protect facilities, materials, operations, or assets referred to in paragraph (1).

(f) Exemption for drug security, drug theft, or drug diversion investigations

(1) In general

Subject to paragraph (2) and sections 2007 and 2009 of this title, this chapter shall not prohibit the use of a polygraph test by any employer authorized to manufacture, distribute, or dispense a controlled substance listed in schedule I, II, III, or IV of section 812 of title 21.

(2) Access

The exemption provided under this subsection shall apply-

(A) if the test is administered to a prospective employee who would have direct access to the manufacture, storage, distribution, or sale of any such controlled substance; or

(B) in the case of a test administered to a current employee, if-

(i) the test is administered in connection with an ongoing investigation of criminal or other misconduct involving, or potentially involving, loss or injury to the manufacture, distribution, or dispensing of any such controlled substance by such employer, and

(ii) the employee had access to the person or property that is the subject of the investigation.

Sec. 2007. Restrictions on use of exemptions

(a) Test as basis for adverse employment action

(1) Under ongoing investigations exemption

Except as provided in paragraph (2), the exemption under subsection (d) of section 2006 of this title shall not apply if an employee is discharged, disciplined, denied employment or promotion, or otherwise discriminated against in any manner on the basis of the analysis of a polygraph test chart or the refusal to take a polygraph test, without additional supporting evidence. The evidence required by such subsection may serve as additional supporting evidence.

(2) Under other exemptions

In the case of an exemption described in subsection (e) or (f) of such section, the exemption shall not apply if the results of an analysis of a polygraph test chart are used, or the refusal to take a polygraph test is used, as the sole basis upon which an adverse employment action described in paragraph (1) is taken against an employee or prospective employee.

(b) Rights of examinee

The exemptions provided under subsections (d), (e), and (f) of section 2006 of this title shall not apply unless the requirements described in the following paragraphs are met:

(1) All phases

Throughout all phases of the test -

(A) the examinee shall be permitted to terminate the test at any time;

(B) the examinee is not asked questions in a manner designed to degrade, or needlessly intrude on, such examinee;

(C) the examinee is not asked any question concerning -

(i) religious beliefs or affiliations,

(ii) beliefs or opinions regarding racial matters,

(iii) political beliefs or affiliations,

(iv) any matter relating to sexual behavior; and

(v) beliefs, affiliations, opinions, or lawful activities regarding unions or labor organizations; and

(D) the examiner does not conduct the test if there is sufficient written evidence by a physician that the examinee is suffering from a medical or psychological condition or undergoing treatment that might cause abnormal responses during the actual testing phase.

(2) Pretest phase

During the pretest phase, the prospective examinee -

(A) is provided with reasonable written notice of the date, time, and location of the test, and of such examinee's right to obtain and consult with legal counsel or an employee representative before each phase of the test;

(B) is informed in writing of the nature and characteristics

of the tests and of the instruments involved;

(C) is informed, in writing -

(i) whether the testing area contains a two-way mirror, a camera, or any other device through which the test can be observed,

(ii) whether any other device, including any device for recording or monitoring the test, will be used, or

(iii) that the employer or the examinee may (with mutual knowledge) make a recording of the test;

(D) is read and signs a written notice informing such examinee -

(i) that the examinee cannot be required to take the test as a condition of employment,

(ii) that any statement made during the test may constitute additional supporting evidence for the purposes of an adverse employment action described in subsection (a) of this section,

(iii) of the limitations imposed under this section,

(iv) of the legal rights and remedies available to the examinee if the polygraph test is not conducted in accordance with this chapter, and

(v) of the legal rights and remedies of the employer under this chapter (including the rights of the employer under section 2008(c)(2) of this title); and

(E) is provided an opportunity to review all questions to be asked during the test and is informed of the right to terminate the test at any time.

(3) Actual testing phase

During the actual testing phase, the examiner does not ask such examinee any question relevant during the test that was not presented in writing for review to such examinee before the test.

(4) Post-test phase

Before any adverse employment action, the employer shall -

(A) further interview the examinee on the basis of the results of the test; and

(B) provide the examinee with -

(i) a written copy of any opinion or conclusion rendered as a result of the test, and

(ii) a copy of the questions asked during the test along with the corresponding charted responses.

(5) Maximum number and minimum duration of tests The examiner shall not conduct and complete more than five polygraph tests on a calendar day on which the test is given, and shall not conduct any such test for less than a 90-minute duration.

(c) Qualifications and requirements of examiners

The exemptions provided under subsections (d), (e), and (f) of section 2006 of this title shall not apply unless the individual who conducts the polygraph test satisfies the requirements under the following paragraphs:

(1) Qualifications

The examiner -

(A) has a valid and current license granted by licensing and regulatory authorities in the State in which the test is to be conducted, if so required by the State; and

(B) maintains a minimum of a $50,000 bond or an equivalent amount of professional liability coverage.

(2) Requirements

The examiner -

(A) renders any opinion or conclusion regarding the test -

(i) in writing and solely on the basis of an analysis of polygraph test charts,

(ii) that does not contain information other than admissions, information, case facts, and interpretation of the charts relevant to the purpose and stated objectives of the test, and

(iii) that does not include any recommendation concerning the employment of the examinee; and

(B) maintains all opinions, reports, charts, written questions, lists, and other records relating to the test for a minimum period of 3 years after administration of the test.

United States
Employee Polygraph Protection Act

Sec. 2008. Disclosure of information

(a) In general

A person, other than the examinee, may not disclose information obtained during a polygraph test, except as provided in this section.

(b) Permitted disclosures

A polygraph examiner may disclose information acquired from a polygraph test only to -

(1) the examinee or any other person specifically designated in writing by the examinee;

(2) the employer that requested the test; or

(3) any court, governmental agency, arbitrator, or mediator, in accordance with due process of law, pursuant to an order from a court of competent jurisdiction.

(c) Disclosure by employer

An employer (other than an employer described in subsection (a), (b), or (c) of section 2006 of this title) for whom a polygraph test is conducted may disclose information from the test only to -

(1) a person in accordance with subsection (b) of this section; or

(2) a governmental agency, but only insofar as the disclosed information is an admission of criminal conduct.

Sec. 2009. Effect on other law and agreements

Except as provided in subsections (a), (b), and (c) of section 2006 of this title, this chapter shall not preempt any provision of any State or local law or of any negotiated collective bargaining agreement that prohibits lie detector tests or is more restrictive with respect to lie detector tests than any provision of this chapter.

TELEPHONE CONSUMER PROTECTION
ACT (1991)

Summary

The Telephone Consumer Protection Act of 1991 (TCPA) amended the Communications Act of 1934 to prohibit any person within the United States from using an automatic telephone dialing system to make a call to any emergency telephone line or to any telephone number for which the called party is charged for the call without the consent of the called party, with specified exceptions. The Act also prohibited the use of a telephone facsimile machine, computer, or other device to send an unsolicited advertisement to a FAX machine. The Act also directs the Federal Communications Commission (FCC) to issue regulations to implement these requirements, and authorizes private actions and the recovery of damages with respect to violations of such requirements.

The Act further directs the FCC to initiate a rulemaking proceeding concerning the need to protect residential telephone subscribers' privacy rights to avoid receiving telephone solicitations to which they object and issue regulations to implement methods and procedures for protecting such privacy rights without the imposition of any additional charge to telephone subscribers. It states that such regulations may require the establishment and operation of a single national database to compile a list of telephone numbers of residential subscribers who object to receiving such solicitations, or to receiving certain classes or categories of solicitations, and to make the compiled list available for purchase. The Act authorizes private actions and the recovery of damages with respect to violations of such privacy rights.

The Act makes it unlawful for any person within the United States to initiate any communication using a FAX that does not comply with certain technical and procedural standards or to use a computer or other electronic device to send any message via FAX unless such person clearly marks on the document the date and time it is sent and identifies the entity sending the message and the telephone number of the sending machine or entity.

The Act permits states to bring civil actions to enjoin calls to residents in violation of the Act and to recover monetary damages. It grants U.S. district courts exclusive jurisdiction over such actions. It prohibits a State, whenever the FCC has instituted a civil action for violation of this Act, from bringing an action against any defendant named in the FCC's complaint.

In 2002, the Federal Trade Commission, followed by the FCC, issued rules to implement a national do-not-call registry which will be fully operational in October 2003. Additionally, the FCC issued new rules regulating unsolicited commercial faxes in order to curb the practices of "fax broadcasters," companies that send massive amounts of fax advertising to individuals. The new rules, which do not take effect until 2005, require the acquisition of written consent from the recipient before individuals can transmit unsolicited commercial faxes.

United States
Telephone Consumer Protection Act

References

> Public Law 102-243 codified at 47 U.S.C. § 227
> [https://www.law.cornell.edu/uscode/text/47/227]
>
> EPIC, Telephone Consumer Protection Act (TCPA)
> [https://www.epic.org/privacy/telemarketing/]

Congressional Statement of Findings

Section 2 of Pub. L. 102-243 provided that: "The Congress finds that:

"(1) The use of the telephone to market goods and services to the home and other businesses is now pervasive due to the increased use of cost-effective telemarketing techniques.

"(2) Over 30,000 businesses actively telemarket goods and services to business and residential customers.

"(3) More than 300,000 solicitors call more than 18,000,000 Americans every day.

"(4) Total United States sales generated through telemarketing amounted to $435,000,000,000 in 1990, a more than four-fold increase since 1984.

"(5) Unrestricted telemarketing, however, can be an intrusive invasion of privacy and, when an emergency or medical assistance telephone line is seized, a risk to public safety.

"(6) Many consumers are outraged over the proliferation of intrusive, nuisance calls to their homes from telemarketers.

"(7) Over half the States now have statutes restricting various uses of the telephone for marketing, but telemarketers can evade their prohibitions through interstate operations; therefore, Federal law is needed to control residential telemarketing practices.

"(8) The Constitution does not prohibit restrictions on commercial telemarketing solicitations.

"(9) Individuals' privacy rights, public safety interests, and commercial freedoms of speech and trade must be balanced in a way that protects the privacy of individuals and permits legitimate telemarketing practices.

"(10) Evidence compiled by the Congress indicates that residential telephone subscribers consider automated or prerecorded telephone calls, regardless of the content or the initiator of the message, to be a nuisance and an invasion of privacy.

"(11) Technologies that might allow consumers to avoid receiving such calls are not universally available, are costly, are unlikely to be enforced, or place an inordinate burden on the consumer.

"(12) Banning such automated or prerecorded telephone calls to the home, except when the receiving party consents to receiving the call or when such calls are necessary in an emergency situation affecting the health and safety of the consumer, is the only effective means of protecting telephone consumers from this nuisance and privacy invasion.

"(13) While the evidence presented to the Congress indicates that automated or prerecorded calls are a nuisance and an invasion of privacy, regardless of the type of call, the Federal Communications Commission should have the flexibility to design different rules for those types of automated or prerecorded calls that it finds are not considered a nuisance or invasion of privacy, or for noncommercial calls, consistent with the free speech protections embodied in the First Amendment of the Constitution.

"(14) Businesses also have complained to the Congress and the Federal Communications Commission that automated or prerecorded telephone calls are a nuisance, are an invasion of privacy, and interfere with interstate commerce.

"(15) The Federal Communications Commission should consider adopting reasonable restrictions on automated or prerecorded calls to businesses as well as to the home, consistent with the constitutional protections of free speech."

47 U.S.C. Sec. 227. Restrictions on use of telephone equipment

(a) Definitions

As used in this section-

(1) The term "automatic telephone dialing system" means equipment which has the capacity-

(A) to store or produce telephone numbers to be called, using a random or sequential number generator; and

(B) to dial such numbers.

(2) The term "established business relationship", for purposes only of subsection (b)(1)(C)(i), shall have the meaning given the term in section 64.1200 of title 47, Code of Federal Regulations, as in effect on January 1, 2003, except that-

(A) such term shall include a relationship between a person or entity and a business subscriber subject to the same terms applicable under such section to a relationship between a person or entity and a residential subscriber; and

(B) an established business relationship shall be subject to any time limitation established pursuant to paragraph (2)(G)).

(3) The term "telephone facsimile machine" means equipment which has the capacity (A) to transcribe text or images, or both, from paper into an electronic signal and to transmit that signal over a regular telephone line, or (B) to transcribe text or images (or both) from an electronic signal received over a regular telephone line onto paper.

(4) The term "telephone solicitation" means the initiation of a telephone call or message for the purpose of encouraging the purchase or rental of, or investment in, property, goods, or services, which is transmitted to any person, but such term does not include a call or message (A) to any person with that person's prior

express invitation or permission, (B) to any person with whom the caller has an established business relationship, or (C) by a tax exempt nonprofit organization.

(5) The term "unsolicited advertisement" means any material advertising the commercial availability or quality of any property, goods, or services which is transmitted to any person without that person's prior express invitation or permission, in writing or otherwise.

(b) Restrictions on use of automated telephone equipment

(1) Prohibitions

It shall be unlawful for any person within the United States, or any person outside the United States if the recipient is within the United States-

(A) to make any call (other than a call made for emergency purposes or made with the prior express consent of the called party) using any automatic telephone dialing system or an artificial or prerecorded voice-

(i) to any emergency telephone line (including any "911" line and any emergency line of a hospital, medical physician or service office, health care facility, poison control center, or fire protection or law enforcement agency);

(ii) to the telephone line of any guest room or patient room of a hospital, health care facility, elderly home, or similar establishment; or

(iii) to any telephone number assigned to a paging service, cellular telephone service, specialized mobile radio service, or other radio common carrier service, or any service for which the called party is charged for the call, unless such call is made solely to collect a debt owed to or guaranteed by the United States;

(B) to initiate any telephone call to any residential telephone line using an artificial or prerecorded voice to deliver a message without the prior express consent of the called party, unless the call is initiated for emergency purposes, is made solely pursuant to the collection of a debt owed to or guaranteed by the United States, or is exempted by rule or order by the Commission under paragraph (2)(B);

(C) to use any telephone facsimile machine, computer, or other device to send, to a telephone facsimile machine, an unsolicited advertisement, unless-

(i) the unsolicited advertisement is from a sender with an established business relationship with the recipient;

(ii) the sender obtained the number of the telephone facsimile machine through-

(I) the voluntary communication of such number, within the context of such established business relationship, from the recipient of the unsolicited advertisement, or

(II) a directory, advertisement, or site on the Internet to which the recipient voluntarily agreed to make available its facsimile number for public distribution, except that this clause shall not apply in the case of an unsolicited advertisement that is sent based on an established business relationship with the recipient that was in existence before July 9, 2005, if the sender possessed the facsimile machine number of the recipient before July 9, 2005; and

(iii) the unsolicited advertisement contains a notice meeting the requirements under paragraph (2)(D), except that the exception under clauses (i) and (ii) shall not apply with respect to an unsolicited advertisement sent to a telephone facsimile machine by a sender to whom a request has been made not to send future unsolicited advertisements to such telephone facsimile machine that complies with the requirements under paragraph (2)(E); or

(D) to use an automatic telephone dialing system in such a way that two or more telephone lines of a multi-line business are engaged simultaneously.

(2) Regulations; exemptions and other provisions

The Commission shall prescribe regulations to implement the requirements of this subsection. In implementing the requirements of this subsection, the Commission-

(A) shall consider prescribing regulations to allow businesses to avoid receiving calls made using an artificial or prerecorded voice to which they have not given their prior express consent;

(B) may, by rule or order, exempt from the requirements of paragraph (1)(B) of this subsection, subject to such conditions as the Commission may prescribe-

(i) calls that are not made for a commercial purpose; and

(ii) such classes or categories of calls made for commercial purposes as the Commission determines-

(I) will not adversely affect the privacy rights that this section is intended to protect; and

(II) do not include the transmission of any unsolicited advertisement;

(C) may, by rule or order, exempt from the requirements of paragraph (1)(A)(iii) of this subsection calls to a telephone number assigned to a cellular telephone service that are not charged to the called party, subject to such conditions as the Commission may prescribe as necessary in the interest of the privacy rights this section is intended to protect;

(D) shall provide that a notice contained in an unsolicited advertisement complies with the requirements under this subparagraph only if-

(i) the notice is clear and conspicuous and on the first page of the unsolicited advertisement;

(ii) the notice states that the recipient may make a request to the sender of the unsolicited advertisement not to send any future unsolicited advertisements to a telephone facsimile machine or machines and that failure to comply, within the shortest reasonable time, as determined by the Commission, with such a request meeting the requirements under subparagraph (E) is unlawful;

(iii) the notice sets forth the requirements for a request under subparagraph (E);

(iv) the notice includes-

(I) a domestic contact telephone and facsimile machine number for the recipient to transmit such a request to the sender; and

(II) a cost-free mechanism for a recipient to transmit a request pursuant to such notice to the sender of the unsolicited advertisement; the Commission shall by rule require the sender to provide such a mechanism and may, in the discretion of the Commission and subject to such conditions as the Commission may prescribe, exempt certain classes of small business senders, but only if the Commission determines that the costs to such class are unduly burdensome given the revenues generated by such small businesses;

(v) the telephone and facsimile machine numbers and the cost-free mechanism set forth pursuant to clause (iv) permit an individual or business to make such a request at any time on any day of the week; and

(vi) the notice complies with the requirements of subsection (d);

(E) shall provide, by rule, that a request not to send future unsolicited advertisements to a telephone facsimile machine complies with the requirements under this subparagraph only if-

(i) the request identifies the telephone number or numbers of the telephone facsimile machine or machines to which the request relates;

(ii) the request is made to the telephone or facsimile number of the sender of such an unsolicited advertisement provided pursuant to subparagraph (D)(iv) or by any other method of communication as determined by the Commission; and

(iii) the person making the request has not, subsequent to such request, provided express invitation or permission to the sender, in writing or otherwise, to send such advertisements to such person at such telephone facsimile machine;

(F) may, in the discretion of the Commission and subject to such conditions as the Commission may prescribe, allow professional or trade associations that are tax-exempt nonprofit organizations to send unsolicited advertisements to their members in furtherance of the association's tax-exempt purpose that do not contain the notice required by paragraph (1)(C)(iii), except that the Commission may take action under this subparagraph only-

(i) by regulation issued after public notice and opportunity for public comment; and

(ii) if the Commission determines that such notice required by paragraph (1)(C)(iii) is not necessary to protect the ability of the members of such associations to stop such associations from sending any future unsolicited advertisements;

(G)

(i) may, consistent with clause (ii), limit the duration of the existence of an established business relationship, however, before establishing any such limits, the Commission shall-

(I) determine whether the existence of the exception under paragraph (1)(C) relating to an established business relationship has resulted in a significant number of complaints to the Commission regarding the sending of unsolicited advertisements to telephone facsimile machines;

(II) determine whether a significant number of any such complaints involve unsolicited advertisements that were sent on the basis of an established business relationship that was longer in duration than the Commission believes is consistent with the reasonable expectations of consumers;

(III) evaluate the costs to senders of demonstrating the existence of an established business relationship within a specified period of time and the benefits to recipients of establishing a limitation on such established business relationship; and

(IV) determine whether with respect to small businesses, the costs would not be unduly burdensome; and

(ii) may not commence a proceeding to determine whether to limit the duration of the existence of an established business relationship before the expiration of the 3-month period that begins on July 9, 2005; and

(H) may restrict or limit the number and duration of calls made to a telephone number assigned to a cellular telephone service to collect a debt owed to or guaranteed by the United States.

(3) Private right of action

A person or entity may, if otherwise permitted by the laws or rules of court of a State, bring in an appropriate court of that State-

(A) an action based on a violation of this subsection or the regulations prescribed under this subsection to enjoin such violation,

(B) an action to recover for actual monetary loss from such a violation, or to receive $500 in damages for each such violation, whichever is greater, or

(C) both such actions.

If the court finds that the defendant willfully or knowingly violated this subsection or the regulations prescribed under this subsection, the court may, in its discretion, increase the amount of the award to an amount equal to not more than 3 times the amount available under subparagraph (B) of this paragraph.

(c) Protection of subscriber privacy rights

(1) Rulemaking proceeding required

Within 120 days after December 20, 1991, the Commission shall initiate a rulemaking proceeding concerning the need to protect residential telephone subscribers' privacy rights to avoid receiving telephone solicitations to which they object. The proceeding shall-

(A) compare and evaluate alternative methods and procedures (including the use of electronic databases, telephone network technologies, special directory markings, industry-based or company-specific "do not call" systems, and any other alternatives, individually or in combination) for their effectiveness in protecting such privacy rights, and in terms of their cost and other advantages and disadvantages;

(B) evaluate the categories of public and private entities that would have the capacity to establish and administer such methods and procedures;

(C) consider whether different methods and procedures may apply for local telephone solicitations, such as local telephone solicitations of small businesses or holders of second class mail permits;

(D) consider whether there is a need for additional Commission authority to further restrict telephone solicitations, including those calls exempted under subsection (a)(3) of this section, and, if such a finding is made and supported by the record, propose specific restrictions to the Congress; and

(E) develop proposed regulations to implement the methods and procedures that the Commission determines are most effective and efficient to accomplish the purposes of this section.

(2) Regulations

Not later than 9 months after December 20, 1991, the Commission shall conclude the rulemaking proceeding initiated under paragraph (1) and shall prescribe regulations to implement methods and procedures for protecting the privacy rights described in such paragraph in an efficient, effective, and economic manner and without the imposition of any additional charge to telephone subscribers.

(3) Use of database permitted

The regulations required by paragraph (2) may require the establishment and operation of a single national database to compile a list of telephone numbers of residential subscribers who object to receiving telephone solicitations, and to make that compiled list and parts thereof available for purchase. If the Commission determines to require such a database, such regulations shall-

(A) specify a method by which the Commission will select an entity to administer such database;

(B) require each common carrier providing telephone exchange service, in accordance with regulations prescribed by the Commission, to inform subscribers for telephone exchange service of the opportunity to provide notification, in accordance with regulations established under this paragraph, that such subscriber objects to receiving telephone solicitations;

(C) specify the methods by which each telephone subscriber shall be informed, by the common carrier that provides local exchange service to that subscriber, of (i) the subscriber's right to give or revoke a notification of an objection under subparagraph (A), and (ii) the methods by which such right may be exercised by the subscriber;

(D) specify the methods by which such objections shall be collected and added to the database;

(E) prohibit any residential subscriber from being charged for giving or revoking such notification or for being included in a database compiled under this section;

(F) prohibit any person from making or transmitting a telephone solicitation to the telephone number of any subscriber included in such database;

(G) specify (i) the methods by which any person desiring to make or transmit telephone solicitations will obtain access to the database, by area code or local exchange prefix, as required to avoid calling the telephone numbers of subscribers included in such database; and (ii) the costs to be recovered from such persons;

(H) specify the methods for recovering, from persons accessing such database, the costs involved in identifying, collecting, updating, disseminating, and selling, and other activities relating to, the operations of the database that are incurred by the entities carrying out those activities;

(I) specify the frequency with which such database will be updated and specify the method by which such updating will take effect for purposes of compliance with the regulations prescribed under this subsection;

(J) be designed to enable States to use the database mechanism selected by the Commission for purposes of administering or enforcing State law;

(K) prohibit the use of such database for any purpose other than compliance with the requirements of this section and any such State law and specify methods for protection of the privacy rights of persons whose numbers are included in such database; and

(L) require each common carrier providing services to any person for the purpose of making telephone solicitations to notify such person of the requirements of this section and the regulations thereunder.

(4) Considerations required for use of database method

If the Commission determines to require the database mechanism described in paragraph (3), the Commission shall-

(A) in developing procedures for gaining access to the database, consider the different needs of telemarketers conducting business on a national, regional, State, or local level;

(B) develop a fee schedule or price structure for recouping the cost of such database that recognizes such differences and-

(i) reflect the relative costs of providing a national, regional, State, or local list of phone numbers of subscribers who object to receiving telephone solicitations;

(ii) reflect the relative costs of providing such lists on paper or electronic media; and

(iii) not place an unreasonable financial burden on small businesses; and

(C) consider (i) whether the needs of telemarketers operating on a local basis could be met through special markings of area white pages directories, and (ii) if such directories are needed as an adjunct to database lists prepared by area code and local exchange prefix.

(5) Private right of action

A person who has received more than one telephone call within any 12-month period by or on behalf of the same entity in violation of the regulations prescribed under this subsection may, if otherwise permitted by the laws or rules of court of a State bring in an appropriate court of that State-

(A) an action based on a violation of the regulations prescribed under this subsection to enjoin such violation,

(B) an action to recover for actual monetary loss from such a violation, or to receive up to $500 in damages for each such violation, whichever is greater, or

(C) both such actions.

It shall be an affirmative defense in any action brought under this paragraph that the defendant has established and implemented, with due care, reasonable practices and procedures to effectively prevent telephone solicitations in violation of the regulations prescribed under this subsection. If the court finds that the defendant willfully or knowingly violated the regulations prescribed under this subsection, the court may, in its discretion, increase the amount of the award to an amount equal to not more than 3 times the amount available under subparagraph (B) of this paragraph.

(6) Relation to subsection (b)

The provisions of this subsection shall not be construed to permit a communication prohibited by subsection (b).

(d) Technical and procedural standards

(1) Prohibition

It shall be unlawful for any person within the United States-

(A) to initiate any communication using a telephone facsimile machine, or to make any telephone call using any automatic telephone dialing system, that does not comply with the technical and procedural standards prescribed under this subsection, or to use any telephone facsimile machine or automatic telephone dialing system in a manner that does not comply with such standards; or

(B) to use a computer or other electronic device to send any message via a telephone facsimile machine unless such person clearly marks, in a margin at the top or bottom of each transmitted page of the message or on the first page of the transmission, the date and time it is sent and an identification of the business, other entity, or individual sending the message and the telephone number of the sending machine or of such business, other entity, or individual.

(2) Telephone facsimile machines

The Commission shall revise the regulations setting technical and procedural standards for telephone facsimile machines to require that any such machine which is manufactured after one year after December 20, 1991, clearly marks, in a margin at the top or bottom of each transmitted page or on the first page of each transmission, the date and time sent, an identification of the business, other entity, or individual sending the message, and the telephone number of the sending machine or of such business, other entity, or individual.

(3) Artificial or prerecorded voice systems

The Commission shall prescribe technical and procedural standards for systems that are used to transmit any artificial or prerecorded voice message via telephone. Such standards shall require that-

(A) all artificial or prerecorded telephone messages (i) shall, at the beginning of the message, state clearly the identity of the business, individual, or other entity initiating the call, and (ii) shall, during or after the message, state clearly the telephone number or address of such business, other entity, or individual; and

(B) any such system will automatically release the called party's line within 5 seconds of the time notification is transmitted to the system that the called party has hung up, to allow the called party's line to be used to make or receive other calls.

United States
Telephone Consumer Protection Act

(e) Prohibition on provision of inaccurate caller identification information

(1) In general

It shall be unlawful for any person within the United States, in connection with any telecommunications service or IP-enabled voice service, to cause any caller identification service to knowingly transmit misleading or inaccurate caller identification information with the intent to defraud, cause harm, or wrongfully obtain anything of value, unless such transmission is exempted pursuant to paragraph (3)(B).

(2) Protection for blocking caller identification information

Nothing in this subsection may be construed to prevent or restrict any person from blocking the capability of any caller identification service to transmit caller identification information.

(3) Regulations

(A) In general

Not later than 6 months after December 22, 2010, the Commission shall prescribe regulations to implement this subsection.

(B) Content of regulations

(i) In general

The regulations required under subparagraph (A) shall include such exemptions from the prohibition under paragraph (1) as the Commission determines is appropriate.

(ii) Specific exemption for law enforcement agencies or court orders

The regulations required under subparagraph (A) shall exempt from the prohibition under paragraph (1) transmissions in connection with-

(I) any authorized activity of a law enforcement agency; or

(II) a court order that specifically authorizes the use of caller identification manipulation.

(4) Report

Not later than 6 months after December 22, 2010, the Commission shall report to Congress whether additional legislation is necessary to prohibit the provision of inaccurate caller identification information in technologies that are successor or replacement technologies to telecommunications service or IP-enabled voice service.

(5) Penalties

(A) Civil forfeiture

(i) In general

Any person that is determined by the Commission, in accordance with paragraphs (3) and (4) of section 503(b) of this title, to have violated this subsection shall be liable to the United States for a forfeiture penalty. A forfeiture penalty under this paragraph shall be in addition to any other penalty provided for by this chapter. The amount of the forfeiture penalty determined under this paragraph shall not exceed $10,000 for each violation, or 3 times that amount for each day of a continuing violation, except that the amount assessed for any continuing violation shall not exceed a total of $1,000,000 for any single act or failure to act.

(ii) Recovery

Any forfeiture penalty determined under clause (i) shall be recoverable pursuant to section 504(a) of this title.

(iii) Procedure

No forfeiture liability shall be determined under clause (i) against any person unless such person receives the notice required by section 503(b)(3) of this title or section 503(b)(4) of this title.

(iv) 2-year statute of limitations

No forfeiture penalty shall be determined or imposed against any person under clause (i) if the violation charged occurred more than 2 years prior to the date of issuance of the required notice or notice or apparent liability.

(B) Criminal fine

Any person who willfully and knowingly violates this subsection shall upon conviction thereof be fined not more than $10,000 for each violation, or 3 times that amount for each day of a continuing violation, in lieu of the fine provided by section 501 of this title for such a violation. This subparagraph does not supersede the provisions of section 501 of this title relating to imprisonment or the imposition of a penalty of both fine and imprisonment.

(6) Enforcement by States

(A) In general

The chief legal officer of a State, or any other State officer authorized by law to bring actions on behalf of the residents of a State, may bring a civil action, as parens patriae, on behalf of the residents of that State in an appropriate district court of the United States to enforce this subsection or to impose the civil penalties for violation of this subsection, whenever the chief legal officer or other State officer has reason to believe that the interests of the residents of the State have been or are being threatened or adversely affected by a violation of this subsection or a regulation under this subsection.

(B) Notice

The chief legal officer or other State officer shall serve written notice on the Commission of any civil action under subparagraph (A) prior to initiating such civil action. The notice shall include a copy of the complaint to be filed to initiate such civil action, except that if it is not feasible for the State to provide such prior notice, the State shall provide such notice immediately upon instituting such civil action.

(C) Authority to intervene

Upon receiving the notice required by subparagraph (B), the Commission shall have the right-

(i) to intervene in the action;

(ii) upon so intervening, to be heard on all matters arising therein; and

(iii) to file petitions for appeal.

(D) Construction

For purposes of bringing any civil action under subparagraph (A), nothing in this paragraph shall prevent the chief legal officer or other State officer from exercising the powers conferred on that officer by the laws of such State to conduct investigations or to administer oaths or affirmations or to compel the attendance of witnesses or the production of documentary and other evidence.

(E) Venue; service or process

(i) Venue

An action brought under subparagraph (A) shall be brought in a district court of the United States that meets applicable requirements relating to venue under section 1391 of title 28.

(ii) Service of process

In an action brought under subparagraph (A)-

(I) process may be served without regard to the territorial limits of the district or of the State in which the action is instituted; and

(II) a person who participated in an alleged violation that is being litigated in the civil action may be joined in the civil action without regard to the residence of the person.

(7) Effect on other laws

This subsection does not prohibit any lawfully authorized investigative, protective, or intelligence activity of a law enforcement agency of the United States, a State, or a political subdivision of a State, or of an intelligence agency of the United States.

(8) Definitions

For purposes of this subsection:

(A) Caller identification information

The term "caller identification information" means information provided by a caller identification service regarding the telephone number of, or other information regarding the origination of, a call made using a telecommunications service or IP-enabled voice service.

(B) Caller identification service

The term "caller identification service" means any service or device designed to provide the user of the service or device with the telephone number of, or other information regarding the origination of, a call made using a telecommunications service or IP-enabled voice service. Such term includes automatic number identification services.

(C) IP-enabled voice service

The term "IP-enabled voice service" has the meaning given that term by section 9.3 of the Commission's regulations (47 C.F.R. 9.3), as those regulations may be amended by the Commission from time to time.

(9) Limitation

Notwithstanding any other provision of this section, subsection (f) shall not apply to this subsection or to the regulations under this subsection.

(f) Effect on State law

(1) State law not preempted

Except for the standards prescribed under subsection (d) and subject to paragraph (2) of this subsection, nothing in this section or in the regulations prescribed under this section shall preempt any State law that imposes more restrictive intrastate requirements or regulations on, or which prohibits-

(A) the use of telephone facsimile machines or other electronic devices to send unsolicited advertisements;

(B) the use of automatic telephone dialing systems;

(C) the use of artificial or prerecorded voice messages; or

(D) the making of telephone solicitations.

(2) State use of databases

If, pursuant to subsection (c)(3), the Commission requires the establishment of a single national database of telephone numbers of subscribers who object to receiving telephone solicitations, a State or local authority may not, in its regulation of telephone solicitations, require the use of any database, list, or listing system that does not include the part of such single national database that relates to such State.

(g) Actions by States

(1) Authority of States

Whenever the attorney general of a State, or an official or agency designated by a State, has reason to believe that any person has engaged or is engaging in a pattern or practice of telephone calls or other transmissions to residents of that State in violation of this section or the regulations prescribed under this section, the State may bring a civil action on behalf of its residents to enjoin such calls, an action to recover for actual monetary loss or receive $500 in damages for each violation, or both such actions. If the court finds the defendant willfully or knowingly violated such regulations, the court may, in its discretion, increase the amount of the award to an amount equal to not more than 3 times the amount available under the preceding sentence.

(2) Exclusive jurisdiction of Federal courts

The district courts of the United States, the United States courts of any territory, and the District Court of the United States for the District of Columbia shall have exclusive jurisdiction over all civil actions brought under this subsection. Upon proper application, such courts shall also have jurisdiction to issue writs of mandamus, or orders affording like relief, commanding the defendant to comply with the provisions of this section or regulations prescribed under this section, including the requirement that the defendant take such action as is necessary to remove the danger of such violation. Upon a proper showing, a permanent or temporary injunction or restraining order shall be granted without bond.

(3) Rights of Commission

The State shall serve prior written notice of any such civil action upon the Commission and provide the Commission with a copy of its complaint, except in any case where such prior notice is not feasible, in which case the State shall serve such notice immediately upon instituting such action. The Commission shall have the right (A) to intervene in the action, (B) upon so intervening, to be heard on all matters arising therein, and (C) to file petitions for appeal.

(4) Venue; service of process

Any civil action brought under this subsection in a district court of the United States may be brought in the district wherein the defendant is found or is an inhabitant or transacts business or wherein the violation occurred or is occurring, and process in such cases may be served in any district in which the defendant is an inhabitant or where the defendant may be found.

(5) Investigatory powers

For purposes of bringing any civil action under this subsection, nothing in this section shall prevent the attorney general of a State, or an official or agency designated by a State, from exercising the powers conferred on the attorney general or such official by the laws of such State to conduct investigations or to administer oaths or affirmations or to compel the attendance of witnesses or the production of documentary and other evidence.

(6) Effect on State court proceedings

Nothing contained in this subsection shall be construed to prohibit an authorized State official from proceeding in State court on the basis of an alleged violation of any general civil or criminal statute of such State.

(7) Limitation

Whenever the Commission has instituted a civil action for violation of regulations prescribed under this section, no State may, during the pendency of such action instituted by the Commission, subsequently institute a civil action against any defendant named in the Commission's complaint for any violation as alleged in the Commission's complaint.

(8) "Attorney general" defined

As used in this subsection, the term "attorney general" means the chief legal officer of a State.

(h) Junk fax enforcement report

The Commission shall submit an annual report to Congress regarding the enforcement during the past year of the provisions of this section relating to sending of unsolicited advertisements to telephone facsimile machines, which report shall include-

(1) the number of complaints received by the Commission during such year alleging that a consumer received an unsolicited advertisement via telephone facsimile machine in violation of the Commission's rules;

(2) the number of citations issued by the Commission pursuant to section 503 of this title during the year to enforce any law, regulation, or policy relating to sending of unsolicited advertisements to telephone facsimile machines;

(3) the number of notices of apparent liability issued by the Commission pursuant to section 503 of this title during the year to enforce any law, regulation, or policy relating to sending of unsolicited advertisements to telephone facsimile machines;

(4) for each notice referred to in paragraph (3)-

(A) the amount of the proposed forfeiture penalty involved;

(B) the person to whom the notice was issued;

(C) the length of time between the date on which the complaint was filed and the date on which the notice was issued; and

(D) the status of the proceeding;

(5) the number of final orders imposing forfeiture penalties issued pursuant to section 503 of this title during the year to enforce any law, regulation, or policy relating to sending of unsolicited advertisements to telephone facsimile machines;

(6) for each forfeiture order referred to in paragraph (5)-

(A) the amount of the penalty imposed by the order;

(B) the person to whom the order was issued;

(C) whether the forfeiture penalty has been paid; and

(D) the amount paid;

(7) for each case in which a person has failed to pay a forfeiture penalty imposed by such a final order, whether the Commission referred such matter for recovery of the penalty; and

(8) for each case in which the Commission referred such an order for recovery-

(A) the number of days from the date the Commission issued such order to the date of such referral;

(B) whether an action has been commenced to recover the penalty, and if so, the number of days from the date the Commission referred such order for recovery to the date of such commencement; and

(C) whether the recovery action resulted in collection of any amount, and if so, the amount collected.

DRIVER'S PRIVACY PROTECTION ACT
(1994)

Summary

The Driver's Privacy Protection Act requires all States to protect the privacy of personal information contained in an individual's motor vehicle record. This information includes the driver's name, address, phone number, Social Security Number, driver identification number, photograph, height, weight, gender, age, certain medical or disability information, and in some states, fingerprints. It does not include information concerning a driver's traffic violations, license status, or accidents.

The Act has a number of exceptions. A driver's personal information may be obtained from the department of motor vehicles for any federal, state or local agency use in carrying out its functions; for any federal, state or local legal proceeding if the proceeding involves a motor vehicle; for automobile and driver safety purposes, such as conducting recall of motor vehicles; and for use in marketing activities if the individual has been given an opportunity to "opt-out."

The Act imposes criminal fines for non-compliance and grants individuals a private right of action including actual and punitive damages as well as attorney's fees and litigation costs.

In 1999 Congress amended the law to give drivers additional privacy protections. The amendment requires State DMVs to obtain a driver's express consent before releasing any personal information, regardless of whether the request is made for a particular individual's information or in bulk for marketing purposes. Previously, such information would be released if the individual had failed to opt out of the disclosure.

In 2000 the Supreme Court upheld the constitutionality of the Drivers Privacy Protection Act following a challenge by the state of South Carolina which alleged that the Act violated principles of federalism. The Court held that the Act is a proper exercise of Congress' authority to regulate interstate commerce under the Commerce Clause.

References

Public Law 103-322 as amended by Public Law 106-69. Codified at 18 U.S.C. § 2721.
[https://www.law.cornell.edu/uscode/text/18/2721]

Condon v. Reno, 528 U.S. 141 (2000)
[https://www.law.cornell.edu/supct/html/98-1464.ZO.html]

EPIC, The Drivers Privacy Protection Act and the Privacy of Your State Motor Vehicle Record
[https://www.epic.org/privacy/drivers/]

18 U.S.C. § 2721. Prohibition on release and use of certain personal information from State motor vehicle records

(a) In General. – A State department of motor vehicles, and any officer, employee, or contractor thereof, shall not knowingly disclose or otherwise make available to any person or entity:

> (1) personal information, as defined in 18 U.S.C. 2725(3), about any individual obtained by the department in connection with a motor vehicle record, except as provided in subsection (b) of this section; or

> (2) highly restricted personal information, as defined in 18 U.S.C. 2725(4), about any individual obtained by the department in connection with a motor vehicle record, without the express consent of the person to whom such information applies, except uses permitted in subsections (b)(1), (b)(4), (b)(6) and (b)(9): Provided, that subsection (a)(2) shall not in any way affect the use of organ donation information on an individual's license or affect the administration of organ donation initiatives in the States.

(b) Permissible Uses. - Personal information referred to in subsection (a) shall be disclosed for use in connection with matters of motor vehicle or driver safety and theft, motor vehicle emissions, motor vehicle product alterations, recalls, or advisories, performance monitoring of motor vehicles and dealers by motor vehicle manufacturers, and removal of non-owner records from the original owner records of motor vehicle manufacturers to carry out the purposes of the Automobile Information Disclosure Act, the Motor Vehicle Information and Cost Saving Act, the National Traffic and Motor Vehicle Safety Act of 1966, the Anti-Car Theft Act of 1992, and the Clean Air Act, and, subject to subsection (a)(2), may be disclosed as follows:

> (1) For use by any government agency, including any court or law enforcement agency, in carrying out its functions, or any private person or entity acting on behalf of a Federal, State, or local agency in carrying out its functions.

> (2) For use in connection with matters of motor vehicle or driver safety and theft; motor vehicle emissions; motor vehicle product alterations, recalls, or advisories; performance monitoring of motor vehicles, motor vehicle parts and dealers; motor vehicle market research activities, including survey research; and removal of non-owner records from the original owner records of motor vehicle manufacturers.

> (3) For use in the normal course of business by a legitimate business or its agents, employees, or contractors, but only -

> > (A) to verify the accuracy of personal information submitted by the individual to the business or its agents, employees, or contractors; and

> > (B) if such information as so submitted is not correct or is no longer correct, to obtain the correct information, but only for the purposes of preventing fraud by, pursuing legal remedies against, or recovering on a debt or security interest against, the individual.

(4) For use in connection with any civil, criminal, administrative, or arbitral proceeding in any Federal, State, or local court or agency or before any self-regulatory body, including the service of process, investigation in anticipation of litigation, and the execution or enforcement of judgments and orders, or pursuant to an order of a Federal, State, or local court.

(5) For use in research activities, and for use in producing statistical reports, so long as the personal information is not published, redisclosed, or used to contact individuals.

(6) For use by any insurer or insurance support organization, or by a self-insured entity, or its agents, employees, or contractors, in connection with claims investigation activities, antifraud activities, rating or underwriting.

(7) For use in providing notice to the owners of towed or impounded vehicles.

(8) For use by any licensed private investigative agency or licensed security service for any purpose permitted under this subsection.

(9) For use by an employer or its agent or insurer to obtain or verify information relating to a holder of a commercial driver's license that is required under the Commercial Motor Vehicle Safety Act of 1986 (49 U.S.C. App. 2710 et seq.)

(10) For use in connection with the operation of private toll transportation facilities.

(11) For any other use in response to requests for individual motor vehicle records if the State has obtained the express consent of the person to whom such personal information pertains.

(12) For bulk distribution for surveys, marketing or solicitations if the State has obtained the express consent of the person to whom such personal information pertains.

(13) For use by any requester, if the requester demonstrates it has obtained the written consent of the individual to whom the information pertains.

(14) For any other use specifically authorized under the law of the State that holds the record, if such use is related to the operation of a motor vehicle or public safety.

(c) Resale or Redisclosure. - An authorized recipient of personal information (except a recipient under subsection (b)(11) or (12)) may resell or redisclose the information only for a use permitted under subsection (b) (but not for uses under subsection (b)(11) or (12)). An authorized recipient under subsection (b)(11) may resell or redisclose personal information for any purpose. An authorized recipient under subsection (b)(12) may resell or redisclose personal information pursuant to subsection (b)(12). Any authorized recipient (except a recipient under subsection (b)(11)) that resells or rediscloses personal information covered by this title must keep for a period of 5 years records identifying each person or entity that receives information and the permitted purpose for which the information will be used and must make such records available to the motor vehicle department upon request.

(d) Waiver Procedures. - A State motor vehicle department may establish and carry out procedures under which the department or its agents, upon receiving a request for personal information that does not fall within one of the exceptions in subsection (b), may mail a copy of the request to the individual about whom the information was requested, informing such individual of the request, together with a statement to the effect that the information will not be released unless the individual waives such individual's right to privacy under this section.

(e) Prohibition on Conditions. - No State may condition or burden in any way the issuance of an individual's motor vehicle record as defined in 18 U.S.C. 2725(1) to obtain express consent. Nothing in this paragraph shall be construed to prohibit a State from charging an administrative fee for issuance of a motor vehicle record.

Sec. 2722. Additional unlawful acts

(a) Procurement for Unlawful Purpose. - It shall be unlawful for any person knowingly to obtain or disclose personal information, from a motor vehicle record, for any use not permitted under section 2721(b) of this title.

(b) False Representation. - It shall be unlawful for any person to make false representation to obtain any personal information from an individual's motor vehicle record.

Sec. 2723. Penalties

(a) Criminal Fine. - A person who knowingly violates this chapter shall be fined under this title.

(b) Violations by State Department of Motor Vehicles. - Any State department of motor vehicles that has a policy or practice of substantial noncompliance with this chapter shall be subject to a civil penalty imposed by the Attorney General of not more than $5,000 a day for each day of substantial noncompliance.

Sec. 2724. Civil action

(a) Cause of Action. - A person who knowingly obtains, discloses or uses personal information, from a motor vehicle record, for a purpose not permitted under this chapter shall be liable to the individual to whom the information pertains, who may bring a civil action in a United States district court.

(b) Remedies. - The court may award - (1) actual damages, but not less than liquidated damages in the amount of $2,500; (2) punitive damages upon proof of willful or reckless disregard of the law; (3) reasonable attorneys' fees and other litigation costs reasonably incurred; and (4) such other preliminary and equitable relief as the court determines to be appropriate.

United States
Driver's Privacy Protection Act

Sec. 2725. Definitions

In this chapter -

(1) "motor vehicle record" means any record that pertains to a motor vehicle operator's permit, motor vehicle title, motor vehicle registration, or identification card issued by a department of motor vehicles;

(2) "person" means an individual, organization or entity, but does not include a State or agency thereof;

(3) "personal information" means information that identifies an individual, including an individual's photograph, social security number, driver identification number, name, address (but not the 5-digit zip code), telephone number, and medical or disability information, but does not include information on vehicular accidents, driving violations, and driver's status.

(4) "highly restricted personal information" means an individual's photograph or image, social security number, medical or disability information; and

(5) "express consent" means consent in writing, including consent conveyed electronically that bears an electronic signature as defined in section 106(5) of Public Law 106-229.

TELECOMMUNICATIONS ACT (1996)
[EXCERPT]

Summary

The Telecommunications Act of 1996 amends the 1934 Communications Act. Section 222 of the Act provides that telecommunications carriers must protect the confidentiality of Consumer Proprietary Network Information (CPNI). CPNI includes calling patterns, billing records, unlisted telephone numbers and home addresses of service subscribers. The Act further provides that carriers receiving CPNI in connection with providing services can use the information only for that purpose and not for their own marketing purposes. Moreover, the Act allows carriers to use, disclose, and permit access to individually identifiable CPNI only when directed by the consumer or in connection with providing services for the consumer.

In 1998 the Federal Communications Commission issued a Second Report and Order and Further Notice of Proposed Rulemaking, which interpreted and implemented Section 222 of the Telecommunications Act of 1996. The FCC's Order adopted an opt-in approach, requiring carriers to obtain express approval before disclosing a customer's CPNI. However, in 1999 a federal appeals court vacated the FCC's Order, holding that the regulations of the FCC violated the First Amendment.

In 1999 the Congress enacted the Wireless Communications and Public Safety Act which promoted the use of 9-1-1, the universal emergency assistance number, and established certain privacy safeguards to limit the use of call location information to the delivery of emergency services and to further limit the use of wireless location information to those circumstances where the customer has provided "express prior authorization."

References

Public Law 104-104 as amended by Public Law 106-81 and Public Law 110-283. Codified at 47 U.S.C. §222.
[https://www.law.cornell.edu/uscode/text/47/222]

"In the Matter of Implementation of the Telecommunications Act of 1996: Telecommunications Carriers' Use of Customer Proprietary Network Information and Other Customer Information," adopted May 21, 1998
[https://transition.fcc.gov/Bureaus/Common_Carrier/Orders/1998/da980971.pdf]

47 U.S.C. Sec. 222. Privacy of customer information

(a) In general

Every telecommunications carrier has a duty to protect the confidentiality of proprietary information of, and relating to, other telecommunication carriers, equipment manufacturers, and customers, including telecommunication carriers reselling telecommunications services provided by a telecommunications carrier.

(b) Confidentiality of carrier information

A telecommunications carrier that receives or obtains proprietary information from another carrier for purposes of providing any telecommunications service shall use such information only for such purpose, and shall not use such information for its own marketing efforts.

(c) Confidentiality of customer proprietary network information

(1) Privacy requirements for telecommunications carriers

Except as required by law or with the approval of the customer, a telecommunications carrier that receives or obtains customer proprietary network information by virtue of its provision of a telecommunications service shall only use, disclose, or permit access to individually identifiable customer proprietary network information in its provision of (A) the telecommunications service from which such information is derived, or (B) services necessary to, or used in, the provision of such telecommunications service, including the publishing of directories.

(2) Disclosure on request by customers

A telecommunications carrier shall disclose customer proprietary network information, upon affirmative written request by the customer, to any person designated by the customer.

(3) Aggregate customer information

A telecommunications carrier that receives or obtains customer proprietary network information by virtue of its provision of a telecommunications service may use, disclose, or permit access to aggregate customer information other than for the purposes described in paragraph (1). A local exchange carrier may use, disclose, or permit access to aggregate customer information other than for purposes described in paragraph (1) only if it provides such aggregate information to other carriers or persons on reasonable and nondiscriminatory terms and conditions upon reasonable request therefor.

(d) Exceptions

Nothing in this section prohibits a telecommunications carrier from using, disclosing, or permitting access to customer proprietary network information obtained from its customers, either directly or indirectly through its agents-

(1) to initiate, render, bill, and collect for telecommunications services;

(2) to protect the rights or property of the carrier, or to protect users of those services and other carriers from fraudulent, abusive, or unlawful use of, or subscription to, such services;

(3) to provide any inbound telemarketing, referral, or administrative services to the customer for the duration of the call, if such call was initiated by the customer and the customer approves of the use of such information to provide such service; and

(4) to provide call location information concerning the user of a commercial mobile service (as such term is defined in section 332(d) of this title) or the user of an IP-enabled voice service (as such term is defined in section 615b of this title)-

> (A) to a public safety answering point, emergency medical service provider or emergency dispatch provider, public safety, fire service, or law enforcement official, or hospital emergency or trauma care facility, in order to respond to the user's call for emergency services;

> (B) to inform the user's legal guardian or members of the user's immediate family of the user's location in an emergency situation that involves the risk of death or serious physical harm; or

> (C) to providers of information or database management services solely for purposes of assisting in the delivery of emergency services in response to an emergency.

(e) Subscriber list information

Notwithstanding subsections (b), (c), and (d), a telecommunications carrier that provides telephone exchange service shall provide subscriber list information gathered in its capacity as a provider of such service on a timely and unbundled basis, under nondiscriminatory and reasonable rates, terms, and conditions, to any person upon request for the purpose of publishing directories in any format.

(f) Authority to use location information

For purposes of subsection (c)(1), without the express prior authorization of the customer, a customer shall not be considered to have approved the use or disclosure of or access to-

> (1) call location information concerning the user of a commercial mobile service (as such term is defined in section 332(d) of this title) or the user of an IP-enabled voice service (as such term is defined in section 615b of this title), other than in accordance with subsection (d)(4); or

> (2) automatic crash notification information to any person other than for use in the operation of an automatic crash notification system.

(g) Subscriber listed and unlisted information for emergency services

Notwithstanding subsections (b), (c), and (d), a telecommunications carrier that provides telephone exchange service or a provider of IP-enabled voice service (as such term is defined in section 615b of this title) shall provide information described in subsection (i)(3)(A) (including information pertaining to subscribers whose information is unlisted or unpublished) that is in its possession or control (including information pertaining to subscribers of other carriers) on a timely and unbundled basis, under nondiscriminatory and reasonable rates, terms, and conditions to providers of emergency services, and providers of emergency support services, solely for purposes of delivering or assisting in the delivery of emergency services.

(h) Definitions

As used in this section:

(1) Customer proprietary network information

The term "customer proprietary network information" means-

(A) information that relates to the quantity, technical configuration, type, destination, location, and amount of use of a telecommunications service subscribed to by any customer of a telecommunications carrier, and that is made available to the carrier by the customer solely by virtue of the carrier-customer relationship; and

(B) information contained in the bills pertaining to telephone exchange service or telephone toll service received by a customer of a carrier; except that such term does not include subscriber list information.

(2) Aggregate information

The term "aggregate customer information" means collective data that relates to a group or category of services or customers, from which individual customer identities and characteristics have been removed.

(3) Subscriber list information

The term "subscriber list information" means any information-

(A) identifying the listed names of subscribers of a carrier and such subscribers' telephone numbers, addresses, or primary advertising classifications (as such classifications are assigned at the time of the establishment of such service), or any combination of such listed names, numbers, addresses, or classifications; and

(B) that the carrier or an affiliate has published, caused to be published, or accepted for publication in any directory format.

(4) Public safety answering point

The term "public safety answering point" means a facility that has been designated to receive emergency calls and route them to emergency service personnel.

(5) Emergency services

The term "emergency services" means 9–1–1 emergency services and emergency notification services.

(6) Emergency notification services

The term "emergency notification services" means services that notify the public of an emergency.

(7) Emergency support services

The term "emergency support services" means information or data base management services used in support of emergency services.

CHILDREN'S ONLINE PRIVACY PROTECTION ACT (1998)

Summary

The Children's Online Privacy Protection Act of 1998 prohibits an operator of a website or online service directed to children, or any operator having actual knowledge that it is doing so, from collecting personal information from a child in a manner that violates regulations required under this title which are designed to protect such children from unlawful and deceptive practices in the collection of personal information. The Act provides an exception for information disclosed to a child's parent.

The Act directs the Federal Trade Commission (FTC) to prescribe regulations requiring such operators to follow specified procedures in connection with the collection and use of personal information from children, including: (1) obtaining verifiable parental consent for the collection, use, or disclosure of such information; and (2) requiring such operators to establish and maintain procedures to protect the confidentiality, security, and integrity of collected information. It provides exceptions to the parental consent requirement. The Act allows an operator to satisfy such regulatory requirements by following a set of FTC-approved self-regulatory guidelines established by appropriate online representatives. The Act directs the FTC to provide incentives for such self-regulation.

The Act authorizes the States to enforce such regulations by bringing actions on behalf of its residents, requiring the appropriate attorney general to first notify the FTC of such action. It authorizes the FTC to intervene in any such action, and it provides for enforcement through the Federal Trade Commission Act. It also directs the FTC to review and report to the Congress on implementation.

References

Public Law 105-277 codified at 15 U.S.C. § 6501.
[https://www.law.cornell.edu/uscode/text/15/6501]

EPIC, Children's Online Privacy Protection Act (COPPA)
[https://www.epic.org/privacy/kids/]

15 U.S.C. § 6501. Definitions

In this title:

(1) Child. The term "child" means an individual under the age of 13.

(2) Operator. The term "operator"–

(A) means any person who operates a website located on the Internet or an online service and who collects or maintains personal information from or about the users of or visitors to such website or online service, or on whose behalf such information is collected or maintained, where such website or online service is operated for commercial purposes, including any person offering products or services for sale through that website or online service, involving commerce–

(i) among the several States or with 1 or more foreign nations;

(ii) in any territory of the United States or in the District of Columbia, or between any such territory and–

(I) another such territory; or

(II) any State or foreign nation; or

(iii) between the District of Columbia and any State, territory, or foreign nation; but

(B) does not include any nonprofit entity that would otherwise be exempt from coverage under section 5 of the Federal Trade Commission Act.

(3) Commission. The term "Commission" means the Federal Trade Commission.

(4) Disclosure. The term "disclosure" means, with respect to personal information–

(A) the release of personal information collected from a child in identifiable form by an operator for any purpose, except where such information is provided to a person other than the operator who provides support for the internal operations of the website and does not disclose or use that information for any other purpose; and

(B) making personal information collected from a child by a website or online service directed to children or with actual knowledge that such information was collected from a child, publicly available in identifiable form, by any means including by a public posting, through the Internet, or through–

(i) a home page of a website;

(ii) a pen pal service;

(iii) an electronic mail service;

(iv) a message board; or

(v) a chat room.

(5) Federal agency. The term "Federal agency" means an agency, as that term is defined in section 551(1) of title 5, United States Code.

(6) Internet. The term "Internet" means collectively the myriad of computer and telecommunications facilities, including equipment and operating software, which comprise the interconnected world-wide network of networks that employ the Transmission Control Protocol/Internet Protocol, or any predecessor or successor protocols to such protocol, to communicate information of all kinds by wire or radio.

(7) Parent. The term "parent" includes a legal guardian.

(8) Personal information. The term "personal information" means individually identifiable information about an individual collected online, including–

(A) a first and last name;

(B) a home or other physical address including street name and name of a city or town;

(C) an e-mail address;

(D) a telephone number;

(E) a Social Security number;

(F) any other identifier that the Commission determines permits the physical or online contacting of a specific individual; or .

(G) information concerning the child or the parents of that child that the website collects online from the child and combines with an identifier described in this paragraph.

(9) Verifiable parental consent. The term "verifiable parental consent" means any reasonable effort (taking into consideration available technology), including a request for authorization for future collection, use, and disclosure described in the notice, to ensure that a parent of a child receives notice of the operator's personal information collection, use, and disclosure practices, and authorizes the collection, use, and disclosure, as applicable, of personal information and the subsequent use of that information before that information is collected from that child.

(10) Website or online service directed to children.

(A) In general. The term "website or online service directed to children" means–

(i) a commercial website or online service that is targeted to children; or

(ii) that portion of a commercial website or online service that is targeted to children.

(B) Limitation. A commercial website or online service, or a portion of a commercial website or online service, shall not be deemed directed to children solely for referring or linking to a commercial website or online service directed to children by using information location tools, including a directory, index, reference, pointer, or hypertext link.

(11) Person. The term "person" means any individual, partnership, corporation, trust, estate, cooperative, association, or other entity.

(12) Online contact information. The term "online contact information" means an e-mail address or another substantially similar identifier that permits direct contact with a person online.

§ 6502. Regulation of unfair and deceptive acts and practices in connection with the collection and use of personal information from and about children on the Internet

(a) Acts prohibited

United States
Children's Online Privacy Protection Act

(1) In general. It is unlawful for an operator of a website or online service directed to children, or any operator that has actual knowledge that it is collecting personal information from a child, to collect personal information from a child in a manner that violates the regulations prescribed under subsection (b).

(2) Disclosure to parent protected. Notwithstanding paragraph (1), neither an operator of such a website or online service nor the operator's agent shall be held to be liable under any Federal or State law for any disclosure made in good faith and following reasonable procedures in responding to a request for disclosure of personal information under subsection (b)(1)(B)(iii) to the parent of a child.

(b) Regulations

(1) In general. Not later than 1 year after the date of the enactment of this Act, the Commission shall promulgate under section 553 of title 5, United States Code, regulations that–

(A) require the operator of any website or online service directed to children that collects personal information from children or the operator of a website or online service that has actual knowledge that it is collecting personal information from a child–

(i) to provide notice on the website of what information is collected from children by the operator, how the operator uses such information, and the operator's disclosure practices for such information; and

(ii) to obtain verifiable parental consent for the collection, use, or disclosure of personal information from children;

(B) require the operator to provide, upon request of a parent under this subparagraph whose child has provided personal information to that website or online service, upon proper identification of that parent, to such parent–

(i) a description of the specific types of personal information collected from the child by that operator;

(ii) the opportunity at any time to refuse to permit the operator's further use or maintenance in retrievable form, or future online collection, of personal information from that child; and

(iii) notwithstanding any other provision of law, a means that is reasonable under the circumstances for the parent to obtain any personal information collected from that child;

(C) prohibit conditioning a child's participation in a game, the offering of a prize, or another activity on the child disclosing more personal information than is reasonably necessary to participate in such activity; and

(D) require the operator of such a website or online service to establish and maintain reasonable procedures to protect the confidentiality, security, and integrity of personal information collected from children.

(2) When consent not required. The regulations shall provide that verifiable parental consent under paragraph (1)(A)(ii) is not required in the case of–

(A) online contact information collected from a child that is used only to respond directly on a one-time basis to a specific request from the child and is not used to recontact the child and is not maintained in retrievable form by the operator;

(B) a request for the name or online contact information of a parent or child that is used for the sole purpose of obtaining parental consent or providing notice under this section and where such information is not maintained in retrievable form by the operator if parental consent is not obtained after a reasonable time;

(C) online contact information collected from a child that is used only to respond more than once directly to a specific request from the child and is not used to recontact the child beyond the scope of that request–

    (i) if, before any additional response after the initial response to the child, the operator uses reasonable efforts to provide a parent notice of the online contact information collected from the child, the purposes for which it is to be used, and an opportunity for the parent to request that the operator make no further use of the information and that it not be maintained in retrievable form; or

    (ii) without notice to the parent in such circumstances as the Commission may determine are appropriate, taking into consideration the benefits to the child of access to information and services, and risks to the security and privacy of the child, in regulations promulgated under this subsection;

(D) the name of the child and online contact information (to the extent reasonably necessary to protect the safety of a child participant on the site)–

    (i) used only for the purpose of protecting such safety;

    (ii) not used to recontact the child or for any other purpose; and

    (iii) not disclosed on the site,

    if the operator uses reasonable efforts to provide a parent notice of the name and online contact information collected from the child, the purposes for which it is to be used, and an opportunity for the parent to request that the operator make no further use of the information and that it not be maintained in retrievable form; or

(E) the collection, use, or dissemination of such information by the operator of such a website or online service necessary–

    (i) to protect the security or integrity of its website;

    (ii) to take precautions against liability;

    (iii) to respond to judicial process; or

(iv) to the extent permitted under other provisions of law, to provide information to law enforcement agencies or for an investigation on a matter related to public safety.

(3) Termination of service. The regulations shall permit the operator of a website or an online service to terminate service provided to a child whose parent has refused, under the regulations prescribed under paragraph (1)(B)(ii), to permit the operator's further use or maintenance in retrievable form, or future online collection, of personal information from that child.

(c) Enforcement. Subject to sections 1304 and 1306, a violation of a regulation prescribed under subsection (a) shall be treated as a violation of a rule defining an unfair or deceptive act or practice prescribed under section 18(a)(1)(B) of the Federal Trade Commission Act *(15 U.S.C. 57a*(a)(1)(B)).

(d) Inconsistent State law. No State or local government may impose any liability for commercial activities or actions by operators in interstate or foreign commerce in connection with an activity or action described in this title that is inconsistent with the treatment of those activities or actions under this section.

§ 6503. Safe harbors

(a) Guidelines. An operator may satisfy the requirements of regulations issued under section 1303(b) by following a set of self-regulatory guidelines, issued by representatives of the marketing or online industries, or by other persons, approved under subsection (b).

(b) Incentives

(1) Self-regulatory incentives. In prescribing regulations under section 1303, the Commission shall provide incentives for self-regulation by operators to implement the protections afforded children under the regulatory requirements described in subsection (b) of that section.

(2) Deemed compliance. Such incentives shall include provisions for ensuring that a person will be deemed to be in compliance with the requirements of the regulations under section 1303 if that person complies with guidelines that, after notice and comment, are approved by the Commission upon making a determination that the guidelines meet the requirements of the regulations issued under section 1303.

(3) Expedited response to requests. The Commission shall act upon requests for safe harbor treatment within 180 days of the filing of the request, and shall set forth in writing its conclusions with regard to such requests.

(c) Appeals. Final action by the Commission on a request for approval of guidelines, or the failure to act within 180 days on a request for approval of guidelines, submitted under subsection (b) may be appealed to a district court of the United States of appropriate jurisdiction as provided for in section 706 of title 5, United States Code.

§ 6504. Actions by States

(a) In general

(1) Civil actions. In any case in which the attorney general of a State has reason to believe that an interest of the residents of that State has been or is threatened or adversely affected by the engagement of any person in a practice that violates any regulation of the Commission prescribed under section 1303(b), the State, as parens patriae, may bring a civil action on behalf of the residents of the State in a district court of the United States of appropriate jurisdiction to–

(A) enjoin that practice;

(B) enforce compliance with the regulation;

(C) obtain damage, restitution, or other compensation on behalf of residents of the State; or

(D) obtain such other relief as the court may consider to be appropriate.

(2) Notice

(A) In general. Before filing an action under paragraph (1), the attorney general of the State involved shall provide to the Commission–

(i) written notice of that action; and

(ii) a copy of the complaint for that action.

(B) Exemption

(i) In general. Subparagraph (A) shall not apply with respect to the filing of an action by an attorney general of a State under this subsection, if the attorney general determines that it is not feasible to provide the notice described in that subparagraph before the filing of the action.

(ii) Notification. In an action described in clause (i), the attorney general of a State shall provide notice and a copy of the complaint to the Commission at the same time as the attorney general files the action.

(b) Intervention

(1) In general. On receiving notice under subsection (a)(2), the Commission shall have the right to intervene in the action that is the subject of the notice.

(2) Effect of intervention. If the Commission intervenes in an action under subsection (a), it shall have the right–

(A) to be heard with respect to any matter that arises in that action; and

(B) to file a petition for appeal.

(3) Amicus curiae. Upon application to the court, a person whose self-regulatory guidelines have been approved by the Commission and are relied upon as a defense by any defendant to a proceeding under this section may file amicus curiae in that proceeding.

(c) Construction. For purposes of bringing any civil action under subsection (a), nothing in this title shall be construed to prevent an attorney general of a State from exercising the powers conferred on the attorney general by the laws of that State to–

(1) conduct investigations;

(2) administer oaths or affirmations; or

(3) compel the attendance of witnesses or the production of documentary and other evidence.

(d) Actions by the Commission. In any case in which an action is instituted by or on behalf of the Commission for violation of any regulation prescribed under section 1303, no State may, during the pendency of that action, institute an action under subsection (a) against any defendant named in the complaint in that action for violation of that regulation.

(e) Venue; service of process.

(1) Venue. Any action brought under subsection (a) may be brought in the district court of the United States that meets applicable requirements relating to venue under section 1391 of title 28, United States Code.

(2) Service of process. In an action brought under subsection (a), process may be served in any district in which the defendant–

(A) is an inhabitant; or

(B) may be found.

§ 6505. Administration and applicability of Act

(a) In general. Except as otherwise provided, this title shall be enforced by the Commission under the Federal Trade Commission Act *(15 U.S.C. 41* et seq.).

(b) Provisions. Compliance with the requirements imposed under this title shall be enforced under–

(1) section 8 of the Federal Deposit Insurance Act *(12 U.S.C. 1818)*, in the case of–

(A) national banks, and Federal branches and Federal agencies of foreign banks, by the Office of the Comptroller of the Currency;

(B) member banks of the Federal Reserve System (other than national banks), branches and agencies of foreign banks (other than Federal branches, Federal agencies, and insured State branches of foreign banks), commercial lending companies owned or controlled by foreign banks, and organizations operating under section 25 or 25(a) of the Federal Reserve Act *(12 U.S.C. 601* et seq. and 611 et seq.), by the Board; and

(C) banks insured by the Federal Deposit Insurance Corporation (other than members of the Federal Reserve System) and insured State branches of foreign banks, by the Board of Directors of the Federal Deposit Insurance Corporation;

(2) section 8 of the Federal Deposit Insurance Act *(12 U.S.C. 1818)*, by the Director of the Office of Thrift Supervision, in the case of a savings association the deposits of which are insured by the Federal Deposit Insurance Corporation;

(3) the Federal Credit Union Act *(12 U.S.C. 1751* et seq.) by the National Credit Union Administration Board with respect to any Federal credit union;

(4) part A of subtitle VII of title 49, United States Code, by the Secretary of Transportation with respect to any air carrier or foreign air carrier subject to that part;

(5) the Packers and Stockyards Act, 1921 *(7 U.S.C. 181* et seq.) (except as provided in section 406 of that Act *(7 U.S.C. 226,* 227)), by the Secretary of Agriculture with respect to any activities subject to that Act; and

(6) the Farm Credit Act of 1971 *(12 U.S.C. 2001* et seq.) by the Farm Credit Administration with respect to any Federal land bank, Federal land bank association, Federal intermediate credit bank, or production credit association.

(c) Exercise of certain powers. For the purpose of the exercise by any agency referred to in subsection (a) of its powers under any Act referred to in that subsection, a violation of any requirement imposed under this title shall be deemed to be a violation of a requirement imposed under that Act. In addition to its powers under any provision of law specifically referred to in subsection (a), each of the agencies referred to in that subsection may exercise, for the purpose of enforcing compliance with any requirement imposed under this title, any other authority conferred on it by law.

(d) Actions by the Commission. The Commission shall prevent any person from violating a rule of the Commission under section 1303 in the same manner, by the same means, and with the same jurisdiction, powers, and duties as though all applicable terms and provisions of the Federal Trade Commission Act *(15 U.S.C. 41* et seq.) were incorporated into and made a part of this title. Any entity that violates such rule shall be subject to the penalties and entitled to the privileges and immunities provided in the Federal Trade Commission Act in the same manner, by the same means, and with the same jurisdiction, power, and duties as though all applicable terms and provisions of the Federal Trade Commission Act were incorporated into and made a part of this title.

(e) Effect on other laws. Nothing contained in the Act shall be construed to limit the authority of the Commission under any other provisions of law.

§ 6506. Review

Not later than 5 years after the effective date of the regulations initially issued under section 6502 of this title, the Commission shall -

(1) review the implementation of this chapter, including the effect of the implementation of this chapter on practices relating to the collection and disclosure of information relating to children, children's ability to obtain access to information of their choice online, and on the availability of websites directed to children; and

(2) prepare and submit to Congress a report on the results of the review under paragraph (1).

IDENTITY THEFT AND ASSUMPTION DETERRENCE ACT (1998)

Summary

Congress passed the Identity Theft and Assumption Deterrence Act in 1998 to address the increasing problem of identity theft. The Act specifically made it a federal crime to "knowingly transfer or use, without lawful authority, a means of identification of another person with the intent to commit, or to aid or abet, any unlawful activity that constitutes a violation of federal law, or that constitutes a felony under any applicable state or local law."

References

Public Law 97-398, as amended by Pub. L. 99-646, Pub. L. 100-90, Pub. L. 101–647; Pub. L. 103–322, Pub. L. 104–208, Pub. L. 104–294, Pub. L. 105–318, Pub. L. 106–578, Pub. L. 108–21, Pub. L. 108–275, Pub. L. 108–458, Pub. L. 109–13, and Pub. L. 109–177. Codified at 18 U.S.C. § 1028.

[https://www.law.cornell.edu/uscode/text/18/1028]

§1028. Fraud and related activity in connection with identification documents, authentication features, and information

(a) Whoever, in a circumstance described in subsection (c) of this section-

(1) knowingly and without lawful authority produces an identification document, authentication feature, or a false identification document;

(2) knowingly transfers an identification document, authentication feature, or a false identification document knowing that such document or feature was stolen or produced without lawful authority;

(3) knowingly possesses with intent to use unlawfully or transfer unlawfully five or more identification documents (other than those issued lawfully for the use of the possessor), authentication features, or false identification documents;

(4) knowingly possesses an identification document (other than one issued lawfully for the use of the possessor), authentication feature, or a false identification document, with the intent such document or feature be used to defraud the United States;

(5) knowingly produces, transfers, or possesses a document-making implement or authentication feature with the intent such document-making implement or authentication feature will be used in the production of a false identification document or another document-making implement or authentication feature which will be so used;

(6) knowingly possesses an identification document or authentication feature that is or appears to be an identification document or authentication feature of the United States or a sponsoring entity of an event designated as a special event of national significance which is stolen or produced without lawful authority knowing that such document or feature was stolen or produced without such authority;

(7) knowingly transfers, possesses, or uses, without lawful authority, a means of identification of another person with the intent to commit, or to aid or abet, or in connection with, any unlawful activity that constitutes a violation of Federal law, or that constitutes a felony under any applicable State or local law; or

(8) knowingly traffics in false or actual authentication features for use in false identification documents, document-making implements, or means of identification;

shall be punished as provided in subsection (b) of this section.

(b) The punishment for an offense under subsection (a) of this section is-

(1) except as provided in paragraphs (3) and (4), a fine under this title or imprisonment for not more than 15 years, or both, if the offense is-

(A) the production or transfer of an identification document, authentication feature, or false identification document that is or appears to be-

(i) an identification document or authentication feature issued by or under the authority of the United States; or

(ii) a birth certificate, or a driver's license or personal identification card;

(B) the production or transfer of more than five identification documents, authentication features, or false identification documents;

(C) an offense under paragraph (5) of such subsection; or

(D) an offense under paragraph (7) of such subsection that involves the transfer, possession, or use of 1 or more means of identification if, as a result of the offense, any individual committing the offense obtains anything of value aggregating $1,000 or more during any 1-year period;

(2) except as provided in paragraphs (3) and (4), a fine under this title or imprisonment for not more than 5 years, or both, if the offense is-

(A) any other production, transfer, or use of a means of identification, an identification document, authentication feature, or a false identification document; or

(B) an offense under paragraph (3) or (7) of such subsection;

(3) a fine under this title or imprisonment for not more than 20 years, or both, if the offense is committed-

(A) to facilitate a drug trafficking crime (as defined in section 929(a)(2));

(B) in connection with a crime of violence (as defined in section 924(c)(3)); or

(C) after a prior conviction under this section becomes final;

(4) a fine under this title or imprisonment for not more than 30 years, or both, if the offense is committed to facilitate an act of domestic terrorism (as defined under section 2331(5) of this title) or an act of international terrorism (as defined in section 2331(1) of this title);

(5) in the case of any offense under subsection (a), forfeiture to the United States of any personal property used or intended to be used to commit the offense; and

(6) a fine under this title or imprisonment for not more than one year, or both, in any other case.

(c) The circumstance referred to in subsection (a) of this section is that-

(1) the identification document, authentication feature, or false identification document is or appears to be issued by or under the authority of the United States or a sponsoring entity of an event designated as a special event of national significance or the document-making implement is designed or suited for making such an identification document, authentication feature, or false identification document;

(2) the offense is an offense under subsection (a)(4) of this section; or

(3) either-

(A) the production, transfer, possession, or use prohibited by this section is in or affects interstate or foreign commerce, including the transfer of a document by electronic means; or

(B) the means of identification, identification document, false identification document, or document-making implement is transported in the mail in the course of the production, transfer, possession, or use prohibited by this section.

(d) In this section and section 1028A-

(1) the term "authentication feature" means any hologram, watermark, certification, symbol, code, image, sequence of numbers or letters, or other feature that either individually or in combination with another feature is used by the issuing authority on an identification document, document-making implement, or means of identification to determine if the document is counterfeit, altered, or otherwise falsified;

(2) the term "document-making implement" means any implement, impression, template, computer file, computer disc, electronic device, or computer hardware or software, that is specifically configured or primarily used for making an identification document, a false identification document, or another document-making implement;

(3) the term "identification document" means a document made or issued by or under the authority of the United States Government, a State, political subdivision of a State, a sponsoring entity of an event designated as a special event of national significance, a foreign government, political subdivision of a foreign government,

an international governmental or an international quasi-governmental organization which, when completed with information concerning a particular individual, is of a type intended or commonly accepted for the purpose of identification of individuals;

(4) the term "false identification document" means a document of a type intended or commonly accepted for the purposes of identification of individuals that-

(A) is not issued by or under the authority of a governmental entity or was issued under the authority of a governmental entity but was subsequently altered for purposes of deceit; and

(B) appears to be issued by or under the authority of the United States Government, a State, a political subdivision of a State, a sponsoring entity of an event designated by the President as a special event of national significance, a foreign government, a political subdivision of a foreign government, or an international governmental or quasi-governmental organization;

(5) the term "false authentication feature" means an authentication feature that-

(A) is genuine in origin, but, without the authorization of the issuing authority, has been tampered with or altered for purposes of deceit;

(B) is genuine, but has been distributed, or is intended for distribution, without the authorization of the issuing authority and not in connection with a lawfully made identification document, document-making implement, or means of identification to which such authentication feature is intended to be affixed or embedded by the respective issuing authority; or

(C) appears to be genuine, but is not;

(6) the term "issuing authority"-

(A) means any governmental entity or agency that is authorized to issue identification documents, means of identification, or authentication features; and

(B) includes the United States Government, a State, a political subdivision of a State, a sponsoring entity of an event designated by the President as a special event of national significance, a foreign government, a political subdivision of a foreign government, or an international government or quasi-governmental organization;

(7) the term "means of identification" means any name or number that may be used, alone or in conjunction with any other information, to identify a specific individual, including any-

(A) name, social security number, date of birth, official State or government issued driver's license or identification number, alien registration number, government passport number, employer or taxpayer identification number;

(B) unique biometric data, such as fingerprint, voice print, retina or iris image, or other unique physical representation;

(C) unique electronic identification number, address, or routing code; or

(D) telecommunication identifying information or access device (as defined in section 1029(e));

(8) the term "personal identification card" means an identification document issued by a State or local government solely for the purpose of identification;

(9) the term "produce" includes alter, authenticate, or assemble;

(10) the term "transfer" includes selecting an identification document, false identification document, or document-making implement and placing or directing the placement of such identification document, false identification document, or document-making implement on an online location where it is available to others;

(11) the term "State" includes any State of the United States, the District of Columbia, the Commonwealth of Puerto Rico, and any other commonwealth, possession, or territory of the United States; and

(12) the term "traffic" means-

(A) to transport, transfer, or otherwise dispose of, to another, as consideration for anything of value; or

(B) to make or obtain control of with intent to so transport, transfer, or otherwise dispose of.

(e) This section does not prohibit any lawfully authorized investigative, protective, or intelligence activity of a law enforcement agency of the United States, a State, or a political subdivision of a State, or of an intelligence agency of the United States, or any activity authorized under chapter 224 of this title.

(f) Attempt and Conspiracy.-Any person who attempts or conspires to commit any offense under this section shall be subject to the same penalties as those prescribed for the offense, the commission of which was the object of the attempt or conspiracy.

(g) Forfeiture Procedures.-The forfeiture of property under this section, including any seizure and disposition of the property and any related judicial or administrative proceeding, shall be governed by the provisions of section 413 (other than subsection (d) of that section) of the Comprehensive Drug Abuse Prevention and Control Act of 1970 (21 U.S.C. 853).

(h) Forfeiture; Disposition.-In the circumstance in which any person is convicted of a violation of subsection (a), the court shall order, in addition to the penalty prescribed, the forfeiture and destruction or other disposition of all illicit authentication features, identification documents, document-making implements, or means of identification.

(i) Rule of Construction.-For purpose of subsection (a)(7), a single identification document or false identification document that contains 1 or more means of identification shall be construed to be 1 means of identification.

FINANCIAL SERVICES
MODERNIZATION ACT (1999)
[EXCERPTS]

Summary

The Financial Services Modernization Act (also known as the Gramm-Leach-Bliley Act or GLBA) is regarded as the most sweeping legislation affecting banks and other financial institutions since the Depression. The passage of GLBA permits banks, insurance companies, and brokerage firms to operate as one entity, transforming them into a "financial supermarket" and enabling them to offer a wider range of products and services.

The consolidation of these financial institutions, however, has great implications for consumer privacy rights. It enables financial institutions to share consumer information with their affiliates (other commonly owned companies) for sales and promotional purposes. Hence, to regulate the disclosure of consumer data amongst affiliates, GLBA requires financial institutions to give consumers a privacy policy notice informing them of the kind of information it collects about the individual and how it uses that information. It also requires financial institutions to give consumers the right to opt-out or prevent the sale of personal data to third parties. Moreover, GLBA requires financial institutions to develop policies to prevent fraudulent access to confidential financial information. July 1, 2001 is the deadline for financial institutions to comply with the notice requirements.

Although GLBA prohibits financial institutions from disclosing nonpublic information, such as an individual's account number or access code to a third party non-affiliated company (an outside company), it does not prevent these institutions from selling publicly available information, that is information the financial institution reasonably believes is lawfully made available to the general public, to a non-affiliated telemarketer. Thus, if the consumer does not opt-out, the institution is free to sell, lease or otherwise disclose almost anything in its files about the consumer, including medical information, to non-affiliates.

Under GLBA the consumer has no private right of action if a financial institution violates GLBA privacy requirements. However, the consumer can complain to one of the seven federal agencies that have jurisdiction and enforcement authority over financial institutions under GLBA. Once a complaint is made the enforcing agency will investigate the complaint and may bring a court action or an administrative case against the company. However, the agency cannot represent or give legal advice to the complaining party.

Seven federal agencies enforce the privacy provisions of the GLBA. They include the Federal Deposit Insurance Corporation (FDIC), the Federal Reserve, the Office of Thrift Supervision, the Office of Comptroller of the Currency (OCC), the National Credit Union Administration (NCUA), the Securities and Exchange Commission (SEC) and the Federal Trade Commission (FTC).

References

Public Law, 106-102, as amended by Public Law 111-203. Codified at 16 U.S.C. §6801 et seq.
[https://www.law.cornell.edu/uscode/text/15/6801

Senate Report, 106-44, Financial Services Modernization Act of 1999
[https://www.congress.gov/congressional-report/106th-congress/senate-report/44/1]

House Report, 106-434, Gramm-Leach-Bliley Act of 1999
[https://www.congress.gov/congressional-report/106th-congress/house-report/434/1]

L. Richard Fischer, *The Law of Financial Privacy* (A.S. Pratt & Sons 2000)

EPIC, Financial Services Modernization Act
[https://www.epic.org/privacy/glba/]

§ 6801. Protection of nonpublic personal information

(a) Privacy obligation policy

It is the policy of the Congress that each financial institution has an affirmative and continuing obligation to respect the privacy of its customers and to protect the security and confidentiality of those customers' nonpublic personal information.

(b) Financial institutions safeguards

In furtherance of the policy in subsection (a), each agency or authority described in section 6805(a) of this title, other than the Bureau of Consumer Financial Protection, shall establish appropriate standards for the financial institutions subject to their jurisdiction relating to administrative, technical, and physical safeguards-

(1) to insure the security and confidentiality of customer records and information;

(2) to protect against any anticipated threats or hazards to the security or integrity of such records; and

(3) to protect against unauthorized access to or use of such records or information which could result in substantial harm or inconvenience to any customer.

§ 6802. Obligations with respect to disclosures of personal information

(a) Notice requirements

Except as otherwise provided in this subchapter, a financial institution may not, directly or through any affiliate, disclose to a nonaffiliated third party any nonpublic personal information, unless such financial institution provides or has provided to the consumer a notice that complies with section 6803 of this title.

(b) Opt out

(1) In general

United States
Financial Services Modernization Act

A financial institution may not disclose nonpublic personal information to a nonaffiliated third party unless-

(A) such financial institution clearly and conspicuously discloses to the consumer, in writing or in electronic form or other form permitted by the regulations prescribed under section 6804 of this title, that such information may be disclosed to such third party;

(B) the consumer is given the opportunity, before the time that such information is initially disclosed, to direct that such information not be disclosed to such third party; and

(C) the consumer is given an explanation of how the consumer can exercise that nondisclosure option.

(2) Exception

This subsection shall not prevent a financial institution from providing nonpublic personal information to a nonaffiliated third party to perform services for or functions on behalf of the financial institution, including marketing of the financial institution's own products or services, or financial products or services offered pursuant to joint agreements between two or more financial institutions that comply with the requirements imposed by the regulations prescribed under section 6804 of this title, if the financial institution fully discloses the providing of such information and enters into a contractual agreement with the third party that requires the third party to maintain the confidentiality of such information.

(c) Limits on reuse of information

Except as otherwise provided in this subchapter, a nonaffiliated third party that receives from a financial institution nonpublic personal information under this section shall not, directly or through an affiliate of such receiving third party, disclose such information to any other person that is a nonaffiliated third party of both the financial institution and such receiving third party, unless such disclosure would be lawful if made directly to such other person by the financial institution.

(d) Limitations on the sharing of account number information for marketing purposes

A financial institution shall not disclose, other than to a consumer reporting agency, an account number or similar form of access number or access code for a credit card account, deposit account, or transaction account of a consumer to any nonaffiliated third party for use in telemarketing, direct mail marketing, or other marketing through electronic mail to the consumer.

(e) General exceptions

Subsections (a) and (b) shall not prohibit the disclosure of nonpublic personal information-

(1) as necessary to effect, administer, or enforce a transaction requested or authorized by the consumer, or in connection with-

(A) servicing or processing a financial product or service requested or authorized by the consumer;

(B) maintaining or servicing the consumer's account with the financial institution, or with another entity as part of a private label credit card program or other extension of credit on behalf of such entity; or

(C) a proposed or actual securitization, secondary market sale (including sales of servicing rights), or similar transaction related to a transaction of the consumer;

(2) with the consent or at the direction of the consumer;

(3)(A) to protect the confidentiality or security of the financial institution's records pertaining to the consumer, the service or product, or the transaction therein; (B) to protect against or prevent actual or potential fraud, unauthorized transactions, claims, or other liability; (C) for required institutional risk control, or for resolving customer disputes or inquiries; (D) to persons holding a legal or beneficial interest relating to the consumer; or (E) to persons acting in a fiduciary or representative capacity on behalf of the consumer;

(4) to provide information to insurance rate advisory organizations, guaranty funds or agencies, applicable rating agencies of the financial institution, persons assessing the institution's compliance with industry standards, and the institution's attorneys, accountants, and auditors;

(5) to the extent specifically permitted or required under other provisions of law and in accordance with the Right to Financial Privacy Act of 1978 [12 U.S.C. 3401 et seq.], to law enforcement agencies (including the Bureau of Consumer Financial Protection a Federal functional regulator, the Secretary of the Treasury with respect to subchapter II of chapter 53 of title 31, and chapter 2 of title I of Public Law 91–508 (12 U.S.C. 1951–1959), a State insurance authority, or the Federal Trade Commission), self-regulatory organizations, or for an investigation on a matter related to public safety;

(6)(A) to a consumer reporting agency in accordance with the Fair Credit Reporting Act [15 U.S.C. 1681 et seq.], or (B) from a consumer report reported by a consumer reporting agency;

(7) in connection with a proposed or actual sale, merger, transfer, or exchange of all or a portion of a business or operating unit if the disclosure of nonpublic personal information concerns solely consumers of such business or unit; or

(8) to comply with Federal, State, or local laws, rules, and other applicable legal requirements; to comply with a properly authorized civil, criminal, or regulatory investigation or subpoena or summons by Federal, State, or local authorities; or to respond to judicial process or government regulatory authorities having jurisdiction over the financial institution for examination, compliance, or other purposes as authorized by law.

United States
Financial Services Modernization Act

§ 6803. Disclosure of institution privacy policy

(a) Disclosure required

At the time of establishing a customer relationship with a consumer and not less than annually during the continuation of such relationship, a financial institution shall provide a clear and conspicuous disclosure to such consumer, in writing or in electronic form or other form permitted by the regulations prescribed under section 6804 of this title, of such financial institution's policies and practices with respect to-

(1) disclosing nonpublic personal information to affiliates and nonaffiliated third parties, consistent with section 6802 of this title, including the categories of information that may be disclosed;

(2) disclosing nonpublic personal information of persons who have ceased to be customers of the financial institution; and

(3) protecting the nonpublic personal information of consumers.

(b) Regulations

Disclosures required by subsection (a) shall be made in accordance with the regulations prescribed under section 6804 of this title.

(c) Information to be included

The disclosure required by subsection (a) shall include-

(1) the policies and practices of the institution with respect to disclosing nonpublic personal information to nonaffiliated third parties, other than agents of the institution, consistent with section 6802 of this title, and including-

(A) the categories of persons to whom the information is or may be disclosed, other than the persons to whom the information may be provided pursuant to section 6802(e) of this title; and

(B) the policies and practices of the institution with respect to disclosing of nonpublic personal information of persons who have ceased to be customers of the financial institution;

(2) the categories of nonpublic personal information that are collected by the financial institution;

(3) the policies that the institution maintains to protect the confidentiality and security of nonpublic personal information in accordance with section 6801 of this title; and

(4) the disclosures required, if any, under section 1681a(d)(2)(A)(iii) of this title.

(d) Exemption for certified public accountants

(1) In general

The disclosure requirements of subsection (a) do not apply to any person, to the extent that the person is-

(A) a certified public accountant;

(B) certified or licensed for such purpose by a State; and

(C) subject to any provision of law, rule, or regulation issued by a legislative or regulatory body of the State, including rules of professional conduct or ethics, that prohibits disclosure of nonpublic personal information without the knowing and expressed consent of the consumer.

(2) Limitation

Nothing in this subsection shall be construed to exempt or otherwise exclude any financial institution that is affiliated or becomes affiliated with a certified public accountant described in paragraph (1) from any provision of this section.

(3) Definitions

For purposes of this subsection, the term "State" means any State or territory of the United States, the District of Columbia, Puerto Rico, Guam, American Samoa, the Trust Territory of the Pacific Islands, the Virgin Islands, or the Northern Mariana Islands.

(e) Model forms

(1) In general

The agencies referred to in section 6804(a)(1) of this title shall jointly develop a model form which may be used, at the option of the financial institution, for the provision of disclosures under this section.

(2) Format

A model form developed under paragraph (1) shall-

(A) be comprehensible to consumers, with a clear format and design;

(B) provide for clear and conspicuous disclosures;

(C) enable consumers easily to identify the sharing practices of a financial institution and to compare privacy practices among financial institutions; and

(D) be succinct, and use an easily readable type font.

(3) Timing

A model form required to be developed by this subsection shall be issued in proposed form for public comment not later than 180 days after October 13, 2006.

(4) Safe harbor

Any financial institution that elects to provide the model form developed by the agencies under this subsection shall be deemed to be in compliance with the disclosures required under this section.

(f) Exception to annual notice requirement

A financial institution that-

(1) provides nonpublic personal information only in accordance with the provisions of subsection (b)(2) or (e) of section 6802 of this title or regulations prescribed under section 6804(b) of this title, and

(2) has not changed its policies and practices with regard to disclosing nonpublic personal information from the policies and practices that were disclosed in the most recent disclosure sent to consumers in accordance with this section, shall not

be required to provide an annual disclosure under this section until such time as the financial institution fails to comply with any criteria described in paragraph (1) or (2).

§ 6804. Rulemaking

(a) Regulatory authority

    (1) Rulemaking

        (A) In general

Except as provided in subparagraph (C), the Bureau of Consumer Financial Protection and the Securities and Exchange Commission shall have authority to prescribe such regulations as may be necessary to carry out the purposes of this subchapter with respect to financial institutions and other persons subject to their respective jurisdiction under section 6805 of this title (and notwithstanding subtitle B of the Consumer Financial Protection Act of 2010 [12 U.S.C. 5511 et seq.]), except that the Bureau of Consumer Financial Protection shall not have authority to prescribe regulations with respect to the standards under section 6801 of this title.

        (B) CFTC

The Commodity Futures Trading Commission shall have authority to prescribe such regulations as may be necessary to carry out the purposes of this subchapter with respect to financial institutions and other persons subject to the jurisdiction of the Commodity Futures Trading Commission under section 7b–2 of title 7.

        (C) Federal Trade Commission authority

Notwithstanding the authority of the Bureau of Consumer Financial Protection under subparagraph (A), the Federal Trade Commission shall have authority to prescribe such regulations as may be necessary to carry out the purposes of this subchapter with respect to any financial institution that is a person described in section 1029(a) of the Consumer Financial Protection Act of 2010 [12 U.S.C. 5519(a)].

        (D) Rule of construction

Nothing in this paragraph shall be construed to alter, affect, or otherwise limit the authority of a State insurance authority to adopt regulations to carry out this subchapter.

    (2) Coordination, consistency, and comparability

Each of the agencies authorized under paragraph (1) to prescribe regulations shall consult and coordinate with the other such agencies and, as appropriate, and with representatives of State insurance authorities designated by the National Association of Insurance Commissioners, for the purpose of assuring, to the extent possible, that the regulations prescribed by each such agency are consistent and comparable with the regulations prescribed by the other such agencies.

(3) Procedures and deadline

Such regulations shall be prescribed in accordance with applicable requirements of title 5.

(b) Authority to grant exceptions

The regulations prescribed under subsection (a) may include such additional exceptions to subsections (a) through (d) of section 6802 of this title as are deemed consistent with the purposes of this subchapter.

§ 6805. Enforcement

(a) In general

Subject to subtitle B of the Consumer Financial Protection Act of 2010 [12 U.S.C. 5511 et seq.], this subchapter and the regulations prescribed thereunder shall be enforced by the Bureau of Consumer Financial Protection, the Federal functional regulators, the State insurance authorities, and the Federal Trade Commission with respect to financial institutions and other persons subject to their jurisdiction under applicable law, as follows:

(1) Under section 1818 of title 12, by the appropriate Federal banking agency, as defined in section 1813(q) of title 12, in the case of-

(A) national banks, Federal branches and Federal agencies of foreign banks, and any subsidiaries of such entities (except brokers, dealers, persons providing insurance, investment companies, and investment advisers);

(B) member banks of the Federal Reserve System (other than national banks), branches and agencies of foreign banks (other than Federal branches, Federal agencies, and insured State branches of foreign banks), commercial lending companies owned or controlled by foreign banks, organizations operating under section 25 or 25A of the Federal Reserve Act [12 U.S.C. 601 et seq., 611 et seq.], and bank holding companies and their nonbank subsidiaries or affiliates (except brokers, dealers, persons providing insurance, investment companies, and investment advisers);

(C) banks insured by the Federal Deposit Insurance Corporation (other than members of the Federal Reserve System), insured State branches of foreign banks, and any subsidiaries of such entities (except brokers, dealers, persons providing insurance, investment companies, and investment advisers); and

(D) savings associations the deposits of which are insured by the Federal Deposit Insurance Corporation, and any subsidiaries of such savings associations (except brokers, dealers, persons providing insurance, investment companies, and investment advisers).

(2) Under the Federal Credit Union Act [12 U.S.C. 1751 et seq.], by the Board of the National Credit Union Administration with respect to any federally insured credit union, and any subsidiaries of such an entity.

(3) Under the Securities Exchange Act of 1934 [15 U.S.C. 78a et seq.], by the Securities and Exchange Commission with respect to any broker or dealer.

(4) Under the Investment Company Act of 1940 [15 U.S.C. 80a–1 et seq.], by the Securities and Exchange Commission with respect to investment companies.

(5) Under the Investment Advisers Act of 1940 [15 U.S.C. 80b–1 et seq.], by the Securities and Exchange Commission with respect to investment advisers registered with the Commission under such Act.

(6) Under State insurance law, in the case of any person engaged in providing insurance, by the applicable State insurance authority of the State in which the person is domiciled, subject to section 6701 of this title.

(7) Under the Federal Trade Commission Act [15 U.S.C. 41 et seq.], by the Federal Trade Commission for any other financial institution or other person that is not subject to the jurisdiction of any agency or authority under paragraphs (1) through (6) of this subsection.

(8) Under subtitle E of the Consumer Financial Protection Act of 2010 [12 U.S.C. 5561 et seq.], by the Bureau of Consumer Financial Protection, in the case of any financial institution and other covered person or service provider that is subject to the jurisdiction of the Bureau and any person subject to this subchapter, but not with respect to the standards under section 6801 of this title.

(b) Enforcement of section 6801

(1) In general

Except as provided in paragraph (2), the agencies and authorities described in subsection (a), other than the Bureau of Consumer Financial Protection, shall implement the standards prescribed under section 6801(b) of this title in the same manner, to the extent practicable, as standards prescribed pursuant to section 1831p–1(a) of title 12 are implemented pursuant to such section.

(2) Exception

The agencies and authorities described in paragraphs (3), (4), (5), (6), and (7) of subsection (a) shall implement the standards prescribed under section 6801(b) of this title by rule with respect to the financial institutions and other persons subject to their respective jurisdictions under subsection (a).

(c) Absence of State action

If a State insurance authority fails to adopt regulations to carry out this subchapter, such State shall not be eligible to override, pursuant to section 1831x(g)(2)(B)(iii) of title 12, the insurance customer protection regulations prescribed by a Federal banking agency under section 1831x(a) of title 12.

(d) Definitions

The terms used in subsection (a)(1) that are not defined in this subchapter or otherwise defined in section 1813(s) of title 12 shall have the same meaning as given in section 3101 of title 12.

§ 6806. Relation to other provisions

Except for the amendments made by subsections (a) and (b), nothing in this chapter shall be construed to modify, limit, or supersede the operation of the Fair Credit Reporting Act [15 U.S.C. 1681 et seq.], and no inference shall be drawn on the basis of the provisions of this chapter regarding whether information is transaction or experience information under section 603 of such Act [15 U.S.C. 1681a].

§ 6807. Relation to State laws

(a) In general

This subchapter and the amendments made by this subchapter shall not be construed as superseding, altering, or affecting any statute, regulation, order, or interpretation in effect in any State, except to the extent that such statute, regulation, order, or interpretation is inconsistent with the provisions of this subchapter, and then only to the extent of the inconsistency.

(b) Greater protection under State law

For purposes of this section, a State statute, regulation, order, or interpretation is not inconsistent with the provisions of this subchapter if the protection such statute, regulation, order, or interpretation affords any person is greater than the protection provided under this subchapter and the amendments made by this subchapter, as determined by the Bureau of Consumer Financial Protection, after consultation with the agency or authority with jurisdiction under section 6805(a) of this title of either the person that initiated the complaint or that is the subject of the complaint, on its own motion or upon the petition of any interested party.

§ 6808. Study of information sharing among financial affiliates

(a) In general

The Secretary of the Treasury, in conjunction with the Federal functional regulators and the Federal Trade Commission, shall conduct a study of information sharing practices among financial institutions and their affiliates. Such study shall include-

   (1) the purposes for the sharing of confidential customer information with affiliates or with nonaffiliated third parties;
   (2) the extent and adequacy of security protections for such information;
   (3) the potential risks for customer privacy of such sharing of information;
   (4) the potential benefits for financial institutions and affiliates of such sharing of information;
   (5) the potential benefits for customers of such sharing of information;
   (6) the adequacy of existing laws to protect customer privacy;

(7) the adequacy of financial institution privacy policy and privacy rights disclosure under existing law;

(8) the feasibility of different approaches, including opt-out and opt-in, to permit customers to direct that confidential information not be shared with affiliates and nonaffiliated third parties; and

(9) the feasibility of restricting sharing of information for specific uses or of permitting customers to direct the uses for which information may be shared.

(b) Consultation

The Secretary shall consult with representatives of State insurance authorities designated by the National Association of Insurance Commissioners, and also with financial services industry, consumer organizations and privacy groups, and other representatives of the general public, in formulating and conducting the study required by subsection (a).

(c) Report

On or before January 1, 2002, the Secretary shall submit a report to the Congress containing the findings and conclusions of the study required under subsection (a), together with such recommendations for legislative or administrative action as may be appropriate.

§ 6809. Definitions

As used in this subchapter:

(1) Federal banking agency

The term "Federal banking agency" has the same meaning as given in section 1813 of title 12.

(2) Federal functional regulator

The term "Federal functional regulator" means-

    (A) the Board of Governors of the Federal Reserve System;

    (B) the Office of the Comptroller of the Currency;

    (C) the Board of Directors of the Federal Deposit Insurance Corporation;

    (D) the Director of the Office of Thrift Supervision;

    (E) the National Credit Union Administration Board; and

    (F) the Securities and Exchange Commission.

(3) Financial institution

    (A) In general

    The term "financial institution" means any institution the business of which is engaging in financial activities as described in section 1843(k) of title 12.

    (B) Persons subject to CFTC regulation

    Notwithstanding subparagraph (A), the term "financial institution" does not include any person or entity with respect to any financial activity that is subject to the jurisdiction of the Commodity Futures Trading Commission under the Commodity Exchange Act [7 U.S.C. 1 et seq.].

(C) Farm credit institutions

Notwithstanding subparagraph (A), the term "financial institution" does not include the Federal Agricultural Mortgage Corporation or any entity chartered and operating under the Farm Credit Act of 1971 [12 U.S.C. 2001 et seq.].

(D) Other secondary market institutions

Notwithstanding subparagraph (A), the term "financial institution" does not include institutions chartered by Congress specifically to engage in transactions described in section 6802(e)(1)(C) of this title, as long as such institutions do not sell or transfer nonpublic personal information to a nonaffiliated third party.

(4) Nonpublic personal information

(A) The term "nonpublic personal information" means personally identifiable financial information-

(i) provided by a consumer to a financial institution;

(ii) resulting from any transaction with the consumer or any service performed for the consumer; or

(iii) otherwise obtained by the financial institution.

(B) Such term does not include publicly available information, as such term is defined by the regulations prescribed under section 6804 of this title.

(C) Notwithstanding subparagraph (B), such term-

(i) shall include any list, description, or other grouping of consumers (and publicly available information pertaining to them) that is derived using any nonpublic personal information other than publicly available information; but

(ii) shall not include any list, description, or other grouping of consumers (and publicly available information pertaining to them) that is derived without using any nonpublic personal information.

(5) Nonaffiliated third party

The term "nonaffiliated third party" means any entity that is not an affiliate of, or related by common ownership or affiliated by corporate control with, the financial institution, but does not include a joint employee of such institution.

(6) Affiliate

The term "affiliate" means any company that controls, is controlled by, or is under common control with another company.

(7) Necessary to effect, administer, or enforce

The term "as necessary to effect, administer, or enforce the transaction" means-

(A) the disclosure is required, or is a usual, appropriate, or acceptable method, to carry out the transaction or the product or service business of which the transaction is a part, and record or service or maintain the consumer's account in the ordinary course of providing the financial service or financial product, or to administer or service benefits or claims relating to the transaction or the product or service business of which it is a part, and includes-

(i) providing the consumer or the consumer's agent or broker with a confirmation, statement, or other record of the transaction, or information on the status or value of the financial service or financial product; and

(ii) the accrual or recognition of incentives or bonuses associated with the transaction that are provided by the financial institution or any other party;

(B) the disclosure is required, or is one of the lawful or appropriate methods, to enforce the rights of the financial institution or of other persons engaged in carrying out the financial transaction, or providing the product or service;

(C) the disclosure is required, or is a usual, appropriate, or acceptable method, for insurance underwriting at the consumer's request or for reinsurance purposes, or for any of the following purposes as they relate to a consumer's insurance: Account administration, reporting, investigating, or preventing fraud or material misrepresentation, processing premium payments, processing insurance claims, administering insurance benefits (including utilization review activities), participating in research projects, or as otherwise required or specifically permitted by Federal or State law; or

(D) the disclosure is required, or is a usual, appropriate or acceptable method, in connection with-

(i) the authorization, settlement, billing, processing, clearing, transferring, reconciling, or collection of amounts charged, debited, or otherwise paid using a debit, credit or other payment card, check, or account number, or by other payment means;

(ii) the transfer of receivables, accounts or interests therein; or

(iii) the audit of debit, credit or other payment information.

(8) State insurance authority

The term "State insurance authority" means, in the case of any person engaged in providing insurance, the State insurance authority of the State in which the person is domiciled.

(9) Consumer

The term "consumer" means an individual who obtains, from a financial institution, financial products or services which are to be used primarily for personal, family, or household purposes, and also means the legal representative of such an individual.

(10) Joint agreement

The term "joint agreement" means a formal written contract pursuant to which two or more financial institutions jointly offer, endorse, or sponsor a financial product or service, and as may be further defined in the regulations prescribed under section 6804 of this title.

(11) Customer relationship

The term "time of establishing a customer relationship" shall be defined by the regulations prescribed under section 6804 of this title, and shall, in the case of a financial institution engaged in extending credit directly to consumers to finance purchases of goods or services, mean the time of establishing the credit relationship with the consumer.

Subtitle B--Fraudulent Access to Financial Information

§ 6821. Privacy protection for customer information of financial institutions

(a) Prohibition on obtaining customer information by false pretenses

It shall be a violation of this subchapter for any person to obtain or attempt to obtain, or cause to be disclosed or attempt to cause to be disclosed to any person, customer information of a financial institution relating to another person-

(1) by making a false, fictitious, or fraudulent statement or representation to an officer, employee, or agent of a financial institution;

(2) by making a false, fictitious, or fraudulent statement or representation to a customer of a financial institution; or

(3) by providing any document to an officer, employee, or agent of a financial institution, knowing that the document is forged, counterfeit, lost, or stolen, was fraudulently obtained, or contains a false, fictitious, or fraudulent statement or representation.

(b) Prohibition on solicitation of a person to obtain customer information from financial institution under false pretenses

It shall be a violation of this subchapter to request a person to obtain customer information of a financial institution, knowing that the person will obtain, or attempt to obtain, the information from the institution in any manner described in subsection (a).

(c) Nonapplicability to law enforcement agencies

No provision of this section shall be construed so as to prevent any action by a law enforcement agency, or any officer, employee, or agent of such agency, to obtain customer information of a financial institution in connection with the performance of the official duties of the agency.

(d) Nonapplicability to financial institutions in certain cases

No provision of this section shall be construed so as to prevent any financial institution, or any officer, employee, or agent of a financial institution, from obtaining customer information of such financial institution in the course of-

(1) testing the security procedures or systems of such institution for maintaining the confidentiality of customer information;

United States
Financial Services Modernization Act

(2) investigating allegations of misconduct or negligence on the part of any officer, employee, or agent of the financial institution; or

(3) recovering customer information of the financial institution which was obtained or received by another person in any manner described in subsection (a) or (b).

(e) Nonapplicability to insurance institutions for investigation of insurance fraud

No provision of this section shall be construed so as to prevent any insurance institution, or any officer, employee, or agency of an insurance institution, from obtaining information as part of an insurance investigation into criminal activity, fraud, material misrepresentation, or material nondisclosure that is authorized for such institution under State law, regulation, interpretation, or order.

(f) Nonapplicability to certain types of customer information of financial institutions

No provision of this section shall be construed so as to prevent any person from obtaining customer information of a financial institution that otherwise is available as a public record filed pursuant to the securities laws (as defined in section 78c(a)(47) of this title).

(g) Nonapplicability to collection of child support judgments

No provision of this section shall be construed to prevent any State-licensed private investigator, or any officer, employee, or agent of such private investigator, from obtaining customer information of a financial institution, to the extent reasonably necessary to collect child support from a person adjudged to have been delinquent in his or her obligations by a Federal or State court, and to the extent that such action by a State-licensed private investigator is not unlawful under any other Federal or State law or regulation, and has been authorized by an order or judgment of a court of competent jurisdiction.

§ 6822. Administrative enforcement

(a) Enforcement by Federal Trade Commission

Except as provided in subsection (b), compliance with this subchapter shall be enforced by the Federal Trade Commission in the same manner and with the same power and authority as the Commission has under the Fair Debt Collection Practices Act [15 U.S.C. 1692 et seq.] to enforce compliance with such Act.

(b) Enforcement by other agencies in certain cases

(1) In general

Compliance with this subchapter shall be enforced under-

(A) section 8 of the Federal Deposit Insurance Act [12 U.S.C. 1818], in the case of-

(i) national banks, and Federal branches and Federal agencies of foreign banks, by the Office of the Comptroller of the Currency;

(ii) member banks of the Federal Reserve System (other than national banks), branches and agencies of foreign banks (other than Federal branches, Federal agencies, and insured State branches of foreign banks), commercial lending companies owned or controlled by foreign banks, and organizations operating under section 25 or 25A of the Federal Reserve Act [12 U.S.C. 601 et seq., 611 et seq.], by the Board;

(iii) banks insured by the Federal Deposit Insurance Corporation (other than members of the Federal Reserve System and national nonmember banks) and insured State branches of foreign banks, by the Board of Directors of the Federal Deposit Insurance Corporation; and

(iv) savings associations the deposits of which are insured by the Federal Deposit Insurance Corporation, by the Director of the Office of Thrift Supervision; and

(B) the Federal Credit Union Act [12 U.S.C. 1751 et seq.], by the Administrator of the National Credit Union Administration with respect to any Federal credit union.

(2) Violations of this subchapter treated as violations of other laws

For the purpose of the exercise by any agency referred to in paragraph (1) of its powers under any Act referred to in that paragraph, a violation of this subchapter shall be deemed to be a violation of a requirement imposed under that Act. In addition to its powers under any provision of law specifically referred to in paragraph (1), each of the agencies referred to in that paragraph may exercise, for the purpose of enforcing compliance with this subchapter, any other authority conferred on such agency by law.

§ 6823. Criminal penalty

(a) In general

Whoever knowingly and intentionally violates, or knowingly and intentionally attempts to violate, section 6821 of this title shall be fined in accordance with title 18 or imprisoned for not more than 5 years, or both.

(b) Enhanced penalty for aggravated cases

Whoever violates, or attempts to violate, section 6821 of this title while violating another law of the United States or as part of a pattern of any illegal activity involving more than $100,000 in a 12-month period shall be fined twice the amount provided in subsection (b)(3) or (c)(3) (as the case may be) of section 3571 of title 18, imprisoned for not more than 10 years, or both.

§ 6824. Relation to State laws

(a) In general

This subchapter shall not be construed as superseding, altering, or affecting the statutes, regulations, orders, or interpretations in effect in any State, except to the extent that such statutes, regulations, orders, or interpretations are inconsistent with the provisions of this subchapter, and then only to the extent of the inconsistency.

(b) Greater protection under State law

For purposes of this section, a State statute, regulation, order, or interpretation is not inconsistent with the provisions of this subchapter if the protection such statute, regulation, order, or interpretation affords any person is greater than the protection provided under this subchapter as determined by the Federal Trade Commission, after consultation with the agency or authority with jurisdiction under section 6822 of this title of either the person that initiated the complaint or that is the subject of the complaint, on its own motion or upon the petition of any interested party.

§ 6825. Agency guidance

In furtherance of the objectives of this subchapter, each Federal banking agency (as defined in section 1813(z) of title 12), the National Credit Union Administration, and the Securities and Exchange Commission or self-regulatory organizations, as appropriate, shall review regulations and guidelines applicable to financial institutions under their respective jurisdictions and shall prescribe such revisions to such regulations and guidelines as may be necessary to ensure that such financial institutions have policies, procedures, and controls in place to prevent the unauthorized disclosure of customer financial information and to deter and detect activities proscribed under section 6821 of this title.

§ 6826. Reports

(a) Report to the Congress

Before the end of the 18-month period beginning on November 12, 1999, the Comptroller General, in consultation with the Federal Trade Commission, Federal banking agencies, the National Credit Union Administration, the Securities and Exchange Commission, appropriate Federal law enforcement agencies, and appropriate State insurance regulators, shall submit to the Congress a report on the following:

(1) The efficacy and adequacy of the remedies provided in this subchapter in addressing attempts to obtain financial information by fraudulent means or by false pretenses.

(2) Any recommendations for additional legislative or regulatory action to address threats to the privacy of financial information created by attempts to obtain information by fraudulent means or false pretenses.

(b) Annual report by administering agencies

The Federal Trade Commission and the Attorney General shall submit to Congress an annual report on number and disposition of all enforcement actions taken pursuant to this subchapter.

§ 6827. Definitions

For purposes of this subchapter, the following definitions shall apply:

(1) Customer

The term "customer" means, with respect to a financial institution, any person (or authorized representative of a person) to whom the financial institution provides a product or service, including that of acting as a fiduciary.

(2) Customer information of a financial institution

The term "customer information of a financial institution" means any information maintained by or for a financial institution which is derived from the relationship between the financial institution and a customer of the financial institution and is identified with the customer.

(3) Document

The term "document" means any information in any form.

(4) Financial institution

(A) In general

The term "financial institution" means any institution engaged in the business of providing financial services to customers who maintain a credit, deposit, trust, or other financial account or relationship with the institution.

(B) Certain financial institutions specifically included

The term "financial institution" includes any depository institution (as defined in section 461(b)(1)(A) of title 12), any broker or dealer, any investment adviser or investment company, any insurance company, any loan or finance company, any credit card issuer or operator of a credit card system, and any consumer reporting agency that compiles and maintains files on consumers on a nationwide basis (as defined in section 1681a(p) of this title).

(C) Securities institutions

For purposes of subparagraph (B)-

(i) the terms "broker" and "dealer" have the same meanings as given in section 78c of this title;

(ii) the term "investment adviser" has the same meaning as given in section 80b–2(a)(11) of this title; and

(iii) the term "investment company" has the same meaning as given in section 80a–3 of this title.

(D) Certain persons and entities specifically excluded

The term "financial institution" does not include any person or entity with respect to any financial activity that is subject to the jurisdiction of the

Commodity Futures Trading Commission under the Commodity Exchange Act [7 U.S.C. 1 et seq.] and does not include the Federal Agricultural Mortgage Corporation or any entity chartered and operating under the Farm Credit Act of 1971 [12 U.S.C. 2001 et seq.].

(E) Further definition by regulation

The Federal Trade Commission, after consultation with Federal banking agencies and the Securities and Exchange Commission, may prescribe regulations clarifying or describing the types of institutions which shall be treated as financial institutions for purposes of this subchapter.

NO CHILD LEFT BEHIND ACT (2001)
[EXCERPT]

Summary

Congress passed the No Child Left Behind Act in December 2001, making significant amendments to the General Education Provisions Act to protect students' privacy. The amendments require educational agencies to give parents annual notice of and access to certain surveys and examinations administered students. Notice is required for student surveys that are performed for marketing purposes, for surveys that collect sensitive information, and for non-emergency invasive physical examinations. Sensitive information includes political and religious beliefs of the student or parent, sexual behavior, mental health information, income, and anti-social or illegal behavior.

Educational agencies must allow parents or adult students to opt-out of surveys administered for marketing purposes and of non-emergency invasive physical examinations. Some marketing activities, such as book clubs, military and college recruitment, and student "recognition" awards, are not subject to the opt-out requirement. Prior consent must be obtained before an educational agency administers a mandatory survey that collects sensitive information. Stricter state laws are not preempted by the privacy amendments.

References

Public Law 107-110 as codified at 20 U.S.C. § 1232h
[https://www.law.cornell.edu/uscode/text/20/1232h]

EPIC, EPIC Student Privacy Project
[https://www.epic.org/privacy/student/]

20 U.S.C. § 1232h

(a) Inspection of instructional materials by parents or guardians

All instructional materials, including teacher's manuals, films, tapes, or other supplementary material which will be used in connection with any survey, analysis, or evaluation as part of any applicable program shall be available for inspection by the parents or guardians of the children.

(b) Limits on survey, analysis, or evaluations

No student shall be required, as part of any applicable program, to submit to a survey, analysis, or evaluation that reveals information concerning-

(1) political affiliations or beliefs of the student or the student's parent;

(2) mental or psychological problems of the student or the student's family;

(3) sex behavior or attitudes;

(4) illegal, anti-social, self-incriminating, or demeaning behavior;

(5) critical appraisals of other individuals with whom respondents have close family relationships;

(6) legally recognized privileged or analogous relationships, such as those of lawyers, physicians, and ministers;

(7) religious practices, affiliations, or beliefs of the student or student's parent; or

(8) income (other than that required by law to determine eligibility for participation in a program or for receiving financial assistance under such program), without the prior consent of the student (if the student is an adult or emancipated minor), or in the case of an unemancipated minor, without the prior written consent of the parent.

(c) Development of local policies concerning student privacy, parental access to information, and administration of certain physical examinations to minors

(1) Development and adoption of local policies

Except as provided in subsections (a) and (b), a local educational agency that receives funds under any applicable program shall develop and adopt policies, in consultation with parents, regarding the following:

(A)(i) The right of a parent of a student to inspect, upon the request of the parent, a survey created by a third party before the survey is administered or distributed by a school to a student; and

(ii) any applicable procedures for granting a request by a parent for reasonable access to such survey within a reasonable period of time after the request is received.

(B) Arrangements to protect student privacy that are provided by the agency in the event of the administration or distribution of a survey to a student containing one or more of the following items (including the right of a parent of a student to inspect, upon the request of the parent, any survey containing one or more of such items):

(i) Political affiliations or beliefs of the student or the student's parent.

(ii) Mental or psychological problems of the student or the student's family.

(iii) Sex behavior or attitudes.

(iv) Illegal, anti-social, self-incriminating, or demeaning behavior.

(v) Critical appraisals of other individuals with whom respondents have close family relationships.

(vi) Legally recognized privileged or analogous relationships, such as those of lawyers, physicians, and ministers.

(vii) Religious practices, affiliations, or beliefs of the student or the student's parent.

(viii) Income (other than that required by law to determine eligibility for participation in a program or for receiving financial assistance under such program).

(C)(i) The right of a parent of a student to inspect, upon the request of the parent, any instructional material used as part of the educational curriculum for the student; and

(ii) any applicable procedures for granting a request by a parent for reasonable access to instructional material within a reasonable period of time after the request is received.

(D) The administration of physical examinations or screenings that the school or agency may administer to a student.

(E) The collection, disclosure, or use of personal information collected from students for the purpose of marketing or for selling that information (or otherwise providing that information to others for that purpose), including arrangements to protect student privacy that are provided by the agency in the event of such collection, disclosure, or use.

(F)(i) The right of a parent of a student to inspect, upon the request of the parent, any instrument used in the collection of personal information under subparagraph (E) before the instrument is administered or distributed to a student; and

(ii) any applicable procedures for granting a request by a parent for reasonable access to such instrument within a reasonable period of time after the request is received.

(2) Parental notification

(A) Notification of policies

The policies developed by a local educational agency under paragraph (1) shall provide for reasonable notice of the adoption or continued use of such policies directly to the parents of students enrolled in schools served by that agency. At a minimum, the agency shall-

(i) provide such notice at least annually, at the beginning of the school year, and within a reasonable period of time after any substantive change in such policies; and

(ii) offer an opportunity for the parent (and for purposes of an activity described in subparagraph (C)(i), in the case of a student of an appropriate age, the student) to opt the student out of participation in an activity described in subparagraph (C).

(B) Notification of specific events

The local educational agency shall directly notify the parent of a student, at least annually at the beginning of the school year, of the specific or approximate dates during the school year when activities described in subparagraph (C) are scheduled, or expected to be scheduled.

(C) Activities requiring notification

The following activities require notification under this paragraph:

(i) Activities involving the collection, disclosure, or use of personal information collected from students for the purpose of marketing or for selling that information (or otherwise providing that information to others for that purpose).

(ii) The administration of any survey containing one or more items described in clauses (i) through (viii) of paragraph (1)(B).

(iii) Any nonemergency, invasive physical examination or screening that is-

(I) required as a condition of attendance;

(II) administered by the school and scheduled by the school in advance; and

(III) not necessary to protect the immediate health and safety of the student, or of other students.

(3) Existing policies

A local educational agency need not develop and adopt new policies if the State educational agency or local educational agency has in place, on January 8, 2002, policies covering the requirements of paragraph (1). The agency shall provide reasonable notice of such existing policies to parents and guardians of students, in accordance with paragraph (2).

(4) Exceptions

(A) Educational products or services

Paragraph (1)(E) does not apply to the collection, disclosure, or use of personal information collected from students for the exclusive purpose of developing, evaluating, or providing educational products or services for, or to, students or educational institutions, such as the following:

(i) College or other postsecondary education recruitment, or military recruitment.

(ii) Book clubs, magazines, and programs providing access to low-cost literary products.

(iii) Curriculum and instructional materials used by elementary schools and secondary schools.

(iv) Tests and assessments used by elementary schools and secondary schools to provide cognitive, evaluative, diagnostic, clinical, aptitude, or achievement information about students (or to generate other statistically useful data for the purpose of securing such tests and assessments) and the subsequent analysis and public release of the aggregate data from such tests and assessments.

(v) The sale by students of products or services to raise funds for school-related or education-related activities.

(vi) Student recognition programs.

(B) State law exception

The provisions of this subsection-

(i) shall not be construed to preempt applicable provisions of State law that require parental notification; and

(ii) do not apply to any physical examination or screening that is permitted or required by an applicable State law, including physical examinations or screenings that are permitted without parental notification.

(5) General provisions

(A) Rules of construction

(i) This section does not supersede section 1232g of this title.

(ii) Paragraph (1)(D) does not apply to a survey administered to a student in accordance with the Individuals with Disabilities Education Act (20 U.S.C. 1400 et seq.).

(B) Student rights

The rights provided to parents under this section transfer to the student when the student turns 18 years old, or is an emancipated minor (under an applicable State law) at any age.

(C) Information activities

The Secretary shall annually inform each State educational agency and each local educational agency of the educational agency's obligations under this section and section 1232g of this title.

(D) Funding

A State educational agency or local educational agency may use funds provided under part A of title IV of the Elementary and Secondary Education Act of 1965 [20 U.S.C. 7101 et seq.] to enhance parental involvement in areas affecting the in-school privacy of students.

(6) Definitions

As used in this subsection:

(A) Instructional material

The term "instructional material" means instructional content that is provided to a student, regardless of its format, including printed or representational materials, audio-visual materials, and materials in electronic or digital formats (such as materials accessible through the Internet). The term does not include academic tests or academic assessments.

(B) Invasive physical examination

The term "invasive physical examination" means any medical examination that involves the exposure of private body parts, or any act during such examination that includes incision, insertion, or injection into the body, but does not include a hearing, vision, or scoliosis screening.

(C) Local educational agency

The term "local educational agency" means an elementary school, secondary school, school district, or local board of education that is the recipient of funds under an applicable program, but does not include a postsecondary institution.

(D) Parent

The term "parent" includes a legal guardian or other person standing in loco parentis (such as a grandparent or stepparent with whom the child lives, or a person who is legally responsible for the welfare of the child).

(E) Personal information

The term "personal information" means individually identifiable information including-

(i) a student or parent's first and last name;

(ii) a home or other physical address (including street name and the name of the city or town);

(iii) a telephone number; or

(iv) a Social Security identification number.

(F) Student

The term "student" means any elementary school or secondary school student.

(G) Survey

The term "survey" includes an evaluation.

(d) Notice

Educational agencies and institutions shall give parents and students effective notice of their rights under this section.

(e) Enforcement

The Secretary shall take such action as the Secretary determines appropriate to enforce this section, except that action to terminate assistance provided under an applicable program shall be taken only if the Secretary determines that-

(1) there has been a failure to comply with such section; and

(2) compliance with such section cannot be secured by voluntary means.

(f) Office and review board

The Secretary shall establish or designate an office and review board within the Department of Education to investigate, process, review, and adjudicate violations of the rights established under this section.

US HOMELAND SECURITY ACT (2002)
[EXCERPTS]

Summary

Congress passed the Department of Homeland Security Act in 2002, combining 22 agencies for the purpose of securing the United States from threats. Four provisions of the bill are excerpted here. First, the Act broadly exempts "critical infrastructure information" voluntarily submitted to the Department of Homeland Security from the Freedom of Information Act. Critical infrastructure information relates to the operation of systems such as the national power grid and telecommunications networks. Once disclosed to the government, the information could not be used against the company in civil litigation, and government agents who disclose the information would be subject to criminal penalties and fines. Second, the Act creates a privacy officer for the Department charged with the responsibility of compliance with the Privacy Act, with formulating privacy impact assessments for rules proposed by the Department, and with preparing an annual report to Congress. Third, the Act prohibits all federal agencies from implementing the Terrorism Information and Prevention System (TIPS). TIPS was a program that encouraged individuals to report the suspicious behaviors of others. Fourth, the Act prohibits the new agency from developing a national identification system or card. The Act also makes certaiu changes to the Electronic Communications Privacy Act (ECPA). Those changes increased prison sentences for computer crimes, lowered burdens for law enforcement access to communications data, and expanded law enforcement authority to use pen register and trap and trace devices. The changes have been incorporated in the ECPA section.

References

Public Law 107-296 , as amended by Public Law 114-113. Codified at 6 U.S.C. § 131 et seq.
[https://www.law.cornell.edu/uscode/text/6/131]

§ 131 Definitions

In this part:

(1) Agency

The term "agency" has the meaning given it in section 551 of title 5.

(2) Covered Federal agency

The term "covered Federal agency" means the Department of Homeland Security.

(3) Critical infrastructure information

The term "critical infrastructure information" means information not customarily in the public domain and related to the security of critical infrastructure or protected systems-

(A) actual, potential, or threatened interference with, attack on, compromise of, or incapacitation of critical infrastructure or protected systems by either physical or computer-based attack or other similar conduct (including the misuse of or unauthorized access to all types of communications and data transmission systems) that violates Federal, State, or local law, harms interstate commerce of the United States, or threatens public health or safety;

(B) the ability of any critical infrastructure or protected system to resist such interference, compromise, or incapacitation, including any planned or past assessment, projection, or estimate of the vulnerability of critical infrastructure or a protected system, including security testing, risk evaluation thereto, risk management planning, or risk audit; or

(C) any planned or past operational problem or solution regarding critical infrastructure or protected systems, including repair, recovery, reconstruction, insurance, or continuity, to the extent it is related to such interference, compromise, or incapacitation.

(4) Critical infrastructure protection program

The term "critical infrastructure protection program" means any component or bureau of a covered Federal agency that has been designated by the President or any agency head to receive critical infrastructure information.

(5) Information Sharing and Analysis Organization

The term "Information Sharing and Analysis Organization" means any formal or informal entity or collaboration created or employed by public or private sector organizations, for purposes of-

(A) gathering and analyzing critical infrastructure information, including information related to cybersecurity risks and incidents, in order to better understand security problems and interdependencies related to critical infrastructure, including cybersecurity risks and incidents, and protected systems, so as to ensure the availability, integrity, and reliability thereof;

(B) communicating or disclosing critical infrastructure information, including cybersecurity risks and incidents, to help prevent, detect, mitigate, or recover from the effects of a interference, compromise, or an incapacitation problem related to critical infrastructure, including cybersecurity risks and incidents, or protected systems; and

(C) voluntarily disseminating critical infrastructure information, including cybersecurity risks and incidents, to its members, State, local, and Federal Governments, or any other entities that may be of assistance in carrying out the purposes specified in subparagraphs (A) and (B).

(6) Protected system

The term "protected system"-

(A) means any service, physical or computer-based system, process, or procedure that directly or indirectly affects the viability of a facility of critical infrastructure; and

(B) includes any physical or computer-based system, including a computer, computer system, computer or communications network, or any component hardware or element thereof, software program, processing instructions, or information or data in transmission or storage therein, irrespective of the medium of transmission or storage.

(7) Voluntary

(A) In general

The term "voluntary", in the case of any submittal of critical infrastructure information to a covered Federal agency, means the submittal thereof in the absence of such agency's exercise of legal authority to compel access to or submission of such information and may be accomplished by a single entity or an Information Sharing and Analysis Organization on behalf of itself or its members.

(B) Exclusions

The term "voluntary"-

(i) in the case of any action brought under the securities laws as is defined in section 78c(a)(47) of title 15-

(I) does not include information or statements contained in any documents or materials filed with the Securities and Exchange Commission, or with Federal banking regulators, pursuant to section 78l(i) of title 15; and

(II) with respect to the submittal of critical infrastructure information, does not include any disclosure or writing that when made accompanied the solicitation of an offer or a sale of securities; and

(ii) does not include information or statements submitted or relied upon as a basis for making licensing or permitting determinations, or during regulatory proceedings.

(8) Cybersecurity risk; incident

The terms "cybersecurity risk" and "incident" have the meanings given those terms in section 148 of this title.

§ 132. Designation of critical infrastructure protection program

A critical infrastructure protection program may be designated as such by one of the following:

(1) The President.

(2) The Secretary of Homeland Security.

§ 133. Protection of voluntarily shared critical infrastructure information

(a) Protection

(1) In general

United States
US Homeland Security Act

Notwithstanding any other provision of law, critical infrastructure information (including the identity of the submitting person or entity) that is voluntarily submitted to a covered Federal agency for use by that agency regarding the security of critical infrastructure and protected systems, analysis, warning, interdependency study, recovery, reconstitution, or other informational purpose, when accompanied by an express statement specified in paragraph (2)-

(A) shall be exempt from disclosure under section 552 of title 5 (commonly referred to as the Freedom of Information Act);

(B) shall not be subject to any agency rules or judicial doctrine regarding ex parte communications with a decision making official;

(C) shall not, without the written consent of the person or entity submitting such information, be used directly by such agency, any other Federal, State, or local authority, or any third party, in any civil action arising under Federal or State law if such information is submitted in good faith;

(D) shall not, without the written consent of the person or entity submitting such information, be used or disclosed by any officer or employee of the United States for purposes other than the purposes of this part, except-

  (i) in furtherance of an investigation or the prosecution of a criminal act; or

  (ii) when disclosure of the information would be-

    (I) to either House of Congress, or to the extent of matter within its jurisdiction, any committee or subcommittee thereof, any joint committee thereof or subcommittee of any such joint committee; or

    (II) to the Comptroller General, or any authorized representative of the Comptroller General, in the course of the performance of the duties of the Government Accountability Office.

(E) shall not, if provided to a State or local government or government agency-

  (i) be made available pursuant to any State or local law requiring disclosure of information or records;

  (ii) otherwise be disclosed or distributed to any party by said State or local government or government agency without the written consent of the person or entity submitting such information; or

  (iii) be used other than for the purpose of protecting critical infrastructure or protected systems, or in furtherance of an investigation or the prosecution of a criminal act; and

(F) does not constitute a waiver of any applicable privilege or protection provided under law, such as trade secret protection.

(2) Express statement

For purposes of paragraph (1), the term "express statement", with respect to information or records, means-

(A) in the case of written information or records, a written marking on the information or records substantially similar to the following: "This information is voluntarily submitted to the Federal Government in expectation of protection from disclosure as provided by the provisions of the Critical Infrastructure Information Act of 2002."; or

(B) in the case of oral information, a similar written statement submitted within a reasonable period following the oral communication.

(b) Limitation

No communication of critical infrastructure information to a covered Federal agency made pursuant to this part shall be considered to be an action subject to the requirements of the Federal Advisory Committee Act.

(c) Independently obtained information

Nothing in this section shall be construed to limit or otherwise affect the ability of a State, local, or Federal Government entity, agency, or authority, or any third party, under applicable law, to obtain critical infrastructure information in a manner not covered by subsection (a), including any information lawfully and properly disclosed generally or broadly to the public and to use such information in any manner permitted by law. For purposes of this section a permissible use of independently obtained information includes the disclosure of such information under section 2302(b)(8) of title 5.

(d) Treatment of voluntary submittal of information

The voluntary submittal to the Government of information or records that are protected from disclosure by this part shall not be construed to constitute compliance with any requirement to submit such information to a Federal agency under any other provision of law.

(e) Procedures

(1) In general

The Secretary of the Department of Homeland Security shall, in consultation with appropriate representatives of the National Security Council and the Office of Science and Technology Policy, establish uniform procedures for the receipt, care, and storage by Federal agencies of critical infrastructure information that is voluntarily submitted to the Government. The procedures shall be established not later than 90 days after November 25, 2002.

(2) Elements

The procedures established under paragraph (1) shall include mechanisms regarding-

(A) the acknowledgement of receipt by Federal agencies of critical infrastructure information that is voluntarily submitted to the Government;

(B) the maintenance of the identification of such information as voluntarily submitted to the Government for purposes of and subject to the provisions of this part;

(C) the care and storage of such information; and

(D) the protection and maintenance of the confidentiality of such information so as to permit the sharing of such information within the Federal Government and with State and local governments, and the issuance of notices and warnings related to the protection of critical infrastructure and protected systems, in such manner as to protect from public disclosure the identity of the submitting person or entity, or information that is proprietary, business sensitive, relates specifically to the submitting person or entity, and is otherwise not appropriately in the public domain.

(f) Penalties

Whoever, being an officer or employee of the United States or of any department or agency thereof, knowingly publishes, divulges, discloses, or makes known in any manner or to any extent not authorized by law, any critical infrastructure information protected from disclosure by this part coming to him in the course of this employment or official duties or by reason of any examination or investigation made by, or return, report, or record made to or filed with, such department or agency or officer or employee thereof, shall be fined under title 18, imprisoned not more than 1 year, or both, and shall be removed from office or employment.

(g) Authority to issue warnings

The Federal Government may provide advisories, alerts, and warnings to relevant companies, targeted sectors, other governmental entities, or the general public regarding potential threats to critical infrastructure as appropriate. In issuing a warning, the Federal Government shall take appropriate actions to protect from disclosure-

(1) the source of any voluntarily submitted critical infrastructure information that forms the basis for the warning; or

(2) information that is proprietary, business sensitive, relates specifically to the submitting person or entity, or is otherwise not appropriately in the public domain.

(h) Authority to delegate

The President may delegate authority to a critical infrastructure protection program, designated under section 132 of this title, to enter into a voluntary agreement to promote critical infrastructure security, including with any Information Sharing and Analysis Organization, or a plan of action as otherwise defined in section 4558 of title 50.

§ 134. No private right of action

Nothing in this subtitle may be construed to create a private right of action for enforcement of any provision of this Act.

§ 142. Privacy officer

(a) Appointment and responsibilities

The Secretary shall appoint a senior official in the Department, who shall report directly to the Secretary, to assume primary responsibility for privacy policy, including-

(1) assuring that the use of technologies sustain, and do not erode, privacy protections relating to the use, collection, and disclosure of personal information;

(2) assuring that personal information contained in Privacy Act systems of records is handled in full compliance with fair information practices as set out in the Privacy Act of 1974 [5 U.S.C. 552a];

(3) evaluating legislative and regulatory proposals involving collection, use, and disclosure of personal information by the Federal Government;

(4) conducting a privacy impact assessment of proposed rules of the Department or that of the Department on the privacy of personal information, including the type of personal information collected and the number of people affected;

(5) coordinating with the Officer for Civil Rights and Civil Liberties to ensure that-

(A) programs, policies, and procedures involving civil rights, civil liberties, and privacy considerations are addressed in an integrated and comprehensive manner; and

(B) Congress receives appropriate reports on such programs, policies, and procedures; and

(6) preparing a report to Congress on an annual basis on activities of the Department that affect privacy, including complaints of privacy violations, implementation of the Privacy Act of 1974 [5 U.S.C. 552a], internal controls, and other matters.

(b) Authority to investigate

(1) In general

The senior official appointed under subsection (a) may-

(A) have access to all records, reports, audits, reviews, documents, papers, recommendations, and other materials available to the Department that relate to programs and operations with respect to the responsibilities of the senior official under this section;

(B) make such investigations and reports relating to the administration of the programs and operations of the Department as are, in the senior official's judgment, necessary or desirable;

(C) subject to the approval of the Secretary, require by subpoena the production, by any person other than a Federal agency, of all information, documents, reports, answers, records, accounts, papers, and other data and documentary evidence necessary to performance of the responsibilities of the senior official under this section; and

(D) administer to or take from any person an oath, affirmation, or affidavit, whenever necessary to performance of the responsibilities of the senior official under this section.

(2) Enforcement of subpoenas

Any subpoena issued under paragraph (1)(C) shall, in the case of contumacy or refusal to obey, be enforceable by order of any appropriate United States district court.

(3) Effect of oaths

Any oath, affirmation, or affidavit administered or taken under paragraph (1)(D) by or before an employee of the Privacy Office designated for that purpose by the senior official appointed under subsection (a) shall have the same force and effect as if administered or taken by or before an officer having a seal of office.

(c) Supervision and coordination

(1) In general

The senior official appointed under subsection (a) shall-

(A) report to, and be under the general supervision of, the Secretary; and

(B) coordinate activities with the Inspector General of the Department in order to avoid duplication of effort.

(2) Coordination with the Inspector General

(A) In general

Except as provided in subparagraph (B), the senior official appointed under subsection (a) may investigate any matter relating to possible violations or abuse concerning the administration of any program or operation of the Department relevant to the purposes under this section.

(B) Coordination

(i) Referral

Before initiating any investigation described under subparagraph (A), the senior official shall refer the matter and all related complaints, allegations, and information to the Inspector General of the Department.

(ii) Determinations and notifications by the Inspector General

(I) In general

Not later than 30 days after the receipt of a matter referred under clause (i), the Inspector General shall-

(aa) make a determination regarding whether the Inspector General intends to initiate an audit or investigation of the matter referred under clause (i); and

(bb) notify the senior official of that determination.

(II) Investigation not initiated

If the Inspector General notifies the senior official under subclause (I)(bb) that the Inspector General intended to initiate an audit or investigation, but does not initiate that audit or investigation within 90 days after providing that notification, the Inspector General shall further notify the senior official that an audit or investigation was not initiated. The further notification under this subclause shall be made not later than 3 days after the end of that 90-day period.

(iii) Investigation by senior official

The senior official may investigate a matter referred under clause (i) if-

    (I) the Inspector General notifies the senior official under clause (ii)(I)(bb) that the Inspector General does not intend to initiate an audit or investigation relating to that matter; or

    (II) the Inspector General provides a further notification under clause (ii)(II) relating to that matter.

(iv) Privacy training

Any employee of the Office of Inspector General who audits or investigates any matter referred under clause (i) shall be required to receive adequate training on privacy laws, rules, and regulations, to be provided by an entity approved by the Inspector General in consultation with the senior official appointed under subsection (a).

(d) Notification to Congress on removal

If the Secretary removes the senior official appointed under subsection (a) or transfers that senior official to another position or location within the Department, the Secretary shall-

    (1) promptly submit a written notification of the removal or transfer to Houses of Congress; and

    (2) include in any such notification the reasons for the removal or transfer.

(e) Reports by senior official to Congress

The senior official appointed under subsection (a) shall-

    (1) submit reports directly to the Congress regarding performance of the responsibilities of the senior official under this section, without any prior comment or amendment by the Secretary, Deputy Secretary, or any other officer or employee of the Department or the Office of Management and Budget; and

    (2) inform the Committee on Homeland Security and Governmental Affairs of the Senate and the Committee on Homeland Security of the House of Representatives not later than-

        (A) 30 days after the Secretary disapproves the senior official's request for a subpoena under subsection (b)(1)(C) or the Secretary substantively modifies the requested subpoena; or

(B) 45 days after the senior official's request for a subpoena under subsection (b)(1)(C), if that subpoena has not either been approved or disapproved by the Secretary.

§ 460. Prohibition of the Terrorism Information and Prevention System

Any and all activities of the Federal Government to implement the proposed component program of the Citizen Corps known as Operation TIPS (Terrorism Information and Prevention System) are hereby prohibited.

§ 554. National identification system not authorized

Nothing in this Act shall be construed to authorize the development of a national identification system or card.

US E-GOVERNMENT ACT (2002)
[EXCERPT]

Summary

Enacted in December 2002, the E-Government Act was intended to make federal agencies more accessible to the public by electronic means. Among other things, the Act created an Office of Electronic Government within the Office of Management and Budget, and requires that regulatory proceedings and other material appear on agency web sites.

The Act also requires agencies to perform Privacy Impact Assessments (PIAs) whenever procuring an information system, or initiating a new collection of personal information. The PIA must include a description of what information is collected, the purpose for the collection, how the information will be shared, intended uses of the information, and security measures for protecting the information. Assessments must be provided to the Office of Management and Budget and made public where possible.

References

P. L. 107-347, as amended by Public Law 106-398, and Public Law 107-217. Excerpt codified at 44 U.S.C. § 3501 note.

[https://www.law.cornell.edu/uscode/text/44/3501]

44 U.S.C. § 3501 Note. Sec. 208. Privacy provisions.

(a) Purpose. The purpose of this section is to ensure sufficient protections for the privacy of personal information as agencies implement citizen-centered electronic Government.

(b) Privacy impact assessments.

(1) Responsibilities of agencies.

(A) In general. An agency shall take actions described under subparagraph (B) before--

(i) developing or procuring information technology that collects, maintains, or disseminates information that is in an identifiable form; or

(ii) initiating a new collection of information that--

(I) will be collected, maintained, or disseminated using information technology; and

(II) includes any information in an identifiable form permitting the physical or online contacting of a specific individual, if identical questions have been posed to, or identical reporting requirements imposed on, 10 or more persons, other than agencies, instrumentalities, or employees of the Federal Government.

(B) Agency activities. To the extent required under subparagraph (A), each agency shall--

(i) conduct a privacy impact assessment;

(ii) ensure the review of the privacy impact assessment by the Chief Information Officer, or equivalent official, as determined by the head of the agency; and

(iii) if practicable, after completion of the review under clause (ii), make the privacy impact assessment publicly available through the website of the agency, publication in the Federal Register, or other means.

(C) Sensitive information. Subparagraph (B)(iii) may be modified or waived for security reasons, or to protect classified, sensitive, or private information contained in an assessment.

(D) Copy to Director. Agencies shall provide the Director with a copy of the privacy impact assessment for each system for which funding is requested.

(2) Contents of a privacy impact assessment.

(A) In general. The Director shall issue guidance to agencies specifying the required contents of a privacy impact assessment.

(B) Guidance. The guidance shall--

(i) ensure that a privacy impact assessment is commensurate with the size of the information system being assessed, the sensitivity of information that is in an identifiable form in that system, and the risk of harm from unauthorized release of that information; and

(ii) require that a privacy impact assessment address--

(I) what information is to be collected;

(II) why the information is being collected;

(III) the intended use of the agency of the information;

(IV) with whom the information will be shared;

(V) what notice or opportunities for consent would be provided to individuals regarding what information is collected and how that information is shared;

(VI) how the information will be secured; and

(VII) whether a system of records is being created under section 552a of title 5, United States Code, (commonly referred to as the "Privacy Act").

(3) Responsibilities of the Director. The Director shall--

(A) develop policies and guidelines for agencies on the conduct of privacy impact assessments;

(B) oversee the implementation of the privacy impact assessment process throughout the Government; and

(C) require agencies to conduct privacy impact assessments of existing information systems or ongoing collections of information that is in an identifiable form as the Director determines appropriate.

(c) Privacy protections on agency websites.

(1) Privacy policies on websites.

(A) Guidelines for notices. The Director shall develop guidance for privacy notices on agency websites used by the public.

(B) Contents. The guidance shall require that a privacy notice address, consistent with section 552a of title 5, United States Code--

(i) what information is to be collected;

(ii) why the information is being collected;

(iii) the intended use of the agency of the information;

(iv) with whom the information will be shared;

(v) what notice or opportunities for consent would be provided to individuals regarding what information is collected and how that information is shared;

(vi) how the information will be secured; and

(vii) the rights of the individual under section 552a of title 5, United States Code (commonly referred to as the "Privacy Act"), and other laws relevant to the protection of the privacy of an individual.

(2) Privacy policies in machine-readable formats. The Director shall issue guidance requiring agencies to translate privacy policies into a standardized machine-readable format.

(d) Definition. In this section, the term "identifiable form" means any representation of information that permits the identity of an individual to whom the information applies to be reasonably inferred by either direct or indirect means.

United States
Do-Not-Call Implementation Act

DO-NOT-CALL IMPLEMENTATION ACT (2003)

Summary

In 2002, the Federal Trade Commission proposed the creation of a national "do-not-call" registry. The rule establishes a presumption that telemarketers may not contact people on the list, unless the telemarketer has either express written authorization or an existing business relationship with the person.

The regulation has been challenged in court several times. On September 23, 2003, a federal district judge held that the registry exceeded the scope of the FTC's statutory authority. Within a week, Congress ratified the list by statute. Telemarketers have also challenged the statute as an unconstitutional restriction on speech; courts have generally rejected that argument on the grounds that the privacy interests of the people on the list outweigh the telemarketers' right to commercial speech.

There are three main pieces of law that make up the Do-Not-Call registry. The FTC's regulation, 16 C.F.R. 310.4(b)(iii)(B), establishes the registry itself and the related prohibitions on telemarketing. Public Law 108-10 authorizes the FTC to collect fees to operate the registry and requires the FTC to report on the progress of the registry. Public Law 108-82, discussed in the previous paragraph, granted statutory authority to the FTC to operate the registry.

References

16 C.F.R. 310.4(b)(iii)(B)
[https://www.law.cornell.edu/cfr/text/16/310.4]

Public Law 108-10 (Do-Not-Call Implementation Act), codified at 15 U.S.C. § 6101 note.
[http://frwebgate.access.gpo.gov/cgi-bin/getdoc.cgi?dbname=108_cong_public_laws&docid=f:publ010.108]

Public Law 108-82 (Act of Sept. 29, 2003), codified at 15 U.S.C. § 6102 note.
[http://frwebgate.access.gpo.gov/cgi-bin/getdoc.cgi?dbname=108_cong_public_laws&docid=f:publ082.108]

FTC's Do-Not-Call Registry
[https://donotcall.gov/]

16 C.F.R. § 310.4

(b) Pattern of calls.

(1) It is an abusive telemarketing act or practice and a violation of this Rule for a telemarketer to engage in, or for a seller to cause a telemarketer to engage in, the following conduct:

. . . .

(iii) Initiating any outbound telephone call to a person when:

(A) That person previously has stated that he or she does not wish to receive an outbound telephone call made by or on behalf of the seller whose goods or services are being offered or made on behalf of the charitable organization for which a charitable contribution is being solicited; or

(B) That person's telephone number is on the "do-not-call" registry, maintained by the Commission, of persons who do not wish to receive outbound telephone calls to induce the purchase of goods or services unless the seller or telemarketer:

(1) Can demonstrate that the seller has obtained the express agreement, in writing, of such person to place calls to that person. Such written agreement shall clearly evidence such person's authorization that calls made by or on behalf of a specific party may be placed to that person, and shall include the telephone number to which the calls may be placed and the signature [FN] of that person; or

(2) Can demonstrate that the seller has an established business relationship with such person, and that person has not stated that he or she does not wish to receive outbound telephone calls under paragraph (b)(1)(iii)(A) of this section. . . .

[FN: For purposes of this Rule, the term "signature" shall include an electronic or digital form of signature, to the extent that such form of signature is recognized as a valid signature under applicable federal law or state contract law.]

Public Law 108-10

§ 1. Short Title.

This Act may be cited as the "Do-Not-Call Implementation Act".

§ 2. Telemarketing Sales Rule; Do-Not-Call Registry Fees.

The Federal Trade Commission may promulgate regulations establishing fees sufficient to implement and enforce the provisions relating to the "do-not-call" registry of the Telemarketing Sales Rule (16 CFR 310.4(b)(1)(iii)), promulgated under the Telemarketing and Consumer Fraud and Abuse Prevention Act (15 U.S.C. 6101 et seq.). Such regulations shall be promulgated in accordance with section 553 of title 5, United States Code. Fees may be collected pursuant to this section for fiscal years 2003 through 2007, and shall be deposited and credited as offsetting collections to the account, Federal Trade Commission--Salaries and Expenses, and shall remain available until expended. No amounts shall be collected as fees pursuant to this section for such fiscal years except to the extent provided in advance in appropriations Acts. Such amounts shall be available for expenditure only to offset the costs of activities and services related to the implementation and enforcement of the Telemarketing Sales Rule, and other activities resulting from such implementation and enforcement.

§ 3. Federal Communications Commission Do-Not-Call Regulations.

Not later than 180 days after the date of enactment of this Act, the Federal Communications Commission shall issue a final rule pursuant to the rulemaking proceeding that it began on September 18, 2002, under the Telephone Consumer Protection Act (47 U.S.C. 227 et seq.). In issuing such rule, the Federal Communications Commission shall consult and coordinate with the Federal Trade Commission to maximize consistency with the rule promulgated by the Federal Trade Commission (16 CFR 310.4(b)).

§ 4. Reporting Requirements.

(a) Report on Regulatory Coordination.--Within 45 days after the promulgation of a final rule by the Federal Communications Commission as required by section 3, the Federal Trade Commission and the Federal Communications Commission shall each transmit to the Committee on Energy and Commerce of the House of Representatives and the Committee on Commerce, Science, and Transportation of the Senate a report which shall include--

(1) an analysis of the telemarketing rules promulgated by both the Federal Trade Commission and the Federal Communications Commission;

(2) any inconsistencies between the rules promulgated by each such Commission and the effect of any such inconsistencies on consumers, and persons paying for access to the registry; and

(3) proposals to remedy any such inconsistencies.

(b) Annual Report.--For each of fiscal years 2003 through 2007, the Federal Trade Commission and the Federal Communications Commission shall each transmit an annual report to the Committee on Energy and Commerce of the House of Representatives and the Committee on Commerce, Science, and Transportation of the Senate a report which shall include--

(1) an analysis of the effectiveness of the "do-not-call" registry as a national registry;

(2) the number of consumers who have placed their telephone numbers on the registry;

(3) the number of persons paying fees for access to the registry and the amount of such fees;

(4) an analysis of the progress of coordinating the operation and enforcement of the "do-not-call" registry with similar registries established and maintained by the various States;

(5) an analysis of the progress of coordinating the operation and enforcement of the "do-not-call" registry with the enforcement activities of the Federal Communications Commission pursuant to the Telephone Consumer Protection Act (47 U.S.C. 227 et seq.); and

(6) a review of the enforcement proceedings under the Telemarketing Sales Rule (16 CFR 310), in the case of the Federal Trade Commission, and under the Telephone Consumer Protection Act (47 U.S.C. 227 et seq.), in the case of the Federal Communications Commission.

CAN-SPAM ACT (2003)

Summary

The "Controlling the Assault of Non- Solicited Pornography and Marketing Act of 2003" (the CAN-SPAM Act) was designed to control the ever-growing influx of unsolicited bulk e-mail. The law requires unsolicited marketing e-mails to contain a mailing address of the sender, an opt-out mechanism, a valid subject line, and a label if the content is adult. It also prohibits certain "aggravated" spamming techniques such as dictionary attacks (in which spammers use a dictionary of common names to blindly send unsolicited messages).

The Act also gave the FTC the authority to implement a Do-Not-Email list. The FTC rejected this proposal, citing security concerns stemming from the unauthenticated nature of the e-mail system.

References

Public Law 108-187, codified at 15 U.S.C. § 7701.
[https://www.law.cornell.edu/uscode/text/15/7701]

15 U.S.C. § 7701. Congressional Findings and Policy

(a) Findings.--The Congress finds the following:

(1) Electronic mail has become an extremely important and popular means of communication, relied on by millions of Americans on a daily basis for personal and commercial purposes. Its low cost and global reach make it extremely convenient and efficient, and offer unique opportunities for the development and growth of frictionless commerce.

(2) The convenience and efficiency of electronic mail are threatened by the extremely rapid growth in the volume of unsolicited commercial electronic mail. Unsolicited commercial electronic mail is currently estimated to account for over half of all electronic mail traffic, up from an estimated 7 percent in 2001, and the volume continues to rise. Most of these messages are fraudulent or deceptive in one or more respects.

(3) The receipt of unsolicited commercial electronic mail may result in costs to recipients who cannot refuse to accept such mail and who incur costs for the storage of such mail, or for the time spent accessing, reviewing, and discarding such mail, or for both.

(4) The receipt of a large number of unwanted messages also decreases the convenience of electronic mail and creates a risk that wanted electronic mail messages, both commercial and noncommercial, will be lost, overlooked, or discarded amidst the larger volume of unwanted messages, thus reducing the reliability and usefulness of electronic mail to the recipient.

(5) Some commercial electronic mail contains material that many recipients may consider vulgar or pornographic in nature.

(6) The growth in unsolicited commercial electronic mail imposes significant monetary costs on providers of Internet access services, businesses, and educational and nonprofit institutions that carry and receive such mail, as there is a finite volume of mail that such providers, businesses, and institutions can handle without further investment in infrastructure.

(7) Many senders of unsolicited commercial electronic mail purposefully disguise the source of such mail.

(8) Many senders of unsolicited commercial electronic mail purposefully include misleading information in the messages' subject lines in order to induce the recipients to view the messages.

(9) While some senders of commercial electronic mail messages provide simple and reliable ways for recipients to reject (or "opt-out" of) receipt of commercial electronic mail from such senders in the future, other senders provide no such "opt-out" mechanism, or refuse to honor the requests of recipients not to receive electronic mail from such senders in the future, or both.

(10) Many senders of bulk unsolicited commercial electronic mail use computer programs to gather large numbers of electronic mail addresses on an automated basis from Internet websites or online services where users must post their addresses in order to make full use of the website or service.

(11) Many States have enacted legislation intended to regulate or reduce unsolicited commercial electronic mail, but these statutes impose different standards and requirements. As a result, they do not appear to have been successful in addressing the problems associated with unsolicited commercial electronic mail, in part because, since an electronic mail address does not specify a geographic location, it can be extremely difficult for law-abiding businesses to know with which of these disparate statutes they are required to comply.

(12) The problems associated with the rapid growth and abuse of unsolicited commercial electronic mail cannot be solved by Federal legislation alone. The development and adoption of technological approaches and the pursuit of cooperative efforts with other countries will be necessary as well.

(b) Congressional Determination of Public Policy.--On the basis of the findings in subsection (a), the Congress determines that--

(1) there is a substantial government interest in regulation of commercial electronic mail on a nationwide basis;

(2) senders of commercial electronic mail should not mislead recipients as to the source or content of such mail; and

(3) recipients of commercial electronic mail have a right to decline to receive additional commercial electronic mail from the same source.

United States
CAN-SPAM Act

15 U.S.C. § 7702. Definitions

In this Act:

    (1) Affirmative consent.--The term "affirmative consent", when used with respect to a commercial electronic mail message, means that--

        (A) the recipient expressly consented to receive the message, either in response to a clear and conspicuous request for such consent or at the recipient's own initiative; and

        (B) if the message is from a party other than the party to which the recipient communicated such consent, the recipient was given clear and conspicuous notice at the time the consent was communicated that the recipient's electronic mail address could be transferred to such other party for the purpose of initiating commercial electronic mail messages.

    (2) Commercial electronic mail message.--

        (A) In general.--The term "commercial electronic mail message" means any electronic mail message the primary purpose of which is the commercial advertisement or promotion of a commercial product or service (including content on an Internet website operated for a commercial purpose).

        (B) Transactional or relationship messages.--The term "commercial electronic mail message" does not include a transactional or relationship message.

        (C) Regulations regarding primary purpose.--Not later than 12 months after the date of the enactment of this Act, the Commission shall issue regulations pursuant to section 13 defining the relevant criteria to facilitate the determination of the primary purpose of an electronic mail message.

        (D) Reference to company or website.--The inclusion of a reference to a commercial entity or a link to the website of a commercial entity in an electronic mail message does not, by itself, cause such message to be treated as a commercial electronic mail message for purposes of this Act if the contents or circumstances of the message indicate a primary purpose other than commercial advertisement or promotion of a commercial product or service.

    (3) Commission.--The term "Commission" means the Federal Trade Commission.

    (4) Domain name.--The term "domain name" means any alphanumeric designation which is registered with or assigned by any domain name registrar, domain name registry, or other domain name registration authority as part of an electronic address on the Internet.

    (5) Electronic mail address.--The term "electronic mail address" means a destination, commonly expressed as a string of characters, consisting of a unique user name or mailbox (commonly referred to as the "local part") and a reference to an Internet domain (commonly referred to as the "domain part"), whether or not displayed, to which an electronic mail message can be sent or delivered.

(6) Electronic mail message.--The term "electronic mail message" means a message sent to a unique electronic mail address.

(7) FTC act.--The term "FTC Act" means the Federal Trade Commission Act (15 U.S.C. 41 et seq.).

(8) Header information.--The term "header information" means the source, destination, and routing information attached to an electronic mail message, including the originating domain name and originating electronic mail address, and any other information that appears in the line identifying, or purporting to identify, a person initiating the message.

(9) Initiate.--The term "initiate", when used with respect to a commercial electronic mail message, means to originate or transmit such message or to procure the origination or transmission of such message, but shall not include actions that constitute routine conveyance of such message. For purposes of this paragraph, more than one person may be considered to have initiated a message.

(10) Internet.--The term "Internet" has the meaning given that term in the Internet Tax Freedom Act (47 U.S.C. 151 nt).

(11) Internet access service.--The term "Internet access service" has the meaning given that term in section 231(e)(4) of the Communications Act of 1934 (47 U.S.C. 231(e)(4)).

(12) Procure.--The term "procure", when used with respect to the initiation of a commercial electronic mail message, means intentionally to pay or provide other consideration to, or induce, another person to initiate such a message on one's behalf.

(13) Protected computer.--The term "protected computer" has the meaning given that term in section 1030(e)(2)(B) of title 18, United States Code.

(14) Recipient.--The term "recipient", when used with respect to a commercial electronic mail message, means an authorized user of the electronic mail address to which the message was sent or delivered. If a recipient of a commercial electronic mail message has one or more electronic mail addresses in addition to the address to which the message was sent or delivered, the recipient shall be treated as a separate recipient with respect to each such address. If an electronic mail address is reassigned to a new user, the new user shall not be treated as a recipient of any commercial electronic mail message sent or delivered to that address before it was reassigned.

(15) Routine conveyance.--The term "routine conveyance" means the transmission, routing, relaying, handling, or storing, through an automatic technical process, of an electronic mail message for which another person has identified the recipients or provided the recipient addresses.

(16) Sender.--

(A) In general.--Except as provided in subparagraph (B), the term "sender", when used with respect to a commercial electronic mail message, means a person who initiates such a message and whose product, service, or Internet web site is advertised or promoted by the message.

(B) Separate lines of business or divisions.--If an entity operates through separate lines of business or divisions and holds itself out to the recipient throughout the message as that particular line of business or division rather than as the entity of which such line of business or division is a part, then the line of business or the division shall be treated as the sender of such message for purposes of this Act.

(17) Transactional or relationship message.--

(A) In general.--The term "transactional or relationship message" means an electronic mail message the primary purpose of which is--

(i) to facilitate, complete, or confirm a commercial transaction that the recipient has previously agreed to enter into with the sender;

(ii) to provide warranty information, product recall information, or safety or security information with respect to a commercial product or service used or purchased by the recipient;

(iii) to provide--

(I) notification concerning a change in the terms or features of;

(II) notification of a change in the recipient's standing or status with respect to; or

(III) at regular periodic intervals, account balance information or other type of account statement with respect to, a subscription, membership, account, loan, or comparable ongoing commercial relationship involving the ongoing purchase or use by the recipient of products or services offered by the sender;

(iv) to provide information directly related to an employment relationship or related benefit plan in which the recipient is currently involved, participating, or enrolled; or

(v) to deliver goods or services, including product updates or upgrades, that the recipient is entitled to receive under the terms of a transaction that the recipient has previously agreed to enter into with the sender.

(B) Modification of definition.--The Commission by regulation pursuant to section 13 may modify the definition in subparagraph (A) to expand or contract the categories of messages that are treated as transactional or relationship messages for purposes of this Act to the extent that such modification is necessary to accommodate changes in electronic mail technology or practices and accomplish the purposes of this Act.

15 U.S.C. § 7703. Prohibition Against Predatory And Abusive Commercial E-Mail.

(a) [Omitted; see 18 U.S.C. § 1037.]

(b) United States Sentencing Commission.--

(1) Directive.--Pursuant to its authority under section 994(p) of title 28, United States Code, and in accordance with this section, the United States Sentencing Commission shall review and, as appropriate, amend the sentencing guidelines and policy statements to provide appropriate penalties for violations of section 1037 of title 18, United States Code, as added by this section, and other offenses that may be facilitated by the sending of large quantities of unsolicited electronic mail.

(2) Requirements.--In carrying out this subsection, the Sentencing Commission shall consider providing sentencing enhancements for--

(A) those convicted under section 1037 of title 18, United States Code, who--

(i) obtained electronic mail addresses through improper means, including--

(I) harvesting electronic mail addresses of the users of a website, proprietary service, or other online public forum operated by another person, without the authorization of such person; and

(II) randomly generating electronic mail addresses by computer; or

(ii) knew that the commercial electronic mail messages involved in the offense contained or advertised an Internet domain for which the registrant of the domain had provided false registration information; and

(B) those convicted of other offenses, including offenses involving fraud, identity theft, obscenity, child pornography, and the sexual exploitation of children, if such offenses involved the sending of large quantities of electronic mail.

(c) Sense of Congress.--It is the sense of Congress that--

(1) Spam has become the method of choice for those who distribute pornography, perpetrate fraudulent schemes, and introduce viruses, worms, and Trojan horses into personal and business computer systems; and

(2) the Department of Justice should use all existing law enforcement tools to investigate and prosecute those who send bulk commercial e-mail to facilitate the commission of Federal crimes, including the tools contained in chapters 47 and 63 of title 18, United States Code (relating to fraud and false statements); chapter 71 of title 18, United States Code (relating to obscenity); chapter 110 of title 18, United States Code (relating to the sexual exploitation of children); and chapter 95 of title 18, United States Code (relating to racketeering), as appropriate.

15 U.S.C. § 7704. Other Protections for Users of Commercial Electronic Mail.

(a) Requirements for Transmission of Messages.--

(1) Prohibition of false or misleading transmission information.--It is unlawful for any person to initiate the transmission, to a protected computer, of a commercial

electronic mail message, or a transactional or relationship message, that contains, or is accompanied by, header information that is materially false or materially misleading. For purposes of this paragraph--

(A) header information that is technically accurate but includes an originating electronic mail address, domain name, or Internet Protocol address the access to which for purposes of initiating the message was obtained by means of false or fraudulent pretenses or representations shall be considered materially misleading;

(B) a "from" line (the line identifying or purporting to identify a person initiating the message) that accurately identifies any person who initiated the message shall not be considered materially false or materially misleading; and

(C) header information shall be considered materially misleading if it fails to identify accurately a protected computer used to initiate the message because the person initiating the message knowingly uses another protected computer to relay or retransmit the message for purposes of disguising its origin.

(2) Prohibition of deceptive subject headings.--It is unlawful for any person to initiate the transmission to a protected computer of a commercial electronic mail message if such person has actual knowledge, or knowledge fairly implied on the basis of objective circumstances, that a subject heading of the message would be likely to mislead a recipient, acting reasonably under the circumstances, about a material fact regarding the contents or subject matter of the message (consistent with the criteria used in enforcement of section 5 of the Federal Trade Commission Act (15 U.S.C. 45)).

(3) Inclusion of return address or comparable mechanism in commercial electronic mail.--

(A) In general.--It is unlawful for any person to initiate the transmission to a protected computer of a commercial electronic mail message that does not contain a functioning return electronic mail address or other Internet-based mechanism, clearly and conspicuously displayed, that--

(i) a recipient may use to submit, in a manner specified in the message, a reply electronic mail message or other form of Internet-based communication requesting not to receive future commercial electronic mail messages from that sender at the electronic mail address where the message was received; and

(ii) remains capable of receiving such messages or communications for no less than 30 days after the transmission of the original message.

(B) More detailed options possible.--The person initiating a commercial electronic mail message may comply with subparagraph (A)(i) by providing the recipient a list or menu from which the recipient may choose the specific types of commercial electronic mail messages the recipient wants to receive or does not want to receive from the sender, if the list or menu includes an option under which the recipient may choose not to receive any commercial electronic mail messages from the sender.

(C) Temporary inability to receive messages or process requests.--A return electronic mail address or other mechanism does not fail to satisfy the requirements of subparagraph (A) if it is unexpectedly and temporarily unable to receive messages or process requests due to a technical problem beyond the control of the sender if the problem is corrected within a reasonable time period.

(4) Prohibition of transmission of commercial electronic mail after objection.--

(A) In general.--If a recipient makes a request using a mechanism provided pursuant to paragraph (3) not to receive some or any commercial electronic mail messages from such sender, then it is unlawful--

(i) for the sender to initiate the transmission to the recipient, more than 10 business days after the receipt of such request, of a commercial electronic mail message that falls within the scope of the request;

(ii) for any person acting on behalf of the sender to initiate the transmission to the recipient, more than 10 business days after the receipt of such request, of a commercial electronic mail message with actual knowledge, or knowledge fairly implied on the basis of objective circumstances, that such message falls within the scope of the request;

(iii) for any person acting on behalf of the sender to assist in initiating the transmission to the recipient, through the provision or selection of addresses to which the message will be sent, of a commercial electronic mail message with actual knowledge, or knowledge fairly implied on the basis of objective circumstances, that such message would violate clause (i) or (ii); or

(iv) for the sender, or any other person who knows that the recipient has made such a request, to sell, lease, exchange, or otherwise transfer or release the electronic mail address of the recipient (including through any transaction or other transfer involving mailing lists bearing the electronic mail address of the recipient) for any purpose other than compliance with this Act or other provision of law.

(B) Subsequent affirmative consent.--A prohibition in subparagraph (A) does not apply if there is affirmative consent by the recipient subsequent to the request under subparagraph (A).

(5) Inclusion of identifier, opt-out, and physical address in commercial electronic mail.--

(A) It is unlawful for any person to initiate the transmission of any commercial electronic mail message to a protected computer unless the message provides--

(i) clear and conspicuous identification that the message is an advertisement or solicitation;

(ii) clear and conspicuous notice of the opportunity under paragraph (3) to decline to receive further commercial electronic mail messages from the sender; and

(iii) a valid physical postal address of the sender.

(B) Subparagraph (A)(i) does not apply to the transmission of a commercial electronic mail message if the recipient has given prior affirmative consent to receipt of the message.

(6) Materially.--For purposes of paragraph (1), the term "materially", when used with respect to false or misleading header information, includes the alteration or concealment of header information in a manner that would impair the ability of an Internet access service processing the message on behalf of a recipient, a person alleging a violation of this section, or a law enforcement agency to identify, locate, or respond to a person who initiated the electronic mail message or to investigate the alleged violation, or the ability of a recipient of the message to respond to a person who initiated the electronic message.

(b) Aggravated Violations Relating to Commercial Electronic Mail.--

(1) Address harvesting and dictionary attacks.--

(A) In general.--It is unlawful for any person to initiate the transmission, to a protected computer, of a commercial electronic mail message that is unlawful under subsection (a), or to assist in the origination of such message through the provision or selection of addresses to which the message will be transmitted, if such person had actual knowledge, or knowledge fairly implied on the basis of objective circumstances, that--

(i) the electronic mail address of the recipient was obtained using an automated means from an Internet website or proprietary online service operated by another person, and such website or online service included, at the time the address was obtained, a notice stating that the operator of such website or online service will not give, sell, or otherwise transfer addresses maintained by such website or online service to any other party for the purposes of initiating, or enabling others to initiate, electronic mail messages; or

(ii) the electronic mail address of the recipient was obtained using an automated means that generates possible electronic mail addresses by combining names, letters, or numbers into numerous permutations.

(B) Disclaimer.--Nothing in this paragraph creates an ownership or proprietary interest in such electronic mail addresses.

(2) Automated creation of multiple electronic mail accounts.--It is unlawful for any person to use scripts or other automated means to register for multiple

electronic mail accounts or online user accounts from which to transmit to a protected computer, or enable another person to transmit to a protected computer, a commercial electronic mail message that is unlawful under subsection (a).

(3) Relay or retransmission through unauthorized access.--It is unlawful for any person knowingly to relay or retransmit a commercial electronic mail message that is unlawful under subsection (a) from a protected computer or computer network that such person has accessed without authorization.

(c) Supplementary Rulemaking Authority.--The Commission shall by regulation, pursuant to section 13--

(1) modify the 10-business-day period under subsection (a)(4)(A) or subsection (a)(4)(B), or both, if the Commission determines that a different period would be more reasonable after taking into account--

(A) the purposes of subsection (a);

(B) the interests of recipients of commercial electronic mail; and

(C) the burdens imposed on senders of lawful commercial electronic mail; and

(2) specify additional activities or practices to which subsection (b) applies if the Commission determines that those activities or practices are contributing substantially to the proliferation of commercial electronic mail messages that are unlawful under subsection (a).

(d) Requirement To Place Warning Labels on Commercial Electronic Mail Containing Sexually Oriented Material.--

(1) In general.--No person may initiate in or affecting interstate commerce the transmission, to a protected computer, of any commercial electronic mail message that includes sexually oriented material and--

(A) fail to include in subject heading for the electronic mail message the marks or notices prescribed by the Commission under this subsection; or

(B) fail to provide that the matter in the message that is initially viewable to the recipient, when the message is opened by any recipient and absent any further actions by the recipient, includes only--

(i) to the extent required or authorized pursuant to paragraph (2), any such marks or notices;

(ii) the information required to be included in the message pursuant to subsection (a)(5); and

(iii) instructions on how to access, or a mechanism to access, the sexually oriented material.

(2) Prior affirmative consent.--Paragraph (1) does not apply to the transmission of an electronic mail message if the recipient has given prior affirmative consent to receipt of the message.

(3) Prescription of marks and notices.-- Not later than 120 days after the date of the enactment of this Act, the Commission in consultation with the Attorney

General shall prescribe clearly identifiable marks or notices to be included in or associated with commercial electronic mail that contains sexually oriented material, in order to inform the recipient of that fact and to facilitate filtering of such electronic mail. The <<NOTE: Federal Register, publication.>> Commission shall publish in the Federal Register and provide notice to the public of the marks or notices prescribed under this paragraph.

(4) Definition.--In this subsection, the term "sexually oriented material" means any material that depicts sexually explicit conduct (as that term is defined in section 2256 of title 18, United States Code), unless the depiction constitutes a small and insignificant part of the whole, the remainder of which is not primarily devoted to sexual matters.

(5) Penalty.--Whoever knowingly violates paragraph (1) shall be fined under title 18, United States Code, or imprisoned not more than 5 years, or both.

15 U.S.C. § 7705. Businesses Knowingly Promoted By Electronic Mail With False Or Misleading Transmission Information.

(a) In General.--It is unlawful for a person to promote, or allow the promotion of, that person's trade or business, or goods, products, property, or services sold, offered for sale, leased or offered for lease, or otherwise made available through that trade or business, in a commercial electronic mail message the transmission of which is in violation of section 5(a)(1) if that person--

(1) knows, or should have known in the ordinary course of that person's trade or business, that the goods, products, property, or services sold, offered for sale, leased or offered for lease, or otherwise made available through that trade or business were being promoted in such a message;

(2) received or expected to receive an economic benefit from such promotion; and

(3) took no reasonable action--

(A) to prevent the transmission; or

(B) to detect the transmission and report it to the Commission.

(b) Limited Enforcement Against Third Parties.--

(1) In general.--Except as provided in paragraph (2), a person (hereinafter referred to as the "third party") that provides goods, products, property, or services to another person that violates subsection (a) shall not be held liable for such violation.

(2) Exception.--Liability for a violation of subsection (a) shall be imputed to a third party that provides goods, products, property, or services to another person that violates subsection

(a) if that third party--

(A) owns, or has a greater than 50 percent ownership or economic interest in, the trade or business of the person that violated subsection (a); or

(B)

(i) has actual knowledge that goods, products, property, or services are promoted in a commercial electronic mail message the transmission of which is in violation of section 5(a)(1); and

(ii) receives, or expects to receive, an economic benefit from such promotion.

(c) Exclusive Enforcement by FTC.--Subsections (f) and (g) of section 7 do not apply to violations of this section.

(d) Savings Provision.--Except as provided in section 7(f)(8), nothing in this section may be construed to limit or prevent any action that may be taken under this Act with respect to any violation of any other section of this Act.

15 U.S.C. § 7706. Enforcement Generally.

(a) Violation Is Unfair or Deceptive Act or Practice.--Except as provided in subsection (b), this Act shall be enforced by the Commission as if the violation of this Act were an unfair or deceptive act or practice proscribed under section 18(a)(1)(B) of the Federal Trade Commission Act (15 U.S.C. 57a(a)(1)(B)).

(b) Enforcement by Certain Other Agencies.--Compliance with this Act shall be enforced--

(1) under section 8 of the Federal Deposit Insurance Act (12 U.S.C. 1818), in the case of--

(A) national banks, and Federal branches and Federal agencies of foreign banks, by the Office of the Comptroller of the Currency;

(B) member banks of the Federal Reserve System (other than national banks), branches and agencies of foreign banks (other than Federal branches, Federal agencies, and insured State branches of foreign banks), commercial lending companies owned or controlled by foreign banks, organizations operating under section 25 or 25A of the Federal Reserve Act (12 U.S.C. 601 and 611), and bank holding companies, by the Board;

(C) banks insured by the Federal Deposit Insurance Corporation (other than members of the Federal Reserve System) and insured State branches of foreign banks, by the Board of Directors of the Federal Deposit Insurance Corporation; and

(D) savings associations the deposits of which are insured by the Federal Deposit Insurance Corporation, by the Director of the Office of Thrift Supervision;

(2) under the Federal Credit Union Act (12 U.S.C. 1751 et seq.) by the Board of the National Credit Union Administration with respect to any Federally insured credit union;

(3) under the Securities Exchange Act of 1934 (15 U.S.C. 78a et seq.) by the Securities and Exchange Commission with respect to any broker or dealer;

(4) under the Investment Company Act of 1940 (15 U.S.C. 80a- 1 et seq.) by the Securities and Exchange Commission with respect to investment companies;

(5) under the Investment Advisers Act of 1940 (15 U.S.C. 80b-1 et seq.) by the Securities and Exchange Commission with respect to investment advisers registered under that Act;

(6) under State insurance law in the case of any person engaged in providing insurance, by the applicable State insurance authority of the State in which the person is domiciled, subject to section 104 of the Gramm-Bliley-Leach Act (15 U.S.C. 6701), except that in any State in which the State insurance authority elects not to exercise this power, the enforcement authority pursuant to this Act shall be exercised by the Commission in accordance with subsection (a);

(7) under part A of subtitle VII of title 49, United States Code, by the Secretary of Transportation with respect to any air carrier or foreign air carrier subject to that part;

(8) under the Packers and Stockyards Act, 1921 (7 U.S.C. 181 et seq.) (except as provided in section 406 of that Act (7 U.S.C. 226, 227)), by the Secretary of Agriculture with respect to any activities subject to that Act;

(9) under the Farm Credit Act of 1971 (12 U.S.C. 2001 et seq.) by the Farm Credit Administration with respect to any Federal land bank, Federal land bank association, Federal intermediate credit bank, or production credit association; and

(10) under the Communications Act of 1934 (47 U.S.C. 151 et seq.) by the Federal Communications Commission with respect to any person subject to the provisions of that Act.

(c) Exercise of Certain Powers.--For the purpose of the exercise by any agency referred to in subsection (b) of its powers under any Act referred to in that subsection, a violation of this Act is deemed to be a violation of a Federal Trade Commission trade regulation rule. In addition to its powers under any provision of law specifically referred to in subsection (b), each of the agencies referred to in that subsection may exercise, for the purpose of enforcing compliance with any requirement imposed under this Act, any other authority conferred on it by law.

(d) Actions by the Commission.--The Commission shall prevent any person from violating this Act in the same manner, by the same means, and with the same jurisdiction, powers, and duties as though all applicable terms and provisions of the Federal Trade Commission Act (15 U.S.C. 41 et seq.) were incorporated into and made a part of this Act. Any entity that violates any provision of that subtitle is subject to the penalties and entitled to the privileges and immunities provided in the Federal Trade Commission Act in the same manner, by the same means, and with the same jurisdiction, power, and duties as though all applicable terms and provisions of the Federal Trade Commission Act were incorporated into and made a part of that subtitle.

(e) Availability of Cease-and-Desist Orders and Injunctive Relief Without Showing of Knowledge.--Notwithstanding any other provision of this Act, in any proceeding or action pursuant to subsection (a), (b), (c), or (d) of this section to enforce compliance, through an order to cease and desist or an injunction, with section 5(a)(1)(C), section 5(a)(2), clause (ii), (iii), or (iv) of section 5(a)(4)(A), section 5(b)(1)(A), or section 5(b)(3), neither the Commission nor the Federal Communications Commission shall be required to allege or prove the state of mind required by such section or subparagraph.

(f) Enforcement by States.--

(1) Civil action.--In any case in which the attorney general of a State, or an official or agency of a State, has reason to believe that an interest of the residents of that State has been or is threatened or adversely affected by any person who violates paragraph (1) or (2) of section 5(a), who violates section 5(d), or who engages in a pattern or practice that violates paragraph (3), (4), or (5) of section 5(a), of this Act, the attorney general, official, or agency of the State, as parens patriae, may bring a civil action on behalf of the residents of the State in a district court of the United States of appropriate jurisdiction--

(A) to enjoin further violation of section 5 of this Act by the defendant; or

(B) to obtain damages on behalf of residents of the State, in an amount equal to the greater of--

(i) the actual monetary loss suffered by such residents; or

(ii) the amount determined under paragraph (3).

(2) Availability of injunctive relief without showing of knowledge.--Notwithstanding any other provision of this Act, in a civil action under paragraph (1)(A) of this subsection, the attorney general, official, or agency of the State shall not be required to allege or prove the state of mind required by section 5(a)(1)(C), section 5(a)(2), clause (ii), (iii), or (iv) of section 5(a)(4)(A), section 5(b)(1)(A), or section 5(b)(3).

(3) Statutory damages.--

(A) In general.--For purposes of paragraph (1)(B)(ii), the amount determined under this paragraph is the amount calculated by multiplying the number of violations (with each separately addressed unlawful message received by or addressed to such residents treated as a separate violation) by up to $250.

(B) Limitation.--For any violation of section 5 (other than section 5(a)(1)), the amount determined under subparagraph (A) may not exceed $2,000,000.

(C) Aggravated damages.--The court may increase a damage award to an amount equal to not more than three times the amount otherwise available under this paragraph if--

(i) the court determines that the defendant committed the violation willfully and knowingly; or

(ii) the defendant's unlawful activity included one or more of the aggravating violations set forth in section 5(b).

(D) Reduction of damages.--In assessing damages under subparagraph (A), the court may consider whether--

(i) the defendant has established and implemented, with due care, commercially reasonable practices and procedures designed to effectively prevent such violations; or

(ii) the violation occurred despite commercially reasonable efforts to maintain compliance the practices and procedures to which reference is made in clause (i).

(4) Attorney fees.--In the case of any successful action under paragraph (1), the court, in its discretion, may award the costs of the action and reasonable attorney fees to the State.

(5) Rights of federal regulators.--The State shall serve prior written notice of any action under paragraph (1) upon the Federal Trade Commission or the appropriate Federal regulator determined under subsection (b) and provide the Commission or appropriate Federal regulator with a copy of its complaint, except in any case in which such prior notice is not feasible, in which case the State shall serve such notice immediately upon instituting such action. The Federal Trade Commission or appropriate Federal regulator shall have the right--

(A) to intervene in the action;

(B) upon so intervening, to be heard on all matters arising therein;

(C) to remove the action to the appropriate United States district court; and

(D) to file petitions for appeal.

(6) Construction.--For purposes of bringing any civil action under paragraph (1), nothing in this Act shall be construed to prevent an attorney general of a State from exercising the powers conferred on the attorney general by the laws of that State to--

(A) conduct investigations;

(B) administer oaths or affirmations; or

(C) compel the attendance of witnesses or the production of documentary and other evidence.

(7) Venue; service of process.--

(A) Venue.--Any action brought under paragraph (1) may be brought in the district court of the United States that meets applicable requirements relating to venue under section 1391 of title 28, United States Code.

(B) Service of process.--In an action brought under paragraph (1), process may be served in any district in which the defendant--

(i) is an inhabitant; or

(ii) maintains a physical place of business.

(8) Limitation on state action while federal action is pending.--If the Commission, or other appropriate Federal agency under subsection (b), has instituted a civil action or an administrative action for violation of this Act, no State attorney general, or official or agency of a State, may bring an action under this subsection during the pendency of that action against any defendant named in the complaint of the Commission or the other agency for any violation of this Act alleged in the complaint.

(9) Requisite scienter for certain civil actions.--Except as provided in section 5(a)(1)(C), section 5(a)(2), clause (ii), (iii), or (iv) of section 5(a)(4)(A), section 5(b)(1)(A), or section 5(b)(3), in a civil action brought by a State attorney general, or an official or agency of a State, to recover monetary damages for a violation of this Act, the court shall not grant the relief sought unless the attorney general, official, or agency establishes that the defendant acted with actual knowledge, or knowledge fairly implied on the basis of objective circumstances, of the act or omission that constitutes the violation.

(g) Action by Provider of Internet Access Service.--

(1) Action authorized.--A provider of Internet access service adversely affected by a violation of section 5(a)(1), 5(b), or 5(d), or a pattern or practice that violates paragraph (2), (3), (4), or (5) of section 5(a), may bring a civil action in any district court of the United States with jurisdiction over the defendant--

(A) to enjoin further violation by the defendant; or

(B) to recover damages in an amount equal to the greater of--

(i) actual monetary loss incurred by the provider of Internet access service as a result of such violation; or

(ii) the amount determined under paragraph (3).

(2) Special definition of "procure".--In any action brought under paragraph (1), this Act shall be applied as if the definition of the term "procure" in section 3(12) contained, after "behalf" the words "with actual knowledge, or by consciously avoiding knowing, whether such person is engaging, or will engage, in a pattern or practice that violates this Act".

(3) Statutory damages.--

(A) In general.--For purposes of paragraph (1)(B)(ii), the amount determined under this paragraph is the amount calculated by multiplying the number of violations (with each separately addressed unlawful message that is transmitted or attempted to be transmitted over the facilities of the provider of Internet access service, or that is transmitted or attempted to be transmitted to an electronic mail address obtained from the provider of Internet access service in violation of section 5(b)(1)(A)(i), treated as a separate violation) by--

(i) up to $100, in the case of a violation of section 5(a)(1); or

(ii) up to $25, in the case of any other violation of section 5.

(B) Limitation.--For any violation of section 5 (other than section 5(a)(1)), the amount determined under subparagraph (A) may not exceed $1,000,000.

(C) Aggravated damages.--The court may increase a damage award to an amount equal to not more than three times the amount otherwise available under this paragraph if--

    (i) the court determines that the defendant committed the violation willfully and knowingly; or

    (ii) the defendant's unlawful activity included one or more of the aggravated violations set forth in section 5(b).

(D) Reduction of damages.--In assessing damages under subparagraph (A), the court may consider whether--

    (i) the defendant has established and implemented, with due care, commercially reasonable practices and procedures designed to effectively prevent such violations; or

    (ii) the violation occurred despite commercially reasonable efforts to maintain compliance with the practices and procedures to which reference is made in clause (i).

(4) Attorney fees.--In any action brought pursuant to paragraph (1), the court may, in its discretion, require an undertaking for the payment of the costs of such action, and assess reasonable costs, including reasonable attorneys' fees, against any party.

15 U.S.C. § 7707. Effect on Other Laws.

(a) Federal Law.—

(1) Nothing in this Act shall be construed to impair the enforcement of section 223 or 231 of the Communications Act of 1934 (47 U.S.C. 223 or 231, respectively), chapter 71 (relating to obscenity) or 110 (relating to sexual exploitation of children) of title 18, United States Code, or any other Federal criminal statute.

(2) Nothing in this Act shall be construed to affect in any way the Commission's authority to bring enforcement actions under FTC Act for materially false or deceptive representations or unfair practices in commercial electronic mail messages.

(b) State Law.--

(1) In general.--This Act supersedes any statute, regulation, or rule of a State or political subdivision of a State that expressly regulates the use of electronic mail to send commercial messages, except to the extent that any such statute, regulation, or rule prohibits falsity or deception in any portion of a commercial electronic mail message or information attached thereto.

(2) State law not specific to electronic mail.--This Act shall not be construed to preempt the applicability of--

(A) State laws that are not specific to electronic mail, including State trespass, contract, or tort law; or

(B) other State laws to the extent that those laws relate to acts of fraud or computer crime.

(c) No Effect on Policies of Providers of Internet Access Service.-- Nothing in this Act shall be construed to have any effect on the lawfulness or unlawfulness, under any other provision of law, of the adoption, implementation, or enforcement by a provider of Internet access service of a policy of declining to transmit, route, relay, handle, or store certain types of electronic mail messages.

15 U.S.C. § 7708. Do-Not-E-Mail Registry

(a) In General.--Not later than 6 months after the date of enactment of this Act, the Commission shall transmit to the Senate Committee on Commerce, Science, and Transportation and the House of Representatives Committee on Energy and Commerce a report that--

(1) sets forth a plan and timetable for establishing a nationwide marketing Do-Not-E-Mail registry;

(2) includes an explanation of any practical, technical, security, privacy, enforceability, or other concerns that the Commission has regarding such a registry; and

(3) includes an explanation of how the registry would be applied with respect to children with e-mail accounts.

(b) Authorization To Implement.--The Commission may establish and implement the plan, but not earlier than 9 months after the date of enactment of this Act.

15 U.S.C. § 7709. Study Of Effects Of Commercial Electronic Mail

(a) In General.--Not later than 24 months after the date of the enactment of this Act, the Commission, in consultation with the Department of Justice and other appropriate agencies, shall submit a report to the Congress that provides a detailed analysis of the effectiveness and enforcement of the provisions of this Act and the need (if any) for the Congress to modify such provisions.

(b) Required Analysis.--The Commission shall include in the report required by subsection (a)--

(1) an analysis of the extent to which technological and marketplace developments, including changes in the nature of the devices through which consumers access their electronic mail messages, may affect the practicality and effectiveness of the provisions of this Act;

(2) analysis and recommendations concerning how to address commercial electronic mail that originates in or is transmitted through or to facilities or computers in other nations, including initiatives or policy positions that the Federal

Government could pursue through international negotiations, fora, organizations, or institutions; and

(3) analysis and recommendations concerning options for protecting consumers, including children, from the receipt and viewing of commercial electronic mail that is obscene or pornographic.

15 U.S.C. § 7710. Improving Enforcement By Providing Rewards For Information About Violations; Labeling.

The Commission shall transmit to the Senate Committee on Commerce, Science, and Transportation and the House of Representatives Committee on Energy and Commerce--

(1) a report, within 9 months after the date of enactment of this Act, that sets forth a system for rewarding those who supply information about violations of this Act, including--

(A) procedures for the Commission to grant a reward of not less than 20 percent of the total civil penalty collected for a violation of this Act to the first person that--

(i) identifies the person in violation of this Act; and

(ii) supplies information that leads to the successful collection of a civil penalty by the Commission; and

(B) procedures to minimize the burden of submitting a complaint to the Commission concerning violations of this Act, including procedures to allow the electronic submission of complaints to the Commission; and

(2) a report, within 18 months after the date of enactment of this Act, that sets forth a plan for requiring commercial electronic mail to be identifiable from its subject line, by means of compliance with Internet Engineering Task Force Standards, the use of the characters "ADV" in the subject line, or other comparable identifier, or an explanation of any concerns the Commission has that cause the Commission to recommend against the plan.

15 U.S.C. § 7711. Regulations.

(a) In General.--The Commission may issue regulations to implement the provisions of this Act (not including the amendments made by sections 4 and 12). Any such regulations shall be issued in accordance with section 553 of title 5, United States Code.

(b) Limitation.--Subsection (a) may not be construed to authorize the Commission to establish a requirement pursuant to section 5(a)(5)(A) to include any specific words, characters, marks, or labels in a commercial electronic mail message, or to include the identification required by section 5(a)(5)(A) in any particular part of such a mail message (such as the subject line or body).

15 U.S.C. § 7712. Application to Wireless

(a) Effect on Other Law.--Nothing in this Act shall be interpreted to preclude or override the applicability of section 227 of the Communications Act of 1934 (47 U.S.C. 227) or the rules prescribed under section 3 of the Telemarketing and Consumer Fraud and Abuse Prevention Act (15 U.S.C. 6102).

(b) FCC Rulemaking.--The Federal Communications Commission, in consultation with the Federal Trade Commission, shall promulgate rules within 270 days to protect consumers from unwanted mobile service commercial messages. The Federal Communications Commission, in promulgating the rules, shall, to the extent consistent with subsection (c)--

(1) provide subscribers to commercial mobile services the ability to avoid receiving mobile service commercial messages unless the subscriber has provided express prior authorization to the sender, except as provided in paragraph (3);

(2) allow recipients of mobile service commercial messages to indicate electronically a desire not to receive future mobile service commercial messages from the sender;

(3) take into consideration, in determining whether to subject providers of commercial mobile services to paragraph (1), the relationship that exists between providers of such services and their subscribers, but if the Commission determines that such providers should not be subject to paragraph (1), the rules shall require such providers, in addition to complying with the other provisions of this Act, to allow subscribers to indicate a desire not to receive future mobile service commercial messages from the provider--

(A) at the time of subscribing to such service; and

(B) in any billing mechanism; and

(4) determine how a sender of mobile service commercial messages may comply with the provisions of this Act, considering the unique technical aspects, including the functional and character limitations, of devices that receive such messages.

(c) Other Factors Considered.--The Federal Communications Commission shall consider the ability of a sender of a commercial electronic mail message to reasonably determine that the message is a mobile service commercial message.

(d) Mobile Service Commercial Message Defined.--In this section, the term "mobile service commercial message" means a commercial electronic mail message that is transmitted directly to a wireless device that is utilized by a subscriber of commercial mobile service (as such term is defined in section 332(d) of the Communications Act of 1934 (47 U.S.C. 332(d))) in connection with such service.

United States
CAN-SPAM Act

15 U.S.C. § 7713. Separability

If any provision of this Act or the application thereof to any person or circumstance is held invalid, the remainder of this Act and the application of such provision to other persons or circumstances shall not be affected.

18 U.S.C. § 1037. Fraud and related activity in connection with electronic mail

(a) In General.--Whoever, in or affecting interstate or foreign commerce, knowingly--

(1) accesses a protected computer without authorization, and intentionally initiates the transmission of multiple commercial electronic mail messages from or through such computer,

(2) uses a protected computer to relay or retransmit multiple commercial electronic mail messages, with the intent to deceive or mislead recipients, or any Internet access service, as to the origin of such messages,

(3) materially falsifies header information in multiple commercial electronic mail messages and intentionally initiates the transmission of such messages,

(4) registers, using information that materially falsifies the identity of the actual registrant, for five or more electronic mail accounts or online user accounts or two or more domain names, and intentionally initiates the transmission of multiple commercial electronic mail messages from any combination of such accounts or domain names, or

(5) falsely represents oneself to be the registrant or the legitimate successor in interest to the registrant of 5 or more Internet Protocol addresses, and intentionally initiates the transmission of multiple commercial electronic mail messages from such addresses, or conspires to do so, shall be punished as provided in subsection (b).

(b) Penalties.--The punishment for an offense under subsection (a) is--

(1) a fine under this title, imprisonment for not more than 5 years, or both, if--

(A) the offense is committed in furtherance of any felony under the laws of the United States or of any State; or

(B) the defendant has previously been convicted under this section or section 1030, or under the law of any State for conduct involving the transmission of multiple commercial electronic mail messages or unauthorized access to a computer system;

(2) a fine under this title, imprisonment for not more than 3 years, or both, if--

(A) the offense is an offense under subsection (a)(1);

(B) the offense is an offense under subsection (a)(4) and involved 20 or more falsified electronic mail or online user account registrations, or 10 or more falsified domain name registrations;

(C) the volume of electronic mail messages transmitted in furtherance of the offense exceeded 2,500 during any 24-hour period, 25,000 during any 30-day period, or 250,000 during any 1-year period;

(D) the offense caused loss to one or more persons aggregating $5,000 or more in value during any 1-year period;

(E) as a result of the offense any individual committing the offense obtained anything of value aggregating $5,000 or more during any 1-year period; or

(F) the offense was undertaken by the defendant in concert with three or more other persons with respect to whom the defendant occupied a position of organizer or leader; and

(3) a fine under this title or imprisonment for not more than 1 year, or both, in any other case.

(c) Forfeiture.--

(1) In general.--The court, in imposing sentence on a person who is convicted of an offense under this section, shall order that the defendant forfeit to the United States--

(A) any property, real or personal, constituting or traceable to gross proceeds obtained from such offense; and

(B) any equipment, software, or other technology used or intended to be used to commit or to facilitate the commission of such offense.

(2) Procedures.--The procedures set forth in section 413 of the Controlled Substances Act (21 U.S.C. 853), other than subsection (d) of that section, and in Rule 32.2 of the Federal Rules of Criminal Procedure, shall apply to all stages of a criminal forfeiture proceeding under this section.

(d) Definitions.--In this section:

(1) Loss.--The term "loss" has the meaning given that term in section 1030(e) of this title.

(2) Materially.--For purposes of paragraphs (3) and (4) of subsection (a), header information or registration information is materially falsified if it is altered or concealed in a manner that would impair the ability of a recipient of the message, an Internet access service processing the message on behalf of a recipient, a person alleging a violation of this section, or a law enforcement agency to identify, locate, or respond to a person who initiated the electronic mail message or to investigate the alleged violation.

(3) Multiple.--The term "multiple" means more than 100 electronic mail messages during a 24-hour period, more than 1,000 electronic mail messages during a 30-day period, or more than 10,000 electronic mail messages during a 1-year period.

(4) Other terms.--Any other term has the meaning given that term by section 3 of the CAN-SPAM Act of 2003 [15 U.S.C. § 7702].

VIDEO VOYEURISM PREVENTION ACT
(2004)

Summary

The Video Voyeurism Prevention Act of 2004 was passed in response to the growing popularity of miniature spy cameras. The Act is very limited in scope: it only covers voyeuristic acts performed on federal lands such as federal parks.

References

Public Law 108-495, codified at 18 U.S.C. § 1801.
[https://www.law.cornell.edu/uscode/text/18/1801]

18 U.S.C. § 1801. Video voyeurism

(a) Whoever, in the special maritime and territorial jurisdiction of the United States, has the intent to capture an image of a private area of an individual without their consent, and knowingly does so under circumstances in which the individual has a reasonable expectation of privacy, shall be fined under this title or imprisoned not more than one year, or both.

(b) In this section--

(1) the term "capture", with respect to an image, means to videotape, photograph, film, record by any means, or broadcast;

(2) the term "broadcast" means to electronically transmit a visual image with the intent that it be viewed by a person or persons;

(3) the term "a private area of the individual" means the naked or undergarment clad genitals, pubic area, buttocks, or female breast of that individual;

(4) the term "female breast" means any portion of the female breast below the top of the areola; and

(5) the term "under circumstances in which that individual has a reasonable expectation of privacy" means--

(A) circumstances in which a reasonable person would believe that he or she could disrobe in privacy, without being concerned that an image of a private area of the individual was being captured; or

(B) circumstances in which a reasonable person would believe that a private area of the individual would not be visible to the public, regardless of whether that person is in a public or private place.

(c) This section does not prohibit any lawful law enforcement, correctional, or intelligence   activity.

IDENTITY THEFT PENALTY ENHANCEMENT ACT (2004)

Summary

The Identity Theft Penalty Enhancement Act of 2004 strengthens the criminal punishments for identity theft. The Act creates a five-year sentence for identity theft committed in relation to terrorism and a two-year sentence for identity theft committed in relation to felonies such as fraud and immigration violations. The Act also prohibits judicial alteration of these sentences or conversion to probation.

References

Public Law No. 108-275, codified at 18 U.S.C. §§ 1028A–1028.
[https://www.law.cornell.edu/uscode/text/18/1028]

18 U.S.C. § 1028A. Aggravated identity theft

(a) Offenses.--

(1) In general.--Whoever, during and in relation to any felony violation enumerated in subsection (c), knowingly transfers, possesses, or uses, without lawful authority, a means of identification of another person shall, in addition to the punishment provided for such felony, be sentenced to a term of imprisonment of 2 years.

(2) Terrorism offense.--Whoever, during and in relation to any felony violation enumerated in section 2332b(g)(5)(B), knowingly transfers, possesses, or uses, without lawful authority, a means of identification of another person or a false identification document shall, in addition to the punishment provided for such felony, be sentenced to a term of imprisonment of 5 years.

(b) Consecutive Sentence.--Notwithstanding any other provision of law--

(1) a court shall not place on probation any person convicted of a violation of this section;

(2) except as provided in paragraph (4), no term of imprisonment imposed on a person under this section shall run concurrently with any other term of imprisonment imposed on the person under any other provision of law, including any term of imprisonment imposed for the felony during which the means of identification was transferred, possessed, or used;

(3) in determining any term of imprisonment to be imposed for the felony during which the means of identification was transferred, possessed, or used, a court shall not in any way reduce the term to be imposed for such crime so as to compensate for, or otherwise take into account, any separate term of imprisonment imposed or to be imposed for a violation of this section; and

(4) a term of imprisonment imposed on a person for a violation of this section may, in the discretion of the court, run concurrently, in whole or in part, only with another term of imprisonment that is imposed by the court at the same time on that person for an additional violation of this section, provided that such discretion shall be exercised in accordance with any applicable guidelines and policy statements issued by the Sentencing Commission pursuant to section 994 of title 28.

(c) Definition.--For purposes of this section, the term "felony violation enumerated in subsection (c)" means any offense that is a felony violation of--

(1) section 641 (relating to theft of public money, property, or rewards), section 656 (relating to theft, embezzlement, or misapplication by bank officer or employee), or section 664 (relating to theft from employee benefit plans);

(2) section 911 (relating to false personation of citizenship);

(3) section 922(a)(6) (relating to false statements in connection with the acquisition of a firearm);

(4) any provision contained in this chapter (relating to fraud and false statements), other than this section or section 1028(a)(7);

(5) any provision contained in chapter 63 (relating to mail, bank, and wire fraud);

(6) any provision contained in chapter 69 (relating to nationality and citizenship);

(7) any provision contained in chapter 75 (relating to passports and visas);

(8) section 523 of the Gramm-Leach-Bliley Act (15 U.S.C. 6823) (relating to obtaining customer information by false pretenses);

(9) section 243 or 266 of the Immigration and Nationality Act (8 U.S.C. 1253 and 1306) (relating to willfully failing to leave the United States after deportation and creating a counterfeit alien registration card);

(10) any provision contained in chapter 8 of title II of the Immigration and Nationality Act (8 U.S.C. 1321 et seq.) (relating to various immigration offenses); or

(11) section 208, 811, 1107(b), 1128B(a), or 1632 of the Social Security Act (42 U.S.C. 408, 1011, 1307(b), 1320a-7b(a), and 1383a) (relating to false statements relating to programs under the Act).

18 U.S.C. § 1028. Fraud and related activity in connection with identification documents and information

(a) Whoever, in a circumstance described in subsection (c) of this section-

. . .

(7) knowingly transfers, possesses, or uses, without lawful authority, a means of identification of another person with the intent to commit, or to aid or abet, or in connection with, any unlawful activity that constitutes a violation of Federal law, or that constitutes a felony under any applicable State or local law; or

(8) knowingly traffics in false or actual authentication features for use in false identification documents, document-making implements, or means of identification;

shall be punished as provided in subsection (b) of this section.

(b) The punishment for an offense under subsection (a) of this section is-

(1) except as provided in paragraphs (3) and (4), a fine under this title or imprisonment for not more than 15 years, or both, if the offense is-

(A) the production or transfer of an identification document, authentication feature, or false identification document that is or appears to be-

(i) an identification document or authentication feature issued by or under the authority of the United States; or

(ii) a birth certificate, or a driver's license or personal identification card;

(B) the production or transfer of more than five identification documents, authentication features, or false identification documents;

(C) an offense under paragraph (5) of such subsection; or

(D) an offense under paragraph (7) of such subsection that involves the transfer, possession, or use of 1 or more means of identification if, as a result of the offense, any individual committing the offense obtains anything of value aggregating $1,000 or more during any 1-year period;

(2) except as provided in paragraphs (3) and (4), a fine under this title or imprisonment for not more than 5 years, or both, if the offense is-

(A) any other production, transfer, or use of a means of identification, an identification document,,1 authentication feature, or a false identification document; or

(B) an offense under paragraph (3) or (7) of such subsection;

(3) a fine under this title or imprisonment for not more than 20 years, or both, if the offense is committed-

(A) to facilitate a drug trafficking crime (as defined in section 929(a)(2));

(B) in connection with a crime of violence (as defined in section 924(c)(3)); or

(C) after a prior conviction under this section becomes final;

(4) a fine under this title or imprisonment for not more than 30 years, or both, if the offense is committed to facilitate an act of domestic terrorism (as defined under section 2331(5) of this title) or an act of international terrorism (as defined in section 2331(1) of this title);

(5) in the case of any offense under subsection (a), forfeiture to the United States of any personal property used or intended to be used to commit the offense; and

(6) a fine under this title or imprisonment for not more than one year, or both, in any other case.

. . .

United States
Identity Theft Penalty Enhancement Act

18 U.S.C. § 641. Public money, property or records

Whoever embezzles, steals, purloins, or knowingly converts to his use or the use of another, or without authority, sells, conveys or disposes of any record, voucher, money, or thing of value of the United States or of any department or agency thereof, or any property made or being made under contract for the United States or any department or agency thereof; or

Whoever receives, conceals, or retains the same with intent to convert it to his use or gain, knowing it to have been embezzled, stolen, purloined or converted—

Shall be fined under this title or imprisoned not more than ten years, or both; but if the value of such property *<in the aggregate, combining amounts from all the counts for which the defendant is convicted in a single case,>* does not exceed the sum of $1,000, he shall be fined under this title or imprisoned not more than one year, or both.

The word "value" means face, par, or market value, or cost price, either wholesale or retail, whichever is greater.

INTELLIGENCE REFORM AND
TERRORISM PREVENTION ACT (2004)
[EXCERPTS]

Summary

The Intelligence Reform and Terrorism Prevention Act, among other things, included provisions to standardize state-issued identification documents such as birth certificates and driver's licenses. The Act creates minimum standards for these documents to be accepted by federal agencies. It also charges the Social Security Administration to improve detection of social security number fraud, and prohibits the display of social security numbers on identification documents. Finally, the Act directs attention to the security of passports and their use for identity verification on airlines.

Note: Some provisions of this act were repealed by the REAL ID Act of 2005.

References

Public Law No. 108-458
[https://www.congress.gov/bill/108th-congress/senate-bill/02845]

§ 7211 (5 U.S.C. § 301 note). Standards for Birth Certificates.

(a) Definition.--In this section, the term "birth certificate" means a certificate of birth--

(1) for an individual (regardless of where born)--

(A) who is a citizen or national of the United States at birth; and

(B) whose birth is registered in the United States; and

(2) that--

(A) is issued by a Federal, State, or local government agency or authorized custodian of record and produced from birth records maintained by such agency or custodian of record; or

(B) is an authenticated copy, issued by a Federal, State, or local government agency or authorized custodian of record, of an original certificate of birth issued by such agency or custodian of record.

(b) Standards for Acceptance by Federal Agencies.--

(1) In general.--Beginning 2 years after the promulgation of minimum standards under paragraph (3), no Federal agency may accept a birth certificate for any official purpose unless the certificate conforms to such standards.

(2) State certification.--

(A) In general.--Each State shall certify to the Secretary of Health and Human Services that the State is in compliance with the requirements of this section.

(B) Frequency.--Certifications under subparagraph (A) shall be made at such intervals and in such a manner as the Secretary of Health and Human Services, with the concurrence of the Secretary of Homeland Security and the Commissioner of Social Security, may prescribe by regulation.

(C) Compliance.--Each State shall ensure that units of local government and other authorized custodians of records in the State comply with this section.

(D) Audits.--The Secretary of Health and Human Services may conduct periodic audits of each State's compliance with the requirements of this section.

(3) Minimum standards.--Not later than 1 year after the date of enactment of this Act, the Secretary of Health and Human Services shall by regulation establish minimum standards for birth certificates for use by Federal agencies for official purposes that--

(A) at a minimum, shall require certification of the birth certificate by the State or local government custodian of record that issued the certificate, and shall require the use of safety paper or an alternative, equally secure medium, the seal of the issuing custodian of record, and other features designed to prevent tampering, counterfeiting, or otherwise duplicating the birth certificate for fraudulent purposes;

(B) shall establish requirements for proof and verification of identity as a condition of issuance of a birth certificate, with additional security measures for the issuance of a birth certificate for a person who is not the applicant;

(C) shall establish standards for the processing of birth certificate applications to prevent fraud;

(D) may not require a single design to which birth certificates issued by all States must conform; and

(E) shall accommodate the differences between the States in the manner and form in which birth records are stored and birth certificates are produced from such records.

(4) Consultation with government agencies.--In promulgating the standards required under paragraph (3), the Secretary of Health and Human Services shall consult with--

(A) the Secretary of Homeland Security;

(B) the Commissioner of Social Security;

(C) State vital statistics offices; and

(D) other appropriate Federal agencies.

(5) Extension of effective date.--The Secretary of Health and Human Services may extend the date specified under paragraph (1) for up to 2 years for birth certificates issued by a State if the Secretary determines that the State made reasonable efforts to comply with the date under paragraph (1) but was unable to do so.

(c) Grants to States.--

(1) Assistance in meeting federal standards.--

(A) In general.--Beginning on the date a final regulation is promulgated under subsection (b)(3), the Secretary of Health and Human Services shall award grants to States to assist them in conforming to the minimum standards for birth certificates set forth in the regulation.

(B) Allocation of grants.--The Secretary shall award grants to States under this paragraph based on the proportion that the estimated average annual number of birth certificates issued by a State applying for a grant bears to the estimated average annual number of birth certificates issued by all States.

(C) Minimum allocation.--Notwithstanding subparagraph (B), each State shall receive not less than 0.5 percent of the grant funds made available under this paragraph.

(2) Assistance in matching birth and death records.--

(A) In general.--The Secretary of Health and Human Services, in coordination with the Commissioner of Social Security and other appropriate Federal agencies, shall award grants to States, under criteria established by the Secretary, to assist States in--

(i) computerizing their birth and death records;

(ii) developing the capability to match birth and death records within each State and among the States; and

(iii) noting the fact of death on the birth certificates of deceased persons.

(B) Allocation of grants.--The Secretary shall award grants to qualifying States under this paragraph based on the proportion that the estimated annual average number of birth and death records created by a State applying for a grant bears to the estimated annual average number of birth and death records originated by all States.

(C) Minimum allocation.--Notwithstanding subparagraph (B), each State shall receive not less than 0.5 percent of the grant funds made available under this paragraph.

(d) Authorization of Appropriations.--There are authorized to be appropriated to the Secretary for each of the fiscal years 2005 through 2009 such sums as may be necessary to carry out this section.

(e) Technical and Conforming Amendment.--Section 656 of the Illegal Immigration Reform and Immigrant Responsibility Act of 1996 (5 U.S.C. 301 note) is repealed.

§ 7212 (49 U.S.C. § 30301 note). Driver's Licenses and Personal Identification Cards.

(a) Definitions.--In this section:

(1) Driver's license.--The term "driver's license" means a motor vehicle operator's license as defined in section 30301(5) of title 49, United States Code.

(2) Personal identification card.--The term "personal identification card" means an identification document (as defined in section 1028(d)(3) of title 18, United States Code) issued by a State.

(b) Standards for Acceptance by Federal Agencies.--

United States
Intelligence Reform and Terrorism Prevention Act

(1) In general.--

(A) Limitation on acceptance.--No Federal agency may accept, for any official purpose, a driver's license or personal identification card newly issued by a State more than 2 years after the promulgation of the minimum standards under paragraph (2) unless the driver's license or personal identification card conforms to such minimum standards.

(B) Date for conformance.--The Secretary of Transportation, in consultation with the Secretary of Homeland Security, shall establish a date after which no driver's license or personal identification card shall be accepted by a Federal agency for any official purpose unless such driver's license or personal identification card conforms to the minimum standards established under paragraph (2). The date shall be as early as the Secretary determines it is practicable for the States to comply with such date with reasonable efforts.

(C) State certification.--

(i) In general.--Each State shall certify to the Secretary of Transportation that the State is in compliance with the requirements of this section.

(ii) Frequency.--Certifications under clause (i) shall be made at such intervals and in such a manner as the Secretary of Transportation, with the concurrence of the Secretary of Homeland Security, may prescribe by regulation.

(iii) Audits.--The Secretary of Transportation may conduct periodic audits of each State's compliance with the requirements of this section.

(2) Minimum standards.--Not later than 18 months after the date of enactment of this Act, the Secretary of Transportation, in consultation with the Secretary of Homeland Security, shall by regulation, establish minimum standards for driver's licenses or personal identification cards issued by a State for use by Federal agencies for identification purposes that shall include--

(A) standards for documentation required as proof of identity of an applicant for a driver's license or personal identification card;

(B) standards for the verifiability of documents used to obtain a driver's license or personal identification card;

(C) standards for the processing of applications for driver's licenses and personal identification cards to prevent fraud;

(D) standards for information to be included on each driver's license or personal identification card, including--

(i) the person's full legal name;

(ii) the person's date of birth;

(iii) the person's gender;

(iv) the person's driver's license or personal identification card number;

(v) a digital photograph of the person;

(vi) the person's address of principal residence; and

(vii) the person's signature;

(E) standards for common machine-readable identity information to be included on each driver's license or personal identification card, including defined minimum data elements;

(F) security standards to ensure that driver's licenses and personal identification cards are--

(i) resistant to tampering, alteration, or counterfeiting; and

(ii) capable of accommodating and ensuring the security of a digital photograph or other unique identifier; and

(G) a requirement that a State confiscate a driver's license or personal identification card if any component or security feature of the license or identification card is compromised.

(3) Content of regulations.--The regulations required by paragraph (2)--

(A) shall facilitate communication between the chief driver licensing official of a State, an appropriate official of a Federal agency and other relevant officials, to verify the authenticity of documents, as appropriate, issued by such Federal agency or entity and presented to prove the identity of an individual;

(B) may not infringe on a State's power to set criteria concerning what categories of individuals are eligible to obtain a driver's license or personal identification card from that State;

(C) may not require a State to comply with any such regulation that conflicts with or otherwise interferes with the full enforcement of State criteria concerning the categories of individuals that are eligible to obtain a driver's license or personal identification card from that State;

(D) may not require a single design to which driver's licenses or personal identification cards issued by all States must conform; and

(E) shall include procedures and requirements to protect the privacy rights of individuals who apply for and hold driver's licenses and personal identification cards.

(4) Negotiated rulemaking.--

(A) In general.--Before publishing the proposed regulations required by paragraph (2) to carry out this title, the Secretary of Transportation shall establish a negotiated rulemaking process pursuant to subchapter IV of chapter 5 of title 5, United States Code (5 U.S.C. 561 et seq.).

(B) Representation on negotiated rulemaking committee.--Any negotiated rulemaking committee established by the Secretary of Transportation pursuant to subparagraph (A) shall include representatives from--

(i) among State offices that issue driver's licenses or personal identification cards;

(ii) among State elected officials;

(iii) the Department of Homeland Security; and

(iv) among interested parties.

(C) Time requirement.--The process described in subparagraph (A) shall be conducted in a timely manner to ensure that--

(i) any recommendation for a proposed rule or report is provided to the Secretary of Transportation not later than 9 months after the date of enactment of this Act and shall include an assessment of the benefits and costs of the recommendation; and

(ii) a final rule is promulgated not later than 18 months after the date of enactment of this Act.

(c) Grants to States.--

(1) Assistance in meeting federal standards.--Beginning on the date a final regulation is promulgated under subsection (b)(2), the Secretary of Transportation shall award grants to States to assist them in conforming to the minimum standards for driver's licenses and personal identification cards set forth in the regulation.

(2) Allocation of grants.--The Secretary of Transportation shall award grants to States under this subsection based on the proportion that the estimated average annual number of driver's licenses and personal identification cards issued by a State applying for a grant bears to the average annual number of such documents issued by all States.

(3) Minimum allocation.--Notwithstanding paragraph (2), each State shall receive not less than 0.5 percent of the grant funds made available under this subsection.

(d) Extension of Effective Date.--The Secretary of Transportation may extend the date specified under subsection (b)(1)(A) for up to 2 years for driver's licenses issued by a State if the Secretary determines that the State made reasonable efforts to comply with the date under such subsection but was unable to do so.

(e) Authorization of Appropriations.--There are authorized to be appropriated to the Secretary of Transportation for each of the fiscal years 2005 through 2009, such sums as may be necessary to carry out this section.

§ 7213 (42 U.S.C. § 405 note). Social Security Cards And Numbers.

(a) Security Enhancements.--The Commissioner of Social Security shall--

(1) not later than 1 year after the date of enactment of this Act--

(A) restrict the issuance of multiple replacement social security cards to any individual to 3 per year and 10 for the life of the individual, except that the Commissioner may allow for reasonable exceptions from the limits under this paragraph on a case-by-case basis in compelling circumstances;

(B) establish minimum standards for the verification of documents or records submitted by an individual to establish eligibility for an original or replacement social security card, other than for purposes of enumeration at birth; and

(C) require independent verification of any birth record submitted by an individual to establish eligibility for a social security account number, other than for purposes of enumeration at birth, except that the Commissioner may allow for reasonable exceptions from the requirement for independent verification under this subparagraph on a case by case basis in compelling circumstances; and

(2) notwithstanding section 205(r) of the Social Security Act (42 U.S.C. 405(r)) and any agreement entered into thereunder, not later than 18 months after the date of enactment of this Act with respect to death indicators and not later than 36 months after the date of enactment of this Act with respect to fraud indicators, add death and fraud indicators to the social security number verification systems for employers, State agencies issuing driver's licenses and identity cards, and other verification routines that the Commissioner determines to be appropriate.

(b) Interagency Security Task Force.--The Commissioner of Social Security, in consultation with the Secretary of Homeland Security, shall form an interagency task force for the purpose of further improving the security of social security cards and numbers. Not later than 18 months after the date of enactment of this Act, the task force shall establish, and the Commissioner shall provide for the implementation of, security requirements, including--

(1) standards for safeguarding social security cards from counterfeiting, tampering, alteration, and theft;

(2) requirements for verifying documents submitted for the issuance of replacement cards; and

(3) actions to increase enforcement against the fraudulent use or issuance of social security numbers and cards.

(c) Enumeration at Birth.--

(1) Improvement of application process.--As soon as practicable after the date of enactment of this Act, the Commissioner of Social Security shall undertake to make improvements to the enumeration at birth program for the issuance of social security account numbers to newborns. Such improvements shall be designed to prevent--

(A) the assignment of social security account numbers to unnamed children;

(B) the issuance of more than 1 social security account number to the same child; and

(C) other opportunities for fraudulently obtaining a social security account number.

(2) Report to congress.--Not later than 1 year after the date of enactment of this Act, the Commissioner shall transmit to each House of Congress a report specifying in detail the extent to which the improvements required under paragraph (1) have been made.

(d) Study Regarding Process for Enumeration at Birth.--

(1) In general.--As soon as practicable after the date of enactment of this Act, the Commissioner of Social Security shall conduct a study to determine the most efficient options for ensuring the integrity of the process for enumeration at birth. This study shall include an examination of available methods for reconciling hospital birth records with birth registrations submitted to agencies of States and political subdivisions thereof and with information provided to the Commissioner as part of the process for enumeration at birth.

(2) Report.--

(A) In general.--Not later than 18 months after the date of enactment of this Act, the Commissioner shall submit a report to the Committee on Ways and Means of the House of Representatives and the Committee on Finance of the Senate regarding the results of the study conducted under paragraph (1).

(B) Contents.--The report submitted under subparagraph (A) shall contain such recommendations for legislative changes as the Commissioner considers necessary to implement needed improvements in the process for enumeration at birth.

(e) Authorization of Appropriations.--There are authorized to be appropriated to the Commissioner of Social Security for each of the fiscal years 2005 through 2009, such sums as may be necessary to carry out this section.

§ 7214. Prohibition Of The Display Of Social Security Account Numbers On Driver's Licenses Or Motor Vehicle Registrations.

(a) In General.--Section 205(c)(2)(C)(vi) of the Social Security Act (42 U.S.C. 405(c)(2)(C)(vi)) is amended--

(1) by inserting "(I)" after "(vi)"; and

(2) by adding at the end the following new subclause:

"(II) Any State or political subdivision thereof (and any person acting as an agent of such an agency or instrumentality), in the administration of any driver's license or motor vehicle registration law within its jurisdiction, may not display a social security account number issued by the Commissioner of Social Security (or any derivative of such number) on any driver's license, motor vehicle registration, or personal identification card (as defined in section 7212(a)(2) of the 9/ 11 Commission Implementation Act of 2004), or include, on any such license, registration, or personal identification card, a magnetic strip, bar code, or other means of communication which conveys such number (or derivative thereof)."

(b) Effective Date.--The amendment made by subsection (a)(2) shall apply with respect to licenses, registrations, and identification cards issued or reissued 1 year after the date of enactment of this Act.

(c) Authorization of Appropriations.--There are authorized to be appropriated to the Commissioner of Social Security for each of the fiscal years 2005 through 2009, such sums as may be necessary to carry out this section.

§ 7217. Study On Allegedly Lost Or Stolen Passports.

(a) In General.--Not later than May 31, 2005, the Secretary of State, in consultation with the Secretary of Homeland Security, shall submit a report, containing the results of a study on the subjects described in subsection (b), to--

(1) the Committee on the Judiciary of the Senate;

(2) the Committee on the Judiciary of the House of Representatives;

(3) the Committee on Foreign Relations of the Senate;

(4) the Committee on International Relations of the House of Representatives;

(5) the Committee on Homeland Security and Governmental Affairs of the Senate; and

(6) the Select Committee on Homeland Security of the House of Representatives (or any successor committee).

(b) Contents.--The study referred to in subsection (a) shall examine the feasibility, cost, potential benefits, and relative importance to the objectives of tracking suspected terrorists' travel, and apprehending suspected terrorists, of establishing a system, in coordination with other countries, through which border and visa issuance officials have access in real-time to information on newly issued passports to persons whose previous passports were allegedly lost or stolen.

(c) Incentives.--The study described in subsection (b) shall make recommendations on incentives that might be offered to encourage foreign nations to participate in the initiatives described in subsection (b).

§ 7218 (22 U.S.C. § 4807). Establishment Of Visa And Passport Security Program In The Department Of State.

(a) Establishment.--There is established, within the Bureau of Diplomatic Security of the Department of State, the Visa and Passport Security Program (in this section referred to as the "Program").

(b) Preparation of Strategic Plan.--

(1) In general.--The Assistant Secretary for Diplomatic Security, in coordination with the appropriate officials of the Bureau of Consular Affairs, the coordinator for counterterrorism, the National Counterterrorism Center, and the Department of Homeland Security, and consistent with the strategy mandated by section 7201,

shall ensure the preparation of a strategic plan to target and disrupt individuals and organizations, within the United States and in foreign countries, that are involved in the fraudulent production, distribution, use, or other similar activity--

(A) of a United States visa or United States passport;

(B) of documents intended to help fraudulently procure a United States visa or United States passport, or other documents intended to gain unlawful entry into the United States; or

(C) of passports and visas issued by foreign countries intended to gain unlawful entry into the United States.

(2) Emphasis.--The strategic plan shall--

(A) focus particular emphasis on individuals and organizations that may have links to domestic terrorist organizations or foreign terrorist organizations (as such term is defined in section 219 of the Immigration and Nationality Act (8 U.S.C. 1189));

(B) require the development of a strategic training course under the Antiterrorism Assistance Training (ATA) program of the Department of State (or any successor or related program) under chapter 8 of part II of the Foreign Assistance Act of 1961 (22 U.S.C. 2349aa et seq.) (or other relevant provisions of law) to train participants in the identification of fraudulent documents and the forensic detection of such documents which may be used to obtain unlawful entry into the United States; and

(C) determine the benefits and costs of providing technical assistance to foreign governments to ensure the security of passports, visas, and related documents and to investigate, arrest, and prosecute individuals who facilitate travel by the creation of false passports and visas, documents to obtain such passports and visas, and other types of travel documents.

(c) Program.--

(1) Individual in charge.--

(A) Designation.--The Assistant Secretary for Diplomatic Security shall designate an individual to be in charge of the Program.

(B) Qualification.--The individual designated under subparagraph (A) shall have expertise and experience in the investigation and prosecution of visa and passport fraud.

(2) Program components.--The Program shall include the following:

(A) Analysis of methods.--Analyze, in coordination with other appropriate government agencies, methods used by terrorists to travel internationally, particularly the use of false or altered travel documents to illegally enter foreign countries and the United States, and consult with the Bureau of Consular Affairs and the Secretary of Homeland Security on recommended changes to the visa issuance process that could combat such methods, including the introduction of new technologies into such process.

(B) Identification of individuals and documents.-- Identify, in cooperation with the Human Trafficking and Smuggling Center, individuals who facilitate travel by the creation of false passports and visas, documents used to obtain such passports and visas, and other types of travel documents, and ensure that the appropriate agency is notified for further investigation and prosecution or, in the case of such individuals abroad for which no further investigation or prosecution is initiated, ensure that all appropriate information is shared with foreign governments in order to facilitate investigation, arrest, and prosecution of such individuals.

(C) Identification of foreign countries needing assistance.--Identify foreign countries that need technical assistance, such as law reform, administrative reform, prosecutorial training, or assistance to police and other investigative services, to ensure passport, visa, and related document security and to investigate, arrest, and prosecute individuals who facilitate travel by the creation of false passports and visas, documents used to obtain such passports and visas, and other types of travel documents.

(D) Inspection of applications.--Randomly inspect visa and passport applications for accuracy, efficiency, and fraud, especially at high terrorist threat posts, in order to prevent a recurrence of the issuance of visas to those who submit incomplete, fraudulent, or otherwise irregular or incomplete applications.

(d) Report.--Not later than 90 days after the date on which the strategy required under section 7201 is submitted to Congress, the Assistant Secretary for Diplomatic Security shall submit to Congress a report containing--

(1) a description of the strategic plan prepared under subsection (b); and

(2) an evaluation of the feasibility of establishing civil service positions in field offices of the Bureau of Diplomatic Security to investigate visa and passport fraud, including an evaluation of whether to allow diplomatic security agents to convert to civil service officers to fill such positions.

§ 7220 (49 U.S.C. § 44901 note). Identification Standards.

(a) Proposed Standards.--

(1) In general.--The Secretary of Homeland Security--

(A) shall propose minimum standards for identification documents required of domestic commercial airline passengers for boarding an aircraft; and

(B) may, from time to time, propose minimum standards amending or replacing standards previously proposed and transmitted to Congress and approved under this section.

(2) Submission to congress.--Not later than 6 months after the date of enactment of this Act, the Secretary shall submit the standards under paragraph (1)(A) to the Senate and the House of Representatives on the same day while each House is in session.

(3) Effective date.--Any proposed standards submitted to Congress under this subsection shall take effect when an approval resolution is passed by the House and the Senate under the procedures described in subsection (b) and becomes law.

(b) Congressional Approval Procedures.--

(1) Rulemaking power.--This subsection is enacted by Congress--

(A) as an exercise of the rulemaking power of the Senate and the House of Representatives, respectively, and as such they are deemed a part of the rules of each House, respectively, but applicable only with respect to the procedure to be followed in that House in the case of such approval resolutions; and it supersedes other rules only to the extent that they are inconsistent therewith; and

(B) with full recognition of the constitutional right of either House to change the rules (so far as relating to the procedure of that House) at any time, in the same manner and to the same extent as in the case of any other rule of that House.

(2) Approval resolution.--For the purpose of this subsection, the term "approval resolution" means a joint resolution of Congress, the matter after the resolving clause of which is as follows: "That the Congress approves the proposed standards issued under section 7220 of the 9/11 Commission Implementation Act of 2004, transmitted by the President to the Congress on _____", the blank space being filled in with the appropriate date.

(3) Introduction.--Not later than the first day of session following the day on which proposed standards are transmitted to the House of Representatives and the Senate under subsection (a), an approval resolution--

(A) shall be introduced (by request) in the House by the Majority Leader of the House of Representatives, for himself or herself and the Minority Leader of the House of Representatives, or by Members of the House of Representatives designated by the Majority Leader and Minority Leader of the House; and

(B) shall be introduced (by request) in the Senate by the Majority Leader of the Senate, for himself or herself and the Minority Leader of the Senate, or by Members of the Senate designated by the Majority Leader and Minority Leader of the Senate.

(4) Prohibitions.--

(A) Amendments.--No amendment to an approval resolution shall be in order in either the House of Representatives or the Senate.

(B) Motions to suspend.--No motion to suspend the application of this paragraph shall be in order in either House, nor shall it be in order in either House for the Presiding Officer to entertain a request to suspend the application of this paragraph by unanimous consent.

(5) Referral.--

(A) In general.--An approval resolution shall be referred to the committees of the House of Representatives and of the Senate with jurisdiction. Each committee shall make its recommendations to the House of Representatives or the Senate, as the case may be, within 45 days after its introduction. Except as provided in subparagraph (B), if a committee to which an approval resolution has been referred has not reported it at the close of the 45th day after its introduction, such committee shall be automatically discharged from further consideration of the resolution and it shall be placed on the appropriate calendar.

(B) Final passage.--A vote on final passage of the resolution shall be taken in each House on or before the close of the 15th day after the resolution is reported by the committee or committees of that House to which it was referred, or after such committee or committees have been discharged from further consideration of the resolution.

(C) Computation of days.--For purposes of this paragraph, in computing a number of days in either House, there shall be excluded any day on which that House is not in session.

(6) Coordination with action of other house.--If prior to the passage by one House of an approval resolution of that House, that House receives the same approval resolution from the other House, then the procedure in that House shall be the same as if no approval resolution has been received from the other House, but the vote on final passage shall be on the approval resolution of the other House.

(7) Floor consideration in the house of representatives.--

(A) Motion to proceed.--A motion in the House of Representatives to proceed to the consideration of an approval resolution shall be highly privileged and not debatable. An amendment to the motion shall not be in order, not shall it be in order to move to reconsider the vote by which the motion is agreed to or disagreed to.

(B) Debate.--Debate in the House of Representatives on an implementing bill or approval resolution shall be limited to not more than 4 hours, which shall be divided equally between those favoring and those opposing the resolution. A motion to further limit debate shall not be debatable. It shall not be in order to move to recommit an approval resolution or to move to reconsider the vote by which an approval resolution is agreed to or disagreed to.

(C) Motion to postpone.--Motions to postpone made in the House of Representatives with respect to the consideration of an approval resolution and motions to proceed to the consideration of other business shall be decided without debate.

(D) Appeals.--All appeals from the decisions of the Chair relating to the application of the Rules of the House of Representatives to the procedure relating to an approval resolution shall be decided without debate.

(E) Rules of the house of representatives.--Except to the extent specifically provided in subparagraphs (A) through (D), consideration of an approval resolution shall be governed by the Rules of the House of Representatives applicable to other resolutions in similar circumstances.

(8) Floor consideration in the Senate.--

(A) Motion to proceed.--A motion in the Senate to proceed to the consideration of an approval resolution shall be privileged and not debatable. An amendment to the motion shall not be in order, nor shall it be in order to move to reconsider the vote by which the motion is agreed to or disagreed to.

(B) Debate on resolution.--Debate in the Senate on an approval resolution, and appeals in connection therewith, shall be limited to not more than 10 hours, which shall be equally divided between, and controlled by, the Majority Leader and the Minority Leader, or their designees.

(C) Debate on motions and appeals.--Debate in the Senate on any debatable motion or appeal in connection with an approval resolution shall be limited to not more than 1 hour, which shall be equally divided between, and controlled by, the mover and the manager of the resolution, except that in the event the manager of the resolution is in favor of any such motion or appeal, the time in opposition thereto, shall be controlled by the Minority Leader or designee. Such leaders, or either of them, may, from time under their control on the passage of an approval resolution, allot additional time to any Senator during the consideration of any debatable motion or appeal.

(D) Limit on debate.--A motion in the Senate to further limit debate is not debatable. A motion to recommit an approval resolution is not in order.

(c) Default Standards.--

(1) In general.--If the standards proposed under subsection (a)(1)(A) are not approved pursuant to the procedures described in subsection (b), then not later than 1 year after rejection by a vote of either House of Congress, domestic commercial airline passengers seeking to board an aircraft shall present, for identification purposes--

(A) a valid, unexpired passport;

(B) domestically issued documents that the Secretary of Homeland Security designates as reliable for identification purposes;

(C) any document issued by the Attorney General or the Secretary of Homeland Security under the authority of the immigration laws (as defined under section 101(a)(17) of the Immigration and Nationality Act (8 U.S.C. 1101(a)(17)); or

(D) a document issued by the country of nationality of any alien not required to possess a passport for admission to the United States that the Secretary designates as reliable for identifications purposes

(2) Exception.--The documentary requirements described in paragraph (1)--

(A) shall not apply to individuals below the age of 17, or such other age as determined by the Secretary of Homeland Security;

(B) may be waived by the Secretary of Homeland Security in the case of an unforeseen medical emergency.

(d) Recommendation to Congress.--Not later than 1 year after the date of enactment of this Act, the Secretary of Homeland Security shall recommend to Congress--

(1) categories of Federal facilities that the Secretary determines to be at risk for terrorist attack and requiring minimum identification standards for access to such facilities; and appropriate minimum identification standards to gain access to those facilities.

HEALTH INFORMATION TECHNOLOGY FOR CLINICAL AND ECONOMIC HEALTH (HITECH) ACT (2009) [EXCERPT]

Summary

The Health Information Technology for Economic and Clinical Health (HITECH) Act was passed in 2009 and sought to promote and expand the adoption of health information technology. The HITECH Act requires entities covered by the Health Insurance Portability and Accountability Act (HIPAA) to report data breaches to affected individuals and to the U.S. Department of Health and Human Services. The Act also sets restrictions on the sale or disclosure of patient health information, and establishes rules on how regulated entities must account for such disclosures.

Reference

Public Law 111–5. Codified at 42 U.S.C. §§ 300jj et seq.; §§ 17901 et seq.
[https://www.law.cornell.edu/uscode/text/42/chapter-156/subchapter-III/part-A]

42 U.S.C. § 17932. Notification in the case of breach

(a) In general

A covered entity that accesses, maintains, retains, modifies, records, stores, destroys, or otherwise holds, uses, or discloses unsecured protected health information (as defined in subsection (h)(1)) shall, in the case of a breach of such information that is discovered by the covered entity, notify each individual whose unsecured protected health information has been, or is reasonably believed by the covered entity to have been, accessed, acquired, or disclosed as a result of such breach.

(b) Notification of covered entity by business associate

A business associate of a covered entity that accesses, maintains, retains, modifies, records, stores, destroys, or otherwise holds, uses, or discloses unsecured protected health information shall, following the discovery of a breach of such information, notify the covered entity of such breach. Such notice shall include the identification of each individual whose unsecured protected health information has been, or is reasonably believed by the business associate to have been, accessed, acquired, or disclosed during such breach.

(c) Breaches treated as discovered

For purposes of this section, a breach shall be treated as discovered by a covered entity or by a business associate as of the first day on which such breach is known to such entity or associate, respectively, (including any person, other than the individual committing the breach, that is an employee, officer, or other agent of such entity or associate, respectively) or should reasonably have been known to such entity or associate (or person) to have occurred.

(d) Timeliness of notification

(1) In general

Subject to subsection (g), all notifications required under this section shall be made without unreasonable delay and in no case later than 60 calendar days after the discovery of a breach by the covered entity involved (or business associate involved in the case of a notification required under subsection (b)).

(2) Burden of proof

The covered entity involved (or business associate involved in the case of a notification required under subsection (b)), shall have the burden of demonstrating that all notifications were made as required under this part, including evidence demonstrating the necessity of any delay.

(e) Methods of notice

(1) Individual notice

Notice required under this section to be provided to an individual, with respect to a breach, shall be provided promptly and in the following form:

(A) Written notification by first-class mail to the individual (or the next of kin of the individual if the individual is deceased) at the last known address of the individual or the next of kin, respectively, or, if specified as a preference by the individual, by electronic mail. The notification may be provided in one or more mailings as information is available.

(B) In the case in which there is insufficient, or out-of-date contact information (including a phone number, email address, or any other form of appropriate communication) that precludes direct written (or, if specified by the individual under subparagraph (A), electronic) notification to the individual, a substitute form of notice shall be provided, including, in the case that there are 10 or more individuals for which there is insufficient or out-of-date contact information, a conspicuous posting for a period determined by the Secretary on the home page of the Web site of the covered entity involved or notice in major print or broadcast media, including major media in geographic areas where the individuals affected by the breach likely reside. Such a notice in media or web posting will include a toll-free phone number where an individual can learn whether or not the individual's unsecured protected health information is possibly included in the breach.

(C) In any case deemed by the covered entity involved to require urgency because of possible imminent misuse of unsecured protected health information, the covered entity, in addition to notice provided under subparagraph (A), may provide information to individuals by telephone or other means, as appropriate.

(2) Media notice

Notice shall be provided to prominent media outlets serving a State or jurisdiction, following the discovery of a breach described in subsection (a), if the unsecured protected health information of more than 500 residents of such State or jurisdiction is, or is reasonably believed to have been, accessed, acquired, or disclosed during such breach.

(3) Notice to Secretary

Notice shall be provided to the Secretary by covered entities of unsecured protected health information that has been acquired or disclosed in a breach. If the breach was with respect to 500 or more individuals than such notice must be provided immediately. If the breach was with respect to less than 500 individuals, the covered entity may maintain a log of any such breach occurring and annually submit such a log to the Secretary documenting such breaches occurring during the year involved.

(4) Posting on HHS public website

The Secretary shall make available to the public on the Internet website of the Department of Health and Human Services a list that identifies each covered entity involved in a breach described in subsection (a) in which the unsecured protected health information of more than 500 individuals is acquired or disclosed.

(f) Content of notification

Regardless of the method by which notice is provided to individuals under this section, notice of a breach shall include, to the extent possible, the following:

(1) A brief description of what happened, including the date of the breach and the date of the discovery of the breach, if known.

(2) A description of the types of unsecured protected health information that were involved in the breach (such as full name, Social Security number, date of birth, home address, account number, or disability code).

(3) The steps individuals should take to protect themselves from potential harm resulting from the breach.

(4) A brief description of what the covered entity involved is doing to investigate the breach, to mitigate losses, and to protect against any further breaches.

(5) Contact procedures for individuals to ask questions or learn additional information, which shall include a toll-free telephone number, an e-mail address, Web site, or postal address.

(g) Delay of notification authorized for law enforcement purposes

If a law enforcement official determines that a notification, notice, or posting required under this section would impede a criminal investigation or cause damage to national security, such notification, notice, or posting shall be delayed in the same manner as provided under section 164.528(a)(2) of title 45, Code of Federal Regulations, in the case of a disclosure covered under such section.

(h) Unsecured protected health information

    (1) Definition

        (A) In general

Subject to subparagraph (B), for purposes of this section, the term "unsecured protected health information" means protected health information that is not secured through the use of a technology or methodology specified by the Secretary in the guidance issued under paragraph (2).

        (B) Exception in case timely guidance not issued

In the case that the Secretary does not issue guidance under paragraph (2) by the date specified in such paragraph, for purposes of this section, the term "unsecured protected health information" shall mean protected health information that is not secured by a technology standard that renders protected health information unusable, unreadable, or indecipherable to unauthorized individuals and is developed or endorsed by a standards developing organization that is accredited by the American National Standards Institute.

    (2) Guidance

For purposes of paragraph (1) and section 17937(f)(3) of this title, not later than the date that is 60 days after February 17, 2009, the Secretary shall, after consultation with stakeholders, issue (and annually update) guidance specifying the technologies and methodologies that render protected health information unusable, unreadable, or indecipherable to unauthorized individuals, including the use of standards developed under section 300jj–12(b)(2)(B)(vi) of this title, as added by section 13101 of this Act.

(i) Report to Congress on breaches

    (1) In general

Not later than 12 months after February 17, 2009, and annually thereafter, the Secretary shall prepare and submit to the Committee on Finance and the Committee on Health, Education, Labor, and Pensions of the Senate and the Committee on Ways and Means and the Committee on Energy and Commerce of the House of Representatives a report containing the information described in paragraph (2) regarding breaches for which notice was provided to the Secretary under subsection (e)(3).

    (2) Information

The information described in this paragraph regarding breaches specified in paragraph (1) shall include-

        (A) the number and nature of such breaches; and

        (B) actions taken in response to such breaches.

(j) Regulations; effective date

To carry out this section, the Secretary of Health and Human Services shall promulgate interim final regulations by not later than the date that is 180 days after February 17,

2009. The provisions of this section shall apply to breaches that are discovered on or after the date that is 30 days after the date of publication of such interim final regulations.

. . .

§17934. Application of privacy provisions and penalties to business associates of covered entities

(a) Application of contract requirements

In the case of a business associate of a covered entity that obtains or creates protected health information pursuant to a written contract (or other written arrangement) described in section 164.502(e)(2) of title 45, Code of Federal Regulations, with such covered entity, the business associate may use and disclose such protected health information only if such use or disclosure, respectively, is in compliance with each applicable requirement of section 164.504(e) of such title. The additional requirements of this subchapter that relate to privacy and that are made applicable with respect to covered entities shall also be applicable to such a business associate and shall be incorporated into the business associate agreement between the business associate and the covered entity.

(b) Application of knowledge elements associated with contracts

Section 164.504(e)(1)(ii) of title 45, Code of Federal Regulations, shall apply to a business associate described in subsection (a), with respect to compliance with such subsection, in the same manner that such section applies to a covered entity, with respect to compliance with the standards in sections 164.502(e) and 164.504(e) of such title, except that in applying such section 164.504(e)(1)(ii) each reference to the business associate, with respect to a contract, shall be treated as a reference to the covered entity involved in such contract.

(c) Application of civil and criminal penalties

In the case of a business associate that violates any provision of subsection (a) or (b), the provisions of sections 1176 and 1177 of the Social Security Act (42 U.S.C. 1320d–5, 1320d–6) shall apply to the business associate with respect to such violation in the same manner as such provisions apply to a person who violates a provision of part C of title XI of such Act [42 U.S.C. 1320d et seq.].

§17935. Restrictions on certain disclosures and sales of health information; accounting of certain protected health information disclosures; access to certain information in electronic format

(a) Requested restrictions on certain disclosures of health information

In the case that an individual requests under paragraph (a)(1)(i)(A) of section 164.522 of title 45, Code of Federal Regulations, that a covered entity restrict the disclosure of the protected health information of the individual, notwithstanding paragraph (a)(1)(ii) of such section, the covered entity must comply with the requested restriction if-

(1) except as otherwise required by law, the disclosure is to a health plan for purposes of carrying out payment or health care operations (and is not for purposes of carrying out treatment); and

(2) the protected health information pertains solely to a health care item or service for which the health care provider involved has been paid out of pocket in full.

(b) Disclosures required to be limited to the limited data set or the minimum necessary

(1) In general

(A) In general

Subject to subparagraph (B), a covered entity shall be treated as being in compliance with section 164.502(b)(1) of title 45, Code of Federal Regulations, with respect to the use, disclosure, or request of protected health information described in such section, only if the covered entity limits such protected health information, to the extent practicable, to the limited data set (as defined in section 164.514(e)(2) of such title) or, if needed by such entity, to the minimum necessary to accomplish the intended purpose of such use, disclosure, or request, respectively.

(B) Guidance

Not later than 18 months after February 17, 2009, the Secretary shall issue guidance on what constitutes "minimum necessary" for purposes of subpart E of part 164 of title 45, Code of Federal Regulation. In issuing such guidance the Secretary shall take into consideration the guidance under section 17953(c) of this title and the information necessary to improve patient outcomes and to detect, prevent, and manage chronic disease.

(C) Sunset

Subparagraph (A) shall not apply on and after the effective date on which the Secretary issues the guidance under subparagraph (B).

(2) Determination of minimum necessary

For purposes of paragraph (1), in the case of the disclosure of protected health information, the covered entity or business associate disclosing such information shall determine what constitutes the minimum necessary to accomplish the intended purpose of such disclosure.

(3) Application of exceptions

The exceptions described in section 164.502(b)(2) of title 45, Code of Federal Regulations, shall apply to the requirement under paragraph (1) as of the effective date described in section 13423 in the same manner that such exceptions apply to section 164.502(b)(1) of such title before such date.

(4) Rule of construction

Nothing in this subsection shall be construed as affecting the use, disclosure, or request of protected health information that has been de-identified.

(c) Accounting of certain protected health information disclosures required if covered entity uses electronic health record

(1) In general

In applying section 164.528 of title 45, Code of Federal Regulations, in the case that a covered entity uses or maintains an electronic health record with respect to protected health information-

(A) the exception under paragraph (a)(1)(i) of such section shall not apply to disclosures through an electronic health record made by such entity of such information; and

(B) an individual shall have a right to receive an accounting of disclosures described in such paragraph of such information made by such covered entity during only the three years prior to the date on which the accounting is requested.

(2) Regulations

The Secretary shall promulgate regulations on what information shall be collected about each disclosure referred to in paragraph (1), not later than 6 months after the date on which the Secretary adopts standards on accounting for disclosure described in the section 300jj–12(b)(2)(B)(iv) of this title, as added by section 13101.2 Such regulations shall only require such information to be collected through an electronic health record in a manner that takes into account the interests of the individuals in learning the circumstances under which their protected health information is being disclosed and takes into account the administrative burden of accounting for such disclosures.

(3) Process

In response to an request from an individual for an accounting, a covered entity shall elect to provide either an-

(A) accounting, as specified under paragraph (1), for disclosures of protected health information that are made by such covered entity and by a business associate acting on behalf of the covered entity; or

(B) accounting, as specified under paragraph (1), for disclosures that are made by such covered entity and provide a list of all business associates acting on behalf of the covered entity, including contact information for such associates (such as mailing address, phone, and email address).

A business associate included on a list under subparagraph (B) shall provide an accounting of disclosures (as required under paragraph (1) for a covered entity) made by the business associate upon a request made by an individual directly to the business associate for such an accounting.

(4) Effective date

(A) Current users of electronic records

In the case of a covered entity insofar as it acquired an electronic health record as of January 1, 2009, paragraph (1) shall apply to disclosures, with respect to protected health information, made by the covered entity from such a record on and after January 1, 2014.

(B) Others

In the case of a covered entity insofar as it acquires an electronic health record after January 1, 2009, paragraph (1) shall apply to disclosures, with respect to protected health information, made by the covered entity from such record on and after the later of the following:

(i) January 1, 2011; or

(ii) the date that it acquires an electronic health record.

(C) Later date

The Secretary may set an effective date that is later that the date specified under subparagraph (A) or (B) if the Secretary determines that such later date is necessary, but in no case may the date specified under-

(i) subparagraph (A) be later than 2016; or

(ii) subparagraph (B) be later than 2013.

(d) Prohibition on sale of electronic health records or protected health information

(1) In general

Except as provided in paragraph (2), a covered entity or business associate shall not directly or indirectly receive remuneration in exchange for any protected health information of an individual unless the covered entity obtained from the individual, in accordance with section 164.508 of title 45, Code of Federal Regulations, a valid authorization that includes, in accordance with such section, a specification of whether the protected health information can be further exchanged for remuneration by the entity receiving protected health information of that individual.

(2) Exceptions

Paragraph (1) shall not apply in the following cases:

(A) The purpose of the exchange is for public health activities (as described in section 164.512(b) of title 45, Code of Federal Regulations).

(B) The purpose of the exchange is for research (as described in sections 164.501 and 164.512(i) of title 45, Code of Federal Regulations) and the price charged reflects the costs of preparation and transmittal of the data for such purpose.

(C) The purpose of the exchange is for the treatment of the individual, subject to any regulation that the Secretary may promulgate to prevent protected health information from inappropriate access, use, or disclosure.

(D) The purpose of the exchange is the health care operation specifically described in subparagraph (iv) of paragraph (6) of the definition of healthcare operations in section 164.501 of title 45, Code of Federal Regulations.

(E) The purpose of the exchange is for remuneration that is provided by a covered entity to a business associate for activities involving the exchange of protected health information that the business associate undertakes on behalf of and at the specific request of the covered entity pursuant to a business associate agreement.

(F) The purpose of the exchange is to provide an individual with a copy of the individual's protected health information pursuant to section 164.524 of title 45, Code of Federal Regulations.

(G) The purpose of the exchange is otherwise determined by the Secretary in regulations to be similarly necessary and appropriate as the exceptions provided in subparagraphs (A) through (F).

(3) Regulations

Not later than 18 months after February 17, 2009, the Secretary shall promulgate regulations to carry out this subsection. In promulgating such regulations, the Secretary-

(A) shall evaluate the impact of restricting the exception described in paragraph (2)(A) to require that the price charged for the purposes described in such paragraph reflects the costs of the preparation and transmittal of the data for such purpose, on research or public health activities, including those conducted by or for the use of the Food and Drug Administration; and

(B) may further restrict the exception described in paragraph (2)(A) to require that the price charged for the purposes described in such paragraph reflects the costs of the preparation and transmittal of the data for such purpose, if the Secretary finds that such further restriction will not impede such research or public health activities.

(4) Effective date

Paragraph (1) shall apply to exchanges occurring on or after the date that is 6 months after the date of the promulgation of final regulations implementing this subsection.

(e) Access to certain information in electronic format

In applying section 164.524 of title 45, Code of Federal Regulations, in the case that a covered entity uses or maintains an electronic health record with respect to protected health information of an individual-

(1) the individual shall have a right to obtain from such covered entity a copy of such information in an electronic format and, if the individual chooses, to direct the covered entity to transmit such copy directly to an entity or person designated

by the individual, provided that any such choice is clear, conspicuous, and specific; and

(2) notwithstanding paragraph (c)(4) of such section, any fee that the covered entity may impose for providing such individual with a copy of such information (or a summary or explanation of such information) if such copy (or summary or explanation) is in an electronic form shall not be greater than the entity's labor costs in responding to the request for the copy (or summary or explanation).

. . .

§17937. Temporary breach notification requirement for vendors of personal health records and other non-HIPAA covered entities

(a) In general

In accordance with subsection (c), each vendor of personal health records, following the discovery of a breach of security of unsecured PHR identifiable health information that is in a personal health record maintained or offered by such vendor, and each entity described in clause (ii), (iii), or (iv) of section 17953(b)(1)(A) of this title, following the discovery of a breach of security of such information that is obtained through a product or service provided by such entity, shall-

(1) notify each individual who is a citizen or resident of the United States whose unsecured PHR identifiable health information was acquired by an unauthorized person as a result of such a breach of security; and

(2) notify the Federal Trade Commission.

(b) Notification by third party service providers

A third party service provider that provides services to a vendor of personal health records or to an entity described in clause (ii), (iii).1 or (iv) of section 17953(b)(1)(A) of this title in connection with the offering or maintenance of a personal health record or a related product or service and that accesses, maintains, retains, modifies, records, stores, destroys, or otherwise holds, uses, or discloses unsecured PHR identifiable health information in such a record as a result of such services shall, following the discovery of a breach of security of such information, notify such vendor or entity, respectively, of such breach. Such notice shall include the identification of each individual whose unsecured PHR identifiable health information has been, or is reasonably believed to have been, accessed, acquired, or disclosed during such breach.

(c) Application of requirements for timeliness, method, and content of notifications

Subsections (c), (d), (e), and (f) of section 17932 of this title shall apply to a notification required under subsection (a) and a vendor of personal health records, an entity described in subsection (a) and a third party service provider described in subsection (b), with respect to a breach of security under subsection (a) of unsecured PHR identifiable health information in such records maintained or offered by such vendor, in a manner specified by the Federal Trade Commission.

(d) Notification of the Secretary

Upon receipt of a notification of a breach of security under subsection (a)(2), the Federal Trade Commission shall notify the Secretary of such breach.

(e) Enforcement

A violation of subsection (a) or (b) shall be treated as an unfair and deceptive act or practice in violation of a regulation under section 57a(a)(1)(B) of title 15 regarding unfair or deceptive acts or practices.

(f) Definitions

For purposes of this section:

(1) Breach of security

The term "breach of security" means, with respect to unsecured PHR identifiable health information of an individual in a personal health record, acquisition of such information without the authorization of the individual.

(2) PHR identifiable health information

The term "PHR identifiable health information" means individually identifiable health information, as defined in section 1320d(6) of this title, and includes, with respect to an individual, information-

(A) that is provided by or on behalf of the individual; and

(B) that identifies the individual or with respect to which there is a reasonable basis to believe that the information can be used to identify the individual.

(3) Unsecured PHR identifiable health information

(A) In general

Subject to subparagraph (B), the term "unsecured PHR identifiable health information" means PHR identifiable health information that is not protected through the use of a technology or methodology specified by the Secretary in the guidance issued under section 17932(h)(2) of this title.

(B) Exception in case timely guidance not issued

In the case that the Secretary does not issue guidance under section 17932(h)(2) of this title by the date specified in such section, for purposes of this section, the term "unsecured PHR identifiable health information" shall mean PHR identifiable health information that is not secured by a technology standard that renders protected health information unusable, unreadable, or indecipherable to unauthorized individuals and that is developed or endorsed by a standards developing organization that is accredited by the American National Standards Institute.

(g) Regulations; effective date; sunset

(1) Regulations; effective date

To carry out this section, the Federal Trade Commission shall promulgate interim final regulations by not later than the date that is 180 days after February 17, 2009. The provisions of this section shall apply to breaches of security that are discovered on or after the date that is 30 days after the date of publication of such interim final regulations.

(2) Sunset

If Congress enacts new legislation establishing requirements for notification in the case of a breach of security, that apply to entities that are not covered entities or business associates, the provisions of this section shall not apply to breaches of security discovered on or after the effective date of regulations implementing such legislation.

. . .

§17939. Improved enforcement

(a) In general

(1) Omitted

(2) Enforcement under Social Security Act

Any violation by a covered entity under this subchapter is subject to enforcement and penalties under section 1176 and 1177 of the Social Security Act [42 U.S.C. 1320d–5, 1320d–6].

(b) Effective date; regulations

(1) The amendments made by subsection (a) shall apply to penalties imposed on or after the date that is 24 months after February 17, 2009.

(2) Not later than 18 months after February 17, 2009, the Secretary of Health and Human Services shall promulgate regulations to implement such amendments.

(c) Distribution of certain civil monetary penalties collected

(1) In general

Subject to the regulation promulgated pursuant to paragraph (3), any civil monetary penalty or monetary settlement collected with respect to an offense punishable under this subchapter or section 1176 of the Social Security Act (42 U.S.C. 1320d–5) insofar as such section relates to privacy or security shall be transferred to the Office for Civil Rights of the Department of Health and Human Services to be used for purposes of enforcing the provisions of this subchapter and subparts C and E of part 164 of title 45, Code of Federal Regulations, as such provisions are in effect as of February 17, 2009.

(2) GAO report

Not later than 18 months after February 17, 2009, the Comptroller General shall submit to the Secretary a report including recommendations for a methodology under which an individual who is harmed by an act that constitutes an offense referred to in paragraph (1) may receive a percentage of any civil monetary penalty or monetary settlement collected with respect to such offense.

(3) Establishment of methodology to distribute percentage of CMPS collected to harmed individuals

Not later than 3 years after February 17, 2009, the Secretary shall establish by regulation and based on the recommendations submitted under paragraph (2), a methodology under which an individual who is harmed by an act that constitutes an offense referred to in paragraph (1) may receive a percentage of any civil monetary penalty or monetary settlement collected with respect to such offense.

(4) Application of methodology

The methodology under paragraph (3) shall be applied with respect to civil monetary penalties or monetary settlements imposed on or after the effective date of the regulation.

(d) Tiered increase in amount of civil monetary penalties

(1) to (3) Omitted

(4) Effective date

The amendments made by this subsection shall apply to violations occurring after February 17, 2009.

(e) Enforcement through State attorneys general

(1), (2) Omitted

(3) Effective date

The amendments made by this subsection shall apply to violations occurring after February 17, 2009.

International Privacy Law

UNIVERSAL DECLARATION OF HUMAN RIGHTS (1948)

Summary

On December 10, 1948 the General Assembly of the United Nations adopted and proclaimed the Universal Declaration of Human Rights. The Declaration sets forth a comprehensive list of the rights to which all people are entitled. Because nations initially resisted the creation of a legally binding instrument defining these human rights and fundamental freedoms, the Universal Declaration of Human Rights at its inception was viewed by the nations as a non-binding agreement, without the force of law. However, with passage of time, the UDHR has acquired the force of law through its incorporation into national laws, and because its language and ideas have been included in subsequent, binding treaties on human rights.

Article 12 of the Universal Declaration recognizes the right to privacy. It states: "No one shall be subjected to arbitrary interference with his privacy, family, home or correspondence, nor to attacks upon his honour and reputation. Everyone has the right to the protection of the law against such interference or attacks." Article 12 was the first statement of privacy as a basic human right that ought to be recognized by all nations.

The privacy right envisioned by the Declaration is a universal right that seeks to safeguard the individual across a wide range of activities, including family life, physical residence, and correspondence. The privacy right is coupled with a right to freedom from attacks upon honor and reputation, thereby linking the idea of privacy with human dignity. It is also worth noting that the second sentence of Article 12 imposes a duty upon states to establish rights in law to protect citizens against arbitrary interference with privacy.

Many subsequent international agreements have recognized the right to privacy outlined in Article 12. Article 17 of the International Covenant on Civil and Political Rights adopts the language verbatim. The European Convention on Human Rights, the U.N. Convention on the Rights of the Child, and the American Convention on Human Rights also incorporate a right to privacy based on Article 12.

References

United Nations, Universal Declaration of Human Rights
[http://www.un.org/en/universal-declaration-human-rights/index.html]

UN, Office of the High Commission for Human Rights
[http://www.ohchr.org/EN/Pages/Home.aspx]

International
Universal Declaration of Human Rights

ADOPTED BY THE UNITED NATIONS GENERAL ASSEMBLY 10 DECEMBER 1948

Whereas recognition of the inherent dignity and of the equal and inalienable rights of all members of the human family is the foundation of freedom, justice and peace in the world,

Whereas disregard and contempt for human rights have resulted in barbarous acts which have outraged the conscience of mankind, and the advent of a world in which human beings shall enjoy freedom of speech and belief and freedom from fear and want has been proclaimed as the highest aspiration of the common people,

Whereas it is essential, if man is not to be compelled to have recourse, as a last resort, to rebellion against tyranny and oppression, that human rights should be protected by the rule of law,

Whereas it is essential to promote the development of friendly relations between nations,

Whereas the peoples of the United Nations have in the Charter reaffirmed their faith in fundamental human rights, in the dignity and worth of the human person and in the equal rights of men and women and have determined to promote social progress and better standards of life in larger freedom,

Whereas Member States have pledged themselves to achieve, in co-operation with the United Nations, the promotion of universal respect for and observance of human rights and fundamental freedoms,

Whereas a common understanding of these rights and freedoms is of the greatest importance for the full realisation of this pledge,

Now, Therefore, THE GENERAL ASSEMBLY proclaims THIS UNIVERSAL DECLARATION OF HUMAN RIGHTS as a common standard of achievement for all peoples and all nations, to the end that every individual and every organ of society, keeping this Declaration constantly in mind, shall strive by teaching and education to promote respect for these rights and freedoms and by progressive measures, national and international, to secure their universal and effective recognition and observance, both among the peoples of the Member States themselves and among the peoples of territories under their jurisdiction.

ARTICLE 1. All human beings are born free and equal in dignity and rights. They are endowed with reason and conscience and should act towards one another in a spirit of brotherhood.

ARTICLE 2. Everyone is entitled to all the rights and freedoms set forth in this Declaration, without distinction of any kind, such as race, colour, sex, language, religion, political or other opinion, national or social origin, property, birth or other status.

Furthermore, no distinction shall be made on the basis of the political, jurisdictional or international status of the country or territory to which a person belongs, whether it be independent, trust, non-self-governing or under any other limitation of sovereignty.

ARTICLE 3. Everyone has the right to life, liberty and security of person.

ARTICLE 4. No one shall be held in slavery or servitude; slavery and the slave trade shall be prohibited in all their forms.

ARTICLE 5. No one shall be subjected to torture or to cruel, inhuman or degrading treatment or punishment.

ARTICLE 6. Everyone has the right to recognition everywhere as a person before the law.

ARTICLE 7. All are equal before the law and are entitled without any discrimination to equal protection of the law. All are entitled to equal protection against any discrimination in violation of this Declaration and against any incitement to such discrimination.

ARTICLE 8. Everyone has the right to an effective remedy by the competent national tribunals for acts violating the fundamental rights granted him by the constitution or by law.

ARTICLE 9. No one shall be subjected to arbitrary arrest, detention or exile.

ARTICLE 10. Everyone is entitled in full equality to a fair and public hearing by an independent and impartial tribunal, in the determination of his rights and obligations and of any criminal charge against him.

ARTICLE 11. (1) Everyone charged with a penal offence has the right to be presumed innocent until proved guilty according to law in a public trial at which he has had all the guarantees necessary for his defence. (2) No one shall be held guilty of any penal offence on account of any act or omission which did not constitute a penal offence, under national or international law, at the time when it was committed. Nor shall a heavier penalty be imposed than the one that was applicable at the time the penal offence was committed.

ARTICLE 12. No one shall be subjected to arbitrary interference with his privacy, family, home or correspondence, nor to attacks upon his honour and reputation. Everyone has the right to the protection of the law against such interference or attacks.

ARTICLE 13. (1) Everyone has the right to freedom of movement and residence within the borders of each State. (2) Everyone has the right to leave any country, including his own, and to return to his country.

ARTICLE 14. (1) Everyone has the right to seek and to enjoy in other countries asylum from persecution. (2) This right may not be invoked in the case of prosecutions genuinely arising from non-political crimes or from acts contrary to the purposes and principles of the United Nations.

ARTICLE 15. (1) Everyone has the right to a nationality. (2) No one shall be arbitrarily deprived of his nationality nor denied the right to change his nationality.

ARTICLE 16. (1) Men and women of full age, without any limitation due to race, nationality or religion, have the right to marry and to found a family. They are entitled to equal rights as to marriage, during marriage and at its dissolution. (2) Marriage shall be entered into only with the free and full consent of the intending spouses. (3) The family is the natural and fundamental group unit of society and is entitled to protection by society and the State.

ARTICLE 17. (1) Everyone has the right to own property alone as well as in association with others. (2) No one shall be arbitrarily deprived of his property.

ARTICLE 18. Everyone has the right to freedom of thought, conscience and religion; this right includes freedom to change his religion or belief, and freedom, either alone or in community with others and in public or private, to manifest his religion or belief in teaching, practice, worship and observance.

ARTICLE 19. Everyone has the right to freedom of opinion and expression; this right includes freedom to hold opinions without interference and to seek, receive and impart information and ideas through any media and regardless of frontiers.

ARTICLE 20. (1) Everyone has the right to freedom of peaceful assembly and association. (2) No one may be compelled to belong to an association.

ARTICLE 21. (1) Everyone has the right to take part in the government of his country, directly or through chosen representatives. (2) Everyone has the right of equal access to public service in his country. (3) The will of the people shall be the basis of the authority of government; this will shall be expressed in periodic and genuine elections which shall be held by universal and equal suffrage and shall be held by secret vote or by equivalent free voting procedures.

ARTICLE 22. Everyone, as a member of society, has the right to social security and is entitled to realisation, through national effort and international co-operation and in accordance with the organisation and resources of each State, of the economic, social and cultural rights indispensable for his dignity and the free development of his personality.

ARTICLE 23. (1) Everyone has the right to work, to free choice of employment, to just and favourable conditions of work and to protection against unemployment. (2) Everyone, without any discrimination, has the right to equal pay for equal work. (3) Everyone has the right to just and favourable remuneration ensuring for himself and his family an existence worthy of human dignity, and supplemented, if necessary, by other means of social protection. (4) Everyone has the right to form and to join trade unions for the protection of his interests.

ARTICLE 24. Everyone has the right to rest and leisure, including reasonable limitation of working hours and periodic holidays with pay.

ARTICLE 25. (1) Everyone has the right to a standard of living adequate for the health and well-being of himself and of his family, including food, clothing, housing and medical care and necessary social services, and the right to security in the event of unemployment, sickness, disability, widowhood, old age and other lack of livelihood in circumstances beyond his control. (2) Motherhood and childhood are entitled to special care and assistance. All children, whether born in or out of wedlock, shall enjoy the same social protection.

ARTICLE 26. (1) Everyone has the right to education. Education shall be free, at least in the elementary and fundamental stages. Elementary education shall be compulsory. Technical and professional education shall be made generally available and higher education shall be equally accessible to all on the basis of merit. (2) Education shall be directed to the full development of the human personality and to the strengthening of respect for human rights and fundamental freedoms. It shall promote understanding, tolerance and friendship among all nations, racial or religious groups, and shall further the activities of the United Nations for the maintenance of peace. (3) Parents have a prior right to choose the kind of education that shall be given their children.

ARTICLE 27. (1) Everyone has the right to freely participate in the cultural life of the community, to enjoy the arts and to share in scientific advancement and its benefits. (2) Everyone has the right to the protection of the moral and material interests resulting from any scientific, literary or artistic production of which he is the author.

ARTICLE 28. Everyone is entitled to a social and international order in which the rights and freedoms set forth in this Declaration can be fully realised.

ARTICLE 29. (1) Everyone has duties to the community in which alone the free and full development of is personality is possible. (2) In the exercise of his rights and freedoms, everyone shall be subject only to such limitations as are determined by law solely for the purpose of securing due recognition and respect for the rights and freedoms of others and of meeting the just requirements of morality, public order and the general welfare in a democratic society. (3) These rights and freedoms may in no case be exercised contrary to the purposes and principles of the United Nations.

ARTICLE 30. Nothing in this Declaration may be interpreted as implying for any State, group or person any right to engage in any activity or to perform any act aimed at the destruction of any of the rights and freedoms set forth herein.

International
Council of Europe Convention on Human Rights

COUNCIL OF EUROPE CONVENTION FOR THE PROTECTION OF HUMAN RIGHTS AND FUNDAMENTAL FREEDOMS (1950)

Summary

The Council of Europe Convention for the Protection of Human Rights was adopted shortly after the Universal Declaration of Human Rights of the United Nations. Article 8 in the Council of Europe Convention addresses the right to respect for private and family life.

References

> Council of Europe, Legal Affairs, Treaty Office
> [http://www.coe.int/en/web/conventions/]
> [http://www.coe.int/en/web/conventions/full-list/-/conventions/treaty/005]

The text of the Convention had been amended according to the provisions of Protocol No. 3 (ETS No. 45), which entered into force on 21 September 1970, of Protocol No. 5 (ETS No. 55), which entered into force on 20 December 1971 and of Protocol No. 8 (ETS No. 118), which entered into force on 1 January 1990, and comprised also the text of Protocol No. 2 (ETS No. 44) which, in accordance with Article 5, paragraph 3 thereof, had been an integral part of the Convention since its entry into force on 21 September 1970. All provisions which had been amended or added by these Protocols are replaced by Protocol No. 11 (ETS No. 155), as from the date of its entry into force on 1 November 1998. As from that date, Protocol No. 9 (ETS No. 140), which entered into force on 1 October 1994, is repealed and Protocol No. 10 (ETS no. 146) has lost its purpose.

The governments signatory hereto, being members of the Council of Europe,

Considering the Universal Declaration of Human Rights proclaimed by the General Assembly of the United Nations on 10th December 1948;

Considering that this Declaration aims at securing the universal and effective recognition and observance of the Rights therein declared;

Considering that the aim of the Council of Europe is the achievement of greater unity between its members and that one of the methods by which that aim is to be pursued is the maintenance and further realisation of human rights and fundamental freedoms;

Reaffirming their profound belief in those fundamental freedoms which are the foundation of justice and peace in the world and are best maintained on the one hand by an effective political democracy and on the other by a common understanding and observance of the human rights upon which they depend;

Being resolved, as the governments of European countries which are like-minded and have a common heritage of political traditions, ideals, freedom and the rule of law, to take the first steps for the collective enforcement of certain of the rights stated in the Universal Declaration,

Have agreed as follows:

Article 1 – Obligation to respect human rights

The High Contracting Parties shall secure to everyone within their jurisdiction the rights and freedoms defined in Section I of this Convention.

Section I – Rights and freedoms

Article 2 – Right to life

1. Everyone's right to life shall be protected by law. No one shall be deprived of his life intentionally save in the execution of a sentence of a court following his conviction of a crime for which this penalty is provided by law.

2. Deprivation of life shall not be regarded as inflicted in contravention of this article when it results from the use of force which is no more than absolutely necessary:

   a) in defence of any person from unlawful violence;

   b) in order to effect a lawful arrest or to prevent the escape of a person lawfully detained;

   c) in action lawfully taken for the purpose of quelling a riot or insurrection.

Article 3 – Prohibition of torture

No one shall be subjected to torture or to inhuman or degrading treatment or punishment.

Article 4 – Prohibition of slavery and forced labour

1. No one shall be held in slavery or servitude.

2. No one shall be required to perform forced or compulsory labour.

3. For the purpose of this article the term "forced or compulsory labour" shall not include:

   a) any work required to be done in the ordinary course of detention imposed according to the provisions of Article 5 of this Convention or during conditional release from such detention;

   b) any service of a military character or, in case of conscientious objectors in countries where they are recognised, service exacted instead of compulsory military service;

   c) any service exacted in case of an emergency or calamity threatening the life or well-being of the community;

   d) any work or service which forms part of normal civic obligations.

Article 5 – Right to liberty and security

1. Everyone has the right to liberty and security of person. No one shall be deprived of his liberty save in the following cases and in accordance with a procedure prescribed by law:

   a) the lawful detention of a person after conviction by a competent court;

   b) the lawful arrest or detention of a person for non- compliance with the lawful order of a court or in order to secure the fulfilment of any obligation prescribed by law;

c) the lawful arrest or detention of a person effected for the purpose of bringing him before the competent legal authority on reasonable suspicion of having committed an offence or when it is reasonably considered necessary to prevent his committing an offence or fleeing after having done so;

d) the detention of a minor by lawful order for the purpose of educational supervision or his lawful detention for the purpose of bringing him before the competent legal authority;

e) the lawful detention of persons for the prevention of the spreading of infectious diseases, of persons of unsound mind, alcoholics or drug addicts or vagrants;

f) the lawful arrest or detention of a person to prevent his effecting an unauthorised entry into the country or of a person against whom action is being taken with a view to deportation or extradition.

2. Everyone who is arrested shall be informed promptly, in a language which he understands, of the reasons for his arrest and of any charge against him.

3. Everyone arrested or detained in accordance with the provisions of paragraph 1.c of this article shall be brought promptly before a judge or other officer authorised by law to exercise judicial power and shall be entitled to trial within a reasonable time or to release pending trial. Release may be conditioned by guarantees to appear for trial.

4. Everyone who is deprived of his liberty by arrest or detention shall be entitled to take proceedings by which the lawfulness of his detention shall be decided speedily by a court and his release ordered if the detention is not lawful.

5. Everyone who has been the victim of arrest or detention in contravention of the provisions of this article shall have an enforceable right to compensation.

Article 6 – Right to a fair trial

1. In the determination of his civil rights and obligations or of any criminal charge against him, everyone is entitled to a fair and public hearing within a reasonable time by an independent and impartial tribunal established by law. Judgment shall be pronounced publicly but the press and public may be excluded from all or part of the trial in the interests of morals, public order or national security in a democratic society, where the interests of juveniles or the protection of the private life of the parties so require, or to the extent strictly necessary in the opinion of the court in special circumstances where publicity would prejudice the interests of justice.

2. Everyone charged with a criminal offence shall be presumed innocent until proved guilty according to law.

3. Everyone charged with a criminal offence has the following minimum rights:

a) to be informed promptly, in a language which he understands and in detail, of the nature and cause of the accusation against him;

b) to have adequate time and facilities for the preparation of his defence;

c) to defend himself in person or through legal assistance of his own choosing or, if he has not sufficient means to pay for legal assistance, to be given it free when the interests of justice so require;

d) to examine or have examined witnesses against him and to obtain the attendance and examination of witnesses on his behalf under the same conditions as witnesses against him;

e) to have the free assistance of an interpreter if he cannot understand or speak the language used in court.

Article 7 – No punishment without law

1. No one shall be held guilty of any criminal offence on account of any act or omission which did not constitute a criminal offence under national or international law at the time when it was committed. Nor shall a heavier penalty be imposed than the one that was applicable at the time the criminal offence was committed.

2. This article shall not prejudice the trial and punishment of any person for any act or omission which, at the time when it was committed, was criminal according to the general principles of law recognised by civilised nations.

Article 8 – Right to respect for private and family life

1. Everyone has the right to respect for his private and family life, his home and his correspondence.

2. There shall be no interference by a public authority with the exercise of this right except such as is in accordance with the law and is necessary in a democratic society in the interests of national security, public safety or the economic well-being of the country, for the prevention of disorder or crime, for the protection of health or morals, or for the protection of the rights and freedoms of others.

Article 9 – Freedom of thought, conscience and religion

1. Everyone has the right to freedom of thought, conscience and religion; this right includes freedom to change his religion or belief and freedom, either alone or in community with others and in public or private, to manifest his religion or belief, in worship, teaching, practice and observance.

2. Freedom to manifest one's religion or beliefs shall be subject only to such limitations as are prescribed by law and are necessary in a democratic society in the interests of public safety, for the protection of public order, health or morals, or for the protection of the rights and freedoms of others.

Article 10 – Freedom of expression

1. Everyone has the right to freedom of expression. This right shall include freedom to hold opinions and to receive and impart information and ideas without interference by public

authority and regardless of frontiers. This article shall not prevent States from requiring the licensing of broadcasting, television or cinema enterprises.

The exercise of these freedoms, since it carries with it duties and responsibilities, may be subject to such formalities, conditions, restrictions or penalties as are prescribed by law and are necessary in a democratic society, in the interests of national security, territorial integrity or public safety, for the prevention of disorder or crime, for the protection of health or morals, for the protection of the reputation or rights of others, for preventing the disclosure of information received in confidence, or for maintaining the authority and impartiality of the judiciary.

Article 11 – Freedom of assembly and association

1. Everyone has the right to freedom of peaceful assembly and to freedom of association with others, including the right to form and to join trade unions for the protection of his interests.

2. No restrictions shall be placed on the exercise of these rights other than such as are prescribed by law and are necessary in a democratic society in the interests of national security or public safety, for the prevention of disorder or crime, for the protection of health or morals or for the protection of the rights and freedoms of others. This article shall not prevent the imposition of lawful restrictions on the exercise of these rights by members of the armed forces, of the police or of the administration of the State.

Article 12 – Right to marry

Men and women of marriageable age have the right to marry and to found a family, according to the national laws governing the exercise of this right.

Article 13 – Right to an effective remedy

Everyone whose rights and freedoms as set forth in this Convention are violated shall have an effective remedy before a national authority notwithstanding that the violation has been committed by persons acting in an official capacity.

Article 14 – Prohibition of discrimination

The enjoyment of the rights and freedoms set forth in this Convention shall be secured without discrimination on any ground such as sex, race, colour, language, religion, political or other opinion, national or social origin, association with a national minority, property, birth or other status.

Article 15 – Derogation in time of emergency

1. In time of war or other public emergency threatening the life of the nation any High Contracting Party may take measures derogating from its obligations under this Convention to the extent strictly required by the exigencies of the situation, provided that such measures are not inconsistent with its other obligations under international law.

2. No derogation from Article 2, except in respect of deaths resulting from lawful acts of war, or from Articles 3, 4 (paragraph 1) and 7 shall be made under this provision.

3. Any High Contracting Party availing itself of this right of derogation shall keep the Secretary General of the Council of Europe fully informed of the measures which it has taken and the reasons therefor. It shall also inform the Secretary General of the Council of Europe when such measures have ceased to operate and the provisions of the Convention are again being fully executed.

Article 16 – Restrictions on political activity of aliens

Nothing in Articles 10, 11 and 14 shall be regarded as preventing the High Contracting Parties from imposing restrictions on the political activity of aliens.

Article 17 – Prohibition of abuse of rights

Nothing in this Convention may be interpreted as implying for any State, group or person any right to engage in any activity or perform any act aimed at the destruction of any of the rights and freedoms set forth herein or at their limitation to a greater extent than is provided for in the Convention.

Article 18 – Limitation on use of restrictions on rights

The restrictions permitted under this Convention to the said rights and freedoms shall not be applied for any purpose other than those for which they have been prescribed.

International
OECD Privacy Guidelines

OECD PRIVACY GUIDELINES (1980)

Summary

On September 23, 1980, the Organization for Economic Cooperation and Development, a group of leading industrial countries concerned with global economic and democratic development, issued guidelines for privacy protection in the transfer of personal information across national borders. These are the Guidelines on the Protection of Privacy and Transborder Flows of Personal Data. The OECD Privacy Guidelines outline an eight-fold path to privacy.

First is the principle of collection limitation. This principle states that there should be limits to the collection of personal data; any such data collected should be obtained by lawful means and with the consent of the data subject, where appropriate. Second is the principle of data quality. This principle embodies the notion that collected data should be relevant to a specific purpose, and be accurate, complete, and up-to-date. Third is the principle of purpose specification; that is, the purpose for collecting data should be settled at the outset. The fourth principle, use limitation, works in tandem with the third. It states that the use of personal data ought be limited to specified purposes, and that data acquired for one purpose ought not be used for others. The fifth principle is security: data must be collected and stored in a way reasonably calculated to prevent its loss, theft, or modification. The sixth principle is openness. There should be a general position of transparency with respect to the practices of handling data. The seventh principle is individual participation: individual should have the right to access, confirm, and demand correction of their personal data. The eighth and last principle is accountability. Those in charge of handling data should be responsible for complying with the principles of the privacy guidelines.

In developing the guidelines, the OECD worked closely with the Council of Europe , which was at that time drafting its own Convention on Privacy. Examination of both the Guidelines and the Convention will show that they have much in common, as well as pointing to the general concern for individual privacy protection that arose in the late 1970s. Since the Guidelines' release, many OECD countries have enacted laws to implement them. In 1985, OECD extended the guidelines to cover transborder data flow. Although the OECD Guidelines are nonbinding on signatories, the eight privacy principles have had a significant impact on the development of privacy law around the globe.

References

OECD, Guidelines on the Protection of Privacy and Transborder Flows of Personal Data (1980)
[http://www.oecd.org/internet/ieconomy/oecdguidelinesontheprotectionofprivacyand transborderflowsofpersonaldata.htm]
OECD, Declaration on Transborder Data Flows (1985)
[http://www.oecd.org/internet/ieconomy/declarationontransborderdataflows.htm]

OECD, Ministerial Declaration on the Protection of Privacy on Global Networks (1998)

[http://acts.oecd.org/Instruments/ShowInstrumentView.aspx?InstrumentID=109&]

OECD RECOMMENDATION CONCERNING AND GUIDELINES GOVERNING THE PROTECTION OF PRIVACY AND TRANSBORDER FLOWS OF PERSONAL DATA RECOMMENDATION OF THE COUNCIL CONCERNING GUIDELINES GOVERNING THE PROTECTION OF PRIVACY AND TRANSBORDER FLOWS OF PERSONAL DATA

The Council, Having regard to articles 1(c), 3(a) and 5(b) of the Convention on the Organisation for Economic Co-operation and Development of 14th December, 1960; Recognising:

that, although national laws and policies may differ, Member countries have a common interest in protecting privacy and individual liberties, and in reconciling fundamental but competing values such as privacy and the free flow of information;

that automatic processing and transborder flows of personal data create new forms of relationships among countries and require the development of compatible rules and practices;

that transborder flows of personal data contribute to economic and social development;

that domestic legislation concerning privacy protection and transborder flows of personal data may hinder such transborder flows;

Determined to advance the free flow of information between Member countries and to avoid the creation of unjustified obstacles to the development of economic and social relations among Member countries;

RECOMMENDS

1. That Member countries take into account in their domestic legislation the principles concerning the protection of privacy and individual liberties set forth in the Guidelines contained in the Annex to this Recommendation which is an integral part thereof;

2. That Member countries endeavour to remove or avoid creating, in the name of privacy protection, unjustified obstacles to transborder flows of personal data;

3. That Member countries co-operate in the implementation of the Guidelines set forth in the Annex;

4. That Member countries agree as soon as possible on specific procedures of consultation and co-operation for the application of these Guidelines.

International
OECD Privacy Guidelines

ANNEX

GUIDELINES GOVERNING THE PROTECTION OF PRIVACY AND TRANSBORDER
FLOWS OF PERSONAL DATA

GENERAL

Definitions

1. For the purposes of these Guidelines:

(a) "data controller" means a party who, according to domestic law, is competent to decide about the contents and use of personal data regardless of whether or not such data are collected, stored, processed or disseminated by that party or by an agent on its behalf;

(b) "personal data" means any information relating to an identified or identifiable individual (data subject);

(c) "transborder flows of personal data" means movements of personal data across national borders.

Scope of Guidelines

2. These Guidelines apply to personal data, whether in the public or private sectors, which, because of the manner in which they are processed, or because of their nature or the context in which they are used, pose a danger to privacy and individual liberties.

3. These Guidelines should not be interpreted as preventing:

(a) the application, to different categories of personal data, of different protective measures depending upon their nature and the context in which they are collected, stored, processed or disseminated;

(b) the exclusion from the application of the Guidelines of personal data which obviously do not contain any risk to privacy and individual liberties; or

(c) the application of the Guidelines only to automatic processing of personal data.

4. Exceptions to the Principles contained in Parts Two and Three of these Guidelines, including those relating to national sovereignty, national security and public policy ("ordre public"), should be:

(a) as few as possible, and

(b) made known to the public.

5. In the particular case of Federal countries the observance of these Guidelines may be affected by the division of powers in the Federation.

6. These Guidelines should be regarded as minimum standards which are capable of being supplemented by additional measures for the protection of privacy and individual liberties.

BASIC PRINCIPLES OF NATIONAL APPLICATION

Collection Limitation Principle

7. There should be limits to the collection of personal data and any such data should be obtained by lawful and fair means and, where appropriate, with the knowledge or consent of the data subject:

Data Quality Principle

8. Personal data should be relevant to the purposes for which they are to be used, and, to the extent necessary for those purposes, should be accurate, complete and kept up-to-date.

Purpose Specification Principle

9. The purposes for which personal data are collected should be specified not later than at the time of data collection and the subsequent use limited to the fulfillment of those purposes or such others as are not incompatible with those purposes and as are specified on each occasion of change of purpose.

Use Limitation Principle

10. Personal data should not be disclosed, made available or otherwise used for purposes other than those specified in accordance with Paragraph 9 except: (a) with the consent of the data subject; or (b) by the authority of law.

Security Safeguards Principle

11. Personal data should be protected by reasonable security safeguards against such risks as loss or unauthorised access, destruction, use, modification or disclosure of data.

Openness Principle

12. There should be a general policy of openness about developments, practices and policies with respect to personal data. Means should be readily available of establishing the existence and nature of personal data, and the main purposes of their use, as well as the identity and usual residence of the data controller.

Individual Participation Principle

13. An individual should have the right:

(a) to obtain from a data controller, or otherwise, confirmation of whether or not the data controller has data relating to him;

(b) to have communicated to him, data relating to him (i) within a reasonable time; (ii) at a charge, if any, that is not excessive; (iii) in a reasonable manner; and (iv) in a form that is readily intelligible to him;

(c) to be given reasons if a request made under subparagraphs (a) and (b) is denied, and to be able to challenge such denial; and

(d) to challenge data relating to him and, if the challenge is successful, to have the data erased, rectified, completed or amended.

Accountability Principle

14. A data controller should be accountable for complying with measures which give effect to the principles stated above.

BASIC PRINCIPLES OF INTERNATIONAL APPLICATION: FREE FLOW AND LEGITIMATE RESTRICTIONS

15. Member countries should take into consideration the implications for other Member countries of domestic processing and re-export of personal data.

16. Member countries should take all reasonable and appropriate steps to ensure that transborder flows of personal data, including transit through a Member country, are uninterrupted and secure.

17. A Member country should refrain from restricting transborder flows of personal data between itself and another Member country except where the latter does not yet substantially observe these Guidelines or where the re-export of such data would circumvent its domestic privacy legislation. A Member country may also impose restrictions in respect of certain categories of personal data for which its domestic privacy legislation includes specific regulations in view of the nature of those data and for which the other Member country provides no equivalent protection.

18. Member countries should avoid developing laws, policies and practices in the name of the protection of privacy and individual liberties, which would create obstacles to transborder flows of personal data that would exceed requirements for such protection.

NATIONAL IMPLEMENTATION

19. In implementing domestically the principles set forth in Parts Two and Three, Member countries should establish legal, administrative or other procedures or institutions for the

protection of privacy and individual liberties in respect of personal data. Member countries should in particular endeavour to:

(a) adopt appropriate domestic legislation;

(b) encourage and support self-regulation, whether in the form of codes of conduct or otherwise;

(c) provide for reasonable means for individuals to exercise their rights;

(d) provide for adequate sanctions and remedies in case of failures to comply with measures which implement the principles set forth in Parts Two and Three; and

(e) ensure that there is no unfair discrimination against data subjects.

INTERNATIONAL CO-OPERATION

20. Member countries should, where requested, make known to other Member countries details of the observance of the principles set forth in these Guidelines. Member countries should also ensure that procedures for transborder flows of personal data and for the protection of privacy and individual liberties are simple and compatible with those of other Member countries which comply with these Guidelines.

21. Member countries should establish procedures to facilitate: (i) information exchange related to these Guidelines, and (ii) mutual assistance in the procedural and investigative matters involved.

22. Member countries should work towards the development of principles, domestic and international, to govern the applicable law in the case of transborder flows of personal data.

APPENDIX

EXPLANATORY MEMORANDUM

Introduction

A feature of OECD Member countries over the past decade has been the development of laws for the protection of privacy. These laws have tended to assume different forms in different countries, and in many countries are still in the process of being developed. The disparities in legislation may create obstacles to the free flow of information between countries. Such flows have greatly increased in recent years and are bound to continue to grow as a result of the introduction of new computer and communication technology.

The OECD, which had been active in this field for some years past, decided to address the problems of diverging national legislation and in 1978 instructed a Group of Experts to develop Guidelines on basic rules governing the transborder flow and the protection of personal data and privacy, in order to facilitate the harmonization of national legislation. The Group has now completed its work.

International
OECD Privacy Guidelines

The Guidelines are broad in nature and reflect the debate and legislative work which has been going on for several years in Member countries. The Expert Group which prepared the Guidelines has considered it essential to issue an accompanying Explanatory Memorandum. Its purpose is to explain and elaborate the Guidelines and the basic problems of protection of privacy and individual liberties. It draws attention to key issues that have emerged in the discussion of the Guidelines and spells out the reasons for the choice of particular solutions.

The first part of the Memorandum provides general background information on the area of concern as perceived in Member countries. It explains the need for international action and summarises the work carried out so far by the OECD and certain other international organisations. It concludes with a list of the main problems encountered by the Expert Group in its work.

Part Two has two subsections. The first contains comments on certain general features of the Guidelines, the second detailed comments on individual paragraphs.

This Memorandum is an information document, prepared to explain and describe generally the work of the Expert Group. It is subordinate to the Guidelines themselves. It cannot vary the meaning of the Guidelines but is supplied to help in their interpretation and application.

I GENERAL BACKGROUND

The Problems

1. The 1970s may be described as a period of intensified investigative and legislative activities concerning the protection of privacy with respect to the collection and use of personal data. Numerous official reports show that the problems are taken seriously at the political level and at the same time that the task of balancing opposing interests is delicate and unlikely to be accomplished once and for all. Public interest has tended to focus on the risks and implications associated with the computerised processing of personal data and some countries have chosen to enact statutes which deal exclusively with computers and computer-supported activities. Other countries have preferred a more general approach to privacy protection issues irrespective of the particular data processing technology involved.

2. The remedies under discussion are principally safeguards for the individual which will prevent an invasion of privacy in the classical sense, i.e. abuse or disclosure of intimate personal data; but other, more or less closely related needs for protection have become apparent. Obligations of record-keepers to inform the general public about activities concerned with the processing of data, and rights of data subjects to have data relating to them supplemented or amended, are two random examples. Generally speaking, there has been a tendency to broaden the traditional concept of privacy ("the right to be left alone") and to identify a more complex synthesis of interests which can perhaps more correctly be termed privacy and individual liberties.

3. As far as the legal problems of automatic data processing (ADP) are concerned, the protection of privacy and individual liberties constitutes perhaps the most widely debated

aspect. Among the reasons for such widespread concern are the ubiquitous use of computers for the processing of personal data, vastly expanded possibilities of storing, comparing, linking, selecting and accessing personal data, and the combination of computers and telecommunications technology which may place personal data simultaneously at the disposal of thousands of users at geographically dispersed locations and enables the pooling of data and the creation of complex national and international data networks. Certain problems require particularly urgent attention, e.g. those relating to emerging international data networks, and to the need of balancing competing interests of privacy on the one hand and freedom of information on the other, in order to allow a full exploitation of the potentialities of modern data processing technologies in so far as this is desirable.

Activities at national level

4. Of the OECD Member countries more than one-third have so far enacted one or several laws which, among other things, are intended to protect individuals against abuse of data relating to them and to give them the right of access to data with a view to checking their accuracy and appropriateness. In federal states, laws of this kind may be found both at the national and at the state or provincial level. Such laws are referred to differently in different countries. Thus, it is common practice in continental Europe to talk about "data laws" or "data protection laws" (lois sur la protection des donneées), whereas in English speaking countries they are usually known as "privacy protection laws". Most of the statutes were enacted after 1973 and the present period may be described as one of continued or even widened legislative activity. Countries which already have statutes in force are turning to new areas of protection or are engaged in revising or complementing existing statutes. Several other countries are entering the area and have bills pending or are studying the problems with a view to preparing legislation. These national efforts, and not least the extensive reports and research papers prepared by public committees or similar bodies, help to clarify the problems and the advantages and implications of various solutions. At the present stage, they provide a solid basis for international action.

5. The approaches to protection of privacy and individual liberties adopted by the various countries have many common features. Thus, it is possible to identify certain basic interests or values which are commonly considered to be elementary components of the area of protection. Some core principles of this type are: setting limits to the collection of personal data in accordance with the objectives of the data collector and similar criteria; restricting the usage of data to conform with openly specified purposes; creating facilities for individuals to learn of the existence and contents of data and have data corrected; and the identification of parties who are responsible for compliance with the relevant privacy protection rules and decisions. Generally speaking, statutes to protect privacy and individual liberties in relation to personal data attempt to cover the successive stages of the cycle, beginning with the initial collection of data and ending with erasure or similar measures, and to ensure to the greatest possible extent individual awareness, participation and control.

6. Differences between national approaches as apparent at present in laws, bills or proposals for legislation, refer to aspects such as the scope of legislation, the emphasis placed on different elements of protection, the detailed implementation of the broad principles indicated above, and the machinery of enforcement. Thus, opinions vary with respect to licensing requirements and control mechanisms in the form of special supervisory bodies ("data inspection authorities"). Categories of sensitive data are defined differently, the means of ensuring openness and individual participation vary, to give just a few instances. Of course, existing traditional differences between legal systems are a cause of disparity, both with respect to legislative approaches and the detailed formulation of the regulatory framework for personal data protection.

International aspects of privacy and data banks

7. For a number of reasons the problems of developing safeguards for the individual in respect of the handling of personal data cannot be solved exclusively at the national level. The tremendous increase in data flows across national borders and the creation of international data banks (collections of data intended for retrieval and other purposes) have highlighted the need for concerted national action and at the same time support arguments in favour of free flows of information which must often be balanced against requirements for data protection and for restrictions on their collection, processing and dissemination.

8. One basic concern at the international level is for consensus on the fundamental principles on which protection of the individual must be based. Such a consensus would obviate or diminish reasons for regulating the export of data and facilitate resolving problems of conflict of laws. Moreover, it could constitute a first step towards the development of more detailed, binding international agreements.

9. There are other reasons why the regulation of the processing of personal data should be considered in an international context: the principles involved concern values which many nations are anxious to uphold and see generally accepted; they may help to save costs in international data traffic; countries have a common interest in preventing the creation of locations where national regulations on data processing can easily be circumvented; indeed, in view of the international mobility of people, goods and commercial and scientific activities, commonly accepted practices with regard to the processing of data may be advantageous even where no transborder data traffic is directly involved.

Relevant international activities

10. There are several international agreements on various aspects of telecommunications which, while facilitating relations and co-operation between countries, recognise the sovereign right of each country to regulate its own telecommunications (The International Telecommunications Convention of 1973). The protection of computer data and programmes has been investigated by, among others, the World Intellectual Property Organisation which

has developed draft model provisions for national laws on the protection of computer software. Specialised agreements aiming at informational co-operation may be found in a number of areas, such as law enforcement, health services, statistics and judicial services (e.g. with regard to the taking of evidence).

11. A number of international agreements deal in a more general way with the issues which are at present under discussion, viz. the protection of privacy and the free dissemination of information. They include the European Convention on Human Rights of 4th November, 1950 and the International Covenant on Civil and Political Rights (United Nations, 19th December, 1966).

12. However, in view of the inadequacy of existing international instruments relating to the processing of data and individual rights, a number of international organisations have carried out detailed studies of the problems involved in order to find more satisfactory solutions.

13. In 1973 and 1974 the Committee of Ministers of the Council of Europe adopted two resolutions concerning the protection of the privacy of individuals vis-á-vis electronic data banks in the private and public sectors respectively. Both resolutions recommend that the governments of the Member states of the Council of Europe take steps to give effect to a number of basic principles of protection relating to the obtaining of data, the quality of data, and the rights of individuals to be informed about data and data processing activities.

14. Subsequently the Council of Europe, on the instructions of its Committee of Ministers, began to prepare an international Convention on privacy protection in relation to data processing abroad and transfrontier data processing. It also initiated work on model regulations for medical data banks and rules of conduct for data processing professionals. According to present plans, work on the Convention is to be completed before 30th June, 1980. The draft Convention seeks to establish basic principles of data protection to be enforced by Member countries, to reduce restrictions on transborder data flows between the Contracting Parties on the basis of reciprocity, to bring about co- operation between national data protection authorities, and to set up a Consultative Committee for the application and continuing development of the convention.

15. The European Community has carried out studies concerning the problems of harmonization of national legislations within the Community in relation to transborder data flows and possible distortions of competition, the problems of data security and confidentiality, and the nature of transborder data flows. A sub-committee of the European Parliament held a public hearing on data processing and the rights of the individual in early 1978. Its work has resulted in a report to the European Parliament in spring 1979. The report, which was adopted by the European Parliament in May 1979, contains a resolution on the protection of the rights of the individual in the face of technical developments in data processing.

Activities of the OECD

International
OECD Privacy Guidelines

16. The OECD programme on transborder data flows derives from computer utilisation studies in the public sector which were initiated in 1969. A Group of Experts, the Data Bank Panel, analysed and studied different aspects of the privacy issue, e.g. in relation to digital information, public administration, transborder data flows, and policy implications in general. In order to obtain evidence on the nature of the problems, the Data Bank Panel organised a Symposium in Vienna in 1977 which provided opinions and experience from a diversity of interests, including government, industry, users of international data communication networks, processing services, and interested intergovernmental organisations.

17. A number of guiding principles were elaborated in a general framework for possible international action. These principles recognised (a) the need for generally continuous and uninterrupted flows of information between countries, (b) the legitimate interests of countries in preventing transfers of data which are dangerous to their security or contrary to their laws on public order and decency or which violate the rights of their citizens, (c) the economic value of information and the importance of protecting "data trade" by accepted rules of fair competition, (d) the needs for security safeguards to minimise violations of proprietary data and misuse of personal information, and (e) the significance of a commitment of countries to a set of core principles for the protection of personal information.

18. Early in 1978 a new ad hoc Group of Experts on Transborder Data Barriers and Privacy Protection was set up within the OECD which was instructed to develop guidelines on basic rules governing the transborder flow and the protection of personal data and privacy, in order to facilitate a harmonization of national legislations, without this precluding at a later date the establishment of an international Convention. This work was to be carried out in close co-operation with the Council of Europe and the European Community and to be completed by 1st July, 1979.

19. The Expert Group, under the chairmanship of the Honourable Mr. Justice Kirby, Australia, and with the assistance of Dr. Peter Seipel (Consultant), produced several drafts and discussed various reports containing, for instance, comparative analyses of different approaches to legislation in this field. It was particularly concerned with a number of key issues set out below.

    (a) The specific, sensitive facts issue The question arises as to whether the Guidelines should be of a general nature or whether they should be structured to deal with different types of data or activities (e.g. credit reporting). Indeed, it is probably not possible to identify a set of data which are universally regarded as being sensitive.

    (b) The ADP issue The argument that ADP is the main cause for concern is doubtful and, indeed, contested. (c) The legal persons issue Some, but by no means all, national laws protect data relating to legal persons in a similar manner to data related to physical persons.

    (d) The remedies and sanctions issue The approaches to control mechanisms vary considerably: for instance, schemes involving supervision and licensing by specially constituted authorities might be compared to schemes involving voluntary compliance by record-keepers and reliance on traditional judicial remedies in the Courts.

(e) The basic machinery or implementation issue The choice of core principles and their appropriate level of detail presents difficulties. For instance, the extent to which data security questions (protection of data against unauthorised interference, fire, and similar occurrences) should be regarded as part of the privacy protection complex is debatable; opinions may differ with regard to time limits for the retention, or requirements for the erasure, of data, and the same applies to requirements that data be relevant to specific purposes. In particular, it is difficult to draw a clear dividing line between the level of basic principles or objectives and lower level "machinery" questions which should be left to domestic implementation.

(f) The choice of law issue The problems of choice of jurisdiction, choice of applicable law and recognition of foreign judgements have proved to be complex in the context of transborder data flows. The question arises, however, whether and to what extent it should be attempted at this stage to put forward solutions in Guidelines of a non-binding nature.

(g) The exceptions issue Similarly, opinions may vary on the question of exceptions. Are they required at all? If so, should particular categories of exceptions be provided for or should general limits to exceptions be formulated?

(h) The bias issue Finally, there is an inherent conflict between the protection and the free transborder flow of personal data. Emphasis may be placed on one or the other, and interests in privacy protection may be difficult to distinguish from other interests relating to trade, culture, national sovereignty, and so forth.

20. During its work the Expert Group has maintained close contacts with corresponding organs of the Council of Europe. Every effort has been made to avoid unnecessary differences between the texts produced by the two organisations; thus, the set of basic principles of protection are in many respects similar. On the other hand, a number of differences do occur. To begin with, the OECD Guidelines are not legally binding, whereas the Council of Europe has produced a convention which, if adopted, would be legally binding among those countries which ratify it. This in turn means that the question of exceptions has been dealt with in greater detail by the Council of Europe. As for the area of application, the Council of Europe Convention deals primarily with the automatic processing of personal data whereas the OECD Guidelines apply to personal data which involve dangers to privacy and individual liberties, irrespective of the methods and machinery used in their handling. At the level of details, the basic principles of protection proposed by the two organisations are not identical and the terminology employed differs in some respects. The institutional framework for continued co-operation is treated in greater detail in the Council of Europe Convention than in the OECD Guidelines.

21. The Expert Group also maintained co-operation with the Commission of the European Communities as required by its mandate.

International
OECD Privacy Guidelines

II. THE GUIDELINES

A. Purpose and Scope
General

22. The Preamble of the Recommendation expresses the basic concerns calling for action. The Recommendation affirms the commitment of Member countries to protect privacy and individual liberties and to respect the transborder flows of personal data.

23. The Guidelines set out in the Annex to the Recommendation consist of five parts. Part One contains a number of definitions and specifies the scope of the Guidelines, indicating that they represent minimum standards. Part Two contains eight basic principles (Paragraphs 7-14) relating to the protection of privacy and individual liberties at the national level. Part Three deals with principles of international application, i.e. principles which are chiefly concerned with relationships between Member countries.

24. Part Four deals, in general terms, with means of implementing the basic principles set out in the preceding parts and specifies that these principles should be applied in a non-discriminatory manner. Part Five concerns matters of mutual assistance between Member countries, chiefly through the exchange of information and by avoiding incompatible national procedures for the protection of personal data. It concludes with a reference to issues of applicable law which may arise when flows of personal data involve several Member countries.

Objectives

25. The core of the Guidelines consists of the principles set out in Part Two of the Annex. It is recommended to Member countries that they adhere to these principles with a view to

    (a) achieving acceptance by Member countries of certain minimum standards of protection of privacy and individual liberties with regard to personal data;

    (b) reducing differences between relevant domestic rules and practices of Member countries to a minimum;

    (c) ensuring that in protecting personal data they take into consideration the interests of other Member countries and the need to avoid undue interference with flows of personal data between Member countries; and

    (d) eliminating, as far as possible, reasons which might induce Member countries to restrict transborder flows of personal data because of the possible risks associated with such flows. As stated in the Preamble, two essential basic values are involved: the protection of privacy and individual liberties and the advancement of free flows of personal data. The Guidelines attempt to balance the two values against one another; while accepting certain restrictions to free transborder flows of personal data, they seek to reduce the need for such restrictions and thereby strengthen the notion of free information flows between countries.

26. Finally, Parts Four and Five of the Guidelines contain principles seeking to ensure:
    (a) effective national measures for the protection of privacy and individual liberties;
    (b) avoidance of practices involving unfair discrimination between individuals; and
    (c) bases for continued international co-operation and compatible procedures in any regulation of transborder flows of personal data.

Level of detail

27. The level of detail of the Guidelines varies depending upon two main factors, viz. (a) the extent of consensus reached concerning the solutions put forward, and (b) available knowledge and experience pointing to solutions to be adopted at this stage. For instance, the Individual Participation Principle (Paragraph 13) deals specifically with various aspects of protecting an individual's interest, whereas the provision on problems of choice of law and related matters (Paragraph 22) merely states a starting-point for a gradual development of detailed common approaches and international agreements. On the whole, the Guidelines constitute a general framework for concerted actions by Member countries: objectives put forward by the Guidelines may be pursued in different ways, depending on the legal instruments and strategies preferred by Member countries for their implementation. To conclude, there is a need for a continuing review of the Guidelines, both by Member countries and the OECD. As and when experience is gained, it may prove desirable to develop and adjust the Guidelines accordingly.

Non-Member countries

28. The Recommendation is addressed to Member countries and this is reflected in several provisions which are expressly restricted to relationships between Member countries (see Paragraphs 15, 17 and 20 of the Guidelines). Widespread recognition of the Guidelines is, however, desirable and nothing in them should be interpreted as preventing the application of relevant provisions by Member countries to non-Member countries. In view of the increase in transborder data flows and the need to ensure concerted solutions, efforts will be made to bring the Guidelines to the attention of non-Member countries and appropriate international organisations.

The broader regulatory perspective

29. It has been pointed out earlier that the protection of privacy and individual liberties constitutes one of many overlapping legal aspects involved in the processing of data. The Guidelines constitute a new instrument, in addition to other, related international instruments governing such issues as human rights, telecommunications, international trade, copyright, and various information services. If the need arises, the principles set out in the Guidelines could be further developed within the framework of activities undertaken by the OECD in the area of information, computer and communications policies.

International
OECD Privacy Guidelines

30. Some Member countries have emphasized the advantages of a binding international Convention with a broad coverage. The Mandate of the Expert Group required it to develop guidelines on basic rules governing the transborder flow and the protection of personal data and privacy, without this precluding at a later stage the establishment of an international Convention of a binding nature. The Guidelines could serve as a starting-point for the development of an international Convention when the need arises.

Legal persons, groups and similar entities

31. Some countries consider that the protection required for data relating to individuals may be similar in nature to the protection required for data relating to business enterprises, associations and groups which may or may not possess legal personality. The experience of a number of countries also shows that it is difficult to define clearly the dividing line between personal and non-personal data. For example, data relating to a small company may also concern its owner or owners and provide personal information of a more or less sensitive nature. In such instances it may be advisable to extend to corporate entities the protection offered by rules relating primarily to personal data.

32. Similarly, it is debatable to what extent people belonging to a particular group (e.g. mentally disabled persons, immigrants, ethnic minorities) need additional protection against the dissemination of information relating to that group.

33. On the other hand, the Guidelines reflect the view that the notions of individual integrity and privacy are in many respects particular and should not be treated in the same way as the integrity of a group of persons, or corporate security and confidentiality. The needs for protection are different and so are the policy frameworks within which solutions have to be formulated and interests balanced against one another. Some members of the Expert Group suggested that the possibility of extending the Guidelines to legal persons (corporations, associations) should be provided for. This suggestion has not secured a sufficient consensus. The scope of the Guidelines is therefore confined to data relating to individuals and it is left to Member countries to draw dividing lines and decide policies with regard to corporations, groups and similar bodies (cf. paragraph 49 below).

Automated and non-automated data

34. In the past, OECD activities in privacy protection and related fields have focused on automatic data processing and computer networks. The Expert Group has devoted special attention to the issue of whether or not these Guidelines should be restricted to the automatic and computer-assisted processing of personal data. Such an approach may be defended on a number of grounds, such as the particular dangers to individual privacy raised by automation and computerised data banks, and increasing dominance of automatic data processing methods, especially in transborder data flows, and the particular framework of information,

computer and communications policies within which the Expert Group has set out to fulfil its Mandate.

35. On the other hand, it is the conclusion of the Expert Group that limiting the Guidelines to the automatic processing of personal data would have considerable drawbacks. To begin with, it is difficult, at the level of definitions, to make a clear distinction between the automatic and non- automatic handling of data. There are, for instance, "mixed" data processing systems, and there are stages in the processing of data which may or may not lead to automatic treatment. These difficulties tend to be further complicated by ongoing technological developments, such as the introduction of advanced semi-automated methods based on the use of microfilm, or microcomputers which may increasingly be used for private purposes that are both harmless and impossible to control. Moreover, by concentrating exclusively on computers the Guidelines might lead to inconsistency and lacunae, and opportunities for record-keepers to circumvent rules which implement the Guidelines by using non- automatic means for purposes which may be offensive.

36. Because of the difficulties mentioned, the Guidelines do not put forward a definition of "automatic data processing" although the concept is referred to in the preamble and in paragraph 3 of the Annex. It may be assumed that guidance for the interpretation of the concept can be obtained from sources such as standard technical vocabularies.

37. Above all, the principles for the protection of privacy and individual liberties expressed in the Guidelines are valid for the processing of data in general, irrespective of the particular technology employed. The Guidelines therefore apply to personal data in general or, more precisely, to personal data which, because of the manner in which they are processed, or because of their nature or context, pose a danger to privacy and individual liberties.

38. It should be noted, however, that the Guidelines do not constitute a set of general privacy protection principles; invasions of privacy by, for instance, candid photography, physical maltreatment, or defamation are outside their scope unless such acts are in one way or another associated with the handling of personal data. Thus, the Guidelines deal with the building-up and use of aggregates of data which are organised for retrieval, decision-making, research, surveys and similar purposes. It should be emphasized that the Guidelines are neutral with regard to the particular technology used; automatic methods are only one of the problems raised in the Guidelines although, particularly in the context of transborder data flows, this is clearly an important one.

B. Detailed Comments
General

39. The comments which follow relate to the actual Guidelines set out in the Annex to the Recommendation. They seek to clarify the debate in the Expert Group.

Paragraph 1: Definitions

40. The list of definitions has been kept short. The term "data controller" is of vital importance. It attempts to define a subject who, under domestic law, should carry ultimate

responsibility for activities concerned with the processing of personal data. As defined, the data controller is a party who is legally competent to decide about the contents and use of data, regardless of whether or not such data are collected, stored, processed or disseminated by that party or by an agent on its behalf. The data controller may be a legal or natural person, public authority, agency or any other body. The definition excludes at least four categories which may be involved in the processing of data, viz. (a) licensing authorities and similar bodies which exist in some Member countries and which authorise the processing of data but are not entitled to decide (in the proper sense of the word) what activities should be carried out and for what purposes; (b) data processing service bureaux which carry out data processing on behalf of others; (c) telecommunications authorities and similar bodies which act as mere conduits; and (d) "dependent users" who may have access to data but who are not authorised to decide what data should be stored, who should be able to use them, etc. In implementing the Guidelines, countries may develop more complex schemes of levels and types of responsibilities. Paragraphs 14 and 19 of the Guidelines provide a basis for efforts in this direction.

41. The terms "personal data" and "data subject" serve to underscore that the Guidelines are concerned with physical persons. The precise dividing line between personal data in the sense of information relating to identified or identifiable individuals and anonymous data may be difficult to draw and must be left to the regulation of each Member country. In principle, personal data convey information which by direct (e.g. a civil registration number) or indirect linkages (e.g. an address) may be connected to a particular physical person.

42. The term "transborder flows of personal data" restricts the application of certain provisions of the Guidelines to international data flows and consequently omits the data flow problems particular to federal states. The movements of data will often take place through electronic transmission but other means of data communication may also be involved. Transborder flows as understood in the Guidelines includes the transmission of data by satellite.

Paragraph 2: Area of application

43. The Section of the Memorandum dealing with the scope and purpose of the Guidelines introduces the issue of their application to the automatic as against non-automatic processing of personal data. Paragraph 2 of the Guidelines, which deals with this problem, is based on two limiting criteria. The first is associated with the concept of personal data: the Guidelines apply to data which can be related to identified or identifiable individuals. Collections of data which do not offer such possibilities (collections of statistical data in anonymous form) are not included. The second criterion is more complex and relates to a specific risk element of a factual nature, viz. that data pose a danger to privacy and individual liberties. Such dangers can arise because of the use of automated data processing methods (the manner in which data are processed), but a broad variety of other possible risk sources is implied. Thus, data which are in themselves simple and factual may be used in a context where they become offensive to a data subject. On the other hand, the risks as expressed in Paragraph 2 of the Guidelines are

intended to exclude data collections of an obviously innocent nature (e.g. personal notebooks). The dangers referred to in Paragraph 2 of the Guidelines should relate to privacy and individual liberties. However, the protected interests are broad (cf. paragraph 2 above) and may be viewed differently by different Member countries and at different times. A delimitation as far as the Guidelines are concerned and a common basic approach are provided by the principles set out in Paragraphs 7 to 13.

44. As explained in Paragraph 2 of the Guidelines, they are intended to cover both the private and the public sector. These notions may be defined differently by different Member countries.

Paragraph 3: Different degrees of sensitivity

45. The Guidelines should not be applied in a mechanistic way irrespective of the kind of data and processing activities involved. The framework provided by the basic principles in Part Two of the Guidelines permits Member countries to exercise their discretion with respect to the degree of stringency with which the Guidelines are to be implemented, and with respect to the scope of the measures to be taken. In particular, Paragraph 3(b) provides for many "trivial" cases of collection and use of personal data (cf. above) to be completely excluded from the application of the Guidelines. Obviously this does not mean that Paragraph 3 should be regarded as a vehicle for demolishing the standards set up by the Guidelines. But, generally speaking, the Guidelines do not presuppose their uniform implementation by Member countries with respect to details. For instance, different traditions and different attitudes by the general public have to be taken into account. Thus, in one country universal personal identifiers may be considered both harmless and useful whereas in another country they may be regarded as highly sensitive and their use restricted or even forbidden. In one country, protection may be afforded to data relating to groups and similar entities whereas such protection is completely non-existent in another country, and so forth. To conclude, some Member countries may find it appropriate to restrict the application of the Guidelines to the automatic processing of personal data. Paragraph 3(c) provides for such a limitation.

Paragraph 4: Exceptions to the Guidelines

46. To provide formally for exceptions in Guidelines which are part of a non- binding Recommendation may seem superfluous. However, the Expert Group has found it appropriate to include a provision dealing with this subject and stating that two general criteria ought to guide national policies in limiting the application of the Guidelines: exceptions should be as few as possible, and they should be made known to the public (e.g. through publication in an official government gazette). General knowledge of the existence of certain data or files would be sufficient to meet the second criterion, although details concerning particular data etc. may have to be kept secret. The formula provided in Paragraph 4 is intended to cover many different kinds of concerns and limiting factors, as it was obviously not possible to provide an exhaustive list of exceptions - hence the wording that they include national sovereignty, national security and public policy ("ordre public"). Another overriding national concern would be, for instance, the financial interests of the State ("credit public"). Moreover,

Paragraph 4 allows for different ways of implementing the Guidelines: it should be borne in mind that Member countries are at present at different stages of development with respect to privacy protection rules and institutions and will probably proceed at different paces, applying different strategies, e.g. the regulation of certain types of data or activities as compared to regulation of a general nature ("omnibus approach").

47. The Expert Group recognised that Member countries might apply the Guidelines differentially to different kinds of personal data. There may be differences in the permissible frequency of inspection, in ways of balancing competing interests such as the confidentiality of medical records versus the individual's right to inspect data relating to him, and so forth. Some examples of areas which may be treated differently are credit reporting, criminal investigation and banking. Member countries may also choose different solutions with respect to exceptions associated with, for example, research and statistics. An exhaustive enumeration of all such situations and concerns is neither required nor possible. Some of the subsequent paragraphs of the Guidelines and the comments referring to them provide further clarification of the area of application of the Guidelines and of the closely related issues of balancing opposing interests (compare with Paragraphs 7, 8, 17 and 18 of the Guidelines). To summarise, the Expert Group has assumed that exceptions will be limited to those which are necessary in a democratic society.

Paragraph 5: Federal countries

48. In Federal countries, the application of the Guidelines is subject to various constitutional limitations. Paragraph 5, accordingly, serves to underscore that no commitments exist to apply the Guidelines beyond the limits of constitutional competence.

Paragraph 6: Minimum standards

49. First, Paragraph 6 describes the Guidelines as minimum standards for adoption in domestic legislation. Secondly, and in consequence, it has been agreed that the Guidelines are capable of being supplemented by additional measures for the protection of privacy and individual liberties at the national as well as the international level.

Paragraph 7: Collection Limitation Principle

50. As an introductory comment on the principles set out in Paragraphs 7 to 14 of the Guidelines it should be pointed out that these principles are interrelated and partly overlapping. Thus, the distinctions between different activities and stages involved in the processing of data which are assumed in the principles, are somewhat artificial and it is essential that the principles are treated together and studied as a whole. Paragraph 7 deals with two issues, viz. (a) limits to the collection of data which, because of the manner in which they are to be processed, their nature, the context in which they are to be used or other circumstances, are regarded as specially sensitive; and (b) requirements concerning data collection methods. Different views are frequently put forward with respect to the first issue. It could be argued that it is both possible and desirable to enumerate types or categories of data which are per se sensitive and the collection of which should be restricted or even prohibited. There are precedents in European legislation to this effect (race, religious beliefs,

criminal records, for instance). On the other hand, it may be held that no data are intrinsically "private" or "sensitive" but may become so in view of their context and use. This view is reflected, for example, in the privacy legislation of the United States.

51. The Expert Group has discussed a number of sensitivity criteria, such as the risk of discrimination, but has not found it possible to define any set of data which are universally regarded as sensitive. Consequently, Paragraph 7 merely contains a general statement that there should be limits to the collection of personal data. For one thing, this represents an affirmative recommendation to lawmakers to decide on limits which would put an end to the indiscriminate collection of personal data. The nature of the limits is not spelt out but it is understood that the limits may relate to:

- data quality aspects (i.e. that it should be possible to derive information of sufficiently high quality from the data collected, that data should be collected in a proper information framework, etc.);
- limits associated with the purpose of the processing of data (i.e. that only certain categories of data ought to be collected and, possibly, that data collection should be restricted to the minimum necessary to fulfil the specified purpose);
- "earmarking" of specially sensitive data according to traditions and attitudes in each Member country;
- limits to data collection activities of certain data controllers;
- civil rights concerns.

52. The second part of Paragraph 7 (data collection methods) is directed against practices which involve, for instance, the use of hidden data registration devices such as tape recorders, or deceiving data subjects to make them supply information. The knowledge or consent of the data subject is as a rule essential, knowledge being the minimum requirement. On the other hand, consent cannot always be imposed, for practical reasons. In addition, Paragraph 7 contains a reminder ("where appropriate") that there are situations where for practical or policy reasons the data subject's knowledge or consent cannot be considered necessary. Criminal investigation activities and the routine up-dating of mailing lists may be mentioned as examples. Finally, Paragraph 7 does not exclude the possibility of a data subject being represented by another party, for instance in the case of minors, mentally disabled persons, etc.

Paragraph 8: Data Quality Principle

53. Requirements that data be relevant can be viewed in different ways. In fact, some members of the Expert Group hesitated as to whether such requirements actually fitted into the framework of privacy protection. The conclusion of the Group was to the effect, however, that data should be related to the purpose for which they are to be used. For instance, data concerning opinions may easily be misleading if they are used for purposes to which they bear no relation, and the same is true of evaluative data. Paragraph 8 also deals with accuracy, completeness and up-to-dateness which are all important elements of the data quality concept. The requirements in this respect are linked to the purposes of data, i.e. they are not intended to

be more far- reaching than is necessary for the purposes for which the data are used. Thus, historical data may often have to be collected or retained; cases in point are social research, involving so-called longitudinal studies of developments in society, historical research, and the activities of archives. The "purpose test" will often involve the problem of whether or not harm can be caused to data subjects because of lack of accuracy, completeness and up-dating.

Paragraph 9: Purpose Specification Principle

54. The Purpose Specification Principle is closely associated with the two surrounding principles, i.e. the Data Quality Principle and the Use Limitation Principle. Basically, Paragraph 9 implies that before, and in any case not later than at the time of data collection it should be possible to identify the purposes for which these data are to be used, and that later changes of purposes should likewise be specified. Such specification of purposes can be made in a number of alternative or complementary ways, e.g. by public declarations, information to data subjects, legislation, administrative decrees, and licences provided by supervisory bodies. According to Paragraphs 9 and 10, new purposes should not be introduced arbitrarily; freedom to make changes should imply compatibility with the original purposes. Finally, when data no longer serve a purpose, and if it is practicable, it may be necessary to have them destroyed (erased) or given an anonymous form. The reason is that control over data may be lost when data are no longer of interest; this may lead to risks of theft, unauthorised copying or the like.

Paragraph 10: Use Limitation Principle

55. This paragraph deals with uses of different kinds, including disclosure, which involve deviations from specified purposes. For instances, data may be transmitted from one computer to another where they can be used for unauthorised purposes without being inspected and thus disclosed in the proper sense of the word. As a rule the initially or subsequently specified purposes should be decisive for the uses to which data can be put. Paragraph 10 foresees two general exceptions to this principle: the consent of the data subject (or his representative - see Paragraph 52 above) and the authority of law (including, for example, licences granted by supervisory bodies). For instance, it may be provided that data which have been collected for purposes of administrative decision-making may be made available for research, statistics and social planning.

Paragraph 11: Security Safeguards Principle

56. Security and privacy issues are not identical. However, limitations on data use and disclosure should be reinforced by security safeguards. Such safeguards include physical measures (locked doors and identification cards, for instance), organisational measures (such as authority levels with regard to access to data) and, particularly in computer systems, informational measures (such as enciphering and threat monitoring of unusual activities and responses to them). It should be emphasized that the category of organisational measures includes obligations for data processing personnel to maintain confidentiality. Paragraph 11 has a broad coverage. The cases mentioned in the provision are to some extent overlapping (e.g. access/disclosure). "Loss" of data encompasses such cases as accidental erasure of data,

destruction of data storage media (and thus destruction of data) and theft of data storage media. "Modified" should be construed to cover unauthorised input of data, and "use" to cover unauthorised copying.

Paragraph 12: Openness Principle

57. The Openness Principle may be viewed as a prerequisite for the Individual Participation Principle (Paragraph 13); for the latter principle to be effective, it must be possible in practice to acquire information about the collection, storage or use of personal data. Regular information from data controllers on a voluntary basis, publication in official registers of descriptions of activities concerned with the processing of personal data, and registration with public bodies are some, though not all, of the ways by which this may be brought about. The reference to means which are "readily available" implies that individuals should be able to obtain information without unreasonable effort as to time, advance knowledge, travelling, and so forth, and without unreasonable cost.

Paragraph 13: Individual Participation Principle

58. The right of individuals to access and challenge personal data is generally regarded as perhaps the most important privacy protection safeguard. This view is shared by the Expert Group which, although aware that the right to access and challenge cannot be absolute, has chosen to express it in clear and fairly specific language. With respect to the individual sub-paragraphs, the following explanations are called for:

59. The right to access should as a rule be simple to exercise. This may mean, among other things, that it should be part of the day-to-day activities of the data controller or his representative and should not involve any legal process or similar measures. In some cases it may be appropriate to provide for intermediate access to data; for example, in the medical area a medical practitioner can serve as a go-between. In some countries supervisory organs, such as data inspection authorities, may provide similar services. The requirement that data be communicated within reasonable time may be satisfied in different ways. For instance, a data controller who provides information to data subjects at regular intervals may be exempted from obligations to respond at once to individual requests. Normally, the time is to be counted from the receipt of a request. Its length may vary to some extent from one situation to another depending on circumstances such as the nature of the data processing activity. Communication of such data "in a reasonable manner" means, among other things, that problems of geographical distance should be given due attention. Moreover, if intervals are prescribed between the times when requests for access must be met, such intervals should be reasonable. The extent to which data subjects should be able to obtain copies of data relating to them is a matter of implementation which must be left to the decision of each Member country.

60. The right to reasons in Paragraph 13(c) is narrow in the sense that it is limited to situations where requests for information have been refused. A broadening of this right to include reasons for adverse decisions in general, based on the use of personal data, met with sympathy in the Expert Group. However, on final consideration a right of this kind was thought to be

too broad for insertion in the privacy framework constituted by the Guidelines. This is not to say that a right to reasons for adverse decisions may not be appropriate, e.g. in order to inform and alert a subject to his rights so that he can exercise them effectively.

61. The right to challenge in 13(c) and (d) is broad in scope and includes first instance challenges to data controllers as well as subsequent challenges in courts, administrative bodies, professional organs or other institutions according to domestic rules of procedure (compare with Paragraph 19 of the Guidelines). The right to challenge does not imply that the data subject can decide what remedy or relief is available (rectification, annotation that data are in dispute, etc.): such matters will be decided by domestic law and legal procedures. Generally speaking, the criteria which decide the outcome of a challenge are those which are stated elsewhere in the Guidelines.

Paragraph 14: Accountability Principle

62. The data controller decides about data and data processing activities. It is for his benefit that the processing of data is carried out. Accordingly, it is essential that under domestic law accountability for complying with privacy protection rules and decisions should be placed on the data controller who should not be relieved of this obligation merely because the processing of data is carried out on his behalf by another party, such as a service bureau. On the other hand, nothing in the Guidelines prevents service bureaux personnel, "dependent users" (see paragraph 40) and others from also being held accountable. For instance, sanctions against breaches of confidentiality obligations may be directed against all parties entrusted with the handling of personal information (cf. Paragraph 19 of the Guidelines). Accountability under Paragraph 14 refers to accountability supported by legal sanctions, as well as to accountability established by codes of conduct, for instance.

Paragraphs 15-18: Basic Principles of International Application

63. The principles of international application are closely interrelated. Generally speaking, Paragraph 15 concerns respect by Member countries for each other's interest in protecting personal data, and the privacy and individual liberties of their nationals and residents. Paragraph 16 deals with security issues in a broad sense and may be said to correspond, at the international level, to Paragraph 11 of the Guidelines. Paragraphs 17 and 18 deal with restrictions on free flows of personal data between Member countries; basically, as far as protection of privacy and individual liberties is concerned, such flows should be admitted as soon as requirements of the Guidelines for the protection of these interests have been substantially, i.e. effectively, fulfilled. The question of other possible bases of restricting transborder flows of personal data is not dealt with in the Guidelines.

64. For domestic processing Paragraph 15 has two implications. First, it is directed against liberal policies which are contrary to the spirit of the Guidelines and which facilitate attempts to circumvent or violate protective legislation of other Member countries. However, such circumvention or violation, although condemned by all Member countries, is not specifically mentioned in this Paragraph as a number of countries felt it to be unacceptable that one Member country should be required to directly or indirectly enforce, extraterritorially, the

laws of other Member countries. - It should be noted that the provision explicitly mentions the re-export of personal data. In this respect, Member countries should bear in mind the need to support each other's efforts to ensure that personal data are not deprived of protection as a result of their transfer to territories and facilities for the processing of data where control is slack or non-existent.

65. Secondly, Member countries are implicitly encouraged to consider the need to adapt rules and practices for the processing of data to the particular circumstances which may arise when foreign data and data on non-nationals are involved. By way of illustration, a situation may arise where data on foreign nationals are made available for purposes which serve the particular interests of their country of nationality (e.g. access to the addresses of nationals living abroad).

66. As far as the Guidelines are concerned, the encouragement of international flows of personal data is not an undisputed goal in itself. To the extent that such flows take place they should, however, according to Paragraph 16, be uninterrupted and secure, i.e. protected against unauthorised access, loss of data and similar events. Such protection should also be given to data in transit, i.e. data which pass through a Member country without being used or stored with a view to usage in that country. The general commitment under Paragraph 16 should, as far as computer networks are concerned, be viewed against the background of the International Telecommunications Convention of Malaga-Torremolinos (25th October, 1973). According to that convention, the members of the International Telecommunications Union, including the OECD Member countries, have agreed, inter alia, to ensure the establishment, under the best technical conditions, of the channels and installations necessary to carry on the rapid and uninterrupted exchange of international telecommunications. Moreover, the members of ITU have agreed to take all possible measures compatible with the telecommunications system used to ensure the secrecy of international correspondence. As regards exceptions, the right to suspend international telecommunications services has been reserved and so has the right to communicate international correspondence to the competent authorities in order to ensure the application of internal laws or the execution of international conventions to which members of the ITU are parties. These provisions apply as long as data move through telecommunications lines. In their context, the Guidelines constitute a complementary safeguard that international flows of personal data should be uninterrupted and secure.

67. Paragraph 17 reinforces Paragraph 16 as far as relationships between Member countries are concerned. It deals with interests which are opposed to free transborder flows of personal data but which may nevertheless constitute legitimate grounds for restricting such flows between Member countries. A typical example would be attempts to circumvent national legislation by processing data in a Member country which does not yet substantially observe the Guidelines. Paragraph 17 establishes a standard of equivalent protection, by which is meant protection which is substantially similar in effect to that of the exporting country, but which need not be identical in form or in all respects. As in Paragraph 15, the re-export of

personal data is specifically mentioned - in this case with a view to preventing attempts to circumvent the domestic privacy legislation of Member countries. - The third category of grounds for legitimate restrictions mentioned in Paragraph 17, concerning personal data of a special nature, covers situations where important interests of Member countries could be affected. Generally speaking, however, Paragraph 17 is subject to Paragraph 4 of the Guidelines which implies that restrictions on flows of personal data should be kept to a minimum.

68. Paragraph 18 attempts to ensure that privacy protection interests are balanced against interests of free transborder flows of personal data. It is directed in the first place against the creation of barriers to flows of personal data which are artificial from the point of view of protection of privacy and individual liberties and fulfil restrictive purposes of other kinds which are thus not openly announced. However, Paragraph 18 is not intended to limit the rights of Member countries to regulate transborder flows of personal data in areas relating to free trade, tariffs, employment, and related economic conditions for international data traffic. These are matters which were not addressed by the Expert Group, being outside its Mandate.

Paragraph 19: National Implementation

69. The detailed implementation of Parts Two and Three of the Guidelines is left in the first place to Member countries. It is bound to vary according to different legal systems and traditions, and Paragraph 19 therefore attempts merely to establish a general framework indicating in broad terms what kind of national machinery is envisaged for putting the Guidelines into effect. The opening sentence shows the different approaches which might be taken by countries, both generally and with respect to control mechanisms (e.g. specially set-up supervisory bodies, existing control facilities such as courts, public authorities, etc.).

70. In Paragraph 19(a) countries are invited to adopt appropriate domestic legislation, the word "appropriate" foreshadowing the judgement by individual countries of the appropriateness or otherwise of legislative solutions. Paragraph 19(b) concerning self-regulation is addressed primarily to common law countries where non-legislative implementation of the Guidelines would complement legislative action. Paragraph 19(c) should be given a broad interpretation; it includes such means as advice from data controllers and the provision of assistance, including legal aid. Paragraph 19(d) permits different approaches to the issue of control mechanisms: briefly, either the setting-up of special supervisory bodies, or reliance on already existing control facilities, whether in the form of courts, existing public authorities or otherwise. Paragraph 19(e) dealing with discrimination is directed against unfair practices but leaves open the possibility of "benign discrimination" to support disadvantaged groups, for instance. The provision is directed against unfair discrimination on such bases as nationality and domicile, sex, race, creed, or trade union affiliation.

Paragraph 20: Information Exchange and Compatible Procedures

71. Two major problems are dealt with here, viz. (a) the need to ensure that information can be obtained about rules, regulations, decisions, etc. which implement the Guidelines, and (b)

the need to avoid transborder flows of personal data being hampered by an unnecessarily complex and disparate framework of procedures and compliance requirements. The first problem arises because of the complexity of privacy protection regulation and data policies in general. There are often several levels of regulation (in a broad sense) and many important rules cannot be laid down permanently in detailed statutory provisions; they have to be kept fairly open and left to the discretion of lower-level decision-making bodies.

72. The importance of the second problem is, generally speaking proportional to the number of domestic laws which affect transborder flows of personal data. Even at the present stage, there are obvious needs for co-ordinating special provisions on transborder data flows in domestic laws, including special arrangements relating to compliance control and, where required, licences to operate data processing systems.

Paragraph 21: Machinery for Co-operation

73. The provision on national procedures assumes that the Guidelines will form a basis for continued co-operation. Data protection authorities and specialised bodies dealing with policy issues in information and data communications are obvious partners in such a co-operation. In particular, the second purpose of such measures, contained in Paragraph 21(ii), i.e. mutual aid in procedural matters and requests for information, is future-oriented: its practical significance is likely to grow as international data networks and the complications associated with them become more numerous.

Paragraph 22: Conflicts of Laws

74. The Expert Group has devoted considerable attention to issues of conflicts of laws, and in the first place to the questions as to which courts should have jurisdiction over specific issues (choice of jurisdiction) and which system of law should govern specific issues (choice of law). The discussion of different strategies and proposed principles has confirmed the view that at the present stage, with the advent of such rapid changes in technology, and given the non-binding nature of the Guidelines, no attempt should be made to put forward specific, detailed solutions. difficulties are bound to arise with respect to both the choice of a theoretically sound regulatory model and the need for additional experience about the implications of solutions which in themselves are possible.

75. As regards the question of choice of law, one way of approaching these problems is to identify one or more connecting factors which, at best, indicate one applicable law. This is particularly difficult in the case of international computer networks where, because of dispersed location and rapid movement of data, and geographically dispersed data processing activities, several connecting factors could occur in a complex manner involving elements of legal novelty. Moreover, it is not evident what value should presently be attributed to rules which by mechanistic application establish the specific national law to be applied. For one thing, the appropriateness of such a solution seems to depend upon the existence of both similar legal concepts and rule structures, and binding commitments of nations to observe certain standards of personal data protection. In the absence of these conditions, an attempt could be made to formulate more flexible principles which involve a search for a "proper law"

and are linked to the purpose of ensuring effective protection of privacy and individual liberties. Thus, in a situation where several laws may be applicable, it has been suggested that one solution could be to give preference to the domestic law offering the best protection of personal data. On the other hand, it may be argued that solutions of this kind leave too much uncertainty, not least from the point of view of the data controllers who may wish to know, where necessary in advance, by which national systems of rules an international data processing system will be governed.

76. In view of these difficulties, and considering that problems of conflicts of laws might best be handled within the total framework of personal and non- personal data, the Expert Group has decided to content itself with a statement which merely signals the issues and recommends that Member countries should work towards their solution.

Follow-up

77. The Expert Group called attention to the terms of Recommendation 4 on the Guidelines which suggests that Member countries agree as soon as possible on specific procedures of consultation and co-operation for the application of the Guidelines.

COUNCIL OF EUROPE CONVENTION
ON PRIVACY (1981)

Summary

The Council of Europe concluded the Convention for the Protection of Individuals with Regard to Automatic Processing of Personal Data in 1981, and it entered into force in 1985. The Council negotiated the Convention in response to the rapid rise of automated data processing, and advances in computer technology that were allowing more and more records to be stored and transferred digitally. The Council also noted that there was a lack of rules generally applicable across Europe for dealing with the legal issues that might arise from computerized data transfer.

The convention's point of departure is that certain rights of the individual may have to be protected vis-à-vis the free flow of information regardless of frontiers, the latter principle being enshrined in international and European instruments on human rights. To this end, the convention consists of three main parts: substantive law provisions in the form of basic principles; special rules on transborder data flows; and mechanisms for mutual assistance and consultation between the Parties.

The Council of Europe worked closely with the OECD in drafting the Convention. The result is that both privacy frameworks are similar.

References

Council of Europe, Legal Affairs, Treaty Office, Convention No. 108 (1981)
[http://www.coe.int/en/web/conventions/full-list/-/conventions/treaty/108]

CONVENTION FOR THE PROTECTION OF INDIVIDUALS WITH REGARD TO
AUTOMATIC PROCESSING OF PERSONAL DATA
ENTERED INTO FORCE OCTOBER 1, 1985

The Member States of the Council of Europe, signatory hereto,

Considering that the aim of the Council of Europe is to achieve greater unity between its members, based in particular on respect for the rule of law, as well as human rights and fundamental freedoms;

Considering that it is desirable to extend the safeguards for everyone's rights and fundamental freedoms, and in particular the right to the respect for privacy, taking account of the increasing flow across frontiers of personal data undergoing automatic processing;

Reaffirming at the same time their commitment to freedom of information regardless of frontiers;

Recognising that it is necessary to reconcile the fundamental values of the respect for privacy and the free flow of information between peoples,

Have agreed as follows:

International
Council of Europe Convention on Privacy

CHAPTER I – GENERAL PROVISIONS

Article 1: Object and purpose

The purpose of this convention is to secure in the territory of each Party for every individual, whatever his nationality or residence, respect for his rights and fundamental freedoms, and in particular his right to privacy, with regard to automatic processing of personal data relating to him ("data protection").

Article 2: Definitions

For the purposes of this convention:

a. "personal data" means any information relating to an identified or identifiable individual ("data subject");

b. "automated data file" means any set of data undergoing automatic processing;

c. "automatic processing" includes the following operations if carried out in whole or in part by automated means: storage of data, carrying out of logical and/or arithmetical operations on those data, their alteration, erasure, retrieval or dissemination;

d. "controller of the file" means the natural or legal person, public authority, agency or any other body who is competent according to the national law to decide what should be the purpose of the automated data file, which categories of personal data should be stored and which operations should be applied to them.

Article 3: Scope

1. The Parties undertake to apply this convention to automated personal data files and automatic processing of personal data in the public and private sectors.

2. Any State may, at the time of signature or when depositing its instrument of ratification, acceptance, approval or accession, or at any later time, give notice by a declaration addressed to the Secretary General of the Council of Europe:

a. that it will not apply this convention to certain categories of automated personal data files, a list of which will be deposited. In this list it shall not include, however, categories of automated data files subject under its domestic law to data protection provisions. Consequently, it shall amend this list by a new declaration whenever additional categories of automated personal data files are subjected to data protection provisions under its domestic law;

b. that it will also apply this convention to information relating to groups of persons, associations, foundations, companies, corporations and any other bodies consisting directly or indirectly of individuals, whether or not such bodies possess legal personality;

c. that it will also apply this convention to personal data files which are not processed automatically.

3. Any State which has extended the scope of this convention by any of the declarations provided for in sub-paragraph 2.b or c above may give notice in the said declaration that such

extensions shall apply only to certain categories of personal data files, a list of which will be deposited.

4. Any Party which has excluded certain categories of automated personal data files by a declaration provided for in sub-paragraph 2.a above may not claim the application of this convention to such categories by a Party which has not excluded them.

5. Likewise, a Party which has not made one or other of the extensions provided for in sub-paragraph 2.b and c above may not claim the application of this convention on these points with respect to a Party which has made such extensions.

6. The declarations provided for in paragraph 2 above shall take effect from the moment of the entry into force of the convention with regard to the State which has made them if they have been made at the time of signature or deposit of its instrument of ratification, acceptance, approval or accession, or three months after their receipt by the Secretary General of the Council of Europe if they have been made at any later time. These declarations may be withdrawn, in whole or in part, by a notification addressed to the Secretary General of the Council of Europe. Such withdrawals shall take effect three months after the date of receipt of such notification.

CHAPTER II - BASIC PRINCIPLES FOR DATA PROTECTION

Article 4: Duties of the Parties

1. Each Party shall take the necessary measures in its domestic law to give effect to the basic principles for data protection set out in this chapter.
2. These measures shall be taken at the latest at the time of entry into force of this convention in respect of that Party.

Article 5: Quality of data

Personal data undergoing automatic processing shall be:
a. obtained and processed fairly and lawfully;
b. stored for specified and legitimate purposes and not used in a way incompatible with those purposes;
c. adequate, relevant and not excessive in relation to the purposes for which they are stored;
d. accurate and, where necessary, kept up to date
e. preserved in a form which permits identification of the data subjects for no longer than is required for the purpose for which those data are stored.

Article 6: Special categories of data

Personal data revealing racial origin, political opinions or religious or other beliefs, as well as personal data concerning health or sexual life, may not be processed automatically unless domestic law provides appropriate safeguards. The same shall apply to personal data relating to criminal convictions.

International
Council of Europe Convention on Privacy

Article 7: Data security

Appropriate security measures shall be taken for the protection of personal data stored in automated data files against accidental or unauthorised destruction or accidental loss as well as against unauthorised access, alteration or dissemination.

Article 8: Additional safeguards for the data subject

Any person shall be enabled:

a. to establish the existence of an automated personal data file, its main purposes, as well as the identity and habitual residence or principal place of business of the controller of the file;

b. to obtain at reasonable intervals and without excessive delay or expense confirmation of whether personal data relating to him are stored in the automated data file as well as communication to him of such data in an intelligible form;

c. to obtain, as the case may be, rectification or erasure of such data if these have been processed contrary to the provisions of domestic law giving effect to the basic principles set out in Articles 5 and 6 of this convention;

d. to have a remedy if a request for confirmation or, as the case may be, communication, rectification or erasure as referred to in paragraphs b and c of this article is not complied with.

Article 9: Exceptions and restrictions

1. No exception to the provisions of Articles 5, 6 and 8 of this convention shall be allowed except within the limits defined in this article.

2. Derogation from the provisions of Articles 5, 6 and 8 of this convention shall be allowed when such derogation is provided for by the law of the Party and constitutes a necessary measure in a democratic society in the interests of:

a. protecting State security, public safety, the monetary interests of the State or the suppression of criminal offences;

b. protecting the data subject or the rights and freedoms of others. 3. Restrictions on the exercise of the rights specified in Article 8, paragraphs b, c and d, may be provided by law with respect to automated personal data files used for statistics or for scientific research purposes when there is obviously no risk of an infringement of the privacy of the data subjects.

Article 10: Sanctions and remedies

Each Party undertakes to establish appropriate sanctions and remedies for violations of provisions of domestic law giving effect to the basic principles for data protection set out in this chapter.

Article 11: Extended protection

None of the provisions of this chapter shall be interpreted as limiting or otherwise affecting the possibility for a Party to grant data subjects of wider measure of protection than that stipulated in this convention.

CHAPTER III – TRANSBORDER DATA FLOWS

Article 12: Transborder flows of personal data and domestic law

1. The following provisions shall apply to the transfer across national borders, by whatever medium, of personal data undergoing automatic processing or collected with a view to their being automatically processed.
2. A Party shall not, for the sole purpose of the protection of privacy, prohibit or subject to special authorisation transborder flows of personal data going to the territory of another Party.
3. Nevertheless, each Party shall be entitled to derogate from the provisions of paragraph 2:
a. insofar as its legislation includes specific regulations for certain categories of personal data or of automated personal data files, because of the nature of those data or those files, except where the regulations of the other Party provide an equivalent protection;
b. when the transfer is made from its territory to the territory of a non-Contracting State through the intermediary of the territory of another Party, in order to avoid such transfers resulting in circumvention of the legislation of the Party referred to at the beginning of this paragraph.

CHAPTER IV – MUTUAL ASSISTANCE

Article 13: Co-operation between Parties

1. The Parties agree to render each other mutual assistance in order to implement this convention.
2. For that purpose:
a. each Party shall designate one or more authorities, the name and address of each of which it shall communicate to the Secretary General of the Council of Europe;
b. each Party which has designated more than one authority shall
specify in its communication referred to in the previous sub-paragraph the competence of each authority.
3. An authority designated by a Party shall at the request of an authority designated by another Party:
a. furnish information on its law and administrative practice in the field of data protection;
b. take, in conformity with its domestic law and for the sole purpose of protection of privacy, all appropriate measures for furnishing factual information relating to specific automatic processing carried out in its territory, with the exception however of the personal data being processed.

International
Council of Europe Convention on Privacy

Article 14: Assistance to data subjects resident abroad

1. Each Party shall assist any person resident abroad to exercise the rights conferred by its domestic law giving effect to the principles set out in Article 8 of this convention. 2. When such a person resides in the territory of another Party he shall be given the option of submitting his request through the intermediary of the authority designated by that Party. 3. The request for assistance shall contain all the necessary particulars, relating inter alia to:

a. the name, address and any other relevant particulars identifying the person making the request;

b. the automated personal data file to which the request pertains, or its controller;

c. the purpose of the request.

Article 15: Safeguards concerning assistance rendered by designated authorities

1. An authority designated by a Party which has received information from an authority designated by another Party either accompanying a request for assistance or in reply to its own request for assistance shall not use that information for purposes other than those specified in the request for assistance.

2. Each Party shall see to it that the persons belonging to or acting on behalf of the designated authority shall be bound by appropriate obligations of secrecy or confidentiality with regard to that information.

3. In no case may a designated authority be allowed to make under Article 14, paragraph 2, a request for assistance on behalf of a data subject resident abroad, of its own accord and without the express consent of the person concerned.

Article 16: Refusal of requests for assistance

A designated authority to which a request for assistance is addressed under Articles 13 or 14 of this convention may not refuse to comply with it unless:

a. the request is not compatible with the powers in the field of data protection of the authorities responsible for replying;

b. the request does not comply with the provisions of this convention

c. compliance with the request would be incompatible with the sovereignty, security or public policy (ordre public) of the Party by which it was designated, or with the rights and fundamental freedoms of persons under the jurisdiction of that Party.

Article 17: Costs and procedures of assistance

1. Mutual assistance which the Parties render each other under Article 13 and assistance they render to data subjects abroad under Article 14 shall not give rise to the payment of any costs or fees other than those incurred for experts and interpreters. The latter costs or fees shall be borne by the Party which has designated the authority making the request for assistance.

2. The data subject may not be charged costs or fees in connection with the steps taken on his behalf in the territory of another Party other than those lawfully payable by residents of that Party.

3. Other details concerning the assistance relating in particular to the forms and procedures and the languages to be used, shall be established directly between the Parties concerned.

CHAPTER V – CONSULTATIVE COMMITTEE

Article 18: Composition of the committee

1. A Consultative Committee shall be set up after the entry into force of this convention.

2. Each Party shall appoint a representative to the committee and a deputy representative. Any member State of the Council of Europe which is not a Party to the convention shall have the right to be represented on the committee by an observer.

3. The Consultative Committee may, by unanimous decision, invite any non-member State of the Council of Europe which is not a Party to the convention to be represented by an observer at a given meeting.

Article 19: Functions of the committee

The Consultative Committee:

a. may make proposals with a view to facilitating or improving the application of the convention;

b. may make proposals for amendment of this convention in accordance with Article 21;

c. shall formulate its opinion on any proposal for amendment of this convention which is referred to it in accordance with Article 21, paragraph 3;

d. may, at the request of a Party, express an opinion on any question concerning the application of this convention.

Article 20: Procedure

1. The Consultative Committee shall be convened by the Secretary General of the Council of Europe. Its first meeting shall be held within twelve months of the entry into force of this convention. It shall subsequently meet at least once every two years and in any case when one-third of the representatives of the Parties request its convocation.

2. A majority of representatives of the Parties shall constitute a quorum for a meeting of the Consultative Committee.

3. After each of its meetings, the Consultative Committee shall submit to the Committee of Ministers of the Council of Europe a report on its work and on the functioning of the convention.

4. Subject to the provisions of this convention, the Consultative Committee shall draw up its own Rules of Procedure.

International
Council of Europe Convention on Privacy

CHAPTER VI – AMENDMENTS

Article 21: Amendments

1. Amendments to this convention may be proposed by a Party, the Committee of Ministers of the Council of Europe or the Consultative Committee.

2. Any proposal for amendment shall be communicated by the Secretary General of the Council of Europe to the member States of the Council of Europe and to every non-member State which has acceded to or has been invited to accede to this convention in accordance with the provisions of Article 23.

3. Moreover, any amendment proposed by a Party or the Committee of Ministers shall be communicated to the Consultative Committee, which shall submit to the Committee of Ministers its opinion on that proposed amendment.

4. The Committee of Ministers shall consider the proposed amendment and any opinion submitted by the Consultative Committee and may approve the amendment.

5. The text of any amendment approved by the Committee of Ministers in accordance with paragraph 4 of this article shall be forwarded to the Parties for acceptance.

6. Any amendment approved in accordance with paragraph 4 of this article shall come into force on the thirtieth day after all Parties have informed the Secretary General of their acceptance thereof.

CHAPTER VII – FINAL CLAUSES

Article 22: Entry into force

1. This convention shall be open for signature by the member States of the Council of Europe. It is subject to ratification, acceptance or approval. Instruments of ratification, acceptance or approval shall be deposited with the Secretary General of the Council of Europe.

2. This convention shall enter into force on the first day of the month following the expiration of a period of three months after the date on which five member States of the Council of Europe have expressed their consent to be bound by the convention in accordance with the provisions of the preceding paragraph.

3. In respect of any member State which subsequently expresses its consent to be bound by it, the convention shall enter into force on the first day of the month following the expiration of a period of three months after the date of the deposit of the instrument of ratification, acceptance or approval.

Article 23: Accession by non-member States

1. After the entry into force of this convention, the Committee of Ministers of the Council of Europe may invite any State not a member of the Council of Europe to accede to this convention by a decision taken by the majority provided for in Article 20.d of the Statute of

the Council of Europe and by the unanimous vote of the representatives of the Contracting States entitled to sit on the committee.

2. In respect of any acceding State, the convention shall enter into force on the first day of the month following the expiration of a period of three months after the date of deposit of the instrument of accession with the Secretary General of the Council of Europe.

Article 24: Territorial clause

1. Any State may at the time of signature or when depositing its instrument of ratification, acceptance, approval or accession, specify the territory or territories to which this convention shall apply.

2. Any State may at any later date, by a declaration addressed to the Secretary General of the Council of Europe, extend the application of this convention to any other territory specified in the declaration. In respect of such territory the convention shall enter into force on the first day of the month following the expiration of a period of three months after the date of receipt of such declaration by the Secretary General. 3. Any declaration made under the two preceding paragraphs may, in respect of any territory specified in such declaration, be withdrawn by a notification addressed to the Secretary General. The withdrawal shall become effective on the first day of the month following the expiration of a period of six months after the date of receipt of such notification by the Secretary General.

Article 25: Reservations

No reservation may be made in respect of the provisions of this convention.

Article 26: Denunciation

1. Any Party may at any time denounce this convention by means of a notification addressed to the Secretary General of the Council of Europe.

2. Such denunciation shall become effective on the first day of the month following the expiration of a period of six months after the date of receipt of the notification by the Secretary General.

Article 27: Notifications

The Secretary General of the Council of Europe shall notify the member States of the Council and any State which has acceded to this convention of

a. any signature;

b. the deposit of any instrument of ratification, acceptance, approval or accession

c. any date of entry into force of this convention in accordance with Articles 22, 23 and 24;

d. any other act, notification or communication relating to this convention.

In witness whereof the undersigned, being duly authorised thereto, have signed this Convention.

International
Council of Europe Convention on Privacy

Done at Strasbourg, the 28th day of January 1981, in English and in French, both texts being equally authoritative, in a single copy which shall remain deposited in the archives of the Council of Europe. The Secretary General of the Council of Europe shall transmit certified copies to each member State of the Council of Europe and to any State invited to accede to this Convention.–

UNITED NATIONS GUIDELINES FOR
THE REGULATION OF COMPUTERIZED
PERSONAL FILES (1990) .

Summary

Adopted December 14, 1990 as General Assembly Resolution 45/95, the Guidelines for the Regulation of Computerized Personal Files provide ten principles concerning the minimum privacy guarantees that ought to be reflected in national privacy laws. These mirror the OECD's eight guidelines, but parse them out in slightly different ways. For example, both instruments contain provisions on lawful collection, accuracy, purpose specification, access and enforcement.

Unlike the OECD guidelines, however, the UN guidelines specify that no data ought to be collected which is likely to give rise to unlawful or arbitrary discrimination, such as information on religion, sex life, and race. The UN guidelines also contain a humanitarian clause stating that a nation may depart from the principles espoused by the guidelines when to do so would promote human rights.

References

United Nations, General Assembly Resolution 45/95, Guidelines for the regulation of computerized personal data files (14 December 1999)
[http://www.un.org/documents/ga/res/45/a45r095.htm]

UN, Report of the Secretary-General on the Follow-up to the Guidelines for the Regulation of Computerized Personal Data Files: [https://documents-dds-ny.un.org/doc/UNDOC/GEN/G98/145/66/PDF/G9814566.pdf?OpenElement]

The procedures for implementing regulations concerning computerized personal data files are left to the initiative of each State subject to the following orientations:

A. PRINCIPLES CONCERNING THE MINIMUM GUARANTEES THAT SHOULD BE PROVIDED IN NATIONAL LEGISLATIONS

1. Principle of lawfulness and fairness

Information about persons should not be collected or processed in unfair or unlawful ways, nor should it be used for ends contrary to the purposes and principles of the Charter of the United Nations.

International
UN Guidelines for Personal Data Files

2. Principle of accuracy

Persons responsible for the compilation of files or those responsible for keeping them have an obligation to conduct regular checks on the accuracy and relevance of the data recorded and to ensure that they are kept as complete as possible in order to avoid errors of omission and that they are kept up to date regularly or when the information contained in a file is used, as long as they are being processed.

3. Principle of the purpose-specification

The purpose which a file is to serve and its utilization in terms of that purpose should be specified, legitimate and, when it is established, receive a certain amount of publicity or be brought to the attention of the person concerned, in order to make it possible subsequently to ensure that:

(a) All the personal data collected and recorded remain relevant and adequate to the purposes so specified;

(b) None of the said personal data is used or disclosed, except with the consent of the person concerned, for purposes incompatible with those specified;

(c) The period for which the personal data are kept does not exceed that which would enable the achievement of the purposes so specified.

4. Principle of interested-person access

Everyone who offers proof of identity has the right to know whether information concerning him is being processed and to obtain it in an intelligible form, without undue delay or expense, and to have appropriate rectifications or erasures made in the case of unlawful, unnecessary or inaccurate entries and, when it is being communicated, to be informed of the addressees. Provision should be made for a remedy, if need be with the supervisory authority specified in principle 8 below. The cost of any rectification shall be borne by the person responsible for the file. It is desirable that the provisions of this principle should apply to everyone, irrespective of nationality or place of residence.

5. Principle of non-discrimination

Subject to cases of exceptions restrictively envisaged under principle 6, data likely to give rise to unlawful or arbitrary discrimination, including information on racial or ethnic origin, colour, sex life, political opinions, religious, philosophical and other beliefs as well as membership of an association or trade union, should not be compiled.

6. Power to make exceptions

Departures from principles 1 to 4 may be authorized only if they are necessary to protect national security, public order, public health or morality, as well as, inter alia, the rights and freedoms of others, especially persons being persecuted (humanitarian clause) provided that such departures are expressly specified in a law or equivalent regulation promulgated in accordance with the internal legal system which expressly states their limits and sets forth appropriate safeguards.

Exceptions to principle 5 relating to the prohibition of discrimination, in addition to being subject to the same safeguards as those prescribed for exceptions to principles I and 4, may be authorized only within the limits prescribed by the International Bill of Human Rights and the other relevant instruments in the field of protection of human rights and the prevention of discrimination.

7. Principle of security

Appropriate measures should be taken to protect the files against both natural dangers, such as accidental loss or destruction and human dangers, such as unauthorized access, fraudulent misuse of data or contamination by computer viruses.

8. Supervision and sanctions

The law of every country shall designate the authority which, in accordance with its domestic legal system, is to be responsible for supervising observance of the principles set forth above. This authority shall offer guarantees of impartiality, independence vis-a-vis persons or agencies responsible for processing and establishing data, and technical competence. In the event of violation of the provisions of the national law implementing the aforementioned principles, criminal or other penalties should be envisaged together with the appropriate individual remedies.

9. Transborder data flows

When the legislation of two or more countries concerned by a transborder data flow offers comparable safeguards for the protection of privacy, information should be able to circulate as freely as inside each of the territories concerned. If there are no reciprocal safeguards, limitations on such circulation may not be imposed unduly and only in so far as the protection of privacy demands.

10. Field of application

The present principles should be made applicable, in the first instance, to all public and private computerized files as well as, by means of optional extension and subject to appropriate adjustments, to manual files. Special provision, also optional, might be made to extend all or part of the principles to files on legal persons particularly when they contain some information on individuals.

B. APPLICATION OF THE GUIDELINES TO PERSONAL DATA FILES KEPT BY GOVERNMENTAL INTERNATIONAL ORGANIZATIONS

International
UN Guidelines for Personal Data Files

The present guidelines should apply to personal data files kept by governmental international organizations, subject to any adjustments required to take account of any differences that might exist between files for internal purposes such as those that concern personnel management and files for external purposes concerning third parties having relations with the organization.

Each organization should designate the authority statutorily competent to supervise the observance of these guidelines.

Humanitarian clause: a derogation from these principles may be specifically provided for when the purpose of the file is the protection of human rights and fundamental freedoms of the individual concerned or humanitarian assistance.

A similar derogation should be provided in national legislation for governmental international organizations whose headquarters agreement does not preclude the implementation of the said national legislation as well as for non-governmental international organizations to which this law is applicable.

EUROPEAN UNION DATA PROTECTION DIRECTIVE (1995)

Summary

The European Union Data Protection Directive of 1995 establishes common rules for data protection among Member States of the European Union in order to facilitate the free flow of personal data within the EU. The Directive imposes obligations on the processors of personal data. It requires technical security and the notification of individuals whose data are being collected, and outlines circumstances under which data transfer may occur. The directive also gives individual substantial rights to control the use of data about themselves. These rights include the right to be informed that their personal data is being transferred, the need to obtain "unambiguous" consent from the individual for the transfer of certain data, the opportunity to make corrections in the data, and the right to object to the transfer. Data regulatory authority, enforcement provisions, and sanctions are also key elements of the directive. Following passage of the directive, the various national governments of the EU amended their own national data protection legislation to bring it into line with the Directive. The Directive extends privacy safeguards to personal data that is transferred outside of the European Union. Article 25 of the Directive states that data can only be transferred to third countries that provide an "adequate level of data protection." As a result implementation focuses on both the adoption of adequate methods for privacy protection in third party countries.

References

EUR-Lex- Community Legislation in Force – Document 395L0046
[http://eur-lex.europa.eu/legal-content/EN/TXT/?uri=celex:31995L0046]

DIRECTIVE OF THE EUROPEAN PARLIAMENT AND THE COUNCIL OF EUROPE ON THE PROTECTION OF INDIVIDUALS WITH REGARD TO THE PROCESSING OF PERSONAL DATA AND ON THE FREE MOVEMENT OF SUCH DATA

[As amended and approved by The Council of the European Union, Brussels, 20 July 1995]

THE EUROPEAN PARLIAMENT AND THE COUNCIL OF THE EUROPEAN UNION,

Having regard to the Treaty establishing the European Community, and in particular Article 100a thereof,

Having regard to the proposal from the Commission (1),

Having regard to the Opinion of the Economic and Social Committee (2),

Acting in accordance with the procedure referred to in Article 189b of the Treaty (3)

(1) Whereas the objectives of the Community, as laid down in the Treaty, as amended by the Treaty on European Union, include establishing an ever closer union among the people of Europe, fostering closer relations between the States belonging to the Community, ensuring economic and social progress by common action to eliminate the barriers which divide

International
European Union Data Protection Directive

Europe, encouraging the constant improvement of the living conditions of its people, preserving and strengthening peace and liberty and promoting democracy on the basis of the fundamental rights recognized in the constitutions and laws of the Member States and in the European Convention for the Protection of Human Rights and Fundamental Freedoms;

(2) Whereas data-processing systems are designed to serve man; whereas they must, whatever the nationality or residence of natural persons, respect the fundamental freedoms and rights of individuals, notably the right to privacy, and contribute to economic and social progress, trade expansion and the well-being of individuals;

(3) Whereas the establishment and functioning of an internal market in which, in accordance with Article 7a of the Treaty, the free movement of goods, persons, services and capital is ensured require not only that personal data should be able to flow freely from one Member State to another, but also that the fundamental rights of individuals should be safeguarded.

(4) Whereas increasingly frequent recourse is being had in the Community to the processing of personal data in the various spheres of economic and social activity; whereas the progress made in information technology is making the processing and exchange of such data considerably easier;

(5) Whereas the economic and social integration resulting from the establishment and functioning of the internal market within the meaning of Article 7a of the Treaty will necessarily lead to a substantial increase in cross-border flows of personal data between all those involved in a private or public capacity in economic and social activity in the Member States; whereas the exchange of personal data between undertakings in different Member States is set to increase; whereas the national authorities in the various Member States are being called upon by virtue of Community law to collaborate and exchange personal data so as to be able to perform their duties or carry out tasks on behalf of an authority in another Member State within the context of the area without internal frontiers as constituted by the Internal Market;

(6) Whereas, furthermore, the increase in scientific and technical cooperation and the coordinated introduction of new telecommunications networks in the Community necessitate and facilitate cross-border flows of personal data;

(7) Whereas the difference in levels of protection of the rights and freedoms of individuals, notably the right to privacy, with regard to the processing of personal data afforded in the Member States may prevent the transmission of such data from the territory of one Member State to that of another Member State; whereas this difference may therefore constitute an obstacle to the pursuit of a number of economic activities at Community level, distort competition and impede authorities in the discharge of their responsibilities under Community law; whereas this difference in levels of protection is due to the existence of a wide variety of national laws, regulations and administrative provisions;

(8) Whereas, in order to remove the obstacles to flows of personal data, the level of protection of the rights and freedoms of individuals with regard to the processing of such data must be equivalent in all the Member States; whereas this objective is vital to the internal market but

cannot be achieved by Member States alone, especially in view of the scale of the divergences which currently exist between the relevant laws in the Member States and the need to coordinate the laws of the Member States so as to ensure that the cross-border flow of personal data is regulated in a consistent manner that is in keeping with the objective of the internal market as provided for in Article 7a of the Treaty; whereas Community action to approximate those laws is therefore needed;

(9) Whereas, given the equivalent protection resulting from the approximation of national laws, the Member States will no longer be able to inhibit the free movement between them of personal data on grounds relating to protection of the rights and freedoms of individuals, and in particular the right to privacy; whereas Member States will be left a margin for manoeuvre, which may, in the context of implementation of the Directive, also be exercised by the business and social partners; whereas Member States will therefore be able to specify in their national law the general conditions governing the lawfulness of data processing; whereas in doing so the Member States shall strive to improve the protection currently provided by their legislation; whereas, within the limits of this margin for manoeuvre and in accordance with Community law, disparities could arise in the implementation of the Directive, and this could have an effect on the movement of data within a Member State as well as within the Community;

(10) Whereas the object of the national laws on the processing of personal data is to protect fundamental rights and freedoms, notably the right to privacy, which is recognized both in Article 8 of the European Convention for the Protection of Human Rights and Fundamental Freedoms and in the general principles of Community law; whereas, for that reason, the approximation of those laws must not result in any lessening of the protection they afford but must, on the contrary, seek to ensure a high level of protection in the Community;

(11) Whereas the principles of the protection of the rights and freedoms of individuals, notably the right to privacy, which are contained in this Directive, give substance to and amplify those contained in the Council of Europe Convention of 28 January 1981 for the Protection of Individuals with regard to Automatic Processing of Personal Data;

(12) Whereas the protection principles must apply to all processing of personal data by any person whose activities are governed by Community law; whereas there should be excluded the processing of data carried out by a natural person in the exercise of activities which are exclusively personal or domestic, such as correspondence and the holding of records of addresses;

(13) Whereas the activities referred to in Titles V and VI of the Treaty on European Union regarding public safety, defence, State security or the activities of the State in the area of criminal law fall outside the scope of Community law, without prejudice to the obligations incumbent upon Member States under Article 56(2), Article 57 or Article 100a of the Treaty establishing the European Community; whereas the processing of personal data that is necessary to safeguard the economic well-being of the State does not fall within the scope of this Directive where such processing relates to State security matters;

(14) Whereas, given the importance of the developments under way, in the framework of the information society, of the techniques used to capture, transmit, manipulate, record, store or communicate sound and image data relating to natural persons, this Directive should be applicable to processing involving such data;

(15) Whereas the processing of such data is covered by this Directive only if it is automated or if the data processed are contained or are intended to be contained in a filing system structured according to specific criteria relating to individuals, so as to permit easy access to the personal data in question;

(16) Whereas the processing of sound and image data, such as in cases of video surveillance, does not come within the scope of this Directive if it is carried out for the purposes of public security, defence, national security or in the course of State activities relating to the area of criminal law or of other activities which do not come within the scope of Community law;

(17) Whereas as far as the processing of sound and image data carried out for purposes of journalism or the purposes of literary or artistic expression is concerned, in particular in the audiovisual field, the principles of the Directive are to apply in a restricted manner according to the provisions laid down in Article 9,

(18) Whereas, in order to ensure that individuals are not deprived of the protection to which they are entitled under this Directive, any processing of personal data in the Community must be carried out in accordance with the law of one of the Member States; whereas, in this connection, processing carried out under the responsibility of a controller who is established in a Member State should be governed by the law of that State;

(19) Whereas establishment on the territory of a Member State implies the effective and real exercise of activity through the means of a stable set-up; whereas the legal form of such an establishment, whether a simple branch or a subsidiary with a legal personality, is not the determinate factor in this respect; whereas, when a single controller is established on the territory of several Member States, particularly be means of a subsidiary, he must ensure, in order to avoid any circumvention of national rules, that each of the establishments fulfils the obligations imposed by the national law applicable to its activities;

(20) Whereas the fact that processing is carried out by a person established in a third country must not stand in the way of the protection of individuals provided for in this Directive; whereas, in these cases, the processing should be governed by the law of the Member State in which the means used are located, and there should be guarantees to ensure that the rights and obligations provided for in this Directive are respected in practice;

(21) Whereas this Directive is without prejudice to the rules of territoriality applicable in criminal matters;

(22) Whereas Member States shall more precisely define in the laws they enact or when bringing into force the measures taken under this Directive, the general circumstances in which processing is lawful; whereas in particular Article 5, in conjunction with Articles 7 and 8, allows Member States, independently of general rules, to provide for special processing conditions for specific sectors and for the various categories of data covered by Article 8;

(23) Whereas Member States are empowered to ensure the implementation of the protection of individuals both by means of a general law on the protection of individuals against the processing of personal data and by sectorial laws such as those relating, for example, to Institutes for Statistics;

(24) Whereas the legislation concerning the protection of legal persons with regard to the processing of data which concern them is not affected by this Directive;

(25) Whereas the principles of protection must be reflected, on the one hand, in the obligations imposed on persons, public authorities, enterprises, agencies or other bodies responsible for processing, in particular regarding data quality, technical security, notification to the supervisory authority, and the circumstances under which processing can be carried out, and, on the other hand, in the rights conferred on individuals, the data on whom are the subject of processing, to be informed that processing is taking place, to consult the data, to request corrections and even to object to processing in certain circumstances;

(26) Whereas the principles of protection must apply to any information concerning an identified or identifiable person; whereas, to determine whether a person is identifiable, account should be taken of all the means likely reasonably to be used either by the controller or by any other person to identify the said person; whereas the principles of protection shall not apply to data rendered anonymous in such a way that the data subject is no longer identifiable; whereas codes of conduct within the meaning of Article 27 may be a useful instrument in providing guidance as to the way in which data may be rendered anonymous and retained in a form in which identification of the data subject is no longer possible;

(27) Whereas the protection of individuals must apply as much to automatic processing of data as to manual processing; whereas the scope of this protection must not in effect depend on the techniques used, otherwise this would create a serious risk of circumvention; whereas, nonetheless, as regards manual processing, this Directive covers only filing systems, not according to specific criteria relating to individuals allowing easy access to the personal data; whereas, in line with the definition in Article 2(c) the different criteria for determining the constituents of a structured set of personal data, and the different criteria governing access to such a set, can be laid down by each Member State; whereas files or sets of files as well as their cover pages, which are not structured according to specific criteria, shall under no circumstances fall within the scope of this Directive;

(28) Whereas any processing of personal data must be lawful and fair to the individual concerned; whereas, in particular, the data must be adequate, relevant and not excessive in relation to the purposes for which they are processed; whereas such purposes must be explicit and legitimate and must be determined at the time of collection of the data; whereas the purposes of processing further to collection shall not be incompatible with the purposes as they were originally specified;

(29) Whereas the further processing of personal data for historical, statistical, or scientific purposes is not generally to be considered incompatible with the purposes for which the data have previously been collected provided that Member States furnish suitable guarantees;

whereas these guarantees must in particular rule out the use of data for taking measures or decisions regarding any particular individual;

(30) Whereas, in order to be lawful, the processing of personal data must in addition be carried out with the consent of the data subject or be necessary with a view to the conclusion or performance of a contract binding on the data subject, or be required by law, by the performance of a task in the public interest or in the exercise of official authority, or by the interest of a natural or legal person provided that the interests or the rights and freedoms of the data subject are not overriding; whereas, in particular, in order to maintain a balance between the interests involved while guaranteeing effective competition, Member States remain free to determine the circumstances in which personal data may be used or disclosed to a third party in the context of the legitimate ordinary business activities of companies and other bodies; whereas Member States may similarly specify the conditions under which personal data may be disclosed to a third party for the purposes of marketing whether carried out commercially or b a charitable organization or by any other association or foundation, of a political nature for example, subject to the provisions allowing a data subject to object to the processing of data regarding him, at no cost and without having to state his reasons;

(31) Whereas the processing of personal data must equally be regarded as lawful where it is carried out in order to protect an interest which is essential for the data subject's life;

(32) Whereas it is for national legislation to determine whether the controller performing a task carried out in the public interest or in the exercise of official authority should be a public administration or another national or legal person governed by public law or by private law or such as a professional association;

(33) Whereas data which are capable by their nature of infringing fundamental freedoms or privacy should not be processed unless the data subject gives his explicit consent; whereas, however, derogation from this prohibition must be explicitly provided for in respect of specific needs, in particular where the processing of these data is carried out for certain health-related purposes by individuals subject to a legal obligation of professional secrecy or in the course of legitimate activities by certain associations or foundations the purpose of which is to permit the exercise of fundamental freedoms;

(34) Whereas Member States must also be authorized, when justified by grounds of important public interest, to derogate from the prohibition on processing sensitive categories of data where important reasons of public interest so justify in areas such as public health and social protection, especially as regards the assurance of quality and cost-effectiveness, and as regards the procedures used for settling claims for benefits and services in the health insurance system, scientific research and government statistics; whereas it is incumbent on them, however, to provide specific and suitable safeguards so as to protect the fundamental rights and the privacy of individuals;

(35) Whereas, moreover, the processing of personal data by official authorities for achieving aims, laid down in constitutional law or international public law, of officially recognized religious associations is carried out on important grounds of public interest;

(36)Whereas where, in the course of electoral activities, the operation of the democratic system requires in certain Member States that political parties compile data on people's political opinions, the processing of such data can be permitted for reasons of important public interest, provided that appropriate safeguards are established;

(37) Whereas the processing of personal data for purposes of journalism or for purposes of literary or artistic expression, in particular in the audiovisual field, should qualify for exemption from the requirements of certain provisions of this Directive insofar as this is necessary to reconcile the fundamental rights of individuals with freedom of information and notably the right to receive and impart information, as guaranteed in particular in Article 10 of the European Convention for the Protection of Human Rights and Fundamental Freedoms; whereas Member States should therefore lay down exemptions and derogations necessary for the purposes of balance between fundamental rights as regards general measures on the legitimacy of data processing, measures on the transfer of data to third countries and the powers of supervisory authority; whereas this should not, however, lead Member States to lay down exemptions from the measures to ensure security of processing; whereas the supervisory authority responsible for this sector should also be provided at least with certain ex-post powers, e.g. to publish a regular report or to refer matters to the judicial authorities;

(38) Whereas, if the processing of data is to be fair, the data subject must be in a position to learn of the existence of a processing operation and, where data are collected from him, must be given accurate and full information, bearing in mind the circumstances of the collection;

(39) Whereas certain processing operations involve data which the controller has not collected directly from the data subject; whereas, furthermore, data can be legitimately disclosed to a third party, even if the disclosure was not anticipated at the time the data were collected from the data subject; whereas, in all these cases, the data subject should be informed when the data are recorded or at the latest when the data are first disclosed to a third party;

(40) Whereas, however, it is not necessary to impose this obligation if the data subject already knows the information; whereas, moreover, this obligation is not provided for if the recording or disclosure are expressly provided for by law or if the provision of information proves impossible or involved disproportionate efforts, which could be the case where processing is for historical, statistical or scientific purposes; whereas, in this regard, the number of data subjects, the age of the data, and any compensatory measures adopted may be taken into consideration;

(41) Whereas any person must be able to exercise the right of access to data relating to him which are being processed, in order to verify in particular the accuracy of the data and the lawfulness of the processing; whereas, for the same reasons, every data subject must also have the right to know the logic involved in the automatic processing of data concerning him, at least in the case of the automated decisions referred to in Article 15(1); whereas this right must not be adversely affect business confidentiality or intellectual property and in particular the copyright protecting the software; whereas these considerations must not, however, result in the data subject being refused all information;

(42) Whereas Member States may, in the interest of the data subject or so as to protect the rights and freedoms of others, restrict rights of access and information; whereas they may, for example, specify that access to medical data may be obtained only through a health professional;

(43) Whereas restrictions on the rights of access and information and on certain obligations of the controller may similarly be imposed by Member States insofar as they are necessary to safeguard, for example, national security, defence, public safety, or important economic or financial interests of a Member State or the Union, as well as criminal investigations and prosecutions and action in respect of breaches of ethics in the regulated professions; whereas the list of exceptions and limitations should include the tasks of monitoring, inspection or regulation necessary in three last-mentioned areas concerning public security, economic or financial interests and crime prevention; whereas the listing of tasks in these three areas does not affect the legitimacy of exceptions or restrictions for reasons of State security or defence;

(44) Whereas Member States may also be led, by virtue of the provisions of Community law, to derogate from the provisions of this Directive concerning the right of access, the obligation to inform individuals and the quality of data, in order to safeguard certain purposes among those referred to above;

(45) Whereas, in cases of processing lawfully data pursued on grounds of public interest, official authority or the legitimate interests of a natural or legal person, any data subject should nevertheless be entitled, on legitimate and compelling grounds relating to his particular situation, to object to the processing of any data relating to himself; whereas Member States nevertheless have the possibility of laying down national provisions to the contrary;

(46) Whereas the protection of the rights and freedoms of data subjects with regard to the processing of personal data requires that appropriate technical and organizational measures be taken, both at the time of the design of the processing system and at the time of the processing itself, particularly in order to maintain security and thereby to prevent any unauthorized processing; whereas it is incumbent on the Member States to ensure that controllers comply with these measures; whereas these measures must ensure an appropriate level of security, taking into account the state of the technology and the cost of its use in view of the risks inherent in the processing and the nature of the data to be protected;

(47) Whereas where a message containing personal data is transmitted by means of a telecommunications or electronic mail service, the sole purpose of which is the transmission of such messages, the controller in respect of the personal data contained in the message will normally be considered to be the person from whom the message originates, rather than the person offering the transmission services; whereas, nevertheless, those offering such services will normally be considered controllers in respect of the processing of the additional personal data necessary for the operation of the service;

(48) Whereas the notification procedures are designed to ensure disclosure of the purposes and main features of any processing operation for the purpose of verification that the operation is in accordance with the national measures taken under this Directive;

(49) Whereas, in order to avoid unsuitable administrative formalities, exemptions from the obligation to notify and simplification of the notification required may be provided for by Member States in cases where processing is unlikely to adversely affect the rights and freedoms of data subjects, provided that it is in accordance with a measure taken by a Member State specifying its limits; whereas in an equivalent way exemption or simplification can similarly be provided for by Member States where a person appointed by the controller ensures that the processing carried out is not likely adversely to affect the rights and freedoms of data subjects; whereas such an official, whether or not an employee of the controller, must be in a position to exercise his functions in complete independence;

(50) Whereas exemption or simplification could be provided for in cases of processing operations whose sole purpose is the keeping of a register intended, according to national law, to provide information to the public and open to consultation by the public or by any person demonstrating a legitimate interest;

(51) Whereas, nevertheless, simplification or exemption from the obligation to notify shall not release the controller from any of the other obligations resulting from this Directive;

(52) Whereas, in this context, ex post facto verification by the competent authorities must be in general be considered a sufficient measure;

(53) Whereas, however, certain processing operations are likely to pose specific risks to the rights and freedoms of data subjects by virtue of their nature, their scope or their purposes, such as the purpose of excluding individuals from a right, benefit or contract, or by virtue of the specific use of new technologies; whereas it is for Member States, if they so wish, to specify such risks in their legislation;

(54) Whereas with regard to all the processing undertaken in society, the amount posing such specific risks should be very limited; whereas Member States must provide that the supervisory authority, or the data protection official in cooperation with the authority, check such processing prior to it being carried out; whereas following this prior check, the supervisory authority may, according to its national law, give an opinion or an authorization regarding the processing; whereas such checking may equally take place in the course of the preparation of a legislative measure adopted by the national parliament or on the basis of such a measure, defining the nature of the processing and specifying suitable safeguards;

(55) Whereas, if the controller fails to respect the rights of data subjects, national legislation must provide for a judicial remedy; whereas any damage which a person may suffer as a result of unlawful processing must be compensated for by the controller, who may be exempted from liability if he proves that he is not responsible for the damage, in particular in cases where he reports an error on the part of the data subject or in a case of force majeure; whereas sanctions must be imposed on any person, whether governed by private or public law, who fails to comply with the national measures taken under this Directive;

(56) Whereas cross-border flows of personal data are necessary to the expansion of international trade; whereas the protection of individuals guaranteed in the Community by this Directive does not stand in the way of transfers of personal data to third countries which

ensure an adequate level of protection; whereas the adequacy of the level of protection afforded by a third country must be assessed in the light of all the circumstances surrounding the transfer operation or set of transfer operations;

(57) Whereas, on the other hand, the transfer of personal data to a third country which does not ensure an adequate level of protection must be prohibited;

(58) Whereas provision should be made for exemptions from this prohibition in certain circumstances where the data subject has given his consent, where the transfer is necessary in relation to a contract or a legal claim, where protection of an important public interest so requires, for example in cases of international transfers of data between tax or customs administrations or between services competent for social security matters, or where the transfer is made from a register established by law and intended for consultation by the public or persons having a legitimate interest; whereas in this case such a transfer should not involve the entirety of the data or entire categories of the data contained in the register and, when the register is intended for consultation by persons having a legitimate interest, the transfer should be made only at the request of the same persons or if the latter are the recipients;

(59) Whereas particular measures may be taken to compensate for the lack of protection in a third country in cases where the person responsible for the processing offers appropriate assurances; whereas, moreover, provision must be made for procedures for negotiations between the Community and such third countries;

(60) Whereas, in any event, transfers to third countries may only be effected in full compliance with the provisions adopted by the Member States pursuant to this Directive, and in particular Article 8 thereof;

(61) Whereas Member States and the Commission, in their respective spheres of competence, must encourage the trade associations and other representative organizations concerned to draw up codes of conduct so far as to facilitate the application of this Directive, taking account of the specific characteristics of the processing carried out in certain sectors, and respecting the national provisions adopted for its implementation;

(62) Whereas the establishment in Member States of supervisory authorities, exercising their functions with complete independence, is an essential component of the protection of individuals with regard to the processing of personal data;

(63) Whereas such authorities must have the necessary means to perform their duties, including powers of investigation and intervention, particularly in cases of complaints from individuals, and powers to engage in legal proceedings; whereas such authorities must help to ensure transparency of processing in the Member States within those jurisdiction they fall;

(64) Whereas the authorities in the different Member States will need to assist one another in performing their duties so as to ensure that the rules of protection are properly respected throughout the European Union;

(65) Whereas, at Community level, a Working Party on the Protection of Individuals with regard to the Processing of Personal Data must be set up and be completely independent in the performance of its functions; whereas, having regard to its specific nature, it must advise the

Commission and, in particular, contribute to the uniform application of the national rules adopted pursuant to this Directive;

(66) Whereas, with regard to the transfer of data to third countries, the application of this Directive calls for the conferment of powers of implementation on the Commission and the establishment of a procedure in accordance with the procedures laid down in Council Decision 87/373/EEC(1);

(67) Whereas an agreement on a "modus vivendi" between the European Parliament, the Council and the Commission concerning the implimenting measures for acts adopted in accordance with the procedure laid down in Article 189b of the EC Treaty was reached on 20 December 1994;

(68) Whereas the principles set out in this Directive regarding the protection of the rights and freedoms of individuals, notably their right to privacy, with regard to the processing of personal data may be supplemented or clarified, in particular as far as certain sectors are concerned, by specific rules based on those principles;

(69) Whereas Member States should be allowed a period of not more than three years from the entry into force of the national measures transposing this Directive in which to apply such new national rules gradually to all processing operations already under way; whereas, in order to facilitate cost-efficient implementation, a further period expiring twelve years after the date on which this Directive is adopted will be allowed to Member States to ensure the conformity of existing manual filing systems with certain of the Directive's provisions; whereas data contained in such filing systems actively processed during this extended transition period should nevertheless be brought into conformity with these provisions at the time of such further active processing;

(70) Whereas it is not necessary for the data subject to give his consent again so as to allow the controller to continue to process, after the national provisions taken pursuant to this Directive enter into force, any sensitive data necessary for the performance of a contract concluded on the basis of free and informed consent before the entry into force of these provisions;

(71) Whereas this Directive does not stand in the way of a Member State's regulating marketing activities aimed at consumers residing in its territory insofar as much as such regulation does not concern the protection of individuals with regard to the processing of personal data;

(72) Whereas the Directive allows the principle of public access to official documents to be taken into account when implementing the principles set out in this Directive,

HAVE ADOPTED THIS DIRECTIVE:

CHAPTER I: GENERAL PROVISIONS

Article 1 Object of the Directive

International
European Union Data Protection Directive

1. In accordance with this Directive, Member States shall protect the fundamental rights and freedoms of natural persons, and in particular their right to privacy, with respect to the processing of personal data.

2. Member States shall neither restrict nor prohibit the free flow of personal data between Member States for reasons connected with the protection afforded under paragraph 1.

Article 2 Definitions

For the purposes of this Directive

(a) "personal data" shall mean any information relating to an identified or identifiable natural person ("data subject"); an identifiable person is one who can be identified, directly or indirectly, in particular by reference to an identification number or to one or more factors specific to his physical, physiological, mental, economic, cultural or social identity;

(b) "processing of personal data" ("processing") shall mean any operation or set of operations which is performed upon personal data, whether or not by automatic means, such as collection, recording, organization, storage, adaptation or alteration, retrieval, consultation, use, disclosure by transmission, dissemination or otherwise making available, alignment or combination, blocking, erasure or destruction;

(c) "personal data filing system" ("filing system") shall mean any structured set of personal data which are accessible according to specific criteria, whether centralized, decentralized or dispersed on a functional or geographical basis;

(d) "controller" shall mean the natural or legal person, public authority, agency or any other body which alone or jointly with others determines the purposes and means of the processing of personal data. Where the purposes and means of processing are determined by national or Community laws or regulations, the controller or the specific criteria for his nomination may be designated by a national or Community law.

(e) "processor" shall mean the natural or legal person, public authority, agency or any other body which processes personal data on behalf of the controller;

(f) "third party" shall mean the natural or legal person, public authority, agency or any other body other than the data subject, the controller, the processor and the persons who, under the direct authority of the controller or the processor, are authorized to process the data;

(g) "recipient" shall mean the natural or legal person, public authority, agency or any other body to whom data are disclosed, whether a third party or not; however, authorities which may receive data in the framework of a particular inquiry shall not be regarded as recipients;

(h) "the data subject's consent" shall mean any freely given specific and informed indication of his wishes by which the data subject signifies his agreement to personal data relating to him being processed.

Article 3 Scope

1. This Directive shall apply to the processing of personal data wholly or partly by automatic means, and to the processing otherwise than by automatic means of personal data which form part of a filing system or are intended to form part of a filing system.

2. This Directive shall not apply to the processing of personal data:

- in the course of an activity which falls outside the scope of community law, such as those provided for by Titles V and VI of the Treaty on European Union and in any case to processing operations concerning public security, defence, State security (including the economic well-being of the State when the processing operation related to State security matters) and the activities of the State in areas of criminal law;

- by a natural person in the course of a purely personal or household activity.

Article 4 National law applicable

1. Each Member State shall apply the national provisions it adopts pursuant to this Directive to the processing of personal data where:

(a) the processing is carried out in the context of the activities of an establishment of the controller on the territory of the Member State; when the same controller is established on the territory of several Member States, he must take the necessary measures to ensure that each of these establishments complies with the obligations laid down by the national law applicable;

(b) the controller is not established on the Member State's territory, but in a place where its national law applies by virtue of international public law;

(c) the controller is not established on Community territory and, for purposes of processing personal data makes use of equipment, automated or otherwise, situated on the territory of said Member State, unless such equipment is used only for purposes of transit through the territory of the Community.

2. In the circumstances referred to in paragraph 1(c), the controller must designate a representative established in the territory of that Member State, without prejudice to legal actions which could be initiated against the controller himself.

CHAPTER II: GENERAL RULES ON THE LAWFULNESS OF THE PROCESSING OF PERSONAL DATA

Article 5

Member States shall, within the limits of the provisions of this Chapter, determine more precisely the conditions under which the processing of personal data is lawful.

International
European Union Data Protection Directive

SECTION I PRINCIPLES RELATING TO DATA QUALITY

Article 6

> 1. Member States shall provide that personal data must be:
>> (a) processed fairly and lawfully;
>> (b) collected for specified, explicit and legitimate purposes and not further processed in a way incompatible with those purposes. Further processing of data for historical, statistical or scientific purposes shall not be considered as incompatible provided that Member States provide appropriate safeguards;
>> (c) adequate, relevant and not excessive in relation to the purposes for which they are collected and/or for which they are further processed;
>> (d) accurate and, where necessary, kept up to date; every reasonable step must be taken to ensure that data which are inaccurate or incomplete, having regard to the purposes for which they were collected or for which they are further processed, are erased or rectified;
>> (e) kept in a form which permits identification of data subjects for no longer that is necessary for the purposes for which the data were collected or for which they are further processed. Member Sates shall lay down appropriate safeguards for personal data stored for longer periods for historical, statistical or scientific use.
> 2. It shall be for the controller to ensure that paragraph 1 is complied with.

SECTION II PRINCIPLES RELATING TO THE REASONS FOR MAKING DATA PROCESSING LEGITIMATE

Article 7

> Member States shall provide that personal data may be processed only if:
>> (a) the data subject has given his consent unambiguously; or
>> (b) processing is necessary for the performance of a contact to which the data subject is party or in order to take steps at the request of the data subject entering into a contract.; or
>> (c) processing is necessary for compliance with a legal obligation to which the controller is subject; or
>> (d) processing is necessary in order to protect the vital interests of the data subject; or
>> (e) processing is necessary for the performance of a task carried out in the public interest or in the exercise of official authority vested in the controller or in a third party to whom the data are disclosed; or
>> (f) processing is necessary for the purposes of the legitimate interests pursued by the controller or by the third party or parties to whom the data are disclosed, except where such interests are overridden by the interests or fundamental rights and freedoms of the data subject which require protection under Article 1(1).

SECTION III SPECIAL CATEGORIES OF PROCESSING

Article 8 The processing of special categories of data

1. Member States shall prohibit the processing of personal data revealing racial or ethnic origin, political opinions, religious or philosophical beliefs, trade-union membership, and the processing of data concerning health or sex life.

2. Paragraph 1 shall not apply where:

(a) the data subject has given his explicit consent to the processing of those data, except where the laws of the Member State provide that the prohibition referred to in paragraph 1 may not be waived by the data subject giving his consent.; or

(b) processing is necessary for the purposes of carrying out the obligations and specific rights of the controller in the field of employment law insofar as it is authorized by national law providing for adequate safeguards; or

(c) processing is necessary to protect the vital interests of the data subject or of another person where the data subject is physically or legally incapable of giving his consent; or

(d) processing is carried out in the course of its legitimate activities with appropriate guarantees by a foundation, association or any other non-profit-seeking body with a political, philosophical, religious or trade-union aim and on condition that the processing relates solely to the members of the body or to persons who have regular contact with it in connection with its purposes and that the data are not disclosed to a third party without the consent of the data subjects; or

(e)the processing relates to data which are manifestly made public by the data subject or is necessary for the establishment, exercise or defense of legal claims.

3. Paragraph 1 shall not apply where processing of the data is required for the purposes of preventive medicine, medical diagnosis, the provision of care or treatment or the management of health-care services, and where those data are processed by a health professional subject under national law or rules established by national competent bodies to the obligation of professional secrecy or by another person also subject to an equivalent obligation of secrecy.

4. Subject to the provision of suitable safeguards, Member States may lay down for reasons of important public interest, exemptions in addition to those laid down in paragraph 2 either by national law or by decision of the supervisory authority.

5. Processing of data relating to offences, criminal convictions or security measures may be carried out only under the control of official authority, or if suitable specific safeguards are provided under national law, subject to derogations which may be granted by the Member State under national provisions providing suitable specific safeguards. However, a complete register of criminal convictions may be kept only under the control of official authority. Member States may provide that data relating to

administrative sanctions or civil trials shall also be processed under the control of official authority.

6. Derogations from paragraph 1 provided for in paragraphs 4 and 5 shall be notified to the Commission.

7. Member States shall determine the conditions under which a national identification number or any other identifier of general application may be processed.

Article 9 Processing of personal data and freedom of expression

Member States shall provide for exemptions or derogations from the provisions of this Chapter, Chapter IV and Chapter VI for the processing of personal data carried out solely for journalistic purposes or the purpose of artistic or literary expression only if they are necessary to reconcile the right to privacy with the rules governing freedom of expression.

SECTION IV INFORMATION TO BE GIVEN TO THE DATA SUBJECT

Article 10 Information in cases of collection of data from the data subject

Member States shall provide that the controller or his representative must provide a data subject from whom data relating to himself are collected with at least the following information, except where he already knows:

(a) the identity of the controller and of his representative, if any,

(b) the purposes of the processing for which the data are intended,

(c) any further information such as - the recipients or categories of recipients of the data; - whether replies to the questions are obligatory or voluntary, as well as the possible consequences of the failure to reply; - the existence of the right of access to and the right to rectify the data concerning him insofar as they are necessary, having regard to the specific circumstances in which the data are collected, to guarantee fair processing in respect of the data subject.

Article 11 Information where the data have not been obtained from the data subject

1. Where the data have not been obtained from the data subject, Member States shall provide that the controller or his representative must at the time of undertaking the recording of personal data or if a disclosure to a third party is envisaged, no later than the time when the data are first disclosed provide the data subject with at least the following information, except where he already knows:

(a) the identity of the controller and of his representative, if any,

(b) the purposes of the processing,

(c) any further information such as

- the categories of data concerned

- the recipients or categories of recipients;

- the existence of the right of access to and the right to rectify the data concerning him insofar as they are necessary, having regard to the specific circumstances in which the data are processed, to guarantee fair processing in respect of the data subject.

2. Paragraph 1 shall not apply where, in particular for processing for statistical purposes or for the purposes of historical or scientific research, the provision of information proves impossible or involves a disproportionate effort or if recording or disclosure is expressly laid down by law. In these cases Member States shall provide appropriate safeguards.

SECTION V THE DATA SUBJECT'S RIGHT OF ACCESS TO DATA

Article 12 Right of access

Member States shall guarantee for every data subject the right to obtain from the controller:

(a). without constraint at reasonable intervals and without excessive delay or expense:

- confirmation as to whether or not data relating to him are processed and information at least as to the purposes of the processing, the categories of data concerned, and the recipients or categories of recipients to whom the data are disclosed;

- communication to him in an intelligible form of the data undergoing processing and of any available information as to their source;

- knowledge of the logic involved in any automatic processing of data concerning him at least in the case of the automated decisions referred to in Article 15(1);

(b). as appropriate the rectification, erasure or blocking of data, the processing of which does not comply with the provisions of this Directive, in particular because of the incomplete or inaccurate nature of the data;

(c). notification to third parties to whom the data have been disclosed of any rectification, erasure or blocking carried out in compliance with paragraph (b), unless this proves impossible or involves a disproportionate effort.

SECTION VI: EXEMPTIONS AND RESTRICTIONS

Article 13: Exemptions and restrictions

1. Member States may adopt legislative measures to restrict the scope of the obligations and rights provided for in Articles 6(1), 10, 11(1), 12 and 21 when such a restriction constitutes a necessary measure to safeguard:

(a) national security;

(b) defence;

(c) public security;

(d) the prevention, investigation, detection and prosecution of criminal offences, or of breaches of ethics for regulated professions;

(e) an important economic or financial interest of a Member State or of the European Union, including monetary, budgetary and taxation matters;

(f) a monitoring, inspection or regulatory function connected, even occasionally, with the exercise of official authority in cases referred to in (c), (d) and (e);

(g) the protection of the data subject or of the rights and freedoms of others.

2. Subject to adequate legal guarantees, in particular that the data are not used for taking measures or decisions regarding any particular individual data subject, Member States may restrict, by a legislative measure, the rights provided for in Article 12 when data are processed solely for purposes of scientific research or are kept in personal form for a period which does not exceed the period necessary for the sole purpose of creating statistics.

SECTION VII: THE DATA SUBJECT'S RIGHT TO OBJECT

Article 14 The data subject's right to object

Member States shall grant the data subject the right:

(a) at least in the cases referred to in Article 7(e) and (f), to object at any time on compelling legitimate grounds relating to his particular situation to the processing of data relating to him, save where otherwise

provided by national legislation. Where there is a justified objection, the processing instigated by the controller may no longer involve those data;

(b) to object, on request and free of charge, to the processing of personal data relating to him which the controller anticipates being processed for the purposes of direct marketing; or to be informed before personal data are disclosed for the first time to third parties or used on their behalf for the purposes of direct marketing, and to be expressly offered the right to object free of charge to such disclosures or uses.

Member States shall take the necessary measures to ensure that data subjects are aware of the existence of the right referred to in the first subparagraph of (b).

Article 15: Automated individual decisions

1. Member States shall grant the right to every person not to be subject to a decision which produces legal effects concerning him or significantly affects him and which is based solely on automated processing of data intended to evaluate certain personal aspects relating to him, such as his performance at work, creditworthiness, reliability, conduct, etc.

2. Subject to the other Articles of this Directive, Member States shall provide that a person may be subjected to a decision of the kind referred to in paragraph 1 if that decision:

(a) is taken in the course of entering into or performance of a contract, provided the request by the data subject has been satisfied, or that there are suitable measures to safeguard his legitimate interests, such as arrangements allowing him to defend his point of view; or

(b) is authorized by a law which also lays down measures to safeguard the data subject's legitimate interests.

SECTION VIII: CONFIDENTIALITY AND SECURITY OF PROCESSING

Article 16 Confidentiality of processing

Any person acting under the authority of the controller or of the processor, including the processor himself, who has access to personal data must not process them except on instructions from the controller, unless he is required to do so by law.

Article 17 Security of processing

1. Member States shall provide that the controller must implement appropriate technical and organizational measures to protect personal data against accidental or unlawful destruction or accidental loss and against unauthorized alteration, disclosure or access, in particular where the processing involves the transmission of data over a network, and against all other unlawful forms of processing. Having regard to the state of the art and the costs of their implementation, such measures shall ensure a level of security appropriate to the risks represented by the processing and the nature of the data to be protected.

2. The Member States shall provide that the controller must, where processing is carried out on his behalf, choose a processor who provides sufficient guarantees in respect of the technical security measures and organizational measures governing the processing to be carried out and must ensure compliance with those measures.

3. The carrying out of processing by way of a processor must be governed by a contract or legal act binding the processor to the controller and stipulating in particular that:

    - the processor shall act only on instructions from the controller;

    - the obligations set out in paragraph 1, as defined by the law of the Member State in which the processor is established, shall also be incumbent on the processor.

4. For the purposes of keeping proof, the parts of the contract or legal act relating to data protection and the requirements relating to the measures referred to in paragraph 1 shall be in writing or in another equivalent form.

SECTION IX: NOTIFICATION

Article 18 Obligation to notify the supervisory authority

1. Member States shall provide that the controller or his representative, if any, must notify the supervisory authority referred to in Article 28 before carrying out any wholly or partly automatic processing operation or set of such operations intended to serve a single purpose or several related purposes.

2. Member States may provide for the simplification of or exemption from notification only in the following cases and under the following conditions:

- where, for categories of processing operations which are unlikely, taking account of the data to be processed, to affect adversely the rights and freedoms of data subjects, they specify the purposes of the processing, the data or categories of data undergoing processing, the category or categories of data subject, the recipients or categories of recipient to whom the data are to be disclosed and the length of time the data are to be stored and/or

- where the controller appoints, in compliance with the national law which governs him, a data protection official, responsible in particular

= for ensuring in an independent manner the internal application of the national provisions taken pursuant to this Directive

= for keeping the register of processing operations carried out by the controller, containing the items of information referred to in Article 21(2), thereby ensuring that the rights and freedoms of the data subjects are unlikely to be adversely affected by the processing operations.

3. Member States may provide that paragraph 1 does not apply to processing whose sole purpose is the keeping of a register, which according to laws or regulations is intended to provide information to the public and which is open to consultation either by the public in general or by any person demonstrating a legitimate interest.

4. Member States may provide for an exemption from the obligation to notify or a simplification of the notification in the case or processing operations referred to in Article 8(2)(d).

5. Member States may stipulate that certain or all non-automatic processing operations involving personal data shall be notified, or provide for these processing operations to be subject to a simplified notification.

Article 19 Contents of notification

1. Member States shall specify the information to be given in the notification. It shall include at least:

(a) the name and address of the controller and of his representative, if any;

(b) the purpose or purposes of the processing;

(c) a description of the category or categories of data subject and of the data or categories of data relating to them;

(d) the recipients or categories of recipient to whom the data might be disclosed;

(e) proposed transfers of data to third countries;

(f) a general description allowing a preliminary assessment to be made of the appropriateness of the measures taken pursuant to Article 17 to ensure security of processing.

2. Member States shall specify the procedures under which any change affecting the information referred to in paragraph 1 must be notified to the supervisory authority.

Article 20 Prior checking

1. Member States shall determine the processing operations likely to present specific risks for the rights and freedoms of data subjects and shall check that these processing operations are examined prior to the start thereof.

2. Such prior checks shall be carried out by the supervisory authority following receipt of a notification from the controller or by the data protection official, who in cases of doubt must consult the supervisory authority.

3. Member States may also carry out such checks in the context of preparation of a measure decided on by the national parliament or based on such a decision, defining the nature of the processing operation and laying down appropriate safeguards.

Article 21 Publicizing of processing operations

1. Member States shall take measures to ensure that processing operations are publicized.

2. Member States shall provide that a register of processing operations notified in accordance with Article 18 shall be kept by the supervisory authority. The register shall contain at least the information listed in Article 19(1)(a) to (e). The register may be inspected by any person.

3. Member States shall provide, in relation to processing operations not subject to notification, that controllers or another body appointed by the Member States make available at least the information referred to in Article 19(1)(a) to (e) in an appropriate fashion to any person on request. Member States may provide that this provision does not apply to processing whose sole purpose is the keeping of a register, which according to laws or regulations is intended to provide information to the public and which is open to consultation either by the public in general or by any person who can provide proof of a legitimate interest.

CHAPTER III JUDICIAL REMEDIES, LIABILITY AND PENALTIES

Article 22 Remedies

Without prejudice to any administrative remedy for which provision may be made, inter alia before the supervisory authority referred to in Article 28, prior to referral to the judicial authority, Member States shall provide for the right of every person to a judicial remedy for any breach of the rights guaranteed him by the national law applicable to the processing in question.

Article 23 Liability

1. Member States shall provide that any person who has suffered damage as a result of an unlawful processing operation or of any act incompatible with the national provisions adopted pursuant to this Directive is entitled to receive compensation from the controller for the damage suffered.

2. The controller may be exempted from this liability, in whole or in part, if he proves that he is not responsible for the event giving rise to the damage.

Article 24 Sanctions

The Member States shall adopt suitable measures to ensure the full implementation of the provisions of this Directive and shall in particular lay down the sanctions to be imposed in case of infringement of the provisions adopted pursuant to this Directive.

CHAPTER IV TRANSFER OF PERSONAL DATA TO THIRD COUNTRIES

Article 25 Principles

1. The Member States shall provide that the transfer to a third country of personal data which are undergoing processing or are intended for processing after transfer may take place only if, without prejudice to compliance with the national provisions adopted pursuant to the other provisions of this Directive, the third country in question ensures an adequate level of protection.

2. The adequacy of the level of protection afforded by a third country shall be assessed in the light of all the circumstances surrounding a data transfer operation or set of data transfer operations; particular consideration shall be given to the nature of the data, the purpose and duration of the proposed processing operation or operations, the country of origin and country of final destination, the rules of law, both general and sectoral, in force in the third country in question and the professional rules and security measures which are complied with in those countries.

3. Member States and the Commission shall inform each other of cases where the consider that a third country does not ensure an adequate level of protection within the meaning of paragraph 2.

4. Where the Commission finds, under the procedure provided for in Article 31(2), that a third country does not ensure an adequate level of protection within the meaning of paragraph 2 of this Article Member States shall take the measures necessary to prevent the transfer of data of the same type to the third country in question.

5. At the appropriate time, the Commission shall enter into negotiations with a view to remedying the situation resulting from the funding made pursuant to paragraph 4.

6. The Commission may find, in accordance with the procedure referred to in Article 31(2), that a third country ensures an adequate level of protection within the meaning of paragraph 2 of this Article, by reason of its domestic law or of the international commitments it has entered into, particularly upon conclusion of the negotiations referred to in paragraph 5, for the protection of the private lives and basic freedoms and

rights of individuals. Member States shall take the measures necessary to comply with the Commission's decision.

Article 26 Derogations

1. By way of derogation from Article 25 and save where otherwise provided by domestic law governing particular cases, Member States shall provide that a transfer or a set of transfers of personal data to a third country which does not ensure an adequate level of protection within the meaning of Article 25(2) may take place on condition that:

(a) the data subject has given his consent unambiguously to the proposed transfer, or

(b) the transfer is necessary for the performance of a contract between the data subject and the controller or the implementation of precontractual measures taken in response to the data subject's request, or

(c) the transfer is necessary for the conclusion or for the performance of a contract concluded in the interest of the data subject between the controller and a third party, or

(d) the transfer is necessary or legally required on important public interest grounds, or for the establishment, exercise or defence of legal claims, or

(e) the transfer is necessary in order to protect the vital interests of the data subject, or

(f) the transfer is made from a register which according to laws or regulations is intended to provide information to the public and which is open to consultation either by the public in general or by any person who can demonstrate legitimate interest, to the extent that the conditions laid down in law for consultation are fulfilled in the particular case.

2. Without prejudice to paragraph 1, a Member State may authorize a transfer or a set of transfers of personal data to a third country which does not ensure an adequate level of protection within the meaning of Article 25(2), where the controller adduces sufficient guarantees with respect to the protection of the privacy and fundamental rights and freedoms of individuals and as regards the exercise of the corresponding rights; such guarantees may in particular result from appropriate contractual clauses.

3. The Member State shall inform the Commission and the other Member States of the authorizations granted pursuant to paragraph 2. If a Member State or the Commission objects on justified grounds involving the protection of the privacy and fundamental rights and freedoms of individuals, the Commission shall take appropriate measures in accordance with the procedure laid down in Article 31(2). Member States shall take the necessary measures to comply with the Commission's decision.

4. Where the Commission decides, in accordance with the procedure referred to in Article 31(2), that certain standard contractual clauses offer sufficient guarantees

required by paragraph 2, Member States shall take the necessary measures to comply with the Commission's decision.

CHAPTER V CODES OF CONDUCT

Article 27

1. The Member States and the Commission shall encourage the drawing up of codes of conduct intended to contribute to the proper implementation of the national provisions adopted by the Member States pursuant to this Directive, taking account of the specific features of the various sectors.

2. Member States shall make provision for trade associations and other bodies representing other categories of controllers which have drawn up draft national codes or which have the intention of amending or extending existing national codes to be able to submit them to the opinion of the national authority. Member States shall make provision for this authority to ascertain, among other things, whether the drafts submitted to it are in accordance with the national provisions adopted pursuant to this Directive. If it sees fit, the authority shall seek the views of data subjects or their representatives.

3. Draft Community codes, and amendments or extensions to existing Community codes, may be submitted to the Working Party referred to in Article 29. This Working Party shall determine, among other things, whether the drafts submitted to it are in accordance with the national provisions adopted pursuant to this Directive. If it sees fit, the authority shall seek the views of data subjects or their representatives. The Commission may ensure appropriate publicity for the codes which have been approved by the Working Party.

CHAPTER VI SUPERVISORY AUTHORITY AND WORKING PARTY ON THE PROTECTION OF INDIVIDUALS WITH REGARD TO THE PROCESSING OF PERSONAL DATA

Article 28 Supervisory authority

1. Each Member State shall provide that one or more public authorities are responsible for monitoring the application within its territory of the provisions adopted by the Member States pursuant to this Directive. These authorities shall act with complete independence in exercising the functions entrusted to them.

2. Each Member State shall provide that the supervisory authorities are consulted when drawing up administrative measures or regulations relating to the protection of individuals' rights and freedoms with regard to the processing of personal data.

3. Each authority shall in particular be endowed with:

- investigative powers, such as powers of access to data forming the subject-matter of processing operations and powers to collect all the information necessary for the performance of its supervisory duties;

- effective powers of intervention, such as, for example, that of delivering opinions in accordance with Article 20, before processing operations are carried out and ensuring appropriate publication of such opinions, or that of ordering the blocking, erasure or destruction of data, or of imposing a temporary or definitive ban on processing, or that of warning or admonishing the controller or that of referring the matter to national parliaments or other political institutions;

- the power to engage in legal proceedings where the national provisions adopted pursuant to this Directive have been violated or to bring these violations to the attention of the judicial authorities. Decisions by the supervisory authority which give rise to complaints may be appealed against through the courts.

4. Each supervisory authority shall hear claims lodged by any person, or by an association representing that person, concerning the protection of his rights and freedoms in regard to the processing of personal data. The person concerned shall be informed of the outcome of the claim. Each supervisory authority shall, in particular, hear claims for checks on the lawfulness of data processing lodged by any person when the national provisions adopted pursuant to Article 13 of this Directive apply. The person shall at any rate be informed that a check has taken place.

5. Each supervisory authority shall draw up a report on its activities at regular intervals. The report shall be made public.

6. Each supervisory authority is competent, whatever the national law applicable to the processing in question, for exercising, on the territory of its own Member State, the powers attributed to it in accordance with paragraph 3. Each authority may be requested to exercise its powers by an authority of another Member State. The supervisory authorities shall cooperate with one another to the extent necessary for the performance of their duties, in particular by exchanging all useful information.

7. Member States shall provide that the members and staff of the supervisory authority, even after their employment has ended, are to be subject to a duty of professional secrecy with regard to confidential information to which they have access.

Article 29 Working Party on the Protection of Individuals with regard to the Processing of Personal Data

1. A Working Party on the Protection of Individuals with regard to the Processing of Personal Data, hereinafter referred to as "the Working Party", is hereby set up. It shall have advisory status and act independently.

2. The Working Party shall be composed of a representative of the supervisory authority or authorities designated by each Member State and of a representative of the authority or authorities established for Community institutions and bodies, and of a representative of the Commission. Each member of the Working Party shall be

designated by the institution, authority or authorities which he represents. Where a Member State designates more than one supervisory authority, they shall nominate a joint representative. The same shall apply for the authorities established for Community institutions and bodies.

3. The Working Party shall take decisions by a simple majority of the representatives of the supervisory authorities.

4. The Working Party shall elect its chairman. The chairman's term of office shall be two years. His appointment shall be renewable.

5. The Working Party's secretariat shall be provided by the Commission.

6. The Working Party shall adopt its own rules of procedure.

7. The Working Party shall consider items placed on its agenda by its chairman, either on his own initiative or at the request of a representative of the supervisory authorities or at the Commission's request.

Article 30

1. The Working Party shall:

(a) examine any question covering the application of the national measures adopted under this Directive in order to contribute to the uniform application of such measures;

(b) give the Commission an opinion on the level of protection in the Community and in third countries;

(c) advise the Commission on any proposed amendment of this Directive, on any additional or specific measures to safeguard the rights and freedoms of natural persons with regard to the processing of personal data and on any other proposed Community measures affecting such rights and freedoms;

(d) give an opinion on codes of conduct drawn up at Community level.

2. If the Working Party finds that divergences likely to affect the equivalence of protection for persons with regard to the processing of personal data in the Community are arising between the laws or practices of Member States, it shall inform the Commission accordingly.

3. The Working Party may, on its own initiative, make recommendations on all matters relating to the protection of persons with regard to the processing of personal data in the Community.

4. The Working Party's opinions and recommendations shall be forwarded to the Commission and to the committee referred to in Article 31.

5. The Commission shall inform the Working Party of the action it has taken in response to its opinions and recommendations. It shall do so in a report which shall also be forwarded to the European Parliament and the Council. The report shall be made public.

6. The Working Party shall draw up an annual report on the situation regarding the protection of natural persons with regard to the processing of personal data in the Community and in third countries, which it shall transmit to the Commission, the European Parliament and the Council. The report shall be made public.

CHAPTER VII COMMUNITY IMPLEMENTING MEASURES

Article 31 The Committee

1. The Commission shall be assisted by a committee composed of the representatives of the Member States and chaired by the representative of the Commission.

2. The representative of the Commission shall submit to the committee a draft of the measures to be taken. The committee shall deliver its opinion on the draft within a time limit which the chairman may lay down according to the urgency of the matter. The opinion shall be delivered by the majority laid down in Article 148(2) of the Treaty. The votes of the representatives of the Member States within the committee shall be weighted in the manner set out in that Article. The chairman shall not vote. The Commission shall adopt measures which shall apply immediately. However, if these measures are not in accordance with the opinion of the committee, they shall be communicated by the Commission to the Council forthwith. In that event: The Commission shall defer application of the measures which it has decided for a period to be laid down in each act adopted by the Council, but which may in on case exceed three months from the date of communication. The Council, acting by a qualified majority, may take a different decision within the time limit referred to in the previous paragraph.

FINAL PROVISIONS

Article 32

1. Member States shall bring into force the laws, regulations and administrative provisions necessary to comply with this Directive at the latest at the end of a period of three years from the adoption of the Directive. When Member States adopt these measures, they shall contain a reference to this Directive or be accompanied by such reference on the occasion of their official publication. The methods of making such reference shall be laid down by the Member States.

2. Member States shall ensure that processing already underway on the date the national provisions adopted pursuant to this Directive enter into force, is brought into conformity with these provisions within 3 years of this date. By way of derogation from the preceding subparagraph, Member States may provide that the processing of data already held in manual filing systems on the date of entry into force of the national provisions adopted in implementation of this Directive shall be brought into conformity with Articles 6,7 and 8 within 12 years of the date on which this Directive is adopted.

Member States shall, however, grant the data subject the right to obtain, at his request and in particular at the time of exercising his right of access, the rectification, erasure or blocking of data which are incomplete, inaccurate or stored in a way incompatible with the legitimate purposes pursued by the controller.

3. By way of derogation from paragraph 2, Member States may provide, subject to suitable safeguards, that data kept for the sole purpose of historical research are not brought into conformity with Articles 6,7 and 8 of this Directive.

4. Member States shall communicate to the Commission the provisions of national law which they adopt in the field covered by this Directive.

Article 33

The Commission shall report to the Council and the European Parliament at regular intervals, starting not later than three years after the date referred to in Article 32(1), on the implementation of this Directive, attaching to its report, if necessary, suitable proposals for amendments. The report shall be made public.

The Commission shall examine, in particular, the application of this Directive to the data processing of sound and image data relating to natural persons and shall submit any appropriate proposals which prove to be necessary, taking account of developments in information technology and in the light of the state of progress in the information society.

Article 34

This Directive is addressed to the Member States.

OECD CRYPTOGRAPHY GUIDELINES
(1997)

Summary

The unprecedented growth of communication networks and associated technologies for privacy and security created a need for an international policy framework to harmonize national policies and promote techniques to safeguard communication networks . In 1997 the OECD, an international body of 29 countries, adopted the Guidelines for Cryptography Policy. The Guidelines are a non-binding agreement identifying the policy goals that countries should implement when drawing up cryptography policies at the national and international levels.

The Guidelines set out eight principles for cryptography policy: (i) Cryptographic methods should be trustworthy in order to generate confidence in the use of information and communications systems; (ii) Users should have a right to choose any cryptographic method, subject to applicable law; (iii) Cryptographic methods should be developed in response to the needs, demands and responsibilities of individuals, businesses and governments; (iv) Technical standards, criteria and protocols for cryptographic methods should be developed and promulgated at the national and international level; (v) The fundamental rights of individuals to privacy, including secrecy of communications and protection of personal data, should be respected in national cryptography policies and in the implementation and use of cryptographic methods; (vi) National cryptography policies may allow lawful access to plaintext, or cryptographic keys, of encrypted data. These policies must respect the other principles contained in the guidelines to the greatest extent possible; (vii) Whether established by contract or legislation, the liability of individuals and entities that offer cryptographic services or hold or access cryptographic keys should be clearly stated; (viii) Governments should co-operate to co-ordinate cryptography policies. As part of this effort, governments should remove, or avoid creating in the name of cryptography policy, unjustified obstacles to trade.

During deliberations a proposal for the adoption of key escrow techniques that would enable routine law enforcement access to computer communications was put forward. The OECD member countries firmly rejected the recommendation. Reasons given disfavoring the proposal were that key escrow would undermine trust and could not be included in a nationwide card system. In the end, member states adopted the OECD Guidelines as a coordinated effort to facilitate the smooth development of an efficient secure information infrastructure and to address issues of privacy, law enforcement, national security, technology development and commerce.

References

OECD, Guidelines for Cryptography Policy
[http://www.oecd.org/internet/ieconomy/guidelinesforcryptographypolicy.htm]

International
OECD Cryptography Guidelines

OECD, *Report on Background and Issues of Cryptography Policy* (1997)
[http://www.oecd.org/internet/ieconomy/reportonbackgroundandissuesofcryptograph
ypolicy.htm]

EPIC, *Cryptography & Liberty 2000: An International Survey of Encryption Policy*,
(EPIC 2000)
[https://www2.epic.org/reports/crypto2000/]

RECOMMENDATION OF THE COUNCIL CONCERNING GUIDELINES FOR
CRYPTOGRAPHY POLICY
27 March 1997

THE COUNCIL, HAVING REGARD TO:

* the Convention on the Organisation for Economic Co-operation and Development of
14 December 1960, in particular, articles 1 b), 1 c), 3 a) and 5 b) thereof;

* the Recommendation of the Council concerning Guidelines Governing the Protection
of Privacy and Transborder Flows of Personal Data of 23 September 1980
[C(80)58(Final)];

* the Declaration on Transborder Data Flows adopted by the Governments of OECD
Member countries on 11 April 1985 [Annex to C(85)139];

* the Recommendation of the Council concerning Guidelines for the Security of
Information Systems of 26-27 November 1992 [C(92)188/FINAL];

* the Directive [95/46/EC] of the European Parliament and of the Council of the
European Union of 24 October 1995 on the protection of individuals with regard to the
processing of personal data and on the free movement of such data;

* the Wassenaar Arrangement on Export Controls for Conventional Arms and Dual-use
Goods and Technologies agreed on 13 July 1996;

* the Regulation [(EC) 3381/94] and the Decision [94/942/PESC] of the Council of the
European Union of 19 December 1994 concerning the control of the export of dual-use
goods;

* and the Recommendation [R(95)13] of the Council of Europe of 11 September 1995
concerning problems of criminal procedural law connected with information
technology;

CONSIDERING:

* that national and global information infrastructures are developing rapidly to provide
a seamless network for world-wide communications and access to data;

* that this emerging information and communications network is likely to have an
important impact on economic development and world trade;

* that the users of information technology must have trust in the security of information and communications infrastructures, networks and systems; in the confidentiality, integrity, and availability of data on them; and in the ability to prove the origin and receipt of data;

* that data is increasingly vulnerable to sophisticated threats to its security, and ensuring the security of data through legal, procedural and technical means is fundamentally important in order for national and international information infrastructures to reach their full potential;

RECOGNISING:

* that, as cryptography can be an effective tool for the secure use of information technology by ensuring confidentiality, integrity and availability of data and by providing authentication and

non-repudiation mechanisms for that data, it is an important component of secure information and communications networks and systems;

* that cryptography has a variety of applications related to the protection of privacy, intellectual property, business and financial information, public safety and national security, and the operation of electronic commerce, including secure anonymous payments and transactions;

* that the failure to utilise cryptographic methods can adversely affect the protection of privacy, intellectual property, business and financial information, public safety and national security and the

operation of electronic commerce because data and communications may be inadequately protected from unauthorised access, alteration, and improper use, and, therefore, users may not trust information and communications systems, networks and infrastructures;

* that the use of cryptography to ensure integrity of data, including authentication and non-repudiation mechanisms, is distinct from its use to ensure confidentiality of data, and that each of these uses presents different issues;

1. that the quality of information protection afforded by cryptography depends not only on the selected technical means, but also on good managerial, organisational and operational procedures;

AND FURTHER RECOGNISING:

* that governments have wide-ranging responsibilities, several of which are specifically implicated in the use of cryptography, including protection of privacy and facilitating information and communications systems security; encouraging economic well-being by, in part, promoting commerce; maintaining public safety; and enabling the enforcement of laws and the protection of national security;

* that although there are legitimate governmental, commercial and individual needs and uses for cryptography, it may also be used by individuals or entities for illegal activities, which can affect public safety, national security, the enforcement of laws, business interests, consumer interests or privacy; therefore governments, together with industry and the general public, are challenged to develop balanced policies;

* that due to the inherently global nature of information and communications networks, implementation of incompatible national policies will not meet the needs of individuals, business and governments and may create obstacles to economic co-operation and development; and, therefore, national policies may require international co-ordination;

* that this Recommendation of the Council does not affect the sovereign rights of national governments and that the Guidelines contained in the Annex to this Recommendation are always subject to the requirements of national law;

On the proposal of the Committee for Information, Computer and Communications Policy;

RECOMMENDS THAT MEMBER COUNTRIES:

1. establish new, or amend existing, policies, methods, measures, practices and procedures to reflect and take into account the Principles concerning cryptography policy set forth in the Guidelines contained in the Annex to this Recommendation (hereinafter "the Guidelines"), which is an integral part hereof; in so doing, also take into account the Recommendation of the Council concerning Guidelines Governing the Protection of Privacy and Transborder Flows of Personal Data of 23 September 1980 [C(80)58(Final)] and the Recommendation of the Council concerning Guidelines for the Security of Information Systems of 26-27 November 1992 [C(92)188/FINAL];

2. consult, co-ordinate and co-operate at the national and international level in the implementation of the Guidelines;

3. act on the need for practical and operational solutions in the area of international cryptography policy by using the Guidelines as a basis for agreements on specific issues related to international cryptography policy;

4. disseminate the Guidelines throughout the public and private sectors to promote awareness of the issues and policies related to cryptography;

5. remove, or avoid creating in the name of cryptography policy, unjustified obstacles to international trade and the development of information and communications networks;

6. state clearly and make publicly available, any national controls imposed by governments relating to the use of cryptography;

7. review the Guidelines at least every five years, with a view to improving international co-operation on issues relating to cryptography policy.

ANNEX
GUIDELINES FOR CRYPTOGRAPHY POLICY

I. AIMS

The Guidelines are intended:
* to promote the use of cryptography:
* to foster confidence in information and communication infrastructures, networks and systems and the manner in which they are used;
* to help ensure the security of data, and to protect privacy, in national and global information and communications infrastructures, networks and systems;
* to promote this use of cryptography without unduly jeopardising public safety, law enforcement, and national security;
* to raise awareness of the need for compatible cryptography policies and laws, as well as the need for interoperable, portable and mobile cryptographic methods in national and global information and communications networks;
* to assist decision-makers in the public and private sectors in developing and implementing coherent national and international policies, methods, measures, practices and procedures for the effective use of cryptography;
* to promote co-operation between the public and private sectors in the development and implementation of national and international cryptography policies, methods, measures, practices and procedures;
* to facilitate international trade by promoting cost-effective, interoperable, portable and mobile cryptographic systems;
* to promote international co-operation among governments, business and research communities, and standards-making bodies in achieving co-ordinated use of cryptographic methods.

II. SCOPE

The Guidelines are primarily aimed at governments, in terms of the policy recommendations herein, but with anticipation that they will be widely read and followed by both the private and public sectors.

It is recognised that governments have separable and distinct responsibilities for the protection of information which requires security in the national interest; the Guidelines are not intended for application in these matters.

III. DEFINITIONS

For the purposes of the Guidelines:
* "Authentication" means a function for establishing the validity of a claimed identity of a user, device or another entity in an information or communications system.

International
OECD Cryptography Guidelines

* "Availability" means the property that data, information, and information and communications systems are accessible and usable on a timely basis in the required manner.

* "Confidentiality" means the property that data or information is not made available or disclosed to unauthorised individuals, entities, or processes.

* "Cryptography" means the discipline which embodies principles, means, and methods for the transformation of data in order to hide its information content, establish its authenticity, prevent its undetected modification, prevent its repudiation, and/or prevent its unauthorised use.

* "Cryptographic key" means a parameter used with a cryptographic algorithm to transform, validate, authenticate, encrypt or decrypt data.

* "Cryptographic methods" means cryptographic techniques, services, systems, products and key management systems.

* "Data" means the representation of information in a manner suitable for communication, interpretation, storage, or processing.

* "Decryption" means the inverse function of encryption.

* "Encryption" means the transformation of data by the use of cryptography to produce unintelligible data (encrypted data) to ensure its confidentiality.

* "Integrity" means the property that data or information has not been modified or altered in an unauthorised manner.

* "Interoperability" of cryptographic methods means the technical ability of multiple cryptographic methods to function together.

* "Key management system" means a system for generation, storage, distribution, revocation, deletion, archiving, certification or application of cryptographic keys.

* "Keyholder" means an individual or entity in possession or control of cryptographic keys. A keyholder is not necessarily a user of the key.

* "Law enforcement" or "enforcement of laws" refers to the enforcement of all laws, without regard to subject matter.

* "Lawful access" means access by third party individuals or entities, including governments, to plaintext, or cryptographic keys, of encrypted data, in accordance with law.

* "Mobility" of cryptographic methods only means the technical ability to function in multiple countries or information and communications infrastructures.

* "Non-repudiation" means a property achieved through cryptographic methods, which prevents an individual or entity from denying having performed a particular action related to data (such as mechanisms for non-rejection of authority (origin); for proof of obligation, intent, or commitment; or for proof of ownership).

* "Personal data" means any information relating to an identified or identifiable individual.

* "Plaintext" means intelligible data.

* "Portability" of cryptographic methods means the technical ability to be adapted and function in multiple systems.

IV. INTEGRATION

The principles in Section V of this Annex, each of which addresses an important policy concern, are interdependent and should be implemented as a whole so as to balance the various interests at stake. No principle should be implemented in isolation from the rest.

V. PRINCIPLES

1. TRUST IN CRYPTOGRAPHIC METHODS

CRYPTOGRAPHIC METHODS SHOULD BE TRUSTWORTHY IN ORDER TO GENERATE CONFIDENCE IN THE USE OF INFORMATION AND COMMUNICATIONS SYSTEMS.

Market forces should serve to build trust in reliable systems, and government regulation, licensing, and use of cryptographic methods may also encourage user trust. Evaluation of cryptographic methods, especially against market-accepted criteria, could also generate user trust.

In the interests of user trust, a contract dealing with the use of a key management system should indicate the jurisdiction whose laws apply to that system.

2. CHOICE OF CRYPTOGRAPHIC METHODS

USERS SHOULD HAVE A RIGHT TO CHOOSE ANY CRYPTOGRAPHIC METHOD, SUBJECT TO APPLICABLE LAW.

Users should have access to cryptography that meets their needs, so that they can trust in the security of information and communications systems, and the confidentiality and integrity of data on those systems. Individuals or entities who own, control, access, use or store data may have a responsibility to protect the confidentiality and integrity of such data, and may therefore be responsible for using appropriate cryptographic methods. It is expected that a variety of cryptographic methods may be needed to fulfil different data security requirements. Users of cryptography should be free, subject to applicable law, to determine the type and level of data security needed, and to select and implement appropriate cryptographic methods, including a key management system that suits their needs.

In order to protect an identified public interest, such as the protection of personal data or electronic commerce, governments may implement policies requiring cryptographic methods to achieve a sufficient level of protection.

Government controls on cryptographic methods should be no more than are essential to the discharge of government responsibilities and should respect user choice to the greatest extent possible. This principle should not be interpreted as implying that governments should initiate legislation which limits user choice.

3. MARKET DRIVEN DEVELOPMENT OF CRYPTOGRAPHIC METHODS

CRYPTOGRAPHIC METHODS SHOULD BE DEVELOPED IN RESPONSE TO THE NEEDS, DEMANDS AND RESPONSIBILITIES OF INDIVIDUALS, BUSINESSES AND GOVERNMENTS.

The development and provision of cryptographic methods should be determined by the market in an open and competitive environment. Such an approach would best ensure that solutions keep pace with changing technology, the demands of users and evolving threats to information and communications systems security. The development of international technical standards, criteria and protocols related to cryptographic methods should also be market driven. Governments should encourage and co-operate with business and the research community in the development of cryptographic methods.

4. STANDARDS FOR CRYPTOGRAPHIC METHODS

TECHNICAL STANDARDS, CRITERIA AND PROTOCOLS FOR CRYPTOGRAPHIC METHODS SHOULD BE DEVELOPED AND PROMULGATED AT THE NATIONAL AND INTERNATIONAL LEVEL.

In response to the needs of the market, internationally-recognised standards-making bodies, governments, business and other relevant experts should share information and collaborate to develop and promulgate interoperable technical standards, criteria and protocols for cryptographic methods. National standards for cryptographic methods, if any, should be consistent with international standards to facilitate global interoperability, portability and mobility. Mechanisms to evaluate conformity to such technical standards, criteria and protocols for interoperability, portability and mobility of cryptographic methods should be developed. To the extent that testing of conformity to, or evaluation of, standards may occur, the broad acceptance of such results should be encouraged.

5. PROTECTION OF PRIVACY AND PERSONAL DATA

THE FUNDAMENTAL RIGHTS OF INDIVIDUALS TO PRIVACY, INCLUDING SECRECY OF COMMUNICATIONS AND PROTECTION OF PERSONAL DATA, SHOULD BE RESPECTED IN NATIONAL CRYPTOGRAPHY POLICIES AND IN THE IMPLEMENTATION AND USE OF CRYPTOGRAPHIC METHODS.

Cryptographic methods can be a valuable tool for the protection of privacy, including both the confidentiality of data and communications and the protection of the identity of individuals. Cryptographic methods also offer new opportunities to minimise the collection of personal data, by enabling secure but anonymous payments, transactions and interactions. At the same time, cryptographic methods to ensure the integrity of data in electronic transactions raise privacy implications. These implications, which include the collection of personal data and the creation of systems for personal identification, should be considered and explained, and, where appropriate, privacy safeguards should be established.

The OECD Guidelines for the Protection of Privacy and Transborder Flows of Personal Data provide general guidance concerning the collection and management of personal information, and should be applied in concert with relevant national law when implementing cryptographic methods.

6. LAWFUL ACCESS

NATIONAL CRYPTOGRAPHY POLICIES MAY ALLOW LAWFUL ACCESS TO PLAINTEXT, OR CRYPTOGRAPHIC KEYS, OF ENCRYPTED DATA. THESE POLICIES MUST RESPECT THE OTHER PRINCIPLES CONTAINED IN THE GUIDELINES TO THE GREATEST EXTENT POSSIBLE.

If considering policies on cryptographic methods that provide for lawful access, governments should carefully weigh the benefits, including the benefits for public safety, law enforcement and national security, as well as the risks of misuse, the additional expense of any supporting infrastructure, the prospects of technical failure, and other costs. This principle should not be interpreted as implying that governments should, or should not, initiate legislation that would allow lawful access.

Where access to the plaintext, or cryptographic keys, of encrypted data is requested under lawful process, the individual or entity requesting access must have a legal right to possession of the plaintext, and once obtained the data must only be used for lawful purposes. The process through which lawful access is obtained should be recorded, so that the disclosure of the cryptographic keys or the data can be audited or reviewed in accordance with national law. Where lawful access is requested and obtained, such access should be granted within designated time limits appropriate to the circumstances. The conditions of lawful access should be stated clearly and published in a way that they are easily available to users, keyholders and providers of cryptographic methods.

Key management systems could provide a basis for a possible solution which could balance the interest of users and law enforcement authorities; these techniques could also be used to recover data, when keys are lost. Processes for lawful access to cryptographic keys must recognise the distinction between keys which are used to protect confidentiality and keys which are used for other purposes only. A cryptographic key that provides for identity or integrity only (as distinct from a cryptographic key that verifies identity or integrity only) should not be made available without the consent of the individual or entity in lawful possession of that key.

International
OECD Cryptography Guidelines

7. LIABILITY

WHETHER ESTABLISHED BY CONTRACT OR LEGISLATION, THE LIABILITY OF INDIVIDUALS AND ENTITIES THAT OFFER CRYPTOGRAPHIC SERVICES OR HOLD OR ACCESS CRYPTOGRAPHIC KEYS SHOULD BE CLEARLY STATED.

The liability of any individual or entity, including a government entity, that offers cryptographic services or holds or has access to cryptographic keys, should be made clear by contract or where appropriate by national legislation or international agreement. The liability of users for misuse of their own keys should also be made clear. A keyholder should not be held liable for providing cryptographic keys or plaintext of encrypted data in accordance with lawful access. The party that obtains lawful access should be liable for misuse of cryptographic keys or plaintext that it has obtained.

8. INTERNATIONAL CO-OPERATION

GOVERNMENTS SHOULD CO-OPERATE TO CO-ORDINATE CRYPTOGRAPHY POLICIES. AS PART OF THIS EFFORT, GOVERNMENTS SHOULD REMOVE, OR AVOID CREATING IN THE NAME OF CRYPTOGRAPHY POLICY, UNJUSTIFIED OBSTACLES TO TRADE.

In order to promote the broad international acceptance of cryptography and enable the full potential of the national and global information and communications networks, cryptography policies adopted by a country should be co-ordinated as much as possible with similar policies of other countries. To that end, the Guidelines should be used for national policy formulation.

If developed, national key management systems must, where appropriate, allow for international use of cryptography.

Lawful access across national borders may be achieved through bilateral and multilateral co-operation and agreement.

No government should impede the free flow of encrypted data passing through its jurisdiction merely on the basis of cryptography policy. In order to promote international trade, governments should avoid developing cryptography policies and practices which create unjustified obstacles to global electronic commerce. Governments should avoid creating unjustified obstacles to international availability of cryptographic methods.

GENERAL AGREEMENT ON TRADE IN SERVICES (1994) [EXCERPT]

Reference

WTO | Legal Texts – The WTO Agreements
[http://www.wto.org/english/docs_e/legal_e/final_e.htm]

Article XIV General Exceptions

Subject to the requirement that such measures are not applied in a manner which would constitute a means of arbitrary or unjustifiable discrimination between countries where like conditions prevail, or a disguised restriction on trade in services, nothing in this Agreement shall be construed to prevent the adoption or enforcement by any Member of measures:

(a) necessary to protect public morals or to maintain public order;[1]

(b) necessary to protect human, animal or plant life or health;

(c) necessary to secure compliance with laws or regulations which are not inconsistent with the provisions of this Agreement including those relating to:

(i) the prevention of deceptive and fraudulent practices or to deal with the effects of a default on services contracts;

(ii) the protection of the privacy of individuals in relation to the processing and dissemination of personal data and the protection of confidentiality of individual records and accounts;

(iii) safety;

(d) inconsistent with Article XVII, provided that the difference in treatment is aimed at ensuring the equitable or effective [2]imposition or collection of direct taxes in respect of services or service suppliers of other Members;

---

[1] The public order exception may be invoked only where a genuine and sufficiently serious threat is posed to one of the fundamental interests of society.

[2] Measures that are aimed at ensuring the equitable or effective imposition or collection of direct taxes include measures taken by a Member under its taxation system which:

(i) apply to non-resident service suppliers in recognition of the fact that the tax obligation of non-residents is determined with respect to taxable items sourced or located in the Member's territory; or

(ii) apply to non-residents in order to ensure the imposition or collection of taxes in the Member's territory; or

(iii) apply to non-residents or residents in order to prevent the avoidance or evasion of taxes, including compliance measures; or

(iv) apply to consumers of services supplied in or from the territory of another Member in order to ensure the imposition or collection of taxes on such consumers derived from sources in the Member's territory; or

(e) inconsistent with Article II, provided that the difference in treatment is the result of an agreement on the avoidance of double taxation or provisions on the avoidance of double taxation in any other international agreement or arrangement by which the Member is bound.

(v) distinguish service suppliers subject to tax on worldwide taxable items from other service suppliers, in recognition of the difference in the nature of the tax base between them; or

(vi) determine, allocate or apportion income, profit, gain, loss, deduction or credit of resident persons or branches, or between related persons or branches of the same person, in order to safeguard the Member's tax base.

Tax terms or concepts in paragraph (d) of Article XIV and in this footnote are determined according to tax definitions and concepts, or equivalent or similar definitions and concepts, under the domestic law of the Member taking the measure.

EUROPEAN UNION DIRECTIVE ON PRIVACY AND ELECTRONIC COMMUNICATIONS (2002)

Reference

The European Union: Official Journal of the European Communities 31.7.2002 L 201/44 [http://eur-lex.europa.eu/legal-content/EN/TXT/HTML/?uri=CELEX:32002L0058&from=EN]

DIRECTIVE 2002/58/EC OF THE EUROPEAN PARLIAMENT
AND OF THE COUNCIL
of 12 July 2002
concerning the processing of personal data and the protection of
privacy in the electronic communications sector
(Directive on privacy and electronic communications)

THE EUROPEAN PARLIAMENT AND THE COUNCIL OF THE EUROPEAN UNION,

Having regard to the Treaty establishing the European Community, and in particular Article 95 thereof,

Having regard to the proposal from the Commission[1],

Having regard to the opinion of the Economic and Social Committee[2],

Having consulted the Committee of the Regions,

Acting in accordance with the procedure laid down in Article 251 of the Treaty (3),

Whereas:

(1) Directive 95/46/EC of the European Parliament and of the Council of 24 October 1995 on the protection of individuals with regard to the processing of personal data and on the free movement of such data (4) requires Member States to ensure the rights and freedoms of natural persons with regard to the processing of personal data, and in particular their right to privacy, in order to ensure the free flow of personal data in the Community.

(2) This Directive seeks to respect the fundamental rights and observes the principles recognised in particular by the Charter of fundamental rights of the European Union. In particular, this Directive seeks to ensure full respect for the rights set out in Articles 7 and 8 of that Charter.

(3) Confidentiality of communications is guaranteed in accordance with the international instruments relating to human rights, in particular the European Convention for the Protection of Human Rights and Fundamental Freedoms, and the constitutions of the Member States.

---

[1] (1) OJ L 178, 17.7.2000, p. 1.

[2] (2) OJ L 91, 7.4.1999, p.10.

International
EU Directive on Privacy and Electronic Communications

(4) Directive 97/66/EC of the European Parliament and of the Council of 15 December 1997 concerning the processing of personal data and the protection of privacy in the telecommunications sector (5) translated the principles set out in Directive 95/46/EC into specific rules for the telecommunications sector. Directive 97/66/EC has to be adapted to developments in the markets and technologies for electronic communications services in order to provide an equal level of protection of personal data and privacy for users of publicly available electronic communications services, regardless of the technologies used. That Directive should therefore be repealed and replaced by this Directive.

(5) New advanced digital technologies are currently being introduced in public communications networks in the Community, which give rise to specific requirements concerning the protection of personal data and privacy of the user. The development of the information society is characterised by the introduction of new electronic communications services. Access to digital mobile networks has become available and affordable for a large public. These digital networks have large capacities and possibilities for processing personal data. The successful cross-border development of these services is partly dependent on the confidence of users that their privacy will not be at risk.

(6) The Internet is overturning traditional market structures by providing a common, global infrastructure for the delivery of a wide range of electronic communications services. Publicly available electronic communications services over the Internet open new possibilities for users but also new risks for their personal data and privacy.

(7) In the case of public communications networks, specific legal, regulatory and technical provisions should be made in order to protect fundamental rights and freedoms of natural persons and legitimate interests of legal persons, in particular with regard to the increasing capacity for automated storage and processing of data relating to subscribers and users.

(8) Legal, regulatory and technical provisions adopted by the Member States concerning the protection of personal data, privacy and the legitimate interest of legal persons, in the electronic communication sector, should be harmonised in order to avoid obstacles to the internal market for electronic communication in accordance with Article 14 of the Treaty. Harmonisation should be limited to requirements necessary to guarantee that the promotion and development of new electronic communications services and networks between Member States are not hindered. 31.7.2002 L 201/37 Official Journal of the European Communities EN (1) OJ C 365 E, 19.12.2000, p. 223. (2) OJ C 123, 25.4.2001, p. 53. (3) Opinion of the European Parliament of 13 November 2001 (not yet published in the Official Journal), Council Common Position of 28 January 2002 (OJ C 113 E, 14.5.2002, p. 39) and Decision of the European Parliament of 30 May 2002 (not yet published in the Official Journal). Council Decision of 25 June 2002. (4) OJ L 281, 23.11.1995, p. 31. (5) OJ L 24, 30.1.1998, p. 1.

(9) The Member States, providers and users concerned, together with the competent Community bodies, should cooperate in introducing and developing the relevant technologies where this is necessary to apply the guarantees provided for by this Directive and taking particular account of the objectives of minimising the processing of personal data and of using anonymous or pseudonymous data where possible.

(10) In the electronic communications sector, Directive 95/ 46/EC applies in particular to all matters concerning protection of fundamental rights and freedoms, which are not specifically covered by the provisions of this Directive, including the obligations on the controller and the rights of individuals. Directive 95/46/EC applies to non-public communications services.

(11) Like Directive 95/46/EC, this Directive does not address issues of protection of fundamental rights and freedoms related to activities which are not governed by Community law. Therefore it does not alter the existing balance between the individual's right to privacy and the possibility for Member States to take the measures referred to in Article 15(1) of this Directive, necessary for the protection of public security, defence, State security (including the economic well-being of the State when the activities relate to State security matters) and the enforcement of criminal law. Consequently, this Directive does not affect the ability of Member States to carry out lawful interception of electronic communications, or take other measures, if necessary for any of these purposes and in accordance with the European Convention for the Protection of Human Rights and Fundamental Freedoms, as interpreted by the rulings of the European Court of Human Rights. Such measures must be appropriate, strictly proportionate to the intended purpose and necessary within a democratic society and should be subject to adequate safeguards in accordance with the European Convention for the Protection of Human Rights and Fundamental Freedoms.

(12) Subscribers to a publicly available electronic communications service may be natural or legal persons. By supplementing Directive 95/46/EC, this Directive is aimed at protecting the fundamental rights of natural persons and particularly their right to privacy, as well as the legitimate interests of legal persons. This Directive does not entail an obligation for Member States to extend the application of Directive 95/46/EC to the protection of the legitimate interests of legal persons, which is ensured within the framework of the applicable Community and national legislation.

(13) The contractual relation between a subscriber and a service provider may entail a periodic or a one-off payment for the service provided or to be provided. Prepaid cards are also considered as a contract.

(14) Location data may refer to the latitude, longitude and altitude of the user's terminal equipment, to the direction of travel, to the level of accuracy of the location information, to the identification of the network cell in which the terminal equipment is located at a certain point in time and to the time the location information was recorded.

(15) A communication may include any naming, numbering or addressing information provided by the sender of a communication or the user of a connection to carry out the communication. Traffic data may include any translation of this information by the network over which the communication is transmitted for the purpose of carrying out the transmission. Traffic data may, inter alia, consist of data referring to the routing, duration, time or volume of a communication, to the protocol used, to the location of the terminal equipment of the sender or recipient, to the network on which the communication originates or terminates, to the beginning, end or duration of a connection. They may also consist of the format in which the communication is conveyed by the network.

(16) Information that is part of a broadcasting service provided over a public communications network is intended for a potentially unlimited audience and does not constitute a communication in

the sense of this Directive. However, in cases where the individual subscriber or user receiving such information can be identified, for example with video-on-demand services, the information conveyed is covered within the meaning of a communication for the purposes of this Directive.

(17) For the purposes of this Directive, consent of a user or subscriber, regardless of whether the latter is a natural or a legal person, should have the same meaning as the data subject's consent as defined and further specified in Directive 95/46/EC. Consent may be given by any appropriate method enabling a freely given specific and informed indication of the user's wishes, including by ticking a box when visiting an Internet website.

(18) Value added services may, for example, consist of advice on least expensive tariff packages, route guidance, traffic information, weather forecasts and tourist information.

(19) The application of certain requirements relating to presentation and restriction of calling and connected line identification and to automatic call forwarding to subscriber lines connected to analogue exchanges should not be made mandatory in specific cases where such application would prove to be technically impossible or would require a disproportionate economic effort. It is important for interested parties to be informed of such cases and the Member States should therefore notify them to the Commission.

(20) Service providers should take appropriate measures to safeguard the security of their services, if necessary in conjunction with the provider of the network, and inform subscribers of any special risks of a breach of the security of the network. Such risks may especially occur for electronic communications services over an open network such as the Internet or analogue mobile telephony. It is particularly important for subscribers and users of such services to be fully informed by their service provider of the existing security risks which lie outside the scope of possible remedies by the service provider. Service providers who offer publicly available electronic communications services over the Internet should inform users and subscribers of measures they can take to protect the security of their communications for instance by using specific types of software or encryption technologies. The requirement to inform subscribers of particular security risks does not discharge a service provider from the obligation to take, at its own costs, appropriate and immediate measures to remedy any new, unforeseen security risks and restore the normal security level of the service. The provision of information about security risks to the subscriber should be free of charge except for any nominal costs which the subscriber may incur while receiving or collecting the information, for instance by downloading an electronic mail message. Security is appraised in the light of Article 17 of Directive 95/46/EC.

(21) Measures should be taken to prevent unauthorised access to communications in order to protect the confidentiality of communications, including both the contents and any data related to such communications, by means of public communications networks and publicly available electronic communications services. National legislation in some Member States only prohibits intentional unauthorised access to communications.

(22) The prohibition of storage of communications and the related traffic data by persons other than the users or without their consent is not intended to prohibit any automatic, intermediate and transient storage of this information in so far as this takes place for the sole purpose of carrying out

the transmission in the electronic communications network and provided that the information is not stored for any period longer than is necessary for the transmission and for traffic management purposes, and that during the period of storage the confidentiality remains guaranteed. Where this is necessary for making more efficient the onward transmission of any publicly accessible information to other recipients of the service upon their request, this Directive should not prevent such information from being further stored, provided that this information would in any case be accessible to the public without restriction and that any data referring to the individual subscribers or users requesting such information are erased.

(23) Confidentiality of communications should also be ensured in the course of lawful business practice. Where necessary and legally authorised, communications can be recorded for the purpose of providing evidence of a commercial transaction. Directive 95/46/EC applies to such processing. Parties to the communications should be informed prior to the recording about the recording, its purpose and the duration of its storage. The recorded communication should be erased as soon as possible and in any case at the latest by the end of the period during which the transaction can be lawfully challenged.

(24) Terminal equipment of users of electronic communications networks and any information stored on such equipment are part of the private sphere of the users requiring protection under the European Convention for the Protection of Human Rights and Fundamental Freedoms. So-called spyware, web bugs, hidden identifiers and other similar devices can enter the user's terminal without their knowledge in order to gain access to information, to store hidden information or to trace the activities of the user and may seriously intrude upon the privacy of these users. The use of such devices should be allowed only for legitimate purposes, with the knowledge of the users concerned.

(25) However, such devices, for instance so-called 'cookies', can be a legitimate and useful tool, for example, in analysing the effectiveness of website design and advertising, and in verifying the identity of users engaged in on-line transactions. Where such devices, for instance cookies, are intended for a legitimate purpose, such as to facilitate the provision of information society services, their use should be allowed on condition that users are provided with clear and precise information in accordance with Directive 95/46/EC about the purposes of cookies or similar devices so as to ensure that users are made aware of information being placed on the terminal equipment they are using. Users should have the opportunity to refuse to have a cookie or similar device stored on their terminal equipment. This is particularly important where users other than the original user have access to the terminal equipment and thereby to any data containing privacy-sensitive information stored on such equipment. Information and the right to refuse may be offered once for the use of various devices to be installed on the user's terminal equipment during the same connection and also covering any further use that may be made of those devices during subsequent connections. The methods for giving information, offering a right to refuse or requesting consent should be made as userfriendly as possible. Access to specific website content may still be made conditional on the well-informed acceptance of a cookie or similar device, if it is used for a legitimate purpose.

(26) The data relating to subscribers processed within electronic communications networks to establish connections and to transmit information contain information on the private life of natural persons and concern the right to respect for their correspondence or concern the legitimate interests of legal persons. Such data may only be stored to the extent that is necessary for the provision of the service for the purpose of billing and for interconnection payments, and for a limited time. Any further processing of such data which the provider of the publicly available electronic communications services may want to perform, for the marketing of electronic communications services or for the provision of value added services, may only be allowed if the subscriber has agreed to this on the basis of accurate and full information given by the provider of the publicly available electronic communications services about the types of further processing it intends to perform and about the subscriber's right not to give or to withdraw his/her consent to such processing. Traffic data used for marketing communications services or for the provision of value added services should also be erased or made anonymous after the provision of the service. Service providers should always keep subscribers informed of the types of data they are processing and the purposes and duration for which this is done.

(27) The exact moment of the completion of the transmission of a communication, after which traffic data should be erased except for billing purposes, may depend on the type of electronic communications service that is provided. For instance for a voice telephony call the transmission will be completed as soon as either of the users terminates the connection. For electronic mail the transmission is completed as soon as the addressee collects the message, typically from the server of his service provider.

(28) The obligation to erase traffic data or to make such data anonymous when it is no longer needed for the purpose of the transmission of a communication does not conflict with such procedures on the Internet as the caching in the domain name system of IP addresses or the caching of IP addresses to physical address bindings or the use of log-in information to control the right of access to networks or services.

(29) The service provider may process traffic data relating to subscribers and users where necessary in individual cases in order to detect technical failure or errors in the transmission of communications. Traffic data necessary for billing purposes may also be processed by the provider in order to detect and stop fraud consisting of unpaid use of the electronic communications service.

(30) Systems for the provision of electronic communications networks and services should be designed to limit the amount of personal data necessary to a strict minimum. Any activities related to the provision of the electronic communications service that go beyond the transmission of a communication and the billing thereof should be based on aggregated, traffic data that cannot be related to subscribers or users. Where such activities cannot be based on aggregated data, they should be considered as value added services for which the consent of the subscriber is required.

(31) Whether the consent to be obtained for the processing of personal data with a view to providing a particular value added service should be that of the user or of the subscriber, will depend on the data to be processed and on the type of service to be provided and on whether it is technically,

procedurally and contractually possible to distinguish the individual using an electronic communications service from the legal or natural person having subscribed to it.

(32) Where the provider of an electronic communications service or of a value added service subcontracts the processing of personal data necessary for the provision of these services to another entity, such subcontracting and subsequent data processing should be in full compliance with the requirements regarding controllers and processors of personal data as set out in Directive 95/46/ EC. Where the provision of a value added service requires that traffic or location data are forwarded from an electronic communications service provider to a provider of value added services, the subscribers or users to whom the data are related should also be fully informed of this forwarding before giving their consent for the processing of the data.

(33) The introduction of itemised bills has improved the possibilities for the subscriber to check the accuracy of the fees charged by the service provider but, at the same time, it may jeopardise the privacy of the users of publicly available electronic communications services. Therefore, in order to preserve the privacy of the user, Member States should encourage the development of electronic communication service options such as alternative payment facilities which allow anonymous or strictly private access to publicly available electronic communications services, for example calling cards and facilities for payment by credit card. To the same end, Member States may ask the operators to offer their subscribers a different type of detailed bill in which a certain number of digits of the called number have been deleted.

(34) It is necessary, as regards calling line identification, to protect the right of the calling party to withhold the presentation of the identification of the line from which the call is being made and the right of the called party to reject calls from unidentified lines. There is justification for overriding the elimination of calling line identification presentation in specific cases. Certain subscribers, in particular help lines and similar organisations, have an interest in guaranteeing the anonymity of their callers. It is necessary, as regards connected line identification, to protect the right and the legitimate interest of the called party to withhold the presentation of the identification of the line to which the calling party is actually connected, in particular in the case of forwarded calls. The providers of publicly available electronic communications services should inform their subscribers of the existence of calling and connected line identification in the network and of all services which are offered on the basis of calling and connected line identification as well as the privacy options which are available. This will allow the subscribers to make an informed choice about the privacy facilities they may want to use. The privacy options which are offered on a per-line basis do not necessarily have to be available as an automatic network service but may be obtainable through a simple request to the provider of the publicly available electronic communications service.

(35) In digital mobile networks, location data giving the geographic position of the terminal equipment of the mobile user are processed to enable the transmission of communications. Such data are traffic data covered by Article 6 of this Directive. However, in addition, digital mobile networks may have the capacity to process location data which are more precise than is necessary for the transmission of communications and which are used for the provision of value added services such as services providing individualised traffic information and guidance to drivers. The

processing of such data for value added services should only be allowed where subscribers have given their consent. Even in cases where subscribers have given their consent, they should have a simple means to temporarily deny the processing of location data, free of charge.

(36) Member States may restrict the users' and subscribers' rights to privacy with regard to calling line identification where this is necessary to trace nuisance calls and with regard to calling line identification and location data where this is necessary to allow emergency services to carry out their tasks as effectively as possible. For these purposes, Member States may adopt specific provisions to entitle providers of electronic communications services to provide access to calling line identification and location data without the prior consent of the users or subscribers concerned.

(37) Safeguards should be provided for subscribers against the nuisance which may be caused by automatic call forwarding by others. Moreover, in such cases, it must be possible for subscribers to stop the forwarded calls being passed on to their terminals by simple request to the provider of the publicly available electronic communications service.

(38) Directories of subscribers to electronic communications services are widely distributed and public. The right to privacy of natural persons and the legitimate interest of legal persons require that subscribers are able to determine whether their personal data are published in a directory and if so, which. Providers of public directories should inform the subscribers to be included in such directories of the purposes of the directory and of any particular usage which may be made of electronic versions of public directories especially through search functions embedded in the software, such as reverse search functions enabling users of the directory to discover the name and address of the subscriber on the basis of a telephone number only.

(39) The obligation to inform subscribers of the purpose(s) of public directories in which their personal data are to be included should be imposed on the party collecting the data for such inclusion. Where the data may be transmitted to one or more third parties, the subscriber should be informed of this possibility and of the recipient or the categories of possible recipients. Any transmission should be subject to the condition that the data may not be used for other purposes than those for which they were collected. If the party collecting the data from the subscriber or any third party to whom the data have been transmitted wishes to use the data for an additional purpose, the renewed consent of the subscriber is to be obtained either by the initial party collecting the data or by the third party to whom the data have been transmitted.

(40) Safeguards should be provided for subscribers against intrusion of their privacy by unsolicited communications for direct marketing purposes in particular by means of automated calling machines, telefaxes, and e-mails, including SMS messages. These forms of unsolicited commercial communications may on the one hand be relatively easy and cheap to send and on the other may impose a burden and/or cost on the recipient. Moreover, in some cases their volume may also cause difficulties for electronic communications networks and terminal equipment. For such forms of unsolicited communications for direct marketing, it is justified to require that prior explicit consent of the recipients is obtained before such communications are addressed to them. The single market requires a harmonised approach to ensure simple, Community-wide rules for businesses and users.

(41) Within the context of an existing customer relationship, it is reasonable to allow the use of electronic contact details for the offering of similar products or services, but only by the same company that has obtained the electronic contact details in accordance with Directive 95/46/EC. When electronic contact details are obtained, the customer should be informed about their further use for direct marketing in a clear and distinct manner, and be given the opportunity to refuse such usage. This opportunity should continue to be offered with each subsequent direct marketing message, free of charge, except for any costs for the transmission of this refusal.

(42) Other forms of direct marketing that are more costly for the sender and impose no financial costs on subscribers and users, such as person-to-person voice telephony calls, may justify the maintenance of a system giving subscribers or users the possibility to indicate that they do not want to receive such calls. Nevertheless, in order not to decrease existing levels of privacy protection, Member States should be entitled to uphold national systems, only allowing such calls to subscribers and users who have given their prior consent.

(43) To facilitate effective enforcement of Community rules on unsolicited messages for direct marketing, it is necessary to prohibit the use of false identities or false return addresses or numbers while sending unsolicited messages for direct marketing purposes.

(44) Certain electronic mail systems allow subscribers to view the sender and subject line of an electronic mail, and also to delete the message, without having to download the rest of the electronic mail's content or any attachments, thereby reducing costs which could arise from downloading unsolicited electronic mails or attachments. These arrangements may continue to be useful in certain cases as an additional tool to the general obligations established in this Directive.

(45) This Directive is without prejudice to the arrangements which Member States make to protect the legitimate interests of legal persons with regard to unsolicited communications for direct marketing purposes. Where Member States establish an opt-out register for such communications to legal persons, mostly business users, the provisions of Article 7 of Directive 2000/31/EC of the European Parliament and of the Council of 8 June 2000 on certain legal aspects of information society services, in particular electronic commerce, in the internal market (Directive on electronic commerce) (1) are fully applicable.

(46) The functionalities for the provision of electronic communications services may be integrated in the network or in any part of the terminal equipment of the user, including the software. The protection of the personal data and the privacy of the user of publicly available electronic communications services should be independent of the configuration of the various components necessary to provide the service and of the distribution of the necessary functionalities between these components. Directive 95/46/EC covers any form of processing of personal data regardless of the technology used. The existence of specific rules for electronic communications services alongside general rules for other components necessary for the provision of such services may not facilitate the protection of personal data and privacy in a technologically neutral way. It may therefore be necessary to adopt measures requiring manufacturers of certain types of equipment used for electronic communications services to construct their product in such a way as to incorporate safeguards to ensure that the personal data and privacy of the user and subscriber are

protected. The adoption of such measures in accordance with Directive 1999/5/EC of the European Parliament and of the Council of 9 March 1999 on radio equipment and telecommunications terminal equipment and the mutual recognition of their conformity (2) will ensure that the introduction of technical features of electronic communication equipment including software for data protection purposes is harmonised in order to be compatible with the implementation of the internal market.

(47) Where the rights of the users and subscribers are not respected, national legislation should provide for judicial remedies. Penalties should be imposed on any person, whether governed by private or public law, who fails to comply with the national measures taken under this Directive.

(48) It is useful, in the field of application of this Directive, to draw on the experience of the Working Party on the Protection of Individuals with regard to the Processing of Personal Data composed of representatives of the supervisory authorities of the Member States, set up by Article 29 of Directive 95/46/EC.

(49) To facilitate compliance with the provisions of this Directive, certain specific arrangements are needed for processing of data already under way on the date that national implementing legislation pursuant to this Directive enters into force,

HAVE ADOPTED THIS DIRECTIVE:

Article 1 - Scope and aim

1. This Directive harmonises the provisions of the Member States required to ensure an equivalent level of protection of fundamental rights and freedoms, and in particular the right to privacy, with respect to the processing of personal data in the electronic communication sector and to ensure the free movement of such data and of electronic communication equipment and services in the Community.

2. The provisions of this Directive particularise and complement Directive 95/46/EC for the purposes mentioned in paragraph 1. Moreover, they provide for protection of the legitimate interests of subscribers who are legal persons. 3. This Directive shall not apply to activities which fall outside the scope of the Treaty establishing the European Community, such as those covered by Titles V and VI of the Treaty on European Union, and in any case to activities concerning public security, defence, State security (including the economic well-being of the State when the activities relate to State security matters) and the activities of the State in areas of criminal law.

Article 2 - Definitions

Save as otherwise provided, the definitions in Directive 95/46/ EC and in Directive 2002/21/EC of the European Parliament and of the Council of 7 March 2002 on a common regulatory framework for electronic communications networks and services (Framework Directive) (1) shall apply. The following definitions shall also apply:

(a) 'user' means any natural person using a publicly available electronic communications service, for private or business purposes, without necessarily having subscribed to this service;

(b) 'traffic data' means any data processed for the purpose of the conveyance of a communication on an electronic communications network or for the billing thereof;

(c) 'location data' means any data processed in an electronic communications network, indicating the geographic position of the terminal equipment of a user of a publicly available electronic communications service;

(d) 'communication' means any information exchanged or conveyed between a finite number of parties by means of a publicly available electronic communications service. This does not include any information conveyed as part of a broadcasting service to the public over an electronic communications network except to the extent that the information can be related to the identifiable subscriber or user receiving the information;

(e) 'call' means a connection established by means of a publicly available telephone service allowing two-way communication in real time;

(f) 'consent' by a user or subscriber corresponds to the data subject's consent in Directive 95/46/EC;

(g) 'value added service' means any service which requires the processing of traffic data or location data other than traffic data beyond what is necessary for the transmission of a communication or the billing thereof;

(h) 'electronic mail' means any text, voice, sound or image message sent over a public communications network which can be stored in the network or in the recipient's terminal equipment until it is collected by the recipient.

Article 3 - Services concerned

1. This Directive shall apply to the processing of personal data in connection with the provision of publicly available electronic communications services in public communications networks in the Community. 2. Articles 8, 10 and 11 shall apply to subscriber lines connected to digital exchanges and, where technically possible and if it does not require a disproportionate economic effort, to subscriber lines connected to analogue exchanges. 3. Cases where it would be technically impossible or require a disproportionate economic effort to fulfil the requirements of Articles 8, 10 and 11 shall be notified to the Commission by the Member States.

Article 4 - Security

1. The provider of a publicly available electronic communications service must take appropriate technical and organisational measures to safeguard security of its services, if necessary in conjunction with the provider of the public communications network with respect to network security. Having regard to the state of the art and the cost of their implementation, these measures shall ensure a level of security appropriate to the risk presented. 2. In case of a particular risk of a breach of the security of the network, the provider of a publicly available electronic communications service must inform the subscribers concerning such risk and, where the risk lies

outside the scope of the measures to be taken by the service provider, of any possible remedies, including an indication of the likely costs involved.

Article 5 - Confidentiality of the communications

1. Member States shall ensure the confidentiality of communications and the related traffic data by means of a public communications network and publicly available electronic communications services, through national legislation. In particular, they shall prohibit listening, tapping, storage or other kinds of interception or surveillance of communications and the related traffic data by persons other than users, without the consent of the users concerned, except when legally authorised to do so in accordance with Article 15(1). This paragraph shall not prevent technical storage which is necessary for the conveyance of a communication without prejudice to the principle of confidentiality.

2. Paragraph 1 shall not affect any legally authorised recording of communications and the related traffic data when carried out in the course of lawful business practice for the purpose of providing evidence of a commercial transaction or of any other business communication.

3. Member States shall ensure that the use of electronic communications networks to store information or to gain access to information stored in the terminal equipment of a subscriber or user is only allowed on condition that the subscriber or user concerned is provided with clear and comprehensive information in accordance with Directive 95/ 46/EC, inter alia about the purposes of the processing, and is offered the right to refuse such processing by the data controller. This shall not prevent any technical storage or access for the sole purpose of carrying out or facilitating the transmission of a communication over an electronic communications network, or as strictly necessary in order to provide an information society service explicitly requested by the subscriber or user.

Article 6 - Traffic data

1. Traffic data relating to subscribers and users processed and stored by the provider of a public communications network or publicly available electronic communications service must be erased or made anonymous when it is no longer needed for the purpose of the transmission of a communication without prejudice to paragraphs 2, 3 and 5 of this Article and Article 15(1).

2. Traffic data necessary for the purposes of subscriber billing and interconnection payments may be processed. Such processing is permissible only up to the end of the period during which the bill may lawfully be challenged or payment pursued.

3. For the purpose of marketing electronic communications services or for the provision of value added services, the provider of a publicly available electronic communications service may process the data referred to in paragraph 1 to the extent and for the duration necessary for such services or marketing, if the subscriber or user to whom the data relate has given his/her consent. Users or subscribers shall be given the possibility to withdraw their consent for the processing of traffic data at any time.

4. The service provider must inform the subscriber or user of the types of traffic data which are processed and of the duration of such processing for the purposes mentioned in paragraph 2 and, prior to obtaining consent, for the purposes mentioned in paragraph 3.

5. Processing of traffic data, in accordance with paragraphs 1, 2, 3 and 4, must be restricted to persons acting under the authority of providers of the public communications networks and publicly available electronic communications services handling billing or traffic management, customer enquiries, fraud detection, marketing electronic communications services or providing a value added service, and must be restricted to what is necessary for the purposes of such activities.

6. Paragraphs 1, 2, 3 and 5 shall apply without prejudice to the possibility for competent bodies to be informed of traffic data in conformity with applicable legislation with a view to settling disputes, in particular interconnection or billing disputes.

Article 7 - Itemised billing

1. Subscribers shall have the right to receive non-itemised bills.

2. Member States shall apply national provisions in order to reconcile the rights of subscribers receiving itemised bills with the right to privacy of calling users and called subscribers, for example by ensuring that sufficient alternative privacy enhancing methods of communications or payments are available to such users and subscribers.

Article 8 - Presentation and restriction of calling and connected line identification

1. Where presentation of calling line identification is offered, the service provider must offer the calling user the possibility, using a simple means and free of charge, of preventing the presentation of the calling line identification on a per-call basis. The calling subscriber must have this possibility on a per-line basis.

2. Where presentation of calling line identification is offered, the service provider must offer the called subscriber the possibility, using a simple means and free of charge for reasonable use of this function, of preventing the presentation of the calling line identification of incoming calls.

3. Where presentation of calling line identification is offered and where the calling line identification is presented prior to the call being established, the service provider must offer the called subscriber the possibility, using a simple means, of rejecting incoming calls where the presentation of the calling line identification has been prevented by the calling user or subscriber.

4. Where presentation of connected line identification is offered, the service provider must offer the called subscriber the possibility, using a simple means and free of charge, of preventing the presentation of the connected line identification to the calling user.

5. Paragraph 1 shall also apply with regard to calls to third countries originating in the Community. Paragraphs 2, 3 and 4 shall also apply to incoming calls originating in third countries.

6. Member States shall ensure that where presentation of calling and/or connected line identification is offered, the providers of publicly available electronic communications services inform the public thereof and of the possibilities set out in paragraphs 1, 2, 3 and 4.

International
EU Directive on Privacy and Electronic Communications

Article 9 - Location data other than traffic data

1. Where location data other than traffic data, relating to users or subscribers of public communications networks or publicly available electronic communications services, can be processed, such data may only be processed when they are made anonymous, or with the consent of the users or subscribers to the extent and for the duration necessary for the provision of a value added service. The service provider must inform the users or subscribers, prior to obtaining their consent, of the type of location data other than traffic data which will be processed, of the purposes and duration of the processing and whether the data will be transmitted to a third party for the purpose of providing the value added service. Users or subscribers shall be given the possibility to withdraw their consent for the processing of location data other than traffic data at any time.

2. Where consent of the users or subscribers has been obtained for the processing of location data other than traffic data, the user or subscriber must continue to have the possibility, using a simple means and free of charge, of temporarily refusing the processing of such data for each connection to the network or for each transmission of a communication.

3. Processing of location data other than traffic data in accordance with paragraphs 1 and 2 must be restricted to persons acting under the authority of the provider of the public communications network or publicly available communications service or of the third party providing the value added service, and must be restricted to what is necessary for the purposes of providing the value added service.

Article 10 - Exceptions

Member States shall ensure that there are transparent procedures governing the way in which a provider of a public communications network and/or a publicly available electronic communications service may override:

(a) the elimination of the presentation of calling line identification, on a temporary basis, upon application of a subscriber requesting the tracing of malicious or nuisance calls. In this case, in accordance with national law, the data containing the identification of the calling subscriber will be stored and be made available by the provider of a public communications network and/or publicly available electronic communications service;

(b) the elimination of the presentation of calling line identification and the temporary denial or absence of consent of a subscriber or user for the processing of location data, on a per-line basis for organisations dealing with emergency calls and recognised as such by a Member State, including law enforcement agencies, ambulance services and fire brigades, for the purpose of responding to such calls.

Article 11 - Automatic call forwarding

Member States shall ensure that any subscriber has the possibility, using a simple means and free of charge, of stopping automatic call forwarding by a third party to the subscriber's terminal.

Article 12 - Directories of subscribers

1. Member States shall ensure that subscribers are informed, free of charge and before they are included in the directory, about the purpose(s) of a printed or electronic directory of subscribers available to the public or obtainable through directory enquiry services, in which their personal data can be included and of any further usage possibilities based on search functions embedded in electronic versions of the directory.

2. Member States shall ensure that subscribers are given the opportunity to determine whether their personal data are included in a public directory, and if so, which, to the extent that such data are relevant for the purpose of the directory as determined by the provider of the directory, and to verify, correct or withdraw such data. Not being included in a public subscriber directory, verifying, correcting or withdrawing personal data from it shall be free of charge.

3. Member States may require that for any purpose of a public directory other than the search of contact details of persons on the basis of their name and, where necessary, a minimum of other identifiers, additional consent be asked of the subscribers.

4. Paragraphs 1 and 2 shall apply to subscribers who are natural persons. Member States shall also ensure, in the framework of Community law and applicable national legislation, that the legitimate interests of subscribers other than natural persons with regard to their entry in public directories are sufficiently protected.

Article 13 - Unsolicited communications

1. The use of automated calling systems without human intervention (automatic calling machines), facsimile machines (fax) or electronic mail for the purposes of direct marketing may only be allowed in respect of subscribers who have given their prior consent.

2. Notwithstanding paragraph 1, where a natural or legal person obtains from its customers their electronic contact details for electronic mail, in the context of the sale of a product or a service, in accordance with Directive 95/46/EC, the same natural or legal person may use these electronic contact details for direct marketing of its own similar products or services provided that customers clearly and distinctly are given the opportunity to object, free of charge and in an easy manner, to such use of electronic contact details when they are collected and on the occasion of each message in case the customer has not initially refused such use.

3. Member States shall take appropriate measures to ensure that, free of charge, unsolicited communications for purposes of direct marketing, in cases other than those referred to in paragraphs 1 and 2, are not allowed either without the consent of the subscribers concerned or in respect of subscribers who do not wish to receive these communications, the choice between these options to be determined by national legislation.

4. In any event, the practice of sending electronic mail for purposes of direct marketing disguising or concealing the identity of the sender on whose behalf the communication is made, or without a valid address to which the recipient may send a request that such communications cease, shall be prohibited.

5. Paragraphs 1 and 3 shall apply to subscribers who are natural persons. Member States shall also ensure, in the framework of Community law and applicable national legislation, that the legitimate interests of subscribers other than natural persons with regard to unsolicited communications are sufficiently protected.

Article 14 - Technical features and standardisation

1. In implementing the provisions of this Directive, Member States shall ensure, subject to paragraphs 2 and 3, that no mandatory requirements for specific technical features are imposed on terminal or other electronic communication equipment which could impede the placing of equipment on the market and the free circulation of such equipment in and between Member States.
2. Where provisions of this Directive can be implemented only by requiring specific technical features in electronic communications networks, Member States shall inform the Commission in accordance with the procedure provided for by Directive 98/34/EC of the European Parliament and of the Council of 22 June 1998 laying down a procedure for the provision of information in the field of technical standards and regulations and of rules on information society services (1).
3. Where required, measures may be adopted to ensure that terminal equipment is constructed in a way that is compatible with the right of users to protect and control the use of their personal data, in accordance with Directive 1999/5/EC and Council Decision 87/95/EEC of 22 December 1986 on standardisation in the field of information technology and communications
(2).

Article 15 - Application of certain provisions of Directive 95/46/EC

1. Member States may adopt legislative measures to restrict the scope of the rights and obligations provided for in Article 5, Article 6, Article 8(1), (2), (3) and (4), and Article 9 of this Directive when such restriction constitutes a necessary, appropriate and proportionate measure within a democratic society to safeguard national security (i.e. State security), defence, public security, and the prevention, investigation, detection and prosecution of criminal offences or of unauthorised use of the electronic communication system, as referred to in Article 13(1) of Directive 95/46/EC. To this end, Member States may, inter alia, adopt legislative measures providing for the retention of data for a limited period justified on the grounds laid down in this paragraph. All the measures referred to in this paragraph shall be in accordance with the general principles of Community law, including those referred to in Article 6(1) and (2) of the Treaty on European Union.
2. The provisions of Chapter III on judicial remedies, liability and sanctions of Directive 95/46/EC shall apply with regard to national provisions adopted pursuant to this Directive and with regard to the individual rights derived from this Directive.
3. The Working Party on the Protection of Individuals with regard to the Processing of Personal Data instituted by Article 29 of Directive 95/46/EC shall also carry out the tasks laid down in Article 30 of that Directive with regard to matters covered by this Directive, namely the protection of fundamental rights and freedoms and of legitimate interests in the electronic communications sector.

Article 16 - Transitional arrangements

1. Article 12 shall not apply to editions of directories already produced or placed on the market in printed or off-line electronic form before the national provisions adopted pursuant to this Directive enter into force.

2. Where the personal data of subscribers to fixed or mobile public voice telephony services have been included in a public subscriber directory in conformity with the provisions of Directive 95/46/EC and of Article 11 of Directive 97/66/EC before the national provisions adopted in pursuance of this Directive enter into force, the personal data of such subscribers may remain included in this public directory in its printed or electronic versions, including versions with reverse search functions, unless subscribers indicate otherwise, after having received complete information about purposes and options in accordance with Article 12 of this Directive.

(1) OJ L 204, 21.7.1998, p. 37. Directive as amended by Directive 98/ 48/EC (OJ L 217, 5.8.1998, p. 18).

(2) OJ L 36, 7.2.1987, p. 31.
Article 17 - Transposition

1. Before 31 October 2003 Member States shall bring into force the provisions necessary to comply with this Directive. They shall forthwith inform the Commission thereof.

Decision as last amended by the 1994 Act of Accession. When Member States adopt those provisions, they shall contain a reference to this Directive or be accompanied by such a reference on the occasion of their official publication. The methods of making such reference shall be laid down by the Member States.

2. Member States shall communicate to the Commission the text of the provisions of national law which they adopt in the field governed by this Directive and of any subsequent amendments to those provisions.

Article 18 - Review

The Commission shall submit to the European Parliament and the Council, not later than three years after the date referred to in Article 17(1), a report on the application of this Directive and its impact on economic operators and consumers, in particular as regards the provisions on unsolicited communications, taking into account the international environment. For this purpose, the Commission may request information from the Member States, which shall be supplied without undue delay. Where appropriate, the Commission shall submit proposals to amend this Directive, taking account of the results of that report, any changes in the sector and any other proposal it may deem necessary in order to improve the effectiveness of this Directive.

Article 19 – Repeal

Directive 97/66/EC is hereby repealed with effect from the date referred to in Article 17(1). References made to the repealed Directive shall be construed as being made to this Directive.

International
EU Directive on Privacy and Electronic Communications

Article 20 - Entry into force

This Directive shall enter into force on the day of its publication in the Official Journal of the European Communities.

Article 21 - Addressees

This Directive is addressed to the Member States.

Done at Brussels, 12 July 2002.

For the European Parliament

The President

P. COX

For the Council

The President

T. PEDERSEN

CHARTER OF FUNDAMENTAL RIGHTS
OF THE EUROPEAN UNION (2000)
[EXCERPT]

Reference

Charter of Fundamental Rights
[http://eur-lex.europa.eu/legal-content/EN/TXT/?uri=CELEX:12012P/TXT]

The European Parliament, the Council and the Commission solemnly proclaim the text below as the Charter of fundamental rights of the European Union.

Done at Nice on the seventh day of December in the year two thousand.

C 364/8 Official Journal of the European Communities 18.12.2000

Incorporated into a Treaty establishing a Constitution for Europe in 2004
C 310/41 Official Journal of the European Communities 16.12.2004

PREAMBLE

The peoples of Europe, in creating an ever closer union among them, are resolved to share a peaceful future based on common values.

Conscious of its spiritual and moral heritage, the Union is founded on the indivisible, universal values of human dignity, freedom, equality and solidarity; it is based on the principles of democracy and the rule of law. It places the individual at the heart of its activities, by establishing the citizenship of the Union and by creating an area of freedom, security and justice.

The Union contributes to the preservation and to the development of these common values while respecting the diversity of the cultures and traditions of the peoples of Europe as well as the national identities of the Member States and the organisation of their public authorities at national, regional and local levels; it seeks to promote balanced and sustainable development and ensures free movement of persons, goods, services and capital, and the freedom of establishment.

To this end, it is necessary to strengthen the protection of fundamental rights in the light of changes in society, social progress and scientific and technological developments by making those rights more visible in a Charter.

This Charter reaffirms, with due regard for the powers and tasks of the Community and the Union and the principle of subsidiarity, the rights as they result, in particular, from the constitutional traditions and international obligations common to the Member States, the Treaty on European Union, the Community Treaties, the European Convention for the Protection of Human Rights and Fundamental Freedoms, the Social Charters adopted by the Community and by the Council of Europe and the case-law of the Court of Justice of the European Communities and of the European Court of Human Rights.

Enjoyment of these rights entails responsibilities and duties with regard to other persons, to the human community and to future generations.

The Union therefore recognises the rights, freedoms and principles set out hereafter.

CHAPTER I DIGNITY

Article 1 - Human dignity

Human dignity is inviolable. It must be respected and protected.

Article 2 - Right to life

1. Everyone has the right to life.
2. No one shall be condemned to the death penalty, or executed.

Article 3 - Right to the integrity of the person

1. Everyone has the right to respect for his or her physical and mental integrity.
2. In the fields of medicine and biology, the following must be respected in particular:

   (a) the free and informed consent of the person concerned, according to the procedures laid down by law,

   (b) the prohibition of eugenic practices, in particular those aiming at the selection of persons,

   (c) the prohibition on making the human body and its parts as such a source of financial gain,

   (d) the prohibition of the reproductive cloning of human beings.

Article 4 - Prohibition of torture and inhuman or degrading treatment or punishment

No one shall be subjected to torture or to inhuman or degrading treatment or punishment.

Article 5 - Prohibition of slavery and forced labour

1. No one shall be held in slavery or servitude.
2. No one shall be required to perform forced or compulsory labour.
3. Trafficking in human beings is prohibited.

CHAPTER II FREEDOMS

Article 6 - Right to liberty and security

Everyone has the right to liberty and security of person.

Article 7 - Respect for private and family life

Everyone has the right to respect for his or her private and family life, home and communications.

Article 8 - Protection of personal data

1. Everyone has the right to the protection of personal data concerning him or her.
2. Such data must be processed fairly for specified purposes and on the basis of the consent of the person concerned or some other legitimate basis laid down by law. Everyone has the right of access to data which has been collected concerning him or her, and the right to have it rectified.
3. Compliance with these rules shall be subject to control by an independent authority.

Article 9 - Right to marry and right to found a family

The right to marry and the right to found a family shall be guaranteed in accordance with the national laws governing the exercise of these rights.

Article 10 - Freedom of thought, conscience and religion

1. Everyone has the right to freedom of thought, conscience and religion. This right includes freedom to change religion or belief and freedom, either alone or in community with others and in public or in private, to manifest religion or belief, in worship, teaching, practice and observance.
2. The right to conscientious objection is recognised, in accordance with the national laws governing the exercise of this right.

Article 11 - Freedom of expression and information

1. Everyone has the right to freedom of expression. This right shall include freedom to hold opinions and to receive and impart information and ideas without interference by public authority and regardless of frontiers.
2. The freedom and pluralism of the media shall be respected.

Article 12 - Freedom of assembly and of association

1. Everyone has the right to freedom of peaceful assembly and to freedom of association at all levels, in particular in political, trade union and civic matters, which implies the right of everyone to form and to join trade unions for the protection of his or her interests.

2. Political parties at Union level contribute to expressing the political will of the citizens of the Union

Article 13 - Freedom of the arts and sciences

The arts and scientific research shall be free of constraint. Academic freedom shall be respected.

Article 14 - Right to education

1. Everyone has the right to education and to have access to vocational and continuing training.
2. This right includes the possibility to receive free compulsory education.
3. The freedom to found educational establishments with due respect for democratic principles and the right of parents to ensure the education and teaching of their children in conformity with their religious, philosophical and pedagogical convictions shall be respected, in accordance with the national laws governing the exercise of such freedom and right.

Article 15 - Freedom to choose an occupation and right to engage in work

1. Everyone has the right to engage in work and to pursue a freely chosen or accepted occupation.
2. Every citizen of the Union has the freedom to seek employment, to work, to exercise the right of establishment and to provide services in any Member State.
3. Nationals of third countries who are authorised to work in the territories of the Member States are entitled to working conditions equivalent to those of citizens of the Union.

Article 16 - Freedom to conduct a business

The freedom to conduct a business in accordance with Community law and national laws and practices is recognised.

Article 17 - Right to property

1. Everyone has the right to own, use, dispose of and bequeath his or her lawfully acquired possessions. No one may be deprived of his or her possessions, except in the public interest and in the cases and under the conditions provided for by law, subject to fair compensation being paid in good time for their loss. The use of property may be regulated by law in so far as is necessary for the general interest.
2. Intellectual property shall be protected.

Article 18 - Right to asylum

The right to asylum shall be guaranteed with due respect for the rules of the Geneva Convention of 28 July 1951 and the Protocol of 31 January 1967 relating to the status of refugees and in accordance with the Treaty establishing the European Community.

Article 19 - Protection in the event of removal, expulsion or extradition

1. Collective expulsions are prohibited.
2. No one may be removed, expelled or extradited to a State where there is a serious risk that he or she would be subjected to the death penalty, torture or other inhuman or degrading treatment or punishment.

* * *

APEC PRIVACY FRAMEWORK

References

APEC Privacy Framework
[http://www.apec.org/Groups/Committee-on-Trade-and-
Investment/~/media/Files/Groups/ECSG/05_ecsg_privacyframewk.ashx]

DECEMBER 2005

Part I. Preamble

1. APEC economies recognize the importance of protecting information privacy and maintaining information flows among economies in the Asia Pacific region and among their trading partners. As APEC Ministers acknowledged in endorsing the 1998 Blueprint for Action on Electronic Commerce, the potential of electronic commerce cannot be realized without government and business cooperation "to develop and implement technologies and policies, which build trust and confidence in safe, secure and reliable communication, information and delivery systems, and which address issues including privacy...". The lack of consumer trust and confidence in the privacy and security of online transactions and information networks is one element that may prevent member economies from gaining all of the benefits of electronic commerce. APEC economies realize that a key part of efforts to improve consumer confidence and ensure the growth of electronic commerce must be cooperation to balance and promote both effective information privacy protection and the free flow of information in the Asia Pacific region.

2. Information and communications technologies, including mobile technologies, that link to the Internet and other information networks have made it possible to collect, store and access information from anywhere in the world. These technologies offer great potential for social and economic benefits for business, individuals and governments, including increased consumer choice, market expansion, productivity, education and product innovation. However, while these technologies make it easier and cheaper to collect, link and use large quantities of information, they also often make these activities undetectable to individuals. Consequently, it can be more difficult for individuals to retain a measure of control over their personal information. As a result, individuals have become concerned about the harmful consequences that may arise from the misuse of their information. Therefore, there is a need to promote and enforce ethical and trustworthy information practices in on- and off-line contexts to bolster the confidence of individuals and businesses.

3. As both business operations and consumer expectations continue to shift due to changes in technology and the nature of information flows, businesses and other organizations require simultaneous input and access to data 24-hours a day in order to meet customer and societal

needs, and to provide efficient and cost-effective services. Regulatory systems that unnecessarily restrict this flow or place burdens on it have adverse implications for global business and economies. Therefore, in promoting and enforcing ethical information practices, there is also a need to develop systems for protecting information privacy that account for these new realities in the global environment.

4. APEC economies endorse the principles-based APEC Privacy Framework as an important tool in encouraging the development of appropriate information privacy protections and ensuring the free flow of information in the Asia Pacific region.

5. This Framework, which aims at promoting electronic commerce throughout the Asia Pacific region, is consistent with the core values of the OECD's 1980 Guidelines on the Protection of Privacy and Trans-Border Flows of Personal Data (OECD Guidelines)[3], and reaffirms the value of privacy to individuals and to the information society.

6. The Framework specifically addresses these foundation concepts, as well as issues of particular relevance to APEC member economies. Its distinctive approach is to focus attention on practical and consistent information privacy protection within this context. In so doing, it balances information privacy with business needs and commercial interests, and at the same time, accords due recognition to cultural and other diversities that exist within member economies.

7. The Framework is intended to provide clear guidance and direction to businesses in APEC economies on common privacy issues and the impact of privacy issues upon the way legitimate businesses are conducted. It does so by highlighting the reasonable expectations of the modern consumer that businesses will recognize their privacy interests in a way that is consistent with the Principles outlined in this Framework.

8. Finally, this Framework on information privacy protection was developed in recognition of the importance of: Developing appropriate privacy protections for personal information, particularly from the harmful consequences of unwanted intrusions and the misuse of personal information; Recognizing the free flow of information as being essential for both developed and developing market economies to sustain economic and social growth; Enabling global organizations that collect, access, use or process data in APEC member economies to develop and implement uniform approaches within their organizations for global access to and use of personal information; Enabling enforcement agencies to fulfill their mandate to protect

---

[3] The 1980 OECD Guidelines were drafted at a high level that makes them still relevant today. In many ways, the OECD Guidelines represent the international consensus on what constitutes honest and trustworthy treatment of personal information.

information privacy; and, Advancing international mechanisms to promote and enforce information privacy and to maintain the continuity of information flows among APEC economies and with their trading partners.

Part II. Scope

The purpose of Part II of the APEC Privacy Framework is to make clear the extent of coverage of the Principles.

Definitions

9. **Personal information** means any information about an identified or identifiable individual.

> The Principles have been drafted against a background in which some economies have well-established privacy laws and/or practices while others may be considering the issues. Of those with already settled policies, not all treat personal information in exactly the same way.Some, for example, may draw distinctions between information that is readily searchable and other information. Despite these differences, this Framework has been drafted to promote a consistent approach among the information privacy regimes of APEC economies.
>
> This Framework is intended to apply to information about natural living persons, not legal persons. The APEC Privacy Framework applies to personal information, which is information that can be used to identify an individual. It also includes information that would not meet this criteria alone, but when put together with other information would identify an individual.

10. **Personal information controller** means a person or organization who controls the collection, holding, processing or use of personal information. It includes a person or organization who instructs another person or organization to collect, hold, process, use, transfer or disclose personal information on his or her behalf, but excludes a person or organization who performs such functions as instructed by another person or organization. It also excludes an individual who collects, holds, processes or uses personal information in connection with the individual's personal, family or household affairs.

> The APEC Privacy Framework applies to persons or organizations in the public and private sectors who control the collection, holding, processing, use, transfer or disclosure of personal information. Individual economies' definitions of personal information controller may vary. However, APEC economies agree that for the purposes of this Framework, where a person or organization instructs another person or organization to collect, hold, use, process, transfer or disclose personal information on its behalf, the instructing person or organization is the personal information controller and is responsible for ensuring compliance with the Principles.

Individuals will often collect, hold and use personal information for personal, family or household purposes. For example, they often keep address books and phone lists or prepare family newsletters.The Framework is not intended to apply to such personal, family or household activities.

11. **Publicly available information** means personal information about an individual that the individual knowingly makes or permits to be made available to the public, or is legally obtained and accessed from:

a) government records that are available to the public;

b) journalistic reports; or

c) information required by law to be made available to the public.

The APEC Privacy Framework has limited application to publicly available information. Notice and choice requirements, in particular, often are superfluous where the information is already publicly available, and the personal information controller does not collect the information directly from the individual concerned. Publicly available information may be contained in government records that are available to the public, such as registers of people who are entitled to vote, or in news items broadcast or published by the news media.

Application

12. In view of the differences in social, cultural, economic and legal backgrounds of each member economy, there should be flexibility in implementing these Principles.

Although it is not essential for electronic commerce that all laws and practices within APEC be identical in all respects, including the coverage of personal information, compatible approaches to information privacy protection among APEC economies will greatly facilitate international commerce. These Principles recognize that fact, but also take into account social, cultural and other differences among economies. They focus on those aspects of privacy protection that are of the most importance to international commerce.

13. Exceptions to these Principles contained in Part III of this Framework, including those relating to national sovereignty, national security, public safety and public policy should be:

a) limited and proportional to meeting the objectives to which the exceptions relate;

b) (i) made known to the public; or,

    (ii) in accordance with law.

The Principles contained in Part III of the APEC Privacy Framework should be interpreted as a whole rather than individually, as there is a close relationship among them. For example, the Use Principle is closely related to both the Notice and Choice Principles. Economies implementing the Framework at a domestic level may adopt suitable exceptions that suit their particular domestic circumstances.

Although recognizing the importance of governmental respect for privacy, this Framework is not intended to impede governmental activities authorized by law when taken to protect national security, public safety, national sovereignty or other public policy. Nonetheless, Economies should take into consideration the impact of these activities upon the rights, responsibilities and legitimate interests of individuals and organizations.

Part III. APEC Information Privacy Principles[4]

I. Preventing Harm

14. Recognizing the interests of the individual to legitimate expectations of privacy, personal information protection should be designed to prevent the misuse of such information. Further, acknowledging the risk that harm may result from such misuse of personal information, specific obligations should take account of such risk, and remedial measures should be proportionate to the likelihood and severity of the harm threatened by the collection, use and transfer of personal information.

> The Preventing Harm Principle recognizes that one of the primary objectives of the APEC Privacy Framework is to prevent misuse of personal information and consequent harm to individuals. Therefore, privacy protections, including self-regulatory efforts, education and awareness campaigns, laws, regulations, and enforcement mechanisms, should be designed to prevent harm to individuals from the wrongful collection and misuse of their personal information. Hence, remedies for privacy infringements should be designed to prevent harms resulting from the wrongful collection or misuse of personal information, and should be proportionate to the likelihood and severity of any harm threatened by the collection or use of personal information.

II. Notice

15. Personal information controllers should provide clear and easily accessible statements about their practices and policies with respect to personal information that should include:

   a) the fact that personal information is being collected;

   b) the purposes for which personal information is collected;

   c) the types of persons or organizations to whom personal information might be disclosed;

---

[4] [In the original copy, the text of Part III was presented as a table of two columns, the left column containing the Principles and the right column commentary on each Principle. In reprinting the document here, commentary appears directly below the corresponding Principle, indented so that it is distinguishable from the Principles themselves. Where commentary pertains to more than one Principle, the numbers of the relevant Principles are denoted before the commentary. –Ed.]

d) the identity and location of the personal information controller, including information on how to contact them about their practices and handling of personal information;

e) the choices and means the personal information controller offers individuals for limiting the use and disclosure of, and for accessing and correcting, their personal information.

16. All reasonably practicable steps shall be taken to ensure that such notice is provided either before or at the time of collection of personal information. Otherwise, such notice should be provided as soon after as is practicable.

17. It may not be appropriate for personal information controllers to provide notice regarding the collection and use of publicly available information.

> 15-17. The Notice Principle is directed towards ensuring that individuals are able to know what information is collected about them and for what purpose it is to be used. By providing notice, personal information controllers may enable an individual to make a more informed decision about interacting with the organization. One common method of compliance with this Principle is for personal information controllers to post notices on their Web sites. In other situations, placement of notices on intranet sites or in employee handbooks, for example, may be appropriate.
>
> The requirement in this Principle relating to when notice should be provided is based on a consensus among APEC member economies. APEC member economies agree that good privacy practice is to inform relevant individuals at the time of, or before, information is collected about them. At the same time, the Principle also recognizes that there are circumstances in which it would not be practicable to give notice at or before the time of collection, such as in some cases where electronic technology automatically collects information when a prospective customer initiates contact, as is often the case with the use of cookies.
>
> Moreover, where personal information is not obtained directly from the individual, but from a third party, it may not be practicable to give notice at or before the time of collection of the information. For example, when an insurance company collects employees' information from an employer in order to provide medical insurance services, it may not be practicable for the insurance company to give notice at or before the time of collection of the employees' personal information.
>
> Additionally, there are situations in which it would not be necessary to provide notice, such as in the collection and use of publicly available information, or of business contact information and other professional information that identifies an individual in his or her professional capacity in a business context. For example, if an individual gives his or her business card to another individual in the context of a

business relationship, the individual would not expect that notice would be provided regarding the collection and normal use of that information.

Further, if colleagues who work for the same company as the individual, were to provide the individual's business contact information to potential customers of that company, the individual would not have an expectation that notice would be provided regarding the transfer or the expected use of that information.

III. Collection Limitation

18. The collection of personal information should be limited to information that is relevant to the purposes of collection and any such information should be obtained by lawful and fair means, and where appropriate, with notice to, or consent of, the individual concerned.

This Principle limits collection of information by reference to the purposes for which it is collected. The collection of the information should be relevant to such purposes, and proportionality to the fulfillment of such purposes may be a factor in determining what is relevant.

This Principle also provides that collection methods must be lawful and fair. So, for example, obtaining personal information under false pretenses (e.g., where an organization uses telemarketing calls, print advertising, or email to fraudulently misrepresent itself as another company in order to deceive consumers and induce them to disclose their credit card numbers, bank account information or other sensitive personal information) may in many economies be considered unlawful. Therefore, even in those economies where there is no explicit law against these specific methods, they may be considered an unfair means of collection.

The Principle also recognizes that there are circumstances where providing notice to, or obtaining consent of, individuals would be inappropriate. For example, in a situation where there is an outbreak of food poisoning, it would be appropriate for the relevant health authorities to collect the personal information of patrons from restaurants without providing notice to or obtaining the consent of individuals in order to tell them about the potential health risk.

IV. Uses of Personal Information

19. Personal information collected should be used only to fulfill the purposes of collection and other compatible or related purposes except:

  a) with the consent of the individual whose personal information is collected;
  b) when necessary to provide a service or product requested by the individual; or,
  c) by the authority of law and other legal instruments, proclamations and pronouncements of legal effect.

The Use Principle limits the use of personal information to fulfilling the purposes of collection and other compatible or related purposes. For the purposes of this

Principle, "uses of personal information" includes the transfer or disclosure of personal information.

Application of this Principle requires consideration of the nature of the information, the context of collection and the intended use of the information. The fundamental criterion in determining whether a purpose is compatible with or related to the stated purposes is whether the extended usage stems from or is in furtherance of such purposes. The use of personal information for "compatible or related purposes" would extend, for example, to matters such as the creation and use of a centralized database to manage personnel in an effective and efficient manner; the processing of employee payrolls by a third party; or, the use of information collected by an organization for the purpose of granting credit for the subsequent purpose of collecting debt owed to that organization.

V. Choice

20. Where appropriate, individuals should be provided with clear, prominent, easily understandable, accessible and affordable mechanisms to exercise choice in relation to the collection, use and disclosure of their personal information. It may not be appropriate for personal information controllers to provide these mechanisms when collecting publicly available information.

The general purpose of the Choice Principle is to ensure that individuals are provided with choice in relation to collection, use, transfer and disclosure of their personal information. Whether the choice is conveyed electronically, in writing or by other means, notice of such choice should be clearly worded and displayed clearly and conspicuously. By the same token, the mechanisms for exercising choice should be accessible and affordable to individuals. Ease of access and convenience are factors that should be taken into account.

Where an organization provides information on available mechanisms for exercising choice that is specifically tailored to individuals in an APEC member economy or national group, this may require that the information be conveyed in an "easily understandable" or particular way appropriate to members of that group (e.g., in a particular language). However if the communication is not directed to any particular economy or national group other than the one where the organization is located, this requirement will not apply.

This Principle also recognizes, through the introductory words "where appropriate", that there are certain situations where consent may be clearly implied or where it would not be necessary to provide a mechanism to exercise choice.

As is specified in the Principle, APEC member economies agree that in many situations it would not be necessary or practicable to provide a mechanism to exercise choice when collecting publicly available information. For example, it would not be necessary to provide a mechanism to exercise choice to individuals when collecting their name and address from a public record or a newspaper.

In addition to situations involving publicly available information, APEC member economies also agreed that in specific and limited circumstances it would not be necessary or practicable to provide a mechanism to exercise choice when collecting, using, transferring or disclosing other types of information. For example, when business contact information or other professional information that identifies an individual in his or her professional capacity is being exchanged in a business context it is generally impractical or unnecessary to provide a mechanism to exercise choice, as in these circumstances individuals would expect that their information be used in this way.

Further, in certain situations, it would not be practicable for employers to be subject to requirements to provide a mechanism to exercise choice related to the personal information of their employees when using such information for employment purposes. For example, if an organization has decided to centralize human resources information, that organization should not be required to provide a mechanism to exercise choice to its employees before engaging in such an activity.

VI. Integrity of Personal Information

21. Personal information should be accurate, complete and kept up-to-date to the extent necessary for the purposes of use.

This Principle recognizes that a personal information controller is obliged to maintain the accuracy and completeness of records and keep them up to date. Making decisions about individuals based on inaccurate, incomplete or out of date information may not be in the interests of individuals or organizations. This Principle also recognizes that these obligations are only required to the extent necessary for the purposes of use.

VII. Security Safeguards

22. Personal information controllers should protect personal information that they hold with appropriate safeguards against risks, such as loss or unauthorized access to personal information, or unauthorized destruction, use, modification or disclosure of information or other misuses. Such safeguards should be proportional to the likelihood and severity of the harm threatened, the sensitivity of the information and the context in which it is held, and should be subject to periodic review and reassessment.

This Principle recognizes that individuals who entrust their information to another are entitled to expect that their information be protected with reasonable security safeguards.

VIII. Access and Correction

23. Individuals should be able to:

    a) obtain from the personal information controller confirmation of whether or not the personal information controller holds personal information about them;

    b) have communicated to them, after having provided sufficient proof of their identity, personal information about them;

        i. within a reasonable time;

        ii. at a charge, if any, that is not excessive;

        iii. in a reasonable manner;

        iv. in a form that is generally understandable; and,

    c) challenge the accuracy of information relating to them and, if possible and as appropriate, have the information rectified, completed, amended or deleted.

24. Such access and opportunity for correction should be provided except where:

    (i) the burden or expense of doing so would be unreasonable or disproportionate to the risks to the individual's privacy in the case in question;

    (ii) the information should not be disclosed due to legal or security reasons or to protect confidential commercial information; or

    (iii) the information privacy of persons other than the individual would be violated.

25. If a request under (a) or (b) or a challenge under (c) is denied, the individual should be provided with reasons why and be able to challenge such denial.

    23-25. The ability to access and correct personal information, while generally regarded as a central aspect of privacy protection, is not an absolute right. This Principle includes specific conditions for what would be considered reasonable in the provision of access, including conditions related to timing, fees, and the manner and form in which access would be provided. What is to be considered reasonable in each of these areas will vary from one situation to another depending on circumstances, such as the nature of the information processing activity. Access will also be conditioned by security requirements that preclude the provision of direct access to information and will require sufficient proof of identity prior to provision of access.

    Access must be provided in a reasonable manner and form. A reasonable manner should include the normal methods of interaction between organizations and individuals. For example, if a computer was involved in the transaction or request, and the individual's email address is available, email would be considered "a reasonable manner" to provide information. Organizations that have transacted with an individual may reasonably be expected to answer requests in a form that is similar to what has been used in prior exchanges with said individual or in the form that is used and available within the organization, but should not be understood to require separate language translation or conversion of code into text.

Both the copy of personal information supplied by an organization in response to an access request and any explanation of codes used by the organization should be readily comprehensible. This obligation does not extend to the conversion of computer language (e.g. machine-readable instructions, source codes or object codes) into text. However, where a code represents a particular meaning, the personal information controller shall explain the meaning of that code to the individual. For example, if the personal information held by the organization includes the age range of the individual, and that is represented by a particular code (e.g., "1" means 18-25 years old, "2" means "26-35 [sic] years old, etc.), then when providing the individual with such a code, the organization shall explain to the individual what age range that code represents.

Where individual requests access to his or her information, that information should be provided in the language in which it is currently held. Where information is held in a language different to the language of original collection, and if the individual requests the information be provided in that original language, an organization should supply the information in the original language if the individual pays the cost of translation. The details of the procedures by which the ability to access and correct information is provided may differ depending on the nature of the information and other interests. For this reason, in certain circumstances, it may be impossible, impracticable or unnecessary to change, suppress or delete records.

Consistent with the fundamental nature of access, organizations should always make good faith efforts to provide access. For example, where certain information needs to be protected and can be readily separated from other information subject to an access request, the organization should redact the protected information and make available the other information. However, in some situations, it may be necessary for organizations to deny claims for access and correction, and this Principle sets out the conditions that must be met in order for such denials to be considered acceptable, which include: situations where claims would constitute an unreasonable expense or burden on the personal information controller, such as when claims for access are repetitious or vexatious by nature; cases where providing the information would constitute a violation of laws or would compromise security; or, incidences where it would be necessary in order to protect commercial confidential information that an organization has taken steps to protect from disclosure, where disclosure would benefit a competitor in the marketplace, such as a particular computer or modeling program.

"Confidential commercial information" is information that an organization has taken steps to protect from disclosure, where such disclosure would facilitate a competitor in the market to use or exploit the information against the business interest of the organization causing significant financial loss. The particular computer program or business process an organization uses, such as a modeling program, or the details of that program or business process may be confidential commercial information. Where confidential commercial information can be readily separated from other information subject to an access request, the organization should redact the confidential commercial information and make available the nonconfidential information, to the extent that such information constitutes personal information of the individual concerned. Organizations may deny or limit access to the extent that it is not practicable to separate the personal information from the confidential commercial information and where granting access would reveal the organization's own confidential commercial information as defined above, or where it would reveal the confidential commercial information of another organization that is subject to an obligation of confidentiality.

When an organization denies a request for access, for the reasons specified above, such an organization should provide the individual with an explanation as to why it has made that determination and information on how to challenge that denial. An organization would not be expected to provide an explanation, however, in cases where such disclosure would violate a law or judicial order.

IX. Accountability

26. A personal information controller should be accountable for complying with measures that give effect to the Principles stated above. When personal information is to be transferred to another person or organization, whether domestically or internationally, the personal information controller should obtain the consent of the individual or exercise due diligence and take reasonable steps to ensure that the recipient person or organization will protect the information consistently with these Principles.

Efficient and cost effective business models often require information transfers between different types of organizations in different locations with varying relationships. When transferring information, personal information controllers should be accountable for ensuring that the recipient will protect the information consistently with these Principles when not obtaining consent. Thus, information controllers should take reasonable steps to ensure the information is protected, in accordance with these Principles, after it is transferred. However, there are certain situations where such due diligence may be impractical or impossible, for example, when there is no on-going relationship between the personal information controller and the third party to whom the information is disclosed. In these types of circumstances, personal information controllers may choose to use other means, such as obtaining consent, to assure that the information is being protected consistently with these Principles. However, in cases where disclosures are required by domestic law, the personal information controller would be relieved of any due diligence or consent obligations.

Part IV. Implementation

27. Part IV provides guidance to Member Economies on implementing the APEC Privacy Framework. Section A focuses on those measures Member Economies should consider in implementing the Framework domestically, while Section B sets out APEC-wide arrangements for the implementation of the Framework's cross-border elements.

A. Guidance for Domestic Implementation

I. Maximizing Benefits of Privacy Protections and Information Flows

28. Economies should have regard to the following basic concept in considering the adoption of measures designed for domestic implementation of the APEC Privacy Framework:

29. Recognizing the interests of economies in maximizing the economic and social benefits available to their citizens and businesses, personal information should be collected, held, processed, used, transferred, and disclosed in a manner that protects individual information privacy and allows them to realize the benefits of information flows within and across borders.

30. Consequently, as part of establishing or reviewing their privacy protections, Member Economies, consistent with the APEC Privacy Framework and any existing domestic privacy protections, should take all reasonable and appropriate steps to identify and remove unnecessary barriers to information flows and avoid the creation of any such barriers.

II. Giving Effect to the APEC Privacy Framework

31. There are several options for giving effect to the Framework and securing privacy protections for individuals including legislative, administrative, industry self- regulatory or a combination of these methods under which rights can be exercised under the Framework. In addition, Member Economies should consider taking steps to establish access point(s) or mechanisms to provide information generally about the privacy protections within its jurisdiction. In practice, the Framework is meant to be implemented in a flexible manner that can accommodate various methods of implementation, including through central authorities, multi-agency enforcement bodies, a network of designated industry bodies, or a combination of the above, as Member Economies deem appropriate.

32. As set forth in Paragraph 31, the means of giving effect to the Framework may differ between Member Economies, and it may be appropriate for individual economies to determine that different APEC Privacy Principles may call for different means of

implementation. Whatever approach is adopted in a particular circumstance, the overall goal should be to develop compatibility of approaches in privacy protections in the APEC region that is respectful of requirements of individual economies.

33. APEC economies are encouraged to adopt non-discriminatory practices in protecting individuals from privacy protection violations occurring in that Member Economy's jurisdiction.

34. Discussions with domestic law enforcement, security, public health, and other agencies are important to identify ways to strengthen privacy without creating obstacles to national security, public safety, and other public policy missions.

III. Educating and publicising domestic privacy protections

35. For all Member Economies, in particular those Member Economies in earlier stages of development of their domestic approaches to privacy protections, the Framework is intended to provide guidance in developing their approaches.

36. For the Framework to be of practical effect, it must be known and accessible. Accordingly, Member Economies should:

    a) publicise the privacy protections it provides to individuals;
    b) educate personal information controllers about the Member Economy's privacy protections; and,
    c) educate individuals about how they can report violations and how remedies can be pursued.

IV. Cooperation between the Public and Private Sectors

37. Active participation of non-governmental entities will help ensure that the full benefits of the APEC Privacy Framework can be realized. Accordingly, Member Economies should engage in a dialogue with relevant private sector groups, including privacy groups and those representing consumers and industry, to obtain input on privacy protection issues and cooperation in furthering the Framework's objectives. Furthermore, especially in the economies where they have not established privacy protection regimes in their domestic jurisdiction, Member Economies should pay ample attention to whether private sector's opinions are reflected in developing privacy protections. In particular, Member Economies should seek the cooperation of non-governmental entities in public education and encourage their referral of complaints to privacy enforcement agencies, as well as their continuing cooperation in the investigation of those complaints.

V. Providing for appropriate remedies in situations where privacy protections are violated

38. A Member Economy's system of privacy protections should include an appropriate array of remedies for privacy protection violations, which could include redress, the ability to stop a violation from continuing, and other remedies. In determining the range of remedies for privacy protection violations, a number of factors should be taken into account by a Member Economy including:

> a) the particular system in that Member Economy for providing privacy protections (e.g., legislative enforcement powers, which may include rights of individuals to pursue legal action, industry self-regulation, or a combination of systems); and
>
> b) the importance of having a range of remedies commensurate with the extent of the actual or potential harm to individuals resulting from such violations.

VI. Mechanism for Reporting Domestic Implementation of the APEC Privacy Framework

39. Member economies should make known to APEC domestic implementation of the Framework through the completion of and periodic updates to the Individual Action Plan (IAP) on Information Privacy.

B. Guidance for International Implementation

I. Information sharing among Member Economies

40. Member Economies are encouraged to share and exchange information, surveys and research in respect of matters that have a significant impact on privacy protection.

41. In furthering the objectives of paragraphs 35 and 36, Member Economies are encouraged to educate one another in issues related to privacy protection and to share and exchange information on promotional, educational and training programs for the purpose of raising public awareness and enhancing understanding of the importance of privacy protection and compliance with relevant laws and regulations.

42. Member Economies are encouraged to share experiences on various techniques in investigating violations of privacy protections and regulatory strategies in resolving disputes involving such violations including, for instance, complaints handling and alternative dispute resolution mechanisms.

43. Member Economies should designate and make known to the other Member Economies the public authorities within their own jurisdictions that will be responsible for facilitating cross-border cooperation and information sharing between economies in connection with privacy protection.

II. Cross-border Cooperation in Investigation and Enforcement

44. Developing cooperative arrangements: Taking into consideration existing international arrangements and existing or developing self-regulatory approaches (including those referenced in Part B. III., below), and to the extent permitted by domestic law and policy, Member Economies should consider developing cooperative arrangements and procedures to facilitate cross-border cooperation in the enforcement of privacy laws. Such cooperative arrangements may take the form of bilateral or multilateral arrangements. This paragraph is to be construed with regard to the right of Member Economies to decline or limit cooperation on particular investigations or matters on the ground that compliance with a request for cooperation would be inconsistent with domestic laws, policies or priorities, or on the ground of resource constraints, or based on the absence of a mutual interest in the investigations in question.

45. In civil enforcement of privacy laws, cooperative cross-border arrangements may include the following aspects:

a) mechanisms for promptly, systematically and efficiently notifying designated public authorities in other Member Economies of investigations or privacy enforcement cases that target unlawful conduct or the resulting harm to individuals in those economies;

b) mechanisms for effectively sharing information necessary for successful cooperation in cross-border privacy investigation and enforcement cases;

c) mechanisms for investigative assistance in privacy enforcement cases;

d) mechanisms to prioritize cases for cooperation with public authorities in other economies based on the severity of the unlawful infringements of personal information privacy, the actual or potential harm involved, as well as other relevant considerations;

e) steps to maintain the appropriate level of confidentiality in respect of information exchanged under the cooperative arrangements.

III. Cooperative Development of Cross-border Privacy Rules

46. Member Economies will endeavor to support the development and recognition or acceptance of organizations' cross-border privacy rules across the APEC region, recognizing that organizations would still be responsible for complying with the local data protection requirements, as well as with all applicable laws. Such cross-border privacy rules should adhere to the APEC Privacy Principles.

47. To give effect to such cross-border privacy rules, Member Economies will endeavor to work with appropriate stakeholders to develop frameworks or mechanisms for the mutual recognition or acceptance of such cross-border privacy rules between and among the economies.

48. Member Economies should endeavor to ensure that such cross-border privacy rules and recognition or acceptance mechanisms facilitate responsible and accountable cross- border

data transfers and effective privacy protections without creating unnecessary barriers to cross-border information flows, including unnecessary administrative and bureaucratic burdens for businesses and consumers.

CAIRO DECLARATION OF HUMAN RIGHTS IN ISLAM [EXCERPT]

References

Organization of Islamic Cooperation, Cairo Declaration on Human Rights in Islam [http://www.oic-oci.org/english/article/human.htm]

The Member States of the Organization of the Islamic Conference,

Reaffirming the civilizing and historical role of the Islamic Ummah which God made the best nation that has given mankind a universal and well-balanced civilization in which harmony is established between this life and the hereafter and knowledge is combined with faith; and the role that this Ummah should play to guide a humanity confused by competing trends and ideologies and to provide solutions to the chronic problems of this materialistic civilization.

Wishing to contribute to the efforts of mankind to assert human rights, to protect man from exploitation and persecution, and to affirm his freedom and right to a dignified life in accordance with the Islamic Shari'ah

Convinced that mankind which has reached an advanced stage in materialistic science is still, and shall remain, in dire need of faith to support its civilization and of a self motivating force to guard its rights;

Believing that fundamental rights and universal freedoms in Islam are an integral part of the Islamic religion and that no one as a matter of principle has the right to suspend them in whole or in part or violate or ignore them in as much as they are binding divine commandments, which are contained in the Revealed Books of God and were sent through the last of His Prophets to complete the preceding divine messages thereby making their observance an act of worship and their neglect or violation an abominable sin, and accordingly every person is individually responsible - and the Ummah collectively responsible - for their safeguard.

Proceeding from the above-mentioned principles,

Declare the following:

ARTICLE 18:

(a) Everyone shall have the right to live in security for himself, his religion, his dependents, his honor and his property.

(b) Everyone shall have the right to privacy in the conduct of his private affairs, in his home, among his family, with regard to his property and his relationships. It is not permitted to spy on him, to place him under surveillance or to besmirch his good name. The State shall protect him from arbitrary interference.

(c) A private residence is inviolable in all cases. It will not be entered without permission from its inhabitants or in any unlawful manner, nor shall it be demolished or confiscated and its dwellers evicted.

Declaration of Principles on Freedom of Expression in Africa

DECLARATION OF PRINCIPLES ON
FREEDOM OF EXPRESSION IN AFRICA
[EXCERPT]

References

> African Commission on Human and Peoples' Rights, Resolution on the Adoption of
> the Declaration of Principles on Freedom of Expression in Africa
> [http://www.achpr.org/sessions/32nd/resolutions/62/]

Preamble

Reaffirming the fundamental importance of freedom of expression as an individual human
right, as a cornerstone of democracy and as a means of ensuring respect for all human rights
and freedoms;

Reaffirming Article 9 of the African Charter on Human and Peoples' Rights;

Desiring to promote the free flow of information and ideas and greater respect for freedom of
expression;

Convinced that respect for freedom of expression, as well as the right of access to information
held by public bodies and companies, will lead to greater public transparency and
accountability, as well as to good governance and the strengthening of democracy;

Convinced that laws and customs that repress freedom of expression are a disservice to
society;
Recalling that freedom of expression is a fundamental human right guaranteed by the African
Charter on Human and Peoples' Rights, the Universal Declaration of Human Rights and the
International Covenant on Civil and Political Rights, as well as other international documents
and national constitutions;

Considering the key role of the media and other means of communication in ensuring full
respect for freedom of expression, in promoting the free flow of information and ideas, in
assisting people to make informed decisions and in facilitating and strengthening democracy;
Aware of the particular importance of the broadcast media in Africa, given its capacity to
reach a wide audience due to the comparatively low cost of receiving transmissions and its
ability to overcome barriers of illiteracy;

Noting that oral traditions, which are rooted in African cultures, lend themselves particularly
well to radio broadcasting;

International
Declaration of Principles on Freedom of Expression in Africa

Noting the important contribution that can be made to the realisation of the right to freedom of expression by new information and communication technologies;

Mindful of the evolving human rights and human development environment in Africa, especially in light of the adoption of the Protocol to the African Charter on Human and Peoples' Rights on the establishment of an African Court on Human and Peoples' Rights, the principles of the Constitutive Act of the African Union, 2000, as well as the significance of the human rights and good governance provisions in the New Partnership for Africa's Development (NEPAD); and

Recognising the need to ensure the right to freedom of expression in Africa, the African Commission on Human and Peoples' Rights declares that:

* * *

IV. Freedom of Information

1. Public bodies hold information not for themselves but as custodians of the public good and everyone has a right to access this information, subject only to clearly defined rules established by law.
2. The right to information shall be guaranteed by law in accordance with the following principles:

> everyone has the right to access information held by public bodies;
> everyone has the right to access information held by private bodies which is necessary for the exercise or protection of any right;
> any refusal to disclose information shall be subject to appeal to an independent body and/or the courts;
> public bodies shall be required, even in the absence of a request, actively to publish important information of significant public interest;
> no one shall be subject to any sanction for releasing in good faith information on wrongdoing, or that which would disclose a serious threat to health, safety or the environment save where the imposition of sanctions serves a legitimate interest and is necessary in a democratic society; and
> secrecy laws shall be amended as necessary to comply with freedom of information principles.

3. Everyone has the right to access and update or otherwise correct their personal information, whether it is held by public or by private bodies.

* * *

THIRTEENTH IBERO-AMERICAN SUMMIT MEETING OF HEADS OF STATE AND HEADS OF GOVERNMENT

DECLARATION OF SANTA CRUZ DE LA SIERRA

References

> Permanent Rep. of Bolivia to the U.N., Letter dated Nov. 18, 2003 from the Permanent Rep. of Bolivia to the Secretary-General, U.N. Doc. A/58/607 (Nov. 18, 2003) (Declaration of Santa Cruz de la Sierra).
> [http://www.un.org/en/ga/search/view_doc.asp?symbol=A/58/607]

NOVEMBER 14 AND 15, 2003

"Social Inclusion, the Driving Force Behind the
Development of the Ibero-American Community"

We, the Heads of State and Heads of Government of the twenty-one Ibero-American countries, gathered at the Thirteenth Ibero-American Summit Meeting in the city of Santa Cruz de la Sierra, Bolivia, reiterate our determination to continue strengthening the Ibero-American Community of Nations as a forum for dialogue, cooperation and political agreement by deepening the historical and cultural ties that bind us together, admitting at the same time the characteristic features of each one of our multiple identities that enable us to recognize ourselves as a unit in diversity.../

* * *

45. Likewise we are aware that the protection of personal data is a fundamental right of all persons, and we highlight the importance of Ibero-American regulatory initiatives for protecting the privacy of citizens contained in the La Antigua Declaration creating the Ibero-American Data-Protection Network, open to all the countries of our Community.

MADRID DECLARATION

References

Madrid Declaration
[http://thepublicvoice.org/madrid-declaration/]

3 November 2009

Affirming that privacy is a fundamental human right set out in the Universal Declaration of Human Rights, the International Covenant on Civil and Political Rights, and other human rights instruments and national constitutions;

Reminding the EU member countries of their obligations to enforce the provisions of the 1995 Data Protection Directive and the 2002 Electronic Communications Directive;

Reminding the other OECD member countries of their obligations to uphold the principles set out in the 1980 OECD Privacy Guidelines;

Reminding all countries of their obligations to safeguard the civil rights of their citizens and residents under the provisions of their national constitutions and laws, as well as international human rights law;

Anticipating the entry into force of provisions strengthening the Constitutional rights to privacy and data protection in the European Union;

Noting with alarm the dramatic expansion of secret and unaccountable surveillance, as well as the growing collaboration between governments and vendors of surveillance technology that establish new forms of social control;

Further noting that new strategies to pursue copyright and unlawful content investigations pose substantial threats to communications privacy, intellectual freedom, and due process of law;

Further noting the growing consolidation of Internet-based services, and the fact that some corporations are acquiring vast amounts of personal data without independent oversight;

Warning that privacy law and privacy institutions have failed to take full account of new surveillance practices, including behavioral targeting, databases of DNA and other biometric identifiers, the fusion of data between the public and private sectors, and the particular risks to vulnerable groups, including children, migrants, and minorities;

Warning that the failure to safeguard privacy jeopardizes associated freedoms, including freedom of expression, freedom of assembly, freedom of access to information, non-discrimination, and ultimately the stability of constitutional democracies;

Civil Society takes the occasion of the 31st annual meeting of the International Conference of Privacy and Data Protection Commissioners to:

(1) Reaffirm support for a global framework of Fair Information Practices that places obligations on those who collect and process personal information and gives rights to those whose personal information is collected;

(2) Reaffirm support for independent data protection authorities that make determinations, in the context of a legal framework, transparently and without commercial advantage or political influence;

(3) Reaffirm support for genuine Privacy Enhancing Techniques that minimize or eliminate the collection of personally identifiable information and for meaningful Privacy Impact Assessments that require compliance with privacy standards;

(4) Urge countries that have not ratified Council of Europe Convention 108 together with the Protocol of 2001 to do so as expeditiously as possible;

(5) Urge countries that have not yet established a comprehensive framework for privacy protection and an independent data protection authority to do so as expeditiously as possible;

(6) Urge those countries that have established legal frameworks for privacy protection to ensure effective implementation and enforcement, and to cooperate at the international and regional level;

(7) Urge countries to ensure that individuals are promptly notified when their personal information is improperly disclosed or used in a manner inconsistent with its collection;

(8) Recommend comprehensive research into the adequacy of techniques that deidentify; data to determine whether in practice such methods safeguard privacy and anonymity;

(9) Call for a moratorium on the development or implementation of new systems of mass surveillance, including facial recognition, whole body imaging, biometric identifiers, and embedded RFID tags, subject to a full and transparent evaluation by independent authorities and democratic debate; and

(10) Call for the establishment of a new international framework for privacy protection, with the full participation of civil society, that is based on the rule of law, respect for fundamental human rights, and support for democratic institutions.

Recent Developments

UN RESOLUTION ON RIGHT TO PRIVACY (2014)

References

G.A. Res. 69/166, The Right to Privacy in the Digital Age (Dec. 18, 2014)
[http://www.un.org/en/ga/search/view_doc.asp?symbol=A/RES/69/166]

U.N. – The Right to Privacy in the Digital Age
[http://www.ohchr.org/EN/Issues/DigitalAge/Pages/DigitalAgeIndex.aspx]

Resolution adopted by the General Assembly on 18 December 2014

69/166. The right to privacy in the digital age

The General Assembly,

Reaffirming the purposes and principles of the Charter of the United Nations,

Reaffirming also the human rights and fundamental freedoms enshrined in the Universal Declaration of Human Rights[5] and relevant international human rights treaties, including the International Covenant on Civil and Political Rights[6] and the International Covenant on Economic, Social and Cultural Rights,[6]

Reaffirming further the Vienna Declaration and Programme of Action,[7]

Recalling its resolution 68/167 of 18 December 2013 on the right to privacy in the digital age,

Welcoming the adoption by the Human Rights Council of resolution 26/13 of 26 June 2014 on the promotion, protection and enjoyment of human rights on the Internet,[8]

---

[5] Resolution 217 A (III).

[6] See resolution 2200 A (XXI), annex.

[7] A/CONF.157/24 (Part I), chap. III.

[8] See *Official Records of the General Assembly, Sixty-ninth Session, Supplement No. 53* (A/69/53), chap. V, sect. A.

Recent Developments
UN Resolution on Right to Privacy

Welcoming also the work of the Office of the United Nations High Commissioner for Human Rights on the right to privacy in the digital age, noting with interest its report on the subject,[9] and recalling the panel discussion on the right to privacy in the digital age held during the twenty-seventh session of the Human Rights Council,

Noting the report of the Special Rapporteur of the Human Rights Council on the promotion and protection of human rights and fundamental freedoms while countering terrorism[10] and the report of the Special Rapporteur of the Council on the promotion and protection of the right to freedom of opinion and expression,[11]

Noting with appreciation general comment No. 16 of the Human Rights Committee on the right to respect of privacy, family, home and correspondence, and protection of honour and reputation, while also noting the vast technological leaps that have taken place since its adoption,[12]

Recognizing the need to further discuss and analyse, based on international human rights law, issues relating to the promotion and protection of the right to privacy in the digital age, procedural safeguards, effective domestic oversight and remedies, the impact of surveillance on the right to privacy and other human rights, as well as the need to examine the principles of non-arbitrariness and lawfulness, and the relevance of necessity and proportionality assessments in relation to surveillance practices,

Noting the holding of the Global Multi-stakeholder Meeting on the Future of Internet Governance, "NETmundial", in São Paulo, Brazil, in April 2014, and recognizing that effectively addressing the challenges relating to the right to privacy in the context of modern communications technology will require an ongoing, concerted multi-stakeholder engagement,

Noting also that the rapid pace of technological development enables individuals all over the world to use new information and communication technologies and at the same time enhances the capacity of governments, companies and individuals to undertake surveillance, interception and data collection, which may violate or abuse human rights, in particular the right to privacy, as set out in article 12 of the Universal Declaration of Human Rights and article 17 of the International Covenant on Civil and Political Rights, and is therefore an issue of increasing concern,

---

[9] A/HRC/27/37.

[10] A/69/397.

[11] A/HRC/23/40 and Corr.1.

[12] Official Records of the General Assembly, Forty-third Session, Supplement No. 40 (A/43/40), annex VI.

Reaffirming the human right to privacy, according to which no one shall be subjected to arbitrary or unlawful interference with his or her privacy, family, home or correspondence, and the right to the protection of the law against such interference, and recognizing that the exercise of the right to privacy is important for the realization of the right to freedom of expression and to hold opinions without interference and the right to freedom of peaceful assembly and association, and is one of the foundations of a democratic society,

Stressing the importance of full respect for the freedom to seek, receive and impart information, including the fundamental importance of access to information and democratic participation,

Noting that while metadata can provide benefits, certain types of metadata, when aggregated, can reveal personal information and can give an insight into an individual's behaviour, social relationships, private preferences and identity,

Emphasizing that unlawful or arbitrary surveillance and/or interception of communications, as well as unlawful or arbitrary collection of personal data, as highly intrusive acts, violate the right to privacy, can interfere with the right to freedom of expression and may contradict the tenets of a democratic society, including when undertaken on a mass scale,

Noting in particular that surveillance of digital communications must be consistent with international human rights obligations and must be conducted on the basis of a legal framework, which must be publicly accessible, clear, precise, comprehensive and non-discriminatory and that any interference with the right to privacy must not be arbitrary or unlawful, bearing in mind what is reasonable to the pursuance of legitimate aims, and recalling that States that are parties to the International Covenant on Civil and Political Rights must undertake the necessary steps to adopt laws or other measures as may be necessary to give effect to the rights recognized in the Covenant,

Emphasizing that States must respect international human rights obligations regarding the right to privacy when they intercept digital communications of individuals and/or collect personal data and when they require disclosure of personal data from third parties, including private companies,

Recalling that business enterprises have a responsibility to respect human rights as set out in the Guiding Principles on Business and Human Rights: Implementing the United Nations "Protect, Respect and Remedy" Framework,[13]

---

[13] A/HRC/17/31, annex.

Recent Developments
UN Resolution on Right to Privacy

Deeply concerned at the negative impact that surveillance and/or interception of communications, including extraterritorial surveillance and/or interception of communications, as well as the collection of personal data, in particular when carried out on a mass scale, may have on the exercise and enjoyment of human rights,

Noting with deep concern that, in many countries, persons and organizations engaged in promoting and defending human rights and fundamental freedoms frequently face threats and harassment and suffer insecurity as well as unlawful or arbitrary interference with their right to privacy as a result of their activities,

Noting that while concerns about public security may justify the gathering and protection of certain sensitive information, States must ensure full compliance with their obligations under international human rights law,

Noting also in that respect that the prevention and suppression of terrorism is a public interest of great importance, while reaffirming that States must ensure that any measures taken to combat terrorism are in compliance with their obligations under international law, in particular international human rights, refugee and humanitarian law,

1. *Reaffirms* the right to privacy, according to which no one shall be subjected to arbitrary or unlawful interference with his or her privacy, family, home or correspondence, and the right to the protection of the law against such interference, as set out in article 12 of the Universal Declaration of Human Rights[5] and article 17 of the International Covenant on Civil and Political Rights;[6]

2. *Recognizes* the global and open nature of the Internet and the rapid advancement in information and communications technologies as a driving force in accelerating progress towards development in its various forms;

3. *Affirms* that the same rights that people have offline must also be protected online, including the right to privacy;

4. *Calls upon* all States:

(*a*) To respect and protect the right to privacy, including in the context of digital communication;

(*b*) To take measures to put an end to violations of those rights and to create the conditions to prevent such violations, including by ensuring that relevant national legislation complies with their obligations under international human rights law;

(*c*) To review their procedures, practices and legislation regarding the surveillance of communications, their interception and the collection of personal data, including mass surveillance, interception and collection, with a view to upholding the right to privacy by ensuring the full and effective implementation of all their obligations under international human rights law;

(*d*) To establish or maintain existing independent, effective, adequately resourced and impartial judicial, administrative and/or parliamentary domestic oversight mechanisms capable of ensuring transparency, as appropriate, and accountability for State surveillance of communications, their interception and the collection of personal data;

(*e*) To provide individuals whose right to privacy has been violated by unlawful or arbitrary surveillance with access to an effective remedy, consistent with international human rights obligations;

5. *Encourages* the Human Rights Council to remain actively seized of the debate, with the purpose of identifying and clarifying principles, standards and best practices regarding the promotion and protection of the right to privacy, and to consider the possibility of establishing a special procedure to that end;

6. *Decides* to remain seized of the matter.

73rd plenary meeting
18 December 2014

EU-US "UMBRELLA AGREEMENT"
(2015)

Summary

The EU-US "Umbrella Agreement" is a framework for transatlantic data transfer between the US and the EU. The proposed goal of the Agreement is to provide data protection safeguards for personal information transferred between the EU and the US.

References

> EU-US "Umbrella Agreement"
> [http://ec.europa.eu/justice/data-protection/files/dp-umbrella-agreement_en.pdf]

> European Data Protection Supervisor Opinion
> [https://secure.edps.europa.eu/EDPSWEB/webdav/site/mySite/shared/Documents/Consultation/Opinions/2016/16-02-12_EU-US_Umbrella_Agreement_EN.pdf]

> EPIC, EU-US "Umbrella Agreement"
> [https://epic.org/privacy/intl/data-agreement/]

Mindful that the United States: and the European Union are committed to ensuring a high level of protection of personal information exchanged in the context of the prevention, investigation, detection, and prosecution of criminal offenses, including terrorism;

Intending to establish a lasting legal framework to facilitate the exchange of information, which is critical to prevent, investigate, detect and prosecute criminal offenses, including terrorism, as a means of protecting their respective democratic societies and common values;

Intending, in particular, to provide standards of protection for exchanges of personal information on the basis of both existing and future agreements between the US and the EU and its Member States, in the field of preventing, investigating, detecting, and prosecuting criminal offenses, including terrorism;

Recognizing that certain existing agreements between the Parties concerning the processing of personal information establish that those agreements provide an adequate level of data protection within the scope of those agreements, the Parties affirm that this Agreement should not be construed to alter, condition, or otherwise derogate from those agreements; noting however, that the obligations established by Article 19 of this Agreement on judicial redress would apply with respect to all transfers that fall within the scope of this Agreement, and that this is without prejudice to any future review or modification of such agreements pursuant to their terms.

Acknowledging both Parties' longstanding traditions of respect for individual privacy including as reflected in the Principles on Privacy and Personal Data Protection for Law Enforcement Purposes elaborated by the EU-U.S. High Level Contact Group on Information Sharing and Privacy and Personal Data Protection, the Charter of Fundamental Rights of the European Union and applicable EU laws, the United States Constitution and applicable U.S. laws, and the Fair Information Practice Principles of the Organization for Economic Cooperation and Development; and

Recognizing the principles of proportionality and necessity, and relevance and reasonableness, as implemented by the Parties in their respective legal frameworks;

THE UNITED STATES OF AMERICA AND THE EUROPEAN UNION HAVE AGREED AS FOLLOWS:

Article 1: Purpose of the Agreement

1. The purpose of this Agreement is to ensure a high level of protection of personal information and enhance cooperation between the United States and the European Union and its Member States, in relation to the prevention, investigation, detection or prosecution of criminal offenses, including terrorism.

2. For this purpose, this Agreement establishes the framework for the protection of personal information when transferred between the United States, on the one hand, and the European Union or its Member States, on the other.

3. This Agreement in and of itself shall not be the legal basis for any transfers of personal information. A legal basis for such transfers shall always be required.

Article 2: Definitions

For purposes of this Agreement:

> 1. "Personal information" means information relating to an identified or identifiable natural person. An identifiable person is a person who can be identified, directly or indirectly, by reference to, in particular, an identification number or to one or more factors specific to his or her physical, physiological, mental, economic, cultural or social identity.

> 2. "Processing of personal information" means any operation or set of operations involving collection, maintenance, use, alteration, organization or structuring, disclosure or dissemination, or disposition.

3. "Parties" means the European Union and the United States of America.

4. "Member State" means a Member State of the European Union.

5. "Competent Authority" means, for the United States, a U.S. national law enforcement responsible for the prevention, investigation, detection or prosecution of criminal offenses, including terrorism and, for the European Union, an authority of the European Union, and an authority of a Member State, responsible for the prevention, investigation, detection or prosecution of criminal offenses, including terrorism.

Article 3: Scope

1. This Agreement shall apply to personal information transferred between the Competent Authorities of one Party and the Competent Authorities of the other Party, or otherwise transferred in accordance with an agreement concluded between the United States and the European Union or its Menlber States, for the prevention, detection, investigation and prosecution of criminal offences, including terrorism.

2. This Agreement does not affect, and is without prejudice to, transfers or other forms of cooperation between the authorities of the Member States and of the United States other than those referred to in Article 2(5), responsible for safeguarding national security.

Article 4: Non-Discrimination

Each Party shall comply with its obligations under this Agreement for the purpose of protecting personal information of its own nationals and the other Party's nationals regardless of their nationality, and without arbitrary and unjustifiable discrimination.

Article 5: Effect of the Agreement

1. This Agreement supplements, as appropriate, but does not replace, provisions regarding the protection of personal infomlation in international agreements between the Parties, or the United States and Member States that address matters within the scope of this Agreement.

2. The Parties shall take all necessary measures to implement this Agreement, including, in particular, their respective obligations regarding access, rectification and administrative and judicial redress for individuals provided herein. The protections and remedies set forth in this Agreement shall benefit individuals and entities in the manner implemented in the applicable domestic laws of each Party. For the United States, its obligations shall apply in a manner consistent with its fundamental principles of federalism.

3. By giving effect to paragraph 2, the processing of personal information by the United States, or the European Union and its Member States, with respect to matters falling within

the scope of this Agreement, shall be deemed to comply with their respective data protection legislation restricting or conditioning international transfers of personal information, and no further authorization under such legislation shall be required.

Article 6: Purpose and Use Limitations

1. The transfer of personal information shall be for specific purposes authorized by the legal basis for the transfer as set forth in Article 1.

2. The further processing of personal information by a Party shall not be incompatible with the purposes for which it was transferred. Compatible processing includes processing pursuant to the terms of existing international agreements and written international frameworks for the prevention, detection, investigation or prosecution of serious crimes. All such processing of personal information by other national law enforcement, regulatory or administrative authorities shall respect the other provisions of this Agreement.

3. This Article shall not prejudice the ability of the transferring Competent Authority to impose additional conditions in a specific case to the extent the applicable legal framework for transfer permits it to do so. Such conditions shall not include generic data protection conditions, that is, conditions imposed that are unrelated to the specific facts of the case. If the information is subject to conditions, the receiving Competent Authority shall comply with them. The Competent Authority providing the information may also require the recipient to give information on the use made of the transferred information.

4. Where the United States, on the one hand, and the European Union or a Member State on the other, conclude an agreement on the transfer of personal information other than in relation to specific cases, investigations or prosecutions, the specified purposes for which the information is transferred and processed shall be further set forth in that agreement.

5. The Parties shall ensure under their respective laws that personal information is processed in a manner that is directly relevant to and not excessive or overbroad in relation to the purposes of such processing.

Article 7: Onward Transfer

1. Where a Competent Authority of one Party has transferred personal information relating to a specific case to a Competent Authority of the other Party, that information may be transferred to a State not bound by the present Agreement or international body only where the prior consent of the Competent Authority originally sending that information has been obtained.

2. When granting its consent to a transfer under paragraph 1, the Competent Authority originally transferring the information shall take due account of all relevant factors, including the seriousness of the offence, the purpose for which the data is initially transferred and whether the State not bound by the present Agreement or international body in question ensures an appropriate level of protection of personal information. It may also subject the transfer to specific conditions.

3. Where the United States, on the one hand, and the European Union or a Member State on the other, conclude an agreement on the transfer of personal information other than in relation to specific cases, investigations or prosecutions, the onward transfer of personal information may only take place in accordance with specific conditions set forth in the agreement that provide due justification for the onward transfer. The agreement shall also provide for appropriate information mechanisms between the Competent Authorities.

4. Nothing in this Article shall be construed as affecting any requirement, obligation or practice pursuant to which the prior consent of the Competent Authority originally transferring the information must be obtained before the information is further transferred to a State or body bound by this Agreement, provided that the level of data protection in such State or body shall not be the basis for denying consent for, or imposing conditions on, such transfers.

Article 8: Maintaining Quality and Integrity of Information

The Parties shall take reasonable steps to ensure that personal information is maintained with such accuracy, relevance, timeliness and completeness as is necessary and appropriate for lawful processing of the inforrnation. For this purpose, the Competent Authorities shall have in place procedures, the object of which is to ensure the quality and integrity of personal information, including the following:

> (a) the measures referred to in Article 17;
> (b) where the transferring Competent Authority becomes aware of significant doubts as to the relevance, trnaeliness, completeness or accuracy of such personal information or an assessment it has transferred, it shall, where feasible, advise the receiving Competent Authority thereof;
> (c) where the receiving Competent Authority becomes aware of significant doubts as to the relevance, timeliness, completeness or accuracy of personal information received from a governmental authority, or of an assessment made by the transferring Competent Authority of the accuracy of information or the reliability of a source, it shall, where feasible, advise the transferring Competent Authority thereof.

Article 9: Information Security

The Parties shall ensure that they have in place appropriate technical, security and organizational arrangements for the protection of personal information against all of the following:

(a) accidental or unlawful destruction;

(b) accidental loss; and

(c) unauthorized disclosure, alteration, access, or other processing.

Such arrangements shall include appropriate safeguards regarding the authorization required to access personal information.

Article 10: Notification of an information security incident

1. Upon discovery of an incident involving accidental loss or destruction, or unauthorized access, disclosure, or alteration of personal information, in which there is a significant risk of damage, the receiving Competent Authority shall promptly assess the likelihood and scale of damage to individuals and to the integrity of the transferring Competent Authority's program, and promptly take appropriate action to mitigate any such damage.

2. Action to mitigate damage shall include notification to the transferring Competent Authority. However, notification may:

a) include appropriate restrictions as to the further transmission of the notification;

b) be delayed or omitted when such notification may endanger national security;

c) be delayed when such notification may endanger public security operations.

3. Action to mitigate damage shall also include notification to the individual, where appropriate given the circumstances of the incident, unless such notification may endanger:

a) public or national security;

b) official inquiries, investigations or proceedings;

c) the prevention, detection, investigation, or prosecution of criminal offenses;

d) rights and freedoms of others, in particular the protection of victims and witnesses.

4. The Competent Authorities involved in the transfer of the personal information may consult concerning the incident and the response thereto.

Recent Developments
EU-US "Umbrella Agreement"

Article 11: Maintaining Records

1. The Parties shall have in place effective methods of demonstrating the lawfulness of processing of personal information, which may include the use of logs, as well as other forms of records.

2. The Competent Authorities may use such logs or records for maintaining orderly operations of the databases or files concerned, to ensure data integrity and security, and where necessary to follow backup procedures.

Article 12: Retention Period

1. The Parties shall provide in their applicable legal frameworks specific retention periods for records containing personal information, the object of which is to ensure that personal information is not retained for longer than is necessary and appropriate. Such retention periods shall take into account the purposes of processing, the nature of the data and the authority processing it, the impact on relevant rights and interests of affected persons, and other applicable legal considerations.

2. Where the United States, on the one hand, and the European Union or a Member State on the other, conclude an agreement on the transfer of personal information other than in relation to specific cases, investigations or prosecutions, such agreement will include a specific and mutually agreed upon provision on retention periods.

3. The Parties shall provide procedures for periodic review of the retention period with a view to determining whether changed circumstances require further modification of the applicable period.

4. The Parties shall publish or otherwise make publicly available such retention periods.

Article 13: Special Categories of Personal Information

1. Processing of personal information revealing racial or ethnic origin, political opinions or religious or other beliefs, trade union membership or personal information concerning health or sexual life shall only take place under appropriate safeguards in accordance with law. Such appropriate safeguards may include: restricting the purposes for which the information may be processed, such as allowing the processing only on a case by case basis; masking, deleting or blocking the information after effecting the purpose for which it was processed; restricting personnel permitted to access the information; requiring specialized training to personnel who access the information; requiring supervisory approval to access the information; or other protective measures. These safeguards shall duly take into account the nature of the information, particular sensitivities of the information, and the purpose for which the information is processed.

2. Where the United States, on the one hand, and the European Union or a Member State on the other, conclude an agreement on the transfer of personal information other than in relation to specific cases, investigations or prosecutions, such agreement will further specify the standards and conditions under which such information can be processed, duly taking into account the nature of the information and the purpose for which it is used.

Article 14: Accountability

1. The Parties shall have in place measures to promote accountability for processing personal information within the scope of this Agreement by their Competent Authorities, and any other of their authorities to which personal information has been transferred. Such measures shall include notification of the safeguards applicable to transfers of personal information under this Agreement, and of the conditions that may have been imposed by the transferring Competent Authority pursuant to Article 6(3). Serious misconduct shall be addressed through appropriate and dissuasive criminal, civil or administrative sanctions.

2. The measures set out in paragraph 1 shall include, as appropriate, discontinuation of transfer of personal information to authorities of constituent territorial entities of the Parties not covered by this Agreement that have not effectively protected personal information, taking into account the purpose of this Agreement, and in particular the purpose and use limitations and onward transfer provisions of this Agreement.

3. In case of allegations of improper implementation of this Article, a Party may request the other Party to provide relevant information, including, where appropriate, regarding the measures taken under this Article.

Article 15: Automated Decisilons

Decisions producing signficant adverse actions concerning the relevant interests of the individual may not be based solely on the automated processing of personal information without human involvement, unless authorized under domestic law, and with appropriate safeguards that include the possibility to obtain human intervention.

Article 16: Access

1. The Parties shall ensure that any individual is entitled to seek access to his or her personal information and, subject to the restrictions set forth in paragraph 2, to obtain it. Such access shall be sought and obtained from a Competent Authority in accordance with the applicable legal framework of the State in which relief is sought.

2. The obtaining of such information in a particular case may be subject to reasonable restrictions provided under domestic law, taking into account legitimate interests of the individual concerned, so as to:

a) protect the rights and freedoms of others, including their privacy;

b) safeguard public and national security;

c) protect law enforcement sensitive information;

d) avoid obstructing official or legal inquiries, investigations or proceedings;

e) avoid prejudicing the prevention, detection, investigation or prosecution of criminal offenses or the execution of criminal penalties;

f) otherwise protect interests provided for in legislation regarding freedom of information and public access to documents.

3. Excessive expenses shall not be imposed on the individual as a condition to access his or her personal information.

4. An individual is entitled to authorize, where permitted under applicable domestic law, an oversight authority or other representative to request access on his or her behalf.

5. If access is denied or restricted, the requested Competent Authority will, without undue delay, provide to the individual, or to his or her duly authorized representative as set forth in paragraph 4, the reasons for the denial or restriction of access.

Article 17: Rectification

1. The Parties shall ensure that any individual is entitled to seek correction or rectification of his or her personal information that he or she asserts is either inaccurate or has been improperly processed. Correction or rectification may include supplementation, erasure, blocking or other measures or methods for addressing inaccuracies or improper processing. Such correction or rectification shall be sought and obtained from a Competent Authority in accordance with the applicable legal framework of the State in which relief is sought.

2. Where the receiving Competent Authority concludes following:

a) a request under paragraph 1;

b) notification by the provider; or

c) its own investigations or inquiries;

that information it has received under this Agreement is inaccurate or has been improperly processed, it shall take measures of supplementation, erasure, blocking or other methods of correction or rectification, as appropriate.

3. An individual is entitled to authorize, where permitted under applicable domestic law, an oversight authority or other representative to seek correction or rectification on his or her behalf.

4. If correction or rectification is denied or restricted, the requested Competent Authority will, without undue delay, provide to the individual, or to his or to her duly authorized representative as set forth in paragraph 3, a response setting forth the basis for the denial or restriction of correction or rectification.

Article 18: Administrative Redress

1. The Parties shall ensure that any individual is entitled to seek administrative redress where he or she believes that his or her request for access pursuant to Article 16 or rectification of inaccurate information or improper processing pursuant to Article 17 has been improperly denied. Such redress shall be sought and obtained from a Competent Authority in accordance with the applicable legal framlework of the State in which relief is sought.

2. An individual is entitled to authorize, where permitted under applicable domestic law, an oversight authority or other representative to seek administrative redress on his or her behalf.

3. The Competent Authority from which relief is sought shall carry out the appropriate inquiries and verifications and without undue delay shall respond in written form, including through electronic means, with the result, including the ameliorative or corrective action taken where applicable. Notice ofthe procedure for seeking any further administrative redress shall be as provided for in Article 20.

Article 19: Judicial Redress

1. The Parties shall provide in their applicable legal frameworks that, subject to any requirements that administrative redress first be exhausted, any citizen of a Party is entitled to seek judicial review with regard to:

a) denial by a Competent Authority of access to records containing his or her personal information;
b) denial by a Competent Authority of amendment of records containing his or her personal information; and
c) unlawful disclosure of such information that has been willfully or intentionally made, which shall include the possibility of compensatory damages.

2. Such judicial review shall be sought and obtained in accordance with the applicable legal framework of the State in which relief is sought.

3. Paragraphs 1 and 2 are without prejudice to any other judicial review available with respect to the processing of an individual's personal informafion under the law of the State in which relief is requested.

4. In the event of the suspension or termination of the Agreement, articles 26(2) or 29(3) shall not create a basis for judicial redress that is no longer available under the law of the Party concerned.

Article 20: Transparency

1. The Parties shall provide notice to an individual, as to his or her personal information, which notice may be effected by the Competent Authorities through publication of general notices or through actual notice, in a form and at a time provided for by the law applicable to the authority providing notice, with regard to the:

(a) purposes of processing of such information by that authority;

(b) purposes for which the information may be shared with other authorities;

(c) laws or rules under which such processing takes place;

(d) third parties to whom such information is disclosed; and

(e) access, correction or rectification, and redress available.

2. Such notice requirement is subject to the reasonable restrictions under domestic law with respect to the matters set forth in Article 16(2) (a) through (t).

Article 21: Effective Oversight

1. The Parties shall have in place one or more public oversight authorities that:

(a) exercise independent oversight functions and powers, including review, investigation and intervention, where appropriate on their own initiative;

(b) have the power to accept and act upon complaints made by individuals relating to the measures implementing this Agreement; and

(c) have the power to refer violations of law related to this Agreement for prosecution or disciplinary action vvhen appropriate.

2. The European Union shall provide for oversight under this Article through its data protection authorities and those ofthe Member States.

3. The United States shall provide for oversight under this Article cumulatively through more than one authority, which may include, inter alia, inspectors general, chief privacy officers, government accountability offices, privacy and civil liberties oversight boards, and other applicable executive and legislative privacy or civil liberties review bodies.

Article 22: Cooperation between oversight authorities

1. Consultations between authorities conducting oversight under Article 21 shall take place as appropriate with respect to carrying out the functions in relation to this Agreement, with a view towards ensuring effective implementation of the provisions of Articles 16, 17, and 18.

2. The Parties shall establish national contact points that will assist with the identification of the oversight authority to be addressed in a particular case.

Article 23: Joint Review

1. The Parties shall conduct periodic joint reviews of the policies and procedures that implement this Agreement and of their effectiveness. Particular attention in the joint reviews shall be paid to the effective implementation of the protections under Article 14 on accountability, Article 16 on access, Article 17 on rectification, Article 18 on administrative redress, and Article 19 on judicial redress.

2. The fIrst joint review shall be conducted no later than three years from the date of entry into force of this Agreement and thereafter on a regular basis. The Parties shall jointly determine in advance the modalities and terms thereof and shall communicate to each other the composition of their respective delegations, which shall include representatives of the public oversight authorities referred to in Article 21 on effective oversight, and of law enforcement and justice authorities. The findings of the joint review will be made public.

3. Where the Parties or the United States and a Member State have concluded another agreement, the subject matter of which is also within the scope of this Agreement, which provides for joint reviews, such joint reviews shall not be duplicated and, to the extent relevant, their findings shall be made part of the findings of the joint review of this Agreement.

Article 24: Notification

1. The United States shall notify the European Union of any designation made by U.S. authorities in relation to Article 19, and any modifications thereto.

2. The Parties shall make reasonable efforts to notify each other regarding the enactment of any laws or the adoption of regulations that materially affect the implementation of this Agreement, where feasible before they become effective.

Article 25: Consultation

Any dispute arising from the interpretation or application of this Agreement shall give rise to consultations between the Parties with a view to reaching a mutually agreeable resolution.

Recent Developments
EU-US "Umbrella Agreement"

Article 26: Suspension

1. In the event of a material breach of this Agreement, either Party may suspend this Agreement in whole or in part by written notification to the other Party through diplomatic channels. Such written notification shall not be made until after the Parties have engaged in a reasonable period of consultation without reaching a resolution and suspension shall take effect twenty days from the date of receipt of such notification. Such suspension may be lifted by the suspending Party upon written notification to the other Party. The suspension shall be lifted immediately upon receipt of such notification.

2. Notwithstanding any suspension of this Agreement, personal data falling within the scope of this Agreement and transferred prior to its suspension shall continue to be processed in accordance with this Agreement.

Article 27: Territorial application

1. This Agreement shall only apply to Denmark, the United Kingdom, or Ireland if the European Commission notifies the United States in writing that Denmark, the United Kingdom, or Ireland has decided that this Agreement applies to its State.

2. If the European Commission notifies the United States before the entry into force of this Agreement that this Agreement will apply to Denmark, the United Kingdom, or Ireland, this Agreement shall apply to such States from the date of entry into force of this Agreement.

3. If the European Commission notifies the United States after the entry into force of this Agreement that it applies to Denmark, the United Kingdom, or Ireland, this Agreement shall apply to such State on the first day of the month following receipt of the notification by the United States.

Article 28: Duration of the Agreement

This Agreement is concluded for an unlimited duration.

Article 29: Entry into force and Termination

1. This Agreement shall enter into force on the first day of the month following the date on which the Parties have exchanged notifications indicating that they have completed their internal procedures for entry into force.

2. Either Party may terminate this Agreement by written notification to the other Party through diplomatic channels. Such termination shall take effect thirty days from the date of receipt of such notification.

3. Notwithstanding any termination of this Agreement, personal information falling within the scope of this Agreement and transferred prior to its termination shall continue to be processed in accordance with this Agreement.

IN WITNESS WHEREOF, the undersigned Plenipotentiaries have signed this Agreement.

Done at _ this _ day of _ 201_., in two originals, in the English language. Pursuant to EU law, this Agreement shall also be drawn up by the EU in the Bulgarian, Croatian, Czech, Danish, Dutch, Estonian, Finnish, French, German, Greek, Hungarian, Italian, Irish, Latvian, Lithuanian, Maltese, Polish, Portuguese, Romanian, Slovak, Slovenian, Spanish and Swedish languages. These additional language versions can be authenticated by an exchange of diplomatic notes between the United States and the European Union. In the case of divergence between authentic language versions, the English language shall prevail.

US CYBERSECURITY INFORMATION
SHARING ACT OF 2015

Summary

The "scrubbing provision" in the Cybersecurity Information Sharing Act requires agencies to develop techniqies that "remove any personal information or information that identifies a specific person not directly related to a cybersecurity threat." The Act also requires the Attorney General to develop privacy guidelines for the use of cyberthreat indicators. The heads of several federal agencies are required to prepare a biennual report that provides, among others, "a quantitative and qualitative assessment of the effect of the sharing of such cyber threat indicators with the Federal Government on privacy and civil liberties of specific persons." The Privacy and Civil Liberties Oversight Board is also required to provide a bienniel report to Congress concerning the privacy and civil liberties impact of the Act.

References

Public Law 114–113, codified at 6 U.S.C. § 1501 et seq.
[https://www.law.cornell.edu/uscode/text/6/1501]

EPIC, Cybersecurity Privacy Practical Implications
[https://epic.org/privacy/cybersecurity/]
[https://epic.org/privacy/cybersecurity/presidential-directives/cybersecurity.html]

§1501. Definitions

In this subchapter:
(1) Agency
The term "agency" has the meaning given the term in section 3502 of title 44.
(2) Antitrust laws
The term "antitrust laws"-
(A) has the meaning given the term in section 12 of title 15;
(B) includes section 45 of title 15 to the extent that section 45 of title 15 applies to unfair methods of competition; and
(C) includes any State antitrust law, but only to the extent that such law is consistent with the law referred to in subparagraph (A) or the law referred to in subparagraph (B).
(3) Appropriate Federal entities
The term "appropriate Federal entities" means the following:
(A) The Department of Commerce.
(B) The Department of Defense.
(C) The Department of Energy.
(D) The Department of Homeland Security.
(E) The Department of Justice.

(F) The Department of the Treasury.

(G) The Office of the Director of National Intelligence.

(4) Cybersecurity purpose

The term "cybersecurity purpose" means the purpose of protecting an information system or information that is stored on, processed by, or transiting an information system from a cybersecurity threat or security vulnerability.

(5) Cybersecurity threat

(A) In general

Except as provided in subparagraph (B), the term "cybersecurity threat" means an action, not protected by the First Amendment to the Constitution of the United States, on or through an information system that may result in an unauthorized effort to adversely impact the security, availability, confidentiality, or integrity of an information system or information that is stored on, processed by, or transiting an information system.

(B) Exclusion

The term "cybersecurity threat" does not include any action that solely involves a violation of a consumer term of service or a consumer licensing agreement.

(6) Cyber threat indicator

The term "cyber threat indicator" means information that is necessary to describe or identify-

(A) malicious reconnaissance, including anomalous patterns of communications that appear to be transmitted for the purpose of gathering technical information related to a cybersecurity threat or security vulnerability;

(B) a method of defeating a security control or exploitation of a security vulnerability;

(C) a security vulnerability, including anomalous activity that appears to indicate the existence of a security vulnerability;

(D) a method of causing a user with legitimate access to an information system or information that is stored on, processed by, or transiting an information system to unwittingly enable the defeat of a security control or exploitation of a security vulnerability;

(E) malicious cyber command and control;

(F) the actual or potential harm caused by an incident, including a description of the information exfiltrated as a result of a particular cybersecurity threat;

(G) any other attribute of a cybersecurity threat, if disclosure of such attribute is not otherwise prohibited by law; or

(H) any combination thereof.

(7) Defensive measure

(A) In general

Except as provided in subparagraph (B), the term "defensive measure" means an action, device, procedure, signature, technique, or other measure applied to an information system or information that is stored on, processed by, or transiting an information system that detects, prevents, or mitigates a known or suspected cybersecurity threat or security vulnerability.

(B) Exclusion

The term "defensive measure" does not include a measure that destroys, renders unusable, provides unauthorized access to, or substantially harms an information system or information stored on, processed by, or transiting such information system not owned by-

(i) the private entity operating the measure; or

(ii) another entity or Federal entity that is authorized to provide consent and has provided consent to that private entity for operation of such measure.

(8) Federal entity

The term "Federal entity" means a department or agency of the United States or any component of such department or agency.

(9) Information system

The term "information system"-

(A) has the meaning given the term in section 3502 of title 44; and

(B) includes industrial control systems, such as supervisory control and data acquisition systems, distributed control systems, and programmable logic controllers.

(10) Local government

The term "local government" means any borough, city, county, parish, town, township, village, or other political subdivision of a State.

(11) Malicious cyber command and control

The term "malicious cyber command and control" means a method for unauthorized remote identification of, access to, or use of, an information system or information that is stored on, processed by, or transiting an information system.

(12) Malicious reconnaissance

The term "malicious reconnaissance" means a method for actively probing or passively monitoring an information system for the purpose of discerning security vulnerabilities of the information system, if such method is associated with a known or suspected cybersecurity threat.

(13) Monitor

The term "monitor" means to acquire, identify, or scan, or to possess, information that is stored on, processed by, or transiting an information system.

(14) Non-Federal entity

(A) In general

Except as otherwise provided in this paragraph, the term "non-Federal entity" means any private entity, non-Federal government agency or department, or State, tribal, or local government (including a political subdivision, department, or component thereof).

(B) Inclusions

The term "non-Federal entity" includes a government agency or department of the District of Columbia, the Commonwealth of Puerto Rico, the United States Virgin Islands, Guam, American Samoa, the Northern Mariana Islands, and any other territory or possession of the United States.

(C) Exclusion

The term "non-Federal entity" does not include a foreign power as defined in section 1801 of title 50.

(15) Private entity

(A) In general

Except as otherwise provided in this paragraph, the term "private entity" means any person or private group, organization, proprietorship, partnership, trust, cooperative, corporation, or other commercial or nonprofit entity, including an officer, employee, or agent thereof.

(B) Inclusion

The term "private entity" includes a State, tribal, or local government performing utility services, such as electric, natural gas, or water services.

(C) Exclusion

The term "private entity" does not include a foreign power as defined in section 1801 of title 50.

(16) Security control

The term "security control" means the management, operational, and technical controls used to protect against an unauthorized effort to adversely affect the confidentiality, integrity, and availability of an information system or its information.

(17) Security vulnerability

The term "security vulnerability" means any attribute of hardware, software, process, or procedure that could enable or facilitate the defeat of a security control.

(18) Tribal

The term "tribal" has the meaning given the term "Indian tribe" in section 5304 of title 25.

§1502. Sharing of information by the Federal Government

(a) In general

Consistent with the protection of classified information, intelligence sources and methods, and privacy and civil liberties, the Director of National Intelligence, the

Recent Developments
US Cybersecurity Information Sharing Act

Secretary of Homeland Security, the Secretary of Defense, and the Attorney General, in consultation with the heads of the appropriate Federal entities, shall jointly develop and issue procedures to facilitate and promote-

(1) the timely sharing of classified cyber threat indicators and defensive measures in the possession of the Federal Government with representatives of relevant Federal entities and non-Federal entities that have appropriate security clearances;

(2) the timely sharing with relevant Federal entities and non-Federal entities of cyber threat indicators, defensive measures, and information relating to cybersecurity threats or authorized uses under this subchapter, in the possession of the Federal Government that may be declassified and shared at an unclassified level;

(3) the timely sharing with relevant Federal entities and non-Federal entities, or the public if appropriate, of unclassified, including controlled unclassified, cyber threat indicators and defensive measures in the possession of the Federal Government;

(4) the timely sharing with Federal entities and non-Federal entities, if appropriate, of information relating to cybersecurity threats or authorized uses under this subchapter, in the possession of the Federal Government about cybersecurity threats to such entities to prevent or mitigate adverse effects from such cybersecurity threats; and

(5) the periodic sharing, through publication and targeted outreach, of cybersecurity best practices that are developed based on ongoing analyses of cyber threat indicators, defensive measures, and information relating to cybersecurity threats or authorized uses under this subchapter, in the possession of the Federal Government, with attention to accessibility and implementation challenges faced by small business concerns (as defined in section 632 of title 15).

(b) Development of procedures

(1) In general

The procedures developed under subsection (a) shall-

(A) ensure the Federal Government has and maintains the capability to share cyber threat indicators and defensive measures in real time consistent with the protection of classified information;

(B) incorporate, to the greatest extent practicable, existing processes and existing roles and responsibilities of Federal entities and non-Federal entities for information sharing by the Federal Government, including sector specific information sharing and analysis centers;

(C) include procedures for notifying, in a timely manner, Federal entities and non-Federal entities that have received a cyber threat indicator or defensive measure from a Federal entity under this subchapter that is known or determined to be in error or in contravention of the requirements of this subchapter or another provision of Federal law or policy of such error or contravention;

(D) include requirements for Federal entities sharing cyber threat indicators or defensive measures to implement and utilize security controls to protect against unauthorized access to or acquisition of such cyber threat indicators or defensive measures;

(E) include procedures that require a Federal entity, prior to the sharing of a cyber threat indicator-

(i) to review such cyber threat indicator to assess whether such cyber threat indicator contains any information not directly related to a cybersecurity threat that such Federal entity knows at the time of sharing to be personal information of a specific individual or information that identifies a specific individual and remove such information; or

(ii) to implement and utilize a technical capability configured to remove any information not directly related to a cybersecurity threat that the Federal entity knows at the time of sharing to be personal information of a specific individual or information that identifies a specific individual; and

(F) include procedures for notifying, in a timely manner, any United States person whose personal information is known or determined to have been shared by a Federal entity in violation of this subchapter.

(2) Consultation

In developing the procedures required under this section, the Director of National Intelligence, the Secretary of Homeland Security, the Secretary of Defense, and the Attorney General shall consult with appropriate Federal entities, including the Small Business Administration and the National Laboratories (as defined in section 15801 of title 42), to ensure that effective protocols are implemented that will facilitate and promote the sharing of cyber threat indicators by the Federal Government in a timely manner.

(c) Submittal to Congress

Not later than 60 days after December 18, 2015, the Director of National Intelligence, in consultation with the heads of the appropriate Federal entities, shall submit to Congress the procedures required by subsection (a).

§1503. Authorizations for preventing, detecting, analyzing, and mitigating cybersecurity threats

(a) Authorization for monitoring

(1) In general

Notwithstanding any other provision of law, a private entity may, for cybersecurity purposes, monitor-

(A) an information system of such private entity;

(B) an information system of another non-Federal entity, upon the authorization and written consent of such other entity;

(C) an information system of a Federal entity, upon the authorization and written consent of an authorized representative of the Federal entity; and

(D) information that is stored on, processed by, or transiting an information system monitored by the private entity under this paragraph.

(2) Construction

Nothing in this subsection shall be construed-

(A) to authorize the monitoring of an information system, or the use of any information obtained through such monitoring, other than as provided in this subchapter; or

(B) to limit otherwise lawful activity.

(b) Authorization for operation of defensive measures

(1) In general

Notwithstanding any other provision of law, a private entity may, for cybersecurity purposes, operate a defensive measure that is applied to-

(A) an information system of such private entity in order to protect the rights or property of the private entity;

(B) an information system of another non-Federal entity upon written consent of such entity for operation of such defensive measure to protect the rights or property of such entity; and

(C) an information system of a Federal entity upon written consent of an authorized representative of such Federal entity for operation of such defensive measure to protect the rights or property of the Federal Government.

(2) Construction

Nothing in this subsection shall be construed-

(A) to authorize the use of a defensive measure other than as provided in this subsection; or

(B) to limit otherwise lawful activity.

(c) Authorization for sharing or receiving cyber threat indicators or defensive measures

(1) In general

Except as provided in paragraph (2) and notwithstanding any other provision of law, a non-Federal entity may, for a cybersecurity purpose and consistent with the protection of classified information, share with, or receive from, any other non-Federal entity or the Federal Government a cyber threat indicator or defensive measure.

(2) Lawful restriction

A non-Federal entity receiving a cyber threat indicator or defensive measure from another non-Federal entity or a Federal entity shall comply with otherwise lawful restrictions placed on the sharing or use of such cyber threat indicator or defensive measure by the sharing non-Federal entity or Federal entity.

(3) Construction

Nothing in this subsection shall be construed-

(A) to authorize the sharing or receiving of a cyber threat indicator or defensive measure other than as provided in this subsection; or

(B) to limit otherwise lawful activity.

(d) Protection and use of information

(1) Security of information

A non-Federal entity monitoring an information system, operating a defensive measure, or providing or receiving a cyber threat indicator or defensive measure under this section shall implement and utilize a security control to protect against unauthorized access to or acquisition of such cyber threat indicator or defensive measure.

(2) Removal of certain personal information

A non-Federal entity sharing a cyber threat indicator pursuant to this subchapter shall, prior to such sharing-

(A) review such cyber threat indicator to assess whether such cyber threat indicator contains any information not directly related to a cybersecurity threat that the non-Federal entity knows at the time of sharing to be personal information of a specific individual or information that identifies a specific individual and remove such information; or

(B) implement and utilize a technical capability configured to remove any information not directly related to a cybersecurity threat that the non-Federal entity knows at the time of sharing to be personal information of a specific individual or information that identifies a specific individual.

(3) Use of cyber threat indicators and defensive measures by non-Federal entities

(A) In general

Consistent with this subchapter, a cyber threat indicator or defensive measure shared or received under this section may, for cybersecurity purposes-

(i) be used by a non-Federal entity to monitor or operate a defensive measure that is applied to-

(I) an information system of the non-Federal entity; or

(II) an information system of another non-Federal entity or a Federal entity upon the written consent of that other non-Federal entity or that Federal entity; and

(ii) be otherwise used, retained, and further shared by a non-Federal entity subject to-

(I) an otherwise lawful restriction placed by the sharing non-Federal entity or Federal entity on such cyber threat indicator or defensive measure; or

(II) an otherwise applicable provision of law.

(B) Construction

Nothing in this paragraph shall be construed to authorize the use of a cyber threat indicator or defensive measure other than as provided in this section.

(4) Use of cyber threat indicators by State, tribal, or local government

(A) Law enforcement use

A State, tribal, or local government that receives a cyber threat indicator or defensive measure under this subchapter may use such cyber threat indicator or defensive measure for the purposes described in section 1504(d)(5)(A) of this title.

(B) Exemption from disclosure

A cyber threat indicator or defensive measure shared by or with a State, tribal, or local government, including a component of a State, tribal, or local government that is a private entity, under this section shall be-

(i) deemed voluntarily shared information; and

(ii) exempt from disclosure under any provision of State, tribal, or local freedom of information law, open government law, open meetings law, open records law, sunshine law, or similar law requiring disclosure of information or records.

(C) State, tribal, and local regulatory authority

(i) In general

Except as provided in clause (ii), a cyber threat indicator or defensive measure shared with a State, tribal, or local government under this subchapter shall not be used by any State, tribal, or local government to regulate, including an enforcement action, the lawful activity of any non-Federal entity or any activity taken by a non-Federal entity pursuant to mandatory standards, including an activity relating to monitoring, operating a defensive measure, or sharing of a cyber threat indicator.

(ii) Regulatory authority specifically relating to prevention or mitigation of cybersecurity threats

A cyber threat indicator or defensive measure shared as described in clause (i) may, consistent with a State, tribal, or local government regulatory authority specifically relating to the prevention or mitigation of cybersecurity threats to information systems, inform the development or implementation of a regulation relating to such information systems.

(e) Antitrust exemption

(1) In general

Except as provided in section 1507(e) of this title, it shall not be considered a violation of any provision of antitrust laws for 2 or more private entities to exchange or provide a cyber threat indicator or defensive measure, or assistance relating to the prevention, investigation, or mitigation of a cybersecurity threat, for cybersecurity purposes under this subchapter.

(2) Applicability

Paragraph (1) shall apply only to information that is exchanged or assistance provided in order to assist with-

(A) facilitating the prevention, investigation, or mitigation of a cybersecurity threat to an information system or information that is stored on, processed by, or transiting an information system; or

(B) communicating or disclosing a cyber threat indicator to help prevent, investigate, or mitigate the effect of a cybersecurity threat to an information system or information that is stored on, processed by, or transiting an information system.

(f) No right or benefit

The sharing of a cyber threat indicator or defensive measure with a non-Federal entity under this subchapter shall not create a right or benefit to similar information by such non-Federal entity or any other non-Federal entity.

§1504. Sharing of cyber threat indicators and defensive measures with the Federal Government

(a) Requirement for policies and procedures

(1) Interim policies and procedures

Not later than 60 days after December 18, 2015, the Attorney General and the Secretary of Homeland Security shall, in consultation with the heads of the appropriate Federal entities, jointly develop and submit to Congress interim policies and procedures relating to the receipt of cyber threat indicators and defensive measures by the Federal Government.

(2) Final policies and procedures

Not later than 180 days after December 18, 2015, the Attorney General and the Secretary of Homeland Security shall, in consultation with the heads of the appropriate Federal entities, jointly issue and make publicly available final policies and procedures relating to the receipt of cyber threat indicators and defensive measures by the Federal Government.

(3) Requirements concerning policies and procedures

Consistent with the guidelines required by subsection (b), the policies and procedures developed or issued under this subsection shall-

(A) ensure that cyber threat indicators shared with the Federal Government by any non-Federal entity pursuant to section 1503(c) of this title through the real-time process described in subsection (c) of this section-

(i) are shared in an automated manner with all of the appropriate Federal entities;

(ii) are only subject to a delay, modification, or other action due to controls established for such real-time process that could impede real-time receipt by all of the appropriate Federal entities when the delay, modification, or other action is due to controls-

(I) agreed upon unanimously by all of the heads of the appropriate Federal entities;

(II) carried out before any of the appropriate Federal entities retains or uses the cyber threat indicators or defensive measures; and

(III) uniformly applied such that each of the appropriate Federal entities is subject to the same delay, modification, or other action; and

(iii) may be provided to other Federal entities;

(B) ensure that cyber threat indicators shared with the Federal Government by any non-Federal entity pursuant to section 1503 of this title in a manner other than the real-time process described in subsection (c) of this section-

(i) are shared as quickly as operationally practicable with all of the appropriate Federal entities;

(ii) are not subject to any unnecessary delay, interference, or any other action that could impede receipt by all of the appropriate Federal entities; and

(iii) may be provided to other Federal entities; and

(C) ensure there are-

(i) audit capabilities; and

(ii) appropriate sanctions in place for officers, employees, or agents of a Federal entity who knowingly and willfully conduct activities under this subchapter in an unauthorized manner.

(4) Guidelines for entities sharing cyber threat indicators with Federal Government

(A) In general

Not later than 60 days after December 18, 2015, the Attorney General and the Secretary of Homeland Security shall jointly develop and make publicly available guidance to assist entities and promote sharing of cyber threat indicators with Federal entities under this subchapter.

(B) Contents

The guidelines developed and made publicly available under subparagraph (A) shall include guidance on the following:

(i) Identification of types of information that would qualify as a cyber threat indicator under this subchapter that would be unlikely to include information that-

(I) is not directly related to a cybersecurity threat; and

(II) is personal information of a specific individual or information that identifies a specific individual.

(ii) Identification of types of information protected under otherwise applicable privacy laws that are unlikely to be directly related to a cybersecurity threat.

(iii) Such other matters as the Attorney General and the Secretary of Homeland Security consider appropriate for entities sharing cyber threat indicators with Federal entities under this subchapter.

(b) Privacy and civil liberties

(1) Interim guidelines

Not later than 60 days after December 18, 2015, the Attorney General and the Secretary of Homeland Security shall, in consultation with heads of the appropriate Federal entities and in consultation with officers designated under section 2000ee–1 of title 42, jointly develop, submit to Congress, and make available to the public interim guidelines relating to privacy and civil liberties which shall govern the receipt, retention, use, and dissemination of cyber threat indicators by a Federal entity obtained in connection with activities authorized in this subchapter.

(2) Final guidelines

(A) In general

Not later than 180 days after December 18, 2015, the Attorney General and the Secretary of Homeland Security shall, in coordination with heads of the appropriate Federal entities and in consultation with officers designated under section 2000ee–1 of title 42 and such private entities with industry expertise as the Attorney General and the Secretary consider relevant, jointly issue and make publicly available final guidelines relating to privacy and civil liberties which shall govern the receipt, retention, use, and dissemination of cyber threat indicators by a Federal entity obtained in connection with activities authorized in this subchapter.

(B) Periodic review

The Attorney General and the Secretary of Homeland Security shall, in coordination with heads of the appropriate Federal entities and in consultation with officers and private entities described in subparagraph (A), periodically, but not less frequently than once every 2 years, jointly review the guidelines issued under subparagraph (A).

(3) Content

The guidelines required by paragraphs (1) and (2) shall, consistent with the need to protect information systems from cybersecurity threats and mitigate cybersecurity threats-

(A) limit the effect on privacy and civil liberties of activities by the Federal Government under this subchapter;

(B) limit the receipt, retention, use, and dissemination of cyber threat indicators containing personal information of specific individuals or information that identifies specific individuals, including by establishing-

(i) a process for the timely destruction of such information that is known not to be directly related to uses authorized under this subchapter; and

(ii) specific limitations on the length of any period in which a cyber threat indicator may be retained;

(C) include requirements to safeguard cyber threat indicators containing personal information of specific individuals or information that identifies specific individuals from unauthorized access or acquisition, including appropriate sanctions for activities by officers, employees, or agents of the Federal Government in contravention of such guidelines;

(D) consistent with this subchapter, any other applicable provisions of law, and the fair information practice principles set forth in appendix A of the document entitled "National Strategy for Trusted Identities in Cyberspace" and published by the President in April 2011, govern the retention, use, and dissemination by the Federal Government of cyber threat indicators shared with the Federal Government under this subchapter, including the extent, if any, to which such cyber threat indicators may be used by the Federal Government;

(E) include procedures for notifying entities and Federal entities if information received pursuant to this section is known or determined by a Federal entity receiving such information not to constitute a cyber threat indicator;

(F) protect the confidentiality of cyber threat indicators containing personal information of specific individuals or information that identifies specific individuals to the greatest extent practicable and require recipients to be informed that such indicators may only be used for purposes authorized under this subchapter; and

(G) include steps that may be needed so that dissemination of cyber threat indicators is consistent with the protection of classified and other sensitive national security information.

(c) Capability and process within the Department of Homeland Security

(1) In general

Not later than 90 days after December 18, 2015, the Secretary of Homeland Security, in coordination with the heads of the appropriate Federal entities, shall develop and implement a capability and process within the Department of Homeland Security that-

(A) shall accept from any non-Federal entity in real time cyber threat indicators and defensive measures, pursuant to this section;

(B) shall, upon submittal of the certification under paragraph (2) that such capability and process fully and effectively operates as described in such paragraph, be the process by which the Federal Government receives cyber threat indicators and defensive measures under this subchapter that are shared by a non-Federal entity with the Federal Government through electronic mail or media, an interactive form on an Internet website, or a real time, automated process between information systems except-

(i) consistent with section 1503 of this title, communications between a Federal entity and a non-Federal entity regarding a previously shared cyber threat indicator to describe the relevant cybersecurity threat or develop a defensive measure based on such cyber threat indicator; and

(ii) communications by a regulated non-Federal entity with such entity's Federal regulatory authority regarding a cybersecurity threat;

(C) ensures that all of the appropriate Federal entities receive in an automated manner such cyber threat indicators and defensive measures shared through the real-time process within the Department of Homeland Security;

(D) is in compliance with the policies, procedures, and guidelines required by this section; and

(E) does not limit or prohibit otherwise lawful disclosures of communications, records, or other information, including-

(i) reporting of known or suspected criminal activity, by a non-Federal entity to any other non-Federal entity or a Federal entity, including cyber threat indicators or defensive measures shared with a Federal entity in furtherance of opening a Federal law enforcement investigation;

(ii) voluntary or legally compelled participation in a Federal investigation; and

(iii) providing cyber threat indicators or defensive measures as part of a statutory or authorized contractual requirement.

(2) Certification and designation

(A) Certification of capability and process

Not later than 90 days after December 18, 2015, the Secretary of Homeland Security shall, in consultation with the heads of the appropriate Federal entities, submit to Congress a certification as to whether the capability and process required by paragraph (1) fully and effectively operates-

(i) as the process by which the Federal Government receives from any non-Federal entity a cyber threat indicator or defensive measure under this subchapter; and

(ii) in accordance with the interim policies, procedures, and guidelines developed under this subchapter.

(B) Designation

Recent Developments
US Cybersecurity Information Sharing Act

(i) In general

At any time after certification is submitted under subparagraph (A), the President may designate an appropriate Federal entity, other than the Department of Defense (including the National Security Agency), to develop and implement a capability and process as described in paragraph (1) in addition to the capability and process developed under such paragraph by the Secretary of Homeland Security, if, not fewer than 30 days before making such designation, the President submits to Congress a certification and explanation that-

(I) such designation is necessary to ensure that full, effective, and secure operation of a capability and process for the Federal Government to receive from any non-Federal entity cyber threat indicators or defensive measures under this subchapter;

(II) the designated appropriate Federal entity will receive and share cyber threat indicators and defensive measures in accordance with the policies, procedures, and guidelines developed under this subchapter, including subsection (a)(3)(A); and

(III) such designation is consistent with the mission of such appropriate Federal entity and improves the ability of the Federal Government to receive, share, and use cyber threat indicators and defensive measures as authorized under this subchapter.

(ii) Application to additional capability and process

If the President designates an appropriate Federal entity to develop and implement a capability and process under clause (i), the provisions of this subchapter that apply to the capability and process required by paragraph (1) shall also be construed to apply to the capability and process developed and implemented under clause (i).

(3) Public notice and access

The Secretary of Homeland Security shall ensure there is public notice of, and access to, the capability and process developed and implemented under paragraph (1) so that-

(A) any non-Federal entity may share cyber threat indicators and defensive measures through such process with the Federal Government; and

(B) all of the appropriate Federal entities receive such cyber threat indicators and defensive measures in real time with receipt through the process within the Department of Homeland Security consistent with the policies and procedures issued under subsection (a).

(4) Other Federal entities

The process developed and implemented under paragraph (1) shall ensure that other Federal entities receive in a timely manner any cyber threat indicators and defensive measures shared with the Federal Government through such process.

(d) Information shared with or provided to the Federal Government

(1) No waiver of privilege or protection

The provision of cyber threat indicators and defensive measures to the Federal Government under this subchapter shall not constitute a waiver of any applicable privilege or protection provided by law, including trade secret protection.

(2) Proprietary information

Consistent with section 1503(c)(2) of this title and any other applicable provision of law, a cyber threat indicator or defensive measure provided by a non-Federal entity to the Federal Government under this subchapter shall be considered the commercial, financial, and proprietary information of such non-Federal entity when so designated by the originating non-Federal entity or a third party acting in accordance with the written authorization of the originating non-Federal entity.

(3) Exemption from disclosure

A cyber threat indicator or defensive measure shared with the Federal Government under this subchapter shall be-

(A) deemed voluntarily shared information and exempt from disclosure under section 552 of title 5 and any State, tribal, or local provision of law requiring disclosure of information or records; and

(B) withheld, without discretion, from the public under section 552(b)(3)(B) of title 5 and any State, tribal, or local provision of law requiring disclosure of information or records.

(4) Ex parte communications

The provision of a cyber threat indicator or defensive measure to the Federal Government under this subchapter shall not be subject to a rule of any Federal agency or department or any judicial doctrine regarding ex parte communications with a decision-making official.

(5) Disclosure, retention, and use

(A) Authorized activities

Cyber threat indicators and defensive measures provided to the Federal Government under this subchapter may be disclosed to, retained by, and used by, consistent with otherwise applicable provisions of Federal law, any Federal agency or department, component, officer, employee, or agent of the Federal Government solely for-

(i) a cybersecurity purpose;

(ii) the purpose of identifying-

(I) a cybersecurity threat, including the source of such cybersecurity threat; or

(II) a security vulnerability;

(iii) the purpose of responding to, or otherwise preventing or mitigating, a specific threat of death, a specific threat of serious bodily harm, or a specific threat of serious economic harm, including a terrorist act or a use of a weapon of mass destruction;

(iv) the purpose of responding to, investigating, prosecuting, or otherwise preventing or mitigating, a serious threat to a minor, including sexual exploitation and threats to physical safety; or

(v) the purpose of preventing, investigating, disrupting, or prosecuting an offense arising out of a threat described in clause (iii) or any of the offenses listed in-

(I) sections 1028 through 1030 of title 18 (relating to fraud and identity theft);

(II) chapter 37 of such title (relating to espionage and censorship); and

(III) chapter 90 of such title (relating to protection of trade secrets).

(B) Prohibited activities

Cyber threat indicators and defensive measures provided to the Federal Government under this subchapter shall not be disclosed to, retained by, or used by any Federal agency or department for any use not permitted under subparagraph (A).

(C) Privacy and civil liberties

Cyber threat indicators and defensive measures provided to the Federal Government under this subchapter shall be retained, used, and disseminated by the Federal Government-

(i) in accordance with the policies, procedures, and guidelines required by subsections (a) and (b);

(ii) in a manner that protects from unauthorized use or disclosure any cyber threat indicators that may contain-

(I) personal information of a specific individual; or

(II) information that identifies a specific individual; and

(iii) in a manner that protects the confidentiality of cyber threat indicators containing-

(I) personal information of a specific individual; or

(II) information that identifies a specific individual.

(D) Federal regulatory authority

(i) In general

Except as provided in clause (ii), cyber threat indicators and defensive measures provided to the Federal Government under this subchapter shall not be used by any Federal, State, tribal, or local government to regulate, including an enforcement action, the lawful activities of any non-Federal entity or any activities taken by a non-Federal entity pursuant to mandatory standards, including activities relating to monitoring, operating defensive measures, or sharing cyber threat indicators.

(ii) Exceptions

(I) Regulatory authority specifically relating to prevention or mitigation of cybersecurity threats

Cyber threat indicators and defensive measures provided to the Federal Government under this subchapter may, consistent with Federal or State regulatory authority specifically relating to the prevention or mitigation of cybersecurity threats to information systems, inform the development or implementation of regulations relating to such information systems.

(II) Procedures developed and implemented under this subchapter

Clause (i) shall not apply to procedures developed and implemented under this subchapter.

§1505. Protection from liability

(a) Monitoring of information systems

No cause of action shall lie or be maintained in any court against any private entity, and such action shall be promptly dismissed, for the monitoring of an information system and information under section 1503(a) of this title that is conducted in accordance with this subchapter.

(b) Sharing or receipt of cyber threat indicators

No cause of action shall lie or be maintained in any court against any private entity, and such action shall be promptly dismissed, for the sharing or receipt of a cyber threat indicator or defensive measure under section 1503(c) of this title if-

(1) such sharing or receipt is conducted in accordance with this subchapter; and

(2) in a case in which a cyber threat indicator or defensive measure is shared with the Federal Government, the cyber threat indicator or defensive measure is shared in a manner that is consistent with section 1504(c)(1)(B) of this title and the sharing or receipt, as the case may be, occurs after the earlier of-

(A) the date on which the interim policies and procedures are submitted to Congress under section 1504(a)(1) of this title and guidelines are submitted to Congress under section 1504(b)(1) of this title; or

(B) the date that is 60 days after December 18, 2015.

(c) Construction

Nothing in this subchapter shall be construed-

(1) to create-

(A) a duty to share a cyber threat indicator or defensive measure; or

(B) a duty to warn or act based on the receipt of a cyber threat indicator or defensive measure; or

(2) to undermine or limit the availability of otherwise applicable common law or statutory defenses.

§1506. Oversight of government activities

(a) Report on implementation

(1) In general

Not later than 1 year after December 18, 2015, the heads of the appropriate Federal entities shall jointly submit to Congress a detailed report concerning the implementation of this subchapter.

(2) Contents

The report required by paragraph (1) may include such recommendations as the heads of the appropriate Federal entities may have for improvements or modifications to the authorities, policies, procedures, and guidelines under this subchapter and shall include the following:

(A) An evaluation of the effectiveness of real-time information sharing through the capability and process developed under section 1504(c) of this title, including any impediments to such real-time sharing.

(B) An assessment of whether cyber threat indicators or defensive measures have been properly classified and an accounting of the number of security clearances authorized by the Federal Government for the purpose of sharing cyber threat indicators or defensive measures with the private sector.

(C) The number of cyber threat indicators or defensive measures received through the capability and process developed under section 1504(c) of this title.

(D) A list of Federal entities that have received cyber threat indicators or defensive measures under this subchapter.

(b) Biennial report on compliance

(1) In general

Not later than 2 years after December 18, 2015 and not less frequently than once every 2 years thereafter, the inspectors general of the appropriate Federal entities, in consultation with the Inspector General of the Intelligence Community and the Council of Inspectors General on Financial Oversight, shall jointly submit to Congress an interagency report on the actions of the executive branch of the Federal Government to carry out this subchapter during the most recent 2-year period.

(2) Contents

Each report submitted under paragraph (1) shall include, for the period covered by the report, the following:

(A) An assessment of the sufficiency of the policies, procedures, and guidelines relating to the sharing of cyber threat indicators within the Federal Government, including those policies, procedures, and guidelines relating to the removal of information not directly related to a cybersecurity threat that is personal information of a specific individual or information that identifies a specific individual.

(B) An assessment of whether cyber threat indicators or defensive measures have been properly classified and an accounting of the number of security clearances authorized by the Federal Government for the purpose of sharing cyber threat indicators or defensive measures with the private sector.

(C) A review of the actions taken by the Federal Government based on cyber threat indicators or defensive measures shared with the Federal Government under this subchapter, including a review of the following:

(i) The appropriateness of subsequent uses and disseminations of cyber threat indicators or defensive measures.

(ii) Whether cyber threat indicators or defensive measures were shared in a timely and adequate manner with appropriate entities, or, if appropriate, were made publicly available.

(D) An assessment of the cyber threat indicators or defensive measures shared with the appropriate Federal entities under this subchapter, including the following:

(i) The number of cyber threat indicators or defensive measures shared through the capability and process developed under section 1504(c) of this title.

(ii) An assessment of any information not directly related to a cybersecurity threat that is personal information of a specific individual or information identifying a specific individual and was shared by a non-Federal government entity with the Federal government in contravention of this subchapter, or was shared within the Federal Government in contravention of the guidelines required by this subchapter, including a description of any significant violation of this subchapter.

(iii) The number of times, according to the Attorney General, that information shared under this subchapter was used by a Federal entity to prosecute an offense listed in section 1504(d)(5)(A) of this title.

(iv) A quantitative and qualitative assessment of the effect of the sharing of cyber threat indicators or defensive measures with the Federal Government on privacy and civil liberties of specific individuals, including the number of notices that were issued with respect to a failure to remove information not directly related to a cybersecurity threat that was personal information of a specific individual or information that identified a specific individual in accordance with the procedures required by section 1504(b)(3)(E) of this title.

(v) The adequacy of any steps taken by the Federal Government to reduce any adverse effect from activities carried out under this subchapter on the privacy and civil liberties of United States persons.

(E) An assessment of the sharing of cyber threat indicators or defensive measures among Federal entities to identify inappropriate barriers to sharing information.

(3) Recommendations

Each report submitted under this subsection may include such recommendations as the inspectors general may have for improvements or modifications to the authorities and processes under this subchapter.

(c) Independent report on removal of personal information

Not later than 3 years after December 18, 2015, the Comptroller General of the United States shall submit to Congress a report on the actions taken by the Federal Government to remove personal information from cyber threat indicators or defensive measures pursuant to this subchapter. Such report shall include an assessment of the sufficiency of the policies, procedures, and guidelines established under this subchapter in addressing concerns relating to privacy and civil liberties.

(d) Form of reports

Each report required under this section shall be submitted in an unclassified form, but may include a classified annex.

(e) Public availability of reports

The unclassified portions of the reports required under this section shall be made available to the public.

§1507. Construction and preemption

(a) Otherwise lawful disclosures

Nothing in this subchapter shall be construed-

(1) to limit or prohibit otherwise lawful disclosures of communications, records, or other information, including reporting of known or suspected criminal activity, by a non-Federal entity to any other non-Federal entity or the Federal Government under this subchapter; or

(2) to limit or prohibit otherwise lawful use of such disclosures by any Federal entity, even when such otherwise lawful disclosures duplicate or replicate disclosures made under this subchapter.

(b) Whistle blower protections

Nothing in this subchapter shall be construed to prohibit or limit the disclosure of information protected under section 2302(b)(8) of title 5 (governing disclosures of illegality, waste, fraud, abuse, or public health or safety threats), section 7211 of title 5 (governing disclosures to Congress), section 1034 of title 10 (governing disclosure to Congress by members of the military), section 3234 of title 50 (governing disclosure by employees of elements of the intelligence community), or any similar provision of Federal or State law.

(c) Protection of sources and methods

Nothing in this subchapter shall be construed-

(1) as creating any immunity against, or otherwise affecting, any action brought by the Federal Government, or any agency or department thereof, to enforce any law, executive order, or procedure governing the appropriate handling, disclosure, or use of classified information;

(2) to affect the conduct of authorized law enforcement or intelligence activities; or

(3) to modify the authority of a department or agency of the Federal Government to protect classified information and sources and methods and the national security of the United States.

(d) Relationship to other laws

Nothing in this subchapter shall be construed to affect any requirement under any other provision of law for a non-Federal entity to provide information to the Federal Government.

(e) Prohibited conduct

Nothing in this subchapter shall be construed to permit price-fixing, allocating a market between competitors, monopolizing or attempting to monopolize a market, boycotting, or exchanges of price or cost information, customer lists, or information regarding future competitive planning.

(f) Information sharing relationships

Nothing in this subchapter shall be construed-

(1) to limit or modify an existing information sharing relationship;

(2) to prohibit a new information sharing relationship;

(3) to require a new information sharing relationship between any non-Federal entity and a Federal entity or another non-Federal entity; or

(4) to require the use of the capability and process within the Department of Homeland Security developed under section 1504(c) of this title.

(g) Preservation of contractual obligations and rights

Nothing in this subchapter shall be construed-

(1) to amend, repeal, or supersede any current or future contractual agreement, terms of service agreement, or other contractual relationship between any non-Federal entities, or between any non-Federal entity and a Federal entity; or

(2) to abrogate trade secret or intellectual property rights of any non-Federal entity or Federal entity.

(h) Anti-tasking restriction

Recent Developments
US Cybersecurity Information Sharing Act

Nothing in this subchapter shall be construed to permit a Federal entity-

(1) to require a non-Federal entity to provide information to a Federal entity or another non-Federal entity;

(2) to condition the sharing of cyber threat indicators with a non-Federal entity on such entity's provision of cyber threat indicators to a Federal entity or another non-Federal entity; or

(3) to condition the award of any Federal grant, contract, or purchase on the provision of a cyber threat indicator to a Federal entity or another non-Federal entity.

(i) No liability for non-participation

Nothing in this subchapter shall be construed to subject any entity to liability for choosing not to engage in the voluntary activities authorized in this subchapter.

(j) Use and retention of information

Nothing in this subchapter shall be construed to authorize, or to modify any existing authority of, a department or agency of the Federal Government to retain or use any information shared under this subchapter for any use other than permitted in this subchapter.

(k) Federal preemption

(1) In general

This subchapter supersedes any statute or other provision of law of a State or political subdivision of a State that restricts or otherwise expressly regulates an activity authorized under this subchapter.

(2) State law enforcement

Nothing in this subchapter shall be construed to supersede any statute or other provision of law of a State or political subdivision of a State concerning the use of authorized law enforcement practices and procedures.

(l) Regulatory authority

Nothing in this subchapter shall be construed-

(1) to authorize the promulgation of any regulations not specifically authorized to be issued under this subchapter;

(2) to establish or limit any regulatory authority not specifically established or limited under this subchapter; or

(3) to authorize regulatory actions that would duplicate or conflict with regulatory requirements, mandatory standards, or related processes under another provision of Federal law.

(m) Authority of Secretary of Defense to respond to malicious cyber activity carried out by foreign powers

Nothing in this subchapter shall be construed to limit the authority of the Secretary of Defense under section 130g of title 10.

(n) Criminal prosecution

Nothing in this subchapter shall be construed to prevent the disclosure of a cyber threat indicator or defensive measure shared under this subchapter in a case of criminal prosecution, when an applicable provision of Federal, State, tribal, or local law requires disclosure in such case.

§1508. Report on cybersecurity threats

(a) Report required

Not later than 180 days after December 18, 2015, the Director of National Intelligence, in coordination with the heads of other appropriate elements of the intelligence community, shall submit to the Select Committee on Intelligence of the Senate and the Permanent Select Committee on Intelligence of the House of Representatives a report on cybersecurity threats, including cyber attacks, theft, and data breaches.

(b) Contents

The report required by subsection (a) shall include the following:

(1) An assessment of the current intelligence sharing and cooperation relationships of the United States with other countries regarding cybersecurity threats, including cyber attacks, theft, and data breaches, directed against the United States and which threaten the United States national security interests and economy and intellectual property, specifically identifying the relative utility of such relationships, which elements of the intelligence community participate in such relationships, and whether and how such relationships could be improved.

(2) A list and an assessment of the countries and nonstate actors that are the primary threats of carrying out a cybersecurity threat, including a cyber attack, theft, or data breach, against the United States and which threaten the United States national security, economy, and intellectual property.

(3) A description of the extent to which the capabilities of the United States Government to respond to or prevent cybersecurity threats, including cyber attacks, theft, or data breaches, directed against the United States private sector are degraded by a delay in the prompt notification by private entities of such threats or cyber attacks, theft, and data breaches.

(4) An assessment of additional technologies or capabilities that would enhance the ability of the United States to prevent and to respond to cybersecurity threats, including cyber attacks, theft, and data breaches.

(5) An assessment of any technologies or practices utilized by the private sector that could be rapidly fielded to assist the intelligence community in preventing and responding to cybersecurity threats.

(c) Form of report

The report required by subsection (a) shall be made available in classified and unclassified forms.

(d) Intelligence community defined

In this section, the term "intelligence community" has the meaning given that term in section 3003 of title 50.

§1509. Exception to limitation on authority of Secretary of Defense to disseminate certain information

Notwithstanding subsection (c)(3) of section 393 of title 10, the Secretary of Defense may authorize the sharing of cyber threat indicators and defensive measures pursuant to the policies, procedures, and guidelines developed or issued under this subchapter.

§1510. Effective period

(a) In general

Except as provided in subsection (b), this subchapter and the amendments made by this subchapter shall be effective during the period beginning on December 18, 2015 and ending on September 30, 2025.

(b) Exception

With respect to any action authorized by this subchapter or information obtained pursuant to an action authorized by this subchapter, which occurred before the date on which the provisions referred to in subsection (a) cease to have effect, the provisions of this subchapter shall continue in effect.

US DRIVER PRIVACY ACT OF 2015

Summary

The Driver Privacy Act of 2015 establishes privacy safeguards for information recorded and stored by an automobile's event data recorder, or "black box." The Act limits the circumstances in which such data may be disclosed, as well as directs the National Highway Traffic Safety Administration to promulgate regulations implementing the Act. The Act also directs NHTSA to prepare a study on the collection of driver information.

References

Public Law 114–94, codified at 49 U.S.C. § 30101 note.
[https://www.congress.gov/114/plaws/publ94/PLAW-114publ94.pdf#page=402]

EPIC, The Drivers Privacy Protection Act (DPPA) and the Privacy of Your State Motor Vehicle Record
[https://epic.org/privacy/drivers/]

SEC. 24301. SHORT TITLE.

This part may be cited as the "Driver Privacy Act of 2015".

SEC. 24302. LIMITATIONS ON DATA RETRIEVAL FROM VEHICLE EVENT DATA RECORDERS

(a) OWNERSHIP OF DATA.—Any data retained by an event data recorder (as defined in section 563.5 of title 49, Code of Federal Regulations), regardless of when the motor vehicle in which it is installed was manufactured, is the property of the owner, or, in the case of a leased vehicle, the lessee of the motor vehicle in which the event data recorder is installed.

(b) PRIVACY.—Data recorded or transmitted by an event data recorder described in subsection (a) may not be accessed by a person other than an owner or a lessee of the motor vehicle in which the event data recorder is installed unless—

(1) a court or other judicial or administrative authority having jurisdiction—

(A) authorizes the retrieval of the data; and

(B) to the extent that there is retrieved data, the data is subject to the standards for admission into evidence required by that court or other administrative authority;

(2) an owner or a lessee of the motor vehicle provides written, electronic, or recorded audio consent to the retrieval of the data for any purpose, including the purpose of diagnosing, servicing, or repairing the motor vehicle, or by agreeing to a subscription that describes how data will be retrieved and used;

(3) the data is retrieved pursuant to an investigation or inspection authorized under section 1131(a) or 30166 of title 49, United States Code, and the personally identifiable information of an owner or a lessee of the vehicle and the vehicle identification number is not disclosed in connection with the retrieved data, except that the vehicle identification number may be disclosed to the certifying manufacturer;

(4) the data is retrieved for the purpose of determining the need for, or facilitating, emergency medical response in response to a motor vehicle crash; or

(5) the data is retrieved for traffic safety research, and the personally identifiable information of an owner or a lessee of the vehicle and the vehicle identification number is not disclosed in connection with the retrieved data.

SEC. 24303. VEHICLE EVENT DATA RECORDER STUDY.

(a) IN GENERAL.—Not later than 1 year after the date of enactment of this Act, the Administrator of the National Highway Traffic Safety Administration shall submit to Congress a report that contains the results of a study conducted by the Administrator to determine the amount of time event data recorders installed in passenger motor vehicles should capture and record for retrieval vehicle-related data in conjunction with an event in order to provide sufficient information to investigate the cause of motor vehicle crashes.

(b) RULEMAKING.—Not later than 2 years after submitting the report required under subsection (a), the Administrator of the National Highway Traffic Safety Administration shall promulgate regulations to establish the appropriate period during which event data recorders installed in passenger motor vehicles may capture and record for retrieval vehicle-related data to the time necessary to provide accident investigators with vehicle-related information pertinent to crashes involving such motor vehicles.

EU-US "PRIVACY SHIELD"

Summary

The "Privacy Shield" is a quasi-legal framework for EU-US data flows that emerged after the Court of Justice of the European Union ruled in 2015 that the Safe Harbor arrangement failed to provide adequate protection for transborder data flows. The basis of the "shield" is a series of representation made by the US government in late 2015 and early 2016 regarding the protection afforded to data that is transferred to the United States, Prior to finalization, substantial opinions were prepared by privacy agencies, including the European Data Protection Supervisor and the Article 29 Working Party.

References

EU-U.S. Privacy Shield Framework
[https://www.privacyshield.gov/EU-US-Framework]

EPIC – Privacy Shield EU-U.S. Data Transfer Agreement
[https://epic.org/privacy/intl/privacy-shield/]

European Commission, Privacy Shield Draft Adequacy Decision
[http://ec.europa.eu/justice/data-protection/files/privacy-shield-adequacy-decision_en.pdf]

European Data Protection Supervisor, Opinion on the EU-U.S. Privacy Shield (May 30, 2016)
[https://secure.edps.europa.eu/EDPSWEB/webdav/site/mySite/shared/Documents/Consultation/Opinions/2016/16-05-30_Privacy_Shield_EN.pdf]

European Commission, Press Release - Restoring trust in transatlantic data flows through strong safeguards: European Commission presents EU-U.S. Privacy Shield (Feb. 29, 2016)
[http://europa.eu/rapid/press-release_IP-16-433_en.htm]

U.S. Department of Commerce, EU-U.S. Privacy Shield (Feb. 2, 2016)
[https://www.commerce.gov/news/fact-sheets/2016/02/eu-us-privacy-shield]

I. OVERVIEW

1.   While the United States and the European Union share the goal of enhancing privacy protection, the United States takes a different approach to privacy from that taken by the European Union.   The United States uses a sectoral approach that relies on a mix of

legislation, regulation, and self-regulation. Given those differences and to provide organizations in the United States with a reliable mechanism for personal data transfers to the United States from the European Union while ensuring that EU data subjects continue to benefit from effective safeguards and protection as required by European legislation with respect to the processing of their personal data when they have been transferred to non-EU countries, the Department of Commerce is issuing these Privacy Shield Principles, including the Supplemental Principles (collectively "the Principles") under its statutory authority to foster, promote, and develop international commerce (15 U.S.C. § 1512). The Principles were developed in consultation with the European Commission, and with industry and other stakeholders, to facilitate trade and commerce between the United States and European Union. They are intended for use solely by organizations in the United States receiving personal data from the European Union for the purpose of qualifying for the Privacy Shield and thus benefitting from the European Commission's adequacy decision. The Principles do not affect the application of national provisions implementing Directive 95/46/EC ("the Directive") that apply to the processing of personal data in the Member States. Nor do the Principles limit privacy obligations that otherwise apply under U.S. law.

2. In order to rely on the Privacy Shield to effectuate transfers of personal data from the EU, an organization must self-certify its adherence to the Principles to the Department of Commerce (or its designee) ("the Department"). While decisions by organizations to thus enter the Privacy Shield are entirely voluntary, effective compliance is compulsory: organizations that self-certify to the Department and publicly declare their commitment to adhere to the Principles must comply fully with the Principles. In order to enter the Privacy Shield, an organization must (a) be subject to the investigatory and enforcement powers of the Federal Trade Commission (the "FTC"), the Department of Transportation or another statutory body that will effectively ensure compliance with the Principles (other U.S. statutory bodies recognized by the EU may be included as an annex in the future); (b) publicly declare its commitment to comply with the Principles; (c) publicly disclose its privacy policies in line with these Principles; and (d) fully implement them. An organization's failure to comply is enforceable under Section 5 of the Federal Trade Commission Act prohibiting unfair and deceptive acts in or affecting commerce (15 U.S.C. § 45(a)) or other laws or regulations prohibiting such acts.

3. The Department of Commerce will maintain and make available to the public an authoritative list of U.S. organizations that have self-certified to the Department and declared their commitment to adhere to the Principles ("the Privacy Shield List"). Privacy Shield benefits are assured from the date that the Department places the organization on the Privacy Shield List. The Department will remove an organization from the Privacy Shield List if it voluntarily withdraws from the Privacy Shield or if it fails to complete its annual re-certification to the Department. An organization's removal from the Privacy Shield List

means it may no longer benefit from the European Commission's adequacy decision to receive personal information from the EU. The organization must continue to apply the Principles to the personal information it received while it participated in the Privacy Shield, and affirm to the Department on an annual basis its commitment to do so, for as long as it retains such information; otherwise, the organization must return or delete the information or provide "adequate" protection for the information by another authorized means. The Department will also remove from the Privacy Shield List those organizations that have persistently failed to comply with the Principles; these organizations do not qualify for Privacy Shield benefits and must return or delete the personal information they received under the Privacy Shield.

4.   The Department will also maintain and make available to the public an authoritative record of U.S. organizations that had previously self-certified to the Department, but that have been removed from the Privacy Shield List. The Department will provide a clear warning that these organizations are not participants in the Privacy Shield; that removal from the Privacy Shield List means that such organizations cannot claim to be Privacy Shield compliant and must avoid any statements or misleading practices implying that they participate in the Privacy Shield; and that such organizations are no longer entitled to benefit from the European Commission's adequacy decision that would enable those organizations to receive personal information from the EU. An organization that continues to claim participation in the Privacy Shield or makes other Privacy Shield-related misrepresentations after it has been removed from the Privacy Shield List may be subject to enforcement action by the FTC, the Department of Transportation, or other enforcement authorities.

5.   Adherence to these Principles may be limited: (a) to the extent necessary to meet national security, public interest, or law enforcement requirements; (b) by statute, government regulation, or case law that creates conflicting obligations or explicit authorizations, provided that, in exercising any such authorization, an organization can demonstrate that its non-compliance with the Principles is limited to the extent necessary to meet the overriding legitimate interests furthered by such authorization; or (c) if the effect of the Directive or Member State law is to allow exceptions or derogations, provided such exceptions or derogations are applied in comparable contexts. Consistent with the goal of enhancing privacy protection, organizations should strive to implement these Principles fully and transparently, including indicating in their privacy policies where exceptions to the Principles permitted by (b) above will apply on a regular basis. For the same reason, where the option is allowable under the Principles and/or U.S. law, organizations are expected to opt for the higher protection where possible.

6.   Organizations are obligated to apply the Principles to all personal data transferred in reliance on the Privacy Shield after they enter the Privacy Shield. An organization that

chooses to extend Privacy Shield benefits to human resources personal information transferred from the EU for use in the context of an employment relationship must indicate this when it self-certifies to the Department and conform to the requirements set forth in the Supplemental Principle on Self-Certification.

7.   U.S. law will apply to questions of interpretation and compliance with the Principles and relevant privacy policies by Privacy Shield organizations, except where such organizations have committed to cooperate with European data protection authorities ("DPAs"). Unless otherwise stated, all provisions of the Principles apply where they are relevant.

8.   Definitions:

   a.   "Personal data" and "personal information" are data about an identified or identifiable individual that are within the scope of the Directive, received by an organization in the United States from the European Union, and recorded in any form.

   b.   "Processing" of personal data means any operation or set of operations which is performed upon personal data, whether or not by automated means, such as collection, recording, organization, storage, adaptation or alteration, retrieval, consultation, use, disclosure or dissemination, and erasure or destruction.

   c.   "Controller" means a person or organization which, alone or jointly with others, determines the purposes and means of the processing of personal data.

9.   The effective date of the Principles is the date of final approval of the European Commission's adequacy determination.

II. PRINCIPLES

1. Notice

   a.   An organization must inform individuals about:

   i.   its participation in the Privacy Shield and provide a link to, or the web address for, the Privacy Shield List,

   ii.   the types of personal data collected and, where applicable, the entities or subsidiaries of the organization also adhering to the Principles,

   iii.   its commitment to subject to the Principles all personal data received from the EU in reliance on the Privacy Shield,

   iv.   the purposes for which it collects and uses personal information about them,

   v.   how to contact the organization with any inquiries or complaints, including any relevant establishment in the EU that can respond to such inquiries or complaints,

   vi.   the type or identity of third parties to which it discloses personal information, and the purposes for which it does so,

   vii.   the right of individuals to access their personal data,

viii.   the choices and means the organization offers individuals for limiting the use and disclosure of their personal data,

ix.   the independent dispute resolution body designated to address complaints and provide appropriate recourse free of charge to the individual, and whether it is: (1) the panel established by DPAs, (2) an alternative dispute resolution provider based in the EU, or (3) an alternative dispute resolution provider based in the United States,

x.   being subject to the investigatory and enforcement powers of the FTC, the Department of Transportation or any other U.S. authorized statutory body,

xi.   the possibility, under certain conditions, for the individual to invoke binding arbitration,

xii.   the requirement to disclose personal information in response to lawful requests by public authorities, including to meet national security or law enforcement requirements, and

xiii.   its liability in cases of onward transfers to third parties.

b.   This notice must be provided in clear and conspicuous language when individuals are first asked to provide personal information to the organization or as soon thereafter as is practicable, but in any event before the organization uses such information for a purpose other than that for which it was originally collected or processed by the transferring organization or discloses it for the first time to a third party.

2. Choice

a.   An organization must offer individuals the opportunity to choose (opt out) whether their personal information is (i) to be disclosed to a third party or (ii) to be used for a purpose that is materially different from the purpose(s) for which it was originally collected or subsequently authorized by the individuals. Individuals must be provided with clear, conspicuous, and readily available mechanisms to exercise choice.

b.   By derogation to the previous paragraph, it is not necessary to provide choice when disclosure is made to a third party that is acting as an agent to perform task(s) on behalf of and under the instructions of the organization. However, an organization shall always enter into a contract with the agent.

c.   For sensitive information (i.e., personal information specifying medical or health conditions, racial or ethnic origin, political opinions, religious or philosophical beliefs, trade union membership or information specifying the sex life of the individual), organizations must obtain affirmative express consent (opt in) from individuals if such information is to be (i) disclosed to a third party or (ii) used for a purpose other than those for which it was originally collected or subsequently authorized by the individuals through the exercise of opt-in choice. In addition, an organization should treat as sensitive any personal information received from a third party where the third party identifies and treats it as sensitive.

3. Accountability for Onward Transfer

a.　To transfer personal information to a third party acting as a controller, organizations must comply with the Notice and Choice Principles. Organizations must also enter into a contract with the third-party controller that provides that such data may only be processed for limited and specified purposes consistent with the consent provided by the individual and that the recipient will provide the same level of protection as the Principles and will notify the organization if it makes a determination that it can no longer meet this obligation. The contract shall provide that when such a determination is made the third party controller ceases processing or takes other reasonable and appropriate steps to remediate.

b.　To transfer personal data to a third party acting as an agent, organizations must: (i) transfer such data only for limited and specified purposes; (ii) ascertain that the agent is obligated to provide at least the same level of privacy protection as is required by the Principles; (iii) take reasonable and appropriate steps to ensure that the agent effectively processes the personal information transferred in a manner consistent with the organization's obligations under the Principles; (iv) require the agent to notify the organization if it makes a determination that it can no longer meet its obligation to provide the same level of protection as is required by the Principles; (v) upon notice, including under (iv), take reasonable and appropriate steps to stop and remediate unauthorized processing; and (vi) provide a summary or a representative copy of the relevant privacy provisions of its contract with that agent to the Department upon request.

4. Security

a.　Organizations creating, maintaining, using or disseminating personal information must take reasonable and appropriate measures to protect it from loss, misuse and unauthorized access, disclosure, alteration and destruction, taking into due account the risks involved in the processing and the nature of the personal data.

5. Data Integrity and Purpose Limitation

a.　Consistent with the Principles, personal information must be limited to the information that is relevant for the purposes of processing.[14] An organization may not

---

[14] Depending on the circumstances, examples of compatible processing purposes may include those that reasonably serve customer relations, compliance and legal considerations, auditing, security and fraud prevention, preserving or defending the organization's legal

process personal information in a way that is incompatible with the purposes for which it has been collected or subsequently authorized by the individual. To the extent necessary for those purposes, an organization must take reasonable steps to ensure that personal data is reliable for its intended use, accurate, complete, and current. An organization must adhere to the Principles for as long as it retains such information.

b.   Information may be retained in a form identifying or making identifiable[15] the individual only for as long as it serves a purpose of processing within the meaning of 5a. This obligation does not prevent organizations from processing personal information for longer periods for the time and to the extent such processing reasonably serves the purposes of archiving in the public interest, journalism, literature and art, scientific or historical research, and statistical analysis. In these cases, such processing shall be subject to the other Principles and provisions of the Framework. Organizations should take reasonable and appropriate measures in complying with this provision.

6. Access

a.   Individuals must have access to personal information about them that an organization holds and be able to correct, amend, or delete that information where it is inaccurate, or has been processed in violation of the Principles, except where the burden or expense of providing access would be disproportionate to the risks to the individual's privacy in the case in question, or where the rights of persons other than the individual would be violated.

7. Recourse, Enforcement and Liability

a.   Effective privacy protection must include robust mechanisms for assuring compliance with the Principles, recourse for individuals who are affected by non-compliance with the Principles, and consequences for the organization when the Principles are not followed. At a minimum such mechanisms must include:

   i.   readily available independent recourse mechanisms by which each individual's complaints and disputes are investigated and expeditiously resolved at no cost to

---

rights, or other purposes consistent with the expectations of a reasonable person given the context of the collection.

[15] In this context, if, given the means of identification reasonably likely to be used (considering, among other things, the costs of and the amount of time required for identification and the available technology at the time of the processing) and the form in which the data is retained, an individual could reasonably be identified by the organization, or a third party if it would have access to the data, then the individual is "identifiable."

the individual and by reference to the Principles, and damages awarded where the applicable law or private-sector initiatives so provide;

ii.   follow-up procedures for verifying that the attestations and assertions organizations make about their privacy practices are true and that privacy practices have been implemented as presented and, in particular, with regard to cases of non-compliance; and

iii.   obligations to remedy problems arising out of failure to comply with the Principles by organizations announcing their adherence to them and consequences for such organizations.   Sanctions must be sufficiently rigorous to ensure compliance by organizations.

b.   Organizations and their selected independent recourse mechanisms will respond promptly to inquiries and requests by the Department for information relating to the Privacy Shield. All organizations must respond expeditiously to complaints regarding compliance with the Principles referred by EU Member State authorities through the Department.   Organizations that have chosen to cooperate with DPAs, including organizations that process human resources data, must respond directly to such authorities with regard to the investigation and resolution of complaints.

c.   Organizations are obligated to arbitrate claims and follow the terms as set forth in Annex I, provided that an individual has invoked binding arbitration by delivering notice to the organization at issue and following the procedures and subject to conditions set forth in Annex I.

d.   In the context of an onward transfer, a Privacy Shield organization has responsibility for the processing of personal information it receives under the Privacy Shield and subsequently transfers to a third party acting as an agent on its behalf. The Privacy Shield organization shall remain liable under the Principles if its agent processes such personal information in a manner inconsistent with the Principles, unless the organization proves that it is not responsible for the event giving rise to the damage.

e.   When an organization becomes subject to an FTC or court order based on non-compliance, the organization shall make public any relevant Privacy Shield-related sections of any compliance or assessment report submitted to the FTC, to the extent consistent with confidentiality requirements.   The Department has established a dedicated point of contact for DPAs for any problems of compliance by Privacy Shield organizations. The FTC will give priority consideration to referrals of non-compliance with the Principles from the Department and EU Member State authorities, and will exchange information regarding referrals with the referring state authorities on a timely basis, subject to existing confidentiality restrictions.

EU GENERAL DATA PROTECTION
REGULATION (2016)

Summary

The General Data Protection Regulation is a comprehensive legal framework for the processing of personal information. It was adopted on April 27, 2016 and will enter into force on May 25, 2018. The regulation will replace the EU Data Protection Directive of 1995. The regulation is directly applicable to the Members States and does not require transposition by means of national law. The aim of the Regulation is to provide a harmonized legal framework for data protection while strengthening enforcement and establishing new privacy rights for data breaches, transparency, data portability, and erasure.

References

Regulation (EU) 2016/679 of the European Parliament and of the Council of 27 April 2016 on the protection of natural persons with regard to the processing of personal data and on the free movement of such data, and repealing Directive 95/46/EC (General Data Protection Regulation)
[http://eur-lex.europa.eu/eli/reg/2016/679/oj]

European Data Protection Supervisor Opinions
[https://secure.edps.europa.eu/EDPSWEB/edps/cache/bypass/Consultation/Opinions C]

Article 29 Working Party Statement on 2016 Action Plan for the Implementation of the GDPR
[http://ec.europa.eu/justice/data-protection/article-29/documentation/opinion-recommendation/files/2016/wp236_en.pdf]

European Commission – Data Protection
[http://ec.europa.eu/justice/data-protection/index_en.htm]

European Commission – Fact Sheet – Data protection reform
[http://europa.eu/rapid/press-release_MEMO-15-6385_en.htm]

CHAPTER I: General provisions

Article 1: Subject-matter and objectives

1. This Regulation lays down rules relating to the protection of natural persons with regard to the processing of personal data and rules relating to the free movement of personal data.
2. This Regulation protects fundamental rights and freedoms of natural persons and in particular their right to the protection of personal data.

3. The free movement of personal data within the Union shall be neither restricted nor prohibited for reasons connected with the protection of natural persons with regard to the processing of personal data.

Article 2: Material scope

1. This Regulation applies to the processing of personal data wholly or partly by automated means and to the processing other than by automated means of personal data which form part of a filing system or are intended to form part of a filing system.

2. This Regulation does not apply to the processing of personal data:

(a) in the course of an activity which falls outside the scope of Union law;

(b) by the Member States when carrying out activities which fall within the scope of Chapter 2 of Title V of the TEU;

(c) by a natural person in the course of a purely personal or household activity;

(d) by competent authorities for the purposes of the prevention, investigation, detection or prosecution of criminal offences or the execution of criminal penalties, including the safeguarding against and the prevention of threats to public security.

3. For the processing of personal data by the Union institutions, bodies, offices and agencies, Regulation (EC) No 45/2001 applies. Regulation (EC) No 45/2001 and other Union legal acts applicable to such processing of personal data shall be adapted to the principles and rules of this Regulation in accordance with Article 98.

4. This Regulation shall be without prejudice to the application of Directive 2000/31/EC, in particular of the liability rules of intermediary service providers in Articles 12 to 15 of that Directive.

Article 3: Territorial scope

1. This Regulation applies to the processing of personal data in the context of the activities of an establishment of a controller or a processor in the Union, regardless of whether the processing takes place in the Union or not.

2. This Regulation applies to the processing of personal data of data subjects who are in the Union by a controller or processor not established in the Union, where the processing activities are related to:

(a) the offering of goods or services, irrespective of whether a payment of the data subject is required, to such data subjects in the Union; or

(b) the monitoring of their behaviour as far as their behaviour takes place within the Union.

3. This Regulation applies to the processing of personal data by a controller not established in the Union, but in a place where Member State law applies by virtue of public international law.

Recent Developments
EU General Data Protection Regulation

Article 4: Definitions

For the purposes of this Regulation:

(1) 'personal data' means any information relating to an identified or identifiable natural person ('data subject'); an identifiable natural person is one who can be identified, directly or indirectly, in particular by reference to an identifier such as a name, an identification number, location data, an online identifier or to one or more factors specific to the physical, physiological, genetic, mental, economic, cultural or social identity of that natural person;

(2) 'processing' means any operation or set of operations which is performed on personal data or on sets of personal data, whether or not by automated means, such as collection, recording, organisation, structuring, storage, adaptation or alteration, retrieval, consultation, use, disclosure by transmission, dissemination or otherwise making available, alignment or combination, restriction, erasure or destruction;

(3) 'restriction of processing' means the marking of stored personal data with the aim of limiting their processing in the future;

(4) 'profiling' means any form of automated processing of personal data consisting of the use of personal data to evaluate certain personal aspects relating to a natural person, in particular to analyse or predict aspects concerning that natural person's performance at work, economic situation, health, personal preferences, interests, reliability, behaviour, location or movements;

(5) 'pseudonymisation' means the processing of personal data in such a manner that the personal data can no longer be attributed to a specific data subject without the use of additional information, provided that such additional information is kept separately and is subject to technical and organisational measures to ensure that the personal data are not attributed to an identified or identifiable natural person;

(6) 'filing system' means any structured set of personal data which are accessible according to specific criteria, whether centralised, decentralised or dispersed on a functional or geographical basis;

(7) 'controller' means the natural or legal person, public authority, agency or other body which, alone or jointly with others, determines the purposes and means of the processing of personal data; where the purposes and means of such processing are determined by Union or Member State law, the controller or the specific criteria for its nomination may be provided for by Union or Member State law;

(8) 'processor' means a natural or legal person, public authority, agency or other body which processes personal data on behalf of the controller;

(9) 'recipient' means a natural or legal person, public authority, agency or another body, to which the personal data are disclosed, whether a third party or not. However, public authorities which may receive personal data in the framework of a particular inquiry in accordance with Union or Member State law shall not be regarded as recipients; the processing of those data by those public authorities shall be in

compliance with the applicable data protection rules according to the purposes of the processing;

(10) 'third party' means a natural or legal person, public authority, agency or body other than the data subject, controller, processor and persons who, under the direct authority of the controller or processor, are authorised to process personal data;

(11) 'consent' of the data subject means any freely given, specific, informed and unambiguous indication of the data subject's wishes by which he or she, by a statement or by a clear affirmative action, signifies agreement to the processing of personal data relating to him or her;

(12) 'personal data breach' means a breach of security leading to the accidental or unlawful destruction, loss, alteration, unauthorised disclosure of, or access to, personal data transmitted, stored or otherwise processed;

(13) 'genetic data' means personal data relating to the inherited or acquired genetic characteristics of a natural person which give unique information about the physiology or the health of that natural person and which result, in particular, from an analysis of a biological sample from the natural person in question;

(14) 'biometric data' means personal data resulting from specific technical processing relating to the physical, physiological or behavioural characteristics of a natural person, which allow or confirm the unique identification of that natural person, such as facial images or dactyloscopic data;

(15) 'data concerning health' means personal data related to the physical or mental health of a natural person, including the provision of health care services, which reveal information about his or her health status;

(16) 'main establishment' means:

(a) as regards a controller with establishments in more than one Member State, the place of its central administration in the Union, unless the decisions on the purposes and means of the processing of personal data are taken in another establishment of the controller in the Union and the latter establishment has the power to have such decisions implemented, in which case the establishment having taken such decisions is to be considered to be the main establishment;

(b) as regards a processor with establishments in more than one Member State, the place of its central administration in the Union, or, if the processor has no central administration in the Union, the establishment of the processor in the Union where the main processing activities in the context of the activities of an establishment of the processor take place to the extent that the processor is subject to specific obligations under this Regulation;

(17) 'representative' means a natural or legal person established in the Union who, designated by the controller or processor in writing pursuant to Article 27, represents the controller or processor with regard to their respective obligations under this Regulation;

(18) 'enterprise' means a natural or legal person engaged in an economic activity, irrespective of its legal form, including partnerships or associations regularly engaged in an economic activity;

(19) 'group of undertakings' means a controlling undertaking and its controlled undertakings;

(20) 'binding corporate rules' means personal data protection policies which are adhered to by a controller or processor established on the territory of a Member State for transfers or a set of transfers of personal data to a controller or processor in one or more third countries within a group of undertakings, or group of enterprises engaged in a joint economic activity;

(21) 'supervisory authority' means an independent public authority which is established by a Member State pursuant to Article 51;

(22) 'supervisory authority concerned' means a supervisory authority which is concerned by the processing of personal data because:

(a) the controller or processor is established on the territory of the Member State of that supervisory authority;

(b) data subjects residing in the Member State of that supervisory authority are substantially affected or likely to be substantially affected by the processing; or

(c) a complaint has been lodged with that supervisory authority;

(23) 'cross-border processing' means either:

(a) processing of personal data which takes place in the context of the activities of establishments in more than one Member State of a controller or processor in the Union where the controller or processor is established in more than one Member State; or

(b) processing of personal data which takes place in the context of the activities of a single establishment of a controller or processor in the Union but which substantially affects or is likely to substantially affect data subjects in more than one Member State.

(24) 'relevant and reasoned objection' means an objection to a draft decision as to whether there is an infringement of this Regulation, or whether envisaged action in relation to the controller or processor complies with this Regulation, which clearly demonstrates the significance of the risks posed by the draft decision as regards the fundamental rights and freedoms of data subjects and, where applicable, the free flow of personal data within the Union;

(25) 'information society service' means a service as defined in point (b) of Article 1(1) of Directive (EU) 2015/1535 of the European Parliament and of the Council (19);

(26) 'international organisation' means an organisation and its subordinate bodies governed by public international law, or any other body which is set up by, or on the basis of, an agreement between two or more countries.

CHAPTER II: Principles

Article 5: Principles relating to processing of personal data

1. Personal data shall be:

(a) processed lawfully, fairly and in a transparent manner in relation to the data subject ('lawfulness, fairness and transparency');

(b) collected for specified, explicit and legitimate purposes and not further processed in a manner that is incompatible with those purposes; further processing for archiving purposes in the public interest, scientific or historical research purposes or statistical purposes shall, in accordance with Article 89(1), not be considered to be incompatible with the initial purposes ('purpose limitation');

(c) adequate, relevant and limited to what is necessary in relation to the purposes for which they are processed ('data minimisation');

(d) accurate and, where necessary, kept up to date; every reasonable step must be taken to ensure that personal data that are inaccurate, having regard to the purposes for which they are processed, are erased or rectified without delay ('accuracy');

(e) kept in a form which permits identification of data subjects for no longer than is necessary for the purposes for which the personal data are processed; personal data may be stored for longer periods insofar as the personal data will be processed solely for archiving purposes in the public interest, scientific or historical research purposes or statistical purposes in accordance with Article 89(1) subject to implementation of the appropriate technical and organisational measures required by this Regulation in order to safeguard the rights and freedoms of the data subject ('storage limitation');

(f) processed in a manner that ensures appropriate security of the personal data, including protection against unauthorised or unlawful processing and against accidental loss, destruction or damage, using appropriate technical or organisational measures ('integrity and confidentiality').

2. The controller shall be responsible for, and be able to demonstrate compliance with, paragraph 1 ('accountability').

Article 6: Lawfulness of processing

1. Processing shall be lawful only if and to the extent that at least one of the following applies:

(a) the data subject has given consent to the processing of his or her personal data for one or more specific purposes;

(b) processing is necessary for the performance of a contract to which the data subject is party or in order to take steps at the request of the data subject prior to entering into a contract;

(c) processing is necessary for compliance with a legal obligation to which the controller is subject;

(d) processing is necessary in order to protect the vital interests of the data subject or of another natural person;

(e) processing is necessary for the performance of a task carried out in the public interest or in the exercise of official authority vested in the controller;

(f) processing is necessary for the purposes of the legitimate interests pursued by the controller or by a third party, except where such interests are overridden by the interests or fundamental rights and freedoms of the data subject which require protection of personal data, in particular where the data subject is a child.

Point (f) of the first subparagraph shall not apply to processing carried out by public authorities in the performance of their tasks.

2.   Member States may maintain or introduce more specific provisions to adapt the application of the rules of this Regulation with regard to processing for compliance with points (c) and (e) of paragraph 1 by determining more precisely specific requirements for the processing and other measures to ensure lawful and fair processing including for other specific processing situations as provided for in Chapter IX.

3.   The basis for the processing referred to in point (c) and (e) of paragraph 1 shall be laid down by:

(a) Union law; or

(b) Member State law to which the controller is subject.

The purpose of the processing shall be determined in that legal basis or, as regards the processing referred to in point (e) of paragraph 1, shall be necessary for the performance of a task carried out in the public interest or in the exercise of official authority vested in the controller. That legal basis may contain specific provisions to adapt the application of rules of this Regulation, inter alia: the general conditions governing the lawfulness of processing by the controller; the types of data which are subject to the processing; the data subjects concerned; the entities to, and the purposes for which, the personal data may be disclosed; the purpose limitation; storage periods; and processing operations and processing procedures, including measures to ensure lawful and fair processing such as those for other specific processing situations as provided for in Chapter IX. The Union or the Member State law shall meet an objective of public interest and be proportionate to the legitimate aim pursued.

4.   Where the processing for a purpose other than that for which the personal data have been collected is not based on the data subject's consent or on a Union or Member State law which constitutes a necessary and proportionate measure in a democratic society to safeguard the objectives referred to in Article 23(1), the controller shall, in order to ascertain whether processing for another purpose is compatible with the purpose for which the personal data are initially collected, take into account, inter alia:

(a) any link between the purposes for which the personal data have been collected and the purposes of the intended further processing;

(b) the context in which the personal data have been collected, in particular regarding the relationship between data subjects and the controller;

(c) the nature of the personal data, in particular whether special categories of personal data are processed, pursuant to Article 9, or whether personal data related to criminal convictions and offences are processed, pursuant to Article 10;

(d) the possible consequences of the intended further processing for data subjects;

(e) the existence of appropriate safeguards, which may include encryption or pseudonymisation.

Article 7: Conditions for consent

1. Where processing is based on consent, the controller shall be able to demonstrate that the data subject has consented to processing of his or her personal data.

2. If the data subject's consent is given in the context of a written declaration which also concerns other matters, the request for consent shall be presented in a manner which is clearly distinguishable from the other matters, in an intelligible and easily accessible form, using clear and plain language. Any part of such a declaration which constitutes an infringement of this Regulation shall not be binding.

3. The data subject shall have the right to withdraw his or her consent at any time. The withdrawal of consent shall not affect the lawfulness of processing based on consent before its withdrawal. Prior to giving consent, the data subject shall be informed thereof. It shall be as easy to withdraw as to give consent.

4. When assessing whether consent is freely given, utmost account shall be taken of whether, inter alia, the performance of a contract, including the provision of a service, is conditional on consent to the processing of personal data that is not necessary for the performance of that contract.

Article 8: Conditions applicable to child's consent in relation to information society services

1. Where point (a) of Article 6(1) applies, in relation to the offer of information society services directly to a child, the processing of the personal data of a child shall be lawful where the child is at least 16 years old. Where the child is below the age of 16 years, such processing shall be lawful only if and to the extent that consent is given or authorised by the holder of parental responsibility over the child.

Member States may provide by law for a lower age for those purposes provided that such lower age is not below 13 years.

2. The controller shall make reasonable efforts to verify in such cases that consent is given or authorised by the holder of parental responsibility over the child, taking into consideration available technology.

3. Paragraph 1 shall not affect the general contract law of Member States such as the rules on the validity, formation or effect of a contract in relation to a child.

Recent Developments
EU General Data Protection Regulation

Article 9: Processing of special categories of personal data

1. Processing of personal data revealing racial or ethnic origin, political opinions, religious or philosophical beliefs, or trade union membership, and the processing of genetic data, biometric data for the purpose of uniquely identifying a natural person, data concerning health or data concerning a natural person's sex life or sexual orientation shall be prohibited.

2. Paragraph 1 shall not apply if one of the following applies:

    (a) the data subject has given explicit consent to the processing of those personal data for one or more specified purposes, except where Union or Member State law provide that the prohibition referred to in paragraph 1 may not be lifted by the data subject;

    (b) processing is necessary for the purposes of carrying out the obligations and exercising specific rights of the controller or of the data subject in the field of employment and social security and social protection law in so far as it is authorised by Union or Member State law or a collective agreement pursuant to Member State law providing for appropriate safeguards for the fundamental rights and the interests of the data subject;

    (c) processing is necessary to protect the vital interests of the data subject or of another natural person where the data subject is physically or legally incapable of giving consent;

    (d) processing is carried out in the course of its legitimate activities with appropriate safeguards by a foundation, association or any other not-for-profit body with a political, philosophical, religious or trade union aim and on condition that the processing relates solely to the members or to former members of the body or to persons who have regular contact with it in connection with its purposes and that the personal data are not disclosed outside that body without the consent of the data subjects;

    (e) processing relates to personal data which are manifestly made public by the data subject;

    (f) processing is necessary for the establishment, exercise or defence of legal claims or whenever courts are acting in their judicial capacity;

    (g) processing is necessary for reasons of substantial public interest, on the basis of Union or Member State law which shall be proportionate to the aim pursued, respect the essence of the right to data protection and provide for suitable and specific measures to safeguard the fundamental rights and the interests of the data subject;

    (h) processing is necessary for the purposes of preventive or occupational medicine, for the assessment of the working capacity of the employee, medical diagnosis, the provision of health or social care or treatment or the management of health or social care systems and services on the basis of Union or Member State law or pursuant to contract with a health professional and subject to the conditions and safeguards referred to in paragraph 3;

(i) processing is necessary for reasons of public interest in the area of public health, such as protecting against serious cross-border threats to health or ensuring high standards of quality and safety of health care and of medicinal products or medical devices, on the basis of Union or Member State law which provides for suitable and specific measures to safeguard the rights and freedoms of the data subject, in particular professional secrecy;

(j) processing is necessary for archiving purposes in the public interest, scientific or historical research purposes or statistical purposes in accordance with Article 89(1) based on Union or Member State law which shall be proportionate to the aim pursued, respect the essence of the right to data protection and provide for suitable and specific measures to safeguard the fundamental rights and the interests of the data subject.

3. Personal data referred to in paragraph 1 may be processed for the purposes referred to in point (h) of paragraph 2 when those data are processed by or under the responsibility of a professional subject to the obligation of professional secrecy under Union or Member State law or rules established by national competent bodies or by another person also subject to an obligation of secrecy under Union or Member State law or rules established by national competent bodies.

4. Member States may maintain or introduce further conditions, including limitations, with regard to the processing of genetic data, biometric data or data concerning health.

Article 10: Processing of personal data relating to criminal convictions and offences

Processing of personal data relating to criminal convictions and offences or related security measures based on Article 6(1) shall be carried out only under the control of official authority or when the processing is authorised by Union or Member State law providing for appropriate safeguards for the rights and freedoms of data subjects. Any comprehensive register of criminal convictions shall be kept only under the control of official authority.

Article 11: Processing which does not require identification

1. If the purposes for which a controller processes personal data do not or do no longer require the identification of a data subject by the controller, the controller shall not be obliged to maintain, acquire or process additional information in order to identify the data subject for the sole purpose of complying with this Regulation.

2. Where, in cases referred to in paragraph 1 of this Article, the controller is able to demonstrate that it is not in a position to identify the data subject, the controller shall inform the data subject accordingly, if possible. In such cases, Articles 15 to 20 shall not apply except where the data subject, for the purpose of exercising his or her rights under those articles, provides additional information enabling his or her identification.

Recent Developments
EU General Data Protection Regulation

CHAPTER III: Rights of the data subject

Section 1: Transparency and modalities

Article 12: Transparent information, communication and modalities for the exercise of the rights of the data subject

1. The controller shall take appropriate measures to provide any information referred to in Articles 13 and 14 and any communication under Articles 15 to 22 and 34 relating to processing to the data subject in a concise, transparent, intelligible and easily accessible form, using clear and plain language, in particular for any information addressed specifically to a child. The information shall be provided in writing, or by other means, including, where appropriate, by electronic means. When requested by the data subject, the information may be provided orally, provided that the identity of the data subject is proven by other means.

2. The controller shall facilitate the exercise of data subject rights under Articles 15 to 22. In the cases referred to in Article 11(2), the controller shall not refuse to act on the request of the data subject for exercising his or her rights under Articles 15 to 22, unless the controller demonstrates that it is not in a position to identify the data subject.

3. The controller shall provide information on action taken on a request under Articles 15 to 22 to the data subject without undue delay and in any event within one month of receipt of the request. That period may be extended by two further months where necessary, taking into account the complexity and number of the requests. The controller shall inform the data subject of any such extension within one month of receipt of the request, together with the reasons for the delay. Where the data subject makes the request by electronic form means, the information shall be provided by electronic means where possible, unless otherwise requested by the data subject.

4. If the controller does not take action on the request of the data subject, the controller shall inform the data subject without delay and at the latest within one month of receipt of the request of the reasons for not taking action and on the possibility of lodging a complaint with a supervisory authority and seeking a judicial remedy.

5. Information provided under Articles 13 and 14 and any communication and any actions taken under Articles 15 to 22 and 34 shall be provided free of charge. Where requests from a data subject are manifestly unfounded or excessive, in particular because of their repetitive character, the controller may either:

> (a) charge a reasonable fee taking into account the administrative costs of providing the information or communication or taking the action requested; or

> (b) refuse to act on the request.

The controller shall bear the burden of demonstrating the manifestly unfounded or excessive character of the request.

6. Without prejudice to Article 11, where the controller has reasonable doubts concerning the identity of the natural person making the request referred to in Articles 15 to 21, the controller

may request the provision of additional information necessary to confirm the identity of the data subject.

7. The information to be provided to data subjects pursuant to Articles 13 and 14 may be provided in combination with standardised icons in order to give in an easily visible, intelligible and clearly legible manner a meaningful overview of the intended processing. Where the icons are presented electronically they shall be machine-readable.

8. The Commission shall be empowered to adopt delegated acts in accordance with Article 92 for the purpose of determining the information to be presented by the icons and the procedures for providing standardised icons.

Section 2: Information and access to personal data

Article 13: Information to be provided where personal data are collected from the data subject

1. Where personal data relating to a data subject are collected from the data subject, the controller shall, at the time when personal data are obtained, provide the data subject with all of the following information:

(a) the identity and the contact details of the controller and, where applicable, of the controller's representative;

(b) the contact details of the data protection officer, where applicable;

(c) the purposes of the processing for which the personal data are intended as well as the legal basis for the processing;

(d) where the processing is based on point (f) of Article 6(1), the legitimate interests pursued by the controller or by a third party;

(e) the recipients or categories of recipients of the personal data, if any;

(f) where applicable, the fact that the controller intends to transfer personal data to a third country or international organisation and the existence or absence of an adequacy decision by the Commission, or in the case of transfers referred to in Article 46 or 47, or the second subparagraph of Article 49(1), reference to the appropriate or suitable safeguards and the means by which to obtain a copy of them or where they have been made available.

2. In addition to the information referred to in paragraph 1, the controller shall, at the time when personal data are obtained, provide the data subject with the following further information necessary to ensure fair and transparent processing:

(a) the period for which the personal data will be stored, or if that is not possible, the criteria used to determine that period;

(b) the existence of the right to request from the controller access to and rectification or erasure of personal data or restriction of processing concerning the data subject or to object to processing as well as the right to data portability;

(c) where the processing is based on point (a) of Article 6(1) or point (a) of Article 9(2), the existence of the right to withdraw consent at any time, without affecting the lawfulness of processing based on consent before its withdrawal;

(d) the right to lodge a complaint with a supervisory authority;

(e) whether the provision of personal data is a statutory or contractual requirement, or a requirement necessary to enter into a contract, as well as whether the data subject is obliged to provide the personal data and of the possible consequences of failure to provide such data;

(f) the existence of automated decision-making, including profiling, referred to in Article 22(1) and (4) and, at least in those cases, meaningful information about the logic involved, as well as the significance and the envisaged consequences of such processing for the data subject.

3. Where the controller intends to further process the personal data for a purpose other than that for which the personal data were collected, the controller shall provide the data subject prior to that further processing with information on that other purpose and with any relevant further information as referred to in paragraph 2.

4. Paragraphs 1, 2 and 3 shall not apply where and insofar as the data subject already has the information.

Article 14: Information to be provided where personal data have not been obtained from the data subject

1. Where personal data have not been obtained from the data subject, the controller shall provide the data subject with the following information:

(a) the identity and the contact details of the controller and, where applicable, of the controller's representative;

(b) the contact details of the data protection officer, where applicable;

(c) the purposes of the processing for which the personal data are intended as well as the legal basis for the processing;

(d) the categories of personal data concerned;

(e) the recipients or categories of recipients of the personal data, if any;

(f) where applicable, that the controller intends to transfer personal data to a recipient in a third country or international organisation and the existence or absence of an adequacy decision by the Commission, or in the case of transfers referred to in Article 46 or 47, or the second subparagraph of Article 49(1), reference to the appropriate or suitable safeguards and the means to obtain a copy of them or where they have been made available.

2. In addition to the information referred to in paragraph 1, the controller shall provide the data subject with the following information necessary to ensure fair and transparent processing in respect of the data subject:

(a) the period for which the personal data will be stored, or if that is not possible, the criteria used to determine that period;

(b) where the processing is based on point (f) of Article 6(1), the legitimate interests pursued by the controller or by a third party;

(c) the existence of the right to request from the controller access to and rectification or erasure of personal data or restriction of processing concerning the data subject and to object to processing as well as the right to data portability;

(d) where processing is based on point (a) of Article 6(1) or point (a) of Article 9(2), the existence of the right to withdraw consent at any time, without affecting the lawfulness of processing based on consent before its withdrawal;

(e) the right to lodge a complaint with a supervisory authority;

(f) from which source the personal data originate, and if applicable, whether it came from publicly accessible sources;

(g) the existence of automated decision-making, including profiling, referred to in Article 22(1) and (4) and, at least in those cases, meaningful information about the logic involved, as well as the significance and the envisaged consequences of such processing for the data subject.

3. The controller shall provide the information referred to in paragraphs 1 and 2:

(a) within a reasonable period after obtaining the personal data, but at the latest within one month, having regard to the specific circumstances in which the personal data are processed;

(b) if the personal data are to be used for communication with the data subject, at the latest at the time of the first communication to that data subject; or

(c) if a disclosure to another recipient is envisaged, at the latest when the personal data are first disclosed.

4. Where the controller intends to further process the personal data for a purpose other than that for which the personal data were obtained, the controller shall provide the data subject prior to that further processing with information on that other purpose and with any relevant further information as referred to in paragraph 2.

5. Paragraphs 1 to 4 shall not apply where and insofar as:

(a) the data subject already has the information;

(b) the provision of such information proves impossible or would involve a disproportionate effort, in particular for processing for archiving purposes in the public interest, scientific or historical research purposes or statistical purposes, subject to the conditions and safeguards referred to in Article 89(1) or in so far as the obligation referred to in paragraph 1 of this Article is likely to render impossible or seriously impair the achievement of the objectives of that processing. In such cases the controller shall take appropriate measures to protect the data subject's rights and freedoms and legitimate interests, including making the information publicly available;

(c) obtaining or disclosure is expressly laid down by Union or Member State law to which the controller is subject and which provides appropriate measures to protect the data subject's legitimate interests; or

(d) where the personal data must remain confidential subject to an obligation of professional secrecy regulated by Union or Member State law, including a statutory obligation of secrecy.

Article 15: Right of access by the data subject

1.   The data subject shall have the right to obtain from the controller confirmation as to whether or not personal data concerning him or her are being processed, and, where that is the case, access to the personal data and the following information:

(a) the purposes of the processing;

(b) the categories of personal data concerned;

(c) the recipients or categories of recipient to whom the personal data have been or will be disclosed, in particular recipients in third countries or international organisations;

(d) where possible, the envisaged period for which the personal data will be stored, or, if not possible, the criteria used to determine that period;

(e) the existence of the right to request from the controller rectification or erasure of personal data or restriction of processing of personal data concerning the data subject or to object to such processing;

(f) the right to lodge a complaint with a supervisory authority;

(g) where the personal data are not collected from the data subject, any available information as to their source;

(h) the existence of automated decision-making, including profiling, referred to in Article 22(1) and (4) and, at least in those cases, meaningful information about the logic involved, as well as the significance and the envisaged consequences of such processing for the data subject.

2.   Where personal data are transferred to a third country or to an international organisation, the data subject shall have the right to be informed of the appropriate safeguards pursuant to Article 46 relating to the transfer.

3.   The controller shall provide a copy of the personal data undergoing processing. For any further copies requested by the data subject, the controller may charge a reasonable fee based on administrative costs. Where the data subject makes the request by electronic means, and unless otherwise requested by the data subject, the information shall be provided in a commonly used electronic form.

4.   The right to obtain a copy referred to in paragraph 3 shall not adversely affect the rights and freedoms of others.

Section 3: Rectification and erasure

Article 16: Right to rectification

The data subject shall have the right to obtain from the controller without undue delay the rectification of inaccurate personal data concerning him or her. Taking into account the purposes of the processing, the data subject shall have the right to have incomplete personal data completed, including by means of providing a supplementary statement.

Article 17: Right to erasure ('right to be forgotten')

1.   The data subject shall have the right to obtain from the controller the erasure of personal data concerning him or her without undue delay and the controller shall have the obligation to erase personal data without undue delay where one of the following grounds applies:

(a) the personal data are no longer necessary in relation to the purposes for which they were collected or otherwise processed;

(b) the data subject withdraws consent on which the processing is based according to point (a) of Article 6(1), or point (a) of Article 9(2), and where there is no other legal ground for the processing;

(c) the data subject objects to the processing pursuant to Article 21(1) and there are no overriding legitimate grounds for the processing, or the data subject objects to the processing pursuant to Article 21(2);

(d) the personal data have been unlawfully processed;

(e) the personal data have to be erased for compliance with a legal obligation in Union or Member State law to which the controller is subject;

(f) the personal data have been collected in relation to the offer of information society services referred to in Article 8(1).

2.   Where the controller has made the personal data public and is obliged pursuant to paragraph 1 to erase the personal data, the controller, taking account of available technology and the cost of implementation, shall take reasonable steps, including technical measures, to inform controllers which are processing the personal data that the data subject has requested the erasure by such controllers of any links to, or copy or replication of, those personal data.

3.   Paragraphs 1 and 2 shall not apply to the extent that processing is necessary:

(a) for exercising the right of freedom of expression and information;

(b) for compliance with a legal obligation which requires processing by Union or Member State law to which the controller is subject or for the performance of a task carried out in the public interest or in the exercise of official authority vested in the controller;

(c) for reasons of public interest in the area of public health in accordance with points (h) and (i) of Article 9(2) as well as Article 9(3);

(d) for archiving purposes in the public interest, scientific or historical research purposes or statistical purposes in accordance with Article 89(1) in so far as the right referred to in paragraph 1 is likely to render impossible or seriously impair the achievement of the objectives of that processing; or

(e) for the establishment, exercise or defence of legal claims.

Article 18: Right to restriction of processing

1. The data subject shall have the right to obtain from the controller restriction of processing where one of the following applies:

(a) the accuracy of the personal data is contested by the data subject, for a period enabling the controller to verify the accuracy of the personal data;

(b) the processing is unlawful and the data subject opposes the erasure of the personal data and requests the restriction of their use instead;

(c) the controller no longer needs the personal data for the purposes of the processing, but they are required by the data subject for the establishment, exercise or defence of legal claims;

(d) the data subject has objected to processing pursuant to Article 21(1) pending the verification whether the legitimate grounds of the controller override those of the data subject.

2. Where processing has been restricted under paragraph 1, such personal data shall, with the exception of storage, only be processed with the data subject's consent or for the establishment, exercise or defence of legal claims or for the protection of the rights of another natural or legal person or for reasons of important public interest of the Union or of a Member State.

3. A data subject who has obtained restriction of processing pursuant to paragraph 1 shall be informed by the controller before the restriction of processing is lifted.

Article 19: Notification obligation regarding rectification or erasure of personal data or restriction of processing

The controller shall communicate any rectification or erasure of personal data or restriction of processing carried out in accordance with Article 16, Article 17(1) and Article 18 to each recipient to whom the personal data have been disclosed, unless this proves impossible or involves disproportionate effort. The controller shall inform the data subject about those recipients if the data subject requests it.

Article 20: Right to data portability

1. The data subject shall have the right to receive the personal data concerning him or her, which he or she has provided to a controller, in a structured, commonly used and machine-readable format and have the right to transmit those data to another controller without hindrance from the controller to which the personal data have been provided, where:

(a) the processing is based on consent pursuant to point (a) of Article 6(1) or point (a) of Article 9(2) or on a contract pursuant to point (b) of Article 6(1); and

(b) the processing is carried out by automated means.

2.   In exercising his or her right to data portability pursuant to paragraph 1, the data subject shall have the right to have the personal data transmitted directly from one controller to another, where technically feasible.

3.   The exercise of the right referred to in paragraph 1 of this Article shall be without prejudice to Article 17. That right shall not apply to processing necessary for the performance of a task carried out in the public interest or in the exercise of official authority vested in the controller.

4.   The right referred to in paragraph 1 shall not adversely affect the rights and freedoms of others.

Section 4: Right to object and automated individual decision-making

Article 21: Right to object

1.   The data subject shall have the right to object, on grounds relating to his or her particular situation, at any time to processing of personal data concerning him or her which is based on point (e) or (f) of Article 6(1), including profiling based on those provisions. The controller shall no longer process the personal data unless the controller demonstrates compelling legitimate grounds for the processing which override the interests, rights and freedoms of the data subject or for the establishment, exercise or defence of legal claims.

2.   Where personal data are processed for direct marketing purposes, the data subject shall have the right to object at any time to processing of personal data concerning him or her for such marketing, which includes profiling to the extent that it is related to such direct marketing.

3.   Where the data subject objects to processing for direct marketing purposes, the personal data shall no longer be processed for such purposes.

4.   At the latest at the time of the first communication with the data subject, the right referred to in paragraphs 1 and 2 shall be explicitly brought to the attention of the data subject and shall be presented clearly and separately from any other information.

5.   In the context of the use of information society services, and notwithstanding Directive 2002/58/EC, the data subject may exercise his or her right to object by automated means using technical specifications.

6.   Where personal data are processed for scientific or historical research purposes or statistical purposes pursuant to Article 89(1), the data subject, on grounds relating to his or her particular situation, shall have the right to object to processing of personal data concerning him or her, unless the processing is necessary for the performance of a task carried out for reasons of public interest.

Recent Developments
EU General Data Protection Regulation

Article 22: Automated individual decision-making, including profiling

1.   The data subject shall have the right not to be subject to a decision based solely on automated processing, including profiling, which produces legal effects concerning him or her or similarly significantly affects him or her.

2.   Paragraph 1 shall not apply if the decision:

> (a) is necessary for entering into, or performance of, a contract between the data subject and a data controller;
>
> (b) is authorised by Union or Member State law to which the controller is subject and which also lays down suitable measures to safeguard the data subject's rights and freedoms and legitimate interests; or
>
> (c) is based on the data subject's explicit consent.

3.   In the cases referred to in points (a) and (c) of paragraph 2, the data controller shall implement suitable measures to safeguard the data subject's rights and freedoms and legitimate interests, at least the right to obtain human intervention on the part of the controller, to express his or her point of view and to contest the decision.

4.   Decisions referred to in paragraph 2 shall not be based on special categories of personal data referred to in Article 9(1), unless point (a) or (g) of Article 9(2) applies and suitable measures to safeguard the data subject's rights and freedoms and legitimate interests are in place.

Section 5: Restrictions

Article 23: Restrictions

1.   Union or Member State law to which the data controller or processor is subject may restrict by way of a legislative measure the scope of the obligations and rights provided for in Articles 12 to 22 and Article 34, as well as Article 5 in so far as its provisions correspond to the rights and obligations provided for in Articles 12 to 22, when such a restriction respects the essence of the fundamental rights and freedoms and is a necessary and proportionate measure in a democratic society to safeguard:

> (a) national security;
>
> (b) defence;
>
> (c) public security;
>
> (d) the prevention, investigation, detection or prosecution of criminal offences or the execution of criminal penalties, including the safeguarding against and the prevention of threats to public security;
>
> (e) other important objectives of general public interest of the Union or of a Member State, in particular an important economic or financial interest of the Union or of a Member State, including monetary, budgetary and taxation a matters, public health and social security;
>
> (f) the protection of judicial independence and judicial proceedings;

(g) the prevention, investigation, detection and prosecution of breaches of ethics for regulated professions;

(h) a monitoring, inspection or regulatory function connected, even occasionally, to the exercise of official authority in the cases referred to in points (a) to (e) and (g);

(i) the protection of the data subject or the rights and freedoms of others;

(j) the enforcement of civil law claims.

2.   In particular, any legislative measure referred to in paragraph 1 shall contain specific provisions at least, where relevant, as to:

(a) the purposes of the processing or categories of processing;

(b) the categories of personal data;

(c) the scope of the restrictions introduced;

(d) the safeguards to prevent abuse or unlawful access or transfer;

(e) the specification of the controller or categories of controllers;

(f) the storage periods and the applicable safeguards taking into account the nature, scope and purposes of the processing or categories of processing;

(g) the risks to the rights and freedoms of data subjects; and

(h) the right of data subjects to be informed about the restriction, unless that may be prejudicial to the purpose of the restriction.

CHAPTER IV: Controller and processor

Section 1: General obligations

Article 24: Responsibility of the controller

1.   Taking into account the nature, scope, context and purposes of processing as well as the risks of varying likelihood and severity for the rights and freedoms of natural persons, the controller shall implement appropriate technical and organisational measures to ensure and to be able to demonstrate that processing is performed in accordance with this Regulation. Those measures shall be reviewed and updated where necessary.

2.   Where proportionate in relation to processing activities, the measures referred to in paragraph 1 shall include the implementation of appropriate data protection policies by the controller.

3.   Adherence to approved codes of conduct as referred to in Article 40 or approved certification mechanisms as referred to in Article 42 may be used as an element by which to demonstrate compliance with the obligations of the controller.

Article 25: Data protection by design and by default

1.   Taking into account the state of the art, the cost of implementation and the nature, scope, context and purposes of processing as well as the risks of varying likelihood and severity for rights and freedoms of natural persons posed by the processing, the controller shall, both at the time of the determination of the means for processing and at the time of the processing

itself, implement appropriate technical and organisational measures, such as pseudonymisation, which are designed to implement data-protection principles, such as data minimisation, in an effective manner and to integrate the necessary safeguards into the processing in order to meet the requirements of this Regulation and protect the rights of data subjects.

2.   The controller shall implement appropriate technical and organisational measures for ensuring that, by default, only personal data which are necessary for each specific purpose of the processing are processed. That obligation applies to the amount of personal data collected, the extent of their processing, the period of their storage and their accessibility. In particular, such measures shall ensure that by default personal data are not made accessible without the individual's intervention to an indefinite number of natural persons.

3.   An approved certification mechanism pursuant to Article 42 may be used as an element to demonstrate compliance with the requirements set out in paragraphs 1 and 2 of this Article.

Article 26: Joint controllers

1.   Where two or more controllers jointly determine the purposes and means of processing, they shall be joint controllers. They shall in a transparent manner determine their respective responsibilities for compliance with the obligations under this Regulation, in particular as regards the exercising of the rights of the data subject and their respective duties to provide the information referred to in Articles 13 and 14, by means of an arrangement between them unless, and in so far as, the respective responsibilities of the controllers are determined by Union or Member State law to which the controllers are subject. The arrangement may designate a contact point for data subjects.

2.   The arrangement referred to in paragraph 1 shall duly reflect the respective roles and relationships of the joint controllers vis-à-vis the data subjects. The essence of the arrangement shall be made available to the data subject.

3.   Irrespective of the terms of the arrangement referred to in paragraph 1, the data subject may exercise his or her rights under this Regulation in respect of and against each of the controllers.

Article 27: Representatives of controllers or processors not established in the Union

1.   Where Article 3(2) applies, the controller or the processor shall designate in writing a representative in the Union.

2.   The obligation laid down in paragraph 1 of this Article shall not apply to:

    (a) processing which is occasional, does not include, on a large scale, processing of special categories of data as referred to in Article 9(1) or processing of personal data relating to criminal convictions and offences referred to in Article 10, and is unlikely to result in a risk to the rights and freedoms of natural persons, taking into account the nature, context, scope and purposes of the processing; or

    (b) a public authority or body.

3.   The representative shall be established in one of the Member States where the data subjects, whose personal data are processed in relation to the offering of goods or services to them, or whose behaviour is monitored, are.

4.   The representative shall be mandated by the controller or processor to be addressed in addition to or instead of the controller or the processor by, in particular, supervisory authorities and data subjects, on all issues related to processing, for the purposes of ensuring compliance with this Regulation.

5.   The designation of a representative by the controller or processor shall be without prejudice to legal actions which could be initiated against the controller or the processor themselves.

Article 28: Processor

1.   Where processing is to be carried out on behalf of a controller, the controller shall use only processors providing sufficient guarantees to implement appropriate technical and organisational measures in such a manner that processing will meet the requirements of this Regulation and ensure the protection of the rights of the data subject.

2.   The processor shall not engage another processor without prior specific or general written authorisation of the controller. In the case of general written authorisation, the processor shall inform the controller of any intended changes concerning the addition or replacement of other processors, thereby giving the controller the opportunity to object to such changes.

3.   Processing by a processor shall be governed by a contract or other legal act under Union or Member State law, that is binding on the processor with regard to the controller and that sets out the subject-matter and duration of the processing, the nature and purpose of the processing, the type of personal data and categories of data subjects and the obligations and rights of the controller. That contract or other legal act shall stipulate, in particular, that the processor:

(a) processes the personal data only on documented instructions from the controller, including with regard to transfers of personal data to a third country or an international organisation, unless required to do so by Union or Member State law to which the processor is subject; in such a case, the processor shall inform the controller of that legal requirement before processing, unless that law prohibits such information on important grounds of public interest;

(b) ensures that persons authorised to process the personal data have committed themselves to confidentiality or are under an appropriate statutory obligation of confidentiality;

(c) takes all measures required pursuant to Article 32;

(d) respects the conditions referred to in paragraphs 2 and 4 for engaging another processor;

(e) taking into account the nature of the processing, assists the controller by appropriate technical and organisational measures, insofar as this is possible, for the fulfilment of the controller's obligation to respond to requests for exercising the data subject's rights laid down in Chapter III;

(f) assists the controller in ensuring compliance with the obligations pursuant to Articles 32 to 36 taking into account the nature of processing and the information available to the processor;

(g) at the choice of the controller, deletes or returns all the personal data to the controller after the end of the provision of services relating to processing, and deletes existing copies unless Union or Member State law requires storage of the personal data;

(h) makes available to the controller all information necessary to demonstrate compliance with the obligations laid down in this Article and allow for and contribute to audits, including inspections, conducted by the controller or another auditor mandated by the controller.

With regard to point (h) of the first subparagraph, the processor shall immediately inform the controller if, in its opinion, an instruction infringes this Regulation or other Union or Member State data protection provisions.

4.   Where a processor engages another processor for carrying out specific processing activities on behalf of the controller, the same data protection obligations as set out in the contract or other legal act between the controller and the processor as referred to in paragraph 3 shall be imposed on that other processor by way of a contract or other legal act under Union or Member State law, in particular providing sufficient guarantees to implement appropriate technical and organisational measures in such a manner that the processing will meet the requirements of this Regulation. Where that other processor fails to fulfil its data protection obligations, the initial processor shall remain fully liable to the controller for the performance of that other processor's obligations.

5.   Adherence of a processor to an approved code of conduct as referred to in Article 40 or an approved certification mechanism as referred to in Article 42 may be used as an element by which to demonstrate sufficient guarantees as referred to in paragraphs 1 and 4 of this Article.

6.   Without prejudice to an individual contract between the controller and the processor, the contract or the other legal act referred to in paragraphs 3 and 4 of this Article may be based, in whole or in part, on standard contractual clauses referred to in paragraphs 7 and 8 of this Article, including when they are part of a certification granted to the controller or processor pursuant to Articles 42 and 43.

7.   The Commission may lay down standard contractual clauses for the matters referred to in paragraph 3 and 4 of this Article and in accordance with the examination procedure referred to in Article 93(2).

8.   A supervisory authority may adopt standard contractual clauses for the matters referred to in paragraph 3 and 4 of this Article and in accordance with the consistency mechanism referred to in Article 63.

9. The contract or the other legal act referred to in paragraphs 3 and 4 shall be in writing, including in electronic form.

10. Without prejudice to Articles 82, 83 and 84, if a processor infringes this Regulation by determining the purposes and means of processing, the processor shall be considered to be a controller in respect of that processing.

Article 29: Processing under the authority of the controller or processor

The processor and any person acting under the authority of the controller or of the processor, who has access to personal data, shall not process those data except on instructions from the controller, unless required to do so by Union or Member State law.

Article 30: Records of processing activities

1. Each controller and, where applicable, the controller's representative, shall maintain a record of processing activities under its responsibility. That record shall contain all of the following information:

(a) the name and contact details of the controller and, where applicable, the joint controller, the controller's representative and the data protection officer;

(b) the purposes of the processing;

(c) a description of the categories of data subjects and of the categories of personal data;

(d) the categories of recipients to whom the personal data have been or will be disclosed including recipients in third countries or international organisations;

(e) where applicable, transfers of personal data to a third country or an international organisation, including the identification of that third country or international organisation and, in the case of transfers referred to in the second subparagraph of Article 49(1), the documentation of suitable safeguards;

(f) where possible, the envisaged time limits for erasure of the different categories of data;

(g) where possible, a general description of the technical and organisational security measures referred to in Article 32(1).

2. Each processor and, where applicable, the processor's representative shall maintain a record of all categories of processing activities carried out on behalf of a controller, containing:

(a) the name and contact details of the processor or processors and of each controller on behalf of which the processor is acting, and, where applicable, of the controller's or the processor's representative, and the data protection officer;

(b) the categories of processing carried out on behalf of each controller;

(c) where applicable, transfers of personal data to a third country or an international organisation, including the identification of that third country or international organisation and, in the case of transfers referred to in the second subparagraph of Article 49(1), the documentation of suitable safeguards;

(d) where possible, a general description of the technical and organisational security measures referred to in Article 32(1).

3.   The records referred to in paragraphs 1 and 2 shall be in writing, including in electronic form.

4.   The controller or the processor and, where applicable, the controller's or the processor's representative, shall make the record available to the supervisory authority on request.

5.   The obligations referred to in paragraphs 1 and 2 shall not apply to an enterprise or an organisation employing fewer than 250 persons unless the processing it carries out is likely to result in a risk to the rights and freedoms of data subjects, the processing is not occasional, or the processing includes special categories of data as referred to in Article 9(1) or personal data relating to criminal convictions and offences referred to in Article 10.

Article 31: Cooperation with the supervisory authority

The controller and the processor and, where applicable, their representatives, shall cooperate, on request, with the supervisory authority in the performance of its tasks.

Section 2: Security of personal data

Article 32: Security of processing

1.   Taking into account the state of the art, the costs of implementation and the nature, scope, context and purposes of processing as well as the risk of varying likelihood and severity for the rights and freedoms of natural persons, the controller and the processor shall implement appropriate technical and organisational measures to ensure a level of security appropriate to the risk, including inter alia as appropriate:

(a) the pseudonymisation and encryption of personal data;

(b) the ability to ensure the ongoing confidentiality, integrity, availability and resilience of processing systems and services;

(c) the ability to restore the availability and access to personal data in a timely manner in the event of a physical or technical incident;

(d) a process for regularly testing, assessing and evaluating the effectiveness of technical and organisational measures for ensuring the security of the processing.

2.   In assessing the appropriate level of security account shall be taken in particular of the risks that are presented by processing, in particular from accidental or unlawful destruction, loss, alteration, unauthorised disclosure of, or access to personal data transmitted, stored or otherwise processed.

3.   Adherence to an approved code of conduct as referred to in Article 40 or an approved certification mechanism as referred to in Article 42 may be used as an element by which to demonstrate compliance with the requirements set out in paragraph 1 of this Article.

4. The controller and processor shall take steps to ensure that any natural person acting under the authority of the controller or the processor who has access to personal data does not process them except on instructions from the controller, unless he or she is required to do so by Union or Member State law.

Article 33: Notification of a personal data breach to the supervisory authority

1. In the case of a personal data breach, the controller shall without undue delay and, where feasible, not later than 72 hours after having become aware of it, notify the personal data breach to the supervisory authority competent in accordance with Article 55, unless the personal data breach is unlikely to result in a risk to the rights and freedoms of natural persons. Where the notification to the supervisory authority is not made within 72 hours, it shall be accompanied by reasons for the delay.

2. The processor shall notify the controller without undue delay after becoming aware of a personal data breach.

3. The notification referred to in paragraph 1 shall at least:

    (a) describe the nature of the personal data breach including where possible, the categories and approximate number of data subjects concerned and the categories and approximate number of personal data records concerned;

    (b) communicate the name and contact details of the data protection officer or other contact point where more information can be obtained;

    (c) describe the likely consequences of the personal data breach;

    (d) describe the measures taken or proposed to be taken by the controller to address the personal data breach, including, where appropriate, measures to mitigate its possible adverse effects.

4. Where, and in so far as, it is not possible to provide the information at the same time, the information may be provided in phases without undue further delay.

5. The controller shall document any personal data breaches, comprising the facts relating to the personal data breach, its effects and the remedial action taken. That documentation shall enable the supervisory authority to verify compliance with this Article.

Article 34: Communication of a personal data breach to the data subject

1. When the personal data breach is likely to result in a high risk to the rights and freedoms of natural persons, the controller shall communicate the personal data breach to the data subject without undue delay.

2. The communication to the data subject referred to in paragraph 1 of this Article shall describe in clear and plain language the nature of the personal data breach and contain at least the information and measures referred to in points (b), (c) and (d) of Article 33(3).

3. The communication to the data subject referred to in paragraph 1 shall not be required if any of the following conditions are met:

(a) the controller has implemented appropriate technical and organisational protection measures, and those measures were applied to the personal data affected by the personal data breach, in particular those that render the personal data unintelligible to any person who is not authorised to access it, such as encryption;

(b) the controller has taken subsequent measures which ensure that the high risk to the rights and freedoms of data subjects referred to in paragraph 1 is no longer likely to materialise;

(c) it would involve disproportionate effort. In such a case, there shall instead be a public communication or similar measure whereby the data subjects are informed in an equally effective manner.

4. If the controller has not already communicated the personal data breach to the data subject, the supervisory authority, having considered the likelihood of the personal data breach resulting in a high risk, may require it to do so or may decide that any of the conditions referred to in paragraph 3 are met.

Section 3: Data protection impact assessment and prior consultation

Article 35: Data protection impact assessment

1. Where a type of processing in particular using new technologies, and taking into account the nature, scope, context and purposes of the processing, is likely to result in a high risk to the rights and freedoms of natural persons, the controller shall, prior to the processing, carry out an assessment of the impact of the envisaged processing operations on the protection of personal data. A single assessment may address a set of similar processing operations that present similar high risks.

2. The controller shall seek the advice of the data protection officer, where designated, when carrying out a data protection impact assessment.

3. A data protection impact assessment referred to in paragraph 1 shall in particular be required in the case of:

(a) a systematic and extensive evaluation of personal aspects relating to natural persons which is based on automated processing, including profiling, and on which decisions are based that produce legal effects concerning the natural person or similarly significantly affect the natural person;

(b) processing on a large scale of special categories of data referred to in Article 9(1), or of personal data relating to criminal convictions and offences referred to in Article 10; or

(c) a systematic monitoring of a publicly accessible area on a large scale.

4. The supervisory authority shall establish and make public a list of the kind of processing operations which are subject to the requirement for a data protection impact assessment pursuant to paragraph 1. The supervisory authority shall communicate those lists to the Board referred to in Article 68.

5.   The supervisory authority may also establish and make public a list of the kind of processing operations for which no data protection impact assessment is required. The supervisory authority shall communicate those lists to the Board.

6.   Prior to the adoption of the lists referred to in paragraphs 4 and 5, the competent supervisory authority shall apply the consistency mechanism referred to in Article 63 where such lists involve processing activities which are related to the offering of goods or services to data subjects or to the monitoring of their behaviour in several Member States, or may substantially affect the free movement of personal data within the Union.

7.   The assessment shall contain at least:

> (a) a systematic description of the envisaged processing operations and the purposes of the processing, including, where applicable, the legitimate interest pursued by the controller;
>
> (b) an assessment of the necessity and proportionality of the processing operations in relation to the purposes;
>
> (c) an assessment of the risks to the rights and freedoms of data subjects referred to in paragraph 1; and
>
> (d) the measures envisaged to address the risks, including safeguards, security measures and mechanisms to ensure the protection of personal data and to demonstrate compliance with this Regulation taking into account the rights and legitimate interests of data subjects and other persons concerned.

8.   Compliance with approved codes of conduct referred to in Article 40 by the relevant controllers or processors shall be taken into due account in assessing the impact of the processing operations performed by such controllers or processors, in particular for the purposes of a data protection impact assessment.

9.   Where appropriate, the controller shall seek the views of data subjects or their representatives on the intended processing, without prejudice to the protection of commercial or public interests or the security of processing operations.

10.   Where processing pursuant to point (c) or (e) of Article 6(1) has a legal basis in Union law or in the law of the Member State to which the controller is subject, that law regulates the specific processing operation or set of operations in question, and a data protection impact assessment has already been carried out as part of a general impact assessment in the context of the adoption of that legal basis, paragraphs 1 to 7 shall not apply unless Member States deem it to be necessary to carry out such an assessment prior to processing activities.

11.   Where necessary, the controller shall carry out a review to assess if processing is performed in accordance with the data protection impact assessment at least when there is a change of the risk represented by processing operations.

Recent Developments
EU General Data Protection Regulation

Article 36: Prior consultation

1.   The controller shall consult the supervisory authority prior to processing where a data protection impact assessment under Article 35 indicates that the processing would result in a high risk in the absence of measures taken by the controller to mitigate the risk.

2.   Where the supervisory authority is of the opinion that the intended processing referred to in paragraph 1 would infringe this Regulation, in particular where the controller has insufficiently identified or mitigated the risk, the supervisory authority shall, within period of up to eight weeks of receipt of the request for consultation, provide written advice to the controller and, where applicable to the processor, and may use any of its powers referred to in Article 58. That period may be extended by six weeks, taking into account the complexity of the intended processing. The supervisory authority shall inform the controller and, where applicable, the processor, of any such extension within one month of receipt of the request for consultation together with the reasons for the delay. Those periods may be suspended until the supervisory authority has obtained information it has requested for the purposes of the consultation.

3.   When consulting the supervisory authority pursuant to paragraph 1, the controller shall provide the supervisory authority with:

    (a) where applicable, the respective responsibilities of the controller, joint controllers and processors involved in the processing, in particular for processing within a group of undertakings;

    (b) the purposes and means of the intended processing;

    (c) the measures and safeguards provided to protect the rights and freedoms of data subjects pursuant to this Regulation;

    (d) where applicable, the contact details of the data protection officer;

    (e) the data protection impact assessment provided for in Article 35; and

    (f) any other information requested by the supervisory authority.

4.   Member States shall consult the supervisory authority during the preparation of a proposal for a legislative measure to be adopted by a national parliament, or of a regulatory measure based on such a legislative measure, which relates to processing.

5.   Notwithstanding paragraph 1, Member State law may require controllers to consult with, and obtain prior authorisation from, the supervisory authority in relation to processing by a controller for the performance of a task carried out by the controller in the public interest, including processing in relation to social protection and public health.

Section 4: Data protection officer

Article 37: Designation of the data protection officer

1.   The controller and the processor shall designate a data protection officer in any case where:

(a) the processing is carried out by a public authority or body, except for courts acting in their judicial capacity;

(b) the core activities of the controller or the processor consist of processing operations which, by virtue of their nature, their scope and/or their purposes, require regular and systematic monitoring of data subjects on a large scale; or

(c) the core activities of the controller or the processor consist of processing on a large scale of special categories of data pursuant to Article 9 and personal data relating to criminal convictions and offences referred to in Article 10.

2. A group of undertakings may appoint a single data protection officer provided that a data protection officer is easily accessible from each establishment.

3. Where the controller or the processor is a public authority or body, a single data protection officer may be designated for several such authorities or bodies, taking account of their organisational structure and size.

4. In cases other than those referred to in paragraph 1, the controller or processor or associations and other bodies representing categories of controllers or processors may or, where required by Union or Member State law shall, designate a data protection officer. The data protection officer may act for such associations and other bodies representing controllers or processors.

5. The data protection officer shall be designated on the basis of professional qualities and, in particular, expert knowledge of data protection law and practices and the ability to fulfil the tasks referred to in Article 39.

6. The data protection officer may be a staff member of the controller or processor, or fulfil the tasks on the basis of a service contract.

7. The controller or the processor shall publish the contact details of the data protection officer and communicate them to the supervisory authority.

Article 38: Position of the data protection officer

1. The controller and the processor shall ensure that the data protection officer is involved, properly and in a timely manner, in all issues which relate to the protection of personal data.

2. The controller and processor shall support the data protection officer in performing the tasks referred to in Article 39 by providing resources necessary to carry out those tasks and access to personal data and processing operations, and to maintain his or her expert knowledge.

3. The controller and processor shall ensure that the data protection officer does not receive any instructions regarding the exercise of those tasks. He or she shall not be dismissed or penalised by the controller or the processor for performing his tasks. The data protection officer shall directly report to the highest management level of the controller or the processor.

4. Data subjects may contact the data protection officer with regard to all issues related to processing of their personal data and to the exercise of their rights under this Regulation.

5. The data protection officer shall be bound by secrecy or confidentiality concerning the performance of his or her tasks, in accordance with Union or Member State law.

6. The data protection officer may fulfil other tasks and duties. The controller or processor shall ensure that any such tasks and duties do not result in a conflict of interests.

Article 39: Tasks of the data protection officer

1. The data protection officer shall have at least the following tasks:

(a) to inform and advise the controller or the processor and the employees who carry out processing of their obligations pursuant to this Regulation and to other Union or Member State data protection provisions;

(b) to monitor compliance with this Regulation, with other Union or Member State data protection provisions and with the policies of the controller or processor in relation to the protection of personal data, including the assignment of responsibilities, awareness-raising and training of staff involved in processing operations, and the related audits;

(c) to provide advice where requested as regards the data protection impact assessment and monitor its performance pursuant to Article 35;

(d) to cooperate with the supervisory authority;

(e) to act as the contact point for the supervisory authority on issues relating to processing, including the prior consultation referred to in Article 36, and to consult, where appropriate, with regard to any other matter.

2. The data protection officer shall in the performance of his or her tasks have due regard to the risk associated with processing operations, taking into account the nature, scope, context and purposes of processing.

Section 5: Codes of conduct and certification

Article 40: Codes of conduct

1. The Member States, the supervisory authorities, the Board and the Commission shall encourage the drawing up of codes of conduct intended to contribute to the proper application of this Regulation, taking account of the specific features of the various processing sectors and the specific needs of micro, small and medium-sized enterprises.

2. Associations and other bodies representing categories of controllers or processors may prepare codes of conduct, or amend or extend such codes, for the purpose of specifying the application of this Regulation, such as with regard to:

(a) fair and transparent processing;

(b) the legitimate interests pursued by controllers in specific contexts;

(c) the collection of personal data;

(d) the pseudonymisation of personal data;

(e) the information provided to the public and to data subjects;

(f) the exercise of the rights of data subjects;

(g) the information provided to, and the protection of, children, and the manner in which the consent of the holders of parental responsibility over children is to be obtained;

(h) the measures and procedures referred to in Articles 24 and 25 and the measures to ensure security of processing referred to in Article 32;

(i) the notification of personal data breaches to supervisory authorities and the communication of such personal data breaches to data subjects;

(j) the transfer of personal data to third countries or international organisations; or

(k) out-of-court proceedings and other dispute resolution procedures for resolving disputes between controllers and data subjects with regard to processing, without prejudice to the rights of data subjects pursuant to Articles 77 and 79.

3.   In addition to adherence by controllers or processors subject to this Regulation, codes of conduct approved pursuant to paragraph 5 of this Article and having general validity pursuant to paragraph 9 of this Article may also be adhered to by controllers or processors that are not subject to this Regulation pursuant to Article 3 in order to provide appropriate safeguards within the framework of personal data transfers to third countries or international organisations under the terms referred to in point (e) of Article 46(2). Such controllers or processors shall make binding and enforceable commitments, via contractual or other legally binding instruments, to apply those appropriate safeguards including with regard to the rights of data subjects.

4.   A code of conduct referred to in paragraph 2 of this Article shall contain mechanisms which enable the body referred to in Article 41(1) to carry out the mandatory monitoring of compliance with its provisions by the controllers or processors which undertake to apply it, without prejudice to the tasks and powers of supervisory authorities competent pursuant to Article 55 or 56.

5.   Associations and other bodies referred to in paragraph 2 of this Article which intend to prepare a code of conduct or to amend or extend an existing code shall submit the draft code, amendment or extension to the supervisory authority which is competent pursuant to Article 55. The supervisory authority shall provide an opinion on whether the draft code, amendment or extension complies with this Regulation and shall approve that draft code, amendment or extension if it finds that it provides sufficient appropriate safeguards.

6.   Where the draft code, or amendment or extension is approved in accordance with paragraph 5, and where the code of conduct concerned does not relate to processing activities in several Member States, the supervisory authority shall register and publish the code.

7.   Where a draft code of conduct relates to processing activities in several Member States, the supervisory authority which is competent pursuant to Article 55 shall, before approving the draft code, amendment or extension, submit it in the procedure referred to in Article 63 to the Board which shall provide an opinion on whether the draft code, amendment or extension complies with this Regulation or, in the situation referred to in paragraph 3 of this Article, provides appropriate safeguards.

8.   Where the opinion referred to in paragraph 7 confirms that the draft code, amendment or extension complies with this Regulation, or, in the situation referred to in paragraph 3, provides appropriate safeguards, the Board shall submit its opinion to the Commission.

9.   The Commission may, by way of implementing acts, decide that the approved code of conduct, amendment or extension submitted to it pursuant to paragraph 8 of this Article have general validity within the Union. Those implementing acts shall be adopted in accordance with the examination procedure set out in Article 93(2).

10.   The Commission shall ensure appropriate publicity for the approved codes which have been decided as having general validity in accordance with paragraph 9.

11.   The Board shall collate all approved codes of conduct, amendments and extensions in a register and shall make them publicly available by way of appropriate means.

Article 41: Monitoring of approved codes of conduct

1.   Without prejudice to the tasks and powers of the competent supervisory authority under Articles 57 and 58, the monitoring of compliance with a code of conduct pursuant to Article 40 may be carried out by a body which has an appropriate level of expertise in relation to the subject-matter of the code and is accredited for that purpose by the competent supervisory authority.

2.   A body as referred to in paragraph 1 may be accredited to monitor compliance with a code of conduct where that body has:

> (a) demonstrated its independence and expertise in relation to the subject-matter of the code to the satisfaction of the competent supervisory authority;

> (b) established procedures which allow it to assess the eligibility of controllers and processors concerned to apply the code, to monitor their compliance with its provisions and to periodically review its operation;

> (c) established procedures and structures to handle complaints about infringements of the code or the manner in which the code has been, or is being, implemented by a controller or processor, and to make those procedures and structures transparent to data subjects and the public; and

> (d) demonstrated to the satisfaction of the competent supervisory authority that its tasks and duties do not result in a conflict of interests.

3.   The competent supervisory authority shall submit the draft criteria for accreditation of a body as referred to in paragraph 1 of this Article to the Board pursuant to the consistency mechanism referred to in Article 63.

4.   Without prejudice to the tasks and powers of the competent supervisory authority and the provisions of Chapter VIII, a body as referred to in paragraph 1 of this Article shall, subject to appropriate safeguards, take appropriate action in cases of infringement of the code by a controller or processor, including suspension or exclusion of the controller or processor concerned from the code. It shall inform the competent supervisory authority of such actions and the reasons for taking them.

5. The competent supervisory authority shall revoke the accreditation of a body as referred to in paragraph 1 if the conditions for accreditation are not, or are no longer, met or where actions taken by the body infringe this Regulation.

6. This Article shall not apply to processing carried out by public authorities and bodies.

Article 42: Certification

1. The Member States, the supervisory authorities, the Board and the Commission shall encourage, in particular at Union level, the establishment of data protection certification mechanisms and of data protection seals and marks, for the purpose of demonstrating compliance with this Regulation of processing operations by controllers and processors. The specific needs of micro, small and medium-sized enterprises shall be taken into account.

2. In addition to adherence by controllers or processors subject to this Regulation, data protection certification mechanisms, seals or marks approved pursuant to paragraph 5 of this Article may be established for the purpose of demonstrating the existence of appropriate safeguards provided by controllers or processors that are not subject to this Regulation pursuant to Article 3 within the framework of personal data transfers to third countries or international organisations under the terms referred to in point (f) of Article 46(2). Such controllers or processors shall make binding and enforceable commitments, via contractual or other legally binding instruments, to apply those appropriate safeguards, including with regard to the rights of data subjects.

3. The certification shall be voluntary and available via a process that is transparent.

4. A certification pursuant to this Article does not reduce the responsibility of the controller or the processor for compliance with this Regulation and is without prejudice to the tasks and powers of the supervisory authorities which are competent pursuant to Article 55 or 56.

5. A certification pursuant to this Article shall be issued by the certification bodies referred to in Article 43 or by the competent supervisory authority, on the basis of criteria approved by that competent supervisory authority pursuant to Article 58(3) or by the Board pursuant to Article 63. Where the criteria are approved by the Board, this may result in a common certification, the European Data Protection Seal.

6. The controller or processor which submits its processing to the certification mechanism shall provide the certification body referred to in Article 43, or where applicable, the competent supervisory authority, with all information and access to its processing activities which are necessary to conduct the certification procedure.

7. Certification shall be issued to a controller or processor for a maximum period of three years and may be renewed, under the same conditions, provided that the relevant requirements continue to be met. Certification shall be withdrawn, as applicable, by the certification bodies referred to in Article 43 or by the competent supervisory authority where the requirements for the certification are not or are no longer met.

8. The Board shall collate all certification mechanisms and data protection seals and marks in a register and shall make them publicly available by any appropriate means.

Article 43: Certification bodies

1. Without prejudice to the tasks and powers of the competent supervisory authority under Articles 57 and 58, certification bodies which have an appropriate level of expertise in relation to data protection shall, after informing the supervisory authority in order to allow it to exercise its powers pursuant to point (h) of Article 58(2) where necessary, issue and renew certification. Member States shall ensure that those certification bodies are accredited by one or both of the following:

> (a) the supervisory authority which is competent pursuant to Article 55 or 56;

> (b) the national accreditation body named in accordance with Regulation (EC) No 765/2008 of the European Parliament and of the Council (20) in accordance with EN-ISO/IEC 17065/2012 and with the additional requirements established by the supervisory authority which is competent pursuant to Article 55 or 56.

2. Certification bodies referred to in paragraph 1 shall be accredited in accordance with that paragraph only where they have:

> (a) demonstrated their independence and expertise in relation to the subject-matter of the certification to the satisfaction of the competent supervisory authority;

> (b) undertaken to respect the criteria referred to in Article 42(5) and approved by the supervisory authority which is competent pursuant to Article 55 or 56 or by the Board pursuant to Article 63;

> (c) established procedures for the issuing, periodic review and withdrawal of data protection certification, seals and marks;

> (d) established procedures and structures to handle complaints about infringements of the certification or the manner in which the certification has been, or is being, implemented by the controller or processor, and to make those procedures and structures transparent to data subjects and the public; and

> (e) demonstrated, to the satisfaction of the competent supervisory authority, that their tasks and duties do not result in a conflict of interests.

3. The accreditation of certification bodies as referred to in paragraphs 1 and 2 of this Article shall take place on the basis of criteria approved by the supervisory authority which is competent pursuant to Article 55 or 56 or by the Board pursuant to Article 63. In the case of accreditation pursuant to point (b) of paragraph 1 of this Article, those requirements shall complement those envisaged in Regulation (EC) No 765/2008 and the technical rules that describe the methods and procedures of the certification bodies.

4. The certification bodies referred to in paragraph 1 shall be responsible for the proper assessment leading to the certification or the withdrawal of such certification without prejudice to the responsibility of the controller or processor for compliance with this Regulation. The accreditation shall be issued for a maximum period of five years and may be renewed on the same conditions provided that the certification body meets the requirements set out in this Article.

5.   The certification bodies referred to in paragraph 1 shall provide the competent supervisory authorities with the reasons for granting or withdrawing the requested certification.

6.   The requirements referred to in paragraph 3 of this Article and the criteria referred to in Article 42(5) shall be made public by the supervisory authority in an easily accessible form. The supervisory authorities shall also transmit those requirements and criteria to the Board. The Board shall collate all certification mechanisms and data protection seals in a register and shall make them publicly available by any appropriate means.

7.   Without prejudice to Chapter VIII, the competent supervisory authority or the national accreditation body shall revoke an accreditation of a certification body pursuant to paragraph 1 of this Article where the conditions for the accreditation are not, or are no longer, met or where actions taken by a certification body infringe this Regulation.

8.   The Commission shall be empowered to adopt delegated acts in accordance with Article 92 for the purpose of specifying the requirements to be taken into account for the data protection certification mechanisms referred to in Article 42(1).

9.   The Commission may adopt implementing acts laying down technical standards for certification mechanisms and data protection seals and marks, and mechanisms to promote and recognise those certification mechanisms, seals and marks. Those implementing acts shall be adopted in accordance with the examination procedure referred to in Article 93(2).

CHAPTER V: Transfers of personal data to third countries or international organisations

Article 44: General principle for transfers

Any transfer of personal data which are undergoing processing or are intended for processing after transfer to a third country or to an international organisation shall take place only if, subject to the other provisions of this Regulation, the conditions laid down in this Chapter are complied with by the controller and processor, including for onward transfers of personal data from the third country or an international organisation to another third country or to another international organisation. All provisions in this Chapter shall be applied in order to ensure that the level of protection of natural persons guaranteed by this Regulation is not undermined.

Article 45: Transfers on the basis of an adequacy decision

1.   A transfer of personal data to a third country or an international organisation may take place where the Commission has decided that the third country, a territory or one or more specified sectors within that third country, or the international organisation in question ensures an adequate level of protection. Such a transfer shall not require any specific authorisation.

2.   When assessing the adequacy of the level of protection, the Commission shall, in particular, take account of the following elements:

(a) the rule of law, respect for human rights and fundamental freedoms, relevant legislation, both general and sectoral, including concerning public security, defence, national security and criminal law and the access of public authorities to personal data, as well as the implementation of such legislation, data protection rules, professional rules and security measures, including rules for the onward transfer of personal data to another third country or international organisation which are complied with in that country or international organisation, case-law, as well as effective and enforceable data subject rights and effective administrative and judicial redress for the data subjects whose personal data are being transferred;

(b) the existence and effective functioning of one or more independent supervisory authorities in the third country or to which an international organisation is subject, with responsibility for ensuring and enforcing compliance with the data protection rules, including adequate enforcement powers, for assisting and advising the data subjects in exercising their rights and for cooperation with the supervisory authorities of the Member States; and

(c) the international commitments the third country or international organisation concerned has entered into, or other obligations arising from legally binding conventions or instruments as well as from its participation in multilateral or regional systems, in particular in relation to the protection of personal data.

3. The Commission, after assessing the adequacy of the level of protection, may decide, by means of implementing act, that a third country, a territory or one or more specified sectors within a third country, or an international organisation ensures an adequate level of protection within the meaning of paragraph 2 of this Article. The implementing act shall provide for a mechanism for a periodic review, at least every four years, which shall take into account all relevant developments in the third country or international organisation. The implementing act shall specify its territorial and sectoral application and, where applicable, identify the supervisory authority or authorities referred to in point (b) of paragraph 2 of this Article. The implementing act shall be adopted in accordance with the examination procedure referred to in Article 93(2).

4. The Commission shall, on an ongoing basis, monitor developments in third countries and international organisations that could affect the functioning of decisions adopted pursuant to paragraph 3 of this Article and decisions adopted on the basis of Article 25(6) of Directive 95/46/EC.

5. The Commission shall, where available information reveals, in particular following the review referred to in paragraph 3 of this Article, that a third country, a territory or one or more specified sectors within a third country, or an international organisation no longer ensures an adequate level of protection within the meaning of paragraph 2 of this Article, to the extent necessary, repeal, amend or suspend the decision referred to in paragraph 3 of this Article by means of implementing acts without retro-active effect. Those implementing acts shall be adopted in accordance with the examination procedure referred to in Article 93(2).

On duly justified imperative grounds of urgency, the Commission shall adopt immediately applicable implementing acts in accordance with the procedure referred to in Article 93(3).

6.   The Commission shall enter into consultations with the third country or international organisation with a view to remedying the situation giving rise to the decision made pursuant to paragraph 5.

7.   A decision pursuant to paragraph 5 of this Article is without prejudice to transfers of personal data to the third country, a territory or one or more specified sectors within that third country, or the international organisation in question pursuant to Articles 46 to 49.

8.   The Commission shall publish in the Official Journal of the European Union and on its website a list of the third countries, territories and specified sectors within a third country and international organisations for which it has decided that an adequate level of protection is or is no longer ensured.

9.   Decisions adopted by the Commission on the basis of Article 25(6) of Directive 95/46/EC shall remain in force until amended, replaced or repealed by a Commission Decision adopted in accordance with paragraph 3 or 5 of this Article.

Article 46: Transfers subject to appropriate safeguards

1.   In the absence of a decision pursuant to Article 45(3), a controller or processor may transfer personal data to a third country or an international organisation only if the controller or processor has provided appropriate safeguards, and on condition that enforceable data subject rights and effective legal remedies for data subjects are available.

2.   The appropriate safeguards referred to in paragraph 1 may be provided for, without requiring any specific authorisation from a supervisory authority, by:

   (a) a legally binding and enforceable instrument between public authorities or bodies;

   (b) binding corporate rules in accordance with Article 47;

   (c) standard data protection clauses adopted by the Commission in accordance with the examination procedure referred to in Article 93(2);

   (d) standard data protection clauses adopted by a supervisory authority and approved by the Commission pursuant to the examination procedure referred to in Article 93(2);

   (e) an approved code of conduct pursuant to Article 40 together with binding and enforceable commitments of the controller or processor in the third country to apply the appropriate safeguards, including as regards data subjects' rights; or

   (f) an approved certification mechanism pursuant to Article 42 together with binding and enforceable commitments of the controller or processor in the third country to apply the appropriate safeguards, including as regards data subjects' rights.

3.   Subject to the authorisation from the competent supervisory authority, the appropriate safeguards referred to in paragraph 1 may also be provided for, in particular, by:

   (a) contractual clauses between the controller or processor and the controller, processor or the recipient of the personal data in the third country or international organisation; or

(b) provisions to be inserted into administrative arrangements between public authorities or bodies which include enforceable and effective data subject rights.

4. The supervisory authority shall apply the consistency mechanism referred to in Article 63 in the cases referred to in paragraph 3 of this Article.

5. Authorisations by a Member State or supervisory authority on the basis of Article 26(2) of Directive 95/46/EC shall remain valid until amended, replaced or repealed, if necessary, by that supervisory authority. Decisions adopted by the Commission on the basis of Article 26(4) of Directive 95/46/EC shall remain in force until amended, replaced or repealed, if necessary, by a Commission Decision adopted in accordance with paragraph 2 of this Article.

Article 47: Binding corporate rules

1. The competent supervisory authority shall approve binding corporate rules in accordance with the consistency mechanism set out in Article 63, provided that they:

(a) are legally binding and apply to and are enforced by every member concerned of the group of undertakings, or group of enterprises engaged in a joint economic activity, including their employees;

(b) expressly confer enforceable rights on data subjects with regard to the processing of their personal data; and

(c) fulfil the requirements laid down in paragraph 2.

2. The binding corporate rules referred to in paragraph 1 shall specify at least:

(a) the structure and contact details of the group of undertakings, or group of enterprises engaged in a joint economic activity and of each of its members;

(b) the data transfers or set of transfers, including the categories of personal data, the type of processing and its purposes, the type of data subjects affected and the identification of the third country or countries in question;

(c) their legally binding nature, both internally and externally;

(d) the application of the general data protection principles, in particular purpose limitation, data minimisation, limited storage periods, data quality, data protection by design and by default, legal basis for processing, processing of special categories of personal data, measures to ensure data security, and the requirements in respect of onward transfers to bodies not bound by the binding corporate rules;

(e) the rights of data subjects in regard to processing and the means to exercise those rights, including the right not to be subject to decisions based solely on automated processing, including profiling in accordance with Article 22, the right to lodge a complaint with the competent supervisory authority and before the competent courts of the Member States in accordance with Article 79, and to obtain redress and, where appropriate, compensation for a breach of the binding corporate rules;

(f) the acceptance by the controller or processor established on the territory of a Member State of liability for any breaches of the binding corporate rules by any member concerned not established in the Union; the controller or the processor shall be exempt from that liability, in whole or in part, only if it proves that that member is not responsible for the event giving rise to the damage;

(g) how the information on the binding corporate rules, in particular on the provisions referred to in points (d), (e) and (f) of this paragraph is provided to the data subjects in addition to Articles 13 and 14;

(h) the tasks of any data protection officer designated in accordance with Article 37 or any other person or entity in charge of the monitoring compliance with the binding corporate rules within the group of undertakings, or group of enterprises engaged in a joint economic activity, as well as monitoring training and complaint-handling;

(i) the complaint procedures;

(j) the mechanisms within the group of undertakings, or group of enterprises engaged in a joint economic activity for ensuring the verification of compliance with the binding corporate rules. Such mechanisms shall include data protection audits and methods for ensuring corrective actions to protect the rights of the data subject. Results of such verification should be communicated to the person or entity referred to in point (h) and to the board of the controlling undertaking of a group of undertakings, or of the group of enterprises engaged in a joint economic activity, and should be available upon request to the competent supervisory authority;

(k) the mechanisms for reporting and recording changes to the rules and reporting those changes to the supervisory authority;

(l) the cooperation mechanism with the supervisory authority to ensure compliance by any member of the group of undertakings, or group of enterprises engaged in a joint economic activity, in particular by making available to the supervisory authority the results of verifications of the measures referred to in point (j);

(m) the mechanisms for reporting to the competent supervisory authority any legal requirements to which a member of the group of undertakings, or group of enterprises engaged in a joint economic activity is subject in a third country which are likely to have a substantial adverse effect on the guarantees provided by the binding corporate rules; and

(n) the appropriate data protection training to personnel having permanent or regular access to personal data.

3. The Commission may specify the format and procedures for the exchange of information between controllers, processors and supervisory authorities for binding corporate rules within the meaning of this Article. Those implementing acts shall be adopted in accordance with the examination procedure set out in Article 93(2).

Article 48: Transfers or disclosures not authorised by Union law

Any judgment of a court or tribunal and any decision of an administrative authority of a third country requiring a controller or processor to transfer or disclose personal data may only be recognised or enforceable in any manner if based on an international agreement, such as a mutual legal assistance treaty, in force between the requesting third country and the Union or a Member State, without prejudice to other grounds for transfer pursuant to this Chapter.

Article 49: Derogations for specific situations

1. In the absence of an adequacy decision pursuant to Article 45(3), or of appropriate safeguards pursuant to Article 46, including binding corporate rules, a transfer or a set of transfers of personal data to a third country or an international organisation shall take place only on one of the following conditions:

(a) the data subject has explicitly consented to the proposed transfer, after having been informed of the possible risks of such transfers for the data subject due to the absence of an adequacy decision and appropriate safeguards;

(b) the transfer is necessary for the performance of a contract between the data subject and the controller or the implementation of pre-contractual measures taken at the data subject's request;

(c) the transfer is necessary for the conclusion or performance of a contract concluded in the interest of the data subject between the controller and another natural or legal person;

(d) the transfer is necessary for important reasons of public interest;

(e) the transfer is necessary for the establishment, exercise or defence of legal claims;

(f) the transfer is necessary in order to protect the vital interests of the data subject or of other persons, where the data subject is physically or legally incapable of giving consent;

(g) the transfer is made from a register which according to Union or Member State law is intended to provide information to the public and which is open to consultation either by the public in general or by any person who can demonstrate a legitimate interest, but only to the extent that the conditions laid down by Union or Member State law for consultation are fulfilled in the particular case.

Where a transfer could not be based on a provision in Article 45 or 46, including the provisions on binding corporate rules, and none of the derogations for a specific situation referred to in the first subparagraph of this paragraph is applicable, a transfer to a third country or an international organisation may take place only if the transfer is not repetitive, concerns only a limited number of data subjects, is necessary for the purposes of compelling legitimate interests pursued by the controller which are not overridden by the interests or rights and freedoms of the data subject, and the controller has assessed all the circumstances surrounding the data transfer and has on the basis of that assessment provided suitable safeguards with regard to the protection of personal data. The controller shall inform the supervisory authority of the transfer. The controller shall, in addition to providing the information referred to in Articles 13 and 14, inform the data subject of the transfer and on the compelling legitimate interests pursued.

2.   A transfer pursuant to point (g) of the first subparagraph of paragraph 1 shall not involve the entirety of the personal data or entire categories of the personal data contained in the register. Where the register is intended for consultation by persons having a legitimate interest, the transfer shall be made only at the request of those persons or if they are to be the recipients.

3.   Points (a), (b) and (c) of the first subparagraph of paragraph 1 and the second subparagraph thereof shall not apply to activities carried out by public authorities in the exercise of their public powers.

4.   The public interest referred to in point (d) of the first subparagraph of paragraph 1 shall be recognised in Union law or in the law of the Member State to which the controller is subject.

5.   In the absence of an adequacy decision, Union or Member State law may, for important reasons of public interest, expressly set limits to the transfer of specific categories of personal data to a third country or an international organisation. Member States shall notify such provisions to the Commission.

6.   The controller or processor shall document the assessment as well as the suitable safeguards referred to in the second subparagraph of paragraph 1 of this Article in the records referred to in Article 30.

Article 50: International cooperation for the protection of personal data

In relation to third countries and international organisations, the Commission and supervisory authorities shall take appropriate steps to:

(a)   develop international cooperation mechanisms to facilitate the effective enforcement of legislation for the protection of personal data;

(b)   provide international mutual assistance in the enforcement of legislation for the protection of personal data, including through notification, complaint referral, investigative assistance and information exchange, subject to appropriate safeguards for the protection of personal data and other fundamental rights and freedoms;

(c)   engage relevant stakeholders in discussion and activities aimed at furthering international cooperation in the enforcement of legislation for the protection of personal data;

(d)   promote the exchange and documentation of personal data protection legislation and practice, including on jurisdictional conflicts with third countries.

CHAPTER VI: Independent supervisory authorities

Section 1: Independent status

Article 51: Supervisory authority

1.   Each Member State shall provide for one or more independent public authorities to be responsible for monitoring the application of this Regulation, in order to protect the

fundamental rights and freedoms of natural persons in relation to processing and to facilitate the free flow of personal data within the Union ('supervisory authority').

2. Each supervisory authority shall contribute to the consistent application of this Regulation throughout the Union. For that purpose, the supervisory authorities shall cooperate with each other and the Commission in accordance with Chapter VII.

3. Where more than one supervisory authority is established in a Member State, that Member State shall designate the supervisory authority which is to represent those authorities in the Board and shall set out the mechanism to ensure compliance by the other authorities with the rules relating to the consistency mechanism referred to in Article 63.

4. Each Member State shall notify to the Commission the provisions of its law which it adopts pursuant to this Chapter, by 25 May 2018 and, without delay, any subsequent amendment affecting them.

Article 52: Independence

1. Each supervisory authority shall act with complete independence in performing its tasks and exercising its powers in accordance with this Regulation.

2. The member or members of each supervisory authority shall, in the performance of their tasks and exercise of their powers in accordance with this Regulation, remain free from external influence, whether direct or indirect, and shall neither seek nor take instructions from anybody.

3. Member or members of each supervisory authority shall refrain from any action incompatible with their duties and shall not, during their term of office, engage in any incompatible occupation, whether gainful or not.

4. Each Member State shall ensure that each supervisory authority is provided with the human, technical and financial resources, premises and infrastructure necessary for the effective performance of its tasks and exercise of its powers, including those to be carried out in the context of mutual assistance, cooperation and participation in the Board.

5. Each Member State shall ensure that each supervisory authority chooses and has its own staff which shall be subject to the exclusive direction of the member or members of the supervisory authority concerned.

6. Each Member State shall ensure that each supervisory authority is subject to financial control which does not affect its independence and that it has separate, public annual budgets, which may be part of the overall state or national budget.

Article 53: General conditions for the members of the supervisory authority

1. Member States shall provide for each member of their supervisory authorities to be appointed by means of a transparent procedure by:

—

their parliament;

—

their government;

—

their head of State; or

—

an independent body entrusted with the appointment under Member State law.

2.   Each member shall have the qualifications, experience and skills, in particular in the area of the protection of personal data, required to perform its duties and exercise its powers.

3.   The duties of a member shall end in the event of the expiry of the term of office, resignation or compulsory retirement, in accordance with the law of the Member State concerned.

4.   A member shall be dismissed only in cases of serious misconduct or if the member no longer fulfils the conditions required for the performance of the duties.

Article 54: Rules on the establishment of the supervisory authority

1.   Each Member State shall provide by law for all of the following:

(a) the establishment of each supervisory authority;

(b) the qualifications and eligibility conditions required to be appointed as member of each supervisory authority;

(c) the rules and procedures for the appointment of the member or members of each supervisory authority;

(d) the duration of the term of the member or members of each supervisory authority of no less than four years, except for the first appointment after 24 May 2016, part of which may take place for a shorter period where that is necessary to protect the independence of the supervisory authority by means of a staggered appointment procedure;

(e) whether and, if so, for how many terms the member or members of each supervisory authority is eligible for reappointment;

(f) the conditions governing the obligations of the member or members and staff of each supervisory authority, prohibitions on actions, occupations and benefits incompatible therewith during and after the term of office and rules governing the cessation of employment.

2.   The member or members and the staff of each supervisory authority shall, in accordance with Union or Member State law, be subject to a duty of professional secrecy both during and after their term of office, with regard to any confidential information which has come to their knowledge in the course of the performance of their tasks or exercise of their powers. During their term of office, that duty of professional secrecy shall in particular apply to reporting by natural persons of infringements of this Regulation.

Recent Developments
EU General Data Protection Regulation

Section 2: Competence, tasks and powers

Article 55: Competence

1. Each supervisory authority shall be competent for the performance of the tasks assigned to and the exercise of the powers conferred on it in accordance with this Regulation on the territory of its own Member State.

2. Where processing is carried out by public authorities or private bodies acting on the basis of point (c) or (e) of Article 6(1), the supervisory authority of the Member State concerned shall be competent. In such cases Article 56 does not apply.

3. Supervisory authorities shall not be competent to supervise processing operations of courts acting in their judicial capacity.

Article 56: Competence of the lead supervisory authority

1. Without prejudice to Article 55, the supervisory authority of the main establishment or of the single establishment of the controller or processor shall be competent to act as lead supervisory authority for the cross-border processing carried out by that controller or processor in accordance with the procedure provided in Article 60.

2. By derogation from paragraph 1, each supervisory authority shall be competent to handle a complaint lodged with it or a possible infringement of this Regulation, if the subject matter relates only to an establishment in its Member State or substantially affects data subjects only in its Member State.

3. In the cases referred to in paragraph 2 of this Article, the supervisory authority shall inform the lead supervisory authority without delay on that matter. Within a period of three weeks after being informed the lead supervisory authority shall decide whether or not it will handle the case in accordance with the procedure provided in Article 60, taking into account whether or not there is an establishment of the controller or processor in the Member State of which the supervisory authority informed it.

4. Where the lead supervisory authority decides to handle the case, the procedure provided in Article 60 shall apply. The supervisory authority which informed the lead supervisory authority may submit to the lead supervisory authority a draft for a decision. The lead supervisory authority shall take utmost account of that draft when preparing the draft decision referred to in Article 60(3).

5. Where the lead supervisory authority decides not to handle the case, the supervisory authority which informed the lead supervisory authority shall handle it according to Articles 61 and 62.

6. The lead supervisory authority shall be the sole interlocutor of the controller or processor for the cross-border processing carried out by that controller or processor.

Article 57: Tasks

1. Without prejudice to other tasks set out under this Regulation, each supervisory authority shall on its territory:

(a) monitor and enforce the application of this Regulation;

(b) promote public awareness and understanding of the risks, rules, safeguards and rights in relation to processing. Activities addressed specifically to children shall receive specific attention;

(c) advise, in accordance with Member State law, the national parliament, the government, and other institutions and bodies on legislative and administrative measures relating to the protection of natural persons' rights and freedoms with regard to processing;

(d) promote the awareness of controllers and processors of their obligations under this Regulation;

(e) upon request, provide information to any data subject concerning the exercise of their rights under this Regulation and, if appropriate, cooperate with the supervisory authorities in other Member States to that end;

(f) handle complaints lodged by a data subject, or by a body, organisation or association in accordance with Article 80, and investigate, to the extent appropriate, the subject matter of the complaint and inform the complainant of the progress and the outcome of the investigation within a reasonable period, in particular if further investigation or coordination with another supervisory authority is necessary;

(g) cooperate with, including sharing information and provide mutual assistance to, other supervisory authorities with a view to ensuring the consistency of application and enforcement of this Regulation;

(h) conduct investigations on the application of this Regulation, including on the basis of information received from another supervisory authority or other public authority;

(i) monitor relevant developments, insofar as they have an impact on the protection of personal data, in particular the development of information and communication technologies and commercial practices;

(j) adopt standard contractual clauses referred to in Article 28(8) and in point (d) of Article 46(2);

(k) establish and maintain a list in relation to the requirement for data protection impact assessment pursuant to Article 35(4);

(l) give advice on the processing operations referred to in Article 36(2);

(m) encourage the drawing up of codes of conduct pursuant to Article 40(1) and provide an opinion and approve such codes of conduct which provide sufficient safeguards, pursuant to Article 40(5);

(n) encourage the establishment of data protection certification mechanisms and of data protection seals and marks pursuant to Article 42(1), and approve the criteria of certification pursuant to Article 42(5);

(o) where applicable, carry out a periodic review of certifications issued in accordance with Article 42(7);

(p) draft and publish the criteria for accreditation of a body for monitoring codes of conduct pursuant to Article 41 and of a certification body pursuant to Article 43;

(q) conduct the accreditation of a body for monitoring codes of conduct pursuant to Article 41 and of a certification body pursuant to Article 43;

(r) authorise contractual clauses and provisions referred to in Article 46(3);

(s) approve binding corporate rules pursuant to Article 47;

(t) contribute to the activities of the Board;

(u) keep internal records of infringements of this Regulation and of measures taken in accordance with Article 58(2); and

(v) fulfil any other tasks related to the protection of personal data.

2.   Each supervisory authority shall facilitate the submission of complaints referred to in point (f) of paragraph 1 by measures such as a complaint submission form which can also be completed electronically, without excluding other means of communication.

3.   The performance of the tasks of each supervisory authority shall be free of charge for the data subject and, where applicable, for the data protection officer.

4.   Where requests are manifestly unfounded or excessive, in particular because of their repetitive character, the supervisory authority may charge a reasonable fee based on administrative costs, or refuse to act on the request. The supervisory authority shall bear the burden of demonstrating the manifestly unfounded or excessive character of the request.

Article 58: Powers

1.   Each supervisory authority shall have all of the following investigative powers:

(a) to order the controller and the processor, and, where applicable, the controller's or the processor's representative to provide any information it requires for the performance of its tasks;

(b) to carry out investigations in the form of data protection audits;

(c) to carry out a review on certifications issued pursuant to Article 42(7);

(d) to notify the controller or the processor of an alleged infringement of this Regulation;

(e) to obtain, from the controller and the processor, access to all personal data and to all information necessary for the performance of its tasks;

(f) to obtain access to any premises of the controller and the processor, including to any data processing equipment and means, in accordance with Union or Member State procedural law.

2.   Each supervisory authority shall have all of the following corrective powers:

(a) to issue warnings to a controller or processor that intended processing operations are likely to infringe provisions of this Regulation;

(b) to issue reprimands to a controller or a processor where processing operations have infringed provisions of this Regulation;

(c) to order the controller or the processor to comply with the data subject's requests to exercise his or her rights pursuant to this Regulation;

(d) to order the controller or processor to bring processing operations into compliance with the provisions of this Regulation, where appropriate, in a specified manner and within a specified period;

(e) to order the controller to communicate a personal data breach to the data subject;

(f) to impose a temporary or definitive limitation including a ban on processing;

(g) to order the rectification or erasure of personal data or restriction of processing pursuant to Articles 16, 17 and 18 and the notification of such actions to recipients to whom the personal data have been disclosed pursuant to Article 17(2) and Article 19;

(h) to withdraw a certification or to order the certification body to withdraw a certification issued pursuant to Articles 42 and 43, or to order the certification body not to issue certification if the requirements for the certification are not or are no longer met;

(i) to impose an administrative fine pursuant to Article 83, in addition to, or instead of measures referred to in this paragraph, depending on the circumstances of each individual case;

(j) to order the suspension of data flows to a recipient in a third country or to an international organisation.

3.   Each supervisory authority shall have all of the following authorisation and advisory powers:

(a) to advise the controller in accordance with the prior consultation procedure referred to in Article 36;

(b) to issue, on its own initiative or on request, opinions to the national parliament, the Member State government or, in accordance with Member State law, to other institutions and bodies as well as to the public on any issue related to the protection of personal data;

(c) to authorise processing referred to in Article 36(5), if the law of the Member State requires such prior authorisation;

(d) to issue an opinion and approve draft codes of conduct pursuant to Article 40(5);

(e) to accredit certification bodies pursuant to Article 43;

(f) to issue certifications and approve criteria of certification in accordance with Article 42(5);

(g) to adopt standard data protection clauses referred to in Article 28(8) and in point (d) of Article 46(2);

(h) to authorise contractual clauses referred to in point (a) of Article 46(3);

(i) to authorise administrative arrangements referred to in point (b) of Article 46(3);

(j) to approve binding corporate rules pursuant to Article 47.

4. The exercise of the powers conferred on the supervisory authority pursuant to this Article shall be subject to appropriate safeguards, including effective judicial remedy and due process, set out in Union and Member State law in accordance with the Charter.

5. Each Member State shall provide by law that its supervisory authority shall have the power to bring infringements of this Regulation to the attention of the judicial authorities and where appropriate, to commence or engage otherwise in legal proceedings, in order to enforce the provisions of this Regulation.

6. Each Member State may provide by law that its supervisory authority shall have additional powers to those referred to in paragraphs 1, 2 and 3. The exercise of those powers shall not impair the effective operation of Chapter VII.

Article 59: Activity reports

Each supervisory authority shall draw up an annual report on its activities, which may include a list of types of infringement notified and types of measures taken in accordance with Article 58(2). Those reports shall be transmitted to the national parliament, the government and other authorities as designated by Member State law. They shall be made available to the public, to the Commission and to the Board.

CHAPTER VII: Cooperation and consistency

Section 1: Cooperation

Article 60: Cooperation between the lead supervisory authority and the other supervisory authorities concerned

1. The lead supervisory authority shall cooperate with the other supervisory authorities concerned in accordance with this Article in an endeavour to reach consensus. The lead supervisory authority and the supervisory authorities concerned shall exchange all relevant information with each other.

2. The lead supervisory authority may request at any time other supervisory authorities concerned to provide mutual assistance pursuant to Article 61 and may conduct joint operations pursuant to Article 62, in particular for carrying out investigations or for monitoring the implementation of a measure concerning a controller or processor established in another Member State.

3. The lead supervisory authority shall, without delay, communicate the relevant information on the matter to the other supervisory authorities concerned. It shall without delay submit a draft decision to the other supervisory authorities concerned for their opinion and take due account of their views.

4. Where any of the other supervisory authorities concerned within a period of four weeks after having been consulted in accordance with paragraph 3 of this Article, expresses a relevant and reasoned objection to the draft decision, the lead supervisory authority shall, if it does not follow the relevant and reasoned objection or is of the opinion that the objection is

not relevant or reasoned, submit the matter to the consistency mechanism referred to in Article 63.

5. Where the lead supervisory authority intends to follow the relevant and reasoned objection made, it shall submit to the other supervisory authorities concerned a revised draft decision for their opinion. That revised draft decision shall be subject to the procedure referred to in paragraph 4 within a period of two weeks.

6. Where none of the other supervisory authorities concerned has objected to the draft decision submitted by the lead supervisory authority within the period referred to in paragraphs 4 and 5, the lead supervisory authority and the supervisory authorities concerned shall be deemed to be in agreement with that draft decision and shall be bound by it.

7. The lead supervisory authority shall adopt and notify the decision to the main establishment or single establishment of the controller or processor, as the case may be and inform the other supervisory authorities concerned and the Board of the decision in question, including a summary of the relevant facts and grounds. The supervisory authority with which a complaint has been lodged shall inform the complainant on the decision.

8. By derogation from paragraph 7, where a complaint is dismissed or rejected, the supervisory authority with which the complaint was lodged shall adopt the decision and notify it to the complainant and shall inform the controller thereof.

9. Where the lead supervisory authority and the supervisory authorities concerned agree to dismiss or reject parts of a complaint and to act on other parts of that complaint, a separate decision shall be adopted for each of those parts of the matter. The lead supervisory authority shall adopt the decision for the part concerning actions in relation to the controller, shall notify it to the main establishment or single establishment of the controller or processor on the territory of its Member State and shall inform the complainant thereof, while the supervisory authority of the complainant shall adopt the decision for the part concerning dismissal or rejection of that complaint, and shall notify it to that complainant and shall inform the controller or processor thereof.

10. After being notified of the decision of the lead supervisory authority pursuant to paragraphs 7 and 9, the controller or processor shall take the necessary measures to ensure compliance with the decision as regards processing activities in the context of all its establishments in the Union. The controller or processor shall notify the measures taken for complying with the decision to the lead supervisory authority, which shall inform the other supervisory authorities concerned.

11. Where, in exceptional circumstances, a supervisory authority concerned has reasons to consider that there is an urgent need to act in order to protect the interests of data subjects, the urgency procedure referred to in Article 66 shall apply.

12. The lead supervisory authority and the other supervisory authorities concerned shall supply the information required under this Article to each other by electronic means, using a standardised format.

Article 61: Mutual assistance

1.   Supervisory authorities shall provide each other with relevant information and mutual assistance in order to implement and apply this Regulation in a consistent manner, and shall put in place measures for effective cooperation with one another. Mutual assistance shall cover, in particular, information requests and supervisory measures, such as requests to carry out prior authorisations and consultations, inspections and investigations.

2.   Each supervisory authority shall take all appropriate measures required to reply to a request of another supervisory authority without undue delay and no later than one month after receiving the request. Such measures may include, in particular, the transmission of relevant information on the conduct of an investigation.

3.   Requests for assistance shall contain all the necessary information, including the purpose of and reasons for the request. Information exchanged shall be used only for the purpose for which it was requested.

4.   The requested supervisory authority shall not refuse to comply with the request unless:

> (a) it is not competent for the subject-matter of the request or for the measures it is requested to execute; or
>
> (b) compliance with the request would infringe this Regulation or Union or Member State law to which the supervisory authority receiving the request is subject.

5.   The requested supervisory authority shall inform the requesting supervisory authority of the results or, as the case may be, of the progress of the measures taken in order to respond to the request. The requested supervisory authority shall provide reasons for any refusal to comply with a request pursuant to paragraph 4.

6.   Requested supervisory authorities shall, as a rule, supply the information requested by other supervisory authorities by electronic means, using a standardised format.

7.   Requested supervisory authorities shall not charge a fee for any action taken by them pursuant to a request for mutual assistance. Supervisory authorities may agree on rules to indemnify each other for specific expenditure arising from the provision of mutual assistance in exceptional circumstances.

8.   Where a supervisory authority does not provide the information referred to in paragraph 5 of this Article within one month of receiving the request of another supervisory authority, the requesting supervisory authority may adopt a provisional measure on the territory of its Member State in accordance with Article 55(1). In that case, the urgent need to act under Article 66(1) shall be presumed to be met and require an urgent binding decision from the Board pursuant to Article 66(2).

9.   The Commission may, by means of implementing acts, specify the format and procedures for mutual assistance referred to in this Article and the arrangements for the exchange of information by electronic means between supervisory authorities, and between supervisory authorities and the Board, in particular the standardised format referred to in paragraph 6 of this Article. Those implementing acts shall be adopted in accordance with the examination procedure referred to in Article 93(2).

Article 62: Joint operations of supervisory authorities

1.   The supervisory authorities shall, where appropriate, conduct joint operations including joint investigations and joint enforcement measures in which members or staff of the supervisory authorities of other Member States are involved.

2.   Where the controller or processor has establishments in several Member States or where a significant number of data subjects in more than one Member State are likely to be substantially affected by processing operations, a supervisory authority of each of those Member States shall have the right to participate in joint operations. The supervisory authority which is competent pursuant to Article 56(1) or (4) shall invite the supervisory authority of each of those Member States to take part in the joint operations and shall respond without delay to the request of a supervisory authority to participate.

3.   A supervisory authority may, in accordance with Member State law, and with the seconding supervisory authority's authorisation, confer powers, including investigative powers on the seconding supervisory authority's members or staff involved in joint operations or, in so far as the law of the Member State of the host supervisory authority permits, allow the seconding supervisory authority's members or staff to exercise their investigative powers in accordance with the law of the Member State of the seconding supervisory authority. Such investigative powers may be exercised only under the guidance and in the presence of members or staff of the host supervisory authority. The seconding supervisory authority's members or staff shall be subject to the Member State law of the host supervisory authority.

4.   Where, in accordance with paragraph 1, staff of a seconding supervisory authority operate in another Member State, the Member State of the host supervisory authority shall assume responsibility for their actions, including liability, for any damage caused by them during their operations, in accordance with the law of the Member State in whose territory they are operating.

5.   The Member State in whose territory the damage was caused shall make good such damage under the conditions applicable to damage caused by its own staff. The Member State of the seconding supervisory authority whose staff has caused damage to any person in the territory of another Member State shall reimburse that other Member State in full any sums it has paid to the persons entitled on their behalf.

6.   Without prejudice to the exercise of its rights vis-à-vis third parties and with the exception of paragraph 5, each Member State shall refrain, in the case provided for in paragraph 1, from requesting reimbursement from another Member State in relation to damage referred to in paragraph 4.

7.   Where a joint operation is intended and a supervisory authority does not, within one month, comply with the obligation laid down in the second sentence of paragraph 2 of this Article, the other supervisory authorities may adopt a provisional measure on the territory of its Member State in accordance with Article 55. In that case, the urgent need to act under Article 66(1) shall be presumed to be met and require an opinion or an urgent binding decision from the Board pursuant to Article 66(2).

Section 2: Consistency

Article 63: Consistency mechanism

In order to contribute to the consistent application of this Regulation throughout the Union, the supervisory authorities shall cooperate with each other and, where relevant, with the Commission, through the consistency mechanism as set out in this Section.

Article 64: Opinion of the Board

1.   The Board shall issue an opinion where a competent supervisory authority intends to adopt any of the measures below. To that end, the competent supervisory authority shall communicate the draft decision to the Board, when it:

   (a) aims to adopt a list of the processing operations subject to the requirement for a data protection impact assessment pursuant to Article 35(4);

   (b) concerns a matter pursuant to Article 40(7) whether a draft code of conduct or an amendment or extension to a code of conduct complies with this Regulation;

   (c) aims to approve the criteria for accreditation of a body pursuant to Article 41(3) or a certification body pursuant to Article 43(3);

   (d) aims to determine standard data protection clauses referred to in point (d) of Article 46(2) and in Article 28(8);

   (e) aims to authorise contractual clauses referred to in point (a) of Article 46(3); or

   (f) aims to approve binding corporate rules within the meaning of Article 47.

2.   Any supervisory authority, the Chair of the Board or the Commission may request that any matter of general application or producing effects in more than one Member State be examined by the Board with a view to obtaining an opinion, in particular where a competent supervisory authority does not comply with the obligations for mutual assistance in accordance with Article 61 or for joint operations in accordance with Article 62.

3.   In the cases referred to in paragraphs 1 and 2, the Board shall issue an opinion on the matter submitted to it provided that it has not already issued an opinion on the same matter. That opinion shall be adopted within eight weeks by simple majority of the members of the Board. That period may be extended by a further six weeks, taking into account the complexity of the subject matter. Regarding the draft decision referred to in paragraph 1 circulated to the members of the Board in accordance with paragraph 5, a member which has not objected within a reasonable period indicated by the Chair, shall be deemed to be in agreement with the draft decision.

4.   Supervisory authorities and the Commission shall, without undue delay, communicate by electronic means to the Board, using a standardised format any relevant information, including as the case may be a summary of the facts, the draft decision, the grounds which make the enactment of such measure necessary, and the views of other supervisory authorities concerned.

5.   The Chair of the Board shall, without undue, delay inform by electronic means:

(a) the members of the Board and the Commission of any relevant information which has been communicated to it using a standardised format. The secretariat of the Board shall, where necessary, provide translations of relevant information; and

(b) the supervisory authority referred to, as the case may be, in paragraphs 1 and 2, and the Commission of the opinion and make it public.

6.   The competent supervisory authority shall not adopt its draft decision referred to in paragraph 1 within the period referred to in paragraph 3.

7.   The supervisory authority referred to in paragraph 1 shall take utmost account of the opinion of the Board and shall, within two weeks after receiving the opinion, communicate to the Chair of the Board by electronic means whether it will maintain or amend its draft decision and, if any, the amended draft decision, using a standardised format.

8.   Where the supervisory authority concerned informs the Chair of the Board within the period referred to in paragraph 7 of this Article that it does not intend to follow the opinion of the Board, in whole or in part, providing the relevant grounds, Article 65(1) shall apply.

Article 65: Dispute resolution by the Board

1.   In order to ensure the correct and consistent application of this Regulation in individual cases, the Board shall adopt a binding decision in the following cases:

(a) where, in a case referred to in Article 60(4), a supervisory authority concerned has raised a relevant and reasoned objection to a draft decision of the lead authority or the lead authority has rejected such an objection as being not relevant or reasoned. The binding decision shall concern all the matters which are the subject of the relevant and reasoned objection, in particular whether there is an infringement of this Regulation;

(b) where there are conflicting views on which of the supervisory authorities concerned is competent for the main establishment;

(c) where a competent supervisory authority does not request the opinion of the Board in the cases referred to in Article 64(1), or does not follow the opinion of the Board issued under Article 64. In that case, any supervisory authority concerned or the Commission may communicate the matter to the Board.

2.   The decision referred to in paragraph 1 shall be adopted within one month from the referral of the subject-matter by a two-thirds majority of the members of the Board. That period may be extended by a further month on account of the complexity of the subject-matter. The decision referred to in paragraph 1 shall be reasoned and addressed to the lead supervisory authority and all the supervisory authorities concerned and binding on them.

3.   Where the Board has been unable to adopt a decision within the periods referred to in paragraph 2, it shall adopt its decision within two weeks following the expiration of the second month referred to in paragraph 2 by a simple majority of the members of the Board. Where the members of the Board are split, the decision shall by adopted by the vote of its Chair.

4.   The supervisory authorities concerned shall not adopt a decision on the subject matter submitted to the Board under paragraph 1 during the periods referred to in paragraphs 2 and 3.

5.   The Chair of the Board shall notify, without undue delay, the decision referred to in paragraph 1 to the supervisory authorities concerned. It shall inform the Commission thereof. The decision shall be published on the website of the Board without delay after the supervisory authority has notified the final decision referred to in paragraph 6.

6.   The lead supervisory authority or, as the case may be, the supervisory authority with which the complaint has been lodged shall adopt its final decision on the basis of the decision referred to in paragraph 1 of this Article, without undue delay and at the latest by one month after the Board has notified its decision. The lead supervisory authority or, as the case may be, the supervisory authority with which the complaint has been lodged, shall inform the Board of the date when its final decision is notified respectively to the controller or the processor and to the data subject. The final decision of the supervisory authorities concerned shall be adopted under the terms of Article 60(7), (8) and (9). The final decision shall refer to the decision referred to in paragraph 1 of this Article and shall specify that the decision referred to in that paragraph will be published on the website of the Board in accordance with paragraph 5 of this Article. The final decision shall attach the decision referred to in paragraph 1 of this Article.

Article 66: Urgency procedure

1.   In exceptional circumstances, where a supervisory authority concerned considers that there is an urgent need to act in order to protect the rights and freedoms of data subjects, it may, by way of derogation from the consistency mechanism referred to in Articles 63, 64 and 65 or the procedure referred to in Article 60, immediately adopt provisional measures intended to produce legal effects on its own territory with a specified period of validity which shall not exceed three months. The supervisory authority shall, without delay, communicate those measures and the reasons for adopting them to the other supervisory authorities concerned, to the Board and to the Commission.

2.   Where a supervisory authority has taken a measure pursuant to paragraph 1 and considers that final measures need urgently be adopted, it may request an urgent opinion or an urgent binding decision from the Board, giving reasons for requesting such opinion or decision.

3.   Any supervisory authority may request an urgent opinion or an urgent binding decision, as the case may be, from the Board where a competent supervisory authority has not taken an appropriate measure in a situation where there is an urgent need to act, in order to protect the rights and freedoms of data subjects, giving reasons for requesting such opinion or decision, including for the urgent need to act.

4.   By derogation from Article 64(3) and Article 65(2), an urgent opinion or an urgent binding decision referred to in paragraphs 2 and 3 of this Article shall be adopted within two weeks by simple majority of the members of the Board.

Article 67: Exchange of information

The Commission may adopt implementing acts of general scope in order to specify the arrangements for the exchange of information by electronic means between supervisory authorities, and between supervisory authorities and the Board, in particular the standardised format referred to in Article 64.

Those implementing acts shall be adopted in accordance with the examination procedure referred to in Article 93(2).

Section 3: European data protection board

Article 68: European Data Protection Board

1. The European Data Protection Board (the 'Board') is hereby established as a body of the Union and shall have legal personality.

2. The Board shall be represented by its Chair.

3. The Board shall be composed of the head of one supervisory authority of each Member State and of the European Data Protection Supervisor, or their respective representatives.

4.   Where in a Member State more than one supervisory authority is responsible for monitoring the application of the provisions pursuant to this Regulation, a joint representative shall be appointed in accordance with that Member State's law.

5.   The Commission shall have the right to participate in the activities and meetings of the Board without voting right. The Commission shall designate a representative. The Chair of the Board shall communicate to the Commission the activities of the Board.

6.   In the cases referred to in Article 65, the European Data Protection Supervisor shall have voting rights only on decisions which concern principles and rules applicable to the Union institutions, bodies, offices and agencies which correspond in substance to those of this Regulation.

Article 69: Independence

1.   The Board shall act independently when performing its tasks or exercising its powers pursuant to Articles 70 and 71.

2.   Without prejudice to requests by the Commission referred to in point (b) of Article 70(1) and in Article 70(2), the Board shall, in the performance of its tasks or the exercise of its powers, neither seek nor take instructions from anybody.

Article 70: Tasks of the Board

1.   The Board shall ensure the consistent application of this Regulation. To that end, the Board shall, on its own initiative or, where relevant, at the request of the Commission, in particular:

(a) monitor and ensure the correct application of this Regulation in the cases provided for in Articles 64 and 65 without prejudice to the tasks of national supervisory authorities;

(b) advise the Commission on any issue related to the protection of personal data in the Union, including on any proposed amendment of this Regulation;

(c) advise the Commission on the format and procedures for the exchange of information between controllers, processors and supervisory authorities for binding corporate rules;

(d) issue guidelines, recommendations, and best practices on procedures for erasing links, copies or replications of personal data from publicly available communication services as referred to in Article 17(2);

(e) examine, on its own initiative, on request of one of its members or on request of the Commission, any question covering the application of this Regulation and issue guidelines, recommendations and best practices in order to encourage consistent application of this Regulation;

(f) issue guidelines, recommendations and best practices in accordance with point (e) of this paragraph for further specifying the criteria and conditions for decisions based on profiling pursuant to Article 22(2);

(g) issue guidelines, recommendations and best practices in accordance with point (e) of this paragraph for establishing the personal data breaches and determining the undue delay referred to in Article 33(1) and (2) and for the particular circumstances in which a controller or a processor is required to notify the personal data breach;

(h) issue guidelines, recommendations and best practices in accordance with point (e) of this paragraph as to the circumstances in which a personal data breach is likely to result in a high risk to the rights and freedoms of the natural persons referred to in Article 34(1).

(i) issue guidelines, recommendations and best practices in accordance with point (e) of this paragraph for the purpose of further specifying the criteria and requirements for personal data transfers based on binding corporate rules adhered to by controllers and binding corporate rules adhered to by processors and on further necessary requirements to ensure the protection of personal data of the data subjects concerned referred to in Article 47;

(j) issue guidelines, recommendations and best practices in accordance with point (e) of this paragraph for the purpose of further specifying the criteria and requirements for the personal data transfers on the basis of Article 49(1);

(k) draw up guidelines for supervisory authorities concerning the application of measures referred to in Article 58(1), (2) and (3) and the setting of administrative fines pursuant to Article 83;

(l) review the practical application of the guidelines, recommendations and best practices referred to in points (e) and (f);

(m) issue guidelines, recommendations and best practices in accordance with point (e) of this paragraph for establishing common procedures for reporting by natural persons of infringements of this Regulation pursuant to Article 54(2);

(n) encourage the drawing-up of codes of conduct and the establishment of data protection certification mechanisms and data protection seals and marks pursuant to Articles 40 and 42;

(o) carry out the accreditation of certification bodies and its periodic review pursuant to Article 43 and maintain a public register of accredited bodies pursuant to Article 43(6) and of the accredited controllers or processors established in third countries pursuant to Article 42(7);

(p) specify the requirements referred to in Article 43(3) with a view to the accreditation of certification bodies under Article 42;

(q) provide the Commission with an opinion on the certification requirements referred to in Article 43(8);

(r) provide the Commission with an opinion on the icons referred to in Article 12(7);

(s) provide the Commission with an opinion for the assessment of the adequacy of the level of protection in a third country or international organisation, including for the assessment whether a third country, a territory or one or more specified sectors within that third country, or an international organisation no longer ensures an adequate level of protection. To that end, the Commission shall provide the Board with all necessary documentation, including correspondence with the government of the third country, with regard to that third country, territory or specified sector, or with the international organisation.

(t) issue opinions on draft decisions of supervisory authorities pursuant to the consistency mechanism referred to in Article 64(1), on matters submitted pursuant to Article 64(2) and to issue binding decisions pursuant to Article 65, including in cases referred to in Article 66;

(u) promote the cooperation and the effective bilateral and multilateral exchange of information and best practices between the supervisory authorities;

(v) promote common training programmes and facilitate personnel exchanges between the supervisory authorities and, where appropriate, with the supervisory authorities of third countries or with international organisations;

(w) promote the exchange of knowledge and documentation on data protection legislation and practice with data protection supervisory authorities worldwide.

(x) issue opinions on codes of conduct drawn up at Union level pursuant to Article 40(9); and

(y) maintain a publicly accessible electronic register of decisions taken by supervisory authorities and courts on issues handled in the consistency mechanism.

2.   Where the Commission requests advice from the Board, it may indicate a time limit, taking into account the urgency of the matter.

3. The Board shall forward its opinions, guidelines, recommendations, and best practices to the Commission and to the committee referred to in Article 93 and make them public.

4. The Board shall, where appropriate, consult interested parties and give them the opportunity to comment within a reasonable period. The Board shall, without prejudice to Article 76, make the results of the consultation procedure publicly available.

Article 71: Reports

1. The Board shall draw up an annual report regarding the protection of natural persons with regard to processing in the Union and, where relevant, in third countries and international organisations. The report shall be made public and be transmitted to the European Parliament, to the Council and to the Commission.

2. The annual report shall include a review of the practical application of the guidelines, recommendations and best practices referred to in point (l) of Article 70(1) as well as of the binding decisions referred to in Article 65.

Article 72: Procedure

1. The Board shall take decisions by a simple majority of its members, unless otherwise provided for in this Regulation.

2. The Board shall adopt its own rules of procedure by a two-thirds majority of its members and organise its own operational arrangements.

Article 73: Chair

1. The Board shall elect a chair and two deputy chairs from amongst its members by simple majority.

2. The term of office of the Chair and of the deputy chairs shall be five years and be renewable once.

Article 74: Tasks of the Chair

1. The Chair shall have the following tasks:
> (a) to convene the meetings of the Board and prepare its agenda;
> (b) to notify decisions adopted by the Board pursuant to Article 65 to the lead supervisory authority and the supervisory authorities concerned;
> (c) to ensure the timely performance of the tasks of the Board, in particular in relation to the consistency mechanism referred to in Article 63.

2. The Board shall lay down the allocation of tasks between the Chair and the deputy chairs in its rules of procedure.

Article 75: Secretariat

1.   The Board shall have a secretariat, which shall be provided by the European Data Protection Supervisor.

2.   The secretariat shall perform its tasks exclusively under the instructions of the Chair of the Board.

3.   The staff of the European Data Protection Supervisor involved in carrying out the tasks conferred on the Board by this Regulation shall be subject to separate reporting lines from the staff involved in carrying out tasks conferred on the European Data Protection Supervisor.

4.   Where appropriate, the Board and the European Data Protection Supervisor shall establish and publish a Memorandum of Understanding implementing this Article, determining the terms of their cooperation, and applicable to the staff of the European Data Protection Supervisor involved in carrying out the tasks conferred on the Board by this Regulation.

5.   The secretariat shall provide analytical, administrative and logistical support to the Board.

6.   The secretariat shall be responsible in particular for:

>   (a) the day-to-day business of the Board;
>
>   (b) communication between the members of the Board, its Chair and the Commission;
>
>   (c) communication with other institutions and the public;
>
>   (d) the use of electronic means for the internal and external communication;
>
>   (e) the translation of relevant information;
>
>   (f) the preparation and follow-up of the meetings of the Board;
>
>   (g) the preparation, drafting and publication of opinions, decisions on the settlement of disputes between supervisory authorities and other texts adopted by the Board.

Article 76: Confidentiality

1.   The discussions of the Board shall be confidential where the Board deems it necessary, as provided for in its rules of procedure.

2.   Access to documents submitted to members of the Board, experts and representatives of third parties shall be governed by Regulation (EC) No 1049/2001 of the European Parliament and of the Council (21).

CHAPTER VIII: Remedies, liability and penalties

Article 77: Right to lodge a complaint with a supervisory authority

1.   Without prejudice to any other administrative or judicial remedy, every data subject shall have the right to lodge a complaint with a supervisory authority, in particular in the Member State of his or her habitual residence, place of work or place of the alleged infringement if the data subject considers that the processing of personal data relating to him or her infringes this Regulation.

2.   The supervisory authority with which the complaint has been lodged shall inform the complainant on the progress and the outcome of the complaint including the possibility of a judicial remedy pursuant to Article 78.

Article 78: Right to an effective judicial remedy against a supervisory authority

1.   Without prejudice to any other administrative or non-judicial remedy, each natural or legal person shall have the right to an effective judicial remedy against a legally binding decision of a supervisory authority concerning them.

2.   Without prejudice to any other administrative or non-judicial remedy, each data subject shall have the right to a an effective judicial remedy where the supervisory authority which is competent pursuant to Articles 55 and 56 does not handle a complaint or does not inform the data subject within three months on the progress or outcome of the complaint lodged pursuant to Article 77.

3.   Proceedings against a supervisory authority shall be brought before the courts of the Member State where the supervisory authority is established.

4.   Where proceedings are brought against a decision of a supervisory authority which was preceded by an opinion or a decision of the Board in the consistency mechanism, the supervisory authority shall forward that opinion or decision to the court.

Article 79: Right to an effective judicial remedy against a controller or processor

1.   Without prejudice to any available administrative or non-judicial remedy, including the right to lodge a complaint with a supervisory authority pursuant to Article 77, each data subject shall have the right to an effective judicial remedy where he or she considers that his or her rights under this Regulation have been infringed as a result of the processing of his or her personal data in non-compliance with this Regulation.

2.   Proceedings against a controller or a processor shall be brought before the courts of the Member State where the controller or processor has an establishment. Alternatively, such proceedings may be brought before the courts of the Member State where the data subject has his or her habitual residence, unless the controller or processor is a public authority of a Member State acting in the exercise of its public powers.

Article 80: Representation of data subjects

1.   The data subject shall have the right to mandate a not-for-profit body, organisation or association which has been properly constituted in accordance with the law of a Member State, has statutory objectives which are in the public interest, and is active in the field of the protection of data subjects' rights and freedoms with regard to the protection of their personal data to lodge the complaint on his or her behalf, to exercise the rights referred to in Articles 77, 78 and 79 on his or her behalf, and to exercise the right to receive compensation referred to in Article 82 on his or her behalf where provided for by Member State law.

2.   Member States may provide that any body, organisation or association referred to in paragraph 1 of this Article, independently of a data subject's mandate, has the right to lodge, in that Member State, a complaint with the supervisory authority which is competent pursuant to Article 77 and to exercise the rights referred to in Articles 78 and 79 if it considers that the rights of a data subject under this Regulation have been infringed as a result of the processing.

Article 81: Suspension of proceedings

1.   Where a competent court of a Member State has information on proceedings, concerning the same subject matter as regards processing by the same controller or processor, that are pending in a court in another Member State, it shall contact that court in the other Member State to confirm the existence of such proceedings.

2.   Where proceedings concerning the same subject matter as regards processing of the same controller or processor are pending in a court in another Member State, any competent court other than the court first seized may suspend its proceedings.

3.   Where those proceedings are pending at first instance, any court other than the court first seized may also, on the application of one of the parties, decline jurisdiction if the court first seized has jurisdiction over the actions in question and its law permits the consolidation thereof.

Article 82: Right to compensation and liability

1.   Any person who has suffered material or non-material damage as a result of an infringement of this Regulation shall have the right to receive compensation from the controller or processor for the damage suffered.

2.   Any controller involved in processing shall be liable for the damage caused by processing which infringes this Regulation. A processor shall be liable for the damage caused by processing only where it has not complied with obligations of this Regulation specifically directed to processors or where it has acted outside or contrary to lawful instructions of the controller.

3.   A controller or processor shall be exempt from liability under paragraph 2 if it proves that it is not in any way responsible for the event giving rise to the damage.

4.   Where more than one controller or processor, or both a controller and a processor, are involved in the same processing and where they are, under paragraphs 2 and 3, responsible for any damage caused by processing, each controller or processor shall be held liable for the entire damage in order to ensure effective compensation of the data subject.

5.   Where a controller or processor has, in accordance with paragraph 4, paid full compensation for the damage suffered, that controller or processor shall be entitled to claim back from the other controllers or processors involved in the same processing that part of the compensation corresponding to their part of responsibility for the damage, in accordance with the conditions set out in paragraph 2.

6. Court proceedings for exercising the right to receive compensation shall be brought before the courts competent under the law of the Member State referred to in Article 79(2).

Article 83: General conditions for imposing administrative fines

1.   Each supervisory authority shall ensure that the imposition of administrative fines pursuant to this Article in respect of infringements of this Regulation referred to in paragraphs 4, 5 and 6 shall in each individual case be effective, proportionate and dissuasive.

2.   Administrative fines shall, depending on the circumstances of each individual case, be imposed in addition to, or instead of, measures referred to in points (a) to (h) and (j) of Article 58(2). When deciding whether to impose an administrative fine and deciding on the amount of the administrative fine in each individual case due regard shall be given to the following:

> (a) the nature, gravity and duration of the infringement taking into account the nature scope or purpose of the processing concerned as well as the number of data subjects affected and the level of damage suffered by them;
>
> (b) the intentional or negligent character of the infringement;
>
> (c) any action taken by the controller or processor to mitigate the damage suffered by data subjects;
>
> (d) the degree of responsibility of the controller or processor taking into account technical and organisational measures implemented by them pursuant to Articles 25 and 32;
>
> (e) any relevant previous infringements by the controller or processor;
>
> (f) the degree of cooperation with the supervisory authority, in order to remedy the infringement and mitigate the possible adverse effects of the infringement;
>
> (g) the categories of personal data affected by the infringement;
>
> (h) the manner in which the infringement became known to the supervisory authority, in particular whether, and if so to what extent, the controller or processor notified the infringement;
>
> (i) where measures referred to in Article 58(2) have previously been ordered against the controller or processor concerned with regard to the same subject-matter, compliance with those measures;
>
> (j) adherence to approved codes of conduct pursuant to Article 40 or approved certification mechanisms pursuant to Article 42; and
>
> (k) any other aggravating or mitigating factor applicable to the circumstances of the case, such as financial benefits gained, or losses avoided, directly or indirectly, from the infringement.

3.   If a controller or processor intentionally or negligently, for the same or linked processing operations, infringes several provisions of this Regulation, the total amount of the administrative fine shall not exceed the amount specified for the gravest infringement.

4.   Infringements of the following provisions shall, in accordance with paragraph 2, be subject to administrative fines up to 10 000 000 EUR, or in the case of an undertaking, up to 2 % of the total worldwide annual turnover of the preceding financial year, whichever is higher:

(a) the obligations of the controller and the processor pursuant to Articles 8, 11, 25 to 39 and 42 and 43;

(b) the obligations of the certification body pursuant to Articles 42 and 43;

(c) the obligations of the monitoring body pursuant to Article 41(4).

5.   Infringements of the following provisions shall, in accordance with paragraph 2, be subject to administrative fines up to 20 000 000 EUR, or in the case of an undertaking, up to 4 % of the total worldwide annual turnover of the preceding financial year, whichever is higher:

(a) the basic principles for processing, including conditions for consent, pursuant to Articles 5, 6, 7 and 9;

(b) the data subjects' rights pursuant to Articles 12 to 22;

(c) the transfers of personal data to a recipient in a third country or an international organisation pursuant to Articles 44 to 49;

(d) any obligations pursuant to Member State law adopted under Chapter IX;

(e) non-compliance with an order or a temporary or definitive limitation on processing or the suspension of data flows by the supervisory authority pursuant to Article 58(2) or failure to provide access in violation of Article 58(1).

6.   Non-compliance with an order by the supervisory authority as referred to in Article 58(2) shall, in accordance with paragraph 2 of this Article, be subject to administrative fines up to 20 000 000 EUR, or in the case of an undertaking, up to 4 % of the total worldwide annual turnover of the preceding financial year, whichever is higher.

7.   Without prejudice to the corrective powers of supervisory authorities pursuant to Article 58(2), each Member State may lay down the rules on whether and to what extent administrative fines may be imposed on public authorities and bodies established in that Member State.

8.   The exercise by the supervisory authority of its powers under this Article shall be subject to appropriate procedural safeguards in accordance with Union and Member State law, including effective judicial remedy and due process.

9.   Where the legal system of the Member State does not provide for administrative fines, this Article may be applied in such a manner that the fine is initiated by the competent supervisory authority and imposed by competent national courts, while ensuring that those legal remedies are effective and have an equivalent effect to the administrative fines imposed by supervisory authorities. In any event, the fines imposed shall be effective, proportionate and dissuasive. Those Member States shall notify to the Commission the provisions of their laws which they adopt pursuant to this paragraph by 25 May 2018 and, without delay, any subsequent amendment law or amendment affecting them.

Recent Developments
EU General Data Protection Regulation

Article 84: Penalties

1.   Member States shall lay down the rules on other penalties applicable to infringements of this Regulation in particular for infringements which are not subject to administrative fines pursuant to Article 83, and shall take all measures necessary to ensure that they are implemented. Such penalties shall be effective, proportionate and dissuasive.

2.   Each Member State shall notify to the Commission the provisions of its law which it adopts pursuant to paragraph 1, by 25 May 2018 and, without delay, any subsequent amendment affecting them.

CHAPTER IX: Provisions relating to specific processing situations

Article 85: Processing and freedom of expression and information

1.   Member States shall by law reconcile the right to the protection of personal data pursuant to this Regulation with the right to freedom of expression and information, including processing for journalistic purposes and the purposes of academic, artistic or literary expression.

2.   For processing carried out for journalistic purposes or the purpose of academic artistic or literary expression, Member States shall provide for exemptions or derogations from Chapter II (principles), Chapter III (rights of the data subject), Chapter IV (controller and processor), Chapter V (transfer of personal data to third countries or international organisations), Chapter VI (independent supervisory authorities), Chapter VII (cooperation and consistency) and Chapter IX (specific data processing situations) if they are necessary to reconcile the right to the protection of personal data with the freedom of expression and information.

3.   Each Member State shall notify to the Commission the provisions of its law which it has adopted pursuant to paragraph 2 and, without delay, any subsequent amendment law or amendment affecting them.

Article 86: Processing and public access to official documents

Personal data in official documents held by a public authority or a public body or a private body for the performance of a task carried out in the public interest may be disclosed by the authority or body in accordance with Union or Member State law to which the public authority or body is subject in order to reconcile public access to official documents with the right to the protection of personal data pursuant to this Regulation.

Article 87: Processing of the national identification number

Member States may further determine the specific conditions for the processing of a national identification number or any other identifier of general application. In that case the national identification number or any other identifier of general application shall be used only under appropriate safeguards for the rights and freedoms of the data subject pursuant to this Regulation.

Article 88: Processing in the context of employment

1.   Member States may, by law or by collective agreements, provide for more specific rules to ensure the protection of the rights and freedoms in respect of the processing of employees' personal data in the employment context, in particular for the purposes of the recruitment, the performance of the contract of employment, including discharge of obligations laid down by law or by collective agreements, management, planning and organisation of work, equality and diversity in the workplace, health and safety at work, protection of employer's or customer's property and for the purposes of the exercise and enjoyment, on an individual or collective basis, of rights and benefits related to employment, and for the purpose of the termination of the employment relationship.

2.   Those rules shall include suitable and specific measures to safeguard the data subject's human dignity, legitimate interests and fundamental rights, with particular regard to the transparency of processing, the transfer of personal data within a group of undertakings, or a group of enterprises engaged in a joint economic activity and monitoring systems at the work place.

3.   Each Member State shall notify to the Commission those provisions of its law which it adopts pursuant to paragraph 1, by 25 May 2018 and, without delay, any subsequent amendment affecting them.

Article 89: Safeguards and derogations relating to processing for archiving purposes in the public interest, scientific or historical research purposes or statistical purposes

1.   Processing for archiving purposes in the public interest, scientific or historical research purposes or statistical purposes, shall be subject to appropriate safeguards, in accordance with this Regulation, for the rights and freedoms of the data subject. Those safeguards shall ensure that technical and organisational measures are in place in particular in order to ensure respect for the principle of data minimisation. Those measures may include pseudonymisation provided that those purposes can be fulfilled in that manner. Where those purposes can be fulfilled by further processing which does not permit or no longer permits the identification of data subjects, those purposes shall be fulfilled in that manner.

2.   Where personal data are processed for scientific or historical research purposes or statistical purposes, Union or Member State law may provide for derogations from the rights referred to in Articles 15, 16, 18 and 21 subject to the conditions and safeguards referred to in paragraph 1 of this Article in so far as such rights are likely to render impossible or seriously impair the achievement of the specific purposes, and such derogations are necessary for the fulfilment of those purposes.

3.   Where personal data are processed for archiving purposes in the public interest, Union or Member State law may provide for derogations from the rights referred to in Articles 15, 16,

18, 19, 20 and 21 subject to the conditions and safeguards referred to in paragraph 1 of this Article in so far as such rights are likely to render impossible or seriously impair the achievement of the specific purposes, and such derogations are necessary for the fulfilment of those purposes.

4.   Where processing referred to in paragraphs 2 and 3 serves at the same time another purpose, the derogations shall apply only to processing for the purposes referred to in those paragraphs.

Article 90: Obligations of secrecy

1.   Member States may adopt specific rules to set out the powers of the supervisory authorities laid down in points (e) and (f) of Article 58(1) in relation to controllers or processors that are subject, under Union or Member State law or rules established by national competent bodies, to an obligation of professional secrecy or other equivalent obligations of secrecy where this is necessary and proportionate to reconcile the right of the protection of personal data with the obligation of secrecy. Those rules shall apply only with regard to personal data which the controller or processor has received as a result of or has obtained in an activity covered by that obligation of secrecy.

2.   Each Member State shall notify to the Commission the rules adopted pursuant to paragraph 1, by 25 May 2018 and, without delay, any subsequent amendment affecting them.

Article 91: Existing data protection rules of churches and religious associations

1.   Where in a Member State, churches and religious associations or communities apply, at the time of entry into force of this Regulation, comprehensive rules relating to the protection of natural persons with regard to processing, such rules may continue to apply, provided that they are brought into line with this Regulation.

2.   Churches and religious associations which apply comprehensive rules in accordance with paragraph 1 of this Article shall be subject to the supervision of an independent supervisory authority, which may be specific, provided that it fulfils the conditions laid down in Chapter VI of this Regulation.

CHAPTER X: Delegated acts and implementing acts

Article 92: Exercise of the delegation

1.   The power to adopt delegated acts is conferred on the Commission subject to the conditions laid down in this Article.

2.   The delegation of power referred to in Article 12(8) and Article 43(8) shall be conferred on the Commission for an indeterminate period of time from 24 May 2016.

3.   The delegation of power referred to in Article 12(8) and Article 43(8) may be revoked at any time by the European Parliament or by the Council. A decision of revocation shall put an end to the delegation of power specified in that decision. It shall take effect the day following

that of its publication in the Official Journal of the European Union or at a later date specified therein. It shall not affect the validity of any delegated acts already in force.

4. As soon as it adopts a delegated act, the Commission shall notify it simultaneously to the European Parliament and to the Council.

5. A delegated act adopted pursuant to Article 12(8) and Article 43(8) shall enter into force only if no objection has been expressed by either the European Parliament or the Council within a period of three months of notification of that act to the European Parliament and the Council or if, before the expiry of that period, the European Parliament and the Council have both informed the Commission that they will not object. That period shall be extended by three months at the initiative of the European Parliament or of the Council.

Article 93: Committee procedure

1. The Commission shall be assisted by a committee. That committee shall be a committee within the meaning of Regulation (EU) No 182/2011.

2. Where reference is made to this paragraph, Article 5 of Regulation (EU) No 182/2011 shall apply.

3. Where reference is made to this paragraph, Article 8 of Regulation (EU) No 182/2011, in conjunction with Article 5 thereof, shall apply.

CHAPTER XI: Final provisions

Article 94: Repeal of Directive 95/46/EC

1. Directive 95/46/EC is repealed with effect from 25 May 2018.

2. References to the repealed Directive shall be construed as references to this Regulation. References to the Working Party on the Protection of Individuals with regard to the Processing of Personal Data established by Article 29 of Directive 95/46/EC shall be construed as references to the European Data Protection Board established by this Regulation.

Article 95: Relationship with Directive 2002/58/EC

This Regulation shall not impose additional obligations on natural or legal persons in relation to processing in connection with the provision of publicly available electronic communications services in public communication networks in the Union in relation to matters for which they are subject to specific obligations with the same objective set out in Directive 2002/58/EC.

Article 96: Relationship with previously concluded Agreements

International agreements involving the transfer of personal data to third countries or international organisations which were concluded by Member States prior to 24 May 2016, and which comply with Union law as applicable prior to that date, shall remain in force until amended, replaced or revoked.

Article 97: Commission reports

1. By 25 May 2020 and every four years thereafter, the Commission shall submit a report on the evaluation and review of this Regulation to the European Parliament and to the Council. The reports shall be made public.

2. In the context of the evaluations and reviews referred to in paragraph 1, the Commission shall examine, in particular, the application and functioning of:

>   (a) Chapter V on the transfer of personal data to third countries or international organisations with particular regard to decisions adopted pursuant to Article 45(3) of this Regulation and decisions adopted on the basis of Article 25(6) of Directive 95/46/EC;
>
>   (b) Chapter VII on cooperation and consistency.

3. For the purpose of paragraph 1, the Commission may request information from Member States and supervisory authorities.

4. In carrying out the evaluations and reviews referred to in paragraphs 1 and 2, the Commission shall take into account the positions and findings of the European Parliament, of the Council, and of other relevant bodies or sources.

5. The Commission shall, if necessary, submit appropriate proposals to amend this Regulation, in particular taking into account of developments in information technology and in the light of the state of progress in the information society.

Article 98: Review of other Union legal acts on data protection

The Commission shall, if appropriate, submit legislative proposals with a view to amending other Union legal acts on the protection of personal data, in order to ensure uniform and consistent protection of natural persons with regard to processing. This shall in particular concern the rules relating to the protection of natural persons with regard to processing by Union institutions, bodies, offices and agencies and on the free movement of such data.

Article 99: Entry into force and application

1. This Regulation shall enter into force on the twentieth day following that of its publication in the Official Journal of the European Union.

2. It shall apply from 25 May 2018.

Selected Bibliography

(available at www.epic.org/bookstore)

Hal Abelson (Author), Ken Ledeen (Author), Harry Lewis (Author), *Blown to Bits: Your Life, Liberty, and Happiness After the Digital Explosion* (Addison-Wesley Professional 2008)

Alessandro Acquisti (Editor), Stefanos Gritzalis (Editor), Costos Lambrinoudakis (Editor), Sabrina di Vimercati (Editor), *Digital Privacy: Theory, Technologies, and Practices* (Auerbach Publications 2007)

Philip E. Agre & Marc Rotenberg, *Technology and Privacy: The New Landscape* (The MIT Press 1998)

Philip E. Agre, *Computation and Human Experience (Learning in Doing: Social, Cognitive and Computational Perspectives)* (Cambridge University Press 1997)

Anita Allen and Marc Rotenberg, *Privacy Law and Society* (West 2015)

Anita Allen, *Unpopular Privacy: What Must We Hide? (Studies in Feminist Philosophy)* (Oxford University Press 2011)

Anita L. Allen, *Why Privacy Isn't Everything: Feminist Reflections on Personal Accountability (Feminist Constructions)* (Rowman & Littlefield Publishers 2003)

Ross J. Anderson, *Security Engineering: A Guide to Building Dependable Distributed Systems* (Wiley 2008)

Jack M. Balkin, *Constitutional Redemption: Political Faith in an Unjust World* (Harvard University Press 2011)

Jack M. Balkin, *Living Originalism* (Belknap Press 2011)

Jack M. Balkin (Editor), Reva B. Siegel (Editor), *The Constitution in 2020* (Oxford University Press 2009)

James Bamford, *The Shadow Factory: The NSA from 9/11 to the Eavesdropping on America* (Anchor 2009)

James Bamford, *A Pretext for War: 9/11, Iraq, and the Abuse of America's Intelligence Agencies* (Anchor 2005)

James Bamford, *Body of Secrets: Anatomy of the Ultra-Secret National Security Agency* (Anchor Books 2001)

Privacy Resources
Selected Bibliography

Michael J. Bazyler and Frank M. Tuerkheimer, *Forgotten Trials of the Holocaust* (NYU Press 2014)

Ori Brafman and Rod Beckstrom, *The Starfish and the Spider* (Portfolio 2006)

Colin Bennett (Editor), Kevin Haggerty (Editor), David Lyon (Editor), Valerie Steeves (Editor), *Transparent Lives: Surveillance in Canada* (Athabasca University Press 2014)

Colin J. Bennett (Editor), Kevin Haggerty (Editor), *Security Games: Surveillance and Control at Mega-Events* (Routledge 2012)

Colin Bennett, *The Privacy Advocates: Resisting the Spread of Surveillance* (The MIT Press 2010)

Christine L. Borgman, *Big Data, Little Data, No Data: Scholarship in the Networked World* (The MIT Press 2015)

Christine L. Borgman, *Scholarship in the Digital Age: Information, Infrastructure, and the Internet* (The MIT Press 2007, 2010)

Christine L. Borgman, *From Gutenberg to the Global Information Infrastructure: Access to Information in the Networked World* (The MIT Press 2000)

danah boyd, *It's Complicated: The Social Lives of Networked Teens* (Yale University Press 2014)

David Burnham, *The Rise of the Computer State* (Random House 1983)

Ryan Calo, A. Michael Froomkin, Ian Kerr , *Robot Law* (Edward Elgar Publishing 2016)

David Chaum, *Advances in Cryptology: Proceedings of Crypto 83* (Springer 2013)

Danielle Keats Citron, *Hate Crimes in Cyberspace* (Harvard University Press 2014)

Ryan Calo, A. Michael Froomkin, Ian Kerr, *Robot Law* (Edward Elgar Publishing 2016)

Julie E. Cohen, *Configuring the Networked Self: Law, Code, and the Play of Everyday Practice* (Yale University Press 2012)

Susan Crawford, *Captive Audience: The Telecom Industry and Monopoly Power in the New Gilded Age* (Yale University Press 2014)

Stephen Goldsmith and Susan Crawford, *The Responsive City: Engaging Communities Through Data-Smart Governance* (Jossey-Bass 2014)

Whitfield Diffie and Susan Landau, *Privacy on the Line: The Politics of Wiretapping and Encryption* (The MIT Press 2010)

Laura K. Donohue, *The Future of Foreign Intelligence: Privacy and Surveillance in a Digital Age* (Oxford University Press 2016)

Laura K. Donohue, *The Cost of Counterterrorism: Power, Politics, and Liberty* (Cambridge University Press 2008)

Cynthia Dwork and Aaron Roth, *The Algorithmic Foundations of Differential Privacy* (Now Publishers 2014)

Niels Ferguson, Bruce Schneier, and Tadayoshi Kohno, *Cryptography Engineering* (John Wiley & Sons 2010)

David H. Flaherty, *Protecting Privacy in Surveillance Societies: The Federal Republic of Germany, Sweden, France, Canada, and the United States* (The University of North Carolina Press 1989)

David H. Flaherty, *Privacy in Colonial New England 1630-1776* (Univ of Virginia Press 1972)

Mary Flanagan (Author), Helen Nissenbaum (Author), *Values at Play in Digital Games* (The MIT Press 2014)

Nancy Gertner, *In Defense of Women: Memoirs of an Unrepentant Advocate* (Beacon Press 2011)

Jack Goldsmith and Tim Wu, *Who Controls the Internet?: Illusions of a Borderless World* (Oxford University Press 2008)

Aziz Z. Huq, *Unchecked And Unbalanced: Presidential Power in a Time of Terror* (New Press 2011)

Deborah Hurley and James Keller, *The First 100 Feet: Options for Internet and Broadband Access* (Mit Press 1999)

Jerry Kang and Alan Butler, *Communications Law and Policy* (Direct Injection Press 2016)

Pamela S. Karlan, *A Constitution for All Times (Boston Review Books)* (The MIT Press 2013)

Goodwin Liu (Author), Pamela S. Karlan (Author), Christopher H. Schroeder (Author), *Keeping Faith with the Constitution (Inalienable Rights)* (Oxford University Press 2010)

Glenn C. Loury (Author), Pamela S. Karlan (Contributor), Lo?c Wacquant (Contributor), Tommie Shelby (Contributor), *Race, Incarceration, and American Values (Boston Review Books)* (The MIT Press 2008)

Ian Kerr (Author), Carole Lucock (Author), Valerie Steeves (Author), *Lessons from the Identity Trail: Anonymity, Privacy and Identity in a Networked Society* (Oxford University Press 2009)

Privacy Resources
Selected Bibliography

Ellen Condliffe Lagemann (Author), Harry Lewis (Author), *What Is College For? The Public Purpose of Higher Education* (Teachers College Press 2013)

Harry Lewis, *Excellence Without a Soul: Does Liberal Education Have a Future?* (PublicAffairs 2007)

Rebecca MacKinnon, *Consent of the Networked: The Worldwide Struggle For Internet Freedom* (Basic Books 2012)

Alice E. Marwick, *Status Update: Celebrity, Publicity, and Branding in the Social Media Age* (Yale University Press 2013)

Gary T. Marx, *Windows into the Soul: Surveillance and Society in an Age of High Technology* (University Of Chicago Press 2016)

Gary T. Marx (Author), Douglas McAdam (Author), *Collective Behavior And Social Movements: Process and Structure* (Pearson 1993)

Gary T. Marx, *Undercover: Police Surveillance in America* (University of California Press 1989)

Gary T Marx, *Protest and Prejudice: A Study of Belief in the Black Community* (Harper & Row 1969)

Gary McGraw and Edward W. Felten, *Securing Java: Getting Down to Business with Mobile Code, 2nd Edition* (Wiley 1999)

Gary McGraw and Edward W. Felten, *Java Security* (Wiley 1996)

Mary Minow, *Library's Legal Answer Book* (American Library Association 2003)

Peter G. Neumann, *Computer-Related Risks* (Addison-Wesley 1994)

Julia Lane (Editor), Victoria Stodden (Editor), Stefan Bender (Editor), Helen Nissenbaum (Editor), *Privacy, Big Data, and the Public Good: Frameworks for Engagement* (Cambridge University Press 2014)

Helen Nissenbaum, *Privacy in Context: Technology, Policy, and the Integrity of Social Life* (Stanford Law Books 2009)

Judith O'Neill (Editor), Eli M. Noam (Editor), Darcy Gerbarg (Editor), *Broadband as a Video Platform* (Springer 2014)

Eli Noam, *Media Ownership and Concentration in America* (Oxford University Press 2009)

Eli M. Noam (Editor), Jo Groebel (Editor), Darcy Gerbarg (Editor), *Internet Television* (Routledge 2003)

Frank Pasquale, *The Black Box Society: The Secret Algorithms That Control Money and Information* (Harvard University Press 2015)

Chip Pitts, *Corporate Social Responsibility - A Legal Analysis* (LexisNexis Canada 2009)

Jeffrey Rosen, *Louis D. Brandeis: American Prophet* (Yale University Press 2016)

Jeffrey Rosen and Benjamin Wittes, *Constitution 3.0: Freedom and Technological Change* (Brookings Institution Press 2013)

Jeffrey Rosen, *The Supreme Court: The Personalities and Rivalries That Defined America* (St. Martins Griffin 2007)

Jeffrey Rosen, *The Most Democratic Branch: How the Courts Serve America* (Oxford University Press 2006)

Marc Rotenberg, *Privacy & Human Rights* (EPIC 2006)

Marc Rotenberg, Julia Horwitz and Jeramie Scott, *Privacy in the Modern Age: The Search for Solutions* (The New Press 2015)

Bruce Schneier, David Banisar, *The Electronic Privacy Papers: Documents on the Battle for Privacy in the Age of Surveillance* (Wiley 1997)

Bruce Schneier, *Carry On: Sound Advice from Schneier on Security* (Wiley 2013)

Bruce Schneier, *Data and Goliath: The Hidden Battles to Collect Your Data and Control Your World* (W.W. Norton & Company 2015)

Bruce Schneier, *Liars and Outliers: Enabling the Trust that Society Needs to Thrive* (Wiley 2012)

Wolfgang Schulz (Editor), Peggy Valcke (Editor), Kristina Irion (Editor), *The Independence of the Media and its Regulatory Agencies* (Intellect Ltd 2014)

Robert Ellis Smith, *Compilation of State and Federal Privacy Laws 2013* (Privacy Journal 2013)

Nadine Strossen, *Defending Pornography: Free Speech, Sex, and the Fight for Women's Rights* (NYU Press 2000)

Sherry Turtle, *Reclaiming Conversation: The Power of Talk in a Digital Age* (Penguin Press 2015)

Sherry Turkle, *Alone Together: Why We Expect More from Technology and Less from Each Other* (Basic Books 2012)

Sherry Turkle, Editor, *Evocative Objects Things We Think With* (The MIT Press 2011)

Privacy Resources
Selected Bibliography

Sherry Turkle, Editor, *Falling for Science Objects in Mind* (The MIT Press 2011)

Willis H. Ware, *RAND and the Information Evolution: A History in Essays and Vignettes* (RAND Corporation 2008)

Tim Wu, *The Master Switch: The Rise and Fall of Information Empires* (Vintage 2011)

Privacy Resources

PRIVACY YEAR IN REVIEW 2015–2016

January

12th – President Obama announced a series of privacy initiatives to protect consumer privacy and cybersecurity. Among the privacy initiatives were proposals for a Student Digital Privacy Act, Personal Data Notification & Protection, and a Consumer Privacy Bill of Rights. However, the initiatives also included proposals that would allow the transfer of personal information from private companies to government agencies and information sharing and analysis organizations to be led by the private sector.

February

5th – The White House releases a new report, "Big Data and Differential Pricing," that examined how new forms of price discrimination were arising resulting from the use of big data analytics. The report highlighted the risk of price discrimination against consumers, acknowledged the failure of self-regulatory efforts, and called for greater transparency and consumer control over personal information.

15th – President Obama issued a Presidential Memorandum that required all agencies to adopt privacy rules for drone use. The purpose of the memorandum was to limit the use of personally identifiable information and required agencies to adopt transparency and accountability procedures, including a publicly available annual report that summarized drone operations from the previous year.

March

16th – The Pew Research Center published a new report, "Americans' Privacy Strategies Post-Snowden." Pew found that about 1/3 of Americans who were aware of the NSA's bulk collection of telephone records had taken steps to hide or shield their information from the government and more than half said that it was unacceptable for the government to monitor the communications of citizens.

19th – The Beneson Strategy Group released a survey on the "Right to be Forgotten." Of those polled 88% said they would support a US law that allowed Internet users to ask search companies to remove links to certain personal information and 2/3 agreed that the federal government had gone too far when it came to collecting information about Americans from technology companies.

April

3rd – The Department of Justice released a final rule governing the agency's Freedom of Information Act practices. The final rule covered many issues including a provisions around documents covered under a "national security exemption" which now requires that the agency must obtain approval before stating that the documents can be excluded from a FOIA request.

21st – The U.S. Supreme Court in *Rodriguez v. United States*, 135 S. Ct. 1609 (2015), held in a 6-3 vote that it is unlawful for a police officer to detain a driver after a traffic stop for the sole purpose of conducting a "sniff" test. The court determined that a traffic stop ends when all tasks related to the stop are, or reasonably should have been, completed and that the stop "could become unlawful if it is prolonged beyond the time reasonably required to complete the [traffic stop]."

May

7th – The U.S. Court of Appeals for the Second Circuit determined that the National Security Agency's "Section 215" telephone record collection program exceeded legal authority. *ACLU v. Clapper*, 785 F.3d 787 (2d. Cir. 2015). Section 215 was a telephone metadata program that required phone companies to turn over records on a daily basis with no end point, relevance to any set of facts, or limitations on the subject matter or individuals covered.

20th – The Pew Research Center published a new poll, "American's Attitudes About Privacy, Security and Surveillance." The poll found that 74% of those polled believed that control over their personal information is "very important' but only 9% believed they actual had that control. The survey also found that Americans supported more limitations on and enhanced oversight of government surveillance programs and wanted limits on how long private companies could retain records about their activities.

21st – Florida passed a new law that exempted any police body camera video with footage from inside a private residence, health care, mental health care, social services facility, or in a place that a reasonable person would expect to be private from public records law. Florida joined other states including North Dakota, Maryland, Arizona, and Colorado on passing laws regarding police body cameras.

22nd – The Obama Administration decides not to renew the legal authority for the National Security Agency's bulk telephone record collection program. The deadline to renew the legal authority for the program had passed and the agency had begun "sundowning" the program.

June

2nd – President Obama signed the USA FREEDOM Act into law, ending the National Security Agency's 14-year practice of bulk collection of domestic phone records under Section 215 of the Patriot Act. However, some controversial NSA programs were untouched by the FREEDOM Act, including programs that are not directed at US citizens but nonetheless collect vast amounts of American communications.

4th–28th – The U.S. Office of Personnel Management announced a massive data breach of the federal government's employee database. The agency believed the breach exposed the personal data of 4 million government workers and later acknowledged that sensitive security clearance information about federal employees and contractors had been breached. Eventually it was determined that the records of more 22 million federal employees, their family members, and friends had been compromised.

18th – The Federal Communications Commission adopted new rules that imposed strict limits on telemarketing practice. The new rules allowed consumers to stop unwanted telemarketing calls and text messages simply telling companies to stop calling and/or textingand allowed phone companies to offer call-blocking services to screen out automated telemarketing calls.

22nd – The U.S. Supreme Court struck down a Los Angeles ordinance that required hotels to collect guest names, length of stay, drivers license, vehicle, and payment information for warrantless police inspection. *City of Los Angeles v. Patel*, 135 S. Ct. 2443 (2015). The Court stated that generally, "searches conducted outside of the judicial process [are] *per se* unreasonable."

29th – The Foreign Intelligence Surveillance Court reauthorized the U.S. government's collection of domestic telephone records for 180 days despite the passage of the USA FREEDOM Act. The Surveillance Court's ruling ignored a decision from the Second Circuit Court of Appeals which held that the National Security Agency's bulk collection program was unlawful.

Privacy Resources
Privacy Year in Review

July

1st – Oregon and Florida join a number of other states in enacting new privacy laws in the areas of student privacy, data breach notifications, and drones. Oregon passed student privacy legislation that restrict the use of student information by website operators, online services, and applications targeting students and prohibits targeted advertising to students. Florida passed the Freedom from Unwanted Surveillance Act which regulates commercial drone use and prohibits using drones to intentionally record images of individuals on private property if a reasonable expectation of privacy exists and applies to both law enforcement and private parties.

August

20th – The U.S. Eighth Circuit Court of Appeals revived several cases brought under the Drivers Privacy Protection Act. *McDonough v. Anoka Cnty.*, 799 F.3d 913 (8th Cir. 2015). The plaintiffs brought suit after learning that their driving records had been accessed hundreds of times by state agencies. In reviving the cases the court noted that the agencies reasons for accessing the records were not convincing enough to undermine the reasonable inference that they were being accessed for an impermissible purpose.

24th – The U.S. Third Circuit Court of Appeals ruled in favor of the Federal Trade Commission in *FTC v. Wyndham Worldwide Corp.*, 799 F.3d 236 (3d. Cir. 2015). The case upheld the Commission's authority to police companies' lax data security practices.

September

3rd – The Department of Justice released new guidance that required the agency's law-enforcements components to obtain search warrants before many uses of "Stingray" cell-site simulators. A cell site simulator operates as a fake cell phone tower and forces nearby cell phones to register with it, divulging identifying information and can triangulate a phone's location. The guidance also exempted delete all data collected by the cell-site simulator once the target device is located and at regular intervals during the investigation.

8th – The United States and European Union signed an agreement for transatlantic data transfers. The agreement left open significant questions about data protection safeguards and was secret at the time of signing with no official public release date.

21st – France's data protection authority, the CNIL, ordered Google to comply with an EU High Court of Justice ruling from 2014 on the "Right to be Forgotten." Google initially complied with the ruling but only removed links from French and British domain names, but the deleted information was available on Google domains outside of the EU. The CNIL noted that Google's actions allowed the ruling to be easily circumvented and removing links from Google search results does not lead to the deletion of information from the Internet.

October

1st – The international Organization for Economic Co-operation and Development published a new "Recommendation on Digital Security Risk Management." The recommendations emphasized digital security risk management in a way that was transparent and consistent with human rights and fundamental values and emphasize security measures that are "commensurate with the risk" and risk assessments that are "carried out as an ongoing and systematic" process.

6th – The Court of Justice of the European Union ruled the transatlantic "Safe Harbor" data framework invalid because it did not provide adequate legal basis to permit the transfer of personal data of Europeans to the United States. The court determined that authorities in the US were able to access personal data that was transferred from EU member states and processed it in a way that was incompatible with the purposes for which is was transferred and that EU citizens had no administrative or judicial means of redress to correct or delete inaccurate information. The "safe Harbor" exempts the US from the European Data Protection Directive and has been criticized for failing to provided adequate data protection for Internet users in the EU.

19th – The U.S. Department of Transportation and the Federal Aviation Administration announced that drone operators will be required to register with a national drone database. Registration in the database is aimed at protecting public safety and promoting accountability but also created new privacy risks. With the announcement both agencies announced that a task force would be developing recommendations for the registration task force but did not mention whether they would include privacy and safety advocates as part of the task force.

19th – The New Mexico Supreme Court ruled that state police violated the 4th Amendment when they conducted warrantless aerial surveillance that interfered with the petitioner's house and property. *State v.* Davis, 360 P.3d 1161 (N.M. 2015). The court determined that "prolonged hovering close enough to the ground to cause interference with Davis' property transformed this surveillance from a lawful observation . . . to an unconstitutional intrusion."

November

12th – US and international human rights and consumer organizations sent a letter to US and EU government officials that offered suggestions for a revised Safe Harbor agreement and urging them to protect the fundamental right to privacy. The groups submitted 13 proposals including conspicuously posted and clearly written privacy policies on all self-certifying company websites, periodic checks on Safe Harbor companies to ensure compliance, and privacy policies that include information on the extent of US data collection and retention.

27th – The Director of National Intelligence announced that the National Security Agency's bulk collection of domestic phone records under the USA Patriot Act had ended. Technical personnel had access to the data for three more months while they verified records produced under the new targeted production by the USA FREEDOM Act. The National Security agency stated they would destroy their collection of records from the program once litigation over it had ended.

December

1st – EU privacy advocate Max Schrems filed a set of coordinated complaints with data protection officials in Ireland, Germany, and Belgium to block Facebook data transfers from Europe to the US. Schrems stated that his complaints were designed to ensure that the European Court of Justice's October 2015 ruling is enforced in practice when it comes to US companies that are "involved in mass surveillance."

13th – The Federal Aviation Administration published a rule requiring registration for small drones (those weighing between .55 lbs. and 55lbs). Owners would be required to pay a small fee, provide their name, physical address, and e-mail address via an online portal in exchange for a unique drone registration number that must be affixed to the drone before use. Operators were also given the option to provide the FAA with the drones serial number. The FAA did no address drones capability for surveillance or data collection or storage.

15th – After more than 4 years of negotiations the EU Commission, Parliament, and Council reached an agreement on the General Data Protection Regulation. The reform consisted of a general regulation and an accompanying directive that covers data transfers between the law enforcement agencies across Europe. The Regulation also establishes common privacy rules across Europe and creates a strong enforcement power for national data protection authorities and includes penalties for noncompliance.

16th – President Obama signed off on the congressional budget bill that included large appropriations bill that includes the Cybersecurity Act of 2015. The Cyber Security Act was negotiated behind closed doors and represents a new version of the controversial Cybersecurity Information Sharing Act. The Act would expand government secrecy by exempting shared information from disclosure under freedom of information, open government, open meetings or similar laws at all levels of government and allow non-federal entities to share information with or receive information from any other non-federal entity or the federal government a cyber threat indicator of defensive measure without judicial oversight.

2016

January

22nd – Privacy organizations in the US filed an amicus brief in support of the Federal Communication in *ACA International v. FCC*. The case concerns a 2015 FCC regulation that strengthened consumer privacy protections by requiring telemarketers to obtain consent from current subscribers to a phone number and allowing consumers to revoke consent through reasonable means. The privacy organizations argued that the role of cell phones in American life mad the nuisance and privacy invasion from unwanted calls and text messages amplified and noted that unsolicited calls and texts facilitate fraud, drain battery life, and take up memory space.

February

9th – President Obama proposed a $19 billion Cybersecurity National Action Plan that aimed to modernize government cyber IT and improve cybersecurity for the federal government and individual Americans. The Plan also includes a new Executive Order to establish a Federal Privacy Council to coordinate federal privacy guidelines across agencies, however, the council would lack the authority to enforce Privacy Act obligations.

11th – In compliance with a European Court of Justice ruling made in 2014, Google announced it would remove links to sensitive personal information across all of its domains, not just those in which the Internet user resided.

16th – Apple opposed a court order that required the company to create a new software to deactivate certain iPhone security features and enable law enforcement to access encrypted files on a phone that was seized during an investigation into the San Bernardino terrorist attack. In response to the order, Apple CEO wrote a letter to Apple customers explaining that the company opposed to order because it would set "a dangerous precedent." In a motion to vacate the order Apple argued that the case was not about access to a single phone, but about whether government could force companies to undermine the security and privacy interests of individuals and that the order was a violation of the 1st and 5th Amendments.

March

15th – The U.S. Senate unanimously passed the Freedom of Information Improvement Act of 2015 which requires federal agencies to operate under a "presumption of openness" and placed limits of FOIA's Exemption5. Exemption 5 is commonly used to protect "deliberative process privilege" of inter- and intra-agency memoranda. A similar bill was passed by the House of Representatives earlier in the year.

24th – Tennessee became the first state to expand data breach notification requirements to encrypted data. Public Chapter Number 962 requires any information holder to notify Tennessee residents of a data breach, even if the data was encrypted, within 45 days of discovering the breach.

April

14th – The European Parliament finalized a historic reform of EU data protection legislation which will have legal force in July 2018. Negotiations for the new General Data Protection Regulation started in January 2012 and involved national governments, Members of the European Parliament, the business sector, academics, and civil society. The new rules include provisions for data breach notification, coordinated enforcement by national data protection authorities, data portability, and new measures to promote privacy innovation.

May

24th – The European Parliament issued a resolution to call for changes in the draft arrangement to allow data transfers between the EU and the U.S. While not legally binding, the resolution puts pressure on the European Commission to reopen negotiations with their American counterpoints before officially adopting a data transfer arrangement.

June

20th – In a 5-3 decision the U.S. Supreme Court overturned a lower court decision that suppressed drug evidence that was found during an illegal stop after a law enforcement officer discovered that the defendant had an outstanding arrest warrant, effectively weakening 4th Amendment protections during police stops. *Utah v. Strieff*, 136 S. Ct. 2056 (2016). The court determined that the warrant "broke the causal chain between an unconstitutional stop" giving the officer a reason to arrest the defendant making his search lawful.

July

12th – The European Commission approved a "Privacy Shield" which will allow companies to transfer the personal data of Europeans to the US without legal protections. The Privacy Shield aims to replace the Safe Harbor framework for commercial data flow between the EU and US that was struck down by the Court of Justice of the European Union in October 2015. Various privacy and consumer organizations had urged the EU and US to strengthen safeguards for transatlantic border flows.

20th – The Fifth Circuit Court of Appeals ruled that a Texas voter ID law violated the Voting Rights Act. *Veasey v.* Abbott, 2016 U.S. App. LEXIS 13255 (5th Cir. 2016). The law required all Texas voters to show one of six forms of photo ID in order to vote and required voters to disclose substantial amounts of personal information to obtain a voter ID. The court determined that the law had a discriminatory effect on minorities' voting rights and remanded the case to the district court to provide interim relief to individuals as soon as possible.

29th – The Federal Trade Commission unanimously reversed an administrative law judge's dismissal of the FTC's complaint against LabMD which found LabMD's poor data security practices are "unfair" under the FTC Act. The Commission determined that LabMD's data security practices were so unreasonable that they constituted an unfair trade practice in violation of Section 5 of the FTC Act and that the administrative law judge had applied the wrong legal standard for unfairness.

Privacy Resources
Privacy Year in Review

August

2nd – The White House Office of Science and Technology hosted a workshop on "Drones and the Future of Aviation." The goal of the workshop was "to accelerate opportunities and address challenges" posed by drones but the workshop declined to address any privacy issues raised by drone use.

September

9th – The EU Competition Commissioner opened an investigation into WhatsApp after the company announced that they intended to transfer data to Facebook in violation of their earlier commitments to US and EU authorities. The two companies had previously been approved for a merger and the commissioner noted that the promise not to merge data was a factor in deciding to approve the merger. Privacy groups in the US also filed complaints with the Federal Trade Commission over WhatsApp's proposed data transfer which includes the disclosure to Facebook.

AGENCIES

Angola

Ministro das Telecomunicações e das Tecnologias de Informação
www.mtti.gov.ao

Argentina

Agencia Nacional de Protección de Datos Personales
Sarmiento 118 5° Piso
C 1041 AAG
Ciudad Autónoma de Buenos Aires
Argentina
5411-5300-4000
http://www.jus.gob.ar/datos-personales.aspx/

Australia

Office of the Australian Information Commissioner
Level 3
175 Pitt Street
Sydney NSW 2000
Australia
1300-363-992 (within Australia)
61 2 9284 9749 (outside Australia)
https://www.oaic.gov.au

Austria

Österreichische Datenschutzbehörde
Hohenstaufengasse 3
1010 Wien
43 1 531 15 / 20252
dsb@dsb.gv.at

Belgium

Commission for the Protection of Privacy
Rue de la Presse 35
1000 Brussels
32 (0)2 274 48 00
commission@privacycommision.be
https://www.privacycommission.be

Bosnia and Herzegovina

Personal Data Protection Agency in Bosnia and Herzegovina
Vilsonovo šetalište broj 10
Sarajevo
00 387 33 726 250
azlpinfo@azlp.gov.ba
www.azlp.gov.ba

Brazil

Brazilian Internet Steering Committee
Av. das Nações Unidas, 11541, 7° andar
04578-000 - São Paulo – SP
55 11 5509 3511
info@cgi.br
www.cgi.br

Bulgaria

Personal Data Protection Commission
2 Professor Tsvetan Larazog
Sofia 1592
Bulgaria
02 / 91-53-518
www.cpdp.bg
kzld@cpdp.bg

Canada

Office of the Privacy Commissioner of Canada
30, Victoria Street
Gatineau, Quebec
K1A 1H3
1-800-282-1376
819-994-5444
https://www.priv.gc.ca/en/?

Privacy Resources
Agencies

Cape Verde

Comissão Nacional de Proteção de Dados
Pessoais
Avenida China
Rampa Terra Branca
Praia, Santiago
CaboVerde
238 5340390
cnpd@cnpd.cv
www.cnpd.cv

Croatia

Croatian Personal Data Protection Agency
Fra Grge Martića 14
HR - 10 000 Zagreb
00385 (0)1 4609-000
azop@azop.hr
www.azop.hr

Cyprus

Office of the Commissioner for Personal
Data Protection
1 Iasonos str.,
1082 Nicosia
357 22818456
commissioner@dataprotection.gov.cy
www.dataprotection.gov.cy

Czech Republic

Office for Personal Data Protection
Pplk. Sochora 27
170 00 Praha 7
Czech Republic
420 234 665 111
https://www.uoou.cz/en

Denmark

Datatilsynet

Borgergade 28, 5.
DK-1300 Copenhagen K.
45 33 19 32 00
dt@datatilsynet.dk
www.datatilsynet.dk

Estonia

Estonian Data Protection Inspectorate
19 Väike-Ameerika St.
10129 Tallinn
Estonia
372 627 4135 (international calls)
http://www.aki.ee/en

Finland

Office of Data Protection Ombudsman
Ministry of Justice
Ratapihantie 9, 6th floor
00520 Helsinki
Finland
358 29 56 16670
tietosuoja@om.fi
http://www.tietosuoja.fi/en/index.html

France

Commission Nationale de l'Informatique
et des Libertés
8 rue Vivienne
CS 30223
75083 Paris cedex 02
France
Tel: +33 (0)1.53.73.22.22
www.cnil.fr

Germany

Die Bundesbeauftragte für den
Datenschutz und die Informationsfreiheit
Husarenstr. 30
53117 Bonn
+49 (0)228-997799-0
poststelle@bfdi.bund.de

http://www.bfdi.bund.de/

Ghana

Data Protection Commission
Ministry of Communications Blk
Ministerial Enclave
Room No. 51, First Floor
P.O. Box CT 7195, Accra
233-(0)30 2631 455
info@ataprotection.org.gh
www.dataprotection.org.gh

Gibraltar

Data Protection Commissioner
Gibraltar Regulatory Authority
Suite 603 Europort
 200 74636
info@gra.gi
www.gra.gi

Greece

Hellenic Data Protection Authority
Kifissias 1-3, 115 23
Athens, Greece
30 210 6475600
contact@dpa.gr
www.dpa.gr

Hong Kong

Privacy Commissioner for Personal Data
12/F, Sunlight Tower,
248 Queen's Road East,
Wanchai,
Hong Kong
2827 2827
enquiry@pcpd.org.hk
https://www.pcpd.org.hk/index.html

Hungary

Hungarian National Authority for Data
Protection and Freedom of Information
H-1125 Budapest
Szilágyi Erzsébet fasor 22/C.
36 (1) 391-1400
privacy@naih.hu
www.naih.hu

Iceland

Persónuvernd
Rauðarárstíg 10
105 Reykjavík
Iceland
510 9606
postur@personuvernd.is
http://www.personuvernd.is

Ireland

Data Protection Commissioner
Canal House
Station Road
Portarlington
R32 AP23 Co. Laois
info@dataprotection.ie
www.dataprotection.ie

Israel

Information and Technology Authority
Ministry of Justice
216 Y'affo st.
Jerusalem
Sha'arei H'air building
Israel
972-2-6595601

Italy

Italian Data Protection Authority
Piazza di Monte Citorio
121 – 00186 Roma
39-06-6967 71
www.granteprivacy.it

Privacy Resources
Agencies

Japan

Consumer Affairs Agency
Sanno Park Tower 11-1
Nagatacho 2-chome
Chiyoda-ku
Tokyo 100-6178

Latvia

Data State Inspectorate
Blaumana Street 11/13-11
Riga, LV-1011
Latvia
info@dvi.gov.lv
www.dvi.gov/lv
67 23 31 31

Luxembourg

National Commission for Data Protectoin
1, avenue du Rock'n'Roll
L-4361 Esch-sur-Alzette
352 26 10 60-1
https://cnpd.public.lu/en/index.html

Lithuania

The State Data Protection Inspectorate
Juozapavičiaus str. 6/Slucko str. 2
LT-09310 Vilnius
Lithuania
370 5 279 1445
www.ada.lt

Macau

Office for Data Protection
Avenida da Praia Grande
n.º 804
Edifício "China Plaza"
13.º andar, A-F
Macau
853 2871 6006
www.gpdp.gov.mo

Macedonia

Directorate for Personal Data Protection
Bulevar Goce Delcev 8
Skopje
www.dlzp.mk
389 (2) 635 3230

Malaysia

Department of Personal Data Protection
Aras   6,   Kompleks   Kementerian
Komunikasi dan Multimedia,
Lot 4G9, Persiaran Perdana, Presint 4
Pusat Pentadbiran Kerajaan Persekutuan
62100 Putrajaya, Malaysia.
03-8000 8000
aduan@pdp.gov.my
www.pdp.gov.my

Malta

Office   of   the   Information   and   Data
Protection Commissioner
Second Floor
High Street
Sliema SLM 1549
356 2328 7100

Mauritius

Data Protection Office
5th Floor, Happy World House
Corner   SSR   and   Sir   William   Newton
Streets,
Port Louis, Mauritius
Tel: +230 212 22 18
www.dataprotection.govmu.gov

Mexico

Instituto   Nacoinal   de   Transparencia,
Accesso a la Información y Protección de
Datos Personales
Av. Insurgentes Sur # 3211
Planta Baja

Colonia Insurgentes Cuicuilco
Delegación Coyoacán, C.P. 04530
Ciudad de México.
www.inicioifai.org.mx
atencion@inia.org.mx
01 800 835 43 24

Monaco

COMMISSION DE CONTROLE DES
INFORMATIONS NOMINATIVES
12, Avenue de Fontvieille
98000 – Monaco
337 92 70 22 44
www.ccin.mc
ccin@ccin.mc

Montenegro

Agency for the Protection of Personal
Data and the Free Access to Information
Kralja Nikole no. 2
Podgorica
382 20 634 894
azlp@t-com.me
www.azlp.me

Morocco

National Control Commission for the
Protection of Personal Data
6 Boulevard Annakhil immeuble Les
Patios
3ème ètage
Hay Riad – Rabat, 10000 Morocco
212 537 57 11 24
contact@cndp.ma
www.cndp.ma

Netherlands

Dutch Data Protection Authority
Autoriteit Persoonsgegevens
Postbus 93374
2509 AJ DEN HAAG

31-(0)70- 888 85 00

New Zealand

Office of the Privacy Commissioner
Level 8, 109 –
111 Featherston Street
Wellington 6011
0800 803 909
https://www.privacy.org.nz

Norway

Datatilsynet
Tollbugata 3
0152 Oslo
Norway
47 22 39 69 00
postkasse@datatilsynet.no
https://www.datatilsynet.no

Peru

The General Agency on Data Protection
Scipión Llona N° 350
Miraflores
Lima, Peru
511 204 8020 (annex 1030)
http://www.minjus.gob.pe/proteccion%20
de%20datos%20personales/

Poland

General Inspector of Personal Data
Protection (Generalny Inspektor Ochrony
Danych Osobowych)
Stawki 2
00-193 Warsaw, Poland
(22) 860 70 86
http://www.giodo.gov.pl

Portugal

Comissão Nacional de Protecção de
Dados
Rua de São Bento n.° 148-3°

Privacy Resources
Agencies

1200-821 Lisboa
(+ 351) 21 392 84 00
https://www.cnpd.pt

Romania

National Authority for the Surveillance of
Personal Data Processing
28-30 Magheru Blvd
District 1, Bucharest
40 318 059 211
www.dataprotection.ro

Russia

Federal Service for Supervision of
Communications, Information
Technologies and Mass Media
Build. 2, 7, Kitaigorodskiy proezd
Moscow, 109074
7 495 987 6800

Serbia

Commissioner for Information of Public
Importance and Personal Data Protection
15 Bulevar Kralja Alksandra str
Belgrade 11000
381 11 3408 900
office@poverenik.rs
www.poverenik.rd

Singapore

Personal Data Protection Commission
460 Alexandra Road
#10-02
PSA Building
Singapore 119963
65 6508 7333
www.pdpc.gov.sg
info@pdpc.gov.sg

Slovak Republic

Office for Personal Data Protection of the
Slovak Republic
Hraničná 12
820 07 Bratislava 27
Slovak Republic
+421/2/32313214
statny.dozor@pdp.gov.sk
https://dataprotection.gov.sk/uoou/en

Spain

Agencia Española de Protección de datos
C/ Jorge Juan, 6
28001-Madrid
901 100 099
www.agpd.es

Sweden

Datainspektionen
Drottninggatan 29, 5th floor
Stockholm
46-70 736 10 80
datainspektionen@datainspektionen.se
www.datainspektionen.se

Switzerland

Federal Data Protection and Information
Commissioner
Feldeggweg 1
CH - 3003 Berne
41 (0)58 462 43 95
https://www.edoeb.admin.ch

Taiwan

The Ministry of Justice
130 Sec 1 Chung Ching
South Road
TAIPEI 100 ROC 100
Tel 886 2 381 39 39
http://www.moj.gov.tw/english/minister.a
spx

United Kingdom

The Office of the Data Protection
Registrar
Water Lane
Wycliffe House
WILMSLOW - CHESHIRE
SK9 5AF
Tel 0303 123 1113
https://ico.org.uk

Uruguay

Unidad Reguladora y de Control de Datos
Personales
Andes No. 1365 piso 7
Montevideo, Uruguay
2901 00 65 option 3
infourcdp@datospersonales.gub.uy
www.datospersonales.gub.uy

NATIONAL LEGISLATION

References

PrivacyExchange, Index of National Law
[http://www.privacyexchange.org/legal/nat/omni/nol.html]

Privacy International, Country Reports
[https://www.privacyinternational.org/reports]

Angola

Data Protection Law (Law no.22/11)
http://www.mtti.gov.ao/verlegislacao.aspx?id=457)

Electronic Communications and Information Society Services Law (Law no. 23/11)
http://www.mtti.gov.ao/verlegislacao.aspx?id=456

Albania

Law No. 8517/1999, on the Protection of Personal Data.

Argentina

Argentina Personal Data Protection Act
http://unpan1.un.org/intradoc/groups/public/documents/un-dpadm/unpan044147.pdf

Australia

The Privacy Amendment (Private Sector) Act (2000)
http://www.privacy.gov.au/act/privacyact/index.html

Privacy Act 1988
https://www.legislation.gov.au/Details/C2016C00838

Austria

Data Protection Act, Federal Law Gazette part I No. 165/1999
http://www.coe.int/t/dghl/standardsetting/dataprotection/National%20laws/Austria%20Federa
l%20Act%20DP.pdf

Belarus

Law on Information, Informatisation and Information Protection of 10 November 2008 No.
455 Z

Belgium

Data Protection Act

https://www.privacycommission.be/sites/privacycommission/files/documents/Privacy_Act_19
92.pdf

Bosnia and Herzegovina
Law on the Protection of Personal Data
http://www.tuzilastvobih.gov.ba/files/docs/zakoni/zakon_o_zastiti_licnih_podataka_49_06_-
_eng.pdf

Brazil
Brazil Internet Act, Federal Law No. 12.965/2014
http://www.planalto.gov.br/ccivil_03/_ato2011-2014/2014/lei/l12965.htm

Bulgaria
Law for the Protection of Personal Data
https://www.cpdp.bg/en/?p=element&aid=373

Canada
The Personal Information Protection and Electronic Documents Act (2000)
http://laws-lois.justice.gc.ca/eng/acts/P-8.6/index.html

Cape Verde
Data Protection Act, law 133/V/2001
http://www.cnpd.cv/leis/DATA%20PROTECTION%20Law%20133.pdf

Chile
Law for the Protection of Private Life of 1999

Croatia
The Act on Personal Data Protection (Official Gazette, No. 103/03)
http://azop.hr/legal-framework/legislation/national-legislation

Cyprus
Processing of Personal Data (Protection of the Individual) Law of 2001
http://www.dataprotection.gov.cy/dataprotection/dataprotection.nsf/697e70c0046f7759c2256
e8c004a0a49/f8e24ef90a27f34fc2256eb4002854e7/$FILE/138(I)-2001_en.pdf

Privacy Resources
National Legislation

Certain Aspects of Information Society and specifically Electronic Commerce and for Relevant Matters Law of 2004 (N.156(I)/2004)
Regulation of Electronic Communications and Posts Law of 2004 (112(I)/2004)
Legal Framework for Electronic Signatures and for Relevant Matters Law of 2004 (N.188(I)/2004)

Czech Republic
Act No. 101/2000 Coll., on the Protection of Personal Data and on Amendment to Some Acts
https://www.uoou.cz/en/vismo/zobraz_dok.asp?id_ktg=1107

Denmark
The Act on Processing of Personal Data (2000)
https://www.datatilsynet.dk/english/the-act-on-processing-of-personal-data/read-the-act-on-processing-of-personal-data/compiled-version-of-the-act-on-processing-of-personal-data/
The Public Authorities' Registers Act (1991)
The Private Registers Act (1987)

Estonia
Personal Data Protection Act
https://www.riigiteataja.ee/en/eli/509072014018/consolide

Finland
Personal Data Act 523/1999 (Henkilötietolaki)
http://www.finlex.fi/en/laki/kaannokset/1999/en19990523.pdf

France
Information Technology, Data Files and Civil Liberty
https://www.cnil.fr/sites/default/files/typo/document/Act78-17VA.pdf

Germany
Federal Data Protection Act
https://www.gesetze-im-internet.de/englisch_bdsg/

Ghana
Data Protection Act (Act 843)
https://www.dataprotection.org.gh/data-protection-act

Gibraltar
Data Protection Act 2004

http://www.gra.gi/data-protection/acts

Greece

Law on the Protection of Individuals with regard to the Processing of Personal Data 1997
http://www.dpa.gr/pls/portal/docs/PAGE/APDPX/ENGLISH_INDEX/LEGAL%20FRAME
WORK/LAW%202472-97-APRIL010-EN%20_2_.PDF

Hong Kong

Personal Data (Privacy) Ordinance
http://www.legislation.gov.hk/blis_pdf.nsf/4f0db701c6c25d4a4825755c00352e35/B4DF8B41
25C4214D482575EF000EC5FF/$FILE/CAP_486_e_b5.pdf

Hungary

Act CXII of 2011 on the Right of Informational Self-Determination and on Freedom of
Information
http://www.naih.hu/files/Privacy_Act-CXII-of-2011_EN_201310.pdf

Iceland

Act on the Protection of Privacy as regards the Processing of Personal Data, No. 77/2000
http://www.personuvernd.is/information-in-english/greinar/nr/438

India

Information Technology Act
http://www.dot.gov.in/act-rules/information-technology-act-2000

Ireland

Data Protection Act (1988)
http://www.irishstatutebook.ie/eli/1988/act/25/enacted/en/html

Israel

Protection of Privacy Law (1981)
http://www.justice.gov.il/En/Units/ILITA/Documents/ProtectionofPrivacyLaw57411981unoff
icialtranslatio.pdf

Italy

Data Protection Code – Legislative Decree no. 196/2003
http://www.garanteprivacy.it/home_en/italian-legislation

Japan

Personal Data Protection Act of 2003

Privacy Resources
National Legislation

http://www.privacyexchange.org/japan/JapanPIPA2003v3_1.pdf

Latvia
Law on Personal Data Protection (2000)
http://www.dvi.gov.lv/eng/legislation/pdp/
Law on Electronic Communications (October 28, 2004)
http://europa.eu.int/idabc/en/document/1167/402
Law on Information Society Services (2004)
http://www.likumi.lv/doc.php?id=96619

Lithuania
Law Amending the Law on State Registers (2004)
http://www3.lrs.lt/cgi-bin/preps2?Condition1=250197&Condition2=
Law on Electronic Communication (2004)
http://www3.lrs.lt/cgi-bin/preps2?Condition1=242679&Condition2=
Law on Legal Protection of Personal Data
https://www.ada.lt/images/cms/File/pers.data.prot.law.pdf

Luxembourg
Data Protection Act of 2002
http://www.cnpd.public.lu/en/legislation/droit-lux/doc_loi02082002mod_en.pdf

Macau
Personal Data Protection Act
http://www.gpdp.gov.mo/uploadfile/2013/1217/20131217120421182.pdf

Macedonia
Law on Personal Data Protection
http://www.dzlp.mk/sites/default/files/Law_on_Personal_Data_Protection_Cleared_version_0
.pdf

Malta
Public Contracts Regulation (2003)
http://www.contracts.gov.mt/documents/LN2992.pdf
Electronic Commerce Act (2001)
http://docs.justice.gov.mt/lom/legislation/english/leg/vol_13/chapt426.pdf
Data Protection Act
http://idpc.gov.mt/en/Legislation/CAP%20440.pdf

Mauritius

Data Protection Act 2004

http://dataprotection.govmu.org/English/Legislation/Pages/Data-Protection-Act-2004.aspx

Mexico

Ley Federal de Protección de Datos Personales en Posesión de los Particulares

http://www.diputados.gob.mx/LeyesBiblio/pdf/LFPDPPP.pdf

Monaco

Act no. 1.165 on the Protection of Personal Data

https://www.ccin.mc/legislation/lois/act-1-165-on-the-protection-of-personal-data.pdf

Netherlands

Personal Data Protection Act of 2000

http://www.coe.int/t/dghl/standardsetting/dataprotection/national%20laws/NL_DP_LAW.pdf

New Zealand

Privacy Act (1993)

http://www.legislation.govt.nz/act/public/1993/0028/latest/DLM296639.html

Norway

Personal Data Act of 2000

https://www.datatilsynet.no/English/Regulations/Personal-Data-Act-/

Paraguay

Law for the Protection of Personal Data in the Private Sector (2000)

http://www.ulpiano.com/habeasdaata_paraguay_Ley.htm (in Spanish)

Peru

Centrales Privadas de Informacion de Riesgo (2001)

Philippines

Republic Act No. 10173, An Act Protecting Individual Personal information in Information and Communications Systems and the Private Sector

http://www.gov.ph/2012/08/15/republic-act-no-10173/

Poland

Law on the Protection of Personal Data, 1997.

http://www.giodo.gov.pl/144/id_art/171/j/en/

Privacy Resources
National Legislation

Act on Electronic Signature (2002)
http://www.mswia.gov.pl/prawo/prawo_bezp_pod_el.html
Act on Public Procurement (2002)
http://www.uzp.gov.pl/english/The_Law_on_PP.html

Portugal
Portuguese Data Protection Law – Law n°. 67/98
https://www.cnpd.pt/english/bin/legislation/Law6798EN.HTM

Romania
Law No. 676/2001 on the Processing of Personal Data and the Protection of Privacy in the Telecommunications Sector (2001)
http://www.riti-internews.ro/lg676.htm
Law No. 677/2001 for the Protection of Persons concerning the Processing of Personal Data and the Free Circulations of Such Data (2001)
http://www.dataprotection.ro/index.jsp?page=legislatie_primara&lang=en

Russia
Federal Law of 27 July 2006 N 152-FZ on Personal Data
https://pd.rkn.gov.ru/authority/p146/p164/

San Marino
Act on Collection, Elaboration and Use of Computerized Personal Data (1983)

Serbia
Data Secrecy Law
www.mpravde.gov.rs/files/DATA%20SECRECY%20LAW_180411.doc

Singapore
Personal Data Protection Act 2012
http://statutes.agc.gov.sg/aol/search/display/view.w3p;page=0;query=DocId%3Aea8b8b45-51b8-48cf-83bf-81d01478e50b%20Depth%3A0%20Status%3Ainforce;rec=0

Slovakia
Act No. 428 on the Protection of Personal Data (2002)
http://www.dataprotection.gov.sk/ (in Slovak)
Act No. 610/2003 on Electronic Communications (2003)
http://www.teleoff.gov.sk/610.pdf
Act No. 215/2002 on Electronic Signatures (2002)
http://www.e-podpis.sk/laws/svk_ep_act215_2002.pdf

Act No. 523/2003 on Public Procurement (2003)
http://www.uvo.gov.sk/download/zakon523_03/act523_03.pdf

Slovenia

Law on the Protection of Personal Data (1999)
http://www.statistics.sk/webdata/english/acts/act5298/act5298.htm
Act Amending Act on Electronic Commerce and Electronic Signature (2004)
http://www.uradni-list.si/1/objava.jsp?urlid=200425&stevilka=1066

South Africa

Protection of Personal Information Act
http://www.gov.za/sites/www.gov.za/files/37067_26-
11_Act4of2013ProtectionOfPersonalInfor_correct.pdf

South Korea

Act on Promotion of Information and Communication Network Utilization and Information
Protection
http://unpan1.un.org/intradoc/groups/public/documents/APCITY/UNPAN025694.pdf

Spain

Data Protection Act (1999)
https://www.agpd.es/index.php (in Spanish)
Royal Decree 1720/2007 relating to Constitutional Act 15/1999 on Personal Data Protection
http://www.mjusticia.gob.es/cs/Satellite/Portal/1292426984243

Sweden

Personal Data Ordinance (1998)
http://www.datainspektionen.se/in_english/
Personal Data Act
http://www.datainspektionen.se/in-english/legislation/the-personal-data-act/

Switzerland

The Swiss Federal Act on Data Protection
https://www.edoeb.admin.ch/org/00129/index.html?lang=en

Taiwan

Computer-Processed Personal Data Protection Law (1995)
http://www.coe.int/T/E/Legal_affairs/Legal_co-
operation/Data_protection/Documents/National_laws/Taiwan-CP-DPLaw.asp
Personal Information Protection Act

Privacy Resources
National Legislation

http://law.moj.gov.tw/Eng/LawClass/LawAll.aspx?PCode=I0050021

Thailand

Thailand Official Information Act

http://www.krisdika.go.th/home.jsp (in Thai)

Trinidad and Tobago

Act No. 13 of 2011, Data Protection Act

http://www.ttparliament.org/legislations/a2011-13.pdf

United Kingdom

The Data Protection Act (1998)

http://www.hmso.gov.uk/acts/acts1998/19980029.htm

Uruguay

Law No. 18.331 Protection of Personal Data

https://www.datospersonales.gub.uy/wps/wcm/connect/urcdp/f085d1b8-0a24-4070-9dad-adc87b7595f2/18.331_con_modificaciones_de_la_19.355..pdf?MOD=AJPERES&CONVERT_TO=url&CACHEID=f085d1b8-0a24-4070-9dad-adc87b7595f2

ORGANIZATIONS

US Organizations

Access Now
P.O. Box 20429
Greeley Square Station
4 East 27th Street
New York, NY 10001-9998
https://www.accessnow.org/

Access Now defends and extends the digital rights of users at risk around the world.

American Civil Liberties Union
125 Broad Street, 18th Floor
New York, New York 10004-2400
212-549-2500
http://www.aclu.org/

The American Civil Liberties Union is the United States foremost advocate of individual rights -- litigating, lobbying, and educating the public on a broad array of issues affecting individual freedom in the United States.

Bill of Right Defense Committee and Defending Dissent Foundation
11431 Amherst Ave #1821
Silver Spring, MD 20915
phone (202) 529-4225
fax (202) 347-1116
email info@bordc.org
http://bordc.org/

The Bill of Rights Defense Committee/Defending Dissent Foundation protects the right of political expression to strengthen participatory democracy, and to fulfill the promise of the Bill of Rights for everyone.

Brennan Center for Justice
161 Avenue of the Americas, 12th Floor
New York, NY 10013
Tel: 646-292-8310
Email: brennancenter@nyu.edu
http://www.brennancenter.org/

Privacy Resources
Organizations

The Brennan Center for Justice at NYU School of Law is a nonpartisan law and policy institute that seeks to improve our systems of democracy and justice. We work to hold our political institutions and laws accountable to the twin American ideals of democracy and equal justice for all. The Center's work ranges from voting rights to campaign finance reform, from ending mass incarceration to preserving Constitutional protection in the fight against terrorism.

Center for Democracy and Technology
1401 K Street NW, Suite 200
Washington, DC 20005
Tel 202-637-9800
Fax 202-637-0968
http://www.cdt.org/

The Center for Democracy and Technology works to support laws, corporate policies, and technology tools that protect the privacy of Internet users, and advocate for stronger legal controls on government surveillance.

Center for Digital Democracy
1621 Connecticut Ave., Suite 550
Washington, DC 20009
202-986-2220

The Center for Digital Democracy (CDD) serves a vitally important mission protecting the privacy and welfare of the public in the "Big Data" digitally driven marketplace. CDD's work helps nonprofits, the news media, policymakers, and concerned citizens/consumers understand and address the online business practices that increasingly influence our lives.

Center on Privacy & Technology
Georgetown Law
600 New Jersey Ave. NW
Washington, DC 20001
202-662-9000
https://www.law.georgetown.edu/academics/centers-institutes/privacy-technology/

The Center on Privacy & Technology at Georgetown Law Center is a think tank focused on privacy and surveillance law and policy.

Consumer Federation of America
1620 I Street, NW, Suite 200
Washington, DC 20006
202-387-6121
cfa@consumerfed.org
http://consumerfed.org/

The Consumer Federation of America (CFA) is an association of non-profit consumer organizations that was established in 1968 to advance the consumer interest through research, advocacy, and education. Today, nearly 300 of these groups participate in the federation and govern it through their representatives on the organization's Board of Directors.

Consumer Watchdog
2701 Ocean Park Blvd., Suite 112
Santa Monica, CA 90405
310-392-0522
http://www.consumerwatchdog.org/

Consumer Watchdog is a nonprofit organization dedicated to providing an effective voice for taxpayers and consumers in an era when special interests dominate public discourse, government and politics. We deploy an in-house team of public interest lawyers, policy experts, strategists, and grassroots activists to expose, confront, and change corporate and political injustice every day, saving Americans billions of dollars and improving countless lives.

Electronic Frontier Foundation
815 Eddy Street
San Francisco CA 94109 USA
Phone: +1 415 436 9333
Fax: +1 415 436 9993
info@eff.org
https://www.eff.org/

Founded in 1990, EFF champions user privacy, free expression, and innovation through impact litigation, policy analysis, grassroots activism, and technology development. We work to ensure that rights and freedoms are enhanced and protected as our use of technology grows.

Privacy Resources
Organizations

Electronic Privacy Information Center
1718 Connecticut Ave., NW Suite 200
Washington, DC 20009
Tel 1 202 483 1140 (tel)
Fax 1 202 483 1248 (fax)
info@epic.org
http://www.epic.org/

EPIC is a public interest research center in Washington, DC. EPIC was established in 1994 to focus public attention on emerging privacy and civil liberties issues and to protect privacy, freedom of expression, and democratic values in the information age.

The Identity Project
https://papersplease.org/wp/

IDP builds public awareness about the effects of ID requirements on fundamental rights. The First Amendment rights of assembly, petition, and speech, our fundamental right to travel, and our basic rights to hold property and transact business are all affected. IDP builds public awareness about the effects of ID requirements on fundamental rights. The First Amendment rights of assembly, petition, and speech, our fundamental right to travel, and our basic rights to hold property and transact business are all affected.

National Consumers League
info@nclnet.org
202-835-3323
1701 K Street, NW
Suite 1200
Washington, DC 20006
http://www.nclnet.org/

NCL provides government, businesses, and other organizations with the consumer's perspective on concerns including child labor, privacy, food safety, and medication information.The mission of the National Consumers League is to protect and promote social and economic justice for consumers and workers in the United States and abroad.

The National Consumers League is a private, nonprofit advocacy group representing consumers on marketplace and workplace issues. We are the nation's oldest consumer organization.

Patient Privacy Rights
1006 Mopac Circle
Suite 102
Austin, Tx 78746
(512) 732-0033
(512) 732-0036 fax
https://patientprivacyrights.org/

PPR's purpose is to honor and empower the individual's right to privacy through personal control of health information wherever such information is collected and used. PPR works to educate, collaborate and partner with people to ensure privacy in law, policy, technology, and maximize the benefits from the use of personal health information with consent.

Privacy Foundation
Mary Reed Building
2199 S. University Blvd.
Denver, CO 80208
Tel 303 871 4971
Fax 303 871 7971
http://www.privacyfoundation.org/

The Privacy Foundation exists to educate the public, in part by conducting research into communications technologies and services that may pose a threat to personal privacy. The foundation will attempt to be fair and objective in its research projects and public reports.

Privacy Rights Clearinghouse
3100 - 5th Ave., Suite B
San Diego CA 92103
Tel 1 619 298 3396
Fax 1 619 298 5681
prc@privacyrights.org
http://www.privacyrights.org/

The Privacy Rights Clearinghouse is a nonprofit consumer information and advocacy program. It offers consumers an opportunity to learn how to protect their personal privacy and publications that provide information on a variety of informational privacy issues, as well as practical tips on safeguarding personal privacy.

Privacy Resources
Organizations

Privacy Forum
lauren@vortex.com
Tel 1 818 225 2800
http://www.vortex.com/privacy.htm

The Privacy Forum includes a moderated e-mail digest for the discussion and analysis of issues relating to the general topic of privacy in the information age of the 1990s and beyond.

Truste
Headquarters

835 Market Street
Suite 800, Box 137
San Francisco, CA 94103
Tel: (415) 520-3490
Fax: (415) 520-3420
http://www.truste.org/

Online privacy seal program. Web site offers advice and information about online privacy. Trustmark program awards seals to Web sites that meet privacy policy requirements and enforcement criteria. Licensed Web sites are required to post privacy statements.

World Privacy Forum
3108 Fifth Avenue, Suite B
San Diego, CA 92103
+1 760. 712. 4281
info@worldprivacyforum.org
https://www.worldprivacyforum.org/

The World Privacy Forum is a nonprofit, non-partisan 501(C)(3) public interest research group. The organization is focused on conducting in-depth research, analysis, and consumer education in the area of privacy. It is the only privacy-focused public interest research group conducting independent, original, longitudinal work.

International Organizations

Article 29 Working Group on Data Protection in Telecommunications
European Commission
B-1049
Brussels, Belgium
http://ec.europa.eu/justice/data-protection/article-29/index_en.htm

The Article 29 Data Protection Working Party was set up under the Directive 95/46/EC of the European Parliament and of the Council of 24 October 1995 on the protection of individuals with regard to the processing of personal data and on the free movement of such data. It has advisory status and acts independently.

BEUC
The European Consumer Organisation
Avenue de Tervueren, 36/
B-1040 Brussels
BELGIUM
Tel 32 2 743 15 90
Fax 32 2 735 74 55
http://www.beuc.eu/

BEUC, the European Consumers' Organisation, is the Brussels based federation of independent national consumer organisations from all the Member States of the EU and from other European countries. BEUC's job is to try to influence, in the consumer interest, the development of EU policy and to promote and defend the interests of all European consumers.

Consumers International
Head Office
24 Highbury Crescent
London
N5 1RX
UNITED KINGDOM
Tel 44 171 226 6663
Fax 44 171 354 0607
consint@consint.org
http://www.consumersinternational.org/

A worldwide non-profit federation of consumer organisations, dedicated to the protection and promotion of consumer interests.

Privacy Resources
Organizations

European Data Protection Supervisory
Rue Montoyer, 30
Brussels, Belgium
https://secure.edps.europa.eu/EDPSWEB/edps/EDPS/cache/offonce?lang=en

The European Data Protection Supervisor (EDPS) is the independent supervisory authority at EU level with responsibility for: monitoring the processing of personal data by the EU institutions and bodies, advising on policies and legislation that affect privacy, cooperating with similar authorities to ensure consistent data protection. The EDPS is a relatively new but increasingly influential independent supervisory authority, with responsibility for monitoring the processing of personal data by the EU institutions and bodies, advising on policies and legislation that affect privacy and cooperating with similar authorities to ensure consistent data protection.

European Digital Rights Initiative (EDRi)
http://www.edri.org/

European Digital Rights is an association in which existing European privacy and civil rights organizations work together in informing decision makers and the public about the upcoming threats to our privacy and civil rights. European Digital Rights will focus its activities towards developments in the European Union and the Council of Europe. European Digital Rights is seated in Brussels.

Human Rights Watch
350 Fifth Ave
34th Floor
New York, N.Y. 10118
http://www.hrw.org/

Human Rights Watch is dedicated to protecting the human rights of people around the world. Web sites includes comprehensive information about human rights campaigns around the globe.

Privacy International
62 Britton Street
EC1M 5UY
London, UK
info@privacyinternational.org
http://www.privacyinternational.org/

Privacy International is a human rights group formed in 1990 as a watchdog on surveillance by governments and corporations. PI is based in London, UK and has an office in Washington, D.C. PI has conducted campaigns in Europe, Asia and North America to counter abuses of privacy by way of information technology such as telephone tapping, ID card systems, video surveillance, data matching, police information systems, and medical records.

International Conference of Data Protection & Privacy Commissioners
New Zealand Office of the Privacy Commissioner
PO Box 10-094, The Terrace
Wellington, New Zealand
ICDPPCExCo@privacy.org.nz
https://icdppc.org/

The International Conference of Data Protection and Privacy Commissioners first met in 1979 and has been the premier global forum for data protection authorities for over 3 decades. The Conference seeks to provide leadership at international level in data protection and privacy. It does this by connecting the efforts of about 110 privacy and data protection authorities from across the globe.

PUBLICATIONS

US Publications

Access Reports, Inc.
1624 Dogwood Lane
Lychnburg, VA 24503
Tel 1 434 384 5334
Fax 1 434 384 8272
hhammitt@accessreports.com
http://www.accessreports.com/

Electronic Commerce & Law Report
Bureau of National Affairs
3 Bethesda Metro Center
Suite 250
Bethesda, MD 20814-5377
Tel 888 560 2529
http://www.bna.com/internet-law-
resource-center-p67aa/

PX Newsflash
Privacy and American Business
Two University Plaza, Suite 414
Hackensack, NJ 07601
Tel 1 201 996 1154
admin@privacyexchange.org
http://www.privacyexchange.org/

Privacy Journal
P.O. Box 28577
Providence, RI 02908
Tel 1 401 274 7861
orders@privacyjournal.net
http://www.privacyjournal.net/

Privacy Times

P.O. Box 302
Cabin John, MD
Tel 1 301 229 7002
evan@privacytimes.com
http://www.privacytimes.com

International Publications

Computer Law & Security Report
Elsevier Advanced Technology
Radarwg 29
1043 NX Amerdam
THE NETHERLANDS
http://www.journals.elsevier.com/compute
r-law-and-security-review/

ISPI Clips
Institute for the Study of Privacy Issues
P.O. Box 201
Crofton, British Columbia
CANADA, V0R 1R0
250 246 2784
ISPI@PrivacyNews.com
http://www.ispiclips.com

Privacy Laws and Business
2nd Floor
Monument House
215 Marsh Road
Pinner
Middx HA5 5NE
UNITED KINGDOM
Tel 44 20 8868 9200
Fax 44 20 8868 5215
Info@privacylaws.co.uk
http://www.privacylaws.co.uk

Reports

Big Data: A tool for Inclusion or Exclusion? Understanding the Issues
Federal Trade Commission Report (January 2016)
https://www.ftc.gov/reports/big-data-tool-inclusion-or-exclusion-understanding-issues-ftc-report

Privacy & Data Security Update (2014)
Federal Trade Commission Report (January 2015)
https://www.ftc.gov/reports/privacy-data-security-update-2014

Federal Trade Commission Staff Report on the November 2013Workshop Entitled The Internet of Things: Privacy and Security in a Connected World (January 2015)
https://www.ftc.gov/reports/federal-trade-commission-staff-report-november-2013-workshop-entitled-internet-things
Data Brokers: A Call For Transparency and Accountability
Federal Trade Commission Report (May 2014)

https://www.ftc.gov/reports/data-brokers-call-transparency-accountability-report-federal-trade-commission-may-2014

Commission Enforcement Policy Statement on Deceptively Formatted Advertisements
Federal Trade Commission Report (December 2015)
https://www.ftc.gov/public-statements/2015/12/commission-enforcement-policy-statement-deceptively-formatted

FTC and FCC Consumer Protection Memorandum of Understanding
Federal Trade Commission (November 2015)
https://www.ftc.gov/news-events/press-releases/2015/11/ftc-fcc-sign-memorandum-understanding-continued-cooperation

Consumer Data Privacy In A Networked World: A Framework for Protecting Privacy and Innovation (Consumer Privacy Bill of Rights)
The White House (February 2012)
https://www.whitehouse.gov/sites/default/files/privacy-final.pdf

Commercial Data Privacy and Innovation in the Internet Economy: A Dynamic Policy Framework
Department of Commerce (December 2010)

Privacy and Civil Liberties Oversight Board Enabling Statute

Privacy Resources
Publications

https://www.pclob.gov/library/42USC200
0ee-PCLOB_Enabling_Statute-2.pdf

Executive Order 13636 – Improving
Critical Infrastructure Cybersecurity
(Febuary 19, 2013)

Recommendations Assessment Report
Privacy and Civil Liberties Oversight
Board (January 29, 2015)
https://www.pclob.gov/library/Recommen
dations_Assessment-Report.pdf

Report on the Surveillance Progam
Operated Pursuant to Section 702 of the
Foreign Intelligence Surveillance Act
Privacy and Civil Liberties Oversight
Board (July 2, 2014)
https://www.pclob.gov/library/702-
Report.pdf

Report on the Telephone Records
Program Conducted under Section 215 of
the USA PATRIOT Act and on the
Operations of the Foreign Intelligence
Surveillance Court
Privacy and Civil Liberties Oversight
Board (January 23, 2014)
https://www.pclob.gov/library/215-
Report_on_the_Telephone_Records_Prog
ram.pdf

WEBSITES

General Interest

Access Reports

http://www.accessreports.com

> *A biweekly newsletter covering the Freedom of Information Act, other federal open government statutes, and information policy issues on both the legislative and administrative level. It also covers case law development on open government issues in the states. Current trends and issues in privacy are also covered.*

EPIC Online Guide to Privacy Resources

http://www.epic.org/privacy/resoucres/

> *This site contains links to printed publications, US and international privacy sites, and electronic mailing lists and newsgroups. It also contains information about upcoming privacy related conference and events.*

EPIC Privacy Archive

http://www.epic.org/privacy/

> *EPIC's Privacy Archive contains an A to Z list of topics relating to privacy, general privacy information, and hot topics as well as new resources relating to privacy.*

EPIC Bookstore

http://www.epic.org/bookstore/

> *At the EPIC Bookstore you will find all of EPIC's past and present publications on issues such as privacy, cryptography, free speech and consumer protection. You will also find links to a wide range of other books recommended by EPIC.*

Law of Information Privacy

http://www.epic.org/misc/gulc/

> *This site contains a description of the Law of Information Privacy course taught at Georgetown University. It contains links to recent privacy cases, privacy articles, and a bibliography of books on privacy and related topics.*

Privacy International - Country Reports

https://www.privacyinternational.org/reports

> *The Privacy International website provides the latest news on privacy issues. It contains a list of country reports concerning privacy laws and online reports. The site also provides information about past conferences and activities.*

Privacy Resources
Index

The Privacy Journal

http://www.privacyjournal.net/

> *Privacy Journal is a monthly newsletter reporting on new technology and its impact on personal privacy. The site gives tips on how to protect privacy and provides an outline of Model Privacy Policies.*

Privacy Law and Society

http://privacylawandsociety.org

> *The Third Edition of Privacy Law and Society is the most comprehensive casebook on privacy law ever produced. The companion website provides updates on recent privacy law developments.*

Privacy Rights Clearinghouse Fact Sheets

https://www.privacyrights.org/Privacy-Rights-Fact-Sheets (in English)

https://www.privacyrights.org/espanol (in Spanish)

> *The site contains fact sheets about workplace privacy, overcoming the emotional impact of identity theft, privacy in Cyberspace, online shopping tips, protecting financial privacy, and much more.*

Schneier on Security

https://www.schneier.com

> *Bruce Schneier is an internationally renowned security technologist, called a "security guru" by The Economist. His influential newsletter "Crypto-Gram" and his blog "Schneier on Security" are read by over 250,000 people.*

Government

International Conference on Privacy and Data Protection Commissioners

https://icdppc.org

> *The ICDPPC is a forum for collaboration between privacy and data protection authorities around the world.*

The European Commission – "Protection of Personal Data"

http://ec.europa.eu/justice/data-protection/

> *Information on data protection efforts in the EU.*

Federal Trade Commission - "Privacy, Identity & Online Security"

https://www.consumer.ftc.gov/topics/privacy-identity-online-security

> *The FTC Privacy page educates consumers and businesses about the importance of personal information privacy. It talks about FTC efforts, what they've learned, and what consumers can do to protect the privacy of their personal information.*

Federal Trade Commission - "ID Theft"

http://www.consumer.gov/idtheft/

> *The FTC's ID Theft page includes resources on what to do if you are the victim of identity theft.*

Federal Trade Commission's National Do Not Call Registry

https://www.donotcall.gov

> *If you've had your dinner interrupted one too many times, this website dedicated to eradicating telemarketers' hold over your time may be for you. The National Do Not Call Registry allows consumers to put their phone number on a "do not call" list for telemarketers.*

Organization for Economic Cooperation and Development - Internet

http://www.oecd.org/internet/

> *The OECD's Internet Policy site offers extensive list of reports released by the OECD about workshops, conferences and activities regarding e-commerce and internet communications.*

United Nations Special Rapporteur on the right to privacy

http://www.ohchr.org/EN/Issues/Privacy/SR/Pages/SRPrivacyIndex.aspx

> *Information from the UN Special Rapporteur on the right to privacy.*

Legal

EUR-Lex: European Union Law

http://eur-lex.europa.eu

> *This site provides links to European treaties, legislation, case law, and documents of interest.*

Legal Information Institute

Cornell Law School

https://www.law.cornell.edu/

> *The Legal Information Institute provides access to constitutions and codes, court opinions, and law directories.*

Library of Congress

https://www.congress.gov/

> *Congress.gov provides extensive information about legislative activities. It contains Library of Congress Web links and information about the legislative process.*